GW00792725

LEADING CASES OF THE TWENTIETH CENTURY

AUSTRALIA

LBC Information Services
Sydney

CANADA AND THE USA

Carswell

NEW ZEALAND

Brooker's
Auckland

SINGAPORE AND MALAYSIA

Thomson Information (S.E. Asia)

Singapore

Leading Cases
of the Twentieth Century

edited by

EOIN O'DELL

DUBLIN
ROUND HALL SWEET & MAXWELL
2000

Published in 2000 by
Round Hall Ltd
43 Fitzwilliam Place
Dublin 2

Typeset by
Gough Typesetting Services
Dublin

Printed by
MPG Books, Cornwall

ISBN 1-85800-208-7

A catalogue record for this book
is available from the British Library.

For Eunice and Andrew

PREFACE

Leading Cases of the Twentieth Century was the theme of the Irish Association of Law Teachers' Annual Conference 1999. The papers in this book are, by and large, the proceedings of that conference, revised to include developments up to the end of 1999, and thus to cover the whole of the century; though, in the nature of things, a few stray 2000 cites have found their way in.

The book does not attempt to be a definitive account of all of the leading cases of the century. That would be too vast an enterprise. Thus, some usual suspects have not been rounded up in this collection. Conversely, not every case discussed in this book would make everyone's list of leading cases of the century. The call for papers for the conference took a deliberately broad view of what constituted a case as leading, and some of the papers presented then and published here are in the nature of arguments for the importance of the cases discussed in them.

There are many people without whom this enterprise would not have reached a successful conclusion. First, I have to thank the Council of the IALT with whom I worked as President in 1998 and 1999 and who ensured the organisational success of the 1999 Conference, held in the Killarney Park Hotel, April 9-11, 1999. Second, I would like to thank all of the contributors to the conference and to this volume; their papers ensured the critical success of the conference, and I am grateful for the opportunity of presenting them to a wider audience in this book. Third, as editor, I have nothing but gratitude for the publishers, Round Hall Sweet & Maxwell, and in particular for the calm efficiency of Thérèse Carrick. Finally, none of this would have been possible without the support and encouragement of my wife, Eunice O'Raw, to whom, with our son, Andrew, this book is dedicated.

Eoin O'Dell
Hallowe'en, 2000

CONTRIBUTORS

Breen, Oonagh, Lecturer in Law, University College, Dublin

Butler, Andrew S., Barrister & Solicitor of the High Court of New Zealand; Senior Lecturer, Victoria University of Wellington

Cahill, Dermot, Lecturer in European Union Law, University College Dublin

Capper, David, Senior Lecturer in Law, Queen's University Belfast; Barrister of the Inn of Court of Northern Ireland

Carney, Tom, Legal Specialist, Office of the Director of Telecommunications Regulation, Ireland

Clark, Robert, Associate Professor of Law, University College Dublin

Clarke, Blanaid, Senior Lecturer in Law, University College Dublin

Cox, Neville, Dr., Lecturer in law, Trinity College, Dublin

de Vries, Dr. Ubaldus, Lecturer, Dublin City University

Fennelly, Nial, Judge of the Supreme Court of Ireland

Griffiths, Gerwyn Ll. H., Senior Lecturer in Law and Head of Legal Research, the University of Glamorgan

Hedley, Steve, Fellow, Christ's College, University Lecturer in Law, University of Cambridge

Hogan, Dr. Gerard, S.C., Fellow, Trinity College, Dublin

Hutchinson, Allan C., Professor of Law, Osgoode Hall School of Law, York University, Toronto

Keane, The Hon. Mr. Justice Ronan, Chief Justice of Ireland

Kennedy, T P, Director of Education, Law Society of Ireland

Mullan, Kenneth, Appeal Tribunal Chairman, Appeals Service, Northern Ireland

O'Connor, Michael P., Attorney at Law; Legal Writing Professor, Arizona State University College of Law

O'Dell, Eoin, Barrister; Lecturer in Law, Trinity College, Dublin

O'Malley, Tom, Lecturer in Law, National University of Ireland, Galway

Pratt, Jr, Walter F., Professor of Law, University of Notre Dame

Rumann, Cella, Assistant Federal Public Defender, District of Arizona; Adjunct Professor of Law, Arizona State University

Scannell, Yvonne, Associate Professor of Law, Trinity College, Dublin

Smith, Sir John, Emeritus Professor of Law, University of Nottingham

Stannard, John E., Dr, Senior Lecturer in Law, School of Law, Queen's University of Belfast

Swan, John, Professor of Law, McGill University; Stikeman, Elliott, Barristers & Solicitors, Montreal

Tunney, James, Senior Lecturer in Law, University of Abertay, Dundee, Scotland

TABLE OF CONTENTS

TABLE OF CASES

IRELAND

ENGLAND

NORTHERN IRELAND

SCOTLAND

EUROPEAN COURT OF JUSTICE

EUROPEAN COURT OF HUMAN RIGHTS

COMMISSION DECISIONS

UNITED STATES

CANADA

AUSTRALIA

NEW ZEALAND

INDIA

GERMANY

CYPRUS

HOLLAND

ITALY

TABLE OF LEGISLATION

IRELAND

STATUTORY INSTRUMENTS

ENGLAND

INTERNATIONAL TREATIES AND CONVENTIONS

EU Directives

THE IMPORTANCE OF LEADING CASES: A CRITICAL ANALYSIS

ALLAN C. HUTCHINSON*

Continuity with the past is only a necessity, not a duty.[1]

1. INTRODUCTION: TRADITION AND TRANSFORMATION IN THE COMMON LAW

One problem that underlies most jurisprudential analyses of the common law is how to explain change in an institution whose controlling motif is still that judges largely apply law rather than create it? Or, how to balance the restraining pull of tradition and the liberating pull of transformation? There is no better symbol of this quandary than the role of leading cases. These are cases – *Hadley v. Baxendale,*[2] *Donoghue v. Stevenson*[3] and their ilk, many of which are included in this volume – that are regarded by almost all lawyers as landmarks of the common law tradition. While their precise import and reach are continuously contested, any credible account of the common law has to be grounded upon such decisions and must be able to incorporate their authoritative intimations. However, the very existence of such cases and particularly the circumstances of their origin seem to confound the legitimacy of the process which they allegedly anchor and from which they purportedly arise. The sceptical might be forgiven for thinking that leading cases appear to be less a continuation of legal tradition and more of a break with existing traditions; they tend to exemplify a deviation from existing commitments, not a derivation from them. Accordingly, while leading cases represent the impressive pragmatic strength of the common law in being able to adapt to fresh challenges and new conditions, they also present jurists with their most pressing jurisprudential challenge in explaining the operation of the common law over time. Insofar as leading cases are the heart and soul of the common law, it must be explained

---

*Professor of Law, Osgoode Hall School of Law, York University, Toronto.

[1] Holmes, *Collected Legal Papers* (Smith, (ed.), University of Chicago Press, Chicago, 1920), 270.

[2] (1854) 23 L.J. Ex. 179; 9 Exch. 341.

[3] [1932] A.C. 562 (H.L.), on which see Hedley *"M'Alister (or Donoghue) (Pauper) v. Stevenson* (1932)", below, 64.

why that common law tradition is considered to extol all the virtues of restraint and caution which the creation and acceptance of leading cases so gloriously flaunt. It is my contention that mainstream efforts to provide such an explanation have failed. Indeed, mindful that the self-imposed task of such jurists is to showcase common law adjudication as a "a rational, disciplined, and constrained process",[4] leading cases seem to reveal the common law to be more of a political, unruly and open-ended process; this is a conclusion that mainstream jurisprudence is committed to resist and refute.

In this essay, I want to take a very different approach from mainstream jurisprudence. At present, perpetuated by a potent combination of institutional self-interest and intellectual naivete, the common law's sense of its own tradition is attenuated and impoverished; there is little appreciation of the organic and evanescent character of tradition and its transformative possibilities. Accordingly, rather than treat leading cases as anomalous occurrences that require special explanations, I will place the incidence, importance and influence of leading cases at the heart of my jurisprudential project. Once this is done, the tradition of the common law is seen to be less about stability and continuity and more about change and transformation. Beginning from the premise that a tradition is best considered and assessed by reference to its great moments rather than its routine practice, I offer an account of the common law tradition, intended to be both descriptively accurate and prescriptively defensible, as an institutional commitment to the notion that "anything might go" that is able to capture both the routine operation of the common law and the radical leaps that transform it.[5] Although lawyers and jurists emphasises the routine, it will be the radical occasions of leading cases that best capture its dynamic spirit. Indeed, contrary to conventional wisdom, it is the relentless critic who most closely grasps and continues the common law tradition than the complacent apologist who insists on a timid acceptance of what has already been decided. To treat the law as static or to adopt an unquestioning posture toward it is to betray, not uphold the common law tradition. As such, I argue that the common law tradition of adjudication is most ably and adequately represented by the work of so-called "bold spirits," not "timorous souls".[6] While leading cases might well

---

[4] Steyn, "Does Legal Formalism Hold Sway in England?" (1996) 49 *C.L.P.* 43, 58.
[5] I have deliberately avoided the slippery and contested term "a theory of . . .". This is because a theory indicates something that is too universal, complete and comprehensive for my sceptical taste or sensibilities; it smacks of the kind of work, with its emphasis on grounded premises and guaranteed procedures, that is antithetical to my whole approach. The idea of a "theory" suggests that jurisprudence is a reflective and first-order enterprise that is to be set against and above a situated and second-order practice. It is exactly that kind of bifurcated thinking that I seek to challenge — theory is another kind of practice that cannot be entirely separated or fully appreciated apart from the historical conditions of its ideological production. See Hutchinson, *It's All in the Game: A Nonfoundationalist Account of Law and Adjudication* (Duke University Press, Durham, N.C., 2000).
[6] *Candler v. Crane, Christmas & Co.* [1951] 2 K.B. 164 (C.A.) 178 *per* Denning L.J. (dissenting).

mark the end of an era and the beginning of another, they also represent the continuation of a tradition in which "anything might go" – "breaking with tradition" is as traditional as it gets.

2. LEADING CASES

Before venturing into deeper and more turbulent jurisprudential water, it seems advisable to begin by saying something about the identity and nature of so-called leading cases. Indeed, insofar as I intend to utilise such decisions as the main grist for my critical mill, such an account seems indispensable. In an important sense, what counts as a leading case is simply whatever people agree to designate as a leading case. There is nothing so self-evidently or intrinsically great about particular cases that automatically guarantees their inclusion in any jurisprudential hall of fame. While this in itself is revealing, there is nothing different about law in this regard from literature or art; it is as much a matter of communal acceptance as conformity with any universal metewand about the virtues of greatness. Or, to put it another way, the quality of greatness is part of the communal debate rather than an external restraint upon it. As such, the debate over what does and does not count as a great or leading case is intimately tied to the informing debate over the nature and purpose of law and adjudication; what qualifies a case as leading depends on the underlying view of law and adjudication being adopted. Consequently, it seems reasonable to utilise such cases as a convenient and compelling way to illuminate that debate and to evaluate contributions to that debate in terms of their capacity to explain the existence and evolution of leading cases. Leading cases – like *Ryland v. Fletcher*,[7] *Donoghue v. Stevenson*, and *Hedley Byrne v. Heller*[8] and many others, some of which are discussed in this collection – are simply those cases that the legal community continues to consider leading.

That having been said, there does seem to be a general consensus on the notion that leading cases are those that have become sufficiently and widely accepted over time as being of such importance that not only must any future development of the law be able to incorporate their holdings, but that such holdings will illuminate the path that such development must take. In this sense,

---

[7] (1868) L.R. 3. H.L. 330 (1868).

[8] *Hedley Byrne & Co. Ltd. v. Heller & Partners Ltd.* [1964] A.C. 467 (H.L.). As these examples suggest, I intend in the main to restrict my discussion to tort cases as this is the area of law that I know best (or, more to the point, least worst). However, this ought not to be taken in any way as a narrowing of my thesis to tort law alone; tort doctrine is simply one illustration of a broader and pervasive feature of the common law. Consequently, many of the leading cases from other areas of law discussed in this volume will also be referred to here. For a convincing account of other areas of law, although from a very different perspective, see Robertson, *Discretion in the House of Lords* (Oxford University Press, Oxford, 1999).

a great or leading case has been elegantly defined as "a fixed star in the juris-prudential firmament".[9]

However, this description suggests that there is something natural or given about their status and that it is more a process of discovery than creation. On the contrary, the recognition and fate of such cases is very much about the willingness of the legal community to sustain faith in the importance of the case. A leading case is only a leading case so long as the lawyers and judges are prepared to treat it as one. It is more that leading cases are lighthouses, designed with a particular purpose in mind, constructed with available materi-als, and with a limited working life. For instance, although *Anns*[10] was consid-ered by many to be a (potential) member of the select elite, its greatness was later denied and its importance rejected in *Murphy*.[11] Again, though *Sinclair v. Brougham*[12] once shone as brightly as any star in the firmament, its light is now rapidly waning.[13] Moreover, because a particular decision has been ac-cepted into the legal canon does not mean that the light it casts is clear or certain. Indeed, as with texts that have received canonical status in literature, the meaning and instruction of such judgments remains indeterminate and un-decided. Precedents do not speak for themselves and their interpretation is an occasion for interested and creative attempts at hermeneutical appropriation; they represent a site for the manufacture of meaning[14] as much as an adequate grounding for its resolution. For some, in law and literature, this richness and opacity are some of the qualities that recommend a text as great. In this sense, both Shakespeare's Hamlet and Lord Atkin's *Donoghue* are great not only be-cause of their profundity, but also because of their profligacy; they lend them-selves to diverse and contestable renderings.[15]

---

[9] Gilmore, *The Death of Contract* (Ohio state University, Columbus, 1974) 83. See also Sunstein, *Legal Reasoning and Political Conflict* (O.U.P., New York, 1996) 82: "judges rely on defining . . . precedents . . . that have a high degree of popular approval and that operate as fixed points for inquiry".

[10] *Anns v. Merton London Borough Council* [1978] A.C. 728; [1977] 2 All E.R. 492 (H.L.)

[11] *Murphy v. Brentwood DC* [1991] 1 A.C. 398; [1990] 2 All E.R. 908 (H.L.); see Hedley, above n.3, text with and in n.23.

[12] [1914] A.C. 398 (H.L.).

[13] See O'Dell, "The Case That Fell to Earth. *Sinclair v. Brougham* (1914)" below, 28.

[14] This is a process to which Tunney, "The Search for Justice. *Mabo* (1992)" below, 445 is quite properly alive; see in particular his section 9.2, headed "The Contest for Meaning". Good exam-ples of this process are provided by Hogan's argument in favour of *State (Ryan) v. Lennon* [1935] I.R. 170 (H.C. and S.C.) as a great case: "A Desert Island Case Set in the Silver Sea. *State (Ryan) v. Lennon* (1935)" below, 80 and by Swan's similar claim for *De Savoye v. Morguard* [1990] 3 S.C.R. 1077 (S.C.C.) in "The Future of the Conflict of Laws. Can *Morguard* (1990) Point the Way?" below, 405.

[15] The issue of canon formation is less about what is contained in a canon and more about how its contents are read. For a good summary of the debate see von Hallberg, (ed.), *Canons* (University of Chicago Press, Chicago, 1984), and Mootz, "Legal Classics: After Constructing the Legal Canon" (1994) 72 *N.Car.L.Rev.* 977.

Because the list of leading cases is simply a matter of communal consensus (although it is a process in which some opinions carry more weight than others), the listing of leading cases is very much an empirical question and, as such, is largely uncontroversial. For instance, few tort scholars would doubt that *Rylands*, *Donoghue*, and *Hedley Byrne* were leading cases. Nevertheless, the recognition of the greatness of these cases does little to explain why such cases have become celebrated as leading cases; the definition is more about the consequences of being designated a leading case rather than an explanation of why they became leading cases in the first place. One possible source of explanation is that such decisions and judgments are feted because of their exemplary stature as embodiments of the common law method through their expert use of legal reasoning and their superlative judicial craft. While such qualities are not irrelevant and are often touted by some jurists as the hallmark of leading cases, such an explanation is unconvincing. If the formal qualities of judgments were determinative, there is little reason to believe that we would have the leading cases that we have; some presently included in the canon would be missing and others might be included. For instance, *Rylands* is hardly the model of legal reasoning; there is little about Lord Cairns's judicial craft that makes his judgment standout as exceptional or excellent. Furthermore, there are myriad examples of judgments that live up to the standard of *Donoghue*'s Lord Atkin or *Hedley Byrne*'s Lord Devlin: the judgement of Lord Buckmaster in *Donoghue* cannot be reasonably said to be the inferior of Lord Atkin's in terms of craft and professionalism.

The greatness of leading cases is less about their formal attributes than it is about their substantive appeal. Decisions like *Donoghue* and *Hedley Byrne* become defining moments in the shifting and developing doctrinal universe not because they are legally correct or analytically sound in that they follow precedent in predictable or prosaic fashion, but because they are considered politically valid and socially acceptable. Indeed, the very strength and singularity of such cases is that they break with the existing tradition of doctrine and carve out a new path for the law to follow. As such, the genesis of leading cases is to be found in strikingly creative and transformative acts of judicial bravado. The difference between *Donoghue* and *Hedley Byrne*, on the one hand, and other less celebrated cases, on the other, has almost nothing to do with interpretative cogency or hermeneutical integrity in legal doctrine. It has everything to do with changing currents and concerns in the political context that frame and condition such germinal and disruptive judicial decisions. As Stanley Fish puts it, "the canon is a very historical, political and social product, something that is fashioned by men and women in the name of certain interests, partisan concerns, and social and political agenda".[16] If this is true for literature, then it

---

[16]Fish, "Canon Busting: The Basic Issues" (1989) *National Forum: Phi Cappa Phi J.* 13. See also

is doubly so for law. For instance, *Winterbottom v. Wright*,[17] which restricted relief for defective products to contractual remedies, ceased to be a fixed point on the legal compass because it no longer enjoyed sufficient political confidence and support among the legal (and political) community; its perception as having an analytically weak (or strong) status was virtually beside the historical point. While the fact that a judgment is crafted in an analytically strong style will facilitate the acceptance of a novel or bold decision, it will not in itself carry the day. Rightness and, therefore, greatness is a matter of social policy and political persuasion, not legal doctrine and logical demonstration.

An illustration of that point can be made in examining the short career of a leading-case-that-never-was, *Junior Books*.[18] The case centred on the much-contested question of whether there could be recovery for pure economic loss which resulted from a negligent act. In short, following *Anns*, it did away with the requirement of related damage to person or property, if there was to be recovery for economic loss, and made the existence of defectively-manufactured property sufficient to trigger tortious liability. As well as appearing to put recovery for economic loss on the same footing as other losses, the House of Lord effectively placed Tort ahead of Contract in the doctrinal hierarchy of civil obligations. Under such a legal regimen, it would no longer be taken for granted that contract was the primary mode of imposing civil obligations or that, without the existence of a contract, people had no legal obligation to safeguard the economic interests of others. In reaching this decision, Lord Fraser maintained that "the present case seems to me to fall well within limits already recognised in principle for this type of claim"[19] and Lord Roskill believed that it represented "the next logical step forward in the development of this branch of the law".[20] In contrast, Lord Brandon's dissenting judgment took the view that, in its treatment of *Donoghue*, the majority had effected "a radical departure from long-established authority"[21] and created "wholly undesirable extensions of the existing law of delict".[22] Of course, the considerable irony of this is that *Donoghue* itself was "a radical departure from long-established authority" and *Hedley Byrne* had been no more a radical departure from *Donoghue* than *Junior Books*. Lord Brandon's disagreement had more to do with the wisdom of introducing a transmissible warranty of quality[23] – a plain-

---

Luban, "Legal Traditionalism" in Luban, (ed.), *Legal Modernism* (University of Michigan Press, Ann Arbour, 1997) 93-124.
[17](1842) M.&.W. 109; 152 E.R. 402.
[18]*Junior Books Ltd. v. Veitchi Co. Ltd.* [1983] 1 A.C. 520 (H.L.). One commentator heralded it as "a landmark decision in the law of torts, representing a development or advance comparable to that which occurred in *Donoghue*." See Starke, "Comment" (1982) 56 *Aust. L.J.* 663, 633.
[19][1983] 1 A.C. 520, 533.
[20][1983] 1 A.C. 520, 546.
[21][1983] 1 A.C. 520, 551.
[22][1983] 1 A.C. 520, 552.
[23][1983] 1 A.C. 520, 551-552.

tiff in tort could be better off than a similar plaintiff with a relevant contract because warranties would run with the product: a subsequent purchaser could have a broader range of legal rights and remedies than the original purchaser.

As is now well-known, this doctrinal transformation did not take place and *Junior Books* did not take its place among the ranks of leading cases. The response to *Junior Books* was decidedly swift and negative. In a series of cases, the courts managed to undermine and cabin the decision without actually over-ruling it. Abandoning Atkin's search for some golden thread that would make general sense of the law's particulars, the judges opted for a less doctrinaire and more pragmatic approach to tort law; there is "no precedent for the appli-cation of strict logic in treading the path leading from the general principle established in *Donoghue v. Stevenson* towards the Pandora's Box of unbridled damages at the end of the path of foreseeability".[24] Indeed, by the end of the decade, Lord Brandon had managed to persuade all his fellow judges to come over to his way of thinking. In *Murphy*, it was held that the loss was purely economic and was more appropriately dealt with under contract, not tort; li-ability based on a "transmissible warranty of quality" was to be strenuously resisted. The rare septet of law lords in *Murphy* overruled *Anns* (and, therefore, *Junior Books*) on the basis that it was not "capable of being reconciled with pre-existing principle" and, again ironically, that it was too big a jump from *Donoghue.*[25] However, any reasonable reading of the *Murphy* decision indi-cates that their rejection of *Anns* has more to do with policy concerns about such a doctrinal innovation than a somewhat belated condemnation of *Anns'* failing as a matter of strict legal analysis; the law lords were unprepared to allow Tort to eclipse Contract as the primary mode of civil obligation. Accord-ingly, *Junior Books'* fate confirms that the status of a case as a leading case has more to do with its substantive desirability than its legal unsoundness. If legal soundness (*i.e.*, whether a decision was a reconcilable extension or modifica-tion of existing principle) is the test, *Donoghue* itself, the epitome of a leading case, would be rendered suspect.

Of course, this judicial effort to defend their work in terms of principled decision-making is made for an eminently good and, at least in traditional terms, compelling reason. Judges are acutely aware that their primary role is sup-

---

[24] *Greater Nottingham Co-operative Society Ltd. v. Cementation Piling and Foundations Ltd.* [1989] Q.B. 21 (C.A.) 95; [1988] 3 W.L.R. 396, 407 *per* Purchas L.J. See also *Muirhead v. Industrial Tank Specialities Ltd.* [1986] Q.B. 507; [1985] 3 All E.R. 705 (C.A). and *Caparo v. Dickman* [1990] 2 A.C. 605 (H.L.) 616-619; [1990] 2 W.L.R. 358, 363-6 *per* Lord Bridge; [1990] 2 A.C. 605, 632-636; [1990] 2 W.L.R. 358, 378-83 *per* Lord Oliver.
[25] *Murphy v. Brentwood DC* [1991] 1 A.C. 398, 460, 466; [1990] 2 All E.R. 908, 914, 919 *per* Lord Keith; *cp.* [1991] 1 A.C. 398, 490-491; [1990] 2 All E.R. 908, 937 *per* Lord Oliver, and [1991] 1 A.C. 398, 497-498; [1990] 2 All E.R. 908, 942 *per* Lord Jauncey. See also *The Aliakmon* [1986] A.C. 785 (H.L.). On the (dubious) retrenchment from *Junior Books*, see Beyleveld and Brownsword, "Privity, Transivity and Rationality" (1991) 54 *M.L.R.* 48 and Logie, "The Final Demise of *Junior Books*?" [1989] *Jur. Rev.* 5.

posed to be to develop and apply the law from existing principles, not to legislate with little regard to the past. A candid confession that leading cases are
less of a principled continuation of existing doctrine and more a radical departure from it puts the jurisprudential defence of the common law into serious
jeopardy. For instance, in *Hedley Byrne*, Lord Reid was adamant that *Donoghue*
"may encourage us to develop existing lines of authority, but it cannot entitle
us to disregard them",[26] and Lord Devlin emphasised that, "as always in English law, the first step in such an inquiry is to see how far the authorities have
gone, for new categories in the law do not spring into existence overnight".[27]
Nonetheless, while this effort is understandable, its convincing performance is
fraught with difficulty. Indeed, attempts to explain the jurisprudential basis of
leading cases are caught between a rock and hard place. On the one hand, if
leading cases are seen to be a continuation of existing doctrine, it is a tradition
that is so ample and generous that it can embrace almost any judicial act. The
reality will be that "anything might go" and that the limits of common law
adjudication are nothing more (and nothing less) than the political limits of the
judges; judgments will stand or fall on the judges' rhetorical ability to persuade their colleagues of their political merit. Such a situation seems anathema
to traditional opinion. However, on the other hand, if leading cases are seen to
be a break with existing doctrine, then their very legitimacy is questionable.
Although law emphasises the routine, it will be the revolutionary occasions of
leading cases that the best capture its dynamic spirit. Either way, the judicial
accounts of the common law's development as incremental and piecemeal concede too much (*i.e.*, almost any case is a routine continuation of common law
tradition) or too little (*i.e.*, all leading cases amount to a revolutionary change
in the common law tradition) for their own jurisprudential good.

   This dilemma can be easily and instructively demonstrated by reference to
the competing judgments in *Donoghue* itself. Lords Buckmaster and Tomlin
took the view that not only were the existing authorities against Mrs. Donoghue,
but that the common law did not evince any principles that would support her
claim: "although [the common law's] principles are capable of application to
meet new conditions not contemplated when the law was laid down, these
principles cannot be changed nor can additions be made to them because any
particular meritorious case seems outside their ambit".[28] Of course, the minority did not rest their disagreement on legal analysis alone, but went on to take
fundamental exception with the substantive wisdom of the majority's decision.
In response, the majority pointed to the inconclusive state of the authorities
and claimed that, although "the neighbour principle" was not the only possible
interpretation of the existing precedents, it was the best substantive outcome.

[26] [1964] A.C. 467, 482.
[27] [1964] A.C. 467, 525.
[28] [1932] A.C. 562, 567 *per* Lord Buckmaster; *cp.*, 599-601 *per* Lord Tomlin.

However, both Lords Atkin and Macmillan were prepared to state that the law must keep pace with prevailing views of justice. Indeed, Lord Macmillan went so far as to approve of the view that "any proposition the result of which would be to show that the common law of England is wholly unreasonable and unjust cannot be part of the common law of England".[29] In short, while the effort to follow principle is to be preferred, such a formal responsibility will not stand in the way of substantive fairness: when push comes to shove, judges should favour justice over precedent. In this classic exchange between *Donoghue*'s minority and majority, the extent of the jurisprudential dilemma with which leading cases confront the common law is revealed. In gallantly attempting to cover all the jurisprudential bases, the majority in *Donoghue* only manage to expose the fragile and, I will argue, illusory foundations of the common law. While Lords Atkin and Macmillan can be applauded for their candour and their willingness to put substantive justice ahead of formal argument, they highlight the fact that the common law is best understood not as a limited, predictable and peculiarly legal mode of decision-making, but as an open, unpredictable and distinctly political process in which "anything might go".

Of course, the efforts by judges to explain what is and is not going on in the development of the common law are only the first, not the last word on such matters. While such pronouncements and rationales cannot be entirely ignored, jurisprudential scholarship is devoted to going beyond and behind such explanations in its own efforts to understand and justify the common law process. Although there is much disagreement among traditional scholars, there remains the unifying commitment to demonstrating that not only can the common law balance the competing demands of stability and change, but that it can do so in a legitimate way that respects the important distinction between law and politics. Accordingly, in the next two sections, I will explore and evaluate the efforts of mainstream jurists to provide a better and more cogent account of the common law. Whereas one group champions the force of tradition in legal decision-making, the other seeks to temper the reliance on tradition with a resort to transformation. In my critical view, both efforts are unconvincing and fail in their stated ambitions – if the common law is a tradition, it is as much one of change and innovation as it is of stability and continuity.

3. THE COMMON LAW TRADITION

Bentham's withering assessment of the common law is as good a place to start as any. After an extended and uncompromising analysis, he came to the firm conclusion that "as a system of rules, the common law is a thing merely imagi-

---

[29] [1932] A.C. 562, 608-609, quoting *Emmens v. Poole* (1885) 16 Q.B.D. 35 , 357-358 *per* Lord Esher.

nary".[30] As an enthusiast for legislation and codification, Bentham was concerned with the fact that the rules of law were nowhere available in any accessible or agreed-upon manner: any effort to enumerate such rules or to pin down their content was doomed to failure, let alone the attempt to apply those putative rules to different fact-situations. Although a perverse few might want to take exception to this charge, almost every jurist would be prepared to concede the general force of Bentham's point. However, theirs is a strategy of confession and avoidance – they acknowledge that the common law cannot be adequately represented as 'a system of rules', but insist that the common law does indeed exist. Moreover, they do not so much take Bentham's point as a criticism of the common law, but more as a compliment – the common law is not static or fixed, but is a flexible and evolving entity. Indeed, it has now become almost trite to acknowledge that law is neither only about rules in the sense in that is supplemented by principles, policies and values nor, even if it is about rules, a system in the sense of being complete, organised, and certain.

Nevertheless, while debate remains intense and hostile over the nature of the common law as a source of institutional norms, very few jurists think about the common law as only an entity. There is considerable agreement over the fact that the common law tradition is as much a process or practice as anything else: "law is something we do, not something we have as a consequence of something we do".[31] Indeed, the depiction of the common law as a practice of law-making is much more important than the body of legal decisions that it produces. Understood as much as an intellectual mind-set to law-making as a technical practice, lawyers have transformed a natural tendency to utilise past performance as a guide to future conduct into an institutional imperative. It is in this sense that the common law is a tradition. However, if law was only thought of as a repository of rules, principles and methods that can be accessed by those sufficiently attuned to its workings, law would be no different than many other traditional practices. What distinguishes the common law is that it is not only a tradition, but is also a practice that embraces the idea of traditionality – the common law accepts that its past has a present authority and significance for its participants in resolving present disputes and negotiating future meaning. By way of the doctrine of *stare decisis*, the common law method insists that past decisions are not only to be considered by future decision-makers, but are to be followed and treated as binding. Judges accept the responsibility to curb their own instincts and to confine themselves to the limits of extant decisions: "the principle of *stare decisis* does not apply only to good decisions: if it did, it would have neither value nor meaning".[32] This means that lawyers and

---

[30]Bentham, *A Comment on the Commentaries* (Everett, (ed.), Clarendon Press, Oxford, 1925) 125.

[31]Bobbitt, *Constitutional Interpretation* (Basil Blackwell, Oxford, 1991) 24.

[32]*Jones v. D.P.P.* [1962 A.C. 635 (H.L.) 711 *per* Lord Devlin. See Brown, "Tradition and Insight" (1993) 103 *Yale L.J.* 177.

judges assume an institutional obligation to justify their present actions and arguments by reference to those results and arguments that are recorded in the official documents and materials of the law. As such, judging is a very traditional practice that gives central importance to the normative force of traditionality; "the past of law . . . is an authoritative significant part of its presence".[33]

This commitment to the traditionality of the common law tradition is often premised on the unstated notion that there is something normatively compelling or worthy about what has come before; the past is not followed simply because it precedes, but because it is superior to present understandings. Accepted by earlier generations and having withstood the test of time, tradition binds not simply because it has not been replaced or altered, but because it has its own normative force. For common lawyers, therefore, the legal past is not simply a store of information and materials, but an obligatory source of value and guidance. In this strong version of traditionality, past decisions possess a moral prestige and accumulated wisdom that are entitled to be given normative preference over present understandings and uninhibited ratiocination; it is an avowedly political stance rather than a hedge against politics. As such, the common law is traditional in the conservative Burkean sense that "we are bound, within whatever limits, to honour the past for its own sake, to respect it just because it is the past we happen to have".[34] When this quality is added to the fact that judges have independent institutional justifications for steering clear of open-ended and creative decision-making, the claims of tradition are very strong in defining the appropriate approach and limits to common law adjudication.

However, while this strong defence of the common law's strictly backward-looking nature receives considerable lip-service in the law reports and academic literature, it offers a very unconvincing account of the common law's actual development generally and the legitimacy of leading cases particularly – the law does change and often in ways that mark a sharp discontinuity with the past. Most importantly, such a strong view misunderstands the whole idea and purpose of traditionality. Understood as a tradition of traditionality, the common law must be distinguished from history and custom. Whereas tradition has

---

[33] Krygier "Law As Tradition" (1986) 5 *Law & Phil.* 237, 245. See also Hobsbawm and Ranger (eds.), *Inventing Tradition* (C.U.P., New York, 1983) and Williams, *Keyword* (Fontana Paperback, London, 1981) 320.

[34] Kronman, "Precedent and Tradition" (1990) 99 *Yale L.J.* 1029, 1037. Burke talks about "the great primeval contract of eternal society" in which "the partnership . . . between those who are living and those who are dead, and those who are to be born". Burke, *Reflections on the Revolution in France* (Pocock (ed.), C.U.P., Cambridge, 1987) 85. See also Hayek, *Law, Legislation and Liberty: The Political Order of Free People* (Routledge and Kegan, London, 1979) 153-176. For more jurisprudential work in this vein, see also Fried, "The Artificial Reason of the Law; or, What Lawyers Know" (1981) 60 *Texas L.Rev.* 35 and Watson *The Evolution of Law* (Johns Hopkins University Press, Baltimore, 1985).

a normative and prescriptive dimension, history and custom tend to be only descriptive. Because tradition has a critical and judgmental character, it is less than the sum total of accumulated decisions and more than the extant practices of the legal. As well as being an attitude to those precedents and how to utilise them in the present process of decision-making, the common law tradition comprises a whole repertoire of techniques for the selection, maintenance, transmission and change of its substantive holdings: it involves an evaluative assessment of what and does not work and what should and should not persist. As Lord Diplock put it, "the common law subsumes a power in judges to adapt its rules to the changing needs of contemporary society – to discard those which have outlived their usefulness, to develop new rules to meet new situations".[35] However, lawyers need not apologise to historians for their poor historical method; they are not trying to be historians, but lawyers. Whereas the historian is interested in understanding the past in its own terms, the lawyer is interested in the past for present purposes. Accordingly, the common law is a tradition that treats its own traditions seriously. By demanding a normative commitment to select and transmit aspects of past practice, the common law decides among and between the different (and often competing) substantive traditions to which the mass of decisions have given rise.

When understood in this way, the common law is more realistically grasped as a tradition-respecting process rather than a past-revering obsession; it is critical tradition that is not averse to change for its own sake, but only change that ignores the past as a matter of course. Moreover, such a posture allows for a more honest and suggestive response to the most pressing challenge that confronts the courts. In a rapidly changing world, the judges must be able to operate the system of precedent so that the need for stability is balanced off against the demand for progress: they must not allow formal certainty to eclipse substantive justice. The success of such an undertaking cannot be judged in technical terms alone, but calls upon the substantive discourse of ideals and ideology. In an important sense, the common law is to be found in the unfolding struggle between the openings of decisional freedom and the closings of precedential constraint. Consequently, in order to ensure that the common law does not grind to a halt and begin to slide into irrelevance and injustice under the weight of its own backward-looking mind-set, the courts have developed a whole series of techniques that allow them to avoid or loosen the binding force of precedent. In a manner of speaking, institutional necessity has been the parent of judicial invention. Some of the more important and acknowledged devices that courts use to circumvent inconvenient or undesirable precedents include: the court that rendered the earlier decision was not a superior court;

---

[35] *Cassell & Co. Ltd. v. Broome* [1972] A.C. 1027 (H.L.) 1127; see also *De Lasala v. De Lasala* [1980] A.C. 546 (P.C.) 557 *per* Lord Diplock. See also Schauer, "Precedent" (1987) 39 *Stan.L.Rev.* 571 and generally Shils, *Tradition* (Faber, London, 1981).

the precedent was given *per incuriam*; the precedent has been subsequently overruled or doubted in other cases; the precedent was based upon a faulty interpretation of earlier cases; the scope of the precedent is unclear; the precedent can be distinguished; social conditions have changed; and the precedent has been criticised by academic commentators (although this may be just wishful thinking by academics).[36]

Nevertheless, the availability of such tradition-cutting techniques threatens to undermine the whole legitimacy of the common law tradition. So powerful are these tools that they are capable of destroying the very tradition which they are designed to protect and enhance. If used without any respect for the legal tradition within which they are supposed to function, they will jeopardise the continued existence of the common law as a tradition of traditionality. Not only will cases and precedents be merely informational rather than influential, but judges will be left to do whatever they think is best in cases before them. Accordingly, the courts and commentators have cultivated an attitude and approach to their usage which is decidedly traditional in orientation and operation. While acknowledging the occurrence and need for change in the substantive law, the pervasive spirit of the common law is that such change will be incremental. The received and prevailing wisdom is that the law advances by evolutionary phases, not by revolutionary moments. The law reports and secondary literature are full of admonitions and sentiments to the effect that "the system is based on precedent, and centres on individual decisions and building up principles by a gradual accretion from case to case".[37] Indeed, in the great bulk of situations and for the greatest part of the time, judges do follow past decisions with little or no reflection on the common law's deeper rationale(s) or its broader structure of fundamental rules; common law decision-making is very much about the routine application of rules and precedents and the belief that this will result in substantive justice in the individual case.

While this is accurate as far as it goes, the problem is that it does not go anywhere near far enough. Leading cases fit only partially, if at all, into this traditional account of the common law. Leading cases are more of a refutation of the incremental hypothesis, not a demonstration of its validity. *Rylands*, *Donoghue* and the like can hardly or reasonably be described as incremental adjustments to the common law body of rules and principles. Again, judges and jurists are left with a stark choice – they can either recognise leading cases as revolutionary moments in the common law's development and revise their

---

[36] See, for example, Cross and Harris, *Precedent in English Law* (4th ed., Clarendon Press, Oxford, 1991); Stone, *Legal System and Lawyers' Reasoning* (Stanford University Press, Stanford, 1964); Dias, *Jurisprudence* (5th ed., Butterworths, London, 1985); Freeman *Lloyd's Introduction to Jurisprudence* (6th ed., Sweet and Maxwell, London, 1994).

[37] Beatson, "Has the Common Law A Future?" [1997] *Camb.L.J.* 291, 295. See also Goff, "The Search for Principle" (1983) 50 *Proc.Brit.Acad.* 169 and Eisenberg, *The Nature of the Common Law* (Harvard University Press, Cambridge, Mass., 1988).

accounts of the common law to accommodate them, with all the subversive consequences that entails, or they can deny that leading cases are revolutionary moments and acknowledge that incremental change encompasses any and every change to the common law, with all its equally subversive consequences. In either case, the result will be both a realisation (no matter how begrudging) that, when it comes to the common law, "anything might go" and an abandon-ment (no matter how reluctant) of the jurisprudential insistence that law and politics are separate. Of course, contemporary jurists have sought to resist this result with all the theoretical means at their disposal. Although their efforts have been spirited and sophisticated, they have failed in this endeavour. In-deed, their attempts to incorporate the genesis and centrality of leading cases into their explanatory frameworks has only managed to support further the claim that "law is politics". If leading cases are the crowning glory of the com-mon law tradition, they are the Achilles heel of its jurisprudential apologists.

4. A PRINCIPLED RESPONSE

It is not so much that contemporary jurisprudential accounts of common law adjudication have abandoned their commitment to the doctrine of precedent, but more that they have relaxed and reworked the nature of law's backward-looking stance. Jurists have recognised that the traditional virtues of precedential authority – it produces certainty, allows reliance, effects equality and encour-ages efficiency – are not be underestimated. They understand that any explana-tion or prescription of what common law judges do or should do in a democratic system of governance must involve a strong attachment to such formal quali-ties. Nevertheless, it is largely recognised that, while the legal past must and should play a central role in the law's present and future development, that resort to the legal past need not be restricted to particular decisions made or a mechanical application of them. Incorporating, but not being restricted to such decisions, the modern perception of common law development emphasises that the most appropriate and respectful use of the legal past is less about a formal and technical enforcement of precedential authorities and more a dynamic and expansive meditation on their underlying rationales and structure. It is accepted that the past matters, but there is considerable disagreement of why and how it matters. Taking as their slogan Holmes' statement that "it is revolting to have no better reason for a rule of law than that it was laid down in the time of Henry IV",[38] modern jurists look as much to the substantive values that animate and integrate the law as to the formal attributes of stare decisis.

---

[38] Holmes, *The Common Law* (Howe, (ed.), Harvard University Press, Cambridge, Mass., 1963) 5. For discussions about the cherished virtues of precedential constraint, see Wasserstrom, *The Judicial Decision. Toward a Theory of Legal Justification* (Stanford University Press, 1961), 56-83; Atiyah and Summers, *Form and Substance in Anglo-American Law* (O.U.P., Oxford, 1987), 116-120; and Schauer, above n.35, 595-602.

Accordingly, common law adjudication is viewed as an exercise in principled justification in which the body of previous legal decisions is treated as an authoritative resource of available arguments, analogies and axioms. Judges are considered to judge best when they distil the principled spirit of the past and rely upon it to develop the law in response to future demands. As Lord Scarman put it in the (semi-)leading case of *McLoughlin v. O'Brian*, "whatever the court decides to do, it starts from a baseline of existing principle and seeks a solution consistent with or analogous to a principle or principles already recognised".[39] From a more theoretical standpoint, the prevailing idea is that it is the task of legal theory and also the responsibility of adjudication to understand the accumulation of legal decisions as fragments of an intelligible, if latent or implicit, plan of social life and to extend law in accordance with the plan so that it becomes less fragmentary and more intelligible. In a dangerously close to boot-strapping argument, the claim is that, although there are recalcitrant areas, the common law is best understood as being the practical expression of connected and abstract principles: the task of the judge is to elucidate those deeper ideals and to extend that structure so as to better render that the common law more practical and coherent. Although there are many advantages to this more sophisticated way of proceeding over an old-style practice of *stare decisis*, the pressing challenge remains the same – how to balance stability and continuity against flexibility and change such that it results in a state of affairs that is neither only a case of stunted development nor a case of "anything might go".

One obvious problem with this neo-formalist approach is that, in elucidating this disciplining structure, jurists (and judges) might be imposing their own personal normative commitments on the law in the name of professional analysis. Indeed, it is telling that the result of applying such a disciplinary method is almost always the same as what the judge or jurist would have done if left to their own legally-untutored devices. However, for our purposes, there is another, more pertinent problem. In adopting such an explanation of the common law's facility for adaptation, what begins its jurisprudential life as a reassuring promise of justifying incremental development runs the risk of quickly and easily turning into a subversive threat of permitting wholesale transformation. In their fragile search for developmental equilibrium between stability and change, defenders of the common law tradition are obliged to tread a precariously thin line between a legitimate practice of unfolding reform and an illegitimate exercise in episodic revolution.[40] In accordance with its self-imposed

---

[39] *McLoughlin v. O'Brian* [1983] A.C. 410 (H.L.) 430 *per* Lord Scarman.

[40] Although I am only concentrating on the common law, this tension is particularly acute in the context of constitutional interpretation and particularly obvious where the constitutional issue is also a major social one; this is the theme of Cox, "Judicial Activism, Constitutional Interpretation and the Problem of Abortion. *Roe v. Wade* (1973) and *A.G. v. X* (1992)" below, 237 and it may also underlie the decision of the U.S. Supreme Court in *Clinton v. Jones* 520 U.S. 681

task, mainstream jurisprudence must be able to show that incremental adaptation is not simply a cover for radical realignment and, as importantly, that the balance between stability and change is neither *ad hoc* nor unpredictable. This is a tall order for any theory and one which the need to explain the emergence and existence of leading cases turns into an almost impossible one.

Undaunted by the enormity of this task, legal scholars have not been slow to accept the challenge. The most prominent and popular of these has been Ronald Dworkin. As the thrust and themes of his ideas are too well-known to warrant extensive elaboration, I will concentrate on only those claims and proposals which are more directly relevant to the explanation of leading cases. Although he is committed to the central notion that law and justice are intimately connected, Dworkin insists that it is incumbent upon judges to treat the legal past "as important for its own sake"[41] because "law as integrity supposes that people are entitled to a coherent and principled extension of past political decisions even when judges profoundly disagree about what is means".[42] Indeed, Dworkin's Hercules, with his "superhuman intellectual power and patience",[43] is lauded much less for his ability to wreak changes in the law's order than his godly capacity to capture the whole tradition of the law in its fullest and most illuminating sense. As very model of the exemplary common law judge, his political obligation is to apply the law dutifully, deferentially, and reliably to present cases. In this way, Dworkin advances an understanding of adjudication as a political practice that works the space between law's institutional past and its future possibilities. For Dworkin, therefore, any interpretation of the legal materials must be able to demonstrate some plausible connection to society's legal history and is, in that important sense, continuous with that past. While the better interpretation is not necessarily the one that accounts for the most decisions, the settled body of legal norms and justifications is claimed to be the motor force of principled adjudication: "law's attitude . . . aims, in the interpretative spirit, to lay principle over practice to show the best route to a better future, keeping the right faith with the past".[44]

In short, Dworkin's interpretative ideal of judicial integrity seeks to combine both backward-looking and forward-looking elements by insisting that judges view what they do as "an unfolding political narrative" which "begins in the present and pursues the past only so far as and in the way . . . that present practice can be organised by and justified in principles sufficiently attractive to

---

(1997) discussed in O'Connor, "Unbalancing the Separation of Powers. *Clinton v. Jones*" below, 507.
[41] Dworkin, *Law's Empire* (Harvard University Press, Cambridge, Mass., 1996) 132 [hereafter Dworkin].
[42] *ibid.*, 134.
[43] *ibid.*, 239.
[44] *ibid.*, 413.

provide an honourable future".[45] Along with the idea of legal continuity, Dworkin maintains that the judges should treat the law as if it were a seamless web, providing complete and determinate guidance on all legal disputes; there is no need or justification to leave the law behind and engage in unconstrained choice. Accordingly, Hercules is most certainly no revolutionary figure and is trusted to uphold the wisdom of the past, albeit in imaginative and innovative ways:

> convictions about fit will provide a rough threshold requirements that an interpretation of some part of the law must meet it is to be eligible as all. . . . That threshold will eliminate interpretations that some judges would otherwise prefer, so the brute facts of legal history will in this way limit the role any judges' personal convictions of justice can play in his decisions. Different judges will set this threshold differently. But anyone who accepts law as integrity must accept that the actual political history of his community will sometimes check his other political convictions in his overall interpretative judgment. If he does not, . . . he is acting from bad faith or self-deception".[46]

Despite the ingenuity of his theory and its robust defence, Dworkin is no better able to provide a convincing account of leading cases than his less theoretically-inclined academic colleagues or his more practically-oriented judicial peers. Indeed, his efforts to do so cause more problems for his general account of common law adjudication than they solve. Dworkin wants it both ways. He wants to demonstrate that the common law is both open and closed: it is open in that the judges are able to develop the law in new and unexpected ways and, at the same time, it is closed in that judges cannot ignore "the brute facts of legal history"[47] in favour of their own political convictions. The fact is that the price of having one is the cost of having the other. This is particularly so in regards to leading cases. If his claims about fidelity to the legal past mean that any constructive account of the law must accommodate leading cases, then his theory is on the mark as an account of adjudication as a partially closed rather than entirely open practice. However, when such a constraining requirement is taken seriously, the birth and acknowledgement of future leading cases – those which represent a radical departure from extant principles, not their incremental development – seems well-nigh impossible. On such an account, leading cases negate rather than exemplify the quintessential character of valid adjudi-

---

[45]Dworkin, 227-228.
[46]*ibid.*, 255. Although I am only concentrating on the common law, Dworkin's theory makes no substantial distinction between how judges deal with this and statutory or constitutional law.
[47]*ibid.*

cation. Such a position is surely a fatal strike against any account that claims, as Dworkin's does, to be a descriptively accurate. However, if the birth and acknowledgement of hard cases are part and parcel of what it means to keep faith with the past, then the law is an entirely open rather than partly closed practice; the common law is a complex of principles that justifies radically different and contradictory readings. As Dworkin himself concedes, how the dimensions of backward-pulling fit and forward-pushing substance relate to each other is "in the last analysis all responsive to [judges'] political judgment".[48] While this is an acceptable conclusion for someone, like me, that maintains that "anything might go", it is a curious and ultimately dissatisfying confession for any theorist devoted to refuting the critical claim that "law is politics".

Nevertheless, aware that his emphasis on fidelity with the past might back him into some politically-unattractive corners, Dworkin tries to provide Hercules and lesser judicial mortals with an escape route. He is rightly concerned with the plight of liberal judges in Nazi Germany or apartheid South Africa. Consequently, he argues that, in exceptional and unusual circumstances, judges are entitled to forgo compliance with even the minimal demands of formal fit: "if a judge's own sense of justice condemned [the grounds of law] as deeply immoral . . ., he would have to consider whether he should actually enforce it . . ., or whether he should lie and say that this was not the law after all, or whether he should resign".[49] While this might seem to extricate Hercules from some tight spots, it actually has him jumping between the frying pan and the fire. On the one hand, if such a radical manoeuvre is only justified in the circumstances of such grotesque societies as Nazi Germany or apartheid South Africa, it is difficult to envision how leading cases meet that standard. Although *Donoghue* might have dealt with instances of consumer injustice that were by no means insignificant, it is a considerable stretch to place such injustice on the same level as what went on in those blighted societies. That being the case, Dworkin's "deeply immoral" exception will have problems incorporating and accounting for leading cases. On the other hand, if the meaning of "deeply immoral" is to be determined by "a judge's own sense justice", the opportunities to finesse the minimal backward-connecting demands of formal fit will be as broad or as narrow as the range of judges' political commitments. Accordingly, provided that judges do so on the basis of sincerely-held beliefs, they are free to "lie", "resign", or "refuse to enforce the law".[50] In short, judges need only keep faith with the past insofar as it accords with their own sense of justice. Or, as Lord

---

[48] *ibid.*, 257.
[49] *ibid.*, 219.
[50] On such refusal, consider, for example, the approach of Kennedy C.J. dissenting, in *State (Ryan) v. Lennon* [1935] I.R. 170 (H.C. and S.C.) 204-205, 209, discussed in Hogan, above n.14, esp. at section 6.

Pearce put it rather more subtly (but no less revealingly) in *Hedley Byrne*, "how wide the sphere of the duty of care in negligence is to be laid depends ultimately upon the courts' assessment of the demands of society for protection from the carelessness of others".[51]

Again, this is a profoundly disturbing conclusion for a mainstream jurist, like Dworkin, who is devoted to justifying the self-sustaining legitimacy and moral force of the judicial enterprise. In particular, Dworkin seems unable to explain leading cases either as part of his general incrementalist account or as an instance of a radical exception to it. Put more positively, Dworkin is only able to explain the genesis of leading cases as the exceptions that prove the rule that "anything might go". This, of course, is the very antithesis of his controlling thesis that law and adjudication are constrained and constraining practices. Indeed, the history of the common law is redolent with judicial pronouncements that support the critical claim that the touchstone of good judging is the strength and sincerity of judge's moral and political beliefs, not the moral force of the extant law or particular judges' fidelity to it. Leading cases give credence to Lord Macmillan's adoption of the maxim in *Donoghue* that "any proposition the result of which would be to show that the common law of England is wholly unreasonable and unjust cannot be part of the common law of England".[52] This is a powerful and appealing notion, but one that eludes the grasp of Dworkin's law-as-integrity and, therefore, undermines its ambition to be a compelling account of the common law.

In the next section, I turn to an account of the common law that is better able to understand and incorporate the rise and role of leading cases in its development. I want to push through on Dworkin's insight that law is an interpretative enterprise in which the task of judges and lawyers is to engage constructively with the past in order to make a better future for society. Although Dworkin does much good work in challenging the static and conservative approach of much legal theory and lawyering, he allows his political instincts to check his intellectual commitments: "anyone who accepts law as integrity must accept that the actual political history of his community will sometimes check his other political convictions in his overall interpretative judgment".[53] Rather than treat leading cases as anomalous occurrences that require special explanations, I will place the incidence, importance and influence of leading cases at the heart of my jurisprudential project. After taking a step back to explore a different and more attractive understanding of tradition and traditionality, I apply such an approach to an appreciation of the common law generally.

---

[51] [1964] A.C. 467, 536.
[52] Above, n.29.
[53] Dworkin, 255.

5. TRANSFORMING TRADITION

We all live in the past. There is no escaping it: the past propels us forward into the future at the same time that it holds us back. Nevertheless, the belief that, if there is to be genuine progress and emancipation, there must be a complete break from that past and that all earlier ideas are corrupted is as paralysing as it is unrealisable; it diverts attention away from the available possibilities for change and transformation that always already exist and cannot be expunged by even the most exhaustive or authoritative analysis. Karl Marx's insistence that "the tradition of all the dead generations weighs like a nightmare on the brains of the living"[54] must be taken seriously. Insofar as the deadening force of tradition can cast a pall over living efforts to improve the future, it is important to remember the danger that the past poses to any progressive initiatives. However, in direct contrast to the tradition-revering approach of Edmund Burke, Marx's anti-traditionalist warning that revolutionary activity "cannot draw its poetry from the past, [but] must let the dead bury their dead"[55] is both impossible and unnecessary. It is impossible in that there is no language or materials from which to imagine a better future that are not passed on to us from the past; there is no way to step outside of ourselves to some elusive site or state of mind that is untouched by the past. However, fortunately, it is unnecessary to attempt such a prodigious feat because the past is neither so dead nor so determined as to occlude its poetic revitalisation in aid of future imaginings; there is no shortage of opportunities for transformative creativity. As such, there is no need to embrace either the traditionalist or the anti-traditionalist stance: the celebration of tradition for its own sake or its condemnation for any other sake is a false dichotomy. On a more critical and suggestive account, tradition and transformation do not stand opposed, but each feeds and feeds off the other.

The fact that we have no choice other than to follow and therefore live, at least in part, in the past says nothing about what it is in the past that we must follow or respect. To uphold a tradition does not mean that it has to done in an uncreative or uncritical way; there is choice and, therefore, there are always politics in play. As Jacques Derrida puts it, "that we *are* heirs does not mean that we *have* or that we *receive* this or that, some inheritance that enriches us one day with this or that, but that the *being* of what we are *is* first of all inheritance, whether we like it or know it or not".[56] Inheritance is an undertaking that those in the present are obliged to perform, but there is no one or only way to fulfil that definitive responsibility. What is given about any tradition is al-

---

[54] Marx, *The Eighteenth Brumaire of Louis Bonaparte* (International Publishers, New York, 1963) 13

[55] *ibid.*, 16.

[56] Derrida, *Spectres of Marx: The State of the Debt, The Work of Mourning, and the New International* (Kamuf, (trans.), Routledge, New York, 1994) 54. See also Shils, above n. 35, 44: "The givenness of a tradition is more problematic than it looks".

ways open to appropriation and contestation; resort to the past is, therefore, always and unavoidably political. There is no one monolithic and unified account of the past that stands in for history or that can claim to be the past's ineffable bruteness. Any attempt to justify a master-narrative of the past (from a materialist right, a socialist left or a liberal centre) is destined to fail; it will be either so abstract as to ignore the contingent and nuanced facts or so detailed as to be little more than a description of those facts. Although the appeal to tradition is only meaningful if that tradition is sufficiently determinate and discrete, history shows that traditions are notoriously imprecise and that they are infuriatingly difficult to pin down. Like anything and everything else, traditions are not so much discovered as constructed in the act of following them. Moreover, because so much of the debate around tradition is less about its heterogeneity and more about the features that are seen to hold it together and which define its homogeneity, the ideas of tradition and transformation have come to be seen as antithetical. However, in most of life (and law), "breaking with tradition" is as traditional as it gets.

In the conventional understanding of tradition, it is held out as a dated accumulation of commitments, customs and practices that are accepted with little room for critical examination or reformulation. On a more critical reading, tradition is not a thing of the past, but something that is vital; people constantly participate and reconstruct as they rely upon it. Indeed, traditions survive by adaptation and change. If they do not change, they become ossified and die. As such, traditions are alive, organic and part of the present; they are not simply the flotsam and jetsam of the forward-moving ship of history as it steams into the future. Moreover, because traditions are understood as organic and social in that they are transmitted from one generation to another, change is at the dynamic heart of a genuine practice of tradition. As participants rely upon the tradition, they are also contributing to and transforming that tradition: "tradition is not simply at a permanent pre-condition; rather, we produce it ourselves inasmuch as we understand, participate in the evolution of tradition, and hence further determine it ourselves".[57] Traditions are not fixed nor bounded and, in being passed on and assumed by individuals, they are constantly re-worked and re-made (as are the individuals who engage with them). As such, the interpretation and application of a tradition is also an act of amending that tradition. This means that tradition is not simply a matter of identifying a fixed continuity between the past and present, but also involves certain rearrangements, ruptures and reversals. This act of reconstruction is both deconstructive and constructive. Although there is always the risk of confirming that which is being deconstructed, the most respectful reaffirmation of the past's traditions is realised in constantly placing them under scrutiny and transforming their

---

[57] Gadamer, *Truth and Method* (Weinsheimer & Marshall, (eds.), 2nd ed., Crossroad, New York, 1989) 293.

substance as their spirit is observed.

This posture of *respectful transformation* is at the heart of great moments in most arenas of human endeavour. In both the arts and sciences, it is not the person who diligently and expertly upholds conventional standards and expectations that will be recognised as great, but those who transform those standard and expectations as they exceed them. The hallmark of truly great artists or scientists is not simply their ability to beat every one at their own game: it is the capacity to envision and dictate a different game to be played. Such persons, like Pablo Picasso, James Joyce, Albert Einstein and Pele, have technical skills in abundance, but they also possess a vision and capacity to reveal possibilities that the rest of their community have not even seen or thought possible. While those rare moments of transformation reject certain traditions and approaches, they operate within a broader tradition of creativity and originality that they reinforce and affirm in their revolutionary contributions. Indeed, such creative geniuses are exemplars of this idea that traditions are upheld by breaking them; it is not the substantive traditions themselves, but the traditionality of change and innovation, that they continue. Even the conservative T.S. Eliot, in his celebration of literary tradition, recognised that, when assessing any individual's contribution, "novelty is better than repetition".[58] Furthermore, the celebrated virtues of traditional education, at least in the university setting, are not restricted to the inculcation of received bodies of knowledge and ideas. While such learning comprises a significant part of the educational process, even traditionalists embrace the notion that such teaching ought to take place within a more critical context in which all knowledge and ideas are exposed to constant scrutiny, criticism and revision. As such, universities adhere to a tradition that demands both conservation and contestation of the past in a transformative tradition.

Once tradition is given such a positive and progressive spin, it becomes much easier and less strained to place leading cases at the heart of the common law tradition. Contrary to more conventional views that emphasise stable continuity and incremental change, placing leading cases at the centre of the jurisprudential inquiry offers both a more convincing description of the common law's development and also a more compelling prescriptive recommendation for future adjudication. Despite the insistence and blindness of its most eminent practitioners and protagonists, the common law is neither firmly grounded, objectively given, incrementally developed nor politically neutral. As evidenced by the emergence and existence of leading cases, the common law is loosely assembled, creatively constructed, unpredictably changeable and ideologically

---

[58] Eliot, "Tradition and the Individual Talent" in *The Sacred Wood: Essays on Poetry and Criticism* (Methuen, London, 1920), 132. In science, the importance of the creative and revolutionary dimensions of the scientific dimensions of the scientific tradition are well-understood. See Kuhn, *The Structure of Scientific Revolutions* (3rd ed., University of Chicago Press, Chicago, 1996). See also Shils, above n.35, 179-184.

loaded. The progress of the common law is marked less by the evolutionary unfolding of an inherent logic and characterised more by its contingent responsiveness to historical circumstances. As such, innovation, not preservation is the quality that most represents the tradition of the common law. Indeed, leading cases change the tradition not only by adding to it, but also by changing common understandings about what the past was and how it can be seen in a new light. Leading cases reinforce the insight that "breaking with tradition" is not only a part of the common law's tradition, but a defining feature of it. They demonstrate that it is not only possible to continue tradition by adapting it, but that such a judicial attitude and approach is in the very best traditions of the common law. Adjudication is treated as a responsibility of both derivation and deviation. By holding up the past to a better image of itself, judges can make changes in the name and furtherance of that image. Such inventiveness is more a reworking of law's substantive traditions in the name and under the tutelage of a more encompassing tradition of creativity and transformation than an abandonment of tradition completely.

Importantly, most of the great innovators of law did not see themselves as "breaking with tradition", they believed that they acted within a continuing larger and more important tradition. Like great artists and scientists, great judges work with a creative tradition and, in so doing, revise the substantive traditions with which they continue to engage. Treading a thin and, at times, non-existent line between heresy and heritage, they occupy a role that is part apostle and part apostate in which they recognise that another present way of understanding the past is to imagine a better future. They accept that the legal past is not a foundation on which to build, but a resource-site from which to draw: past legal decisions combine to form a valuable institutional almanac of experimental strategies whose relevance and results are to be tested and re-tested in the service of making society a better place to live. While good judges are lauded for their technical abilities in parsing cases and rooting out inconsistencies, great judges are celebrated for their vision and inventiveness. Those judges that take most seriously the experimental imperative are those that flaunt conventional standards in the process of re-formulating them; their judgments are the exceptions that prove the rule. Indeed, some of the great judges of the common law tradition, like *Donoghue*'s Lord Atkin and *Hedley Byrne's* Lord Reid, are precisely those who refuse to be hampered by customary habits of judicial mind. Although they often fail or refuse to accept the force and measure of their own behaviour, such judges confound the idea that the judicial resort to tradition can be less a timid and conservative act and more a progressive and bold intervention. Rather than think of themselves as only actors in another's story, they become "joyful poets of the story that continues to originate what they cannot finish".[59]

---

[59]Carse, *Finite and Infinite Games: A Vision of Life as Play and Responsibility* (Free Press, New

In this way of thinking, all decisions are political in that even allegedly rigid deferences to tradition are more realistically characterised as normative approval of the tradition because it jibes with the present critical commitment of the judge. Moreover, under my depiction of the common law tradition, not only is there no compelling justification why judges should reign in their own critical judgments in supposed deference to those implicit in law's substantive traditions, but there is a cogent reason why they should give full and open expression to them: judges respect the common law tradition best when they scrutinise, interrogate, challenge and make it conform with justice. This idea is perfectly captured by Derrida when he states that, "for a decision to be just and responsible, it must, in its proper moment if there is one, be both regulated and without regulation: it must conserve the law and destroy it or suspend it enough to reinvent it in each case, rejustifying it, at least reinvent it in the reaffirmation and the new and free confirmation of it principles".[60] Accordingly, the style of judging that captures most faithfully the cherished traditions of the common law is one that involves both a constant reinterpretation of past decisions and a perpetual openness to future reinterpretation. If it is to be given its due, each new case is entitled to more than an unthinking reliance on existing doctrine or rules: it is requires the judge to make a fresh judgement that actively re-appraises as it re-affirms the traditions of legal doctrine. Indeed, contrary to conventional wisdom, it is the relentless critic who most closely grasps and continues the common law tradition than those who insist on a timid acceptance of what has already been decided. To treat the law as static or to adopt an unquestioning posture toward it is to betray, not uphold the common law tradition.

One objection to focussing on leading cases might be that leading cases, by their nature and status, are more the exception than the rule and, as the proverbial wisdom has it, prove the rule (*i.e.*, the common law is by and large a disciplined process that is exemplified by the routine and uncreative application of existing law). While the claim is true insofar as much adjudication is mundane and prosaic, such a characterisation cannot carry the jurisprudential day. There is never a situation in which judges do not have the opportunity or responsibility to be creative; whether they choose to utilise that chance is a different matter. Once it is conceded, as it must be, that leading cases are a valid feature and

---

York, 1986) 149. See also Balkin, "Tradition, Betrayal, and the Politics of Deconstruction" (1990) 11 *Cardozo L.Rev.* 1612. It would be remiss of me not to acknowledge that the recently-deceased Lord Denning was the pre-eminent great judge of his generation and the boldest of "bold spirits". See text with n. 5 above; for discussion of two of his more successful experiments, see Breen, "Dusting Down Equity's Armour. *High Trees* (1947) in Perspective" below, 164 and Capper, "The *Mareva* Injunction – From Birth to Adulthood. *Mareva Compania Naviera S.A. v. International Bulkcarriers S.A.* (1975)" below, 255. Nevertheless, as his career so amply demonstrates, there is no necessary or consistent relationship between boldness and progressiveness.

[60] Derrida, "Force of Law: The 'Mystical Foundation of Authority'" (1990) 11 *Cardozo L.Rev.* 919, 962.

product of the common law process, the quotidian operation of the adjudicative function has to be viewed in a more expansive way. When judges appear to be following precedent and to be framing their judgments in terms of legal authority, it is more the case that they are approving the substantive desirability of the outcome that arises from a reasonably traditional reliance on existing case-law; it is the end-result, not the reasoning-means, that is controlling. The spectre of leading cases – the possibility that judges can reject traditional approaches, set off in new directions, and still be acting in an appropriately legitimate manner – suggests that, because there is always the choice to do something else, judges must opt for a precedent-directed decision. As it is the substantive values rather than the formal logic of the law that govern, the judges in routine instances are choosing not to be radical or transformative. Accordingly, by giving priority to institutional stability over individualised justice or wholesale reform, the courts are engaging in a very political exercise: conservatism is no less ideological than progressivism.[61]

6. IN PRAISE OF LEADING CASES

In this essay, I have sought to defend the claim that any account of the common law's development must put leading cases at its explanatory heart and that, when this is done, it is hard to resist the conclusion that the common law tradition is more an open and creative one in which "anything might go" than a bounded and cautious one. The development of the common law is better explained as contingent responsiveness to historical circumstances rather than characterised as the evolutionary unfolding of an inherent logic. By different measures at different times, the development of law is a mix of the *logical* — in the sense of attempted compliance with law's own generated (and indeterminate) rationality — and the *expedient* — in the sense of responsiveness to society's own political (and indeterminate) demands. This idea of the interplay of the logical and the expedient fits nicely with the more sophisticated and sound judicial accounts of the common law's development. For instance, while judges are fond of stating that "the common law is tolerant of much illogicality, especially on the surface; but no system of law can be workable if it has not got logic at the root of it"[62] they are also adamant that "it will be an advantage to

---

[61] Two important riders need to be offered to the claim that law and adjudication are political in the sense that "anything might go". One is that there is no necessary connection between being transformative and being progressive. The other is that asserting that the common law's development is better explained as contingent responsiveness to historical circumstances rather than as an evolutionary unfolding of an inherent logic is very different to the claim that law conforms with some external deep-logic, like Marxism. See Hutchinson, above, n. 5, 325-330, 245-250.

[62] *Hedley Byrne v. Heller* [1964] A.C. 467, 516 *per* Lord Devlin. Hence, perhaps, the strength of

make it clear that the law in this matter, as in most others, is in accordance with sound common sense".[63]

However, there should be no mistake that, when the logical push comes to the expedient shove, it is the political that will eclipse the doctrinal. As the leading cases attest, the bottom-line is that, as *Hedley Byrne's* Lord Pearce put it, the force and reach of legal principle "depends ultimately upon the courts' assessment of the demands of society"[64] and that, as *Donoghue's* Lord Macmillan put it, "any proposition the result of which would be to show that the common law of England is wholly unreasonable and unjust cannot be part of the common law of England".[65] Of course, what passes as substantive justice will not be to everyone's liking, but this only serves to underline the contested and political nature of common law adjudication. Moreover, there is no better evidence for that conclusion than the career of leading cases. The courts will follow doctrinal logic and formal authority only so far and for so long; it is political expediency and substantive justice that will win the day. And that includes the fall as well as the rise of leading cases. As is shown by the fate of *Anns* or *Sinclair v. Brougham*, a leading case is only leading for so long as historical circumstances and political currents support its continued prominence. Once the political winds change, the leading case will lose its hallowed status and become one more precedent on the legal scrapheap. Although *Donoghue* seems unassailable in its greatness, the day will come when the general consensus around carelessness as the ruling principle in tort erodes and another commitment (*e.g.* strict liability or intentional harm) wins the day. Legal greatness is as eternal or as ephemeral as the political will that sustains it.

The countless efforts by judges and jurists to resist this claim do as much to confirm the political quality of law and adjudication as to deny it. Indeed, one of few constants in law and adjudication is that change and stability are maintained through constant acts of revision: transformation is the life-blood of the common law's vibrant tradition. Faced with this situation, academic commentators and judicial participants are given a Hobson's choice. On the one hand, they can recognise leading cases as routine illustrations of how the common law develops incrementally and logically; this is a stance that most reject because, amongst other things, it would make it extremely difficult to explain why leading cases were in any way leading. On the other hand, they can concede that leading cases are radical instances of how the law develops by breaking with its past; this is a stance that most reject because, amongst other things, it confounds the idea that the common law develops incrementally and logically. Accordingly, any acclamation of leading cases is also a celebration of the

---

the pull of "inexorable logic" on the judicial mind; for an example in this collection, see Smith, "The Triumph of 'Inexorable Logic'. *D.P.P. v. Morgan* (1976)" below, 294.

[63] *Donoghue v. Stevenson* [1932] A.C. 562, 579 *per* Lord Atkin.

[64] *Hedley Byrne v. Heller* [1964] A.C. 467, 536 *per* Lord Pearce.

[65] Above, n.29.

critical insight that "law is politics". To be in praise of leading cases is a tribute to the force of the observation that "continuity with the past is only a necessity, not a duty".[66] And, judging from the history of its development through leading cases, the common law has and continues to impose a duty on its personnel to respect the past best by revolutionising it in regular acts of continuing transformation.

---

[66] Above, n.1.

THE CASE THAT FELL TO EARTH
Sinclair v. Brougham (1914)

EOIN O'DELL*

Whom the Mad would destroy, they first make Gods.[1]

1. INTRODUCTION. THE LOVE OF MONEY IS THE ROOT OF ALL EVIL?[2]

Some are born great, some achieve greatness, and some have greatness thrust upon them.[3] As with people, so with cases. *Sinclair v. Brougham*[4] was probably born to greatness; something of a *cause célèbre* of its time,[5] it reached a division of the House of Lords of exceptional ability, who produced forthright speeches of elegance and style, characterised by legal precision tempered with an equitable eye to a just outcome. In many ways, therefore, it was a virtuoso performance which deserved its plaudits and the pre-eminence which it enjoyed for more than eighty years.[6]

---

*Barrister; Lecturer in Law, Trinity College, Dublin.

[1] Reworking the more traditional rendering, this is Bernard Levin, of Mao Zedong, *The Times*, September 21, 1987.

[2] 1 Timothy 6.10.

[3] Shakespeare, *Twelfth Night* II:5.

[4] [1914] A.C. 398; [1914-1915] All E.R. Rep. 622 (H.L.); see Lord Wright of Durley, *"Sinclair v. Brougham"* in *Legal Essays and Addresses* (C.U.P., Cambridge, 1939) 1 [hereafter Wright, *Sinclair*; reprinting (1938) 6 *C.L.J.* 305]; Stoljar, "Re-Examining *Sinclair v. Brougham*" (1959) 22 *M.L.R.* 21 [hereafter Stoljar].

[5] There were full reports of the arguments and speeches in *The Times* (see *The Times*, December 9, 10, 11, 13 and 16, 1913 and February 13, 1914). See also the notes (brief and unsigned in the contemporary style) at (1914) 48 *I.L.T.* 294; (1914) 30 *L.Q.R.* 263 and 385.

[6] For example, Stevens has written that it was part of a "clear" trend in private law adjudication in the House of Lords at the time in which: "[a]fter a shaky beginning, the House of Lords moved into a golden period in private law" (Stevens, *Law and Politics. The House of Lords as a Judicial Body, 1800-1976* (Wildenfeld and Nicolson, London, 1979) 20. Again, Lord Wright wrote that it "has been generally regarded as an authority of first-rate importance" (Wright, *Sinclair*, 1); for Hanbury, it was "the great case of *Sinclair v. Brougham*" (Hanbury, "The Recovery of Money" in *Essays in Equity* (Clarendon Press, Oxford, 1934) 1 [hereafter Hanbury; reprinting (1924) 40 *L.Q.R.* 31] 12); and Stoljar wrote that *"Sinclair v. Brougham* has always, and rightly, been thought as of fundamental importance" (Stoljar, 21). In Ireland, Barton J. was of a similar opinion: the "celebrated" speeches are "the most remarkable illustration . . . of the meticulous care with which that House approaches the task of reconciling what is called 'abstract justice' with the strict rule of law" *In re Cummins: Barton v. Bank of Ireland* [1939] I.R. 60 (H.C.) 71.

History teaches us that, however they have achieved greatness, the mighty can fall, and often do, for reasons as Shakespearean as hubris or as mundane as the vagaries of fashion. Again, as with people, so with cases. *Sinclair v. Brougham*, from its great height, had far to fall, and, over the last decade or so, it has fallen far. From a perspective which sees the decline as merited, the influence of the case, though profound, was at best coquettish, at worst malign. On this view, then, it has been not so much a leading case as a misleading[7] or even a bad one. Bad cases, Dworkin says, have no staying power; they don't fit, and the law – eventually – works itself pure.[8] Even if there are problems with this analysis,[9] discussed in this volume by Allen Hutchinson,[10] nevertheless, in many ways it is an excellent description of the rise and fall of *Sinclair v. Brougham*. Decided in 1914, early in the twentieth century but displaying a distinctly nineteenth century cast of mind, its comeuppance eventually arrived in the shape of the decision of the House of Lords in the *Westdeutsche*,[11] decided in 1996, late in the twentieth century but heralding for the twenty-first a fresh start and a firmer footing for the law.[12]

There are many similarities between the England of Queen Victoria and that of Margaret Thatcher. In Victorian England, what we now call classical economics were then newly in vogue and application; Thatcher's England saw the apotheosis of neo-classical economics. As a consequence, both periods saw the growth of financial markets and investment products, sophisticated by contemporary standards: investing in a building society in the former era was as sophisticated a financial transaction as investing in interest rate swaps would be in the latter.[13] Unsurprisingly, the similarity of economic background gave rise to similarity of economic legal problems: in each case, some of these flagship modes of investment would founder on the rock of legal incapacity: in

---

[7] With apologies to A.P. Herbert, *Uncommon Law. Being Sixty Six Misleading Cases* (Methnen, London, 1935; reissued, 1969, 1977).

[8] Dworkin, *Taking Rights Seriously* (Duckworth, 1977) chapter 4; *Laws Empire* (Fontana, 1986); *A Matter of Principle* (O.U.P., 1986) chapter 6.

[9] See, *e.g.*, Cohen, (ed.), *Ronald Dworkin and Contemporary Jurisprudence* (Duckworth, 1984); for a more sympathetic treatment, see Guest, *Ronald Dworkin* (2nd ed., Edinburgh U.R., 1997).

[10] Hutchinson, "The Importance of Leading Cases. A Critical Analysis" above, 7. See also Hutchinson, "The Last Emperor?" in Hunt, (ed.), *Reading Dworking Critically* (Berg, N.Y. and Oxford, 1992) 45.

[11] *Westdeutsche Landesbank Girozentrale v. Islington L.B.C.* [1996] A.C. 669; [1996] 2 All E.R. 961 (H.L.).

[12] It might be said that, in this area of the law at least, there has been, as in history, a short twentieth century; see Hobsbawm, *The Age of Extremes. The Short Twentieth Century 1914-1991* (Abacus, London, 1995) 5-11.

[13] "The impetus leading to the formation of these societies was not so much the desire of the 'industrious class' to obtain funds by 'periodical subscriptions' (as stated in the preamble of the Building Societies Act, 1836), but the desire on the part of capitalists to invest at a higher rate of interest than the usury laws then allowed". Stoljar, 21-22, n.5 referring to Lord Cranworth L.C. in *Fleming v. Self* (1854) 3 De G.M.&G. 997; 43 E.R. 390.

Sinclair v. Brougham, a building society operated as an *ultra vires* bank; in *Westdeutsche*, a local authority had entered into *ultra vires* interest rate swaps.

Sinclair v. Brougham and *Westdeutsche* have it in common, therefore, that they arise out of, and seek solutions for, sophisticated financial transactions which went wrong. Operating successfully, such sophisticated financial instruments can generate untold wealth; George Soros famously made a fortune on the European currency markets at a time of great volatility in 1992.[14] When things go wrong, there is great scope for financial destruction; Nick Leeson famously lost a fortune on the Far Eastern derivatives markets and bankrupted Barings Bank in the process in 1995.[15] There are many who would see in these cautionary tales some support for the biblical injunction[16] that the love of money is the root of all evil. Unlike Leeson and Barings, however, the transactions underlying *Sinclair v. Brougham* and *Westdeutsche* went wrong, not because of financial incompetence, but because of the legal incapacity of a major player in each transaction. The problem was of the law's making, and, on this view, it was incumbent upon the law to find an appropriate solution. *Sinclair v. Brougham* was its first attempt, denying a legal and personal remedy to the depositors in the *ultra vires* bank, but giving them a partial equitable propri-etary one. In truth, this was not a particularly good solution; indeed, in some quarters, it came to be demonised as the root – if not of all evil – then at least of much legal error. *Westdeutsche*, on the other hand, seems to have made a much better fist of things, affording a legal and personal remedy to the local authority but denying an equitable proprietary one, and in the process correcting many of the errors perpetuated by *Sinclair v. Brougham* though not without arousing controversies in its turn.

The controversies of *Sinclair v. Brougham* are the theme of this paper, and the approach is purely formal:[17] to demonstrate the decline of a once-great case by considering the course of the litigation in the case (section 2) the un-

---

[14]Betting against sterling, he made US$1billion when the pound collapsed on September 16, 1992. See, *e.g.*, "Turning Dollars Into Change" *Time Magazine*, September 1, 1997.

[15]Trading derivatives on the Singapore International Monetary Exchange, Nick Leeson lost more than US$1billion of Barings' money. See, *e.g.*, "Going for Broke" Cover Story, *Time Magazine*, March 13, 1995. Less than three months earlier, Orange County, California, having suffered a US$1.5 billion loss in a US$20 billion derivatives investment pool, had filed for bankruptcy protection in the largest municipal collapse in U.S. history. See, *e.g.*, "The California Wipe-out" *Time Magazine*, December 19, 1994.

[16]On the legal fate of another, more famous, "biblical injunction [that] you should love your neighbour" ([1932] A.C. 562, 580 *per* Lord Atkin) see Hedley "*M'Alister (or Donoghue) (Pauper) v. Stevenson* (1932)" below, 64.

[17]Though, I hope, not formalist. Although I am more convinced by the theories which have re-placed it than by those embodied in the case itself, the decline of *Sinclair v. Brougham*, like its original rise, was by no means inevitable.

[18]Though see, generally, Birks and Rose, (eds.), *Lessons of the Swaps Litigation* (Mansfield/ L.L.P., London, 2000).

successful personal claim (section 3) and the successful proprietary one (section 4), and assessing the greatness to which the case was born but from which it has been decisively evicted (section 5), all the while considering the corrective impact of the *Westdeutsche* case but leaving for another day (and perhaps for the leading cases of the twenty-first century[18]) the resolution of many of the replacement *Westdeutsche* controversies.

2. THE *SINCLAIR V. BROUGHAM* LITIGATION. DIARY OF A MADMAN?[19]

It all began innocuously enough with the formation, in 1851, of a building society, the Birkbeck Permanent Benefit Building Society. As its business expanded, it increased its deposits and began also to operate what soon became "an extensive banking business".[20] Hence, from 1871, it began to call itself the Birkbeck Bank, and by 1910 the bank was "much the larger part of the enterprise".[21] However, for a building society to carry on the business of a bank was contrary to the provisions of the Building Societies Act, 1836, and its borrowing from its depositors was therefore *ultra vires*.[22] That became apparent in 1911 when the Society was wound up.[23] The outside creditors,[24] and those shareholders whose shares were to have matured, were paid off. What remained was enough to pay either the permanent shareholders or the depositors, but not both; and the liquidator sought directions.

The depositors argued that their deposits were money had and received by the society to their use or represented money which they had always owned and so had never properly formed part of the society's assets and could be traced into the hands of the society's liquidator; the intended effect of these arguments was to constitute the depositors as creditors who would then be paid off ahead of the shareholders. On the other hand, the shareholders argued that the deposits were *ultra vires* and invalid and could therefore give rise to no

---

[19]With apologies to Gogol, *Diary of a Madman* (Wilks (trans.), Penguin, 1972) and de Maupassant, *The Diary of a Madman, and Other Tales of Horror* (Kellett, (trans.), Pan Books, 1976).

[20][1914] A.C. 398, 439; [1914-1915] All E.R. Rep. 622, 641 *per* Lord Parker.

[21][1914] A.C. 398, 411; [1914-1915] All E.R. Rep. 622, 627 *per* Viscount Haldane LC.

[22][1914] A.C. 398, 411; [1914-1915] All E.R. Rep. 622, 627 *per* Viscount Haldane LC; [1914] A.C. 398, 418; [1914-1915] All E.R. Rep. 622, 636 *per* Lord Dunedin; [1914] A.C. 398, 439; [1914-1915] All E.R. Rep. 622, 641 *per* Lord Parker; [1914] A.C. 398, 451; [1914-1915] All E.R. Rep. 622, 648 *per* Lord Sumner.

[23]"In 1911, however, there was a run on the bank which drove it into liquidation" (Stoljar, 21); "Heavy losses were incurred and the society went into liquidation" (Wright, *Sinclair*, 4); see [1912] 2 Ch. 183, 187.

[24]These outside creditors were "inconsiderable in number and value" ([1914] A.C. 398, 427; [1914-1915] All E.R. Rep. 622, 635 *per* Lord Dunedin) and, as such "they were rightly paid, under the circumstances of the actual case, and had they not been, they would stand, after the expenses of the liquidation, at first in the ranking" ([1914] A.C. 398, 437; [1914-1915] All E.R. Rep. 622, 640 *per* Lord Dunedin).

obligation on the part of the Society to repay them. At first instance and in the Court of Appeal,[25] the remaining shareholders prevailed over the depositors,[26] but the House of Lords divided the spoils between them, ordering that the liquidator should apportion the entirety of the remaining assets between depositors and remaining shareholders in proportion to the amounts originally paid by them.[27] They reached this conclusion, not on the basis of the depositors' legal personal claim, the money had and received argument, which was dismissed, but on the basis of the depositors' equitable proprietary claim, the tracing argument.

The outcome in *Sinclair v. Brougham* seems fair. The means by which it was reached seemed unimpeachable at the time; but, after *Westdeutsche*, very little, if anything, of the reasoning in the speeches, now remains. That case also began innocuously enough, with local authorities seeking to take advantage of the financial markets, and in particular of interest rate swaps, to generate extra income at a time when other sources of funding were capped. In *Hazell v. Hammersmith and Fulham L.B.C.*[28] the House of Lords held that interest rate swaps transactions were *ultra vires* local authorities. In *Westdeutsche*, at first instance,[29] Hobhouse J. held that a net payor on such an *ultra vires* swap – in this case, a bank – was entitled to restitution of the net payment. He reached this conclusion on the basis of a legal personal claim, notwithstanding *Sinclair v. Brougham*. The Court of Appeal affirmed.[30] The defendant local authority did not appeal this matter to the House of Lords, but their Lordships plainly considered this to be right, and overruled *Sinclair v. Brougham* on this point.

---

[25] *Re Birkbeck Permanent Benefit Building Society* [1912] 2 Ch. 183 (Neville J., and C.A.).

[26] At first instance, Neville J. ordered that the assets be applied: first, in payment of costs; second, in paying outside creditors; third, in paying off the shareholders; and fourth, what remained, proportionately, to depositors. The Court of Appeal, by a majority, affirmed. "This order ha[d]the effect, so far as the . . . shareholders are concerned, of paying them in full" ([1914] A.C. 398, 428; [1914-1915] All E.R. Rep. 622, 636 *per* Lord Dunedin). As Lord Wright pointed out, this "was clearly illogical . . . Logically the shareholders if entitled to priority would have been entitled to divide up *all* the remaining assets of the society" (Wright, *Sinclair*, 5; emphasis added). He is followed in this by Oakley who also thought it "difficult to follow the logic of this order" (Oakley, "The Prerequisites of an Equitable Tracing Claim" (1975) 28 *C.L.P.* 64 [hereafter Oakley] 75 n.47). However, Neville J. had followed the earlier decision of *Re Guardian Permanent Benefit Building Society* (1883) 23 Ch.D. 440 (C.A.) [varied in part, *sub nom. Murray v. Scott* (1883-1884) 9 App. Cas. 519 (H.L.) but not in any particular which would affect Neville J.'s order] and he must have been influenced by the concern that that would later motivate the House of Lords that, to have held entirely in favour of the shareholders and entirely against the depositors, though logical, would have been unjust.

[27] After the decision in the Court of Appeal, the liquidator had made payments accordingly; after the decision of the House of Lords, it was clear that they were overpayments, and in a subsequent action, Neville J. held that he was entitled to recover them as mistaken payments: *Re Birkbeck Permanent Building Society* [1915] 1 Ch. 91.

[28] [1992] 2 A.C. 1 (H.L.).

[29] [1994] 4 All E.R. 890 (Hobhouse J., and C.A.).

[30] [1994] 4 All E.R. 890 (Hobhouse J., and C.A.); [1994] 1 W.L.R. 938 (C.A.).

Such a personal action carried an award of only simple interest; but the bank wanted compound interest, which would have been available had there been an equitable claim. So it sought to rely on the successful equitable claim in *Sinclair v. Brougham*. This hare had been started in the Court of Appeal,[31] was given added legs in the House of Lords by the enthusiasm of Viscount Haldane L.C. in particular,[32] and the argument prevailed at first instance and in the Court of Appeal in *Westdeutsche*. However, the local authority did appeal this matter to the House of Lords, and succeeded in having *Sinclair v. Brougham* overruled on this point as well.

It is clear, therefore, that *Sinclair v. Brougham* made two entries in the diary of legal madness: denying a legal personal claim, and awarding an equitable proprietary one instead. They – and their quite proper repudiation in *Westdeutsche* – are treated in the next two sections.

3. THE PERSONAL CLAIM. THE ONCE AND FUTURE KING

The depositors claimed that they had paid the society on foot both of a mistaken belief in the society's capacity to accept deposits as a bank and for a consideration which had wholly failed, so that their deposits amounted to money had and received by the society to their use, and the society was thus under a duty to repay the sums deposited. They relied upon a tradition which conceived of the action for money had and received as a means of achieving restitution and preventing unjust enrichment. It drew its inspiration from the judgment of Lord Mansfield in *Moses v. Macferlan*[33] who took an open-textured and flexible approach to the action,[34] and the tradition constructed upon it saw the implied contract as no more than a fiction which should have faded away with the mid-nineteenth century reforms of the procedure[35] to which it had given rise, to be replaced with an obligation imposed by law to make restitution, just as the obligation to compensate for tortious behaviour is imposed by law.

Such arguments were not necessarily doomed to failure.[36] Indeed, just be-

---

[31] The Court of Appeal, in having recourse to equity, "started a line of reasoning which was to become most troublesome" (Stoljar, 23) and would attain "new levels of complexity" (*ibid.*, 27) in the House of Lords.

[32] [1914] A.C. 398, 404 *arguendo* (the arguments of counsel, and Viscount Haldane's interjection, do not appear in the report at [1914-1915] All E.R. Rep. 522).

[33] (1760) 2 Burr. 1005; 97 E.R. 676.

[34] (1760) 2 Burr. 1005, 1008-1010; 97 E.R. 676, 678-679; see also n.128 below.

[35] *e.g.* the Common Law Procedure Act,1852; the Judicature Act, 1873.

[36] "Brice, the nineteenth-century English authority, in his treatise on *Ultra Vires*, acknowledged that no action could be brought to enforce an *ultra vires* agreement, but then went on to state as a general proposition of English law that benefits received by the corporation under such agreements must be restored" Maddaugh and McCamus, *The Law of Restitution* (Canada Law Book Inc., Ontario, 1991) [hereafter Maddaugh and McCamus] 327, citing Brice, *Ultra Vires* (3rd ed., Stevens & Haynes, London, 1895) 641 *et seq.* Thus, for example, in *Re Phoenix Life Assur-*

fore the House of Lords came to decide *Sinclair v. Brougham*, in *In re Irish Provident Assurance Co.*,[37] the Court of Appeal in Ireland held that an insurance company which had carried on an *ultra vires* life assurance business could, in principle, recover back *ultra vires* payments, subject to making counter-restitution of premia received, which was a complete defence on the facts. But this view of the law was never going to command the assent of Lord Sumner. As Hamilton L.J. in the Court of Appeal the previous year, he had dismissed this view of the action for money had and received: "whatever had been the case 146 years ago [when *Moses v. Macferlan* was decided], we are not now free in the twentieth century to administer that vague jurisprudence which is sometimes attractively styled 'justice as between man and man'."[38] And in the House of Lords in *Sinclair v. Brougham*, he returned to this theme:

> I cannot but think that Lord Mansfield's language has been completely misunderstood. . . . I think it is evident that Lord Mansfield did not conceive himself to be deciding that this action was on in which the courts of common law administered 'an equity' in the sense in which it was understood in the Courts of Chancery. . . . There is no ground left for suggesting as a recognisable 'equity' the right to recover money *in personam* merely because it would be the right and fair thing that it should be refunded to the payer.[39]

Rejecting the open-textured view of the action for money had and received should not of itself have necessarily been fatal to the depositors' claim. Yet the House of Lords unanimously held that it could not be maintained. On their Lordships' view, the common law of obligations had only two branches – tort and contract – within which an obligation to repay of the sort relied upon by the depositors against the society had to be accommodated. Such an obligation, described as *quasi-contractual*, could only be imposed on the society by

---

ance (1862) 2 J.&H. 441; 70 E.R. 1131 and *Flood v. Irish Provident Assurance* (1912) 46 I.L.T.R. 214; [1912] 2 Ch. 597n (C.A., Ir.) it was held that *premia* paid to an insurance company on *ultra vires* policies were recoverable for total failure of consideration. See also *Confederation Life Association v. Howard* (1894) 25 O.R. 197 where money paid on *ultra vires* debentures was recovered as money had and received.

[37] [1913] 1 I.R. 352 (C.A., Ir.); see O'Dell, "Incapacity" in Birks and Rose, (eds.), *Lessons of the Swaps Litigation* (Mansfield/L.L.P., London, 2000) 113 [hereafter O'Dell "Incapacity"] 146-150.

[38] *Baylis v. Bishop of London* [1913] 1 Ch. 127 (C.A.) 140; *cp.* his comments just a short time later sitting in the Court of Appeal in *R. Leslie v. Sheill* [1914] 3 K.B. 607 (C.A.) 613; though *cf.* some less critical views on his part as Hamilton J. in *Evanson v. Crooks* (1911) 106 L.T. 264, 269.

[39] [1914] A.C. 398, 454-456; [1914-1915] All E.R. Rep. 622, 649-650 *per* Lord Sumner; as a consequence, Scrutton L.J. described the history of the action for money had and received as a "history of well-meaning sloppiness of thought" *Holt v. Markham* [1923] 1 K.B. 504 (C.A.) 513.

means of a contract implied by the law; and since the society could not in fact make such a contract, one could not be imposed by the law. The point is summed up best in a sentence in the speech of Lord Parker of Waddington: "The implied promise on which the action for money had and received is based would be precisely that promise which the company or association could not lawfully make".[40] Other speeches were more expansive. Viscount Haldane L.C., with whom Lord Atkinson concurred, put it thus:

> . . . so far as proceedings *in personam* are concerned the law of England really recognises (unlike the Roman law) only actions of two classes, those founded on contract and those founded on tort. When it speaks of actions arising *quasi ex contractu* it refers merely to a class of action in theory based on a contract which is imputed to the defendant by a fiction of law. The fiction can really only be set up with effect if such a contract would be valid if it really existed. . . . Consideration of the authorities has led me to the conclusion that the action [for money had and received] was in principle one which rested on a promise to pay, either actual or imputed by law. . . . I think that it must be taken to have been given only . . . where the law could consistently impute to the defendant at least the fiction of a promise.[41]

Lord Dunedin's reasoning on this point was similar:

> The English common law has various actions which . . . are divided into actions in respect of contract and of tort. . . . the English law, having no *quasi contract*, got over the difficulty in such cases as the action for money had and received by the fiction of a contract. . . . That there can be no resulting proper contractual obligation [in the case of an *ultra vires* contract] is clear . . . It is here that the difficulty comes in extending the action for money had and received to such a case. . . . how is it possible to say that there is a fictional contract which is binding in circumstances in which a real contract is not binding? . . . I have come to the conclusion that the action for money had and received cannot be stretched to meet the situation.[42]

But the most strident and striking rhetoric rejecting the common law actions was that of Lord Sumner:

---

[40][1914] A.C. 398, 440; [1914-1915] All E.R. Rep. 622, 642 *per* Lord Parker.
[41][1914] A.C. 398, 415-417; [1914-1915] All E.R. Rep. 622, 629-630 *per* Viscount Haldane LC. Heuston described this speech as "an authoritative survey of the scope of the doctrine of restitution or quasi-contract". Heuston, *Lives of the Lord Chancellors* (Clarendon Press, Oxford, 1964) 239.
[42][1914] A.C. 398, 432-434; [1914-1915] All E.R. Rep. 622, 638-639 *per* Lord Dunedin.

All these causes of action are common species of the genus assumpsit.
All now rest, and long have rested, upon a notional or imputed promise
to repay. The law cannot *de jure* impute promises to repay, whether for
money had and received or otherwise, which, if made *de facto*, it would
inexorably avoid.[43]

The persuasive power of an opinion is an important factor in establishing a
judgment as leading,[44] and this passage has an epigrammatic[45] quality rendering it instantly memorable and quotable. I remember being struck by this passage as a student, and it has never failed to grab my attention whenever I have
encountered it since. I do not believe myself to be alone in this: many of my
own students quote it as easily as they remind me that promissory estoppel acts
as a shield and not a sword;[46] it has been followed in the House of Lords,[47] and
it was chosen as representative of the reasoning of the House on this point by
Hobhouse J. at first instance[48] and by Lord Goff in the House of Lords[49] in
Westdeutsche.[50] This passage is by no means the whole of the reason for the
importance of *Sinclair v. Brougham*, but it must surely have played a not insignificant part.

The speeches are working on many levels: the rejection of a flexible approach to unjust enrichment, the denial of restitution as a third head of obligations separate from contract and tort, the insistence on restitutionary obligations
being imposed by means of an implied contract, and the reification of the implied contract fiction in the conclusion that if a valid contract could not have
existed in fact, one could not be implied in law. Even though each conclusion
does not flow inexorably from the one before – the rejection of a flexible approach to unjust enrichment does not necessarily entail the denial of restitution

---

[43] [1914] A.C. 398, 652; [1914-1915] All E.R. Rep. 622, 648 *per* Lord Sumner.
[44] See, *e.g.*, Twining, *Rethinking Evidence* (Blackwell, London, 1990) 219, especially his discussion of Lord Denning (232-238). Lord Denning's staccato style is legendary and used to good
effect in the two cases by which he is represented in this volume: see Breen, "Dusting Down
Equity's Armour. *High Trees* (1947) in Perspective" below, 164; and Capper, "The *Mareva*
Injunction – From Birth to Adulthood. *Mareva Compania Naviera S.A. v. International
Bulkcarriers S.A.* (1975)" below, 255. Again, that Gavan Duffy J.'s language is memorable no
doubt helped to establish *Grealish v. Murphy* [1946] I.R. 35 (H.C.) as a leading case on
unconscionability at Irish law; see Clark "An Everyday Story of Country Folk (Not!). *Grealish
v. Murphy* (1946)" below, 149).
[45] Wright, *Sinclair*, 24.
[46] *Combe v. Combe* [1951] 2 K.B. 215 (C.A.) 224; [1951] 1 All E.R. 767, 772 *per* Birkett L.J.
adopting the "vivid" description given by counsel for the husband; on which see Breen "Dusting
Down Equity's Armour. *High Trees* (1947) in Perspective" below, 164, text with n.39.
[47] *Boissevain v. Weil* [1950] A.C. 327 (H.L.) 341; [1950] 1 All E.R. 728, 734-735 *per* Lord Radcliffe.
[48] [1994] 4 All E.R. 980, 919.
[49] [1996] A.C. 669, 687; [1996] 2 All E.R. 960, 971, describing it as "a much-quoted passage".
[50] See also *United Australia v. Barclays Bank* [1941] A.C. 1 (H.L.) 45; [1940] 4 All E.R. 20, 47
per Lord Porter; *Fibrosa Spolka Akcyjna v. Fairbairn Lawson Combe Barbour*[1943] A.C. 32
(H.L.) 64; [1942] 4 All E.R. 122, 137 *per* Lord Wright (on which see text after n.68 below);

as a third head of obligations, any more than subscribing to an implied contract explanation for the obligation to make restitution does not necessarily entail the conclusion that that a contract cannot be implied if it could not have existed in fact – they have come to be regarded as a package deal: buy one, get the others free. And their heady mix proved extraordinarily potent: there were many buyers at the time and subsequently. Thus, its rejection of *Moses v. Macferlan* and its strong version of the implied contract theory were sometimes enthusiastically embraced, as in *Holt v. Markham*,[51] and, in more temperate language, in *Morgan v. Ashcroft.*[52] Hanbury, for example, wrote that to "allow an action for money had and received here would be unhistorical and nonsensical".[53]

Sinclair v. Brougham seemed, therefore, to have put paid to the possibility of restitutionary remedies for *ultra vires* contracts, and many subsequent cases simply set up a dichotomy between enforceability and non-enforceability of the *ultra vires* transaction, without asking whether there are any legal alternatives to enforceability. Remedies consequent upon non-enforceability are simply not considered. Indeed, this has led, on at least one occasion, to the *non sequitur* that because the contract is unenforceable, there must be no remedy. In the Irish case of *Re Cummins*[54] Johnston J. held that the "theory of the law is that the whole transaction is null and void and can give rise to no legal rights or claims whatever".[55]

But these conclusions did not go unchallenged. Lord Wright led the counter-charge against this aspect of *Sinclair v. Brougham*,[56] defending the concept of unjust enrichment,[57] arguing for restitution as a third head of obligations,[58]

---

[51][1923] 1 KB 504 (C.A.) 513 *per* Scrutton L.J. And, in an excellent example of the reification of the implied contract, it became common to includes claims based upon so called *quasi contracts* within those paragraphs of Order 11 R.S.C. covering contracts: *Bowling v. Cox* [1926] A.C. 751 (P.C.); see Briggs, "Jurisdiction under Traditional Rules" in Rose, (ed.), *Restitution and the Conflict of Laws* (Mansfield Press, Oxford, 1995) 49.

[52][1938] 1 K.B. 49 (C.A.) 62 *per* Lord Green M.R; *cp. Re Cleadon Trust* [1939] Ch. 286 (C.A.) 299-300 *per* Lord Green M.R., 315 *per* Scott L.J., 319 *per* Clauson L.J.; *Re Diplock; Diplock v. Wintle* [1948] Ch. 465 (C.A.) 480; [1948] 2 All E.R. 318, 326 *per* Lord Greene M.R. Similarly, in cases such as *Hirsch v. Zinc Corp* (1917) 24 C.L.R. 34 (H.C.A.), *Smith v. William Charlick* (1924) 34 C.L.R. 38 (H.C.A.) and *Turner v. Bladin* (1951) C.L.R. 463 (H.C.A.), the implied "contract theory was dutifully adopted by the High Court of Australia" (Erbacher, *Restitution Law. Text, Cases and Materials* (Cavendish, London & Sydney, 1998) 7; see also Mason and Carter, *Restitution Law in Australia* (Butterworths, Sydney, 1995) [hereafter Mason and Carter] 20, para. 118).

[53]Hanbury, 12.

[54]*In Re Cummins: Barton v. Bank of Ireland* [1939] I.R. 60 (H.C.).

[55][1939] I.R. 60, 70.

[56]In Wright, *Sinclair*; which Lord Atkin subsequently described as "a valuable contribution to the discussion" *United Australia v. Barclays Bank* [1941] A.C. 1 (H.L.) 26; [1940] 4 All E.R. 20, 35.

[57]Lord Wright of Durley "The Study of Law" in *Legal Essays and Addresses* (C.U.P., Cambridge, 1939) 387 [hereafter Wright, "Study"] 404: "not implied contract but unjust enrichment". Similarly, a "careful study of the English reported cases at law or in equity will, I think, show that the

and deprecating the misuse of the language of *quasi-contract*[59] and of the implied contract fiction[60] as

> ... such unfortunate and misleading terminology. The room of the fiction is better than its company. Not only is it undesirable that English law should be defaced by superfluous solecisms and illogical phrases, but the ghost of this fiction has, I fear, actually delayed and hindered in England the systematic and scientific study of this important branch of law. I should like to see it forgotten for good and all here and now. But it is certainly doomed. Another generation of lawyers will have forgotten it, or if they ever remember it, will wonder why people troubled to discuss it except as a matter of obsolete history.[61]

He cited authorities from 1699[62] to 1908[63] in which the obligation to make restitution was seen simply as one imposed by law and not by means of an

---

basis of the doctrine of unjust enrichment is, as has been so often here stated, that the defendant has received some property of the plaintiff or received some benefit from the plaintiff, for which it is just (as shown in the precedents) that he should make restitution" (Wright, *Sinclair*, 26).

[58]"[U]njust enrichment has no relation as a juristic conception with contract at all. . . . the dichotomy [of contract and tort] does not correspond to any juristic classification. . . . even if the term 'contract implied by law' is retained as meaning quasi-contract, and if the equitable rights and remedies are ignored, still 'contracts implied by law' signify a third head apart from contract and tort. The specific character of restitution as a legal category may be disguised but cannot be destroyed by confusing and inappropriate terminology" (Wright, *Sinclair*, 15-16). "I cannot understand why it is not more generally recognised that *quasi-contract* or restitution involves a definite system of rules, just like the rules of contract or tort" (*ibid.*, 26; see also Lord Wright of Durley, "The Common Law in its Old Home" in *Legal Essays and Addresses* (C.U.P., Cambridge, 1939) 327 [hereafter Wright, "Old Home"] 345-346; Wright, "Study", 403.)

[59]The term *quasi-contract* "is not very apt, but it does no harm if it is understood to be a label, and to refer to the peculiarity of the action, though there is no promise in fact, the defendant is ordered by the court to pay the money just as much as if he had promised to pay it" (Wright, "Old Home", 356; see also *ibid.*, 384); that is, the substance is the prevention of unjust enrichment (*ibid.*, 358).

[60]"The old common lawyers [who utilised the fiction] were a robust people, and if a fiction was convenient under the old rigid forms of pleading they did not worry about its correspondence to reality or to juristic concepts. But it does not follow that they did not realise the true nature of the concept" (Wright, *Sinclair*, 20). Again, "the old common lawyers did not always take their fictions seriously. They used them for their practical value" (Wright, *Sinclair*, 30). Hence, "a fiction was adopted in the past merely as a device to justify a court in less enlightened days when it was applying a novel doctrine and was doing so on the analogy of, and by way of extending, a familiar rule. Hence the crop of absurd and outrageous fictions, now mostly forgotten, which it is almost indecent to exhume, fictions which can never have deceived anybody." (Wright, "Old Home", 384-385; see also (1949) 65 L.Q.R. 295). See now, generally, Baker "The History of *Quasi-Contract* in English Law" in Cornish, Nolan, O'Sullivan & Virgo, (eds.), *Restitution. Past, Present and Future* (Hart Publishing, Oxford, 1998) 37, 40-42; and Ibbetson, *A Historical Introduction to the Law of Obligations* (O.U.P., Oxford, 1999) cHapter 14..

[61]Wright, *Sinclair*, 33.

[62]*Starke v. Cheeseman* (1699) 1 Ld. Raym. 538; 91 E.R. 1259 (Holt C.J.).

[63]*Nash v. Inman* [1908] 2 K.B. 1 (C.A.).

implied contract, and he continued, rather disingenuously, that he did not believe "that the House of Lords in *Sinclair v. Brougham* had any intention of overruling these authorities";[64] and he sought to limit the fallout from the speeches in *Sinclair v. Brougham*:

> it is the decision which is the precedent. Here no decision was based on the Lords' views about legal history or about the old forms of action. It was already settled that in such a case as that before them the legal claim did not lie.[65] . . . Decisions, I repeat, are decisions. Views on legal history are not legal decisions. They may form the basis of decisions, though they did not in *Sinclair v Brougham*.[66]

In *Fibrosa v. Fairbairn*,[67] he went even further:

> . . . serious legal writers have seemed to say that the[] words of Lord Sumner in *Sinclair v. Brougham* closed the door to any theory of unjust enrichment in English law. I do not understand why or how. It would indeed be a *reductio ad absurdum* of the doctrine of precedents. In the fact the common law still employs the action for money had and received as a practical and useful, if not complete or ideally perfect, instrument to prevent unjust enrichment, . . .[68]

There is a large measure of wishful thinking in all of this. Lord Wright's essay

---

[64] Wright, *Sinclair*, 22, see also *ibid.*, 24: "the House of Lords cannot have intended to overrule the established authorities . . .". He also referred to the later House of Lords decision of *Jones v. Waring & Gillow* [1926] A.C. 670 (H.L.) as not setting the restitutionary obligation imposed in that case on an implied contract; ironically, he relies in particular on Lord Sumner's speech in that case (see [1926] A.C. 670, 696) and he even manages to extract some solace from *Baylis v. Bishop of London* [1913] 1 Ch. 127 (C.A.) 140 *per* Hamilton L.J. despite the comments from that case set out text with n. 38 above. As Tunney points out in "The Search For Justice. *Mabo* (1992)" below, 445, text after n. 9, the devil can cite scripture for his purpose, and there is something of that in Lord Wright's selective citation of Lord Sumner's views in *Baylis*, *Jones* and the later *Hirji Mulji v. Cheong Yue Steamship Co.* [1926] A.C. 497 (P.C.) 510 and even *Sinclair v. Brougham* itself (!) (Wright, *Sinclair*, 25, citing [1914] A.C. 398, 458; [1914-1915] All E.R. Rep. 622, 651).

[65] Wright, *Sinclair*, 19; that the legal personal claim did not lie had been settled in *Re National Permanent Building Society ex p Williamson* (1869) 5 Ch. App. 309; *Cunliffe Brooks & Co. v. Blackburn and District Benefit Building Society* (1884) 9 App. Cas. 857; *Baroness Wenlock v. River Dee Co.* (1885) 10 App. Cas. 354 (H.L.) discussed by Lord Parker in *Sinclair v. Brougham* at [1914] A.C. 398, 440; [1914-1915] All E.R. Rep. 622, 642 and referred to by Lord Wright earlier in the essay: *Sinclair*, 16. However, in the consequent remedy fashioned in *Cunliffe Brooks v. Blackburn*, it was overruled in *Sinclair v. Brougham*, and this entire line of authority, holding against the presonal claim, is no longer good law after *Westdeutsche*.

[66] Wright, *Sinclair*, 32.

[67] *Fibrosa Spolka Akcyjna v. Fairbairn Lawson Combe Barbour* [1943] A.C. 32 (H.L.); [1942] 4 All E.R. 122.

[68] [1943] A.C. 32, 64; [1942] 4 All E.R. 122, 137.

on the case had drawn from Holdsworth's pen[69] a strong defence of *Sinclair v. Brougham* in all its rigour, and, from his reference to "serious legal writers", Lord Wright must have had Holdsworth's defence in mind in that passage from *Fibrosa*. In fact, Lord Sumner's words do fairly bear the interpretation rejected by Lord Wright but defended by Holdsworth. Whether the law ought to maintain that position is an entirely different matter. It is now clear that it has decided not to. First, in England, there are some examples of restitution of benefits transferred pursuant to an *ultra vires* contract notwithstanding *Sinclair v. Brougham*.[70] More than that, an alternative view of the history of the implied contract has judicially prospered,[71] the fiction has been rejected in favour of a

---

[69] See Holdsworth "Unjustifiable Enrichment" in Goodhart and Hanbury, (eds.), *Essays in Law and History* (Clarendon Press, Oxford, 1946) 238 [reprinting (1939) 55 L.Q.R. 37; see also (1932) *J.S.P.T.L.* 41; (1937) 53 *L.Q.R.* 302, 304]. The editors of the collection of Holdsworths' papers point out in their Preface that "this article . . . is in the nature of reply to Lord Wright's paper on *Sinclair v. Brougham* . . ." (Editors' Preface, xiii). And Lord Wright seems to have been taken aback by it. In his Preface to his *Legal Essays and Addresses* (C.U.P., Cambridge, 1939) he confessed that he had not "appreciate[d] what criticism and opposition my humble extra-judicial expression of opinion would provoke" (xii). He went on that "in the United States, as I understand, it is generally accepted that *quasi-contract*, or restitution as the Restatement calls it, is a separate category in the law. . . . Why, I wonder, is the view so strongly held in England that in the Common Law there are not three but only two categories of civil liability, contract and tort ? That view has recently received its most complete expression in a recent article in the *Law Quarterly Review*, but, with all the respect that I feel for that great lawyer, I cannot in this matter agree with his arguments" (xiv).

[70] See, generally, Street, *The Doctrine of Ultra Vires* (Sweet & Maxwell, London, 1930) [hereafter Street] 376-389: ". . . restitution is a wholly distinct relief. It is, if possible, granted in all cases of true *ultra vires* to all parties affected by the finding of nullity" (376). Hence, "[p]arties to an *ultra vires* transaction will so far as possible be restored to their original position" (377, citing, *inter alia*, *In re Irish Provident Assurance Co.* [1913] 1 I.R. 352 (C.A. Ir.); on which see n.37, above). Thus for example, in *Craven Ellis v. Canons* [1936] 2 K.B. 403; [1936] 2 All E.R. 1066 (C.A.) a Managing Director whose appointment was *ultra vires* nevertheless got a *quantum meruit*; in *Linz v. Electric Wire Co. of Palestine*, Lord Simonds for the Privy Council did not "question the general proposition that, where an *ultra vires* issue of shares has been made, the subscribers are entitled to recover their money" in action for money had and received for total failure of consideration ([1948] A.C. 371 (P.C.) 377); in *Bell Houses Ltd. v. City Wall Properties* [1966] 1 Q.B. 207, 226; [1965] 3 All E.R. 427, 436 Mocatta J. at first instance affirmed the availability of both the *quantum meruit* and the action for money had and received; and in *Simmonds v. Heffer* [1983] B.C.L.C. 298 an *ultra vires* political donation was recovered. And a peculiar species of subrogation – of which the leading Irish example is *In Re Lough Neagh Ship Company; Ex parte Workman* [1895] 1 I.R. 533 (C.A., Ir.) – has also been pressed into service; see Street, 379-383; Goff and Jones *The Law of Restitution* (5th ed., Sweet & Maxwell, London, 1998) [hereafter Goff and Jones] 153-169; Mitchell, *The Law of Subrogation* (O.U.P., Oxford, 1994) 154-161.

[71] See, especially, the speech of Lord Atkin in *United Australia v. Barclays Bank* (rejecting "fantastic resemblances of contracts" ([1941] A.C. 1 (H.L.) 29; [1940] 4 All E.R. 20, 37); the speech of Lord Wright in *Fibrosa Spolka Akcyjna v. Fairbairn Lawson Combe Barbour* [1943] A.C. 32 (H.L.); [1942] 4 All E.R. 122; and the judgments of the High Court of Australia in *Pavey & Matthews v. Paul* (1986) 162 C.L.R. 221 (H.C.A.) on which, for this point, see Ibbetson, "Implied Contracts and Restitution: History in the High Court of Australia" (1988) 8 *O.J.L.S.* 312.

largely descriptive principle against unjust enrichment, and restitution has become established as a third head of obligations alongside contract and tort. [72]
As Keane J. put in the *Bricklayers' Hall* case:[73]

> It is clear that, under our law, a person can in certain circumstances be
> obliged to effect restitution of money or other property to another where
> it would be unjust for him to retain the property. Moreover, as Henchy J.
> noted in *East Cork Foods v. O'Dwyer Steel*,[74] this principle no longer
> rests on the fiction of an implied promise to return the property which, in
> the days when the forms of action still ruled English law, led to its tortu-
> ous rationalisation as being *"quasi-contractual"* in nature.
>
> The modern authorities in this and other common law jurisdictions,
> of which *Murphy v. Attorney General*[75] is a leading Irish example have
> demonstrated that unjust enrichment exists as a distinctive legal concept,
> separate and distinct from contract and tort, which in the words of Deane
> J. in the High Court of Australia in *Pavey & Matthews v. Paul*[76]
>
>> . . . explains why the law recognises, in a variety of distinct catego-
>> ries of cases, an obligation on the part of the defendant to make fair
>> and just restitution for a benefit derived at the expense of a plaintiff
>> and which assists in the determination, by the ordinary process of
>> legal reasoning, of the question of whether the law should, in justice,
>> recognise the obligation in a new and developing category of case.[77]
>
> . . . the law, as it has developed, has avoided the dangers of 'palm tree
> justice' by identifying whether the case belongs in a specific category
> which justifies . . . describing the enrichment [as unjust]: possible in-
> stances are money paid under duress or as a result of a mistake of fact or
> law or accompanied by a total failure of consideration. [78]

Such a development undercuts all of the main planks of the denial of the per-

---

[72]I have attempted elsewhere to describe this process: see O'Dell, "The Principle Against Unjust
Enrichment" (1993) 15 *D.U.L.J.* (*n.s.*) 50; "Birks and Stones and the Structure of the Law of
Restitution" (1998) 20 *D.U.L.J.* (*n.s.*) 101 [hereafter O'Dell "Bricks and Stones . . ."].
[73]*Dublin Corporation v. Building and Allied Trades Union* [1996] 1 I.R. 468; [1996] 2 I.L.R.M.
547 (S.C.); on which see O'Dell [1996] *Restitution Law Review* §134; "Restitution and *Res
Judicata* in the Irish Supreme Court" (1997) 113 *L.Q.R.* 245; and O'Dell "Bricks and
Stones . . .".
[74][1978] I.R. 103 (S.C.): the implied contract fiction was no more than "a pleader's stratagem ...
it would be an affront to truth and reality to say that the basis of that cause of action is an implied
promise to repay the money" ([1978] I.R. 103, 110 *per* Henchy J.).
[75][1982] I.R. 241 (S.C.), on which see, generally, Scannell, "The Taxation of Married Women.
Murphy v. A.G. (1982)" below, 327.
[76](1986) 162 C.L.R. 221 (H.C.A.).
[77](1986) 162 C.L.R. 221, 256-257 *per* Deane J.
[78][1996] 1 I.R. 468, 483-484; [1996] 2 I.L.R.M. 547, 557-558.

sonal action at law in *Sinclair v. Brougham*. In retrospect, its overruling by the House of Lords in *Westdeutsche* has an aura of inevitability about it,[79] not least because there were Canadian and Irish harbingers.

Canadian courts "have demonstrated a remarkable capacity for finding excuses for failing to follow"[80] *Sinclair v. Brougham*: it was almost immediately doubted,[81] and it was soon held that "the principle that a corporation which has received benefit from an *ultra vires* contract must account for the benefit received . . . [is] long and firmly established . . . [and] applicable to any case in which by reason of an *ultra vires* engagement, a corporation has received benefit".[82] This recovery is now explained on the basis of "the recent revival of the law related to restitution based on unjust enrichment".[83] Consequently, *Sinclair v. Brougham* does not seem to form part of the law in Canada.[84]

As to the Irish harbinger, in the *P.M.P.A.* case,[85] Murphy J. pointed out that the significance of the development of a law of restitution predicated upon the principle against unjust enrichment and not the implied contract fiction "is that by eliminating the need for an express or imputed promise to pay as an ingredient of the action for money had and received it overcomes the problem faced by the House of Lords in *Sinclair v. Brougham*".[86]

Unsurprisingly, therefore, for Lord Browne-Wilkinson in *Westdeutsche*, the development of the law of restitution demonstrated that the reasoning in *Sinclair*

---

[79] *Westdeutsche Landesbank Girozentrale v. Islington L.B.C.* [1996] A.C. 669; [1996] 2 All E.R. 961 (H.L.).

[80] Maddaugh and McCamus, 28 and generally, Chap. 14. The case "had no effect on American Law" (Wade, *Restitution. Cases and Materials* (2nd ed., Foundation Press, N.Y., 1966) 852).

[81] *Trades Hall Co. v. Erie Tobacco* (1916) 29 D.L.R. 779, 794 *per* Cameron J.A.; *Gnaedinger v. Turtleford Grain Growers* (1922) 63 D.L.R. 498; *Re General Finance Corp. (Yarmouth)* [1941] 1 D.L.R. 754; *Machrays Department Store v. Zionist Labour* (1965) 53 D.L.R. (2d.) 657.

[82] *Halton County v. Trafalgar Township* [1927] 4 D.L.R. 134, 142 *per* Grant J. Similarly, a borrower under an *ultra vires* contract must return the money so borrowed to prevent unjust enrichment: *Caledonia Community Credit Union Ltd. v. Haldimand Feed Mill* (1974) 45 D.L.R. (3d) 676 (H.C., Ontario) 679 *per* Van Camp J. See also *La Caisse Populaire Notre Dame Limitée v. Moyen* (1967) 61 D.L.R. (2d) 118, Tucker J, (Sask. Q.B.); *Breckenridge Speedway v. The Queen in right of Alberta* (1970) 9 D.L.R. (3d) 142 (S.C.C.); *Provincial Treasurer of Alberta v. Long* (1975) 49 D.L.R. (3d) 695; *cp. Re K.L. Tractors* (1961) 106 C.L.R. 318 (H.C.A.).

[83] *First City Development Corp. v. Regional Municipality of Durham* (1989) 67 O.R. (2d.) 655, 689 *per* Craig J.

[84] *Parkland Mortgage Corporation Ltd. v. Therevan Developments* (1981) 130 D.L.R. (3d.) 682, 696 *per* Feehan J. However, Maddaugh and McCamus are more circumspect, merely commenting that it has been confined to its own particular facts; see Maddaugh and McCamus, 324 *et seq.*

[85] *In re P.M.P.A. Garage (Longmile) Ltd. (No. 2)* [1992] 1 I.R. 332; [1992] I.L.R.M. 349 (H.C); on which see O'Dell, "Estoppel and *Ultra Vires* Contracts" (1992) 14 *D.U.L.J. (n.s.)* 123, and O'Dell "Incapacity", 140-141. Hence, Murphy J. could avoid the "monstrous injustice" which would flow from the "audacious" and "unattractive" proposition ([1992] 1 I.R. 332, 336; [1992] I.L.R.M. 349, 351) that there could be no remedy; thereby correcting the error in *Re Cummins*, above, n.55.

[86] [1992] 1 I.R. 332, 336; [1992] I.L.R.M. 349, 352.

v. Brougham was no longer sound and ought to be overruled, so that the depositors should have been entitled to restitution of their deposits on the ground of failure of consideration.[87] Lord Slynn agreed that *Sinclair v. Brougham* should be departed from,[88] and Lord Lloyd agreed that it was wrongly decided.[89] Lord Woolf expressed no opinion on the point. Only Lord Goff demurred, thinking *Sinclair v. Brougham* "basically irrelevant to the decision of the present appeal",[90] for two reasons. First, he identified "the problem which arose in *Sinclair v. Brougham*"[91] as the exclusion of a personal remedy in restitution "on the grounds of public policy"[92] and held that it did not arise in the present case as it was not concerned with a borrowing contract.[93] Second, he regarded the decision in *Sinclair v. Brougham* as confined to "*ultra vires* borrowing contracts, and as not intended to create a principle of general application".[94] Consequently, he was not for overruling *Sinclair v. Brougham*.

There is a respectable pedigree for Lord Goff's first point that the personal remedy in restitution was excluded in *Sinclair v. Brougham* on the grounds of public policy. There is support in the speeches in the case itself. Viscount Haldane L.C. was of the opinion that to "hold that a remedy will lie *in personam* of a statutory society, which by hypothesis cannot in the case in question have become a debtor, or entered into any contract for repayment, is to strike at the root of the doctrine of *ultra vires* as established in the jurisprudence of this country".[95] Lord Sumner and Lord Parker of Waddington were of the same opinion.[96] Indeed, Hobhouse J. at first instance and Leggatt L.J. in the Court of Appeal in *Westdeutsche*[97] were prepared to support the result in *Sinclair v.*

---

[87][1996] A.C. 669, 710; [1996] 2 All E.R. 961, 993.

[88][1996] A.C. 669, 718; [1996] 2 All E.R. 961, 1000.

[89][1996] A.C. 669, 738; [1996] 2 All E.R. 961, 1018.

[90][1996] A.C. 669, 686; [1996] 2 All E.R. 961, 970.

[91][1996] A.C. 669, 688; [1996] 2 All E.R. 961, 972.

[92]*ibid.*; see generally Arrowsmith, "Ineffective Transactions, Unjust Enrichment and Problems of Policy" (1989) 9 *L.S.* 307.

[93]*ibid.*

[94]*ibid.*

[95][1914] A.C. 398, 414; [1914-1915] All E.R. Rep. 622, 628 *per* Viscount Haldane LC. Similarly, "the law of England cannot now, consistently with the interpretation which the courts have placed on the statutes which determine the society the capacity of statutory societies, impute the fiction of such a promise where it would have been *ultra vires* to give it" ([1914] A.C. 398, 417; [1914-1915] All E.R. Rep. 622, 630 *per* Viscount Haldane L.C.).

[96]"To hold otherwise would be indirectly to sanction an *ultra vires* borrowing" ([1914] A.C. 398, 452; [1914-1915] All E.R. Rep. 622, 648 *per* Lord Sumner). "It is not . . . open to the House to hold that in such a case the lender has an action against the company or association for money had and received. To do so would in effect validate the transaction so far as it embodied a contract to repay the money lent" ([1914] A.C. 398, 440; [1914-1915] All E.R. Rep. 622, 642 *per* Lord Parker). This line of reasoning seems to have commenced with the judgment of Cozens-Hardy M.R. in *Re Guardian Permanent Benefit Building Society* (1883) 23 Ch.D. 440; see Stoljar, 28 n.35.

[97][1994] 4 All E.R. 890, 918 *per* Hobhouse J.; [1994] 4 All E.R. 890, 968; [1994] 1 W.L.R. 938, 952 *per* Leggatt L.J; see also Birks, *An Introduction to the Law of Restitution* (rev. ed., Clarendon

Brougham on that ground. But the policy underlying the *ultra vires* rule must be carefully excavated. It is not monolithic, but instead has two aspects, each designed to increase the funds available for disbursement to company share-holders or local authority ratepayers: there is the retention policy at issue in *Sinclair v. Brougham* which allows the retention of *ultra vires* receipts by the company or local authority acting *ultra vires*, and there is a parallel restitution policy which allows restitution of *ultra vires* expenditure by the company or local authority acting *ultra vires*; in both cases, the effect of that policy is to swell the coffers of the *ultra vires* company or local authority.[98]

The retention policy has its critics. Goff and Jones observe that, at times, "the courts have tended too readily to deny a restitutionary claim on this ground".[99] Even in *Sinclair v. Brougham* itself, Lord Dunedin thought that the *ultra vires* doctrine could not allow an *ultra vires* borrower to retain the bor-rowing: to do so would be "to run the doctrine mad. It was a doctrine which was introduced in order to let societies keep their own money, not to appropri-ate other people's".[100] The rigour of other rules for the maintenance of capital has been much mitigated;[101] and if the law is not strict on capital maintenance even where the capital is validly obtained, there can be little if any justification for its retention where it is invalidly obtained.

By contrast, there is no such objection to a restitution policy which allows societies to recover their own money paid away *ultra vires* – indeed, in *Brougham v. Dwyer*,[102] the liquidator of the Birkbeck Building Society succeeded in just such an action – and every reason in principle to support it.

Moreover, it seems that the retention policy is being supplanted by a resti-tution policy even in the case of *ultra vires* receipts: it was canvassed briefly by Birks in his discussion of Hobhouse J.'s judgment in *Westdeutsche*[103] and taken up by Waller L.J. in *Guinness Mahon v. Kensington L.B.C.* who suggested that there was therefore "no injustice in the council [the receiving incapax] being

---

Press, Oxford, 1989) 396: restitution would have "flatly contradicted the *ultra vires* rule". *Cp. Kasumu v. Baba-Egbe* [1956] A.C. 539 (P.C.) 551; [1956] 3 All E.R. 266, 271 *per* Lord Radcliffe.

[98] See O'Dell "Incapacity", 162-167.

[99] Goff and Jones, 68 criticising *Sinclair v. Brougham* on this ground, but defending *R. Leslie v. Sheill* [1914] 3 K.B. 607 (C.A.); *cf.* Burrows, *An Introduction to the Law of Restitution* (Butterworths, London, 1993) convincingly refuting the reliance by the House of Lords on such policy in the former case (458-460) and seeing a consequently "overwhelming" case to overrule the latter (452).

[100] [1914] A.C. 398, 438; [1914-1915] All E.R. Rep 622, 641.

[101] For example, the rule in *Trevor v. Whitworth* (1887) 12 A.C. 409 (H.L.) has been progressively relaxed (see, in Ireland, the Companies Act, 1990, Part XI, and, in England, the Companies Act 1985, chapter VII). On the modern justifications, if any, for such rules, see Armour, "Share Capital and Creditor Protection: Efficient Rules for a Modern Company Law" (2000) 63 *M.L.R.* 355.

[102] (1913) 108 L.T. 504 (Lush J.); see also *In Re Coltman: Coltman v. Coltman* (1881) 19 Ch.D. 64; *cp. In re Irish Provident Assurance* [1913] 1 I.R. 352 (C.A., Ir.).

[103] Birks "No Consideration. Restitution After Void Contracts" (1993) 23 *U.W.A.L.R.* 195, 206, *semble* changing his mind from n.97 above.

bound to repay".[104] As a co-author of a commentary upon *Guinness Mahon,*[105] Birks has returned the compliment: for him, the proper basis for restitution after an *ultra vires* swap is now "to be found by asking whether the policy behind the nullity dictates that there must be restitution",[106] and he finds various passages in *Guinness Mahon* – and in the subsequent decision of the House of Lords in *Kleinwort Benson v. Lincoln City Council*[107] – which imply that there has to be restitution in order to uphold the policy behind the *ultra vires* rule.[108] These passages are significant because they appear in cases in which it is the defendant which seeks to retain what has been received *ultra vires*, circumstances in which the retention policy would previously have denied restitution. If this is correct, then the focus of policy in the context of *ultra vires* receipts will have flipped from justifying retention to justifying restitution. Hence, the tide of policy seems now to be running strongly in favour of restitution not only of payments made *ultra vires* the payor but also of payments received *ultra vires* the payee. In both cases, by allowing restitution to unwind any performance of the *ultra vires* contract, the void nature of the contract is emphasised and the policy of the *ultra vires* rule is supported and not subverted. Consequently, the ground has been cut out from under Lord Goff's first point in defence of *Sinclair v. Brougham.*

His second, intimately bound up with his first,[109] was that it is confined to the narrow context of precluding the indirect enforcement of *ultra vires* borrowing contracts. It, too, has a respectable pedigree, and support in the speeches in *Sinclair v. Brougham.* For example, Lord Parker of Waddington, was of the opinion that if "the *ultra vires* contract . . . was not a contract of borrowing . . . the implied promise on which the action for money had and received depends would form no part of, but would be merely collateral to, the *ultra vires* contract".[110] In truth, this offers two routes by which to escape the shackles of

---

[104] [1998] 2 All E.R. 272 (C.A.) 287-288; [1998] 3 W.L.R. 829, 843-844, relying on Leggatt L.J. in *Westdeutsche* ([1994] 4 All E.R. 890, 967; [1994] 1 W.L.R. 938, 951.

[105] Birks and Swadling, "Restitution" 393-395 and see also Birks, "Private Law" in Birks and Rose, (eds.), *Lessons of the Swaps Litigation* (Mansfield/L.L.P., London, 2000) 1, 17-18 making the same point.

[106] [1998] *All E.R. Rev.* 390, 394.

[107] [1999] 2 A.C. 349 (H.L.) 382; [1998] 4 All E.R. 513, 543 *per* Lord Goff; [1999] 2 A.C. 349, 415; [1998] 4 All E.R. 513, 567 *per* Lord Hope.

[108] [1998] *All E.R. Rev.* 390, 394.

[109] For example, the comments of Viscount Haldane L.C., Lord Sumner and Lord Parker in nn.95 and 96 above and those of Hobhouse J. and Leggatt L.J. in n.97 above might as easily be cited here.

[110] [1914] A.C. 398, 440; [1914-1915] All E.R. Rep. 622, 642; on which see Wright, *Sinclair,* 14-15. See also *Westdeutsche* [1994] 4 All E.R. 890, 919 *per* Hobhouse J. However, though confined, the policy can still catch the unwary, as seems to have occurred in *South Tyneside B.C. v. Svenska International* [1995] 1 All E.R. 454 (Q.B.). Clarke J. held that where a net payor on a void swap was entitled to restitution, the net payee could not rely on payments in advance as constituting a change of position because to do so "would in effect be relying upon the supposed validity of a void transaction" [1995] 1 All E.R. 454, 565). However, the decline of this

Sinclair v. Brougham's denial of restitution: a plaintiff can argue that the contract in the instant case is not a borrowing one, or that the policy against indirect enforcement is inapplicable. The judgment of Murphy J. in the *P.M.P.A.* case[111] provides an excellent example of the first route: in *Sinclair v. Brougham* "their Lordships had to consider problems which by coincidence bear an extraordinary resemblance to the facts of the present case with the crucial distinction that in *Sinclair v. Brougham* it was the borrowing which was *ultra vires* whereas in the instant case it is the lending which was incompetent".[112] As to the second route – that the policy against indirect enforcement of *ultra vires* borrowing is inapplicable – it is no more than a consideration in the specific context of *ultra vires* borrowing of the general question already discussed of whether the policy underlying the *ultra vires* rule is better served by retention or restitution. The judgment of Lardner J. in the High Court in *In re Frederick Inns*[113] seems to provide an example: in the case of a company making an *ultra vires* payment to the Revenue Commissioners in attempted settlement of a debt of related companies, Lardner J. held that an action for money had and received lay against the Revenue on the ground of their unjust enrichment, and that "the considerations relating to the *ultra vires* nature of the transaction of deposit-taking which existed in *Sinclair v. Brougham* . . . do not exist in the present case".[114] Before *Westdeutsche*, it was an increasingly common strategy.[115] However, in truth, it is an unnecessary one. Restitution of an outstanding balance is very different from repayment according to the detailed repayment schedule and other terms of a contract. More generally, even if the value of the defendant's enrichment and the contract price correspond,[116] then restitution

---

policy (discussed text with nn.115-118 below) must call this reason for rejecting the defence into question: if restitution of benefits transferred does not amount to enforcing a borrowing contract, then *a fortiori* neither does a change of position defence.

[111] [1992] 1 I.R. 332; [1992] I.L.R.M. 349 (H.C.).

[112] [1992] 1 I.R. 332, 336; [1992] I.L.R.M. 349, 352; see also [1992] 1 I.R. 332, 339; [1992] I.L.R.M. 349, 354; indeed, he had noticed this at an earlier stage in the proceedings when he determined the *ultra vires* point: see *In re P.M.P.A. Garage (Longmile) Ltd. (No.1)* [1992] 1 I.R. 315 (H.C.) 331; [1992] I.L.R.M. 337, 349 *per* Murphy J. The same distinction is drawn in *La Caisse Populaire Notre Dame Limitée v. Moyen* (1967) 61 D.L.R. (2d.) 118, 147-151 *per* Tucker J.

[113] [1991] I.L.R.M. 582 (H.C.)

[114] [1991] I.L.R.M. 582, 593. In an extraordinarily selective citation from *Sinclair v. Brougham*, Lardner J. simply set out Viscount Haldane L.C.'s quotation of *Moses v. Macferlan* ([1914] A.C. 398, 415; [1913-1914] All E.R. Rep. 622, 629) without referring to its fate in the Lord Chancellor's speech or to the views on the action for money had and received set forth in all of the speeches. However, Lardner J. had also held that the Revenue held the *ultra vires* payment on constructive trust ([1991] I.L.R.M. 582, 591-592); on appeal, this was the only mechanism of recovery discussed: [1994] 1 I.L.R.M. 387 (S.C.).

[115] See, *e.g. Dynevor v. The Proprietors, Centre Point Building Units Plan No 4327* (Qld C.A., unreported, 12 May 1995) [1996] *Restitution Law Review* § 20.

[116] As they often will, but not invariably: if the benefit is a service, its value may be different from any contract price.

in the amount of the benefit transferred under an invalid contract may look like enforcing the contract,[117] but emphatically it is not, it is giving a remedy in restitution. Since the contract is not being enforced, there is no conflict with the *ultra vires* doctrine. Indeed, in the House of Lords in *Westdeutsche*, Lord Goff himself "incline[d] to the opinion that a personal claim in restitution would not indirectly enforce the *ultra vires* contract . . .".[118] The ground therefore seems also to have been cut out from under the second of Lord Goff's reasons for not overruling *Sinclair v. Brougham*.

Neither of Lord Goff's reasons to support *Sinclair v. Brougham* holds. Nothing beside remains. Its overruling in *Westdeutsche* is therefore to be welcomed as placing the law, at last, upon a sounder footing. On this point at least, a once-great case has therefore quite properly fallen. Though hubris may be a realistic aspersion to cast upon the speeches in *Sinclair v Brougham*, the displacement of the implied contract theory by the principle against unjust enrichment, described in the long extract from the *Bricklayers' Hall* case set out above,[119] is much more likely to be a result of the changing winds of academic and judicial

---

[117] There is another context in which such concerns have been articulated. In the context of an *ultra vires* contract performed, or partly so, on one side, while *Sinclair v. Brougham* obscured the availability of restitution of the benefits transferred in that purported performance, the question was raised whether the party who had performed could prevent the other from taking the *ultra vires* point and so in effect enforce the contract to have a remedy for that performance (see, *e.g.*, Furmston, "Who Can Plead That a Contract is *Ultra Vires* ?" (1961) 24 *M.L.R.*. 715). This view had some attraction (see, *e.g.*, *Cabaret Holdings v. Meeanee Sports and Rodeo Club*[1982] 1 N.Z.L.R. 673 (H.C. N.Z.) 675 *per* Somers J.; *In re P.M.P.A. Garage (Longmile) Ltd. (No. 2)* [1992] 1 I.R. 332, 341-343; [1992] I.L.R.M. 349, 356-357 *per* Murphy J.) but was ultimately rejected as inconsistent with the *ultra vires* doctrine (see, e.g. *Kathleen Investments v. Australian Atomic Energy Commission* (1976-1977) 139 C.L.R. 117 (H.C.A.) 148-149 *per* Stephen J.; *cp. Commonwealth Homes and Investment Co. v. Smith* (1937) 59 C.L.R. 443 (H.C.A.) 460 *per* Dixon J.). This was the position taken by Mocatta J. at first instance in *Bell Houses Ltd. v. City Wall Properties* [1966] 1 Q.B. 207, 224-226; [1965] 3 All E.R. 427, 435-436; on appeal, Salmon LJ. was attracted to the distinction, but found it unnecessary to "to consider the interesting, important and difficult question which would arise were the contract *ultra vires*, namely, whether, the plaintiff company having fully performed its part under the contract and the defendants having obtained all the benefit of the contract, the defendants could successfully take the point that the contract was *ultra vires* the plaintiff company and so avoid payment. It seems strange that third parties could take advantage of a doctrine, manifestly for the protection of shareholders, in order to deprive the company of money which in justice should be paid to it by the third parties" ([1966] 2 Q.B. 656, 693-694; [1966] 2 All E.R. 674, 687). Consistently with the *ultra vires* doctrine, there is no contract, and, on Salmon L.J.'s example, the defendant could so plead, but a remedy in restitution would prevent the injustice he identified. Had it been appreciated that restitution does not amount to the enforcement of the contract, it would not have been necessary to flirt with the heresy of enforcing an *ultra vires* contract to provide an appropriate remedy in the context of a performed or partly-performed *ultra vires* contract.

[118] [1996] A.C. 669, 688; [1996] 2 All E.R. 961, 972; *cp.* Street, 376: ". . . restitution is a *wholly distinct* relief" (emphasis added). And in Canada, where *Sinclair v. Broughan* had been rejected, there seems to be no difficulty with restitution of benefits transferred under an *ultra vires* borrowing contract: see n.82 above.

[119] Text with nn.73-78.

fashion and a judicial adoption of the principle against unjust enrichment as the flavour of the month theory. More profoundly, it may be that the principle against unjust enrichment is an idea whose time has come.

There may be nothing so powerful as an idea whose time has come. It must, first, however, displace the idea whose time has passed. Thus has the principle against unjust enrichment displaced the implied contract theory. But once the time for the idea has come, it must defend itself against other ideas or in turn be vanquished. Thus must the principle against unjust enrichment defended itself against various charges: that it does not organise the subject of restitution, because unjust enrichment ideas are broadly dispersed throughout the realm of private law, or because the law of restitution does not have an organising principle, or because, if it does, it is something other than the principle against unjust enrichment, or because, if the principle does organise the subject, it does not do so in an exclusive way but shares that function with other principles.[120] As Lord Wright found support for the principle against unjust enrichment in the speeches in *Sinclair v. Brougham*, so also – and with perhaps greater justification – may some support for another competing idea be found in them.

Stoljar has suggested that in the action for money had and received, the plaintiff recovers "on what is in effect a proprietary basis"[121] by asserting that the money in defendant's hands belongs to him (*i.e.*, the plaintiff) and that the defendant came to it without the plaintiff's consent.[122] Lord Haldane may have taken a similar approach in *Sinclair v. Brougham* when he said that the "common law looked simply to the question whether the property had passed".[123] Certainly, this is how it is represented by Lord Wright: "Lord Haldane puts the remedy of law as being based on the fact that no property in the money had passed".[124] The property explanation is attractive, but modern writers[125] do not ground their theories upon *Sinclair v. Brougham*. Lord Wright, having discerned in *Sinclair v. Brougham* a theory other than the implied contract fiction, nevertheless, rejected it as an insufficiently comprehensive explanation of the decided cases in favour of the principle against unjust enrichment,[126] and the

---

[120] These alternative theories are considered and rejected in the articles cited in n.72 above.

[121] Stoljar, *The Law of Quasi-Contract* (2nd ed., Law Book Co., Sydney, 1989) 18; see also, 20.

[122] *ibid.*, 6.

[123] [1914] A.C. 398, 420; [1914-1915] All E.R. Rep. 622, 631.

[124] Wright, *Sinclair*, 11; and he finds further support for this in the speech of Lord Dunedin (*ibid.*, 12).

[125] It has been taken up not only by Stoljar, but in various ways by Watts, "A Property Principle and a Services Principle" [1995] *R.L.R.* 49; McBride and McGrath, "The Nature of Restitution" (1995) 15 *O.J.L.S.* 33; and, to a lesser extent Dietrich, *Restitution. A New Perspective* (Federation Press, Sydney, 1998).

[126] Wright, *Sinclair*, 12-13; see also 24: "However, I feel a difficulty in limiting the concept to ideas of property. The cases of services rendered or debts discharged certainly afford frequent examples of unjust enrichment. I think it is safer to state the claim for unjust enrichment in such cases as depending on an obligation imposed by law in all the circumstances of the case in

modern versions of the proprietory theory do not entirely meet these objections. However, even if a modern version were to displace the principle against unjust enrichment, *Sinclair v. Brougham* is not necessary for this displacement.[127]

Under Lord Mansfield, who professed himself a great friend of the action for money had and received,[128] it prospered mightily. If it was not king of all it surveyed, it was certainly a prince among actions. If, by circumscribing the action, *Sinclair v. Brougham* did not quite commit regicide, it certainly consummated a successful coup. And if *P.M.P.A.* and *Westdeutsche* did nothing else, they have helped to restore the law of restitution, incorporating the action for money had and received, to its rightful place among the heads of obligations at common law.

4. THE PROPRIETARY CLAIM. BAD CASES MAKE HARD LAW?

Not only did the denial of the personal claim in *Sinclair v. Brougham* set the law on the wrong path, but it also had the potential to work an injustice on the facts. If the case had rested with the depositors' loss on the personal claim, then the permanent shareholders would have got everything. This would have resulted in a five-fold windfall for them.[129] For the House of Lords, this was unthinkable. When the common law finds itself in times of trouble, principles of equity come to it, speaking words of wisdom, (frequently). Unsurprisingly, therefore, their Lordships appealed to equity to mitigate the harshness of their decision on the common law point. Thus, Lord Sumner thought that "the present case must be decided upon equitable principles upon which there is no direct authority";[130] while for Lord Dunedin, it was not "necessary that the claim should be one capable of being made good by action at common law. It will suffice if there is an equitable remedy. Precisely the same difficulty was felt and met in the Roman law. . . . Is English Equity to retire defeated from the task which other systems of Equity have conquered?"[131] Rousing rhetoric; stirring

---

order to satisfy the requirements of justice, that is, to avoid what is unconscionable or unconscientious . . .".

[127] Even more, Lord Haldane's speech may not be a secure basis for the property theory of the action for money had and received, because Lord Haldane was not in the passage cited at n.123 dealing with the depositors' personal claim at law, but with their tracing claim.

[128] *Weston v. Downes* (1778) 1 Doug. 23, 24; 99 E.R. 19, 20.

[129] "The appalling result in this very case would be that the society shareholders having got the proceeds of the depositors' money in the form of investment, . . . [would be] enriched to the extent of 500 per cent". [1914] A.C. 398, 436; [1914-1915] All E.R. Rep. 622, 640 *per* Lord Dunedin.

[130] [1914] A.C. 398, 458; [1914-1915] All E.R. Rep. 622, 651 *per* Lord Sumner.

[131] [1914] A.C. 398, 434; [1914-1915] All E.R. Rep. 622, 639 *per* Lord Dunedin. On the Roman learning discussed by Lord Dunedin, and intended by him as a guide to the solution of the problem in Scots law, see Rodger "Recovering Payments under Void Contracts in Scots Law" in Jones and Swadling, (eds.), *The Search For Principle. Essays in Honour of Lord Goff of Chieveley* (O.U.P., Oxford, 1999) 1, 5-7, 10-14.

stuff. Unfortunately, it is difficult to discern precisely what the equitable remedy was.[132] Lord Sumner called it "the 'tracing' equity",[133] and the word "tracing" appears in the other speeches,[134] but this seems to have been the occasion upon which this child of equity was christened.[135] Like all infants, it suffered somewhat from its lack of maturity.[136] Indeed, it is only in recent years that it has become clear that the tracing exercise proceeds in two stages: a plaintiff must first identify his property or its exchange product in the defendant's hands, and then, second, make a claim to it.[137] It is commonplace in this context to distinguish between tracing at law and tracing in equity.[138] However, this ought to be understood as applicable not to the identification stage of the tracing exercise but to the claiming stage; there is no justification for having two sets of identification rules,[139] either the plaintiff's property or its exchange product

---

[132] Nevertheless, it has been applied not only generally in subsequent tracing cases, but also in the context of *ultra vires* contracts; see, *e.g. In re P.M.P.A. Garage (Longmile) Ltd. (No. 2)* [1992] 1 I.R. 332; [1992] I.L.R.M. 349 (H.C); *Tauranga Borough v. Tauranga Electric Power Board* [1944] N.Z.L.R. 155 (N.Z. C.A.).

[133] [1914] A.C. 398, 460; [1914-1915] All E.R. Rep. 622, 652 *per* Lord Sumner.

[134] [1914] A.C. 398, 412, 418; [1914-1915] All E.R. Rep. 622, 6627, 630 *per* Viscount Haldane L.C.; [1914] A.C. 398, 437; [1914-1915] All E.R. Rep. 622, 640 *per* Lord Dunedin; [1914] A.C. 398, 441; [1914-1915] All E.R. Rep. 622, 642 *per* Lord Parker.

[135] Winfield, "Equity and *Quasi-Contract*" in *Select Legal Essays* (Sweet & Maxwell, London, 1952) 226 [reprinting (1948) 64 *L.Q.R.* 46] commented (235) that a curious feature of the "tracing order" was that "although it is well represented in Equity, there is an almost total lack of reference to it *eo nomine* in the treatises and textbooks on equity, in which its baptismal name is some phrase like 'following trust property'. In the law reports its christening as a 'tracing order' seems to be as modern as the decision of the House of Lords in *Sinclair v. Brougham*".

[136] For Hanbury, it represented a "somewhat rough-and-ready principle" (Hanbury, 13); while for Lord Wright, though it worked substantial justice (Wright, "Home", 358), it was also "a sort of rough justice, in the form of a tracing order" (Wright, *Sinclair*, 2), even "a rough sort of tracing order" (*ibid.,* 5).

[137] Smith, *The Law of Tracing* (O.U.P., Oxford, 1997) chapter 1. See *Boscawen v. Bajwa* [1996] 1 W.L.R. 328 (C.A.) 334; [1995] 4 All E.R. 769, 776 *per* Millett L.J.; *Trustees of the Property of F.C. Jones & Co. v. Jones* [1997] Ch. 159 (C.A.) 169-170 *per* Millett L.J.; *Foskett v. McKeown* [2000] 2 W.L.R. 1299 (H.L.) 1305 *per* Lord Browne-Wilkinson, 1308 *per* Lord Steyn, 1322-1324 *per* Lord Millett (Lord Hoffmann concurring). Indeed, there would seem to be some measure of support for this separation of the tracing exercise into identification and claiming in the speech of Viscount Haldane L.C. in *Sinclair v. Brougham*: "So long as the money . . . can be *traced* into what has been procured with it, the principal can . . . *claim* that his money is invested in a specific thing" ([1914] A.C. 398, 419; [1914-1915] All E.R. Rep. 622, 631; emphasis added; discussed by Smith, 12).

[138] This distinction is drawn in the speeches in *Sinclair v. Brougham*: see [1914] A.C. 398, 420; [1914-1915] All E.R. Rep. 622, 632 *per* Viscount Haldane L.C.; [1914] A.C. 398, 436-437; [1914-1915] All E.R. Rep. 622, 640 *per* Lord Dunedin.

[139] Smith, 120-130, 277-279, 342-347; Birks "The Need of a Unitary Law of Tracing" in Cranston, (ed.), *Making Commercial Law. Essays in Honour of Roy Goode* (O.U.P., Oxford, 1997) 239; *Trustees of the Property of F.C. Jones & Co. v. Jones* [1997] Ch. 159, 169-170 *per* Millett L.J.; *Foskett v. McKeown* [2000] 2 W.L.R. 1299, 1308-1309 *per* Lord Steyn, 134 *per* Lord Millett (Lord Hoffmann concurring); *cf.* 1305 *per* Lord Browne-Wilkinson reserving the question.

is to be found in the defendant's hands or it is not; once it has been identified, the plaintiff's claim to it can then be made either at law or in equity. Not only do these separations bring order to a notoriously chaotic field of law, but they supply a useful tool with which to analyse the speeches in *Sinclair v. Brougham* on this point.

The House of Lords ordered that the depositors and remaining shareholders should share in the proceeds *pari passu*, and then congratulated themselves on a job well done. It has been left to subsequent generations to work out whether such a conclusion is justifiable. It is not enough simply to assert that the depositors and shareholders were able to trace their money into the society's funds; it is necessary to show both that such money was identifiable in the society's hands and that it could be claimed by the depositors and shareholders.

In the course of argument,[140] Viscount Haldane L.C. suggested that the principle in *Re Hallett's Estate*[141] would help in this regard. In that case, Hallett, a solicitor, died insolvent. Upon his death, it was discovered that by selling bonds, he had misappropriated funds first from his marriage settlement and then from a client, and lodged the proceeds to his bank account. Fry J. at first instance took the view that Hallett had misapplied trust funds in both cases, and that the client and the trustees of the settlement could, in principle, identify the proceeds of their bonds in the bank account and claim accordingly. However, he applied the rule in *Clayton's Case*,[142] and concluded that the trustees' claim was completely defeated by subsequent withdrawals, and the client's claim was partially so.

The Court of Appeal affirmed that Hallett's misappropriation of the client's bonds was a misapplication of trust funds, and that the client could, in principle, claim in the bank account the identifiable proceeds of her misapplied bonds. Jessel M.R. laid down some basic principles of identification and claiming. First, if the misappropriated trust funds are applied to a purchase, the beneficial owner "is entitled at his election either to take the property, or to have a charge on the property for the amount of the trust money".[143] Second, if the misappropriated trust funds are mixed with the trustee's own funds for the purchase, the beneficial owner is "entitled to a charge on the property purchased, for the amount of the trust money laid out in the purchase; and that charge is quite independent of the facts of the amount laid out by the trustee".[144] Furthermore, he confirmed that these rules applied not only where the

---

[140] See above, n.32.

[141] (1880) 13 Ch.D. 696; [1874-1880] All E.R. Rep. 793 (C.A.).

[142] *Devaynes v. Noble*; *Clayton's Case* (1816) 1 Mer. 529; 35 E.R. 767. The rule presumes that, in the absence of contrary intention or countervailing circumstances, the first debt in time is discharged by the first incoming credits, and so on, and *vice versa*. See, generally, McConville "Tracing and the Rule in *Clayton's Case* " (1963) 79 *L.Q.R.* 388.

[143] (1880) 13 Ch.D. 696, 709; [1874-1880] All E.R. Rep. 793, 796 *per* Jessel M.R.

[144] *ibid.*

trustee purchased land or goods with the misappropriated funds, but also where he lodged them in his bank account,[145] and applied not only to express trustees, such as the trustees of the marriage settlement, but also to other fiduciary relationships, such as that between the solicitor and his client.[146]

In a separate judgment on the applicability of the rule in *Clayton's Case*, Jessel M.R. held that "where a man does an act which may be rightfully performed, he cannot say that the act was intentionally and in fact done wrongly".[147] Applying this to Hallett's lodgement of trust money to his bank account from which he subsequently made drawings, it was to Jessel M.R. "perfectly plain that he cannot be heard to say that he [*i.e.,* Hallett] took away the trust money when he had a right to take away his own money".[148] The rule in *Clayton's Case*, though a very convenient one, applied "unless there is evidence either of agreement to the contrary, or of circumstances from which a contrary intention must be presumed and then, of course, that which is a mere presumption of law gives way to those other considerations"[149] as in this case. Since the account at all times had sufficient credit to meet the claim both of the trustees and of the client, the trustees' appeal was allowed.

Quite what all this has to with identifying in the society's hands money which could be claimed by the depositors and shareholders in *Sinclair v. Brougham* is unclear. *Re Hallett's Estate* states two rules to be applied when an errant trustee misapplies trust funds to aid in the identification of the beneficiary's funds, and uses a presumption against a wrongdoer to decline to apply the rule in *Clayton's Case* in the same identification process. On the other hand, in *Sinclair v. Brougham*, trust funds may have been mixed but they were not misapplied; there was no wrongdoer; and *Clayton's Case* would have been unusable on the facts.[150]

---

[145] (1880) 13 Ch.D. 696, 771; [1874-1880] All E.R. Rep. 793, 797; *Pennell v. Deffell* (1853) DeG.M.&G. 372; 43 E.R. 551 approved; *ex p Dale* (1879) 11 Ch.D. 772 doubted; see also (1880) 13 Ch.D. 696, 721-722; [1874-1880] All E.R. Rep. 793, 802-803 *per* Baggallay L.J. concurring.

[146] (1880) 13 Ch.D. 696, 720, 709-710; [1874-1880] All E.R. Rep. 793, 796, 802 *per* Jessel M.R.; see also (1880) 13 Ch.D. 696, 721; [1874-1880] All E.R. Rep. 793, 802 *per* Baggallay L.J. concurring.

[147] (1880) 13 Ch.D. 696, 727; [1874-1880] All E.R. Rep. 793, 805. Again, "[w]henever an act can be done rightfully the man who has done it is not allowed to say, as against the persons entitled to the property or the right, that he has done it wrongfully. That is the universal law" (*ibid.*).

[148] *ibid.* See also *Shanahan's Stamp Auctions v. Farrelly* [1962] I.R. 386 (H.C.) 425-429, 443 *per* Budd J.; *In re Irish Shipping* [1986] I.L.R.M. 518 (H.C.) 521, 523 *per* Carroll J.

[149] (1880) 13 Ch.D. 696, 728; [1874-1880] All E.R. Rep. 793, 806 *per* Jessel M.R.; see also (1880) 13 Ch.D. 696, 738-739; [1874-1880] All E.R. Rep. 793, 811 *per* Baggallay L.J. concurring. See also *In re Chute's Estate* [1914] 1 I.R. 180, 185 *per* Ross J.; *Re Hughes* [1970] I.R. 237, 243 *per* Kenny J.; *In re Money Markets International* High Court, unreported, July 20, 1999, Laffoy J. at 13.

[150] *Barlow Clowes International v. Vaughan* [1992] 4 All E.R. 22 (C.A.); see also *Re Securitibank Ltd.* [1978] 1 N.Z.L.R. 97 (H.C. N.Z.); McConville, "Tracing and the Rule in *Clayton's* Case" (1963) 79 L.Q.R. 388, 406-407. For Viscount Haldane C.L., the enthusiast for *Hallett* in the

Sinclair v. Brougham boils down simply to a case in which two funds were mixed through no fault of either of the contributors.[151] Where property has been mixed through no fault of the contributors to the mixture, the general rules seem to be that each party "can assert that her contribution exists in any part of the mixture, *subject to* the right of other contributors to do likewise"[152] and reductions in the mixture are borne in proportion to the original contribution.[153] Assuming that these principles apply not only to mixtures but also to bank accounts and applying them to the facts of *Sinclair v. Brougham*, it is plain that, in principle, the depositors and shareholders could each identify the proceeds of their money in the society; and the House of Lords readily – perhaps too readily – concluded that they could in fact so identify their money.[154]

On the question of whether they could then claim the money so identified, Viscount Haldane L.C. was of the view that if property in the money had not passed at law, the owners of the money could claim at law.[155] But money being currency,[156] property passes easily – as it does when it is lodged into a bank account and is therefore replaced with a debt owed by the banker to the customer – and the basis of this claim at law disappears.[157] Where there was a

---

House of Lords in *Sinclair v. Brougham*, "the really relevant part of the judgment in *Hallett's Case* is that which stress how the difficulty of following money into a debtor and creditor account like a banker's is got over in equity" [1914] A.C. 398, 422; [1914-195] All E.R. Rep. 622, 633); that is, he regarded *Hallett* as relevant on the identification stage of the process, whereas the analysis above demonstrates otherwise.

[151] [1914] A.C. 398, 000; [1914-1915] All E.R. Rep. 622, 641 *per* Lord Dunedin; *cp. Re Diplock; Diplock v. Wintle* [1948] Ch. 465, 532; [1948] 2 All E.R. 318, 353 *per* Lord Greene M.R.

[152] Smith, 73; emphasis in original.

[153] *ibid. Hallett* is relevant to neither principle. But Smith posits a third – that "when a contributor withdraws from a mixture, his contribution is followed into his withdrawal; in other words, what he takes out is counted first against his contribution" (Smith, 76) – of which he instances *Hallett* (see above, n.147) as an example. But, as has already been said, the facts of *Sinclair v. Brougham* do not come within the terms of this principle.

[154] The application to bank accounts of general principles relating to mixtures is a large and controversial matter, but it is the correct position in principle: see Smith, 183-215. As to the overly easy application of identification principles by the House, see Smith, 227-234.

[155] "The common law . . . looks simply to the question whether the property had passed, and if it had not, for instance, where no relationship of debtor and creditor had intervened, the money could be followed, notwithstanding its normal character as currency, provided that it could be earmarked or traced into assets acquired with it" [1914] A.C. 398, 420; [1914-1915] All E.R. Rep. 622, 631-632 *per* Viscount Haldane L.C. If by this he meant, as it seems he did, that the plaintiff could make a proprietary claim to the money paid, it is at best an overstatement: "Specific relief, as distinct from damages (the normal remedy at common law), was confined to a very limited range of claims . . ." (*Re Diplock; Diplock v. Wintle* [1948] Ch. 465, 519; [1948] 2 All E.R. 318, 346; see also Stoljar, 28-30, and more generally, Smith, 320-338.

[156] Where it is not currency, then it is treated like any other chattel. Furthermore, "if money in a bag is stolen, and can be identified in the form in which it was stolen, it can be recovered *in specie*" ([1914] A.C. 398, 418; [1914-1915] All E.R. Rep. 622, 631). This seemingly simple case of the stolen bag of coins in fact causes great difficulties of analysis: see n.192-193 below.

[157] "But while the common law gave the remedy I have stated, it gave no remedy when the money had been paid by the wrongdoer into his account with his banker, who simply owed him a debt,

claim at law, equity "exercised a concurrent jurisdiction based upon trust"; [158]
where there was no claim at law, equity

> gave a further remedy. The Court of Chancery could and would declare,
> even against the general creditors of the wrongdoer, that there was what
> it called a charge on the banker's debt to the person whose money had
> been paid in to the latter's account in favour of the person whose money
> it really was. And as Jessel M.R. pointed out in *Re Hallett's Estate*, this
> equity was not confined to cases of trust in the strict sense, but applied at
> all events, to every case where there was a fiduciary relationship. . . . I see
> no reason why the remedy explained by Jessel M.R. in *Re Hallett's Es-
> tate* of declaring a charge on the investment in a debt due from bankers
> on balance, or on any mass of money or securities with which the plain-
> tiff's money had been mixed, should not apply in the case of a transaction
> that is *ultra vires*. The property was never converted into a debt, in equity
> at all events, and there has been throughout a resulting trust, not of an
> active character, but sufficient, in my opinion, to bring the transaction
> within the general principle.[159]

However, the funds to be distributed by the liquidator represented money which
not only the depositors but also the society (and thus its shareholders) were
entitled to follow; and, since the depositors could "only claim the depreciated
assets which represent[ed] their money, and nothing more"[160] it followed that
"the principle to be adopted in the distribution must be apportionment on the
footing [that] depreciation and loss are to be borne *pro rata*".[161] Lord Sumner
"agree[d], without recapitulating reasons, that the principle upon which *Re
Hallett's Estate* is founded justifies an order allowing the appellants [the de-
positors] to follow the assets"[162] and make a claim, subject to the equal rights
of the shareholders similarly to identify and claim.

It is difficult to make sense of these passages, but they seem to come to this.
In *Hallett*, Jessel M.R. had held that once the client could identify the proceeds
of the sale of her bonds in Hallett's bank account, since he stood in a fiduciary

---

so that no money was or could be, in the contemplation of a court of law, earmarked" ([1914]
A.C. 398, 420; [1914-1915] All E.R. Rep. 622, 632).
[158] *ibid.*
[159] [1914] A.C. 398, 420-421; [1914-1915] All E.R. Rep. 622, 632.
[160] [1914] A.C. 398, 424; [1914-1915] All E.R. Rep. 622, 633.
[161] [1914] A.C. 398, 424; [1914-1915] All E.R. Rep. 622, 633-634. Heuston comments that in
"the field of equity Haldane was particularly strong . . . [especially] in the uncertain area where
the principle of common law and equity overlap . . . [and in this speech] he expounded with
masterly learning the circumstances in which equity would permit a beneficiary to trace
misapplied trust funds . . ." (Heuston, *Lives of the Lord Chancellors* (Clarendon Press, Oxford,
1964) 215-216); *cf.* below, n.209.
[162] [1914] A.C. 398, 459; [1914-1915] All E.R. Rep. 622, 652.

relation to her and was bailee of the bonds, she could claim such proceeds in the account. Similarly, here, since the society owed fiduciary duties to the depositors – who could identify the proceeds of their money in the society – they could claim those proceeds. Hence, though it was not relevant on the identification leg of the tracing exercise, *Hallett* proved relevant on the claiming leg of the exercise.

So much is tolerably clear from these passages. However, they contain at least three difficulties. First, the *pro rata* distribution of the funds to the depositors and shareholders is made to sound like it was a consequence of the claiming rules at issue. On the reading presented here, it was just as much if not more so a consequence of the identification rules at issue. The fiduciary relationship asserted to subsist between the depositors and the society allowed the depositors to claim in equity the proportion of the funds which had already been identified; both the depositors and shareholders could identify proceeds of their money in the society, and since each group can in such circumstances assert that its contribution exists in any part of the mixture, *subject to* the right of the other group to do likewise,[163] what the depositors could identify and therefore claim was limited by what the shareholders could similarly identify and claim.

Second, Viscount Haldane L.C. seemed to hold that the society owed fiduciary duties to the depositors.[164] This proposition is startling, because the relationship of banker and customer is usually one of debtor and creditor, and not fiduciary in nature,[165] and there was nothing more on the facts of the relation-

---

[163] See text with n.152 above; *cp.* [1914] A.C. 398, 438; [1914-1915] All E.R. Rep. 622, 641 *per* Lord Dunedin; [1914] A.C. 398, 448-449; [1914-1915] All E.R. Rep. 622, 646 *per* Lord Parker.

[164] In allowing the parties to trace and claim, he based himself on *Re Hallett's Estate* which he held "applied to all events to every case where there was a fiduciary relationship" [1914] A.C. 398, 421; [1914-1915] All E.R. Rep. 622, 632) and since he held that *Hallett* applied, it follows that he must have regarded the relationship between the parties as fiduciary, though he was careful to hold that the society had not breached its fiduciary duty [1914] A.C. 398, 422-423; [1914-1915] All E.R. Rep. 622, 633). Lord Atkinson concurred, and Lord Parker delivered a speech to similar effect (see *e.g.* [1914] A.C. 398, 441; [1914-1915] All E.R. Rep. 622, 643 (fiduciary relationship). Lord Sumner agreed that *Hallett* justified the tracing order [1914] A.C. 398, 459; [1914-1915] All E.R. Rep. 622, 652), which presumably amounts to a concurrence that a fiduciary relationship subsisted on the facts. Only Lord Dunedin disagreed: "[n]either party is here in any fiduciary position to the other" [1914] A.C. 398, 438; [1914-1915] All E.R. Rep. 622, 641)

[165] *Foley v. Hill* (1848) 2 H.L.C. 28; *Kinlen v. Ulster Bank* [1928] I.R. 171 (S.C.). See, *e.g.*, Oakley: "The relationship between the depositors and the society was clearly that of creditor and debtor and, therefore, it is difficult to see how the depositors retained any legal or equitable proprietary interest in the money deposited – a creditor retains no proprietary interest in the money advanced" (76-77). Again, "it is by no means clear why the directors of the building society owed fiduciary duties to members, let alone to lenders of money borrowed *ultra vires*", that is, let alone to the depositors (Meaghar, Gummow and Lehane, *Equity. Doctrines and Remedies* (3rd ed., Butterworths, Sydney, 1992) 134, para. 505).

ship between the depositors and the society[166] to alter this conclusion.[167] Hence, it is, as Chambers notes:

> difficult to understand why the directors were in a fiduciary relationship with the depositors, and, if so, why they were in breach of their duties when the depositors had consented to the investment of their money. It is also difficult to accept the classification of shareholders as innocent recipients and directors as fiduciaries in breach, when the . . . shareholders included all of the directors of the society.[168]

The third difficulty arises from the fact that Viscount Haldane L.C. justified the depositors' equitable claim not only on the basis of the fiduciary relationship but also because the facts gave rise to "a resulting trust" – though it was "not of an active character". In *Westdeutsche*, the bank latched on to this, and claimed that the net payments on the *ultra vires* swaps were held by the local authority on resulting trust. Lord Goff concluded that there was no basis for imposing a resulting trust,[169] as did Lord Browne-Wilkinson, who described the inactive resulting trust posited by Viscount Haldane L.C. as an unconventional one of which there was no trace in any other authority[170] and for which there was no justification in principle.[171] Whether or not their Lordships in *Westdeutsche* were correct in rejecting a resulting trust in principle,[172] they were surely right

---

[166] Indeed, Donnelly, *The Law of Banks and Credit Institutions* (Round Hall Sweet & Maxwell, Dublin, 1999) 127-128 sees the principle in *Foley v. Hill* as applicable as between customer and credit institutions generally, and she includes building societies (chapter 3) within that category of credit institution.

[167] However, in *Re Diplock*, the Court of Appeal argued that in *Sinclair v. Brougham*, "a sufficient fiduciary relationship was found to exist between the depositors and the directors by reason of the fact that the purposes for which the depositors had handed their money to the directors were by law incapable of fulfilment" (*Re Diplock, Diplock v. Wintle* [1948] Ch. 465, 540-541; [1948] 2 All E.R. 318, 357).

[168] Chambers, *Resulting Trusts* (O.U.P., Oxford, 1997) [hereafter Chambers] 156, citing [1914] A.C. 398, 422-423, 458 for the proposition that the depositors had consented to the investment, and [1912] 2 Ch. 183, 222-223 for the directors' status as shareholders! See also Mason and Carter, 100, para. 328, n.228.

[169] [1996] A.C. 669, 690; [1996] 2 All E.R. 961, 974.

[170] [1996] A.C. 669, 712; [1996] 2 All E.R. 961, 994.

[171] [1996] A.C. 669, 712-713; [1996] 2 All E.R. 961, 994-995. Lord Slynn agreed that "no resulting trust could arise" ([1996] A.C. 669, 718; [1996] 2 All E.R. 961, 1000); *cp.* Lord Lloyd ([1996] A.C. 669, 738; [1996] 2 All E.R. 961, 1018). Similarly, it "is hard to see how a resulting trust, even one of an inactive character, whatever that may be, can arise in a situation where a person intentionally places money on deposit with another, both parties intending that the property in the money should pass to the depositee" (Oakley, 77; see also Stoljar, 32; and Chambers, 156-163, 167; *cf.* Worthington, *Proprietory Interests in Commercial Transactions* (O.U.P., Oxford, 1996) [hereafter Worthington] 148-161).

[172] On the nature of the resulting trust after *Westdeutsche*, see O'Dell "Bricks and Stones . . .", 170-171 with references, to which should now be added Swadling, "The Law of Property" in Birks and Rose, (eds.), *Lessons of the Swaps Litigation* (Mansfield/L.L.P., London, 2000) 242;

to hold that the reasoning in *Sinclair v. Brougham* provides no support for such a trust.

If neither a fiduciary relationship nor a resulting trust justified the depositors' claim, the question arises: What else in the case – if anything – does?[173] Another equitable proprietary interest was touched on by Viscount Haldane L.C. when he said that he could see "no reason why the remedy explained by Jessel M.R. in *Re Hallett's Estate* of declaring a charge . . . should not apply in the case of a transaction that is *ultra vires*".[174] Lord Parker[175] and Lord Sumner[176] spoke to the same effect.[177] In this identification of a charge[178] there is a credible equitable proprietary base for the depositors' claim. And, as a matter of Irish law, it is clear that a plaintiff who can identify and claim in equity "has a charge on the account to which the money or cheques have been lodged or on property on which the monies received have been spent".[179] Certainly, a charge was imposed in *Hallett*, and this aspect of it may finally provide the reason for Viscount Haldane L.C.'s championing of it in *Sinclair v. Brougham*; but if *Hallett* is secure as an authority justifying such a charge, the deeply problematic speech of Viscount Haldane L.C. is unnecessary for this purpose. In the end, therefore, although a charge might justify the depositors' equitable claim in *Sinclair v. Brougham*, that decision is not necessary to justify the availability of a charge in equity's armoury.

Much else has been taken from the speeches in *Sinclair v. Brougham* on the tracing issue. For example, it has been said that, as a consequence in "England, at least, it is apparently clearly established . . . that a subsisting fiduciary relationship is a necessary precondition of the equitable right to trace":[180] that is,

---

and Birks and Rose, (eds.), *Restitution and Equity. Resulting Trusts and Equitable Compensation* (Mansfield/L.L.P., London, 2000).

[173] See also Virgo, *Principles of the Law of Restitution* (O.U.P., Oxford, 1999) 634 who speculates that a constructive trust might be appropriate on the facts; whether or not that it is correct in principle, it was not canvassed in the case.

[174] [1914] A.C. 398, 421; [1914-1915] All E.R. Rep. 622, 632; though, in fact, this was more by way of prelude, than of alternative, to the resulting trust point.

[175] [1914] A.C. 398, 441-442; [1914-1915] All E.R. Rep. 622, 642-643.

[176] [1914] A.C. 398, 459-460; [1914-1915] All E.R. Rep. 622, 652.

[177] Hence, the House of Lords in *Sinclair v. Brougham* based "the remedy available in equity on a right of property recognised by equity as vested in the plaintiff throughout, not lost by payment into a banking account, nor by the mixture of moneys, nor by merger in a mass of assets. In all these cases the equitable remedy by way of declaration of charge is available" (*Re Diplock, Diplock v. Wintle* [1948] Ch. 465, 540; [1948] 2 All E.R. 318, 357).

[178] Lord Wright called it a lien: "Equity in such cases gives a partial right, which has been called an equitable lien, on the total property to the extent that the total property represents the plaintiff's property" (Wright, *Sinclair*, 7). On whether it should more properly be called a lien, see Worthington, 175. On the accuracy of the concept, see Smith, 200-201; as to when it is appropriate and possible for a plaintiff to claim such a charge or lien, see Smith, 347-351, and, generally, *Foskett v. McKeown* [2000] 2 W.L.R. 1299 (H.L.).

[179] *In re Shannon Travel Ltd.* High Court, unreported, May 8, 1972, Kenny J. at 8-9 of the transcript.

[180] Meaghar, Gummow and Lehane, *Equity. Doctrines and Remedies* (3rd ed., Butterworths, Syd-

in *Sinclair v. Brougham* "Lord Parker and Viscount Haldane both predicate the existence of a right of property recognised by equity which depends on there having existed at some stage a fiduciary relationship of some kind . . .".[181] The requirement of a subsisting fiduciary relationship is often easily satisfied,[182] as it was at first instance in *Westdeutsche* by Hobhouse J.[183] and in the Court of Appeal.[184] But for so long at it persists, it will preclude an equitable claim in support of a purely legal interest, and if strictly interpreted could preclude an equitable claim in support of another species of equitable interest, such as one subsequently raised to reverse an unjust enrichment in a relationship which is not fiduciary. If however, the fiduciary limitation is not found in *Sinclair v. Brougham*, or if it is no longer to be followed on this point, then these limitations can fall away, though it will then be a separate question as to whether they should.

The fiduciary requirement seems to have had no friends since Lord Greene M.R.'s decision in *Re Diplock*.[185] Oakley argues that *Hallett* supported the right of the holder of *any* equitable proprietary interest to identify his property in its exchange product and claim it on the basis of an equitable proprietary interest,[186] and that properly interpreted, apart from Lord Dunedin,[187] the House

---

ney, 1992) 134, para. 505, commenting that it is clearly established by *"Re Diplock* relying on the speech of Lord Parker in *Sinclair v. Brougham"*. To like effect, see Delany, *Equity and the Law of Trusts in Ireland* (2nd ed., Round Hall Sweet & Maxwell, Dublin, 1999), 634-635, 643-647, and Goff and Jones, 103. The requirement seems to have been rejected in Canada and Australia (see Smith, 128), but the position in New Zealand is unclear (see Smith, 120, n.2, and 128, n.33).

[181] *Re Diplock; Diplock v. Wintle* [1948] Ch. 465, 540; [1948] 2 All E.R. 318, 357; *cp.* the earlier defence of "the necessity of establishing as a starting point the existence of a fiduciary or a quasi-fiduciary relationship or of a continuing right of property recognised in equity" ([1948] Ch. 465, 520; [1948] 2 All E.R. 318, 346-347).

[182] See, *e.g., Chase Manhattan Bank N.A. v. Israel British Bank (London) Ltd.,* [1981] Ch. 105 (Goulding J.); *Re Irish Shipping* [1986] I.L.R.M. 518 (H.C.); *Agip (Africa) Ltd. v. Jackson* [1990] Ch. 265 (Ch.) 280 *per* Millett J. (a point not taken on appeal: [1991] Ch. 547 (C.A.)).

[183] [1994] 4 All E.R. 890, 937: "the present case is indistinguishable from *Sinclair v. Brougham.* The fiduciary relationship comes into existence and the equity is created at the time that the payee receives the money".

[184] [1994] 4 All E.R. 890, 964; [1994] 1 W.L.R. 938, 949 *per* Dillon L.J.; [1994] 4 All E.R. 890, 969; [1994] 1 W.L.R. 938, 953 *per* Leggatt L.J. The objections to the finding of a fiduciary relationship in *Sinclair v. Brougham*, nn.165-168 above, apply with equal if not greater force here.

[185] See the careful analysis in Smith, 120-130 (demonstrating that the requirement is founded upon misunderstanding) and 340-347; see also Worthington, 184-185.

[186] Oakley, 72. In this respect, in *Hallett*, the fiduciary relationship was a *sufficient* basis for an equitable proprietary claim, but not a *necessary* one: see Smith, 124-125.

[187] Who simply looked to a "superfluity" ([1914] A.C. 398, 437; [1914-1915] All E.R. Rep. 622, 640) in the defendant's hands. This "unworkable principle" (Oakley, 80), as Oakley rightly points out, is "extraordinarily difficult to apply – what constitutes a superfluity for these purposes ?" (Oakley, 79), and Lord Browne-Wilkinson was very wary of it in *Westdeutsche* ([1996] A.C. 669, 711; [1996] 2 All E.R. 961, 993).

of Lords in *Sinclair v. Brougham*[188] did likewise.[189] On this reading, having identified their money in the society, the depositors' equitable proprietary claim was based simply upon an equitable proprietary interest in the money, of which not one species (the fiduciary relationship) but three (that relationship, resulting trust, and charge) were identified,[190] and there is nothing in the speeches to confine the claim to only one species or source of equitable proprietary interest such as a fiduciary relationship.[191] In *Westdeutsche*, Lord Browne-Wilkinson accepted that the owner of a stolen bag of coins lodged in a bank account could trace into the bank account, *i.e.*, identify the coins in their exchange product and claim accordingly, notwithstanding the absence of a fiduciary relationship between plaintiff and thief.[192] This has probably, and quite rightly, sounded the death-knell for the fiduciary requirement as a matter of English law.[193] Similarly, in Ireland Budd J. in the *Bricklayers' Hall* case in the High Court commented that "[i]t is questionable whether *Sinclair v. Brougham* is authority for the proposition that a fiduciary relationship is essential before property can be followed in equity".[194] This should similarly sound the death-knell for the fiduciary requirement as a matter of Irish law.

It is therefore difficult to abstract anything of value from *Sinclair v. Brougham* on the so-called "tracing" issue. Indeed, for Stoljar, it "cannot be really explained on the basis of the tracing doctrine. What was here called 'tracing' or 'following' property, was nothing more than a question-begging

---

[188] Oakley, 76-77; see also Oakley, "Proprietary Claims and Their Priority in Insolvency" [1995] *C.L.J.* 377; and Smith, 123-125.

[189] *E.g.* Viscount Haldane L.C. commented that the depositors' money "was never converted into a debt, in equity at all events" ([1914] A.C. 398, 421; [1914-1915] All E.R. Rep. 622, 632 and Lord Parker expressed his approach to be based upon the creation by equity of "rights of property, though not recognised as such by the common law" ([1914] A.C. 398, 422; [1914-1915] All E.R. Rep. 622, 643).

[190] A similar argument as to *Diplock* is also more than possible (Oakley, 80-82; [1995] *C.L.J.* 377, 383-384; Pearse, "A Tracing Paper" (1976) 40 *Conv. (n.s.)* 277) but it is probably rather more sound to argue instead that if the fiduciary limitation is not properly to be found in *Sinclair*, or if it is but *Sinclair* is no longer regarded as good law on the point, that limitation should wither away (notwithstanding *Diplock*: *cp.* Jones, *"Ultra Vires* Swaps: The Common Law and Equitable Fall-Out" [1996] *C.L.J.* 432, 435; *cf.* Lord Browne-Wilkinson in *Westdeutsche* [1996] A.C. 669, 714; [1996] 2 All E.R. 961, 996).

[191] *Cp.* Smith, 125-126; Worthington, 184.

[192] [1996] A.C. 669, 716; [1996] 2 All E.R. 961, 974.

[193] See Virgo, 649, and Smith, "Tracing" in Birks and Rose, (eds.), *Lessons of the Swaps Litigation* (Mansfield/L.L.P., London, 2000) 233, 234-235.

[194] High Court, unreported, March 6, 1996, at 41 of the transcript. The point did not arise on appeal: [1996] 1 I.R. 468; [1996] 2 I.L.R.M. 547 (S.C.). It might be objected that Budd J. was bound by the contrary authority of his father's judgment on the point in *Shanahan's Stamp Auctions v. Farrelly* [1962] I.R. 386 (H.C.). However, this may not necessarily be so. In *Shanahan's*, though he quoted them extensively, the elder Budd J. did not consider *Sinclair v. Brougham* and *Re Diplock* for what they themselves might have held but only for whether they supported his interpretation of *Re Hallett's Estate* (see, *e.g.* [1962] I.R. 386, 428, 438, 443).

method to make the society return some of the lenders' money".[195] It comes as no surprise then that it did not survive *Westdeutsche* on this issue either: Lord Browne-Wilkinson held that "the decision as to rights *in rem* in *Sinclair v. Brougham* should . . . be overruled".[196] Lord Slynn agreed that *Sinclair v. Brougham* should be departed from,[197] and Lord Lloyd agreed that it was wrongly decided.[198] Given the infirmity of *Sinclair v. Brougham* on the whole tracing process, both as to identification and as to claiming, this must be right. Furthermore, to my late twentieth century eyes, raised on the distinction between ownership and obligation,[199] it is strange indeed that, where a personal action failed, a proprietary one should have succeeded! This outcome has been described as "somewhat irrational",[200] not least because, in the case of an insolvency, it could result in an unfair priority other creditors, and this was one of the concerns relied upon by Lord Browne-Wilkinson to justify overruling *Sinclair v. Brougham* on this point.[201]

Lord Goff, however, was reluctant to adopt this course, not least because "Lord Wright, who wrote in such strong terms indorsing the just result in *Sinclair v. Brougham*, would turn in his grave at any such suggestion".[202] For Lord Wright, "[t]he importance of the substantial and affirmative decision and of the actual discussion in the judgments lies in the exposition of the *equity* of restitution".[203] Pointing to passages from the speeches of Lord Dunedin and Lord Parker[204] in which the so-called "tracing" claim was justified to prevent the unjust enrichment of the shareholders at the expense of the depositors,[205] he

---

[195] Stoljar, 32.
[196] [1996] A.C. 669, 713; [1996] 2 All E.R. 961, 996.
[197] [1996] A.C. 669, 718; [1996] 2 All E.R. 961, 1000.
[198] [1996] A.C. 669, 738; [1996] 2 All E.R. 961, 1018.
[199] *e.g.* Goode, "Ownership and Obligation in Commercial Transactions" (1987) 103 *L.Q.R.* 433.
[200] Maudsley, "Proprietary Remedies for the Recovery of Money" (1959) 75 *L.Q.R.* 234, 234-235.
[201] [1996] A.C. 669, 713-714; [1996] 2 All E.R. 961, 994-995; a similar point motivated Lord Goff's more limited rejection of the resulting trust: [1996] A.C. 669, 690; [1996] 2 All E.R. 961, 974.
[202] [1996] A.C. 669, 689; [1996] 2 All E.R. 961, 973.
[203] Wright, *Sinclair*, 19, emphasis added; *cp. Fibrosa* [1943] A.C. 32, 64; [1942] 4 All E.R. 122, 137.
[204] "Of the four speeches, I have found those of Lord Parker and Lord Dunedin most illuminating" (Wright, *Sinclair*, 6). Notice, he says that there were four speeches, of which two were illuminating, trying to create a spurious equality between these favoured views and the disfavoured views in the other two speeches. He glosses over the point that one of the other two speeches – that of Viscount Haldane L.C. – commanded the assent of Lord Atkinson, so that the disfavoured views were in fact not equal but in the majority.
[205] "The shareholders are entitled to share among them the proper assets of the society. But they are not entitled to be made rich at the expense of the depositors by swelling the assets of the society by means of the proceeds of moneys to which they themselves never contributed" [1914] A.C. 398, 437-438; [1914-1915] All E.R. Rep. 622, 641 *per* Lord Dunedin. "The equity lay in this, that it would be unconscionable for the society to retain the amount by which its assets had been increased by, and in fact still represented, the borrowed money" [1914] A.C. 398, 444; [1914-1915] All E.R. Rep. 622, 644 *per* Lord Parker.

tries to spin *Sinclair v. Brougham* as supportive of unjust enrichment reasoning, if not at common law, then at least in equity: "I regard the case as primarily significant as embodying the leading principles on which the Court acts in exercising its equitable jurisdiction to give relief in order to prevent unjust enrichment, or to achieve restitution . . .".[206] There this just as much wishful thinking in this, however, as there is in Lord Wright's attempts to spin the common law. The common law has subsequently developed a coherent law of restitution based upon the principle against unjust enrichment, its unfinished business is the integration of equity,[207] and it would better achieve that integration without the distorting effects of *Sinclair v. Brougham.*

Bad cases make hard law.[208] *Sinclair v. Brougham* is doubly hard; first, hard in the sense that it is difficult to follow,[209] and second, hard in the sense of unfair, not necessarily to the parties, but potentially to creditors in subsequent cases in which it is cited.[210] As Burrows and McKendrick observe, "the obscurity of the reasoning of their Lordships in *Sinclair v. Brougham* on the finding of a proprietary interest means that few will mourn its passing".[211]

5. CONCLUSION. *SINCLAIR V. BROUGHAM*: MAD, BAD AND DANGEROUS TO KNOW[212]

Apart from getting things so comprehensively wrong, all that the litigation in *Sinclair v. Brougham* achieved was to dissipate in legal fees a large portion of the money otherwise available for disbursement to the depositors and the remaining shareholders:[213] the litigation only benefited the lawyers in the case

---

[206] Wright, *Sinclair*, 1.

[207] Beatson, "Unfinished Business. Integrating Equity" in *The Use and Abuse of Unjust Enrichment* (O.U.P., Oxford, 1991) 244.

[208] *Sinclair v. Brougham* also demonstrates that hard cases make bad law. This is a maxim almost as much beloved of lawyers as those referred to in n.46 above. See Heuston, "Hard Cases Make Bad Law" (1978) *D.U.L.J.* 31; Dworkin, n.8 above; *cp. Sadler v. Evans* (1766) 4 Burr. 1984, 1990 98 E.R. 34, 37 *per* Lord Mansfield: ". . . the granting [of] this rule would be a bad precedent; though in a favourable case. Favourable cases make bad precedents".

[209] "We should, however, be lacking in candour rather than showing respect if we refrained from saying that we find the opinions in *Sinclair v. Brougham* in many respects not only difficult to follow but difficult to reconcile with one another" (*Re Diplock, Diplock v. Wintle* [1948] 1 Ch. 465, 518; [1948] 2 All E.R. 318, 345). "Like others before me, I find Lord Haldane L.C.'s reasoning difficult, if not impossible, to follow" (*Westdeutsche* [1996] A.C. 669, 712; [1996] 2 All E.R. 961, 994).

[210] Of course, the proprietary remedy is limited to the identifiability of the claimed *res*. As Lord Sumner is reported to have observed in the course of argument (*The Times*, Dec. 11, 1913, 3a) if there is no personal claim, and the proprietary one is lost because the money is no longer identifiable, "the way to get rich quick is to act *ultra vires*, and keep no accounts"!

[211] Burrows and McKendrick, *Cases and Materials on the Law of Restitution* (O.U.P., Oxford, 1997) 676.

[212] This is Lady Caroline Lamb's description in her *Journal* of Lord Byron.

[213] Costs came first out of the fund, even in the House of Lords: [1914] A.C. 398, 427; [1914-1915] All E.R. Rep. 622, 635 *per* Viscount Haldane L.C.

itself, and baffled generations of lawyers since.

The contrast between their Lordships' insistence upon detailed precision (and misguided if not misunderstood detail at that) at law, and their tolerance of (even revelling in) untrammelled discretion in equity is decidedly odd. It is all the more odd when it is realised that the precision was applied to the relatively puny legal personal claim, whilst the discretion was applied to the vastly potentially more powerful equitable proprietary claim. Indeed, the woolliness on the proprietary claim is a whirlwind still being reaped in subsequent attempts to generate unwarranted proprietary claims to gain priority over outside creditors on an insolvency. In neither *Sinclair* nor *Westdeutsche* was this reason in play – the outside creditors in *Sinclair v. Brougham* had already been paid off, and in *Westdeutsche*, the local authority, though strapped for cash, was not insolvent – in both cases the important point was that it was equitable, the fact that it was proprietary was somewhat beside the point. It is difficult to escape the conclusion that if they had got it right on the personal claim at law, the House of Lords would not have had to distort the proprietary claim in equity to achieve a just result.

Part of the problem on the equitable point seems to have been that Viscount Haldane L.C. wanted to talk about *Hallett*, and manufactured the opportunity to do so in *Sinclair v. Brougham*,[214] thereby managing to given it "something of a new mystique, as if it held untold possibilities".[215] In fact, it added very little to the outcome, apart from supplying the source for the charge as one of the three equitable proprietary claims canvassed in the speeches.

For all its problems, however, if *Sinclair v. Brougham* hadn't happened, we'd probably have had it to invent it. Its statement of a hard-line thesis generated as an antithesis the modern principle against unjust enrichment. Strange though it is to say, the modern law of restitution needed *Sinclair v. Brougham*. Without it, the law could have gone the way of discretion rather than principle and been all the less important for that. But this having occurred, its usefulness is now past. Holmes, according to Lord Wright, thought that cases have a shelf-life of about half a century.[216] This might explain why, from the perspective of the end of the twentieth century, there are more than twice as many leading cases in this volume from the second half of the century than from the first.[217]

---

[214] In much the same way, Lord Browne-Wilkinson manufactured an opportunity to discuss constructive trusts in *Westdeutsche*, and having helped to still the controversies surrounding *Sinclair v. Brougham*, thereby constructed a whole new set: see O'Dell, "Bricks and Stones . . .", 170-180.

[215] Stoljar, 30.

[216] "That great American lawyer, Mr Justice Holmes, said that every half-century the case-law is rewritten so that earlier cases may be put aside" (Wright, "Study", 400; see also Wright, "Old Home", 345; and Wright, "Study", 382, 387).

[217] There are 27 cases discussed in this volume; 8 were decided before 1950 (*i.e.* about 30%), 19 were decided after (*i.e.* about 70%).

In this light, the eighty or so years of the *Sinclair v. Brougham* hegemony is a very good innings, and it is unsurprising that this once-great case should have fallen to earth.

The decline of *Sinclair v. Brougham* is an excellent example of the tradition of transformation which Hutchinson argues is at the heart of the common law.[218] But it can also be pressed into other jurisprudential service. For those who disagree with the reasoning in the speeches, the decline of *Sinclair v. Brougham* could be seen as an important example of the law working itself pure.[219] Whether one agrees with it or not, as a matter of observation, its decline provides an example of narrative which did not prove compelling.[220] The story of that decline is one of the displacement of the implied contract fiction and the rise of the principle against unjust enrichment, which could be presented as an important paradigm shift[221] in the alignment of the common law of obligations.

The Chief Justice has written that *Sinclair v Brougham* "must share with *Donoghue v. Stevenson* the distinction of being the most intensively raked over judicial decision of the [twentieth] century".[222] But whilst it can confidently be predicted that *Donoghue* will retain its iconic status in the twenty-first, *Sinclair v. Brougham* – as the case that fell to earth – quite properly will not.

---

[218] Hutchinson, "The Importance of Hearing Cases: A Critical Analysis", above, 1.

[219] Above, text with nn.8-10.

[220] A central concern of branches of the law and literature movement. For various views on this issue, see, *e.g.*, White, *The Legal Imagination* (University of Chicago Press, 1985); Brooks and Gewirtz (eds.), *Law's Stories, Narrative and Rhetoric in the Law* (Yale U.P., New Haven, Conn., 1996); Freeman and Lewis, (eds.), *Law and Literature* (O.U.P., Oxford, 1999); *contra* Posner, *Law and Literature* (rev. ed., Harvard U.P., Mass., 1998); Posner, "Relations between Law and Literature" (1999) XXXIV *Ir. Jur. (n.s.)* 18.

[221] Kuhn, *The Structure of Scientific Revolutions* (3rd ed., University of Chicago Press, 1996).

[222] Keane, *Equity and the Law of Trusts in the Republic of Ireland* (Butterworths, Dublin, 1988) 282, para. 20.09.

M'ALISTER (OR DONOGHUE) (PAUPER) V. STEVENSON (1932)

STEVE HEDLEY[*]

> The only safe rule is to confine the right to recover to those
> who enter into the contract; if we go one step beyond that,
> there is no reason why we should not go fifty.[1]
>
> And the people shall be oppressed, every one by another,
> and everyone by his neighbour.[2]

1. THE CASE ITSELF

It is hard to see signs of incipient greatness on a mere recitation of the facts of
Donoghue v. Stevenson.[3] We know little about the case, but it does not appear
that there is very much to be known.[4] After considerable research, we can say
with some certainty that we now know at least the names of the parties, and

---

[*]Fellow, Christ's College, University Lecturer in Law, University of Cambridge.

[1] *Winterbottom v. Wright* (1842) 10 M.&W. 109, 115 *per* Alderson B.

[2] Isaiah 3:5.

[3] *M'Alister (or Donoghue) (Pauper) v. Stevenson* [1932] A.C. 562 (H.L.).

[4] Significant writings on the case itself include: Lewis, *Lord Atkin* (Butterworths, London, 1983)
51ff; Taylor "The Good Neighbour on Trial: A Message From Scotland" (1983) 17 *U.B.C.L.R.*
59; Linden, "The Good Neighbour On Trial: A Fountain of Sparkling Wisdom" (1983) 17
U.B.C.L.R. 67; Rodger, "Mrs Donoghue and Alfenus Varus" [1988] *C.L.P.* 1; Burns and Lyons
(eds.), *Donoghue v. Stevenson and The Modern Law of Negligence: The Paisley Papers* (Continuing Legal Education Society for British Columbia, Vancouver, 1991); McBryde, "*Donoghue
v. Stevenson*: The Story of the 'Snail in The Bottle' Case" in Gamble (ed.), *Obligations in
Context – Essays in Honour of Professor DM Walker* (Green, Edinburgh, 1990) 13; Rodger,
"Lord Macmillan's Speech in *Donoghue v. Stevenson*" (1992) 108 *L.Q.R.* 236. The detail in the
following paragraphs derives mainly from these writings. To list literature on the principle in
the case would merely be to produce a general reading list on the tort of negligence. There is
however a specific strand of the literature focussing closely on the case itself, nearly all of
which argues that the modern law cannot be (and/or should not have been) derived from the
case: Heuston, "*Donoghue v. Stevenson* in Retrospect" (1957) 20 *M.L.R.* 1; Smith and Burns,
"The Good Neighbour on Trial: Good Neighbours Make Bad Law" (1983) 17 *U.B.C.L.R.* 93;
Smith and Burns, "*Donoghue v. Stevenson* – The Not So Golden Anniversary" (1983) 46 *M.L.R.*
147; Smith, "The Good Neighbour Still on Trial: Is Paisley's Decayed Snail the Pilgrim's Holy
Grail?" in Burns and Lyons (eds.), *Donoghue v. Stevenson and The Modern Law of Negligence:
The Paisley Papers* (Continuing Legal Education Society for British Columbia, Vancouver,
1991) 251.

how to spell them.[5] And certainly the main facts about the circumscribed economic opportunities open to the central character, Mrs May Donoghue, are apparent enough. A shop assistant, a 30-year-old married woman recently separated from her husband, bringing up a 12-year-old son, and, by the time of the hearing before the Lords at least, a pauper. That is, that all of her assets amounted to no more than £5 in value – excluding the clothes she stood up in, and the value of any legal claim she might have, as the certificate of poverty put it.

And how did Mrs Donoghue start the chain of events which proved so consequential for the common law? Well, at about 8:50pm on Sunday August 26th, 1928, she consumed – or at least, started to consume – a bottle of ginger beer, which a friend had just bought for her. The gruesome consequences of this minor act of self-indulgence are well known. Yet still it is not apparent why such an incident had such great legal potential. What is so special about it, that it should lead to a great case, perhaps *the* great case of the 20th century?

Commentators have struggled hard to make more of the facts than is actually there, to seek some harbinger of coming greatness, to see in the entrails of the snail some portent of later fame. Yet attempts to liven the facts up, to make them seem more interesting perhaps than they are, have been mere ineffective speculation. Perhaps the mysterious friend who bought May Donoghue her ginger beer was a man? Well, at this distance in time, who can say. If it was a man, certainly everyone went to great lengths to avoid saying so.[6] Or again, perhaps there never was a snail in the bottle, and the whole affair was the invention of a desperate woman and a dishonest accomplice. Certainly there is good anecdotal evidence that Stevenson would have denied the presence of the snail had he fought the case further; for that matter, the pleadings leave the way open for a denial even that it was Stevenson's bottle. So these exciting possibilities certainly cannot be dismissed out of hand. Perhaps the case is a secret scandal set in 1920s Paisley. But if so, the parties have taken their secret to their graves; and whatever their secret was, it is not the reason for the case's greatness.

Nor is the case any great advertisement for the skills of the plaintiff's lawyers. It is hard to say whether the initial stages of May Donoghue's legal action show the workings of inspired strategic legal genius, or simply everyday legal incompetence. If we judge by the eventual result I suppose we would have to say the former. But for all that, they do not inspire confidence. Two years into the action, her solicitor, Walter Leechman, had secured victory on the preliminary point before the Lord Ordinary, Lord Moncrieff; but this ruling been over-

---

[5] The plaintiff was Mrs May (not Mary) Donoghue, *neé* McAllister (not M'Alister or McAlister). On this detail, as on so many others, the law report is inaccurate. The defendant was David ("Davie") Stevenson.

[6] The friend is referred to as "she" in the Lords, but as McBryde points out (above, n.4, 19) there are "sufficient inaccuracies" in the record generally to cast doubt on it as a source.

turned on appeal. This reverse can hardly have been a surprise to Leechman, as it involved the very same point which he had lost before the same tribunal only a few weeks before he had started the proceedings in *Donoghue* – the earlier case differing only in that it involved dead mice rather than a dead snail.[7] His client therefore stood liable for £44 costs. Moreover, Leechman had seen fit to join the café owner, Francis Minghella, as party, but then soon realised that this was a mistake and discontinued that action – a move which made his client liable for Minghella's costs, adding another £66 to May Donoghue's liabilities. So the best news that Leechman had for his client after the Court of Session had finished with the case was that, as she was now technically a pauper, she could invoke the *in forma pauperis* procedure, and appeal to the Lords without adding anything further to her liabilities.[8]

A case can certainly be made, then, that the appeal to London was one last desperate throw by a lawyer who had failed his client almost completely, who had already pauperised her in theory and was on the verge of doing so in practice — but who had the wit to see that the dire financial straits to which he had brought his client could yet be turned to their joint advantage. If so, it was a great victory indeed. But that was not what he himself said about the matter, at any rate in retrospect. Leechman claimed that he had intended all along to escape the clutches of the Scottish judiciary, for whom he had no particularly high regard, and to seek the "equity" that was to be had in English courts. So for Leechman, if his account is the truth, the road the case took was always meant to end in London. If true, this is ironical indeed, for it was not the English lords that found in his client's favour, but the two Scots, Lord Thankerton and Lord Macmillan, and the cosmopolitan Lord Atkin, whose father was from Kilgariff in County Cork and whose mother was from Merioneth, and who himself was born in Brisbane.[9]

---

[7] *Mullen v. AG Barr & Co Ltd, M'Gowan v. AG Barr & Co Ltd* 1929 S.C. 461. Leechman's firm acted as Edinburgh agent for the two plaintiffs' solicitors. The same panel as later heard *Donoghue* heard the appeals in *Mullen* and *M'Gowan*, and it splits in precisely the same manner: Lords Alness, Ormidale and Anderson for the defendants, Lord Hunter for the plaintiffs.

[8] It appears that May Donoghue only pleaded poverty for the final stage of the proceedings, before the House of Lords; her certificate of poverty is dated February 1931. See McBryde above, n.4, 23. It seems unlikely that Leechman would have obtained very much from Donoghue had the action failed completely; so it seems likely that, *de facto* if not *de iure*, this was a "no foal no fee" arrangement.

[9] Whether the case is properly to be regarded as "Scottish" or "English" is itself a matter that has produced a considerable literature; dissatisfaction, which in England would take the form of complaints against the legal craftsmanship in the case, tends in Scotland to take the form of complaints that it is English. See Brodie, "In Defence of *Donoghue*" [1997] *J.R.* 65. One of the many puzzles about the case is why Lord Macmillan abandoned his draft opinion relating the issues solely to Scots authorities and substituted one dealing with English authorities as well. See Rodger, "Lord Macmillan's Speech in *Donoghue v. Stevenson*" (1992) 108 *L.Q.R.* 236. For the Irish legal system's acceptance of *Donoghue* despite its "Englishness", see Byrne and McCutcheon, *The Irish Legal System* (3rd ed., Butterworths Ireland, Dublin, 1996) (hereafter Byrne and McCutcheon) 376 *et seq.*

So while in one sense we know a great deal about the case, the reason for its greatness is highly elusive. What is so great about the case? Can we not simply say that it was an important contribution to consumer law, and leave it at that? Alas, we cannot, for in Ireland and in Britain at least, consumer law is not a very important subject.[10] There is no such thing as a great consumer law case, that is a contradiction in terms. Indeed, so unimpressed have the nations of Europe been with the common law on the subject that they have swept it all away in favour of strict liability. *Donoghue* is not law on its own facts any more.[11] It is not, then, the excellence of the Lords' resolution of the case in front of them that constitutes its greatness.

The case itself, then, in all its baffling particularity, does not seem an obvious candidate for greatness.

2. THE "NEIGHBOUR" PRINCIPLE

So to look at the background to the case is to miss what is important about it, for the triumph of the "neighbour" principle has been precisely in eschewing particulars, in ignoring details, and focussing on a broad general principle. But surely, at least, the principle itself must be fairly definite? Surely such a fine-sounding principle must have some definite content? Alas, the answer appears to be that it does not.

The "neighbour" formula certainly has resonance, and Atkin would certainly in his own time have been understood as making a reference to Biblical morality – indeed, many later commentators have, without very much thought, have repeated that the "neighbour" principle was derived by Atkin from his Christian beliefs. Those of a more analytical bent might be more suspicious, realising that this great legal craftsman wasn't too particular about *which* Biblical precept he was applying. Only a year before, indeed, he had been solemnly arguing that Tort was based on the notion that you should do to your neighbour as you would be done by.[12] There has to be a suspicion that Atkin

---

[10] For rare examples of a consumer claim at common law see Nash, "A Lady in Litigation" (1996) 14 *I.L.T. (n.s.)* 67; Slapper, "Dangerous Product Litigation" (1998) 148 *N.L.J.* 345.

[11] The principle of strict liability was introduced by the Directive on Products Liability 1985, implemented in Ireland as the Defective Products Act 1991, and in the UK as the Consumer Protection Act 1987. The Directive does not cover all cases, and so *Donoghue* is (in theory) not quite obsolete in this area. Just like the common law remedies, the remedies under the Directive seem to be little used: see *House of Commons Written Answers*, March 24, 1999, col. 270, "Product liability"; Brahams, "Advantage to the plaintiff" *Law Society's Gazette* July 13, 1994, 23.

[12] Atkin, "Law as an Educational Subject" [1932] *J.S.P.T.L.* 27, 30. That principle can be traced to Luke 6:31. On Atkin's religious views generally see Lewis, *Lord Atkin* (Butterworths, London, 1983) 20-22.

simply wanted a tag which vaguely hinted that his principle was a moral one, without tying him to anything very specific.

In fact, there is nothing Biblical about Atkin's principle, as is obvious enough from Luke 10, where the parable of the Good Samaritan is set out.[13] And indeed it is a parable aimed directly at lawyers. A lawyer having asked Jesus how he could attain eternal life, Jesus forces the lawyer to answer the question himself. The lawyer gives the stock answer he has been taught: That he should love God, and should also love his neighbour as himself. The lawyer realises that he is being rebuked for doing what lawyers are always doing – namely, asking questions to which they already know the answer. In an attempt to justify himself, he pretends that his enquiry was merely an introduction to his real question, a more difficult one. *Who is my neighbour?* he asks. But Jesus knows what lawyers are really like, and sets the lawyer to a parable which explains why this is the wrong question to ask. *Everyone* is your neighbour, he says, even people from races and nations generally held in contempt. The lawyer's attempt to get "a restricted reply" to the question was an error. He had no business placing limits on who he is prepared to regard as his neighbour. Atkin was doing much what the lawyer in the story did, and was rebuked for doing: namely, narrowing the range of those who deserve respect as a neighbour. And indeed, anyone who wants to know what Jesus thought about lawyers generally need only read the next chapter of Luke, which contains remarks which would certainly have drawn protest from the Law Society's Press Office, had it then existed.[14]

The invocation of "neighbourliness" in this context, then, is decidedly odd, if not indeed downright perverse. There might be a case for regarding everyone you encounter as your neighbour, but the relationship Atkin describes seems to be based principally on the potential people have for *harming* one another. It is as if Atkin had heard the famous saying that there is no such thing as a stranger, only a friend you haven't met yet; and that he morbidly reformulated it by saying that we are never as isolated and alone as we may think, that in fact we have neighbours all around us, but that some of them have yet to cause us actionable damage.

Does the "neighbour" principle, then, have any moral content at all? It is usually assumed today that if there is a moral basis to it, it is on a basis to which Atkin made no direct reference, namely, a principle of personal responsibility for one's actions and their consequences. And in theory, that is what the "neighbour" principle has led to. But in practice, certain disadvantages become apparent as soon as we try to implement any principle of personal responsibility in personal injury law. Some injured persons will discover that they that they

---

[13]Luke 10:25 *et seq.*
[14]See especially Luke 11:45 *et seq.* For another view see Spiers, "Who is my Neighbour?" in Burns and Lyons (eds.), *Donoghue v. Stevenson and the Modern Law of Negligence: The Paisley Papers* (Continuing Legal Education Society for British Columbia, Vancouver, 1991) 279.

cannot establish precisely what happened, or they cannot locate the person who harmed them, or that that person has no money. Of course, if we were *really* interested in personal responsibility, none of this would bother us. Just as it is hard luck, so far as the law of tort is concerned, if you are struck by lightning, so it would be hard luck if the person who negligently ran you down turned out to have no money to compensate you with.

What the development of the "neighbour" principle shows quite clearly is that while *in form* the law of negligence is about personal responsibility, in practice lawyers are very, very unhappy that legal remedies should be so restricted. That someone who was injured should go without compensation, merely because they were unlucky in the identity of their defendant, seems very unfair. The moment the law begins to apply the principle of personal responsibility, we start to realise that it actually believes in something else, something much more in the direction of a social security principle to protect those injured through no fault of their own – though it is hard to pin down precisely what. And so many devices are used to avoid the consequences of the notion of personal responsibility.

The law avoids the effects of personal responsibility in many ways. It makes full use of liability insurance when it is there, and makes it compulsory in many situations. It adopts high, often unreachable, standards of care, which are bound to be broken on a regular basis even by model citizens. It avoids the difficult matter of attributing blame to companies, by treating the fault of employees in the course of their employment as the fault of the company.[15] The result is a curiously schizophrenic discourse, where for the most part we proceed as if we were discussing the personal responsibility of the parties; yet any officious bystander who points out that this is not so, is testily suppressed with a common "Oh, of course!"[16] As Lord Denning put it, the apparent parties before the courts are not the real parties. "If you lift up the mask, you will usually find the legal aid funds or an insurance company or the taxpayer ..." Yet while the courts know very well who is behind the mask, they dare not lift it, for fear of the financial consequences. If we admitted that personal responsibility was not really the criterion, society would be flooded with demands, which we cannot

---

[15] The standard critique of "fault" in negligence law is Cane, *Atiyah's Accidents, Compensation and the Law* (5th ed., London, Butterworths, 1993) chap. 7; see also Atiyah, *The Damages Lottery* (Hart Publishing, Oxford, 1997), 33-38. What one makes of this depends entirely on what one thinks negligence law is for.

[16] Astonishing as it now seems, for some decades the English courts did not regard themselves as free even to mention insurance issues in the context of tort claims. The Lords have now granted official permission to take insurance issues into account, but we will be a long time recovering from the earlier ban. Undoubtedly, many writers prefer matters the way they were, for it is not yet clear what "taking insurance into account" entails. It is as if discussions of chocolate eggs had until recently assumed the reality of the Easter bunny, and we had now been told that our discussions might, in appropriate circumstances, give some weight to the fact that the bunny is mythical.

afford to meet. The legal system therefore adheres, in theory, to the dogma of personal responsibility, because it cannot afford to do anything else. In practice, of course, it makes multiple departures from it.[17]

The striking thing about the "neighbour" principle is, therefore, not its aptness to the circumstances in which it arose. It wasn't particular apt for them. Nor it is a particularly striking assertion of important values. Insofar as it asserts any values at all, they are not ones which the law prizes. The striking thing about the principle is, as Conaghan and Mansell note, its extraordinary emptiness.[18] What is amazing is that the principle has bite *despite* its evident vacuity. To ask whether two people, the plaintiff and the defendant, are "neighbours" in law is to do nothing less than to reconsider the legal relations between those two people, to throw into the legal melting pot the whole question of what they owe one another. The principle gives freedom, to those judges bold enough to use it, to re-write the legal relations between the parties, and to impose those duties which seem fair, reasonable, and in accord with sound public policy. The inherent vagueness on the principle, on matters both big and small, leaves the court free to do what seems appropriate. And it leaves judges free to expand the tort of negligence as seems to them appropriate.

Historically, it has always been those who have opposed the "neighbour" principle that have seen most clearly what it does – that it is a tool for *expanding* the reach of the tort of negligence. You can see this in the opinions in *Donoghue* itself. The majority focus narrowly on the claim actually made. Even Lord Atkin, with his famous statement of principle, claimed only to be describing how the law actually was, not setting out a manifesto for expansion. It is the minority lords – Buckmaster and Tomlin – who so clearly saw what the issue really was. The question was *not* whether May Donoghue should succeed in her claim, but whether plaintiffs in general should be left free to argue for novel heads of liability. It is not May Donoghue's snail that struck terror in their breasts, but the prospect of a whole army of snails, snail upon snail, stretching out to the crack of doom. Buckmaster and Tomlin may not have given the right answer in the case, but they at least understood the question. "If one step, why not fifty?"[19] They outlined some of the novel claims which they thought would soon be made if the majority got their way, and which the courts would have difficulty resisting; and every single one of their predictions was right.[20]

---

[17] Lord Denning, *The Discipline of Law* (Butterworths, London, 1979), 280. Denning concludes that "I sometimes wonder whether the time has not come – may indeed be already with us – when the Courts should cry Halt ! Enough has been done for the sufferer. Now remember the man who has to foot the bill– even though he be only one of many" (280-281).

[18] Conaghan and Mansell, *The Wrongs of Tort* (2nd ed., Pluto Press, London, 1999) 14.

[19] [1932] A.C. 562, 577 *per* Lord Buckmaster.

[20] So, for example, Buckmaster noted that if May Donoghue could succeed against David Stevenson, then presumably someone injured by the collapse of a house could sue the builder ([1932] A.C. 562, 577-578) — which turns out to be quite true (*Gallagher v. N McDowell Ltd* [1961] N.I. 26 (C.A.)).

It is always a doubtful matter to label particular judges as "progressive" or "conservative" on the basis of a single set of opinions. Even assuming that those terms have clear meanings, a difference of view may mean rather that the different judges had different understandings of what their judgement would entail. So the true division in *Donoghue* may perhaps have been not between conservatives and progressives, but between those who understood what they were really being asked and those who didn't – the latter being, as it turned out, slightly more numerous. Indeed, we might say that true progressives on this issue are hard to find, most of those claiming to be progressives really being conservatives who haven't realised how fast we are expanding liability.

This, then, is the glory of the "neighbour" principle. It establishes a base-line of liability, that we expect those who can foresee harm to others to take reasonable steps to avoid it – whoever they are, and whoever the others are. In the hands of the more timid judges, of course, this principle is somewhat inert. In the hands of bolder spirits, whose cynicism and whose 20:20 hindsight tells them that nothing is ever truly unforeseeable, it is a tool for re-making the law. And the strength of the principle is that it allows bold judges to go forward. Lawyers do not prize originality, but the "neighbour" formula hides from us how original we are being. If the "neighbour" principle is the general rule and all departures from it the exception, then the spot-light is turned on the defence: it is for the defendant to explain why the "neighbour" principle *should not* be applied, not for the plaintiff to explain why it *should*.[21] So the triumph of the neighbour principle is a tale of the outward drift of the law, each successive expansion being seen as the removal of an indefensible anomaly. The siren call to treat all cases alike, unless cause is shown for doing otherwise, leads to a slow but steady expansion of the law.

The "neighbour principle" has therefore expanded the law of negligence beyond all measure, by repeated assertion that liability for foreseeable damage is the general rule, and that limiting principles deserve close scrutiny before they can be accepted. In the process, many distinctions which in earlier times were regarded as crucial have simply faded away, or have been abolished by lawyer-inspired reforming statutes. In relation to personal injury liability and liability for property damage, the "neighbour" principle reigns supreme, having swept away anomalies such as the special defences open to employers as defendants[22] and the old, convoluted law of occupiers' liability.[23] There are

---

[21] In the (very) few areas where the common law had groped towards strict liability, the contrary movement has taken place. See especially Lord Goff's insistence that while the courts are free to develop negligence principle, the imposition of strict liability is for Parliament: *Cambridge Water Co v. Eastern Counties Leather* [1994] 2 A.C. 264, 305; [1994] 1 All E.R. 53 (H.L.) 76.

[22] On the abolition of the old defences, see especially the (U.K.) Law Reform (Personal Injuries) Act 1948 and the (Irish) Law Reform (Personal Injuries) Act 1958.

[23] In the U.K. the old law has almost (but not entirely, see *McGeown v. Northern Ireland Housing Executive* [1995] 1 A.C. 233; [1994] 3 All E.R. 53 (H.L.)) been replaced by a statutory version

still some who insist that economic loss is different, and that omissions need to be treated differently from acts.[24] Yet the boundaries of liability are pushed back year on year.[25] And this new, expanded negligence is increasingly moving into areas where one might not have expected to find it. A relaxed attitude to pure economic loss means that negligence is increasingly doing contract's work for it.[26] And a relaxed attitude to omissions means that negligence comes more and more into public law, to demand compensation for failure to live up to the standards in the state's own legislation. Increasingly, the old argument, that the State needs to be immune from claims brought by aggrieved citizens, is being replaced by the argument that the State owes its citizens at least as much as they owe each other, at least unless very clear exempting circumstances are shown to be present.[27]

Another factor leading to the application of the "neighbour" principle to more and more facts is the development of new facts for it to apply to; specifically, new *medical* facts. Better knowledge of the causes of harm, and indeed of new types of harm, has given the negligence lawyers more grist for their mill. It is *because* competent medical evidence can convincingly show, for example, that the plaintiff's back pain is the result of damage sustained at work, that action in negligence is possible.[28] Better understanding of stress,[29] repeti-

---

of the "neighbour" principle. See especially Occupiers' Liability Act 1957. Much the same result was achieved in Ireland by case law: see McMahon and Binchy, *Irish Law of Torts* (2nd ed., Butterworths Ireland, Dublin, 1990) [hereafter McMahon and Binchy] chap. 12; the common law has now been replaced by the Occupiers' Liability Act 1995.

[24] See especially articles by Heuston, Smith and Burns, above, note 4.

[25] Just about the only major reversal has been the overturning of *Anns v. Merton BC* [1978] A.C. 728; [1977] 2 All E.R. 492 (H.L.) by the House of Lords in *Murphy v. Brentwood DC* [1991] 1 A.C. 398; [1990] 2 All E.R. 908 (H.L.) – though few other Supreme courts have followed them (see, *e.g.* *Ward v. McMaster* [1988] I.R. 337 (S.C.); *Kamloops (City of) v. Nielsen* [1984] 2 S.C.R. 2; (1984) 10 D.L.R. (4th) 651 (S.C.C.)), not even the Privy Council in its capacity as court of final appeal for the New Zealand jurisdiction (*Invercargill C.C. v. Hamlin* [1996] A.C. 624; [1996] 1 All E.R. 756 (P.C.)). Otherwise, while of course not every attempt to push back the boundaries of liability succeeds, ground taken for the tort of negligence seems not to be surrendered in later cases.

[26] See for example McMahon and Binchy, 19. Indeed, even in a contractual situation, Lord Goff at least has been happy to assert that "the law of tort is the general law, out of which the parties can, if they wish, contract ..." (*Hendersen v. Merrett Syndicates* [1995] 2 A.C. 145 (H.L.) 193; [1994] 3 All E.R. 506, 532c).

[27] See especially Gaughran, "Tort, Public Policy and the Protection of Constitutional Rights" (1998) 16 *I.L.T.* (n.s.) 88 (a note on the Brendan Smyth case, *W. v. Ireland (No.2)* [1997] 2 I.R. 141 (H.C.)); *Osman v. United Kingdom* (1998) 29 E.H.R.R. 245. Note that in *Osman* the E.C.H.R.'s objection to U.K. law was not so much that the plaintiff lost his negligence action, but that the blanket ban on actions against the police infringed Article 6.1 (right to an impartial tribunal). Again, the demand is not so much for any particular result, as that the same rules be applied to everyone.

[28] See, *e.g.*, *Barclay v. An Post* [1998] 2 I.R.L.M. 385 (H.C.) (injury sustained through posting to low letter boxes).

[29] See, *e.g.*, *Walker v. Northumberland C.C.* [1995] I.C.R. 702; [1995] 1 All E.R. 737 (Q.B.D.).

tive strain injury,[30] and post-traumatic shock disorder[31] has also lead to legal actions based on that understanding. And, as the doctors complain, it is *because* they can do so much today that they risk being sued if they don't. A century ago, every intelligent person knew how little doctors could do, and indeed punishing those who raised unreasonable expectations was a significant object of legal policy.[32] Today, a fair degree of sophistication is needed to know which expectations are realistic and which are not.[33]

Finally, but not insignificantly, the effective scope of the "neighbour" principle has been expanded by greater ease in commencing legal action. It has become progressively easier to sue, and more and more people have been prepared to do it. Compulsory liability insurance for car drivers has been a factor since the 1930s. Most tort litigation takes place against an insurance background, dealing with claims that could hardly be met by the individuals against whom they are nominally directed.[34] Nor, for that matter, could many plaintiffs meet their initial legal expenses but for state support for legal action or "no foal no fee" funding arrangements. May Donoghue could not, and nor could most plaintiffs today. It should not be forgotten that most of the steps that made it easier to sue were deliberate acts of policy, if not always very carefully-thought-out acts of policy. And it is the authors of these policies that are far more responsible for the importance of the "neighbour" principle than is any number of law lords.

Academics like to imagine themselves at the pinnacle of the legal system, looking over the law lords' shoulders, helping them towards acceptable legal conclusions, even (as some of the testier case notes do) correcting their written opinions and telling them they'll never come to anything if they continue to write like that. This is all very fine. But to ignore how cases come before the law lords at all is to ignore much that is important about the legal system. Many of the more important innovations in tort law have come from the legal professions, who did not derive them from the law reports or from statute but from other sources entirely. There is a whole community of hungry lawyers, with their own view of the world, their own mouths to feed, their own powers of invention, and their own sources of ideas. It was no Supreme Court which

---

[30] See Pheasant, "R.S.I. — Towards a clarification of the points in issue" [1994] *Journal of Personal Injury Litigation* 223.

[31] For a short history of the legal acceptance of "nervous shock" see Robertson, "Review Article: Liability in Negligence For Nervous Shock" (1994) 57 *M.L.R.* 649.

[32] Simpson, "Quackery and Contract Law: The Case of the Carbolic Smoke Ball" (1985) 14 *J.L.S.* 345.

[33] An interesting counterpoint to this is the cigarette litigation (*e.g. Dean v. Gallaher* [1995] N.I. 229 (C.A.)), the substantive issue of which turns precisely on when the dangers of smoking ceased to be the dirty little secret of the cigarette manufacturers and became common knowledge.

[34] On the rise of liability insurance see Davies, "The End of the Affair: Duty of Care and Liability Insurance" (1989) 9 *L.S.* 67.

suggested to some practitioners that they should specialise in cases of clients who had fallen over defective paving stones; they thought of this for themselves.[35] These and other, still weirder specialisms are simply the natural effect of such a large number of cases. It was no Royal Commission that suggested that the British legal system should institute the system of mass actions, where hundreds or even thousands of plaintiffs should club together to sue over the same complaint; but rather a lowly young solicitor called Roger Pannone, who had some experience of how these matters worked in the States and saw no reason not to try it in Manchester.[36] Nor would any public official have been seen dead urging greater use of the media in personal injuries work, either by advertising for clients, or as a tool for pressuring defendants who care about their public image.[37] Yet this too is now a regular feature of personal injury law. When we consider the principle of *Donoghue v. Stevenson* today, we are considering a mighty legal machine, with a whole army of specialist lawyers and insurance companies to keep it running.

And with the greater ease of suing, more and more people have done so. The reach of the "neighbour" principle is thus very great indeed. It reaches into the farmer's field in Carrickmore, to tell the farmer how he should drive his tractor.[38] It reaches onto the rugby pitches of Sutton Coldfield, to say how referees should manage scrums.[39] It reaches into the premises of the West Belfast Pigeon Club, to say how much of a load they should expect their barman to carry.[40] It reaches into the classrooms of Birmingham, to lay down the law to 15-year-olds about appropriate standards of care when fencing with plastic rulers.[41] And it reaches into the breakfast-rooms of Cork, to tell mothers not to leave the tea-pot within reach of their inquisitive two-year-old daughters.[42]

But the reach of the "neighbour" principle today can best be illustrated by a single example, and that is the example of the armed services. Here we see how an array of factors – some strictly legal, some more social – have led to an explosion of litigation where there was no litigation before. For most of history, soldiers have been regarded as the scum of the earth, and the protection of their health and safety has been low indeed on the Government's list of priori-

---

[35] See especially Foster, "Many a slip" *Solicitors Journal* September 16, 1994, 933; "'Trip and slip' injuries to cost councils £130m" *Sunday Times* July 30, 1995. For a typical "trip and fall" case see *e.g. Feely v. Stonard Ltd* (1999) 17 *I.L.T. (n.s.)* 13.

[36] See Hedley, "Group Personal Injury Litigation and Public Opinion" (1994) 14 *L.S.* 70. Legal Aid is not available in Ireland for test cases or group actions (see Byrne and McCutcheon, 298) which may explain why growth of such actions has been slower in Ireland.

[37] Governments are of course particularly vulnerable in this regard.

[38] *Tanny v. Shields* (Queen's Bench Division, unreported, June 16, 1992).

[39] *Smoldon v. Whitworth Times,* December 18, 1996.

[40] *Kinner v. McKeown* (Court of Appeal, unreported, August 5, 1998).

[41] *Mullin v. Richards* [1998] 1 W.L.R. 1304; [1998] 1 All E.R. 920 (C.A.).

[42] *Moynihan v. Moynihan* [1975] I.R. 192 (S.C.).

ties. Yet for a number of reasons, over the course of the twentieth century greater and greater investment in their well-being has been made. And with the concurrent expansion of negligence law, it has become less and less obvious that no duty of care is owed to them.

A century ago, it would all have been obvious to a court of law that no such action should be allowed. All the precedents would have been against. The question is thoroughly tied up with the conduct of defence, which is a matter for Government not the courts. And anyway, the judges wouldn't have wanted to encourage the soldiery to think they could question their orders, in the courts or anywhere else. Yet all of this is now ancient history. As ever, the question has been put, why should these plaintiffs have fewer rights than anyone else? And in the absence of any very convincing reply, they have duly been held to have the same rights as anyone else.[43]

The results, on both sides of the Irish Sea, are well enough known by now. And certainly there is more than enough remarkable material for lawyers. Seeing the court of appeal in London trying to puzzle out what constitutes a reasonably safe working environment, when the work in question consists using a mop to clean howitzers in the middle of a battle, is odd enough.[44] The fact that about a quarter of the Irish Army, including most of their military bands, are suing their employers for hearing loss, is another remarkable fact.[45] And what is truly amazing is to watch the English courts decide on what constitutes "reasonable behaviour", in a case set at a combined birthday celebration and "Hawaiian party event", on an isolated Norwegian naval base where 3 duty-free bars were the principal places of entertainment.[46] Merely to contemplate such an event brings to mind Kipling's observation, that "single men in barricks don't grow into plaster saints"; and to ask what then constitutes reasonable behaviour suggests to me that anyone with any sense would already have left town. At one level, this certainly has humorous aspects. But neither the Irish nor the British authorities are laughing.[47]

---

[43]In the U.K., the old bar on action was removed by private members' Bill (see now the Crown Proceedings (Armed Forces) Act 1987). In Ireland, the Supreme Court held that the common law bar no longer existed (*Ryan v. Ireland* [1989] I.R. 177 (S.C.)).

[44]*Mulcahy v. Ministry of Defence* [1996] Q.B. 732 (C.A.).

[45]By December 1997, something like 10,000 claims in respect of hearing impairment had been made: see "Chief of Staff seeks urgent standard to tackle claims for hearing compensation" *Irish Times* December 6, 1997, 1.

[46]*Barrett v. Ministry of Defence* [1995] 1 W.L.R. 1217; [1995] 3 All E.R. 87 (C.A.).

[47]Personal injury actions are not the only concern of the armed services' legal departments. The British authorities are certainly worried by recent claims, including the looming threat of mass action over "Gulf War Syndrome", but they equally if not more worried about pension disputes and discrimination cases. Rather late in the day, their supporters are re-discovering the argument that, in legal matters, they are a special case: see debate on "Armed Forces: Policy Changes" *Lords Debates*, March 26, 1998, col. 1402 *et seq.* The Irish authorities seem to be gritting their teeth for a very long and very expensive ride over hearing loss claims: in 1998, the Minister of

3. LORD ATKIN'S LEGACY – "IF IT ISN'T HURTING, IT ISN'T WORKING"

With such a broad expansion of doctrine, it was only a matter of time before the wider reaches of society noticed what was going on. The great public have, of course, by-and-large not heard of May Donoghue, or her snail. But it is common knowledge that personal injury compensation is much more broadly available today than it ever has been, and that someone who wishes to pursue a claim will, without much difficulty, find a solicitor ready to press their case. And when someone complains that we live in a "compensation culture", they are suggesting that everyone who is injured has May Donoghue as their heroine and role-model. And it is a common viewpoint that this is not a good thing.[48]

Political pressure to do something about this has been intense in both Ireland and in the UK, though from the tort lawyer's perspective the line taken in each has seemed lacking in rationality. In Ireland, recent attention at least seems to have concentrated on lawyers' advertisements, with attempts to prevent personal injury practitioners from announcing their services too blatantly, or for placing too much emphasis on their willingness to contract on contingent fee terms. It is as if the legislators had no objection to the "neighbour" principle so long as it remains the legal professions' little secret, and so long as they wait for business to come to them rather than doing anything to stimulate demand. The Solicitors (Amendment) Bill 1998 provides for the most frightful penalties on solicitors who are too enthusiastic in their advertising;[49] its effects have yet to be seen.

In the UK, *that* battle was lost a long time ago. Legislative attention has turned rather towards reform of procedure and of the legal aid system. This too seems odd from the tort lawyer's perspective. If it is *too much* tort liability that we are worried about, why make legal procedures *quicker* and *cheaper*, rather than the reverse? The truth seems to be that the Government has decided to promote speed and cheapness in the legal system as ends good in themselves, *even though* the result cannot but be to increase the amount of litigation.

In assessing the merits of the "neighbour" principle today, then, we have to start from the basis that any such principle is bound to be unpopular in some quarters. A system for deterring those who cause harm, and compensating their

---

Defence estimated that, at the current rate of progress, it would take until 2015 for the legal system to resolve claims *already* made (*Ministry of Defence Statement*, July 21, 1998).

[48] For arguments pro and con the "Compo Culture", see Byrne and McCutcheon, 150-152. Argument has been rather more low-key in the UK, but see for example Furedi, *Courting Mistrust — The Hidden Growth of a Culture of Litigation in Britain* (Centre for Policy Studies, London, 1999).

[49] Unveiled to the public gaze on June 2, 1998, the Bill attempts to place sharp limits on advertisements by solicitors, and treats contraventions as professional misconduct. This Bill put an earlier tendency to liberalise advertising rules into very sharp reverse, allowing advertisements to specify only contact information, qualifications, areas of practice and fees. At the time of going to press, it is at final stage.

victims, cannot but be unpopular with those who actually have to pay. As the saying goes, "if it isn't hurting, it isn't working". So some complaints should be expected, even welcomed. A principle so broad and all-embracing as the "neighbour" principle is bound to attract comment, much of it adverse. And we cannot say whether a particular type of liability is good or bad without knowing how many people will seek to take advantage of it. One litigant from Paisley suing over her ginger beer is not a problem; a million consumers complaining in this way is quite another matter.[50]

When considering the merits of the "neighbour" principle, then, there are various items to notice on the debit side, points which undoubtedly go against it, whatever may be said for it. One is that because the "neighbour" principle has so many different objectives, it can perform none of them well.[51] As a system of compensation, it is arbitrary, indeed almost random, and exceedingly wasteful. Of all the sums of money circulating as a result of the principle, a large proportion is bound to be swallowed up in the lawyer's operating budgets – the figure for the English legal system seems to be in the order of 50 per cent of the money.[52] As a system of deterrence, the "neighbour" principle is rather selective about whom it deters – it can only deter through the wallet, and so cannot affect those too rich or too poor to be affected this way. To be sure, most of the criticisms that are made of the deterrence aspects of negligence are rather self-interested. Those whose activities threaten the health and safety of others are always ready to plead that they should not be deterred from economically valuable conduct, relying on the need for economic flexibility. But the fact of the matter is that deterrence is a nasty process. It is the deliberate infliction of financial pain on potential tortfeasors to discourage them from ever becoming *actual* tortfeasors. It is not too surprising if the cost of this sometimes causes resentment, particularly if (as may possibly be the case with Irish car liability insurance) premiums are only so high because a significant number chose not to pay their share of the cost.[53] It may be that, so far as deterrence is concerned, it is no bad thing if people *think* that tort is vicious and unreasonably broad –

---

[50] On why people might *not* claim in tort, see Cane, *Atiyah's Accidents Compensation and the Law* (5th ed., Butterworths, London, 1993) 171 *et seq*. On effects of greater willingness to take legal action see Galanter, "Law Abounding: Legalisation around the North Atlantic" (1992) 55 *M.L.R.* 1.

[51] For general discussion see Harris, "Evaluating the Goals of Personal Injury Law: Some Empirical Evidence" in Cane and Stapleton (eds.), *Essays for Patrick Selim Atiyah* (Oxford, Clarendon Press, 1991) 289.

[52] Possibly the Irish legal system is more efficient, though the evidence is patchy: see Pierse, "Irish Insurance Costs and Damages" (1997) 15 *I.L.T. (n.s.)* 15.

[53] It has been estimated that between 10% and 15% of Irish drivers are not covered by insurance; figures for the UK are lower but still substantial. For the workings of the systems see Campbell, "The uninsured driver, the M.I.B. and the insurance disk system" *Jour Law Soc Scotland* May 1994, 170; Madden, "The Uninsured or Untraceable Driver: M.I.B.I. Litigation" (1995) 13 *I.L.T. (n.s.)* 52.

unless, of course, they are actually right. The best of all worlds may be where potential defendants are worried sick that they will be sued, but where in fact it is rather difficult to do commence a legal action. And at times, the "neighbour" principle has come quite close to achieving this ideal. But perhaps not close enough.

It is also the case that negligence law, as with any established institution of the law, risks eventually succumbing to corruption on a massive scale. This is so in quite a literal sense. It is not a secret, though it is not emphasised in legal discussions of the "neighbour" principle, that a significant number of those who claim its protection are out-and-out con-men, and that any organisation which regularly finds itself a defendant in personal injury matters will nowadays certainly have considered what it can do to reduce the risk of fraud.[54] And in a looser sense, while not corrupt in any ordinary sense, nonetheless the army of lawyers and insurers necessary to administer the "neighbour" principle is itself a body of professionals with its own interests to serve and its own reasons for attachment to the status quo. If the "neighbour" principle is good then we are very fortunate, for it would be very hard to shift even if we were so minded. If there is a law requiring drivers and employers to purchase particular policies from insurers, it would be surprising if insurers were in a hurry to change that law; if lawyers control the only means of achieving compensation in certain situations where compensation will be desperately required on a regular basis, it would be surprising if the lawyers were in a hurry to change those arrangements.[55] And if (as is now clearly the case in the UK) government too takes its cut from the money which personal injury actions generate, then that is one more important player with an incentive not to change the current arrangements.[56] This is not, of course, in itself corruption; it will not necessarily even lead to corruption. But anyone tempted to say that the persistence and expansion of the "neighbour" principle is proof of its excellence should think again. I like to think that, if good and clear case for its abolition were shown, it would be abolished. But it might take a *very* clear case before that would happen.

Yet for all that, there is an up-side to the principle. In its flexibility and its

---

[54] See, *e.g.*, "Investigators excavate profits from potholes" *Irish Times*, March 14, 1998, 12. For general discussion, see especially Joseph, *Lawyers Can Seriously Damage Your Health* (London, Michael Joseph, 1984) chap. 10; Slesenger, "Something For Nothing" (1997) 147 *N.L.J.* 1124.

[55] For the vested interests involved in any reform of personal injury law see Lewis, "Legislation: Lobbying and the Damages Act 1996" (1997) 60 *M.L.R.* 230.

[56] Where, as is almost certainly the case with any significant injury, the plaintiff claims social security benefits in consequence of the injury, then those benefits are included in the plaintiff's damages but then paid to the state: see Social Security (Recovery of Benefits) Act 1997. Over £150m was so recovered in 1997-1998: see "Compensation Recovery Unit" *Commons Written Answers* March 24, 1998 col. 122. Additionally, the cost of treating the plaintiff in National Health Service hospitals is recoverable by the state in road traffic cases, and the provision to that effect has recently been strengthened: see Road Traffic (NHS Charges) Act 1999.

ability to meet new situations; in the scope it allows for creativity, in an age where judicial creativity is usually frowned upon, there is much to be said for it. It is a means for doing something quickly about rogue snails, before the other institutions of government get on the case. It is the state's anti-snail rapid reaction force. And if the idea that the response of civil justice to anything can be described as "rapid" raises a laugh, then I can only say that you should see how quickly the rest of the government reacts. . . .

A DESERT ISLAND CASE SET IN THE SILVER SEA
The State (Ryan) v. Lennon (1934)

DR. GERARD HOGAN S.C.[*]

1. Introduction

If one were to be fastidious about the title of this book, then *The State (Ryan) v. Lennon*[1] probably ought not to qualify as a "leading case" of this century. It is not a "leading case" in the sense in which – to take the most obvious example – *Donoghue v. Stevenson*[2] is a leading case. But, by any standards, is a great case raising profound issues and for that reason it deserves inclusion in this series. It was a great favourite of the late Professor John Kelly who, in his own inimitable fashion, used to describe this case as a "desert island" case, so that if one were the proverbial castaway forced to choose a limited selection of cases to read for intellectual stimulation and enjoyment, this certainly would be one of them.

The decision not only raises a host of novel and difficult issues – including the validity of two separate constitutional amendments; the question of whether any provisions of the Constitution of the Irish Free State had been placed beyond the amending power of the Oireachtas (Parliament); the role of natural law and the response of the courts to extreme legal measures, and the nature of the sovereignty of the Irish Free State – but it is also notable for two judgments – from Kennedy C.J. and FitzGibbon J. – of extraordinary virtuosity and power. The practical dimensions of this case could not have been more important:

> . . . the bill of rights provisions of the Constitution, the document to which Kennedy had contributed so notably, were to be virtually swept away by the Supreme Court itself three years later in *The State (Ryan) v. Lennon*. Kennedy was an isolated dissentient as FitzGibbon and Murnaghan in judgments redolent of Austinian positivism proclaimed the courts pow-

---

[*]Fellow, Trinity College, Dublin.

[1] [1935] I.R. 170 (H.C. and S.C.). For contemporary comment, see Hood Philips, *"Ryan's* Case" (1936) 52 *L.Q.R.* 241; Jennings, "The Statute of Westminster and Privy Council Appeals" (1936) 52 *L.Q.R.* 173; Anon. "The Amendment of the Saorstát Constitution" (1935) 69 *I.L.T.S.J.* 55.

[2] [1932] A.C. 562 (H.L.), on which see Hedley, *"M'Alister (or Donoghue) (Pauper) v. Stevenson* (1932)" above, p. 64–79.

erless in the face of executive and legislative intent on enacting draconian "law and order" measures.[3]

2. The Constitutional Background

To understand the complex constitutional background to this case, it is important to draw attention to some of the key provisions of the Constitution of the Irish Free State. Article 70 of the 1922 Constitution had originally provided in relevant part that:

> ... extraordinary tribunals shall not be established, save only such Military Tribunals as may be authorised by law for dealing with military offences against military law.

Against the backdrop of the Civil War of 1922-3 and the continued disturbed conditions which prevailed thereafter, this guarantee was not, unfortunately, a very realistic one.[4] Throughout the 1920s the Oireachtas found itself forced to pass a variety of Public Safety legislation providing either for a power of internment or, alternatively, for trial by standing military tribunal. Despite the fact that such swinging legislation generally rested uneasily with the solemn guarantees (ranging from Article 6 (personal liberty) to Article 70) contained in that Constitution, the constitutionality of such legislation was upheld in a series of cases, chiefly on the remarkable ground that during the initial eight year period following the entry into force of the Constitution, any legislation enacted by the Oireachtas which was found in conflict with the Constitution had the effect, *ipso facto*, of amending that Constitution, whether on a permanent[5] or temporary basis.[6]

This form of reasoning seems to modern eyes to be so extraordinary that it requires an elaborate explanation. One of the innovatory features of the 1922 Constitution was that it provided that future amendments would have to be subjected to a referendum. Article 50 of the 1922 Constitution originally provided that:

> Amendments of this Constitution within the terms of the Scheduled Treaty may be made by the Oireachtas, but no such amendment, passed by both

---

[3] Keane, "The Voice of the Gael: Chief Justice Kennedy and the Emergence of the New Irish Court System 1921-1936" (1996) XXXI *Ir. Jur. (n.s.)* 205, 223.

[4] As Dodd J. put it – speaking of the enactment of the Constitution in 1922 – what "was supposed to herald an era of settled government turned out to be the harbinger of unrest and rebellion": *R. (O'Connell) v. Military Governor of Hare Park* [1924] 2 I.R. 104, 115 (H.C.).

[5] *R. (Cooney) v. Clinton* [1935] I.R. 245 (C.A.) (decided in 1924, but belatedly reported).

[6] *Attorney General v. McBride* [1928] I.R. 451 (H.C.).

Houses of the Oireachtas, after the expiration of a period of eight years from the date of the coming into operation of this Constitution, shall become law, unless the same shall, after it has been passed or deemed to have been passed by the said two Houses of the Oireachtas, have been submitted to a Referendum of the people, and unless a majority of voters on the register, or two-thirds of the vote recorded, shall have been cast in favour of such amendment.

Had the drafters' original intentions in this regard been fulfilled, the path of constitutional development in the 1920s and 1930s would surely have taken a different route. In particular, the radical constitutional changes of the 1930s might not have been possible had each amendment been subject to the referendum process and which would have required a majority of voters on the register or two-thirds of the voters who actually voted.[7] However, a last-minute alteration to the text of Article 50 allowed amendments by ordinary legislation during an initial eight year period from the date the Constitution came into force, *i.e.*, until December 6, 1930.[8] As Chief Justice Kennedy (himself a member of that Constitution's drafting committee) was later to explain:

It was originally intended, as appears by the draft, that amendment of the Constitution should not be possible without the consideration due to so important a matter affecting the fundamental law and framework of the State, and the draft provided that the process of amendment should be such as to require full and general consideration [*sc.* by means of referendum]. At the last moment, however, it was agreed that a provision be added to Article 50, allowing amendment by way of ordinary legislation during a limited period so that drafting or verbal amendments, not altogether unlikely to appear necessary in a much debated text, might be made without the more elaborate process proper for the purpose of more important amendments. This clause was, however, afterwards used for effecting alterations of a radical and far-reaching character, some of them

---

[7] It will be noted that this was a far more restrictive requirement than that required of amendments to the present Constitution, as Article 47.1 merely requires a majority of the votes actually cast at that referendum. Indeed, the 1937 Constitution would not have been passed had it been required to satisfy the conditions stipulated by Article 50 of the 1922 Constitution. As O'Sullivan, *The Irish Free State and its Senate. A Study in Contemporary Politics* (Faber, London, 1940; facsimile reprint: Arno Press, New York, 1972) [hereafter O'Sullivan] observed:

Under Article 62 of the [1937 Constitution] only a bare majority of those actually voting was required, and so the new Constitution had been enacted by the people. But if the conditions laid down in Article 50 had been incorporated in Article 62 it would have been decisively rejected (O'Sullivan, 502).

[8] This consisted of an addition of the following words at the very end of Article 50:

Any such amendment may be made within the said period of eight years by way of ordinary legislation.

far removed in principle from the ideas and ideals before the minds of the first authors of the instrument.[9]

The eight year clause – originally intended simply to cover minor and technical amendments – ultimately proved to be the means whereby the entire 1922 Constitution was undone.[10] Unfortunately, however, no one foresaw at the time the amendment was accepted by the Dáil that this power could be used to undermine the Constitution in several ways. In particular, there was the prospect that the eight year period might itself be extended by the Oireachtas, so that the Constitution would be rendered entirely vulnerable to legislative abrogation. This is what happened and this ultimately led to the complete undermining of that Constitution.

3. THE DECISION IN *THE STATE (RYAN) V. LENNON*

On March 13, 1929 the Dáil debated the second stage of the Constitution (Amendment No. 16) Bill 1928. The object of this Bill was to extend the eight year transitional period for a further eight years from December 1930 until December 1938. While the debate in the Dáil was perfunctory, the Bill subsequently passed all stages in the Seanad without debate. It seems extraordinary that a Bill with such radical implications should pass through the Oireachtas virtually without comment. The extension of the time during which amendments to the Constitution might be effected by ordinary legislation was to pave the way for even more radical measures during the 1930s.

In late 1931 the Constitution (Amendment No. 17) Act 1931 was enacted and inserted a radical amendment, Article 2A, into the Constitution. Section 2 of the new Article 2A provided that:

---

[9] Preface to Kohn, *The Constitution of the Irish Free State* (Allen and Unwin, London, 1932) [hereafter Kohn] xiii. *Cf.* his comments in dissent on this point in *The State (Ryan) v. Lennon* [1935] I.R. 170, 216-219 and the observations of Murnaghan J. (who was also a member of the 1922 drafting committee) by way of rejoinder ([1935] I.R. 170, 244):

> I am ready to conjecture that when Article 50 was framed it was not considered probable that any such use of the power would be made as has been made, but the terms in which Article 50 is framed does authorise the amendment made and there is not in the Article any express limitation which excludes Article 50 itself from the power of amendment.

[10] See generally 1 *Dáil Debates* at 1235–1239 (October 5, 1922). As FitzGibbon J. later remarked in the Supreme Court in *Ryan* [1935] I.R. 170, 234:

> The framers of our Constitution may have intended "to bind man down from mischief by the chains of the Constitution" but if they did, they defeated their object by handing him the key of the padlock in Article 50.

As it happened, FitzGibbon J. had been a T.D. (representing Dublin University) during the period 1922-1924 immediately before his appointment directly to the Supreme Court and, thus, had been a member of the Constituent Assembly which had approved the amendments to Article 50.

Article 3 and every subsequent Article of this Constitution shall be read and construed subject to the provisions of this Article and, in the case of inconsistency between this Article and the said Article 3 or any subsequent Article, this Article shall prevail.[11]

This device was open to the objection that the provisions of the Constitution were effectively contingent on the making of executive orders bringing these amendments or quasi-amendments into force. This was illustrated in the case of Article 2A, since it was brought into force, later suspended and subsequently brought into force once again. At all events, there was no doubt as to the radical and draconian character of Article 2A: it provided for a standing military court[12] (from which there was to be no appeal[13]) which was empowered to impose any penalty (including the death penalty) in respect of any offence, even if such a penalty was greater than that provided by the ordinary law! In a prohibition application decided a few months before *Ryan's* case, *The State (O'Duffy) v. Bennett*, Hanna J. did not mince his words about the nature of Article 2A: he described the amendment as creating "a kind of intermittent martial law under the harmless name of a constitutional amendment".[14]

The validity of both Constitution (Amendment No. 16) Act 1929 and Constitution (Amendment No. 17) Act 1931 were the key issues in *Ryan*. In this

---

[11] In contemporary times the Supreme Court has re-emphasised the radical character of Article 2A. In *The State (McCarthy) v. Lennon* [1936] I.R. 485 (S.C.) a majority of the Supreme Court held that Article 2A had abrogated the applicant's common law rights against self-incrimination. In *In re National Irish Bank Ltd.(No. 1)* [1999] 3 I.R. 145; [1999] 1 I.L.R.M. 321 (H.C. and S.C.) the Court held that the situation had been significantly altered following the enactment of the Constitution which prohibited the admission in a criminal trial of a confession extracted under statutory compulsion. Barrington J. stressed the difficulties which the former Supreme Court had encountered in *McCarthy*:

At the time of the enactment of the 17th Amendment to the Constitution of the Irish Free State the Oireachtas was in a position to amend the Constitution without reference to the people. The Oireachtas was, for the time being, in the position of a sovereign Parliament. Article 2A was to prevail over subsequent provisions of the Constitution in the event of an inconsistency between it and them. There was no point therefore in appealing to such inconsistency between it and them. The Judges were virtually in the same position as Judges under the British Constitution. It was simply a question of working out what Parliament meant from what Parliament said ([1999] 3 I.R. 145, 176; [1999] 1 I.L.R.M. 321, 349-350).

[12] The then President of the Executive Council (W.T. Cosgrave T.D.) informed the Dáil in the course of the debate on Article 2A that the two judges of the Supreme Court had intimated to him that they would resign if they were required to preside over a non-jury court: 40 *Dáil Debates* at Col. 45 (October 14, 1931).

[13] Article 2A did not, however, have the effect of preventing judicial review of the Tribunal's decision: see *The State (Hughes) v. Lennon* [1935] I.R. 128 (H.C.); *The State (O'Duffy) v. Bennett* [1935] I.R. 70 (H.C.). In *Hughes* a Divisional High Court held that the Tribunal's conviction was invalid in that it did not sufficiently show jurisdiction on its face and as a result the Government was obliged to release 37 (mainly I.R.A.) prisoners: *The Irish Times*, July 25, 1934.

[14] [1935] I.R. 70, 96.

case four prisoners challenged the legality of their detention and sought orders of prohibition restraining the Constitution (Special Powers) Tribunal from proceeding to try them in respect of a variety of offences, including attempting to shoot with intent to murder and unlawful possession of firearms. Their applications were first dismissed by a unanimous Divisional High Court[15] and, subsequently, by a majority of the Supreme Court.[16] In the High Court it was conceded on behalf of the Attorney General that the Constitution (Amendment No. 17) Act 1931 was inconsistent with the Constitution as originally enacted.

As the validity of Constitution (Amendment No. 17) Act 1931 in turn depended on whether Article 50 itself had been validly amended by Constitution (Amendment No. 16) Act 1929, Sullivan P. first considered whether this amendment was itself valid. Having stated that a constitutional statute such as this should receive a liberal interpretation, the President continued:

> I cannot accept the view that the word "amendment" when used in reference to an Act of Parliament, is, as Mr. Costello suggested, limited in its meaning to the removal of faults, corrections in matters of detail but not of substance. I think the ordinary and natural meaning of the word when so used includes alterations of any kind. It will not, I think, be disputed that where the word "amend" occurs in the title of a statute . . . its usual if not invariable meaning is "alter" in the widest sense of the word and I think that we have on the face of the Constitution itself an indication that the word "amend" is used in that sense.[17]

Sullivan P. then gave examples of other provisions of the Constitution – such as Article 38 and Article 73 – in which the power to amend was used in this sense. He then continued:

> I am, therefore, of opinion that Article 50 conferred upon the Oireachtas the power to amend and later the Constitution by way of ordinary legislation passed within a period of eight years from the date on which the Constitution itself came into operation, and that, in the absence of any indication in the statute of an intention to the contrary, the power so conferred is unrestricted, and authorises the alteration of any Article of the Constitution, including Article 50 itself.[18]

From this judgment the applicants appealed to the Supreme Court which dismissed the appeals by a majority. These judgments are notable for the range of

---

[15] Sullivan P., Meredith and O'Byrne JJ.
[16] FitzGibbon and Murnaghan JJ., Kennedy C.J. dissenting.
[17] [1935] I.R. 170, 177-178.
[18] [1935] I.R. 170, 178. The other members of the Divisional High Court – Meredith and O'Byrne JJ. – delivered judgments to similar effect.

issues which they traverse. The key issue facing the Court on appeal, however, was whether the Oireachtas had an unlimited power of amendment of the Constitution during the transitory period. The Court was divided on this question and it may be convenient to turn first to the reasoning of the majority judges, FitzGibbon and Murnaghan JJ.

FitzGibbon J. first rejected the argument that the power to amend the Constitution should confined to circumstances where the amendment effected an "improvement" of the Constitution. If this construction were correct, then the validity of an amendment would depend upon the decision of the High Court that it effected such an improvement, so that:

> . . . the Judges and not the Oireachtas would be made the authority to decide upon the advisability of any particular amendment of the Constitution, and this would involve a direct contravention of the principles [of the separation of powers].[19]

The judge then turned to consider the wider question of whether the power to amend the Constitution included the power to amend Article 50 itself. While he observed that "however undesirable it may appear to some" that the Oireachtas should have the power to extend the period during which the Constitution might be amended by ordinary legislation, nevertheless "if this be the true construction of Article 50, this Court is bound to give effect to that construction".[20] He continued by noting that whereas both the Constituent Act and Article 50 contained restrictions on the power of amendment – they both precluded amendments which were in conflict with the terms of the Treaty – the *expressio unius* principle came into play, suggesting that no further restrictions on the power to amend were thereby intended:

> It is conceded that there is no express prohibition against amendment of Article 50 to be found in the Constitution. It is not unusual to find that Constitutions or Constituents Acts impose such restrictions upon the legislative bodies set up by them, and the omission of any such restriction in regard to amendments of Article 50 is at least a negative argument that Dáil Éireann as a Constituent Assembly did not intend to impose any such restriction upon the Oireachtas. This negative argument is supported by the fact that both the Constituent Act and Article 50 itself do contain an express restriction upon the powers of the Oireachtas to amend the Constitution, and it is a legitimate inference that, when certain restrictions were expressly imposed, it was not intended that certain other undefined restrictions should be imposed by implication".[21]

---

[19][1935] I.R. 170, 223.
[20][1935] I.R. 170, 224.
[21]*ibid.*

FitzGibbon J. then emphasised the fact that it was Dáil Éireann sitting as a Constituent Assembly which had created the Oireachtas and had limited its powers in particular ways:

> Therefore the supreme legislative authority, speaking as the mouthpiece of the people, expressly denied to the Oireachtas the power of enacting *any* legislation, by way of amendment of the Constitution or otherwise, which might be "in any respect repugnant to any of the provisions of the Scheduled Treaty" and it reiterated this prohibition in Article 50, which empowered the Oireachtas to make *"amendments of this Constitution with the terms of the Scheduled Treaty."* It is further observed that this power to make amendments is limited to "amendments of this Constitution", and that the Constituent Assembly did not confer upon the Oireachtas any power to amend the Constituent Act itself. These express limitations, imposed by the mouthpiece of the people upon the legislative powers of the Oireachtas which it set up, support the view that the Oireachtas was intended to have full power of legislation and amendment outside the prohibited area, and as there was no prohibition against amendment of Article 50, I am of opinion that Amendment No. 10 in 1928, and Amendment No. 16 in 1929, were within the powers conferred upon the Oireachtas by the Constituent Act.[22]

FitzGibbon J. concluded by noting that the Constitutions of other jurisdictions often contained express restrictions upon the power of the Legislature to amend the amendment power itself[23] so that it followed that:

> Our Constituent Assembly could in like manner have exempted Article 50 from the amending powers conferred upon the Oireachtas, but it did not do so, and in my opinion the Court has no jurisdiction to read either into the Constituent Act or into Article 50 a proviso excepting it, and it alone, from these powers.[24]

Murnaghan J. spoke in similar terms and concluded that:

---

[22] [1935] I.R. 170, 226-227. Emphasis in the original. FitzGibbon J. added that an amendment of Article 50 by the deletion of the words "within the terms of the Scheduled Treaty" would be "totally ineffective", as effect was given to those words by the Constituent Act itself, "which the Oireachtas has no power to amend".

[23] He instanced s. 152 of the South Africa Act 1909 which provided that no "repeal or alteration of the provisions contained in this section . . . shall, be valid" unless the Bill embodying such an amendment to the amending power itself shall have been passed in a particular way or by a specified majority. Article V of the U.S. Constitution also contained certain restrictions on the power of amendment of certain clauses of Article I prior to 1808.

[24] [1935] I.R. 170, 227.

... the terms in which Article 50 is framed does authorise the amendment made and there is not in the Article any express limitation which excludes Article 50 itself from the power of amendment. I cannot, therefore, find any ground upon which the suggested limitation can be properly based. It must also be remembered that in this country the Referendum was an untried political experiment and it cannot be assumed that the Referendum should be capable of alteration or removal. I feel bound by the words of Article 50, which allows amendment of the Constitution as a whole, of which Article 50 is declared to be a part.[25]

Kennedy C.J.'s dissent on this point contains echoes of his later natural law argument:

The Third Dáil Éireann has, therefore, as Constituent Assembly, of its own supreme authority, proclaimed its acceptance of and declared, in relation to the Constitution which it enacted, certain principles, and in language which shows that beyond doubt that they are stated as governing principles which are fundamental and absolute (except as expressly qualified) and, so, necessarily immutable. Can the power of amendment given to the Oireachtas be lawfully exercised in such a manner as to violate these principles which, as principle, the Oireachtas has no power to change? In my opinion there can be only one to that question, namely, that the Constituent Assembly cannot be supposed to have in the same breadth declared certain principles to be fundamental and immutable, or conveyed that sense in other words, as by a declaration of inviolability, and at the same time to have conferred upon the Oireachtas power to violate them or to alter them. In my opinion, any amendment of the Constitution, purporting to be made under the power given by the Constituent Assembly, which would be a violation of, or inconsistent with, any fundamental principle so declared, is necessarily outside the scope of the power and invalid and void.[26]

4. SOME PRACTICAL CONSEQUENCES OF *RYAN*

Ryan's case gave the imprimatur to a development which was already gathering speed, namely, the wholescale dismantling of the 1922 Constitution by ordinary legislation. Had this decision been otherwise, every amendment after December 1930 would have had to have been by way of referendum. We can only conjecture how a deeply divided electorate would have responded to ref-

---

[25][1935] I.R. 170, 244.
[26][1935] I.R. 170, 209.

erenda on such topics as Article 2A and the successive abolition of the oath, the appeal to the Privy Council, the Senate, the Governor General and all references to the Crown in the Constitution. In this respect, it must be recalled that Article 50 of the 1922 Constitution required for a valid amendment of the Constitution either *a majority of the voters on the register*[27] *or two-thirds of the votes recorded.* These conditions are far more stringent than apply in the case of referenda on constitutional amendments under the present Constitution, where Article 47.1 simply requires a majority of the voters who actually voted. Indeed, the stringency of this requirement can be gauged by the fact that if this rule were to have been continued after 1937, quite a number of amendments would have fallen, including the divorce amendment and the referenda on the Single European Act and the Maastricht and Amsterdam Treaties, not to speak of the enactment of the Constitution itself.[28] While the Government would have probably secured a majority of the voting electorate had referenda on all of the above topics taken place, whether any given referendum would have satisfied the more stringent requirements of the then Article 50 must be open to doubt. Undoubtedly, had the result in *Ryan's* case gone the other way, it would have had huge implications for the constitutional changes of the 1930s which were otherwise facilitated by the fact that the Constitution was rendered entirely vulnerable to constitutional change.[29]

5. ASSESSING THE JUDGMENTS IN *RYAN*

Which, then, of these differing judicial views was correct? In the first place, the Court of Appeal in *Cooney* was clearly wrong to hold that the Constitution could be implicitly amended by ordinary legislation during the eight year period. It is true that the Constitution of the Irish Free State was enacted by means of ordinary legislation by Dáil Éireann sitting as a constituent assembly, but it was not an ordinary piece of legislation. Quite apart from the provisions entrenched by the Treaty, the whole tenor of the Constitution presupposed that it would have a higher legal status than that of ordinary legislation. If it were otherwise, Article 65 would not have expressly empowered the High Court

---

[27] This makes the percentage required to carry the Bill contingent on the actual turn-out. Thus, for example, in a 70% turnout, the majority for the Bill would need to approach 72% in order to constitute a majority of the voters on the register.

[28] See O'Sullivan, 502-3.

[29] *Cf.* the comments of Donaldson, *Some Comparative Aspects of Irish Law* (Duke, 1957) 146-147 in respect of the aftermath of *Ryan's* case:

> One can only speculate on what would have happened if the original eight-year period had not been extended, for it is possible that the constitutional amendments of the 1930s would not have been accomplished so easily if the referendum procedure had been applied to them.

with the power of judicial review of legislation. The entire fallacy of this case was that it invested the Constitution with the same status as that of ordinary legislation. Moreover, had the December 1930 deadline remained unchanged, one would have had the curious situation inasmuch as constitutional amendments could only take effect by means of referendum, yet the repeal after that date by subsequent ordinary legislation of an Act which had impliedly amended the Constitution during the initial eight year period would have had the effect of restoring the Constitution to its original position, *i.e.*, the Constitution would thus have been amended without the necessity for a referendum. The unacceptability of such a conclusion merely highlights the absurdities inherent in the implicit amendment doctrine.

At the same time, the Supreme Court was probably correct in its conclusion in *Ryan* that, subject to the entrenched provisions safeguarded by the Treaty, the Oireachtas had a full power of amendment of the Constitution by ordinary legislation during the initial eight year period. It followed that as Article 50 did not fall within these entrenched provisions, it itself could also be amended. It is also worth recalling that *Ryan's* case involved express amendments to the Constitution: there was no question here of any amendments by implication. It is certainly true that – as both Kennedy C.J. and FitzGibbon J. were to observe – the power of amendment contained in Article 50 was employed in a manner not foreseen by the drafters, but that is not in itself a reason for holding that the Oireachtas did not have the power to amend this provision by ordinary legislation prior to the expiration of the original eight year period.

At all events, Kennedy C.J.'s dissent has proved to be influential. It was at the heart of the famous decision of the Indian Supreme Court in *Kesavandra v. State of Kerala*,[30] where it was frequently cited – generally with approval – in the diverse judgments of the 13 member Supreme Court bench running to 566 printed pages. In this case a majority of that Court held that the "essential features" of the Indian Constitution were beyond the amending power of that Constitution. The majority then went on to hold that a constitutional amendment which sought to immunise the constitutionality of legislation from challenge on the ground that it did not give effect to the Directive Principles of Social Policy contained in Article 37 of the Indian Constitution was itself invalid.[31]

Similar thinking has prevailed in some continental jurisprudence. Thus, in

---

[30] [1973] A.I.R. 1461 (S.C.India). See generally, Gwynn Morgan, "The Indian Essential Features Case" (1981) 30 *I.C.L.Q.* 307 and Whelan, "Constitutional Amendments in Ireland: The Competing Claims of Democracy" in Quinn, Ingram and Livingstone, (eds.), *Justice and Legal Theory in Ireland* (Oak Tree Press, Dublin, 1995) 45.

[31] A provision which itself is clearly modelled on Article 45 of our own Constitution. In *Gandhi v. Raj Narain* (1975) A.S.C. 2299 (S.C.India) the "essential features" doctrine was applied by Indian Supreme Court to invalidate a constitutional amendment which was designed to interfere with a pending appeal to that Court.

the first major case in which it invalidated a Federal statute, the *Southwest State Case*,[32] the German Constitutional Court said that "a Constitution reflects certain overarching principles and fundamental decisions to which individual provisions of the Basic Law are subordinate". The Court added by way of an *obiter dictum* that German constitutional law protects certain suprapositivist norms, so that a constitutional amendment which violated these "overarching principles and fundamental decisions" would be itself void.[33]

6. KENNEDY C.J. AND NATURAL LAW

Ryan's case is also justly famous for the fact that the Chief Justice Kennedy was willing to invalidate a constitutional amendment by reference to natural law or higher law principles. In contrast to the language of the personal rights provisions of Articles 40, 41, 42 and 43 of the present Constitution – where, on one view, at least, there is almost an open invitation to the judiciary to apply natural law reasoning – it must be said that the Chief Justice in his references to the natural law had "to pull his antecedent principles out of the air, so to speak".[34] However, Kennedy C.J. stressed that the Constitution was subject to the certain immutable limitations:

> The Constituent Assembly declared in the forefront of the Constitution Act (an Act which it is not within the power of the Oireachtas to alter, or amend or repeal) that all lawful authority comes from God to the people, and that it is declared by Article 2 of the Constitution that 'all powers of government and all authority, whether legislative, executive or judicial, in order to be lawful under the Constitution, must be capable of being justified under the authority thereby declared to be derived from God. From this it seems clear that, if any legislation of the Oireachtas (including any purported amendment of the Constitution) were to offend against that acknowledged ultimate Source from which the legislative authority has come through the people to the Oireachtas, as, if, for instance, it were repugnant to the Natural Law, such legislation would be necessarily unconstitutional and invalid, and it would be, therefore, absolutely null and void and inoperative. I find it very difficult to reconcile with the Natural

---

[32](1951) 1 BVerfGE 14. Here legislation providing for the compulsory amalgamation of three small Länder into the amalgamated Land of Baden-Württemberg was found to be unconstitutional on the ground that it violated fundamental principles of democracy and federalism.

[33]The nearest that the Constitutional Court has come to applying these principles is the *Klass* case (1970) 30 BverfGE 1, where the dissenting members of the Court considered that amendments to Article 10 of the Basic Law (protecting the "inviolability" of the posts and telegraphs were themselves void on the ground they violated these "overarching principles.")

[34]Hogan and Whyte, *Kelly's The Irish Constitution* (3rd ed., Butterworths, Dublin, 1994) 676.

Law actions and conduct which would appear to be within the legalising intendment of the provisions of the new Article 2A relating to interrogation. I find it impossible to reconcile as compatible with the Natural Law the vesting in three military servants of the Executive, power to impose as punishment for any offence within the indefinite, but certainly extensive, ambit of the Appendix, the penalty of death, whenever these three persons are of opinion that it is *expedient*. Finally, the judicial power has been acknowledged and declared (and the acknowledgement is expedient. Finally, the judicial power has been acknowledged and declared (and the acknowledgement of the judiciary and the Courts of the State. While they can fulfil that trust, dare any say that the Natural Law permits it, or any part of it, to be transferred to the Executive or their military or other servants.[35]

The two majority judges responded to this issue in slightly different ways. It brought forth in FitzGibbon J. a withering, contemptuous response, full of savage and biting irony. He noted first that the appellants had argued that there are:

certain rights, inherent in every individual, which are so sacred that no legislature has authority to deprive him of them. It is useless to speculate upon the origin of a doctrine which may be founded in the writings of Rosseau, Thomas Paine, William Godwin and other philosophical writers, but we have not to decide between their theories and those of Delolme and Burke, not to mention Bentham and Locke, upon what Leslie Stephen described as a "problem which has not yet been solved, nor are even the appropriate methods definitely agreed upon" as we are concerned, not with the principles which might or ought to have been adopted by the framers of our Constitution, but with the powers which have actually been entrusted by it to the Legislature and Executive which it set up.[36]

He then went on to reject the argument that the Constitution, like its American counterpart on which it was to some degree modelled, had attempted to enshrine fundamental principles, since the American experience had been founded upon historical considerations which did not obtain in the case of the Irish Free State:

I can find no justification for the inference which the counsel for the appellants ask us to draw from the provisions of the American Declaration of Independence and the Constitution founded thereon, or from the fact that some of these provisions have been embodied in other Constitu-

---

[35][1935] I.R. 170, 204-5.
[36][1935] I.R. 170, 230-1.

tions, including our own, that the rights thereby secured are universal and inalienable rights of all citizens in all countries or even in the Saorstát which, we have been assured, was, or is, our ought to be, Gaelic and Catholic, attributes to either of which few other States can claim a title, while there is no other which can even suggest a claim to both. There is no ground for surprise, therefore, that this State should, as the Chief Justice has said, "point new ways" in its "pioneer Constitution draftsmanship" or that it should prefer to secure liberty and justice to its citizens by the simple processes of Amendment No. 17 in preference to the complicated British and American machinery of an independent judiciary, trial by jury and *habeas corpus*.

I cannot presume, either, that rights and privileges which the inhabitants of England have always enjoyed, either by virtue of their common law . . . or under the provisions of special statutes, are also indigenous to the citizens of this Gaelic and Catholic State in the sense in which the American colonists claimed them as their birthright by virtue of *their* status as British subjects – a status which I understand to be repudiated by our legislators – or that our national conceptions of liberty and justice must necessarily coincide with those of citizens of any other State.[37]

FitzGibbon J. continued by harking back to the all-embracing power of amendment in Article 50:

Unless, therefore, those rights appear plainly from the express provisions of our Constitution to be inalienable and incapable of being modified or taken away by legislative act, I cannot accede to the argument that the Oireachtas cannot alter, modify or repeal them. The framers of the Constitution may have intended 'to bind man down from mischief by the chains of the Constitution', but if they did, they defeated their object by handing him the key of the padlock in Article 50.[38]

But this remarkable judgment had yet to reach its apotheosis. FitzGibbon J. next surveyed the Constitutions as diverse as those of Poland and Mexico,

---

[37] [1935] I.R. 170, 233-4.
[38] [1935] I.R. 170, 234. As Hood Phillips remarked, this case confirmed that there are no "fundamental laws or 'natural rights' in the Constitution of the Irish Free State whatever continental observers who read that document may have thought" ((1936) 52 *L.Q.R.* 241, 242-3). The reference to "continental observers" is, of course, to Kohn, above n.9. Kohn had, of course, been heavily influenced by the thinking of Kennedy. The two had become friendly and the Chief Justice had written the foreword to Kohn's masterly work: see generally Hand, "A re-consideration of a German study (1927-1932) of the Irish Constitution" in Bieber and Nickel, (eds.), *Das Europa der zweiten Generation: Gedächtnisschrift fur Christoph Sasse* (Nomos, Baden-Baden, 1981) vol. 2, 855.

demonstrating the extraordinary lengths to which to such provisions protected fundamental liberty and then continued:

> But the fact that the Constitutions of other countries prohibit such inva-
> sions of the rights of liberty and property and such extraordinary innova-
> tions in the methods of administering justice in criminal cases as have
> been introduced by Amendment No. 17 affords no ground for condemn-
> ing as unconstitutional in *this* country, or as contrary to any inalienable
> rights of an Irish citizen, an enactment which appears to have received
> the almost unanimous support of the Oireachtas, for we have been told
> that those of our legislators by whom it was opposed most vehemently as
> unconstitutional and oppressive, when it was first introduced, and now
> accord it their unqualified approval.[39] It is true that even a unanimous
> vote of the Legislature does not decide the validity of a law, but it is some
> evidence that none of those whose duty it is to make the laws see any-
> thing in it which they regard as exceptionally iniquitous, or as derogating
> from the standard of civilisation which they deem, adequate for Saorstát
> Éireann. Indeed, it possible that our Constituent Assembly may have fol-
> lowed too slavishly the constitutional models of other nationalities, and
> that, just as the constitutional safeguards of Freedom of Speech, Trial by
> Jury, Security of the Person and Property were only introduced into the
> Constitution of the United States by way of amendment a year after the
> original Constitution had been adopted, so the amendments of our Con-
> stitution which have been enacted during recent years, whereby these
> and similar safeguards have been minimised or abrogated, more truly
> represent our national ideals. If this be so, we find the Briton's concep-
> tion of liberty and justice set forth in his Magna Charta and his Bill of
> Rights; those of the American in his Declaration of Independence and his
> Constitution; while those of the Gael are enshrined in Amendment No.
> 17 (which is to prevail in case of inconsistency, over everything in the
> Constitution, except Articles 1 and 2) and subsequent amendments. How-
> ever this may be, I can find no justification for a declaration that there
> was some "spirit" embodied in our original Constitution which is so sac-
> rosanct and immutable that nothing antagonistic to it may be enacted by
> the Oireachtas.[40]

---

[39] This, of course, is an intentionally ironic reference to the fact that while Fianna Fáil in opposition had vehemently opposed Article 2A and suspended it as soon as they came into Government
in March 1932, they were forced to re-introduce it in 1933: see generally O'Sullivan, 334-335.
[40] [1935] I.R. 170, 235-6. FitzGibbon J. quoted two American decisions at State court level to
illustrate this point, including the following quotation from *Walker v. Cincinnati* 21 Ohio 41:
> Courts cannot nullify an Act of the State Legislature on the vague ground that they think it
> opposed to a general latent spirit supposed to pervade or underlie the Constitution where
> neither the terms nor the implications of the instrument disclose any such restriction.

The judgment of the other majority judge – Murnaghan J. – was more muted. While he acknowledged that the "extreme rigour" of the provisions of Article 2A passed "far beyond anything having the semblance of legal procedure" and that the "judicial mind is staggered at the very complete departure from legal methods in use in these courts",[41] like FitzGibbon J. he evinced no sympathy whatever for the natural law arguments of the appellants:

> . . . the view contended for by the appellants must go to this extreme point, *viz.*, that certain Articles or doctrines of the Constitution are utterly incapable of alteration at any time, even if demanded by an absolute majority of the voters.[42]

While the dissent of Kennedy C.J. is often cited as the foundation of the modern Irish jurisprudential natural law tradition, one cannot help but wondering whether such reliance may be misplaced. It would seem to have little in common with the specifically religiously inspired version of the natural law which is most closely associated with the views of O'Hanlon J. in the general context of the abortion debate;[43] certainly, there does not appear to be anything in the Ten Commandments or the Sermon on the Mount or even in the writings of St. Thomas Acquinas which even remotely addresses matters such as the mode of a criminal trial or the need for such trials to be in the hands of an independent judiciary in times of peace. Nor does it seem to much in common with contemporary secular versions of natural law or substantive due process, since the starting point for this strand of jurisprudence – ostensibly, at least – is the actual wording of the Constitution. In any event, as Murnaghan J. perceptively anticipated in his own judgment, this modern version of natural law jurisprudence recognises the ultimate supremacy of the Constitution and, crucially, the capacity of the People to amend the Constitution by referendum in any way that they deem fit.[44]

The reality is that Kennedy C.J.'s dissent on the natural law issue – magnificent though it was – must really be regarded as a personal judicial response to an extreme and draconian constitutional amendment which had been en-

---

[41] [1935] I.R. 170, 237-8.

[42] *ibid.*, 240.

[43] For this debate, see O'Hanlon, "Natural Rights and the Irish Constitution" (1993) 11 *I.L.T.* (*n.s.*) 8; Murphy, "Democracy, Natural Law and the Irish Constitution" (1993) 11 *I.L.T.* (*n.s.*) 81; O'Hanlon, "The Judiciary and the Moral Law" (1993) 11 *I.L.T.* (*n.s.*) 129; Twomey, "The Death of Natural Law" (1995) 13 *I.L.T.* (*n.s.*) 270; see also, generally, Cox "Judicial Activism, Constitutional Interpretation and the Problem of Abortion. *Roe v. Wade* (1973) and *A.G. v. X* (1992)" below, 237.

[44] See, *e.g.*, *Re Article 26 and the Regulation of Information (Services outside the State for Termination of Pregnancies) Bill 1995* [1995] 1 I.R. 1; *Hanafin v. Minister for Environment* [1996] 2 I.R. 321; *Riordan v. An Taoiseach (No. 1)* [1999] 4 I.R. 325; *Riordan v. An Taoiseach (No. 2)* [1999] 4 I.R. 347.

acted almost by a legislative sleight of hand without the sanction of the electorate in the manner in which the Constitution had originally intended.[45] This
dissent also reflected a sharp clash in judicial attitude. Kennedy had clearly
hoped for:

> the creation of an indigenous legal system [and] for the development of a
> vibrant constitutional law, augmented by judicial review of legislation . .
> . This profound clash in judicial attitude – between what might conven-
> iently be described as the enthusiastic nationalism of Kennedy C.J. and
> the pessimistic scepticism of FitzGibbon J. – ultimately came to a head
> publicly in cases such as [*Ryan*].[46]

The key question is whether Kennedy C.J. would have taken the same view
had Article 2A been approved by way of referendum. As that question was not
before the Court, we can only speculate on the answer. However, given Kennedy
C.J.'s own beliefs about the nature of popular sovereignty, it would have been
surprising if he felt that the courts had jurisdiction in this regard. In other words,
it is likely that he would have adopted the approach taken by a later Supreme
Court in a trilogy of cases in the 1990s whereby the Court affirmed the supremacy of popular sovereignty as the key principle of the Constitution, so that
there are (almost) no limits to the people's right to amend that document by
way of referendum. As Hamilton C.J. said in *In re Article 26 and the Information (Termination of Pregnancies) Bill*[47] in response to the argument that the
people's power of amendment at a referendum did not extend to violating fundamental natural law principles:

> From a consideration of all of the cases which recognised the existence
> of a personal right which was not specifically enumerated in the Consti-
> tution, it is manifest that the Court in each such case had satisfied itself
> that such personal right was one which could be reasonably implied from
> and guaranteed by the provisions of the Constitution, interpreted in ac-
> cordance with its ideas of prudence, justice and charity. The courts, as
> they were and are bound to, recognised the Constitution as the funda-
> mental law of the State to which the organs of the State were subject and
> at no stage recognised the provisions of the natural law as superior to the
> Constitution. The People were entitled to amend the Constitution in ac-
> cordance with the provisions of Article 46 of the Constitution and the
> Constitution as so amended by the Fourteenth Amendment is the funda-

---

[45] See the extract from Kennedy's preface to Kohn set out, text with n.9, above.
[46] Hogan, "Chief Justice Kennedy and Sir James O'Connor's Application" (1988) XXIII *Ir. Jur.*
(*n.s.*) 144, 156.
[47] [1995] 1 I.R. 1 (S.C.).

mental and supreme law of the State representing as it does the will of the People.[48]

Similar views may be found in the various judgments of the Supreme Court in *Hanafin v. Minister for Environment*.[49] In an echo of his comments for the Court in the *Information Bill* reference, Hamilton C.J. observed:

> No organ of State is entitled to review or interfere with the will of the people as expressed in their votes cast in a referendum to consider a proposal for the amendment of the Constitution because the will of the people as so expressed is binding on all organs of the State, as it is the fundamental right of the people to decide all questions of national policy via the referendum process. While the judicial arm of government is not entitled to interfere with the right of the people to cast their votes at a referendum or with the results of the referendum, it is entitled to intervene in order to protect the rights of the citizens to exercise freely their constitutional right to vote if the constitutional rights of the citizens in regard thereto are violated by any body or individual. The will of the people as expressed in a referendum providing for the amendment of the Constitution is sacrosanct and if freely given, cannot be interfered with. The decision is theirs and theirs alone.[50]

Likewise, in *Riordan v. An Taoiseach (No. 1)*[51] (where the plaintiff had challenged, *inter alia*, the 15th Amendment of the Constitution Act 1996 providing for divorce) Barrington J. was emphatic on this question:

> There can be no question of a constitutional amendment properly placed before the people and approved by them being itself unconstitutional. . . . A proposed amendment to the Constitution will usually be designed to change something in the Constitution and will therefore, until enacted, be inconsistent with the existing text of the Constitution, but once approved by the people under Article 46 and promulgated by the President as law, it will form part of the Constitution and cannot be attacked as unconstitutional.[52]

While these judgments acknowledge the supremacy of the Constitution and the referendum process, one wonders what the contemporary judicial reaction

---

[48][1995] 1 I.R. 1, 43.
[49][1996] 2 I.R. 321 (S.C.).
[50][1996] 2 I.R. 321, 425.
[51][1999] 4 I.R. 325.
[52][1999] 4 I.R. 325, 339.

might be if the electorate were by referendum to sanction an alteration of fundamental constitutional values in a manner which was positively hostile to ordinary human rights standards? In a sense this is but a variation of the problem which confronted the Supreme Court in *Ryan*. However, once the court was satisfied that the referendum was duly passed it seems that it could have no concern with its merits, save, of course, that the courts would probably strive to place the most benign interpretation possible on the provision in question. In this regard, it is interesting that neither the Indian nor the German Constitution provides for the referendum process for constitutional amendments. If these Constitutions had provided for the supremacy of popular sovereignty as the key constitutional value – as appears to be the case with the Irish Constitution – perhaps, then, the doctrine of "essential features" or "supra-positivist" norms would not hold sway.

7. THE SOVEREIGNTY OF SAORSTÁT ÉIREANN

The other major question addressed in *Ryan* concerned the nature of the sovereignty of the Irish Free State. While by any standards the Irish Free State was an independent, sovereign State at the time of its establishment, the Sinn Féin negotiators had been forced following the 1921 Treaty negotiations to accept an unusual abridgement of that sovereignty in that the then Oireachtas was precluded from enacting legislation which was in conflict with that Treaty. This was provided for in section 2 of the Constitution of the Irish Free State (Saorstát Éireann) Act 1922:

> The said Constitution shall be construed with reference to the Articles of Agreement for a Treaty between Great Britain and Ireland set forth in the Second Schedule hereto annexed . . . which are hereby given the force of law, and if any provision of the said Constitution or of any amendment thereof or of any law made thereunder is in any respect repugnant to any of the provisions of the Scheduled Treaty, it shall, to the extent only of such repugnancy, be absolutely void and inoperative and the Parliament and the Executive Council of the Irish Free State (Saorstát Éireann) shall respectively pass such further legislation and do all such other things as may be necessary to implement the Scheduled Treaty.

Article 50 of the Constitution provided that any amendments to the Constitution had to be "within the terms of the Scheduled Treaty." Following Mr. De Valera's accession to power in March 1932, he immediately set about dismantling those elements of the Constitution (such as the Oath of Allegiance, the appeal to the Privy Council and the Governor-General) to which he was so resolutely opposed. The was done in the first instance by the Constitution (Removal of Oath) Act 1933. As the provision for the Oath of Allegiance had been incorporated in Article 4 of the Treaty, as well as in Article 17 of the Constitution, it would not have sufficed simply for the Oireachtas to have attempted to delete Article 17.[53] The 1933 Act therefore took the opportunity to delete section 2 of the 1922 Constitution Act and the reference in Article 50 to "within the terms of the Scheduled Treaty".

The Supreme Court was agreed in *Ryan* that the Oireachtas had no power whatever to amend the terms of the Constituent Act and the Scheduled Treaty, although, of course, there was no suggestion that Article 2A violated the terms of the Scheduled Treaty.[54] But a further extraordinary dimension of the *Ryan* case is that the Supreme Court completely ignored the 1933 Act – which had been in force for over a year[55] – and treated section 2 of the 1922 Act as if it had not been amended! There is simply no other precedent for a court purporting to ignore and treat a constitutional amendment as a complete nullity.

A further complication was provided by the Privy Council's decision some six months later in June 1935 in *Moore v. Attorney General of the Irish Free State*.[56] Here the issue was whether the Constitution (Amendment No. 22) Act 1933 – which had purported to abolish the right of appeal from the Supreme Court to the Privy Council – was valid. As this right of appeal was held to have been protected by the Treaty,[57] the Judicial Committee was thus confronted directly with the issue of whether the Oireachtas had power to amend the Constitution in a manner inconsistent with the Treaty. The Statute of Westminster

---

[53] None of the earlier constitutional amendments – however radical – had attempted unilaterally to alter the provisions of the Treaty.

[54] See, for example, the comments of Murnaghan J.:

The only limitation specified in the text of Article 50 itself is that the amendment of the Constitution must be within the terms of the Scheduled Treaty. This limitation is emphasised by the Constituent Act itself, which provides that if any amendment of the Constitution is in any respect repugnant to any of the provisions of the Scheduled Treaty it shall to the extent only of such repugnancy be absolutely void and inoperative. This conception of the power of amendment as entertained by the framers of the Constitution of the Constitution does not at all accord with the limitation now attempted to be put forward. As a matter of construction I am satisfied that the power of amendment extends to any limits other than those specified in the Article and in the Constituent Act, and it is not argued that the Act of 1931 is in any way inconsistent with the Scheduled Treaty. ([1935] I.R. 170, 241).

[55] The 1933 Act had become law on May 3, 1933.

[56] [1935] I.R. 472 (P.C.).

[57] Article 2 of the Treaty provided that the position of the Irish Free State "in relation to the Imperial Parliament and Government . . . shall be that of the Dominion of Canada" and the "law, practice and constitutional usage governing the relationship of the Crown or the representative of the Crown and of the Imperial Parliament to the Dominion of Canada shall govern their relationship to the Irish Free State". In *Performing Right Society v. Bray Urban District Council* [1930] I.R. 509 (P.C.), the Privy Council held that Article 2 of the Treaty specifically ensured the right to petition the Judicial Committee for leave to appeal, because the right was part of the law, practice and constitutional usage then governing the relationship of the Crown and of the Imperial Parliament to the Dominion of Canada.

1931 had provided that a Dominion Parliament had power to abrogate an enactment of the Imperial Parliament. Although the Irish Free State had never
purported to legislate by reference to the Statute of Westminster, Viscount
Sankey L.C. held that the Constitution (Amendment No. 22) Act was valid. As
he put it pithily:

> The simplest way of stating the situation is that the Statute of Westmin-
> ster gave to the Irish Free State a power under which they could abrogate
> the Treaty, and that, as a matter of law, they have availed themselves of
> that power.[58]

In so doing, the Privy Council held that the Irish Free State derived its authority
from an Act of the Imperial Parliament and rejected the contrary views expressed in *Ryan*. Of course, in more recent times the Supreme Court has reaffirmed the views expressed in *Ryan's* case to the view that the Constitution of
1922 derived its authority from an Act of Dáil Éireann and not from an Act of
the Imperial Parliament.[59] While this conclusion is understandable having regard to the overall Irish political culture, it is not without its difficulties. As
Lenihan has convincingly argued:

> The view in *Ryan's* case also involves accepting that the British Parlia-
> ment no longer had the power to legislate for Ireland after the establish-
> ment of the First Dáil in 1919. This would mean that legislation passed
> by the British Parliament between 1919 and 1922 was not carried over
> into the new legal order, contrary to the presumed purpose behind Article
> 73 of the 1922 Constitution, which provides that subject to the Constitu-
> tion and to the extent that they are not inconsistent therewith, the laws in
> force in Saorstát Éireann at the date of the coming into force of the Con-
> stitution shall continue to be of full force and effect until the same or any
> of them shall have been repealed or amendment by enactment of the
> Oireachtas.[60]

8. FitzGibbon J. and *Richard II*

It remains, penultimately, to examine the extraordinary language used by
FitzGibbon J. at the conclusion of his judgment:

---

[58][1935] I.R. 472, 486-7.
[59]*Re Article 26 and Criminal Law (Jurisdiction) Bill 1976* [1977] I.R. 129 (S.C.) 146-7 *per*
O'Higgins C.J.
[60]Lenihan, "Royal Prerogatives and the Constitution" (1989) XXIV *Ir. Jur. (n.s.)* 1, 10.

The last contention of Mr. Overend [counsel for the applicants], that every person who accepted citizenship of the Irish Free State when it was first established, or at any subsequent date, did so upon the faith of an undertaking, express or implied, on the part of the State, embodied in the Constitution, that no alteration of the Constitution to his detriment would thereafter be made, is so manifestly untenable upon any ground of law or principle, that I mention it only to show that it has not been overlooked.

Equally unfounded is the suggestion that the power of amendment introduced in Article 50 should be treated by analogy to a proviso in small print at the end of a fraudulent prospectus, or to a condition on the back of a railway ticket handed to an illiterate traveller. Such arguments show the desperate straits to which the appellants have been reduced. Article 50 seems to me to occupy its appropriate place, at the end of the group of clauses which deal with the creation, composition, and powers of the Legislature, and every person who became a citizen must be presumed to have accepted citizenship upon the terms therein set forth.

Fortunately, it can never again be suggested that the Saorstát has obtained citizens by false pretences, now that the Oireachtas has promulgated, *urbi et orbi*, to Czechoslovak and the Mexican, to our kinsmen in the United States of America and, above all, to our fellow-countrymen in Northern Ireland, whose co-operation we profess to desire, as well as all those who seek or acquire, or have thrust upon them, rights under our new Irish Nationality and Citizenship Act, Amendment No. 17 as an integral part of our Constitution, setting forth in the clearest language, in the forefront of that document, the conditions under which liberty is enjoyed and justice may be administered in "this other Eden demi-Paradise, this precious stone, set in the silver sea, this blessed plot, this earth, this realm, this" Saorstát.[61]

It can be stated with confidence that this is the most remarkable language ever to be found in a judgment of the Irish Supreme Court and it is hard to see how it would not have given considerable offence.[62] In this respect, our judges

---

[61][1935] I.R. 170, 236-7. The parody – reflected in the title to this article – is, of course, from Shakespeare's *Richard II*.

[62]See Hogan "Chief Justice Kennedy and Sir James O'Connor's Application" (1988) XXIII *Ir. Jur.* (*n.s.*) 144, 156: "FitzGibbon J.'s judgment is remarkable for its sustained invective and sarcasm, largely directed at the new State and its institutions". An "old friend" wrote of FitzGibbon J. following his retirement in (1938) 72 *I.L.T.S.J.* 324, 324 that he had not adopted a "die-hard" attitude when the Irish Free State began its chequered career". That is doubtless so, but his judgment in *Ryan* cannot be interpreted otherwise than displaying considerable unhappiness with the post-1922 state of affairs.

have followed the English tradition which is, of course, that "personal attacks are politely concealed".[63] Nevertheless, FitzGibbon J.'s final peroration has a majestic eloquence which lifts it beyond the boorish petulance sometimes seen in dissents in the US Supreme Court.[64] Of course, great cases and profound issues often call out for memorable language and quite often it is the use of such language which contributes to elevating the decision into the ranks of the truly great. This is certainly true of the famous dissenting judgments of Holmes J. and Brandeis J. in the post-World War I American free speech cases[65] and of Lord Atkin's celebrated dissent in *Liversidge v. Anderson.*[66]

9. CONCLUSION

If *Ryan's* case effectively heralded the collapse of the 1922 Constitution, since it established that, the terms of the Scheduled Treaty aside, there were no legislative barriers to amendments of that Constitution, that process was completed by *Moore's* case, since, in the wake of the Privy Council's interpretation of the Statute of Westminster, the Oireachtas was now free to dismantle the Treaty as well. Writing shortly afterwards in the *Law Quarterly Review*, Hood Phillips thought that it followed that the Oireachtas was free to repeal "*ex post facto* Article 65 and part of Article 66 of the Constitution which give the Courts their power to review legislation".[67] Yet, unbeknownst to him, events were already moving decisively in a different direction. By May 1934 Mr. De Valera had established a top-level Committee whose task was to examine the existing Constitution with a view:

> to ascertaining what Articles should be regarded as fundamental, on the grounds that they safeguard democratic rights, and to make recommendations as to steps which should be taken to ensure that such Articles should not be capable of being altered by ordinary processes of legislation.[68]

---

[63] Blom-Cooper and Drewery, *Final Appeal – A Study of the House of Lords in its Judicial Capacity* (Clarendon Press, Oxford, 1972) 86-7.

[64] See, *e.g.*, Rehnquist J.'s dissent in *United Steelworkers of America v. Weber* 443 U.S. 193 (1979) where he denounced the majority judgments saying that "by a *tour de force* reminiscent not of jurists such as Hale, Holmes and Hughes, but of escape artists such as Houdini, the Court eludes clear statutory language . . . legislative history and uniform precedent" (443 U.S. 193, 222).

[65] See, *e.g.*, Lewis, *Make No Law: The Sullivan case and the First Amendment* (Random House, New York, 1991) 67-89.

[66] [1942] A.C. 406 (H.L.). For the fascinating account of how Lord Atkin's remarks caused him to be cold-shouldered by his fellow Law Lords, see the late Professor Heuston's definitive account: "*Liversidge v. Anderson* in Retrospect" (1970) 86 *L.Q.R.* 33.

[67] (1936) 52 *L.Q.R.* 241, 244.

[68] SPO file 2979.

The recommendations of this Committee were to form the nucleus of the drafts for the present Constitution, which work began in earnest a few months after the Supreme Court's judgment in *Ryan*.[69] What is notable is that a memorandum to his fellow committee-members, the Secretary of the Department of Justice admitted that "in form" Article 2A was "grotesque as an Article of the Constitution. It must go"[70] and the Committee's recommendations anticipated the present provisions of the Constitution relating to the Special Criminal Court. The Committee also recommended the re-introduction of the referendum procedure. Further lessons from *Ryan* and the entire Article 2A experience were clearly learnt by the drafters of the new Constitution, as during the three year transitory period during which the Constitution could be amended by ordinary legislation, Article 51 was careful to ensure that the referendum provisions of Article 46 and the three year period itself were beyond the reach of ordinary legislation. This was a vital step in ensuring the stability and success of the new Constitution, since it ensured that, thereafter, a referendum would be necessary to effect constitutional change. And so thus, the practical lessons of *Ryan* having being learnt and as the endless debates over the Treaty and the 1922 Constitution were effectively ended by the new Constitution, the practical significance of this remarkable decision began to wane. But even if its practical significance is nowadays slight, *Ryan's* case raises profound jurisprudential issues about the nature of law and constitutional change and it produced remarkable and interesting judgments. For all of these reasons, if not nowadays a "leading case", it surely deserves inclusion in a catalogue of the "great" cases of this century.

---

[69] Hogan, "The Constitution Review Committee of 1934" in O'Muircheartaigh (ed.), *Ireland in the Coming Times: Essays to Celebrate T.K. Whitaker's 80 Years* (Dublin, 1997) 342.
[70] *ibid.*, 350.

A PRESUMPTION AND FOUR BURDENS
WOOLMINGTON V. D.P.P. (1935)

DR. JOHN E. STANNARD[*]

1. INTRODUCTION

Leading cases can be of different types. One dictionary defines a leading case as "a judicial decision or precedent settling the principles of a branch of law";[1] another speaks of "cases which have had the most influence in settling the law";[2] another of "a judicial decision always regarded as the chief precedent or judicial statement of principle on a particular point".[3] The third of these definitions is preferable to the first two, for this reason: leading cases may indeed be chief precedents, and they may state principles, but they do not always settle the law.

If a choice were to be made as to the leading case of the twentieth century in the field of criminal law and evidence, most people would opt without hesitation for *Woolmington v. D.P.P.*[4] At one level, no doubt, this "settled" the criminal law by laying down one of its most fundamental principles, namely the presumption of innocence; yet even after sixty years its implications have still not fully been worked out. The aim of this paper is to examine the present status of the presumption of innocence in England and Wales and in Northern Ireland, with reference to the jurisprudence of the courts in the Republic of Ireland and of the European Convention on Human Rights. The current law on the topic can best be expressed in terms of a presumption (the presumption of innocence itself as set out in *Woolmington*) and four burdens (the so-called exceptions to *Woolmington*, which are generally termed "burdens" on the defence). We shall see how these different burdens relate to one another, and in doing so we shall ask to what extent, if at all, it is either right or necessary to place a burden on the defence in a criminal trial.

Senior Lecturer in Law, Queen's University of Belfast. Thanks are due to Jenny McEwan for her helpful comments on earlier drafts. A version of this article also appears in (2000) 51 *N.I.L.Q.*

[1] *Jowitt's Dictionary of English Law* (2nd ed., Sweet & Maxwell, London, 1977).
[2] *Mozley and Whiteley's Law Dictionary* (11th ed., Butterworths, London, 1993).
[3] *The Oxford Companion to Law* (Clarendon Press, Oxford, 1980).
[4] [1935] A.C. 462 (H.L.).

2. THE PRESUMPTION

The crucial point at issue in *Woolmington v. D.P.P.*, as is well known, was as to
the incidence of the burden and standard of proof in a case where the accused
admitted the act of killing the deceased but claimed in evidence that it was an
accident. In giving his summing-up at Taunton Assizes, Swift J. had made use
of a statement in Foster's *Crown Law* which, though originally penned in 1762,
had been adopted as a correct statement of the law by virtually every textbook
or abridgement since.[5] This is what Sir Michael Foster wrote:

> In every charge of murder, the fact of killing being first proved, all the
> circumstances of accident, necessity, or infirmity are to be satisfactorily
> proved by the prisoner, unless they arise out of the evidence produced
> against him; for the law presumeth the fact to have been founded in mal-
> ice, unless the contrary appeareth.[6]

Having quoted this passage to the jury, the judge concluded his summing-up as
follows:

> The Crown has got to satisfy you that this woman . . . died at the prison-
> er's hands. They must satisfy you of that beyond any reasonable doubt. If
> they satisfy you of that, then he has to show that there are circumstances
> to be found in the evidence which has been given from the witness-box in
> this case which alleviate the crime so that it is only manslaughter or which
> excuse the homicide altogether by showing that it was a pure accident.[7]

In sum, the judge was telling the jury: "The accused admits the killing. He
claims that it was an accident? Let him prove it!" Upon this basis, Woolmington
was convicted and duly sentenced to death. An appeal to the Court of Criminal
Appeal failed, which is hardly surprising, given that as we have just seen, the
passage in *Foster* relied on by the judge had been regarded as a correct statement of the law for over a hundred and fifty years.[8] In any event, said the court,
the misdirection, if misdirection it had been, had caused no substantial miscarriage of justice.[9]

The House of Lords, however, took a different view. Giving the unanimous
opinion of their Lordships, Viscount Sankey declared that if Sir Michael Foster
was meaning to say that in cases of accident the burden was on the accused to

---

[5] [1935] A.C. 462, 474.

[6] Foster, *Crown Law* (Folio edition, Clarendon Press, Oxford, 1762) 255.

[7] [1935] A.C. 462, 473.

[8] See *Jayasena v. R.* [1970] A.C. 618 (P.C.) 625 (Lord Devlin).

[9] Section 4 of the Criminal Appeal Act 1907 (now repealed) allowed an appeal to be dismissed on
this ground even if there had been a misdirection of the jury.

prove his defence to the satisfaction of the jury,[10] the statement was wrong and should no longer be followed. The appeal was allowed and the conviction quashed.

> Throughout the web of the English Criminal Law one golden thread is always to be seen, that it is the duty of the prosecution to prove the prisoner's guilt subject to...the defence of insanity and subject also to any statutory exception. If, at the end of and on the whole of the case, there is a reasonable doubt, created by the evidence given by either the prosecution or the prisoner, as to whether the prisoner killed the deceased with a malicious intention, the prosecution has not made out the case and the prisoner is entitled to an acquittal. No matter what the charge or where the trial, the principle that the prosecution must prove the guilt of the prisoner is part of the common law of England and no attempt to whittle it down can be entertained.[11]

Few people would disagree with the view of Sir John Smith that this was the finest day's work ever done by the House of Lords in the field of criminal law,[12] even though some would argue that the subsequent side-effects of the case have not been entirely benign.[13] After all, to impose a burden of proof on the defendant, as was done prior to *Woolmington*, involves telling a jury or a bench of magistrates that they are to convict even if they think that it is as likely as not that the defendant was innocent, a situation which makes a mockery of the law.[14] The presumption of innocence has been held by the Supreme Court of the Republic of Ireland to be a principle protected by the Constitution,[15] and it is also enshrined in Article 6(2) of the European Convention of Human Rights.

---

[10]Whether he was meaning to say any such thing is open to argument. As Lord Sankey himself pointed out on page 478, the law of evidence at the time was in a very fluid state, and on one interpretation Sir Michael Foster was referring only to an "evidential" burden of the type discussed below, nn. 60-81; see the comments of Davitt P. in *McGowan v. Carville* [1960] I.R. 330 (H.C.) 337 and of Lord Devlin in *Jayasena v. R.* [1970] A.C. 628 (P.C.) 623. This has been the interpretation adopted in the Irish Republic since it was held that the presumption of innocence was protected by the Constitution: see *Hardy v. Ireland* [1994] I.R. 550 (S.C.) and *O'Leary v. Attorney-General* [1995] 1 I.R. 254 (S.C.): below, nn. 43-48.

[11][1935] A.C. 462, 481-482.

[12]"The Presumption of Innocence" (1987) 38 *N.I.L.Q.* 223 [hereafter Smith] 224.

[13]Thus in his 1997 Hamlyn Lectures Lord Cooke of Thorndon argued that the English courts had subsequently found the *Woolmington* principle to be a useful excuse for their failure to temper other unjust features of the criminal law, notably the doctrine of strict liability: *Turning Points of the Common Law* (Sweet & Maxwell, London, 1997) 28-48.

[14]Smith, 224. *Woolmington* was applied in the Republic of Ireland by *The People (Attorney General) v. McMahon* [1946] I.R. 267 (C.C.A.) and *The People (Attorney General) v. Quinn.* [1965] I.R. 366 (C.C.A.): see also *The People (Attorney General) v. Oglesby* [1966] I.R. 162 (C.C.A.); *The People (Attorney General) v. Dwyer* [1972] I.R. 416 (S.C.); *The People (Attorney General) v. Byrne* [1974] I.R. 1 (C.C.A.); *The People (D.P.P.) v. Clarke* [1994] 3 I.R. 289 (C.C.A.).

[15]*Hardy v. Ireland* [1994] I.R. 550 (S.C.); below, nn. 43-46.

Woolmington is therefore a case of the highest importance, not only in England and Wales, but throughout the whole island of Ireland. Indeed, it has been described as the foundation of the presumption of innocence for the entire common law world.[16]

3. THE FOUR BURDENS

The main controversy centres, not on *Woolmington* itself, but on the so-called exceptions to it. Even Lord Sankey, as we have seen, had to concede two of these: the defence of insanity, and other "statutory exceptions".[17] The precise scope of these exceptions, and the extent to which they are true exceptions at all, is open to some doubt, as is the relationship between them. The main thrust of *Woolmington* is clear; in the terms used by evidence lawyers, the burden of proof in a criminal case is on the prosecution throughout. In some cases, however, there is a burden of some sort, if not always a full burden of proof, on the defence. It is on these burdens that the rest of this paper will focus. There are no less than four different types of burden that can lie on the defence. These are termed for the purposes of this paper as follows:[18] (1) the probative burden; (2) the evidential burden; (3) the tactical burden; and (4) the personal burden. As we shall see, the distinction between these different burdens is sometimes not easy to draw.

3.1 The Probative Burden

The first type of burden which the defence may have to bear is the probative burden, or "persuasive" burden as it is sometimes called.[19] Where this arises, we see a true exception to *Woolmington*: in effect, the defendant has to prove his or her innocence.[20] Lord Sankey in *Woolmington* refers to two cases where this burden arises in English law, one being the defence of insanity and the other "any statutory exception".[21] The first of these has always been recognised as an exception to the *Woolmington* principle, and it gives rise to no

---

[16] Smith, 223.

[17] Above, n. 11.

[18] Some of these labels are traditional: others are borrowed from other authors or invented for the purpose. As Sir Rupert Cross pointed out, there is nothing in the nature of an agreed terminology, so that it is not always clear as to the sense in which a particular term is being used by a writer or judge: *Cross and Tapper on Evidence* (9th ed., Butterworths, London, 1999) [hereafter *Cross and Tapper*] 107-108.

[19] *Cross and Tapper*, 108.

[20] The standard of proof here is on the balance of probabilities: *R. v. Carr-Briant* [1943] 2 All E.R. 156 (C.C.A.); *The People (D.P.P.) v. O'Mahony* [1985] I.R. 51 (S.C.); *Convening Authority v. Doyle* [1996] 2 I.L.R.M. 213 (C.M.A.C.).

[21] Above, n. 11.

problems of analysis.[22] The second exception can be further subdivided into two categories, "express" and "implied" statutory exceptions. The former category encompasses those statutory defences which expressly place a burden of proof on the accused. These are often found in regulatory offences, and in relation to firearms and explosives, offensive weapons, dangerous drugs and so on. Like insanity, they give rise to few if any problems of analysis.

The category of implied exceptions is more problematical. In England, section 101 of the Magistrates' Courts Act 1980 provides as follows:

> Where the defendant to an information or complaint relies for his defence on any exception, exemption, proviso, excuse or qualification, whether or not it accompanies the description of the offence or matter of complaint in the enactment creating the description of the offence or on which the complaint is founded, the burden of proving the exception, exemption, proviso, excuse or qualification shall be on him; and this notwithstanding that the information or complaint contains an allegation negativing the exception, exemption, proviso, excuse or qualification.

Similar provisions are to be found in Northern Ireland,[23] in the Republic of Ireland,[24] in Scotland[25] and throughout the common law world.[26] At first sight, the provision may seem to relate merely to an esoteric issue of summary jurisdiction, but in fact it gives rise to problems on a much wider scale. The scope of section 101 and its relationship to the *Woolmington* principle has already been the subject of extensive analysis by scholars, not least by Sir John Smith,[27] and it is therefore unnecessary to give more than a bare summary in the present context. Though section 101 and its kindred provisions in other jurisdictions are in terms limited to cases where the offence is created by an "enactment", its origins lie in a common law principle going back to the seventeenth century, whereby certain matters which were thought to be peculiarly within the knowledge of the accused did not have to be pleaded and negatived in the indictment, but were left to be raised by the defence.[28] The exact scope of this rule, and the extent to which it affected the burden of proof, is a matter which needs no further discussion in the present context.[29] Suffice it to say that the English

---

[22]See *R. v. M'Naghten* (1843) 10 Cl.&F. 200 (H.L.) 210; *Attorney-General v. Boylan* [1937] I.R. 449 (S.C.); *Doyle v. Wicklow County Council* [1974] I.R.55 (S.C.); Criminal Justice Act (N.I.) 1966, s. 2(1).

[23]Magistrates' Courts (N.I.) Order 1981, art. 124.

[24]County Officers and Courts (Ireland) Act 1877, s. 78.

[25]Criminal Procedure (Scotland) Act 1995, sch. 3, para. 16.

[26]Smith, 223.

[27]*op. cit.*

[28]The development of this rule was traced by Lawton L.J. in *R. v. Edwards* [1975] 1 Q.B. 27 (C.A.) 32-33.

[29]See Zuckerman, "The Third Exception to the Woolmington Rule" (1976) 92 *L.Q.R.* 402.

Court of Appeal in *R. v. Edwards*,[30] the Irish High Court in *Attorney-General v. Duff* [31] and the House of Lords in *R. v. Hunt*[32] all agreed that section 101 was paralleled by an equivalent common law principle[33] which was not confined to summary trials but extended also to trials on indictment,[34] since the burden and standard of proof could hardly vary depending on the court in which the case was being tried.[35]

There has been much discussion in the cases and elsewhere as to what constitutes an "exception, exemption, proviso, excuse or qualification". Obviously this will not be so where the accused is relying on a general common law defence such as duress, self-defence or provocation, where the law as we shall see clearly puts the burden of proof on the prosecution.[36] The situation is more problematic where the defence in question is a special one contained in the statute setting out the crime. Here the starting point is the notoriously tricky distinction between defences which negative one of the essential ingredients of the offence and those which set up other facts by way of confession and avoidance.[37] As we shall see, this distinction is both controversial and a tricky one to draw.[38] Even if it can be maintained, it does not conclude the matter, for the question is not merely one of grammar but of policy. Thus it has been held that where the words of the statute do not clearly indicate upon whom the burden is meant to lie the court has to look to other considerations, such as the mischief at which the Act is aimed and practical considerations affecting the burden of proof; in particular, the ease or difficulty that the respective parties would encounter in discharging the burden.[39] Thus in *R v. Hunt*[40] it was held that regulation 4(1) and Schedule 1 of the Misuse of Drugs Regulations 1973, which exempted from criminal liability the possession of any morphine preparation containing not more than 0.2 per cent of morphine, placed the burden of proof on the prosecution to show that the contents of the preparation in ques-

---

[30] [1975] 1 Q.B. 27, 31, 36.
[31] [1941] I.R. 406.
[32] [1987] A.C. 352, 369-373, 385-386.
[33] See *R. v. Turner* (1816) 5 M. & S. 206 (K.B.); *Apothecaries' Co. v. Bentley* (1824) C. & P. 538 (Nisi Prius); *R. (Sheahan) v. Justices of Cork* [1907] 2 I.R. 5 (K.B.D.); *R. v. Scott* (1921) 86 J.P. 69 (C.C.A.); *R. v. Oliver* [1944] K.B. 68 (C.C.A.); *The People (Attorney-General) v. Shribman and Samuels* [1946] I.R. 431 (C.C.A.); *R. v. Putland and Sorrell* [1946] 1 All E.R. 85 (C.C.A.); *Minister for Industry and Commerce v. Steele* [1952] I.R. 304 (S.C.); *John v. Humphreys* [1955] 1 W.L.R. 325 (Q.B.D.); *McGowan v. Carville* [1960] I.R. 330 (H.C.); *Robertson v. Bannister* [1973] R.T.R. 109 (Q.B.D.).
[34] Smith, 231.
[35] [1987] 1 A.C. 352, 373, 385.
[36] Below, nn. 76-79.
[37] Smith, 230.
[38] Below, n. 95
[39] *Attorney-General v. Duff* [1941] I.R. 406 (H.C.); *People (A-G) v. Shribman and Samuels* [1946] I.R. 431 (C.C.A.); *R. v. Oliver* [1944] KB 68 (C.C.A.); *R.. v. Putland and Sorrell* [1946] 1 All E.R. 85 (C.C.A.); *Nimmo v. Alexander Cowan and Sons Ltd* [1968] A.C. 107 (H.L.).
[40] [1987] 1 A.C. 352 (H.L.).

tion exceeded the specified amount, and that it was not up to the defence to prove that they did not. Despite the clear structure of the statutory provision, the matter was one upon which it was easier for the prosecution – who, after all, would normally have an analyst's report – to give evidence than the defence. The court should be slow, it was said, to conclude in the absence of the clearest words that Parliament had placed the burden of proof on the defence in an offence of this gravity.[41]

In sum, it seems that the burden of proof will be held to lie on the accused in relation to a statutory defence of this sort only where the defence in question can plausibly be described as an exception to a main head of liability prescribed by the statute, and then only where it relates to matters in relation to which it is reasonable to expect him to produce evidence rather than the prosecution. In the light of this, it may well be, as Tapper says, that the effects of *Hunt* are unlikely to prove so deleterious as its critics assert, nor so beneficial as its supporters may hope.[42]

There is no injustice in a principle which compels the accused to produce evidence in support of a defence involving facts which are peculiarly within his own knowledge. Whether it is either necessary or desirable to go further and impose a full burden of *proof* is a different matter altogether. The validity of reverse onus provisions of this sort has been questioned in the Irish Republic in the light of Article 38.1 of the Constitution, whereby no person is to be tried on a criminal charge save in due course of law. In *Hardy v. Ireland*[43] the applicant was charged under section 4 of the Explosive Substances Act 1883, which reads as follows:

> Any person who . . . knowingly has in his possession . . . any explosive substance, under such circumstances as to give rise to a reasonable suspicion . . . that he . . . does not have it in his possession . . . for a lawful object, shall, unless he can show that he . . . had it in his possession . . . for a lawful object, be guilty of felony.

Challenging the validity of this provision, the applicant argued that it required him to prove his innocence, and as such was contrary to Article 38.1. The High Court and the Supreme Court both rejected the application, but different reasons were given by the various judges involved in the case. According to Flood J. in the High Court, section 4 did no more than place an evidential burden on the accused.[44] In the Supreme Court, Egan and Murphy JJ. conceded that the provision required the defence to prove a lawful object on the balance of prob-

---

[41] [1987] 1 A.C. 352, 378 (Lord Griffiths).
[42] *Cross and Tapper*, 135.
[43] [1994] I.R. 550 (S.C.).
[44] [1994] I.R. 550, 559.

abilities, but said that such provisions did not necessarily infringe the Constitution.[45] The question came up again in *O'Leary v. Attorney General*[46] two years later. Here the accused was charged with IRA membership contrary to section 21 of the Offences Against the State Act 1939. Various documents emanating from the I.R.A. had been found in his possession, and the prosecution sought to rely on section 24 of the Act, whereby such possession constituted evidence of membership "until the contrary is proved". Applying the presumption of constitutionality, whereby a statute of the Oireachtas, the Irish Parliament, is to be interpreted if at all possible in a manner compatible with the Constitution,[47] the Supreme Court unanimously held that section 24 did no more than place an evidential burden on the defence, since to impose a full burden of proof would have been contrary to Article 38.1. The upshot of this is that the use of the word "prove" in Irish legislation of this sort no longer necessarily imports a requirement that the defence be made out on the balance of probabilities. This is in line with the proposals of the English Criminal Law Revision Committee back in 1972,[48] and does not seem, so far at any rate, to have caused any great problems in the administration of the law.

As we have seen, the presumption of innocence is also enshrined in Article 6(2) of the European Convention on Human Rights. A common lawyer might suppose that reverse onus provisions of this sort would inevitably be contrary to Article 6(2), but this is by no means the case.[49] The matter has rarely been discussed in the jurisprudence of the Convention: firstly because questions of this sort have less relevance in the inquisitorial systems of continental Europe,[50] and secondly because the courts prefer to decide cases on an individual basis rather than judge the validity of legislation in the abstract. In *Salabiaku v. France*[51] the applicant was convicted of smuggling under Article 392(1) of the Customs Code, whereby persons found in possession of goods brought into France without being declared to Customs were presumed to be criminally liable unless they could prove a specific event of *force majeure* by way of exculpation.[52] The European Court of Human Rights held that the presumption of innocence had not been infringed. This was in essence a crime of strict

[45][1994] I.R. 550, 566 *per* Egan J, 568 *per* Murphy J.
[46][1995] 1 I.R. 254; [1995] 1 I.L.R.M. 259 (S.C.); *cf. R. v. Oakes* [1986] 1 S.C.R. 103 (S.C.C.). See, generally, Ní Raifeartaigh, "Revising the Burden of Proof in a Criminal Trial: Canadian and Irish Perspectives on the Presumption of Innocence" (1995) 5 *I.C.L.J.* 135.
[47]*East Donegal Co-operative Livestock Marts Ltd v. Attorney-General* [1970] I.R. 317 (S.C.). The basis of the argument is that the Oireachtas must be presumed to have passed legislation that is compatible with the Constitution.
[48]See the Eleventh Report of the Committee (Cmnd. 4991, 1972), paras. 137-142: Smith, 242-243.
[49]See Lewis, "The Human Rights Act 1998: Shifting the Burden" [2000] *Crim. L.R.* 667 [hereafter Lewis].
[50]Jacobs, *The European Convention on Human Rights* (Clarendon Press, Oxford, 1975), 113.
[51]Series A, No. 141-A; (1991) 13 E.H.R.R. 379 (E.C.H.R.).
[52](1991) 13 E.H.R.R. 379, 381-382, para. 14.

liability, and it was perfectly permissible under the Convention for Contracting States to penalise a simple or objective fact as such, irrespective of whether it resulted from criminal intent or from negligence.[53] Moreover, presumptions of fact or of law were a feature of every legal system, and whilst Contracting States were obliged under the Convention to confine them within reasonable limits,[54] there was nothing in the present case to show that the courts had applied the contested provision in a manner incompatible with the presumption of innocence.[55] In *R.P. v. United Kingdom*,[56] the Commission considered section 30(2) of the Sexual Offences Act 1956, whereby a man who lives with or is habitually in the company of a prostitute, or who exercises control, direction or influence over a prostitute's movements in a way which shows he is aiding, abetting or compelling her prostitution with others, shall be presumed to be knowingly living on the earnings of prostitution unless he proves the contrary. It was held that the use of this provision to convict the applicant did not infringe the presumption of innocence; rather, it merely created a rebuttable presumption of fact which it was open to the defence to disprove. Moreover, that presumption was not an unreasonable one to draw in the circumstances, given the difficulty of proving offences of this sort by direct evidence.[57] The matter was considered more recently by the House of Lords in *R. v. D.P.P. ex parte Kebilene*.[58] This was a case involving section 16A of the Prevention of Terrorism (Temporary Provisions) Act 1989, a complex provision which dealt with the possession of articles for purposes of terrorism and which contained several reverse onus provisions which the applicant contended were contrary to the Convention. In an exhaustive analysis of the law, Lord Hope said that provisions of this sort had to be judged in the light of three questions. What does the prosecution have to prove in order to transfer the onus? What is the burden on the accused; in particular, does it relate to something which is likely to be difficult for him to prove, or does it relate to something which is readily in his knowledge or to which he readily has access? What is the nature of the threat faced by society which the provision is designed to combat?[59] It seems, therefore, that a balancing exercise is required, and that reverse onus provisions will not infringe the Convention, provided that the presumption created by the provision is a reasonable one in itself, can be rebutted by appropriate evidence, and is applied so as to give the accused the benefit of any doubt in the individual case.

---

[53](1991) 13 E.H.R.R. 379, 387-388, para. 27; *Schneider v. France* (1993) 36 Ybk.E.C.H.R. 76 (Commission).
[54] (1991) 13 E.H.R.R. 379, 388, para. 28.
[55](1991) 13 E.H.R.R. 379, 390-39, para 30; *Pham Hoang v. France* (1992) 35 Ybk.E.C.H.R. 181.
[56]Decision 5124/71, 42 C.D. 135, 1972.
[57]Decision 5124/71, para. 135.
[58][1999] 3 W.L.R. 972 (H.L.); see Lewis, 671.
[59][1999] 3 W.L.R. 972, 998-999.

3.2 The Evidential Burden

The prosecution have to prove the defendant's guilt, but this does not mean having to disprove every possible defence in advance. As Lord Devlin said in *Jayasena v. R.*,

> [*Woolmington v. D.P.P.*] does not mean, as the House made clear in subsequent cases, that a jury must always be told that before it can convict, it must consider and reject provocation and self-defence and all other matters that might be raised as an answer to a charge of murder. Some evidence in support of such an answer must be adduced before the jury is directed to consider it; but the only burden laid upon the accused in this respect is to collect from the evidence enough material to make it possible for a reasonable jury to acquit.[60]

Here Lord Devlin is doing no more than to apply to the defendant in a criminal case the general principle whereby in a trial by jury a party may be required to adduce some evidence in support of his case, whether on the general issue or on a particular issue, before that issue is left to the jury.[61] There must, in Wigmore's graphic phrase, be enough evidence to get past the judge.[62] Similarly, the defence will not be allowed to succeed on a submission of no case to answer on the grounds that the prosecution have not disproved self-defence, duress, provocation and so on. Before these defences can come into play, a proper foundation must be laid, as it is said; there must be some evidence in the case, either from the accused in person or from some other witness, which points towards the defence in question. If there is none, the judge need not leave it to the jury.

The evidential burden has two effects, the first arising in the event of a submission of no case to answer and the second when the judge sums up to the jury.[63] The former effect results from the *existence* of the evidential burden on a particular party; since two opposing parties cannot both bear an evidential burden on the same issue,[64] the existence of an evidential burden on one side absolves the other side from having to produce evidence on that issue unless and until the burden is discharged; this is why a submission of no case to an-

---

[60][1970] A.C. 618 (P.C.) 623.

[61]*Cross and Tapper*, 108.

[62]Wigmore, *A Treatise on the Anglo-American System of Evidence* (Little, Brown & Co., Boston, 1940) para. 2487.

[63]Williams, "Placing the Burden of Proof" in Waller and Campbell, (eds.), *Well and Truly Tried: Essays on Evidence in Honour of Sir Richard Eggleston* (Law Book Company, Sydney,1982) 271 [hereafter Williams].

[64]Glanville Williams, "The Evidential Burden: Some Common Misapprehensions" (1977) 127 *N.L.J.* 156 [hereafter Glanville Williams] 158.

swer can be rejected in the circumstances discussed above.[65] The latter effect, in contrast, concerns the *discharge* of the burden; once this happens, the party upon whom the burden lies is entitled to have the issue left to the jury. This is what is meant by "getting past the judge". In effect, the evidential burden acts as a filter to prevent the jury being sent on a wild goose chase by having to consider baseless issues.

There is a very great difference between the evidential burden and the probative burden. It is not merely that the former requires proof to a certain standard and the latter the mere raising of a doubt, as is sometimes said. Rather, the two burdens are, as Glanville Williams says, radically different in function; the probative burden is about what the judge *says* (telling the jury when they may or may not find themselves satisfied as to a particular issue in the case), whereas the evidential burden is all about what the judge *does* (refusing a submission of no case to answer, or allowing a defence to go forward to the jury).[66] Nor need the probative and evidential burdens necessary be on the same party. Sometimes they are; thus for instance in a criminal trial the prosecution is said to bear both the evidential and the probative burden with regard to the main elements of the crime, whilst in relation to the defence of insanity both burdens are on the defence.[67] However, there are cases where the evidential burden lies on the defence in the first instance, but the probative burden lies on the prosecution if the evidential burden is discharged; thus as we shall see, in relation to most general defences the accused bears the evidential burden, but if this is discharged the prosecution must prove beyond reasonable doubt that the defence is not made out.

Evidential burdens are not confined to the defence, or to criminal trials. In a civil case involving a jury, the plaintiff has to convince the judge that there is a case fit to go to the jury (the evidential burden), and then at the end of the day the jury must be satisfied on the balance of probabilities that the case is made out (the probative burden).[68] In the same way the prosecution in a criminal trial has to discharge the evidential burden to avoid a successful submission of no case to answer, and must then go on to discharge the probative burden to win a conviction.[69] In theory, the defence is in the same position as regards getting past the judge when they have the evidential burden; if the judge does not find the burden satisfied, the issue may be withdrawn from the jury.[70] However, the practical effect of this is very limited, for it takes very little by way of evidence to discharge the burden in this situation.[71] There is also a fundamen-

---

[65] This is also the effect of the tactical burden, as we shall see: below, nn. 89-90.

[66] Glanville Williams, 156.

[67] *Cross and Tapper*, 116-117.

[68] Williams, 280.

[69] *Cross and Tapper*, 116.

[70] Glanville Williams, "Evidential Burdens on the Defence" (1977) 127 *N.L.J.* 182.

[71] Thus, for instance, an evidential burden on the defence can be satisfied by the exculpatory part of a "mixed" statement: *R. v. Duncan* (1981) 73 Cr. App. R. 359 (C.A.) (provocation); *R. v.*

tal difference in the way the burden impinges on the defence. In a civil case, or where the prosecution fails to discharge the burden in a criminal case, the judge can truly in the words of Glanville Williams "censor the evidence"[72] by withdrawing the issue altogether from the hands of the jury. But the judge in a criminal trial cannot, even if he is brave enough to withdraw a defence from the jury,[73] direct them to convict. This means that one cannot be sure, even if a defence has been withdrawn from the jury, that they will not go ahead and consider it anyway; indeed, the judge's instructions may make them only all the more determined so to do.[74]

So when does the defence bear an evidential burden? Four different areas are identified by Glanville Williams:[75] (1) cases where the defence has the burden of proof; (2) general defences; (3) cases where the prosecution are required to prove a negative averment, such as the lack of a licence or of lawful excuse; and (4) the defence of automatism. Of these by far the most important is the second category. Thus it has been established that such defences as self-defence,[76] duress[77] and provocation[78] need not be left to the jury unless there is some evidence in the case worth considering,[79] but that if such evidence has been produced the jury must be told not to convict unless satisfied beyond reasonable doubt that the defence has not been made out. For this reason, provisions which merely place an evidential burden on the accused do not contravene the "due process" requirements of the Irish Constitution,[80] and they give rise to no problems with the European Convention on Human Rights.[81]

Hamand (1986) 82 Cr. App. R. 65 (C.A.) (self-defence); and see *R. v. Sharp* (1988) 86 Cr. App. R. 274 (H.L.).

[72] Glanville Williams, 157.

[73] As Tapper points out, judges will be reluctant to withdraw a defence from the jury where there is even a scintilla of evidence to support the defence, not least because they fear the possibility of an appeal: *Cross and Tapper*, 117. Conversely, the Irish Supreme Court has confirmed that it would be unconstitutional for a judge to direct a jury to convict: *The People (D.P.P.) v. Davis* [1993] 2 I.R. 1 (S.C.) (directed verdict of guilty of murder overturned).

[74] The hallowed principle of jury secrecy, backed up throughout the UK by the draconian provisions in s.8 of the Contempt of Court Act 1981, prohibits any research being done into the extent to which juries obey instructions given to them by the judge, and even prevents any enquiry by the courts into what goes on in the jury room. Perhaps this is just as well; it has been suggested recently by Sir John Smith that public confidence in the jury system would be unlikely to survive too much scrutiny of its workings: "Is ignorance bliss? Could jury trial survive investigation?" (1998) 38 *Med. Sci. Law* 98.

[75] (1977) 127 *N.L.J.* 182.

[76] *R. v. Lobell* [1957] 1 Q.B. 547 (C.C.A.).

[77] *R.. v. Gill* [1963] 1 W.I. R. 841 (C.C.A.).

[78] *Mancini v. D.P.P.* [1942] A.C. 1 (H.L.).

[79] It does not matter whether that evidence has been produced by the defence or by the prosecution. Nor does it matter whether the defence has been specifically argued for by counsel, or whether for tactical reasons, it has not been mentioned. If there is any evidence in the case to indicate that the defence in question might be available, the judge must draw it to the attention of the jury: see Doran, "Alternative Defences: The Invisible Burden on the Trial Judge" [1991] *Crim. L.R.* 878.

[80] *O'Leary v. Attorney General* [1995] 1 I.R. 254 (S.C.); above, n. 46.

[81] *R. v. D.P.P. ex parte Kebilene* [1999] 3 W.L.R. 972 (H.L.) 990 *per* Lord Hope.

Most of the defences to which this rule relates have been described as "confession and avoidance" defences. The accused is not denying any basic element of the crime, but is raising further matters by way of justification or excuse; in a nutshell, he is not saying "I didn't do it", but "I did do it, but . . .". But in some cases a defence raised by the accused may deny an element of the crime charged. One example of this is *Woolmington* itself, where the defence was one of accident, which is no more than another way of saying that the necessary malice aforethought was lacking. Does the defence bear any sort of burden here too? This brings us on to the question of the "tactical" or "provisional" burden.

3.3 The Tactical Burden

There is some authority for saying that an evidential burden only rests on the defence in the "confession and avoidance" situation just described, where the basic elements of the crime charged are admitted but further facts are put forward which, if true, entitle the defendant to an acquittal.[82] Where the defendant denies an element of the crime, it is said, there is not even an evidential burden to be discharged.[83] Now, this cannot mean that there can never be any burden on the defence *at all* in this situation. Sir John Smith cites in this connection the American case of *State v. Horton*,[84] a case from North Carolina in which the defendant claimed that he thought he was shooting a turkey. If there was any evidence that this was so, well and good; the jury would have to be directed to acquit if they thought that there was a reasonable possibility that the defendant was telling the truth; but it would be absurd to allow a submission of no case to answer on a murder charge because the prosecution have not disproved in advance the possibility that the defendant might have thought he was shooting at a turkey. The fact of the killing itself will sometimes[85] demand an explanation from the defendant. As Lord Sankey said in *Woolmington* itself, if it is proved that the conscious act of the prisoner killed a man and nothing else appears in the case, there is evidence upon which the jury may, not must, find him guilty of murder.[86] The question then is *why* the jury may find him guilty, in the absence of any direct evidence of malice aforethought and there being, *ex hypothesi*, no evidential burden on the defence. The answer given by Glanville Williams and others is that in cases of this sort the defendant has a "tactical" or

---

[82] *R. v. Morgan* [1976] A.C. 182 (H.L.) 200 *per* Lord Cross; see Glanville Williams, *passim*; see also Williams, 289-290.

[83] Glanville Williams, 156.

[84] 51 S.E. 945 (1905), discussed by Smith, 226.

[85] Whether it does in any given case will depend of course on the manner of the killing. As Glanville Williams points out, there is all the difference in the world between proving a fatal traffic accident and proving that the defendant drove his car straight at the victim: Glanville Williams, 158.

[86] [1935] A.C. 462, 480.

"provisional" burden. This has been described as the burden which is borne by a party after the other has discharged an evidential burden.[87] In such a case it wrong to say that he was *obliged* to call evidence in order to succeed, as would be the case if the evidential burden had been on him, for at the end of the day he will still win the case if the jury are not satisfied to the requisite standard. He is certainly under a risk of losing if he does not do so, but one cannot put it any more strongly than that.[88]

How does the effect of this "tactical" burden differ from that of the evidential burden? As we have seen,[89] the effects of the latter are seen at two stages in the trial, namely, when there is a submission of no case to answer and when the judge seeks to withdraw a defence from the jury. In the first case, there is no difference at all between the evidential and tactical burdens; if the defence bears either of them in relation to a particular issue they cannot submit that there is no case to answer on the ground that the prosecution have not led evidence to disprove that issue. In the second case, however, there is a difference; the judge may withdraw a defence from the jury if an evidential burden has not been met, but cannot do this in the case of a mere tactical burden. Thus it is said that a defence of provocation or of duress may be withdrawn from the jury, but not a defence of accident or mistake, since the latter defences go to negative the constituent elements of the crime charged.[90]

That the legal concept of the tactical burden exists cannot be denied, but the distinction drawn by Glanville Williams and others between defences upon which the accused bears the evidential burden and those where he merely bears the tactical burden has not met with universal acceptance. Thus it has been argued by Tapper that even where the accused raises a defence such as alibi or mistake there is no logical reason why he should not bear a full evidential burden, since he is raising a fresh specific issue within the general issue, and that on policy grounds there is something to be said for preventing the jury from considering these defences if no reasonable foundation for them exists.[91] Nor does the distinction square with all the authorities. It is clear that the accused bears the evidential burden in relation to the defence of automatism,[92] even though this is tantamount to a denial not merely of the *mens rea* but of the *actus reus* as well, and there are similar *dicta* in relation to mistake[93] and to alibi.[94] Moreover, the distinction between definitional elements of a crime and

---

[87] *Cross and Tapper*, 113.
[88] In the words of Sir Alfred Denning, as he then was, he must call evidence or take the consequences, which may not [*sic*] necessarily be adverse: "Presumptions and Burdens" (1945) 61 *L.Q.R.* 379, 380; *Cross and Tapper*, 113.
[89] Above, nn. 63-65.
[90] Glanville Williams, 158; Williams, 289.
[91] *Cross and Tapper*, 118.
[92] *Bratty v. Attorney-General for Northern Ireland* [1963] A.C. 386 (H.L.).
[93] *Sweet v. Parsley* [1970] A.C. 132 (H.L.) 164 *per* Lord Diplock.
[94] *R. v. Johnson* [1961] 1 W.L.R. 1478 (C.C.A.).

defences is one which has been rejected as unworkable by many eminent scholars.[95] Whilst it may be true to say that the distinction in question is no more difficult than a lot of others that the law obliges us to draw,[96] there are good reasons for not trying to do so unless we really have to.

We have just seen that the only distinction between a defence on which the accused bears the evidential burden and one where he bears the tactical burden is that in theory the judge can in the former case withdraw the defence from the jury if there is insufficient evidence to support it. But judges are understandably reluctant to do this in practice, and as we have seen the impact of evidential burdens on the defence in a criminal trial is a limited one.[97] Given the artificiality of withdrawing defences from the jury when it is not possible to direct them to convict, it may be asked whether at the end of the day the distinction between the evidential and the tactical burden is one really worth drawing in this context.

3.4 The Personal Burden

In none of the cases so far discussed is there any burden on the accused to give evidence in person. Whether the burden on the defence is probative, evidential or tactical it can be discharged either by the accused in person, or by other defence witnesses, or even by admissions elicited from the prosecution witnesses in cross-examination. The defendant has never been obliged in the common law system to give evidence; indeed, he was not even entitled to do so until relatively recent times.[98] But now that the accused can give evidence, can adverse inferences be drawn if he fails to do so? The extent to which a court or jury could do this at common law was open to argument,[99] but the matter was put on a statutory footing in Northern Ireland by article 4 of the Criminal Evidence (NI) Order 1988, which was followed in England by section 35 of the Criminal Justice and Public Order Act 1994. The effect of these provisions is to allow for a court or jury to draw "such inferences as appear proper" from a defendant's failure to testify without good reason. No particular label has been

---

[95] See Stone, "Burden of Proof and the Judicial Process" (1944) 60 *L.Q.R.* 415; Zuckerman, "The Third Exception to the Woolmington Rule" (1976) 92 *L.Q.R.* 402, 415. Even Glanville Williams himself eventually came round to the view that "what we think of as the definition of an offence and what we call a defence can only be regarded as depending largely upon the accidents of language, the convenience of legal drafting, or the unreasoning force of tradition": "Offences and Defences" (1982) 2 *L.S.* 233, 256.

[96] Smith, 230.

[97] Above, nn. 70-74.

[98] The prohibition on the accused giving evidence was removed in England and Wales by s.1 of the Criminal Evidence Act 1898, in the Republic of Ireland by s.1 of the Criminal Justice (Evidence) Act, 1924, and in Northern Ireland by s.1 of the Criminal Evidence Act (N.I.) 1923.

[99] See *R. v. Bathurst* [1968] 2 Q.B. 99 (C.A.); *R. v. Mutch* (1973) 57 Cr. App. R. 96 (C.A.); *R. v. Sparrow* [1973] 1 W.L.R. 488 (C.A.); *R. v. Martinez-Tobon* [1994] 1 W.L.R. 388 (C.A.).

given by the commentators to the burden thus placed on the accused, but it may conveniently be called the personal burden.

The legislation gives no indication as to what inferences are "proper" in this context, but it was held by the House of Lords in *Murray v. D.P.P.*[100] that the scope of the statutory provision is wider than that of the old common law, and that the drawing of adverse inferences is not confined to the drawing of specific inferences from specific facts, but can include in an appropriate case the general inference that the accused is guilty as charged. The only limitations to this are that a defendant cannot be convicted purely on the basis of the statutory inference;[101] indeed, it has been held that there is no scope for drawing the inference at all unless the prosecution has made out a *prima facie* case against the accused.[102] This means a case strong enough to go to the jury, so if there is no case to answer, the statutory inference can never come into play.[103]

In formal terms, the changes made by article 4 and section 35 do not have much effect on the existing structure of exceptions to the *Woolmington* principle. The burden of proof is not affected; the prosecution still have to prove their case beyond reasonable doubt, with or without the aid of the statutory inference.[104] The defendant is not even subjected to any evidential burden; as we have just seen, the prosecution probably still has to show a good case to answer without having any recourse to the statutory inference,[105] and there is nothing in the legislation allowing a judge to withdraw defences from the jury on the grounds that the accused has not gone into the witness box. All that the statutory inference does is to strengthen the tactical burden which already existed on the accused when the prosecution has made out a *prima facie* case. Before the new legislation, the accused knew that he was at risk of conviction if he did not produce some evidence to challenge the prosecution case,[106] but it

---

[100] [1994] 1 W.L.R. 1 (H.L.). This was a case on the Northern Ireland provision, article 4 of the Criminal Evidence (NI) Order 1988.

[101] Criminal Evidence (NI) Order 1988, art. 2(4); Criminal Justice and Public Order Act 1994, s. 38(3).

[102] *R. v. Cowan* [1996] Q.B. 373 (C.A.), affirming the *dicta* of Lord Mustill in *Murray v. D.P.P.* [1994] 1 W.L.R. 1, 4.

[103] It is however suggested by Murphy (*Murphy on Evidence*, (6th ed., Blackstone Press, London, 1997), 423) that on the basis of s.38(3) (article 2(4) of the 1988 Order) a judge may ask whether the accused is prepared to give evidence *before* making a ruling as to whether there is a case to answer, and may take any refusal to do so into account in coming to a decision on the point. If this is right, the accused is hit with the proverbial "double whammy"; his silence is taken into account both in deciding whether he has a case to answer and then in deciding whether he had answered it. The legislation is ambiguous on this point, and such a result would be clean contrary to the proposals of the Criminal Law Revision Committee, upon which the legislation was based (see Cmnd. 4991 (1972) para. 111), and the observations of Lord Mustill in *Murray* cited above.

[104] This is made clear by the English Court of Appeal in *R. v. Cowan* [1996] Q.B. 373 (C.A.).

[105] Though see n. 103 above.

[106] Above, n. 88.

was not clear to what extent this required him to testify in person. Now he
knows that if he does not do so the consequences are likely to be fatal.

Strengthening an already-existing tactical burden may not seem to be a
matter of very great moment, but in practical terms the effect of this legislation
is profound. In effect, the prosecution need no longer necessarily prepare a
case which will prove the defendant's guilt beyond all reasonable doubt; they
can simply present a *prima facie* case, and then rely on the accused to make up
the difference. If he goes into the witness box, they can elicit damaging admissions from him in cross-examination.[107] If he does not, they can invoke the
statutory inference. Either way, they are using the accused to do their job for
them. We are a long way from *Woolmington* here. As Jackson argues, the traditional conception of the accusatorial criminal trial demands not so much an
inquiry into the guilt of the accused but a *demonstration* of that guilt by the
prosecution.[108] He adds that it is surely inconsistent with that principle to expect the accused to contribute to the demonstration, or to allow his refusal to
participate in the trial by testifying to play a part in the proof of his guilt. All in
all, the personal burden may make little difference to the law in theory, but in
practice it is probably the most significant of all the exceptions to the
Woolmington principle.[109]

There is no equivalent provision in the Irish Republic, which is hardly surprising given the constitutional significance of the so-called right of silence in
this jurisdiction.[110] According to the analysis of Costello J. in *Heaney v. Ireland*,[111] the common law right of silence embraces two discrete immunities
against self-incrimination, the first being the immunity of the suspect in the
context of the investigation, and the second being the immunity of the accused
in the context of the trial. As to the immunity of the suspect in the context of
the investigation, Keane J. in the Supreme Court in the more recent case of
People (D.P.P.) v. Finnerty held that:

> the right of suspects in custody to remain silent, recognised by the com-
> mon law, is also a constitutional right. . . . Absent any express statutory
> provisions entitling a court or jury to draw inferences from such silence,
> the conclusion follows inevitably that the right is left unaffected by the

---

[107] *R. v. Bingham* (1999) 1 W.L.R. 598 (H.L.).
[108] "Inferences from Silence" (1993) 44 *N.I.L.Q.* 103, 108.
[109] In this context Peter Murphy's trenchant comments on the 1994 Act are well worth reading: n.
103 above, xiii-xiv.
[110] See *The People (Director of Public Prosecutions) v. Quilligan* [1986] I.R. 495 (S.C.); *Heaney
v. Ireland* [1994] 3 I.R. 593 (H.C.); [1996] 1 I.R. 580 (S.C.); *Rock v. Ireland* [1997] 3 I.R. 484;
[1998] 2 I.L.R.M. 35 (S.C.); *In re National Irish Bank (No. 1)* [1999] 3 I.R. 145 (S.C.) 177-
180; [1999] I.L.R.M. 321, 350-353 *per* Barrington J.
[111] [1994] 3 I.R. 593 (H.C.) 603-604; he based the right on the due process provisions of Article
38.1, but in the Supreme Court in that case O'Flaherty J. preferred to base it on Article 40.6.1
and the right to freedom of expression: [1996] 1 I.R. 580 (S.C.).

[Criminal Justice Act, 1984] save in cases coming within ss. 18 and 19, and must be upheld by the courts.[112]

The defendant had been detained under the 1984 Act but had refused to answer questions or to make a statement; he had been cross-examined as to this refusal, and the trial judge had commented on upon it in his charge to the jury. The Supreme Court held that, in the light of the conditional protection of his right of silence, there should have been no such cross-examination or comment, and quashed his conviction. As to the immunity of the accused in the context of the trial, Costello J. in *Heaney* explained this immunity as having developed out of the objections taken by the common law courts to the abuses arising from procedures involving the judicial interrogation of accused persons, and points out that it has been long established in the common law world and has been a basic concept of criminal law trials in the Irish criminal process for many years.[113] It is an immunity enshrined in the Fifth Amendment to the United States Constitution, in the United Nations International Covenant on Civil and Political Rights,[114] and in the jurisprudence of the European Convention of Human Rights.[115]

Given the tremendous significance of the right of silence in the common law system, it is not surprising that the provisions discussed above were vigorously challenged not only in academic circles but also before the European Court of Human Rights in *Murray v. U.K.*[116] There the applicant was convicted of terrorist offences before a judge sitting alone under section 7 of the Northern Ireland (Emergency Provisions) Act 1978.[117] In giving reasons for the conviction as required by section 7(5) of the Act,[118] the judge said that he had drawn adverse inferences under the Criminal Evidence (NI) Order 1988, both from the applicant's failure to answer police questions and from his failure to testify at the trial. The applicant had been denied access to a solicitor for the first 48 hours of his detention, and it was held by the Court that this factor,

---

[112] [2000] 1 I.LR.M. 197, 207. The constitutionality of ss. 18 and 19 of the 1984 Act, by which inferences may be drawn at trial from the accused's failure, when asked at the time of his arrest, to account for his possession of "any object, substance or mark" attributable to the offence in respect of which he was arrested (s.18) or for his presence at the scene of the offence in respect of which he was arrested (s.19), had been sustained in *Rock*. Although *Finnerty* makes it clear that, in the absence of a statutory basis, the drawing of an inference from an accused's silence is unconstitutional, it says nothing about the question of whether any statutory basis similar to the provisions in the UK or Northern Ireland would be constitutional. In the light of *Heaney* and *Rock*, however, they could very well be.

[113] [1994] 3 I.R. 593, 603-604.

[114] See Article 14.8(3)(g).

[115] See Article 6.1 of the Convention, as interpreted in *Funke v. France* Series A, No. 256-A; (1993) 16 E.H.R.R. 297.

[116] (1996) 22 E.H.R.R. 29.

[117] See now s. 75 of the Terrorism Act 2000.

[118] See now Terrorism Act 2000, s. 75(7).

taken together with the drawing of adverse inferences from his silence under questioning, amounted to the denial of a fair trial under Article 6(1) of the Convention.[119] In relation to the right of silence generally, the Court made it clear that, though not specifically mentioned in the Convention, the right to remain silent under police questioning and the privilege against self-incrimination were both recognised international standards which lay at the heart of Article 6.[120] However, these standards were not absolute. Whilst it would be incompatible with Article 6 to base a conviction solely on the silence of the accused or on his refusal to answer questions or give evidence, where a situation clearly called for an explanation such silence could legitimately be taken into account in assessing the persuasiveness of the prosecution evidence.[121] In the present case, given the safeguards provided by the legislation,[122] the inferences reasonably drawn against the applicant did not of themselves infringe either the presumption of innocence or his right to a fair trial.[123] It is not without significance that as we have seen this was a trial before a judge sitting alone, who is obliged to give reasons for a conviction. Had a jury been involved, the outcome of the case might well have been different.[124]

4. REFORM OF THE LAW

Woolmington v. D.P.P. was decided over sixty years ago, and it would not be reasonable to expect its precepts to be set in stone for all time. But the case is one of such fundamental constitutional importance that we should at least expect any departure from it to be properly thought through and justified by the most rigorous analysis. Unfortunately this is far from being so, partly because some of the exceptions to *Woolmington* are older than the case itself, and partly because the sheer complexity of this branch of the law makes it difficult to see the wood for the trees. Even so, reform of the law in this area is no mere technical matter, but should depend on principle. Four basic questions need to be answered in this context.

The first question is whether a jury or other finder of fact should be expected to convict when it is of the opinion that as likely as not the accused is innocent. There can surely be only one answer to this question, but if it is accepted it would mean the abolition of all probative burdens on the defendant. The main argument in favour of imposing a burden of proof on the defence is

---

[119] (1996) 22 E.H.R.R. 29, 67, paras. 66-68.
[120] (1996) 22 E.H.R.R. 29, 60, paras. 44-45.
[121] (1996) 22 E.H.R.R. 60-61, para. 47.
[122] (1996) 22 E.H.R.R. 29, 61, para. 48.
[123] (1996) 22 E.H.R.R. 29, 63, para. 54.
[124] See the commentary by Diana Birch to *R. v. Birchall* [1999] *Crim. L.R.* 311 (C.A.) 313; see also *Condron v. U.K.* [2000] *Crim. L.R.* 679 (E.C.H.R.).

that such burdens relate to matters of which the defendant has the best knowledge, and that the law would be unenforceable if such matters had to be proved by the prosecution in the normal way.[125] But this is a fallacy;[126] certainly it is an argument for imposing *some* sort of burden on the defence, but there is no reason why this has to be a full burden *of proof*. It is for this reason that the Criminal Law Revision Committee recommended as long ago as 1972 that all probative burdens on the accused be converted into mere evidential burdens.[127] As we have seen, this is currently the position under the Irish Constitution in any case.[128]

The second question is whether the judge should be entitled to withdraw defences from the jury if they are not backed by sufficient evidence. The arguments are more evenly balanced here. It is argued by Tapper that there is something to be said for preventing the jury from considering the possibility of defences which lack any reasonable foundation,[129] and that the mere facile mouthing, in the words of Lord Morris,[130] of some easy phrase or excuse should not be enough to place a duty on the jury to consider a particular issue. As against this we have seen[131] that the practical effect of withdrawing a defence from the jury may not amount to very much, given that the law knows no such thing as a directed conviction. There is also a fundamental point of principle at stake here. Allowing a judge to withdraw a defence from the jury is open to the same criticism as was levelled by Lord Sankey against the prosecution case in *Woolmington*; it is tantamount to allowing the judge to decide the case and not the jury, which is not the common law.[132] Should such a fundamental constitutional principle as that of trial by one's peers be watered down for the sake of convenience and tidiness? After all, if a jury is trusted to deliver a true verdict on the evidence,[133] it can surely be trusted to reject baseless defences. If this argument is accepted, it leads to the surprising conclusion that the Criminal Law Revision Committee did not go far enough in proposing that probative burdens should be converted into evidential burdens. It may be that there is no need even for an evidential burden on the accused in this sort of case.

---

[125] See *R. v. Ewens* [1967] 1 Q.B. 322 (C.C.A) 473 *per* Melford Stevenson J.

[126] See the Eleventh Report of the Criminal Law Revision Committee (Cmnd. 4991, 1972), paras. 137-142, and the comments of Davitt P. in *McGowan v. Carville* [1960] I.R. 330 (H.C.) 337.

[127] As Smith points out, these provisions fell by the wayside not because of any intrinsic flaws but because of the controversy over the other recommendations of the Committee with regard to the right of silence (Smith, 242). It is one of the ironies of legal history that the latter provisions have now come into effect but not the former.

[128] Above, n.48.

[129] *Cross and Tapper*, 118.

[130] *Bratty v. Attorney General for Northern Ireland* [1963] A.C. 386 (H.L.) 417.

[131] Above, nn. 70-74.

[132] [1935] A.C. 462, 480; see also *The People (D.P.P.) v. Davis* [1993] 2 I.R. 1, 13-15 *per* Finlay C.J.

[133] Whether such trust is justified is a different matter: see Smith, above, n.74.

The third question is whether the prosecution should be obliged to negative in advance any possible defence that the accused might raise, at the risk of a successful submission of no case to answer if this is not done. Clearly this would be absurd, and there must therefore be some sort of burden on the accused here. But it need not be a burden of proof, or even an evidential burden. All that is needed is a rule placing a tactical burden on the defence not only in relation to defences in the strict sense but also where there is a denial of *mens rea*; indeed, the tactical burden should lie on the accused in relation to all matters peculiarly within his or her knowledge.[134] This is probably already the law, and it involves no injustice to the accused; as we have seen, all that a tactical burden prevents is an unmeritorious submission of no case to answer.[135] At the end of the day, the jury will still have to consider the issue, and will have to be satisfied beyond reasonable doubt before they may convict the accused.

The fourth question relates to the existence and scope of what we have termed the personal burden. This is a more difficult issue, for questions about the scope of the so-called "right to silence" are as much political as legal. Certainly there is a lot of force in Bentham's famous aphorism that innocence invokes the right of speaking as guilt invokes the privilege of silence,[136] and there can be no doubt that the right of silence has been a boon and a blessing to rogues and blackguards of all kinds. But that is the nature of fundamental rights; if they are only to be invoked in deserving cases, they are utterly worthless.[137]

At the beginning of this paper it was said that *Woolmington v. D.P.P.* was one of those leading cases which, so far from settling the law once and for all, led to continuing discussion and debate. The debate about the presumption of innocence is one which needs to be carried on not only in the courtroom but in the wider political sphere, for the principles laid down in *Woolmington* are not mere "lawyer's law"; on the contrary, they go to the heart of our historic constitutional liberties.

---

[134] This is a very ancient principle, as we have seen (above, n.28).

[135] Above, nn. 89-90.

[136] See *R. v. Gilbert* (1977) Cr. App. R. 237 (C.A.) 243; Jackson, above, n. 108, 110.

[137] As Sir Thomas More said in Robert Bolt's play *A Man for all Seasons*, even the Devil himself must have the benefit of law: see Murphy, n. 109 above.

A NEW VOCABULARY FOR A NEW CONSTITUTIONAL LAW
UNITED STATES V. CAROLENE PRODUCTS (1938)

WALTER F. PRATT, JR.[*]

1. INTRODUCTION

This essay is about a time when the Supreme Court of the United States *did not* declare a law unconstitutional – a bit like Sherlock Holmes's dog who didn't bark.

To compress history just a bit: I begin with the collapse of the stock market in 1929; I conclude in 1938 with the Supreme Court's decision in *United States v. Carolene Products*. The focal point is the final abdication of the Court in matters of regulation of commerce, effectively ending for at least two generations the conversations about that aspect of the relationship between the states and the federal government. As arbiters of both the grammar and the vocabulary of that conversation, the Court had conducted a dialogue between past and present for a century and a half. Bound by a rich tradition of precedent, the justices tended to rely on the taxonomy of the eighteenth-century nation. Slowly, however, they discovered that those categories were inadequate for the crises of the twentieth century. After attempting to translate, the justices eventually abandoned the older vocabulary in favour of a modern lexicon. In doing so, they set the Court on a new path, one that shaped the twentieth-century debate as much as the older vocabulary shaped that of the nineteenth century. A different perspective would reveal the origins of the discussion and would see the canvas rent apart in the Civil War (*Dred Scott*), culminating in the relegation of African-Americans to a position of racial inferiority (*Plessy*). With *Carolene Products* we see the final resolution of the struggle to define "commerce"; and we see the beginning of the idiom that leads to *Brown v. Board of Education*, and the core of twentieth-century American constitutional debate.[1]

---

[*]Professor of Law, University of Notre Dame.

[1] The citations for cases mentioned in the paragraph are these: *United States v. Carolene Products*, 304 U.S. 144 (1938); *Dred Scott v. Sanford*, 60 U.S. (19 How.) 393 (1857); *Plessy v. Ferguson*, 163 U.S. 537 (1896); and *Brown v. Board of Education*, 347 U.S. 483 (1954).

2. The New Deal Responds to the Depression

But that is to get ahead of the story. The stock market collapsed in 1929, plunging the country into an economic depression. In the absence of a generally accepted theory for dealing with an economic crisis of such magnitude, President Herbert Hoover's suggestions for intervention by the federal government were largely ignored. The economy continued to spiral downward, the sharpest in the nation's history. The fundamental point is that the extent of the Depression (combined with the challenges from totalitarian governments overseas[2]) demonstrated convincingly that the economy was a national one. The transcendence of the depression emphasised the national character of the economy, thereby reinforcing what had been growing feelings that only the federal government could effectively regulate economic activities, whether they be railroads or the general health of the economy. Franklin D. Roosevelt began his term as president much like Thomas Jefferson had done in 1801, finding political opponents everywhere. One of FDR's closest advisors, Raymond Moley, said, "We stood in the city of Washington on March 4th [1933] like a handful of marauders in a hostile territory".[3]

Roosevelt began the restoration of the nation's morale with an inaugural address in which he asserted that "the only thing we have to fear is fear itself". But beyond that memorable phrase, the speech contained another observation, one often overlooked, even though it foretold the struggle which is the subject of this essay. Responding to the increasing activism of the Supreme Court, Roosevelt glossed over the difficulties with soothing ease, saying, "Our Constitution is so simple and practical that it is possible always to meet extraordinary needs by changes in emphasis and arrangement without loss of essential form".[4] His was not an attack on the Supreme Court as an institution; neither was it a criticism of the language of the Constitution. He merely suggested a change in emphasis here, a minor rearrangement there.

Almost overnight the nation's mood changed from one of pessimism to one of optimism. FDR acted quickly to declare a national bank holiday and to support legislation to promote recovery. He called a special session of Congress to

---

[2] Leuchtenburg, *Franklin D. Roosevelt and the New Deal, 1932-1940* (Harper & Row, New York, 1963) 275-98 [hereafter Leuchtenburg, *Roosevelt and the New Deal*].

[3] Quoted in Leuchtenburg, "The Case of the Contentious Commissioner: *Humphreys'* [*sic*] *Executor v. United States*," in Hyman & Levy, (eds.), *Freedom and Reform: Essays in Honor of Henry Steele Commager* (Harper & Row, New York, 1967) 307 [hereafter Leuchtenburg, "Case of the Contentious Commissioner"]; and in Leuchtenburg, *The Supreme Court Reborn: The Constitutional Revolution in the Age of Roosevelt* (O.U.P., New York, 1995) 77-78 [hereafter Leuchtenburg, *Supreme Court Reborn*].

[4] Quoted in Leuchtenburg, *Supreme Court Reborn*, 84. For a series of scholarly papers contemporaneous with the FDR battle, though actually written for the sesquicentennial of the Constitution, see Read (ed.), *The Constitution Reconsidered* (Columbia University Press, New York, 1938).

meet on March 9, 1934. By March 15, over half of the nation's banks were allowed to reopen, thereby proving that there was cause for optimism. Then came a series of new statutes as FDR raced through the first days of the administration. Each new agency – known by their acronyms, and therefore as "alphabet soup" agencies – was clearly understood to be experimental, but at least Roosevelt was seen to be doing something. Congress's struggle to cope with the economic depression had an international component as well – to show the world that a democracy could work.[5] As Roosevelt himself later said, in a fireside chat in March 1937, "'[I]n a world in which democracy is under attack, I seek to make American democracy succeed'".[6]

All of that activity came before the centerpiece of the New Deal, the National Industrial Recovery Act (NIRA). FDR predicted: "History probably will record the National Industrial Recovery Act as the most important and far-reaching legislation ever enacted by the American Congress".[7] The NIRA authorised the National Recovery Administration (NRA) to supervise the writing of "codes" for every industry. Reflecting the compromises required to enact the legislation, the act suspended the antitrust laws to permit code agreements to raise prices and to restrict production, as a concession to industry. Then, as a concession to labour, the act required all codes to fix maximum hours and minimum wages and to recognise the right of workers to organise collectively. The initial hope was to achieve results through social pressure rather than legal enforcement – modelled after the sale of Liberty Bonds during World War I. Thus, the Blue Eagle came to be the symbol of those who adhered to the NIRA (even the *Harvard Law Review* displayed a Blue Eagle).

Concern about the constitutionality of the legislation, however, gave the administration pause. As the *New Republic* noted on November 15, 1933, "One of the deepest weaknesses of the administration in Washington, ever since the Agricultural Act and the Recovery Act went into effect, has arisen from its fears that these laws, or parts of them, would be declared unconstitutional if allowed to be tested in the courts".[8] The administrator of the NRA admitted to

---

[5] See Leuchtenburg, *Roosevelt and the New Deal*, 275-298 (chapter entitled "The Fascist Challenge").

[6] Quoted in Alton, "Loyal Lieutenant, Able Advocate: The Role of Robert H. Jackson in Franklin D. Roosevelt's Battle with the Supreme Court" (1997) 5 *William & Mary Bill of Rights Journal* 527 [hereafter Alton, "Loyal Lieutenant"] 566. For more on the concern about the possibility of turning to fascism and other totalitarian solutions, see Hulsebosch, "The New Deal Court: Emergence of a New Reason" (1990) 90 *Colub.L.Rev.* 1973, 1977-1978, 2002.

[7] Roosevelt, *The Public Papers and Addresses of Franklin D. Roosevelt* (Rosenman (ed.), Random House, New York, 1938-1950) vol. 2, 246 [hereafter *Public Papers of FDR*] (quoted in Swisher, *American Constitutional Development*, (2nd ed., Houghton Mifflin, Boston, Mass., 1954) [hereafter Swisher, *Constitutional Development*] 894.

[8] "Take the New Deal to Court!" 77 *The New Republic* 5 (15 November 1933); quoted in Mason, *Harlan Fiske Stone: Pillar of the Law* (Viking Press, New York, 1956) [hereafter Mason, *Stone*] 385.

refraining from seeking a court test of the NIRA, lest enforcement provoke a challenge in court.[9]

The apprehension about how the Supreme Court of the United States might rule arose from the presence on the Court of a perceived block of conservative justices, Pierce Butler, James C. McReynolds, George Sutherland, and Willis Van Devanter – dubbed the "Four Horsemen" – who could be counted on to vote against most reform legislation. There were but three justices who presumptively favoured the New Deal – Louis D. Brandeis, Benjamin N. Cardozo, and Harlan Fiske Stone. The other two, Chief Justice Charles Evans Hughes and Associate Justice Owen Roberts, were swing votes, who might vote one way or another, depending upon the case.[10] The ideological split seemed to extend even to personal relations: Joseph Rauh, a law clerk for Cardozo, recounted that the four conservative justices often travelled together to and from the Court.[11] As with most bivalent labels, there is a tendency to slide toward caricature. The "Four Horsemen" did indeed vote together more often than they voted with the "liberals". But they also voted to sustain reform legislation.[12] That the labels have stuck is a measure of the power of political rhetoric from the hectic days of FDR's first term. Moreover, FDR's efforts to allay the nation's fears were well served by portraying his opponents (political as well as judicial) as a "hostile" enemy.

The spurt in legislative activity brought an apparent upturn in the economy. But late in 1933 the economy turned downward again. The new agencies seemed unable to cope with the enormity of the crises. As the depression worsened through 1934, and after the Democrats strengthened their control in Congress in the elections of that year, FDR changed his tactics. His original legislation sought to provide higher prices for industry and agriculture. His new tactic was to increase purchasing power and provide social security for the people.

3. THE SUPREME COURT'S REACTION

With the change in tactics and the recognition that some of the initial New Deal programs were failing, it was not entirely with regret that the White House

---

[9] Irons, *The New Deal Lawyers* (Princeton University Press, Princeton, N.J., 1982) [hereafter Irons, *New Deal Lawyers*] 35.

[10] For an analysis of the voting blocs during this period see Galloway, "The Roosevelt Court: The Liberals Conquer (1937-1941) and Divide (1941-1946)" (1983) 23 *Santa Clara L.Rev.* 491; Galloway, "The Court that Challenged the New Deal" (1984) 24 *Santa Clara L.Rev.* 65.

[11] Rauh, "An Unabashed Liberal Looks at a Half-Century of the Supreme Court" (1990) 69 *North Carolina L.Rev.* 213, 214. Part of this essay is reprinted as Rauh, "A Personalized View of the Court-Packing Episode" (1990) *Journal of Supreme Court History* 93.

[12] For an essay properly (and cleverly) warning against caricatures, see Cushman, "The Secret Lives of the Four Horsemen" (1997) 83 *Virginia L.Rev.* 559.

learned in January 1935 that part of the NIRA had been declared unconstitutional by the Supreme Court.[13] Early in the oral argument counsel for the government had conceded that the provision establishing a criminal penalty for violation of the code had been omitted from the relevant executive order. Put simply, the government had to admit that there was no practical way for the industry to discover the provisions of the rules. So it came as no real surprise when the Court held part of the act unconstitutional on a procedural ground. In addition, there was no consternation when the Court ruled that the act constituted an unconstitutional delegation of powers (the first time the Court had used that rationale to strike down a law[14]) – it seemed that the act could simply be rewritten to provide adequate notice and appropriate standards.

Shortly after that decision the Court, by a 5-4 vote, afforded a slight glimmer of hope to the New Dealers in the *Gold Clause Cases*.[15] The decision upheld a joint resolution of Congress which banned gold clauses from all existing contracts of public or private debt. For the future, contracts had to be "discharged upon payment, dollar for dollar, in any coin or currency which at the time of payment is legal tender for public and private debts".[16]

The Court allowed some reform measures to stand,[17] but to a country fearful of its economic survival and especially to an administration consumed with maintaining political advantage, the Court seemed intent on overturning more than it allowed. But even the glimmer of hope soon dimmed, for shortly thereafter the Court in another 5-4 decision held that the Railway Pension Act was unconstitutional.[18] Justice Roberts provided the additional vote for the conservatives. The close vote provoked this observation from a staunch supporter of New Deal programs, *The New Republic*: "One wonders how many more such decisions touching the very foundation of national power in a modern industrial society can be absorbed without destroying the very Constitution the odd man on the Court thinks he is preserving".[19] Like Roosevelt, the magazine

---

[13] *Panama Refining Co. v. Ryan*, 293 U.S. 388 (1935).

[14] See Corwin, Testimony before the Senate Judiciary Committee, "Reorganization of the Federal Judiciary," *Hearings before the Committee on the Judiciary United States Senate on S. 1392*, 75th Cong, 1st Sess., pt. 2, 169 (March 17, 1937) [hereafter Corwin, Testimony].

[15] The *Gold Clause Cases* were a group of four cases, the results of which were reported in three opinions: *Norman v. Baltimore & Ohio Railroad Co.*, 294 U.S. 240 (1935); *Nortz v. United States*, 294 U.S. 317 (1935); *Perry v. United States*, 294 U.S. 330 (1935). The fourth case, *United States v. Bankers Trust Co.*, was decided along with *Norman*.

[16] Congressional Joint Resolution of June 5, 1933, ch. 48, § 1, 48 Stat. 112, 113 (1933); quoted in Mason, *Stone*, 388.

[17] For examples, see *Home Building and Loan Association v. Blaisdell*, 290 U.S. 398 (1934) (Minnesota's mortgage moratorium law upheld); *Nebbia v. New York*, 291 U.S. 502 (1934) (New York's regulation of milk prices upheld).

[18] *Railroad Retirement Board v. Alton Railroad Co.*, 295 U.S. 330 (1935). For discussion of Justice Roberts' role in this decision see "Mr. Justice Roberts and the Railroaders" in Leuchtenburg, *Supreme Court Reborn*, 26-51.

[19] "A *Dred Scott* Decision" 83 *The New Republic* 34 (22 May 1935); quoted in Leuchtenburg,

personalised the conflict, deflecting attention from the language of the Constitution.

The justices seemed to belie that personalisation later in the month, on Monday, May 27, 1935, termed at the time, "Black Monday," when the Court struck down three of the statutes most desired by FDR. What made the day all the worse for FDR was that the Court was unanimous in each of its decisions. The most important of the three decisions was *A. L. A. Schechter Poultry Corp. v. United States*, in which the Court held that the NIRA was unconstitutional.[20] As one revisionist historian has recently reminded us, "When the Supreme Court invalidated the NIRA in May of 1935, the program had few friends, and prospects for congressional extension of its two-year charter were gloomy".[21] Or, in the words of another historian, "In its administration, the NIRA was an economic nightmare and a political embarrassment".[22] Even so, this *was* the centerpiece of FDR's program – the "most important . . . legislation ever enacted by the American Congress".

4. SCHECHTER POULTRY DECISION

Schechter involved a dispute about the implementation of the NRA through the "Code of Fair Competition for the Live Poultry Industry of the Metropolitan Area in and about the City of New York". The City as a whole provided the largest live-poultry market in the United States – ninety-six percent of the live poultry marketed in New York City came from other states. The Schechter brothers usually bought the poultry live at the market in New York City, buying from dealers who had dealt with out-of-state suppliers. The Schechter brothers then slaughtered the chickens, and sold them to retail poultry dealers in New York City. They did not sell in interstate commerce.

The case originated with indictments of the A.L.A. Schechter Poultry Corporation and the Schechter Live Poultry Market for violations of the Code of Fair Competition, including a charge that they had sold diseased chicken – thus the name by which the case is known, the "sick chicken case". The Second Circuit Court of Appeals sustained the convictions on all counts except those charging violations of the minimum wage and maximum hours provisions. Those

---

Supreme Court Reborn, 45 (Professor Leuchtenburg attributes the unsigned editorial to Felix Frankfurter and Henry Hart, both professors at Harvard Law School).

[20] 295 U.S. 495 (1935). The other two decisions were *Louisville Joint Stock Land Bank v. Radford*, 295 U.S. 555 (1935); *Humphrey's Executor v. United States*, 295 U.S. 602 (1935).

[21] Cushman, "Rethinking the New Deal Court" (1994) 80 *Virginia L.Rev.* 201, 242. Professor Cushman subsequently published his work as *Rethinking the New Deal Court: The Structure of a Constitutional Revolution* (O.U.P., New York, 1998) [hereafter Cushman, *Rethinking the New Deal Court*].

[22] Gordon, "Rethinking the New Deal" (1998) 98 *Colum.L.Rev.* 2029, 2038 (reviewing Ackerman, *We the People: Transformations* (Harvard University Press, Cambridge, Mass., 1998)).

provisions, the court held, were outside of Congress' power. Both sides sought review by the Supreme Court.

Chief Justice Hughes began his opinion for the Court with what he called a preliminary matter: As though responding to Roosevelt's first inaugural address, he noted that "extraordinary conditions do not create or enlarge constitutional power".[23] Then, moving on to the substance of the case, he announced that the NIRA constituted an unconstitutional delegation of legislative power. The particular problem was that there was no congressional definition of standards to be applied under the act. Instead, the act permitted private organisations to set the standards. The Court also held that the delegation to the president to approve the codes was unconstitutional because lacking in standards.

Although some might have thought that the Court had sufficiently dismantled the NIRA, the Court went further to discuss the power of Congress to regulate intrastate commerce. The Court was emphatic in its conclusion that the interstate commerce had ceased in the case of the chickens. Furthermore, in the now familiar vocabulary, there was no "direct" effect on interstate commerce, thus Congress had no power over the transactions.

Then Hughes wrote as though he was responding to those who argued that only a national solution would suffice. Echoing the Anti-federalists' concerns of 150 years earlier, he identified the structural concerns behind the verbal sparring, illustrating how the Constitution's word "commerce" had already been translated to "direct" and "indirect": "If the commerce clause were construed to reach all enterprises and transactions which could be said to have an indirect effect upon interstate commerce, the federal authority would," he warned, "embrace practically all the activities of the people and the authority of the State over its domestic concerns would exist only by sufferance of the federal government".[24] He later emphasised that "the distinction between direct and indirect effects of intrastate transactions upon interstate commerce must be recognised as a fundamental one, essential to the maintenance of our constitutional system".[25]

Brandeis, who had not been happy with the direction of the New Deal, thought that this was the greatest day in the history of the Court because the

---

[23] 295 U.S. at 528.

[24] 295 U.S. at 546. *Cf.* Chief Justice Fuller's opinion in *United States v. E.C. Knight*, 156 U.S. 1 (1895).

[25] 295 U.S. at 548. In the later words of Robert Jackson, the Court had dealt the "corpse a second blow". *Struggle for Judicial Supremacy*, 114. The Court "not merely decided the case before it but drew into doubt the capacity of the Federal Government by use of the commerce power to accomplish many other things that the emergency seemed to require". *ibid.* The Court also declared that the Frazier-Lemke Act was unconstitutional, *Louisville Joint Stock Land Bank v. Radford*, 295 U.S. 555 (1935). As Professor Leuchtenburg notes, this act was not supported by the New Deal, having been introduced by two Republicans. Leuchtenburg, "When the People Spoke, What Did They Say?: The Election of 1936 and the Ackerman Thesis" (1999) 108 *Yale L.J.* 2077, 2088 n.69 [hereafter Leuchtenburg, "When the People Spoke"].

decisions promised to get the country back on the right track. The label "liberal" never rested well on Brandeis. He favoured small over large, in both public and private enterprises. He wanted Harvard Law School professor Felix Frankfurter to come to the Supreme Court so that Brandeis could explain the day's decisions and have Frankfurter report to FDR. He summoned another of FDR's advisors, Tommy Cocoran, to the justices' robing room with a message for Roosevelt: "This is the end of this business of centralisation, and I want you to go back and tell the President that we're not going to let this government centralise everything. It's come to an end".[26]

In its next term, the Court continued its repudiation of the New Deal programs, beginning with decisions in January 1936, when it invalidated the Agricultural Adjustment Act, in *United States v. Butler*.[27] In May of that year it struck down the Guffey Coal Act, in *Carter v. Carter Coal Co*.[28] The Court also decided (5-4) that New York's minimum wage law was unconstitutional,[29] prompting FDR to respond the next day that the Court had created a "'no-man's land' where no Government – State or Federal – can function".[30]

Attorney General Homer Cummings echoed that thought in his diary, where he recorded these comments:

> [T]he Court has seemed to be moving in two parallel lines, one to restrict the States within such narrow margins that the States cannot deal effectively with economic conditions and, at the same time, limiting the power of the Congress so to do by cutting down the full import of the General Welfare Clause, and arrogating to the Court the power, in the last analysis, to say what was for the General Welfare.
>
> In these hectic days when there is so much talk about usurpation of authority, it is astounding to find the Supreme Court reaching out in that direction. All these things seem to be converging upon a real constitutional struggle that may effect the destinies of our people for generations yet to come.[31]

---

[26]Quoted in Irons, *New Deal Lawyers*, 104.

[27]297 U.S. 1 (1936) (6-3 vote). Professor Leuchtenburg describes this act as "the second of the two most important New Deal recovery programs". Leuchtenburg, "The Origins of Franklin D. Roosevelt's 'Court-Packing' Plan" (1966) *Supreme Court Review* 347, 365 [hereafter Leuchtenburg, "Origins"].

[28]298 U.S. 238 (1936).

[29]*Morehead v. New York* ex rel. *Tipaldo*, 298 U.S. 587 (1936).

[30]Quoted in Leuchtenburg, "Origins," 377-378.

[31]Quoted in Alton, "Rosenkrantz and Guildenstern are Dead: The Role of Robert H. Jackson in FDR's Court-Packing Plan" (LL.M. Thesis, Columbia University, 1992) [hereafter Alton, LLM Thesis], 17 (Homer S. Cummings, Diary, Box 235, Homer S. Cummings Papers, University of Virginia (January 13, 1936)).

5. *Carter Coal* Decision

The most revealing of the decisions, *Carter v. Carter Coal Co.*,[32] involved a statute, the Guffey Coal Act, that had been carefully drafted in response to the Court's decision in *Schechter*. The act sought to provide the same sorts of regulations that would have applied had the NIRA been upheld. Not surprisingly, the debate in Congress, after the *Schechter* decision, focused on the constitutionality of the bill. FDR sent a letter to a member of the House asking that the bill be passed in spite of any doubts about its constitutionality. FDR's message reflected his belief in the malleability of language, saying in part: "Manifestly, no one is in a position to give assurance that the proposed act will withstand constitutional tests, for the simple fact that you can get not 10 but 1,000 different legal opinions on the subject". The rhetorical uncertainty did not distract Roosevelt from his political goal, for he continued: "But the situation is so urgent and the benefits of the legislation so evident that all doubts should be resolved in favour of the bill, leaving to the courts, in an orderly fashion, the ultimate question of constitutionality". He concluded with an element of disingenuous optimism: "A decision by the Supreme Court relative to this measure would be helpful as indicating with increasing clarity the constitutional limits within which this Government must operate. The proposed bill has been carefully drafted by employers and employees working co-operatively. An opportunity should be given to the industry to attempt to work out some of its major problems. I hope your committee will not permit doubts as to constitutionality, however reasonable, to block the suggested legislation".[33]

As enacted, the key provision of the Guffey Coal Act provided a "tax" of fifteen percent on the gross profits of all companies in the coal industry. Companies that adhered to the provisions of the act received a rebate of 13½%; those that did not received nothing. The same day that the bill passed, the board of the Carter Coal Company met and voted 3-2 to accept the Guffey Act. The president of the company voted in the minority; he then sought an injunction against his father and the two other majority directors. The case was rushed to the Supreme Court, on a writ of certiorari granted before oral argument in the court of appeals. The two-month delay in announcing a decision thus seemed to hint that the Court might uphold the Act. But on May 18, 1936, to the dismay of the New Dealers, Justice Sutherland announced the decision of the Court. In spite of the care taken in drafting the statute, the Court declared the act unconstitutional.

---

[32] 298 U.S. 238 (1936).

[33] 79 Congressional Record 13449 (quoted in Swisher, *Constitutional Development*, 935). For approval of Roosevelt's efforts on this point see Corwin, "Curbing the Court" (1936) 185 *The Annals of the American Academy of Political and Social Science* 45 [hereafter Corwin, "Curbing the Court"] 54.

After preliminary matters Sutherland continued the script penned by Hughes in *Schechter*: "The proposition, often advanced and as often discredited, that the power of the federal government inherently extends to purposes affecting the nation as a whole with which the states severally cannot deal or cannot adequately deal, and the related notion that Congress, entirely apart from those powers delegated by the Constitution, may enact laws to promote the general welfare, have never been accepted but always definitely rejected by this court".[34] Likewise following the dialogue of Hughes, Sutherland emphasised the relationship between the states and the federal government. Among his warnings was this: "Every journey to a forbidden end begins with the first step; and the danger of such a step by the federal government in the direction of taking over the powers of the states is that the end of the journey may find the states so despoiled of their powers . . . as to reduce them to little more than geographical subdivisions of the national domain".[35]

After an extensive examination of precedents, replete with vocabulary from the structural portion of the Constitution, Sutherland reached the conclusion: "Plainly, the incidents leading up to and culminating in the mining of coal do not constitute such intercourse [for the purposes of trade – the definition of 'commerce']".[36] To emphasise his point, he added curtly that the "relation of employer and employee is a local relation".[37] Even though Sutherland wrote with confidence, the starkness of that conclusion hinted that he realised that the end was near. In its rhetorical overkill, the decision seems to acknowledge that the constitutional vocabulary of "commerce" was waning in vitality.

Chief Justice Hughes wrote a "separate opinion". He too indicated a concern that to permit Congress to exceed its constitutional power would destroy the functions of the states. And he added, echoing the then-current political debate, that if the people wanted to amend the Constitution they could do so, but that it was not for the Court to provide the amendment.[38]

At the end of the Term, in June 1936, Justice Stone wrote his sister: "We finished the term of court yesterday. I think in many ways one of the most disastrous in its history. At any rate it seems to me that the Court has been needlessly narrow and obscurantic in its outlook. I suppose no intelligent person likes very well the way the New Deal does things, but that ought not to make us forget that ours is a nation which should have the powers ordinarily possessed by governments, and that the framers of the Constitution intended that it should have".[39]

---

[34]298 U.S., at 291.
[35]298 U.S., at 295-296.
[36]298 U.S., at 303.
[37]298 U.S., at 308.
[38]298 U.S., at 318.
[39]Quoted in Mason, *Stone*, 425-426.

Roosevelt's own later recollection nicely captured the dispute over meaning:

> By June, 1936, the Congressional program, which had pulled the nation
> out of despair, had been fairly completely undermined. What was worse,
> the language and temper of the decisions indicated little hope for the
> future. Apparently [Chief Justice] Marshall's conception of our Consti-
> tution as a flexible instrument – adequate for all times, and, therefore,
> able to adjust itself as the new needs of new generations arose – had been
> repudiated. . . .
>
> But was it really the fault of our Constitution? Or was it the fault of
> the human beings who, in our generation, were torturing its meaning,
> twisting its purposes, to make it conform to the mould of their own out-
> moded economic beliefs?[40]

6. ROOSEVELT'S "COURT-PACKING" PLAN

In sum what had occurred in four years was the greatest spate of activity by the
federal legislature in creating new, national programs, followed by seemingly
comparable effort by the Supreme Court in striking down much of that same
legislation. FDR, though dismayed, had withheld public comment, other than a
press conference four days after the *Schechter* opinion, in May 1935. FDR
calmly reflected that the issue was a non-partisan one of whether the nation
would have the powers that existed in every other national government throughout the world. This refrain, common throughout American history, was made
acute by the apparent success of Hitler and other totalitarian rulers in responding to the Depression. There was, however, bite to Roosevelt's comments, when
he observed that the "implications of this decision are . . . more important than
any since the *Dred Scott* case".[41] And, he added an acerbic comment that became a headline throughout the nation when he charged that the *Schechter*
decision had relegated the nation to "the horse-and-buggy definition of interstate commerce".[42]

The president did little else publicly during the remainder of the year, remaining silent in the face of growing calls for some form of curb on the Court.
He even declined to make the Court an issue in the election of 1936 – though
his political opponents did so, as did any number of other people.[43] In spite of

---

[40]Quoted in Alton, LLM Thesis, 32.

[41]4 *Public Papers of FDR*, 205. No doubt, Roosevelt's reference to *Dred Scott* was influenced by
the editorial in the *New Republic* attributed to Frankfurter and Hart.

[42]Quoted in Leuchtenburg, "Origins" 357 (4 *Public Papers of FDR*, 221).

[43]The most complete discussion of the extent to which the Court was an issue in the 1936 election

early polls suggesting that FDR would lose the election, he achieved the greatest electoral landslide in the nation's history to that time, winning all but two of the forty-eight states.[44] After the election the New Deal saw still more of its statutes facing review by the Court – the Social Security Act, the Wagner Act, the Railway Labor Act, to name but three of the major pieces of legislation.

FDR then re-energised his private consultations with Attorney General Homer Cummings. Cummings assigned small portions of memoranda to various people within the Justice Department, hoping that no one could guess what the program was about.[45] Ignoring the success of five recent amendments to the Constitution, FDR concluded that an amendment could not be passed in time. He focused instead on the child-labour amendment to confirm his doubts, – thirteen years had elapsed and the amendment still languished in the state legislatures. Moreover, he doubted that the conservative-oriented legislatures of the states would approve an amendment, though he apparently gave little thought to the alternative of ratification by state conventions specially called to vote on the amendment. Finally, Roosevelt realised that even an amendment would be subject to interpretation by the Court.[46]

The final proposal emerged from several sources, including Professor Edward Corwin of Princeton University. In correspondence between Cummings and Corwin, Corwin suggested that the president consider appointing a new justice for each sitting justice over the age of 70.[47] Six of the justices were then over 70. Some critics complained that the justices lived on merely to thwart FDR.[48] In the words of Robert Jackson, "The Court seemed to have declared the mortality table unconstitutional".[49] The truth may well have been that some of the justices were deterred from retiring by Congress' action in reducing Holmes' retirement pay in 1932.[50]

Corwin's accusations were strongly worded, including this: "That nine elderly gentlemen holding office for life should exercise, without considerable responsibility and responsiveness to the political forces of the Nation, the sweeping powers which the Court today exercises over the national legislative power, would be a preposterous idea and one in nowise to be reconciled with the notion of 'a government of the people, by the people, and for the people.'"[51]

---

is Leuchtenburg, "When the People Spoke". See also Baker, *Back to Back: The Duel between FDR and the Supreme Court* (Macmillan, New York, 1967), 43: Alton, LLM Thesis, 33-38.

[44] The exceptions were Maine and Vermont. In electoral votes, the count was 523-8.

[45] For a description of the process as well as criticism of Roosevelt's strategy concerning the plan, see Nelson, "The President and the Court: Reinterpreting the Court-packing Episode of 1937" (1988) 103 *Political Science Quarterly* 267 (1988).

[46] For a critique of Roosevelt's view, see Kyvig, "The Road Not Taken: FDR, the Supreme Court, and Constitutional Amendment" (1989) 104 *Political Science Quarterly*, 463.

[47] Leuchtenburg, *Supreme Court Reborn*, 115-121.

[48] Jackson, *Struggle for Judicial Supremacy*, 185.

[49] *ibid.*, 187.

[50] Mason, *Stone*, 454; Pusey, *Charles Evans Hughes* (Macmillan, New York, 1951), vol. 2, 760.

[51] Corwin, "Curbing the Court", 53-54.

Later, in testimony before a Senate committee, Corwin criticised the Court for seeking to elevate a particular economic bias of its own into the Constitution. Emphasising that adequate vocabulary already existed to support the reform legislation, he chided the justices for entering what was essentially a political debate: "There is no doubt but that many parts of the New Deal could have been sustained on the basis of doctrines which have been approved by the Court in the past, doctrines equally reputable – more reputable – than the doctrines by which it was overthrown". His comments continued with a subtle shift in language, suggesting that the Court was dabbling in politics: "Modern principles of constitutional law confront the Court with great political questions. It is desirable that they should be decided by men whose social philosophy is modern; at least, by men who are willing to pursue a hands-off policy unless clearly agreed principles leave them no option but to interfere". That shift allowed him to cut the justices off from reliance on precedent. Instead, politics demanded contemporaneity: "Elderly men look backward. The experience that elderly judges have had in life is inapplicable to changing conditions. There ought to be constant refreshment of knowledge of life and of new currents of thought available to the entire bench. . . . The pressure a judge is subjected to from his own personal experience, his own education, his own training, is a pressure which is exceedingly difficult to withstand".[52]

Some years later, Robert Jackson echoed Corwin's comments. During the court-packing debate, Jackson had been one of the most effective defenders of the proposal, in spite of being only a junior attorney in the Department of Justice. Roosevelt appointed him to the Supreme Court in 1941, the same year that his book appeared. In the preface Jackson emphasised the fading importance of the past (and, consequently, the lessening significance of the historic vocabulary): "The peculiar character of judicial tenure had enabled a past that was dead and repudiated in the intellectual and political world to keep a firm grip on the judicial world. What we demanded for our generation was the right consciously to influence the evolutionary process of constitutional law, as other generations had done".[53] That suggestion reflected a refrain among the critics of the Court: The justices were simply too old to understand the needs of a modern nation. A less eloquent version of the refrain appeared in October 1936 as the title of a book by Drew Pearson and Robert Allen – *The Nine Old Men*. The title proved to be a popular slogan for the press in its criticism of the Court.

Meanwhile, Attorney General Cummings and his staff continued their research. When Cummings learned that Justice McReynolds, as attorney general, had suggested to President Wilson that judges of federal courts be allowed to retire at age 70, or have the president empowered to appoint a new judge, he knew that he had found the answer. McReynolds was a mean-spirited anti-

---

[52]Corwin, Testimony, 168, 173, 174.
[53]Jackson, *Struggle for Judicial Supremacy*, xiv.

Semite who refused to sit with Brandeis for the Court's annual photograph.[54] He had referred to FDR as "that crippled son-of-a-bitch in the White House".[55] Thus it is understandable that according to the distinguished historian of the New Deal, William E. Leuchtenburg, FDR giggled when he read McReynolds' generation-old sentence about the justices not being able to perceive their own infirmities.

Even though FDR agreed with the proposal, he still did not make it public until he discovered that parts of the plan were becoming public knowledge. On February 2, 1937, he entertained the members of the Court at a White House dinner, as was his custom. Three days later, on Friday, February 5, 1937, he sent Congress a proposal to reform federal judicial procedures.[56] The centerpiece of that proposal would permit the president to nominate as many as six new justices, one for each of the sitting justices who did not retire within six months after reaching his 70th birthday. The six justices were these: Brandeis, at 80 the oldest; next came Van Devanter, 77; then Chief Justice Hughes, McReynolds, and Sutherland, all 74; the youngest of the six septuagenarians was Butler, who had turned 70 the previous year.

In his accompanying message, FDR disingenuously justified the proposal by pointing to overcrowded courts and delays in litigation. One cause of those problems, he asserted, was the declining capacity of the judges as they became older. "A lower mental or physical vigour leads men to avoid an examination of complicated and changed conditions. Little by little, new facts become blurred through old glasses fitted, as it were, for the needs of another generation; older men, assuming that the scene is the same as it was in the past, cease to explore or inquire into the present or the future. . . . A constant and systematic addition of younger blood will vitalize the courts and better equip them to recognize

---

[54]Bond, *I Dissent: The Legacy of Chief Justice James Clark McReynolds* (George Mason University Press, Fairfax, Va., 1992) 56 [the title is a misprint] [hereafter Bond, *I Dissent*] (the source is Abraham, *Justices and Presidents: A Political History of Appointments to the Supreme Court* (O.U.P., New York, 1974), 167 n.49). "Because McReynolds could not tolerate those who disagreed with him, he had stormy relationships with many of his fellow justices. From the beginning he disliked Justice Clarke, whom he thought stupid, and for years would not even speak to him. He did not sign the letter of regret which his brethren sent Clarke upon his resignation, and he likewise refused to sign similar letters sent to Justices Brandeis and Cardozo when they retired. McReynolds was so implacably hostile to Brandeis that he would turn his back when Brandeis spoke in conference" (Bond, *I Dissent*, 53). Bond also reports an interview account of Chief Justice Hughes having to have two initial dinners, because McReynolds refused to socialize with Jewish colleagues (*ibid.*, 56 n.39).

[55]Quoted in Leuchtenburg, *Supreme Court Reborn*, 121. Bond quotes McReynolds as saying he would never "retire 'as long as that crippled jackass is in the White House'" (Bond, *I Dissent*, 84) [The source given for that quotation, *Time* (December 4, 1939), 14, was actually more discreet, reporting that Justice McReynolds had said, "'I'll never resign as long as that crippled —— —— is in the White House!.'"]. Bond also quotes from an interview with McReynolds' nephew, saying that "'jackass' was McReynolds' favorite appellation for anyone he disliked" (Bond, *I Dissent*, 93 n.72).

[56]H. Doc. No. 142, 75th Cong., 1st Sess. See also 6 *Public Papers of FDR*, 63.

and apply the essential concepts of justice in the light of the needs and the facts of an ever-changing world".[57] Additional support came from Attorney General Cummings, who captured the domestic as well as the international aspect of the debate when he said, "If we are to defend successfully our institutions against all comers from the Right and from the Left we must make democracy work".[58]

Although the plan provoked an outpouring of comment, the early indicators pointed toward approval in both houses of Congress, where the Democrats had substantial majorities. The nation's press, however, generally opposed the plan.[59] The surprise leader of the opposition was Senator Burton Wheeler, a liberal Democrat from Montana. Wheeler had campaigned with Robert La Follette in 1924 on a platform that called for reform of the Court. Nevertheless, Wheeler presented the opposition's case in two radio addresses in February 1937. In the second he revealed the emergence of a new vocabulary, for he spoke not in terms of states and federalism but in terms of minorities: "Make the Court subservient to one man or make it subservient to mob rule and you destroy the liberties of the minorities of this country. Though I am in the majority now, I remember when I was with the minority, and I am just as anxious to preserve the rights of minorities now as I was to have my rights preserved when I was in the minority".[60]

Roosevelt spoke only twice in favour of the bill. Once, on March 4, 1937, he repeated his earlier characterisation of the Court as having created "a no-man's land" in which neither state nor federal government could deal with the country's problems.[61] The second time was March 9, the initial fireside chat of his second term, when he explicitly criticised the Court for straying into the political arena:

> The Court in addition to the proper use of its judicial function has improperly set itself up as a third House of Congress – a super-legislature, as one of the justices has called it – reading into the Constitution words

---

[57]H. Doc. No. 142, 75th Cong., 1st Sess., 4; quoted in Leuchtenburg, "Franklin D. Roosevelt's Supreme Court 'Packing' Plan" in Hollingsworth and Holmes (eds.), *Essays on the New Deal* (University of Texas Press, Austin, 1969) [hereafter Leuchtenburg, "Franklin D. Roosevelt's Supreme Court 'Packing' Plan"] 69, 70. (The full message is quoted in Jackson, *The Struggle for Judicial Supremacy*, 328). For an account of the internal disagreements among FDR's advisors over the appropriate strategy see Alton, LLM Thesis, 80 *et seq.*

[58]Quoted in Barnes and Littlefield (eds.), *The Supreme Court Issue and the Constitution* (Barnes & Noble, New York, 1937) 31.

[59]See Alton, "Loyal Lieutenant," 580, n.376.

[60]81 Cong. Rec. App. pt. 9, 309-11 (75th Cong., 1st Sess.). Joseph Lash quotes Wheeler as saying to Tom Corcoran that Roosevelt seemed intent on making "'himself the boss of us all. . . . Well he's made the mistake we've been waiting for a long time – and this is our chance to cut him down to size.'" Lash, *Dealers and Dreamers: A New Look at the New Deal* (Doubleday, New York, 1988) 298.

[61]6 *Public Papers of FDR*, 118 (quoted in Alton, LLM Thesis, 91).

and implications which are not there, and which were never intended to be there.

We have, therefore, reached the point as a Nation where we must take action to save the Constitution from the Court and the Court from itself. . . . We want a Supreme Court which will do justice under the Constitution – not over it. In our Courts we want a government of laws and not of men.[62]

Roosevelt continued:

During the past half century the balance of power between the three great branches of the Federal Government, has been tipped out of balance by the Courts in direct contradiction of the high purposes of the framers of the Constitution. It is my purpose to restore that balance. You who know me will accept my solemn assurance that in a world in which democracy is under attack, I seek to make American democracy succeed.[63]

The contrast between Wheeler and Roosevelt is noteworthy. Wheeler alluded to an emerging concern (both nationally and internationally) to protect minorities. By contrast, Roosevelt (like Corwin) saw the Court as an unwelcome participant in the sport of national and international politics.

In testimony before the Senate Judiciary Committee, Wheeler astonished the nation when he produced a letter from Chief Justice Charles Evans Hughes denying that the Court was behind in its docket. In fact, the chief justice asserted, more justices would only delay the work of the Court, "there would be more judges to hear, more judges to confer, more judges to discuss, more judges to be convinced and to decide".[64]

Even so, in spite of the opposition, it seemed that FDR would still win approval of his proposal. But then, on March 29, the Court announced *West Coast Hotel Co. v. Parrish*, upholding a minimum-wage law from Washington state.[65] In so doing, the Court reversed itself on the very point that had provoked FDR's "no-man's land" expletive only the year before.[66]

---

[62] 6 *Public Papers of FDR*, 126 (quoted in Alton, LLM Thesis, 93). Justice Brandeis had been the first to use the term "super-legislature," in his dissent in *Jay Burns Baking Co. v. Bryan*, 264 U.S. 504, 534 (1924). He also used it in a dissent in *New State Ice Co. v. Liebmann*, 285 U.S. 262, 300 (1932); and he joined Justice Stone's dissent using the term in *Colgate v. Harvey*, 296 U.S. 404, 441 (1935).

[63] 6 *Public Papers of FDR*, 133 (quoted in Alton, LLM Thesis, 94).

[64] Quoted in Leuchtenburg, *Supreme Court Reborn*, 140-141; Leuchtenburg, "Franklin D. Roosevelt's Supreme Court 'Packing' Plan" 90 (S. Rep. No. 711, 75th Cong., 1st Sess., 38-40).

[65] 300 U.S. 379 (1937) (overruling *Adkins v. Children's Hospital*, 261 U.S. 525 (1923)).

[66] The earlier case was *Morehead v. New York* ex rel. *Tipaldo*, 298 U.S. 587 (1936). In turn, *Morehead* had relied on *Adkins v. Children's Hospital*, 261 U.S. 525 (1923).

Writing for the 5-4 Court, Hughes began with the observation that the liberty guaranteed by the due process clause was not liberty without restriction. Rather, the liberty was "subject to the restraints of due process"; and, introducing a note of relativity, he added that "regulation which is reasonable in relation to its subject and is adopted in the interests of the community is due process".[67] He quoted from a number of cases which had held that liberty could be limited, if in the public interest. Most importantly, he pointed to the fact that the statute was limited to women and minors as reflecting an appropriate state interest.[68] All of his thoughts led to the conclusion that recent decisions had been a "departure from the true application of the principles governing the regulation by the State of the relation of employer and employed".[69]

Justice Sutherland wrote a dissent for the Four Horsemen, who not unexpectedly would adhere to those decisions. Sutherland had written in *Carter Coal* that the "relation of employer and employee is a local relation". Now, seeing that conclusion rejected, he fell back on admonitions of the importance of fidelity to the language of the Constitution. He rebuffed FDR's inaugural suggestion that words could have different emphases, chosen to fit the needs of an era. In particular, Sutherland warned that changed economic conditions could not alter the meaning of the Constitution. For him, the vocabulary of the debate was unchanging – "The judicial function is that of interpretation; it does not include the power of amendment under the guise of interpretation". Then he added, showing his awareness of the political debate swirling about the Court, "If the Constitution, intelligently and reasonably construed in the light of these principles, stands in the way of desirable legislation, the blame must rest upon that instrument, and not upon the court for enforcing it according to its terms. The remedy in that situation – and the only true remedy – is to amend the Constitution".[70]

It is now known that the justices reached their decision in *Parrish* before Roosevelt announced his court-packing plan.[71] In 1937, however, the chronology appeared to reflect the Court's bending to political pressure – termed at the time, the "switch in time that saved nine". That bending seemed all the more pronounced when, two weeks later, April 12, 1937, the Court upheld the Wagner Act in a series of five opinions, the most important of which was *NLRB v. Jones & Laughlin Steel Corp.*[72] Finally, on May 24 the Court upheld the Social

---

[67] 300 U.S., at 391.
[68] 300 U.S., at 394 (citing *Muller v. Oregon*, 208 U.S. 412 (1908)). For discussion of this point see Erickson, "*Muller v. Oregon* Reconsidered: The Origins of a Sex-Based Doctrine of Liberty of Contract" 30 *Labor History* 228 (1989).
[69] 300 U.S., at 397.
[70] 300 U.S., at 404. See Chambers, "*The Big Switch*: Justice Roberts and the Minimum-Wage Cases" (1969) 10 *Labor History* 44, 54.
[71] See, for example, Mason, *Stone*, 456; Leuchtenburg, *Supreme Court Reborn*, 311 n.17.
[72] 301 U.S. 1 (1937).

Security Act.[73] Possibly of greatest significance though, was the announcement on May 18, that one of the stolid lexicographers, Justice Van Devanter, would retire at the end of the term.[74]

Although the events of the spring did not assure the defeat of the court-packing plan, they certainly lessened its chances for success. Later, following the death of Senator Joseph Robinson, Roosevelt's leader in the Senate, it became clear that the plan would fail.[75] The result was that FDR won a Court that would uphold his laws – beginning with Hugo Black, who replaced Van Devanter.[76] The transformation was not complete until Reed replaced Sutherland; Douglas replaced Brandeis; and Murphy replaced Butler. Within thirty months, Roosevelt would appoint five justices; before he left office, he appointed eight, and elevated Stone to the chief justiceship. In spite of those judicial appointments, the battle over the plan led to a split in the New Deal's legislative coalition from which FDR never recovered.[77]

We cannot be certain about what happened within the Court. The familiar account, told with different degrees of emphasis, is that the justices bowed to the political winds, including the gust from the court-packing plan. Recently, however, a revision has suggested that the justices relied more on the internal logic of their own opinions, evolving since the turn of the century. This revision further suggests that poorly worded statutes and sloppy lawyering contributed more to the New Deal's early failures than did a clique of conservative justices.[78] Wherever along the continuum of historical explanation one falls, it does seem clear that Roberts switched his vote – or at least changed the emphasis of his analysis. His comment in a 1951 lecture at Harvard is illuminating: "Looking back, it is difficult to see how the Court could have resisted the popular urge for uniform standards throughout the country – for what in effect was a unified economy. . . . An insistence by the Court on holding federal power to

---

[73] *Steward Machine Co. v. Davis*, 301 U.S. 548 (1937).

[74] The decision was at least in part the result of more liberal retirement allowances, enacted by Congress shortly after Roosevelt announced his court-packing plan. Act of March 1, 1937, ch. 21, 50 Stat. 24.

[75] Leuchtenburg, *Supreme Court Reborn*, 145-154.

[76] Leuchtenburg, *Supreme Court Reborn*, 154.

[77] See Leuchtenburg, *Supreme Court Reborn*, 156-162; Leuchtenburg, "FDR's Court-Packing Plan: A Second Life, A Second Death" (1985) *Duke L.J.* 673.

[78] For support of the revision, see Cushman, *Rethinking the New Deal Court*, and Irons, *New Deal Lawyers*. Professor Michael Parrish suggests that Chief Justice Hughes "may have been the original architect of this theory" (Parrish, "The Hughes Court, the Great Depression, and the Historians" (1978) 40 *The Historian* 286, 289 n.13. Professor Parrish characterizes the argument as "curious," given the caliber of the attorneys who argued the cases before the Supreme Court). For opposition to the revision, see Leuchtenburg, *Supreme Court Reborn*. Professor Leuchtenburg has also promised a two-volume study of the court-packing crisis. Professor Laura Kalman nicely summarizes the differences between Cushman and Leuchtenburg in her article, "Law, Politics, and the New Deal(s)" (1999) 108 *Yale L.J.* 2165, esp., 2165 n.3. *See also* Griffin, "Constitutional Theory Transformed" (1999) 108 *Yale L.J.* 2115.

what seemed its appropriate orbit when the Constitution was adopted might have resulted in even more radical changes in our dual structure than those which have been gradually accomplished through the extension of the limited jurisdiction conferred on the federal government".[79]

Regardless of the explanation, it is clear that by the late 1930s, the Court had changed. The past recorded a court speaking the vocabulary of commerce and states in an effort to describe the boundaries of federal power. The future had only begun to appear, voiced by Wheeler and others in terms of minorities threatened by majorities, as well as by dictators abroad. Revealing hints of the Court's future came on April 25, 1938, when the Court announced two decisions – *Erie Railroad v. Tompkins*[80] and *United States v. Carolene Products Co.*[81] As one scholar wrote, "Taken together, these two opinions left the Supreme Court almost without function in what had previously been an important part of its docket. If *Erie* mandated deference to state common law decisions and if the *Carolene Products* rationality test meant that the Court would hold constitutionally infirm only those laws that no one could reasonably have enacted, then the Court's role would be significant only in policing federal-state relationships, interpreting and elaborating federal statutes, and developing areas of law that, like patent and admiralty law, the Constitution proscribed to the states".[82]

7. THE *CAROLENE PRODUCTS* DECISION

The second decision did, however, point to what would become a significant role for the Court. The judgment upheld the conviction of the Carolene Products Company for shipping Milnut, a milk and coconut oil product, in interstate commerce, in violation of the Federal Filled Milk Act of 1923,[83] which

---

[79]Roberts, *The Court and the Constitution* (Harvard University Press, Cambridge, Mass., 1951) 61-62. Roberts' "switch" has been the subject of much commentary, see especially Frankfurter, "Mr. Justice Roberts" (1955) 104 *U.Penn.L.Rev.* 311; Ariens, "A Thrice-Told Tale, or Felix the Cat" (1994) 107 *Harv.L.Rev.* 620; Friedman, "A Reaffirmation: The Authenticity of the Roberts Memorandum, or Felix the Non-Forger" (1994) 142 *U.Penn.L.Rev.* 1985.

[80]304 U.S. 64 (1938). For a contemporaneous defense of *Erie*, by Roosevelt's first appointee to the Court, Justice Hugo Black, see Black, "Address" (1942) 13 *Missouri Bar Journal* 173.

[81]304 U.S. 144 (1938).

[82]Danzig, "Justice Frankfurter's Opinions in the Flag Salute Cases: Blending Logic and Psychologic in Constitutional Decisionmaking" (1984) 36 *Stan.L.Rev.* 675, 685. Compare Ackerman, *We the People: Foundations* (The Belknap Press of Harvard University Press, Cambridge, Mass. 1991) 119: "Of the early efforts at redefinition, the single most significant is contained in a footnote whose provocative character has made it the most famous in Supreme Court history: footnote four of the *Carolene Products* case". Professor Ackerman focuses on footnote four in chap. five, "The Modern Republic" *ibid.*, 105-130. The entire June 1999 issue of the *Yale Law Journal* contains a valuable discussion of Professor Ackerman's thesis: (1999) 108 *Yale L.J.* 1917-2349.

[83]The law is still in the U.S. Code, 21 U.S.C. §§ 61-64 (1995).

prohibited the interstate transportation of skimmed milk to which vegetable oil had been added.[84] In the opinion for the Court, Justice Stone confirmed that the Court had surrendered the field of economic regulation to Congress:[85] "The existence of facts supporting the legislative judgment is to be presumed, for regulatory legislation affecting ordinary commercial transactions is not to be pronounced unconstitutional unless in the light of the facts made known or generally assumed it is of such a character as to preclude the assumption that it rests on some rational basis within the knowledge and experience of the legislators". In effect, the constitutional discussion of the meaning of "commerce" was to be left to the political process. But it was to be a process overwatched by the judiciary. For, as Stone added in footnote numbered four:[86]

> There may be narrower scope for operation of the presumption of constitutionality when the legislation appears on its face to be within a specific prohibition of the Constitution, such as those of the first ten amendments, which are deemed equally specific when held to be embraced within the Fourteenth.
>
>   It is unnecessary to consider now whether legislation which restricts those political processes which can ordinarily be expected to bring about repeal of undesirable legislation, is to be subjected to more exacting judicial scrutiny under the general prohibitions of the Fourteenth Amendment than are most other types of legislation.
>
>   Nor need we inquire whether similar considerations into the review of statutes directed at particular religious . . . or national . . . or racial minorities . . . whether prejudice against discrete and insular minorities

---

[84] The case was not seen as posing a particularly difficult issue at the time. One commentator, writing in 1945, had this to say: "The court here merely followed its precedents since its first decision on oleomargarine. Whether the shipment of the product was injurious to public health, morals, or welfare, it insisted, was a Congressional matter. Since the product had been so classified by Congress, the company could claim no vested rights and Congress could choose its method for regulating the product". Ganoe, "The Roosevelt Court and the Commerce Clause" (1945) 24 *Oregon L.Rev.* 71, 77.

[85] See Ely, "Property Rights and Liberty: Allies or Enemies?" (1992) 22 *Presidential Studies Quarterly* 703, 707: "The Supreme Court signaled its new direction in *Carolene Products* by creating a dichotomy between property rights and personal liberties". Then, the next paragraph begins: "With its generous understanding of legislative authority over economic matters, *Carolene Products* marked the end of reliance on property rights as a means of safeguarding individual liberty by limiting the reach of government. ... It is difficult to square *Carolene Products* with the framers' belief that protection of property rights was essential to the enjoyment of individual liberty".

[86] According to Stone's biographer, the note was drafted substantially by Stone's law clerk Louis Lusky. Mason, *Stone*, 513. For Lusky's account, see Lusky, "Footnote Redux: A *Carolene Products* Reminiscence" (1982) 82 *Colum.L.Rev.* 1093; Lusky, *Our Nine Tribunes: the Supreme Court in Modern America* (Praeger, Westport, Conn., 1993), 119-132, 177-190. See also Linzer, "The *Carolene Products* Footnote and the Preferred Position of Individual Rights: Louis Lusky and John Hart Ely vs. Harlan Fiske Stone" (1995) 12 *Constitutional Commentary* 277.

may be a special condition, which tends seriously to curtail the operation of those political processes ordinarily to be relied upon to protect minorities, and which may call for a correspondingly more searching judicial inquiry.[87]

Mr. Justice Black concurred in the result and in all of the opinion except the part marked *"Third"*.[88] Thus only a plurality of four supported the footnote. (McReynolds would affirm; Cardozo and Reed did not participate; Butler concurred only in the result).

The day after the decision was announced, Justice Stone wrote Judge Irving Lehman of the United States Court of Appeals for the Second Circuit. The letter nicely illustrates the link between domestic and international concerns. "I have been deeply concerned about the increasing racial and religious intolerance which seems to bedevil the world, and which I greatly fear may be augmented in this country. For that reason I was greatly disturbed by the attacks on the Court and the Constitution last year, for one consequence of the program of 'judicial reform' might well result in breaking down the guarantees of individual liberty".[89]

The extent of the Court's surrender becomes apparent only after considering the Filled Milk statute's origins. One scholar has aptly described the 1923 act as "an utterly unprincipled example of special interest legislation".[90] If ever there was a statute "of such a character as to preclude the assumption that it rests on some rational basis," this was it.

"Filled milk" was a canned milk, marketed for its long shelf-life, an important characteristic at a time when many homes, especially in poorer areas, lacked adequate refrigeration to keep whole milk. The chief competitor was evaporated milk, which also had a long life, but had a very high sugar content, as high as 40%. Filled milk, by contrast, was skimmed milk to which vegetable oils (primarily coconut oil) had been added to replace the butterfat.[91] Canned milk had a history dating at least to 1853.[92] Filled milk was first marketed in the years immediately before the Civil War.[93] The First World War, however, saw a marked increase in production, spurred on by the Food Administration's

---

[87] 304 U.S., at 152-154 n.4 (citations omitted). For an article emphasizing that the note was merely *dictum*, see Powell, *"Carolene Products* Revisited" (1982) 82 *Colum.L.Rev.* 1087.

[88] 304 U.S., at 155.

[89] Quoted in Mason, *Stone*, 515. For further discussion of this point, see Perry, "Justice Stone and Footnote 4" (1996) 6 *George Mason University Civil Rights Law Journal* 35, 49-63.

[90] Miller, "The True Story of Carolene Products" (1987) *Supreme Court Review* 397, 398. Miller also notes that filled milk is now sold in most supermarkets (*ibid.*, 399, n.18).

[91] Senate Rep. No. 987, 67th Cong., 4th Sess., 1923 (Committee on Agriculture & Forestry).

[92] 1921 FTC Report 35. For more information see Hunziker, *Condensed Milk and Milk Powder* (published privately by the author in several editions between 1918 and 1949, La Grange, Ill.)

[93] For a survey of the market see *Report of the Federal Trade Commission on Milk and Milk Products, 1914-1918*, 34-62 (1921).

admonition that citizens "Do Without Butter-fat" to allow the butter-fats to be sent to the troops fighting in Europe.[94] By the time of the federal statute, filled milk had a significant price advantage over evaporated milk, largely because skimmed milk was considered to be almost worthless. Since coconut oil was cheaper than butterfat, the entire product was cheaper than its competitor. At retail, filled milk sold for 25% less than evaporated milk.[95]

The end of the First World War saw a substantial decline in the American economy – a decline that was all the more severe in agriculture which had witnessed increased demand for its products during the war. In those conditions, farmers began to view filled milk as a product that took money away from their pockets.[96] Filled milk replaced butter and butterfat, largely through the use of coconut products. Even though filled milk required skimmed milk, the gain there did not outweigh the losses elsewhere. Joining the farmers in opposition was the Borden Company, which had yet to enter the market with a filled milk product of its own. Supporters of filled milk were represented by Carnation.[97]

But even before Congress acted, legal battles reached the Supreme Court, beginning in 1919, with a case challenging Ohio's ban on the manufacture or sale of condensed skimmed milk.[98] Writing for the Court, Justice Holmes left the matter entirely to the state legislature. That conclusion, along with the continuing depression in the agricultural markets, led others to think that legislative action might be their economic salvation. By 1923, seventeen states had laws that prohibited or restricted sales of filled milk.[99] In spite of that success, opponents of filled milk recognised that the product could still be shipped into their states from states without the restrictions. Following the pattern of banning transport of alcohol, the opponents of filled milk turned to federal legislation.[100]

---

[94] See 73 *Literary Digest* 24 (May 27, 1922), 24; for summaries of the growth of the canned-milk industry during the War see *Report of the Federal Trade Commission on Milk and Milk Products, 1914-1918*, 16, 17-21 (1921).

[95] Senate Rep. No. 987, 67th Cong., 4th Sess., 2 (1923 Committee on Agriculture & Forestry). The wholesale prices were $3.50 vs. $5.00 for a case of 48 cans. At retail, a single can of filled milk cost 7½¢ vs. 10¢ for evaporated milk.

[96] For an account of the production which suggests that farmers were short-sighted to oppose filled milk, see "Filled Milk," 13 *American Journal of Public Health* 310 (Apr. 23, 1923), 310. There was a British embargo on canned milk in 1918, see *Report of the Federal Trade Commission on Milk and Milk Products, 1914-1918*, 33 (1921).

[97] See "Filled Milk," 13 *American Journal of Public Health* 310 (Apr. 23, 1923), 310 ("It is charged that the whole matter is a trade fight between two large milk companies, one of which is putting out filled milk in addition to its other business, and it is almost impossible to read the transcript of these hearings without gaining the impression that this is a fact".).

[98] *Hebe Co. v. Shaw*, 248 U.S. 297 (1919).

[99] Brief for the United States in *United States v. Carolene Products Co.*, Oct. Term 1937, 60-68.

[100] One of the earliest responses from Congress was Senate Resolution 431, 65th Cong., 3d Sess, January 31, 1919, calling on the FTC to study the milk industry. The FTC's report, *Milk and Milk Products: 1914-1918*, was issued June 6, 1921.

The bill, HR 8086, first passed the House in May 1922;[101] after hearings in both houses during the summer of 1922, the bill was introduced in the Senate in February 1923, nearing the end of the legislative session.[102] Supporters of the bill did not claim that filled milk was unhealthy; rather, they pointed to possible misuse by feeding it to children, thereby robbing them of needed nutrients, which were supposedly contained only in the butterfat of milk.[103] A statement common to both the House and the Senate reports on the bill attempted to emphasise the dangers in passing filled milk off as condensed milk, a product which had uncritical acceptance: "[Filled milk] is an exact imitation of pure evaporated or condensed milk; it has the same consistency, the same color, the same taste, and the difference in the two products can only be detected by an expert or by chemical analysis. The compound can be made more cheaply than the regular article, and, in view of the fact that the imitation is perfect, many people buy it in the belief that they are getting full condensed or evaporated milk".[104]

But the fundamental point of supporters was that the bill was required to support the dairy industry. As the Senate report asserted:

> [W]e can not afford to let a few manufacturers in this country for an additional profit to them strike a blow which will do irreparable injury to our entire dairying industry. Dairying represents the highest point reached in farm economy. Wherever dairying is extensively practized, the entire community reflects its benefits.
>
> . . . .
>
> The civilisation of our country is dependent upon the dairying industry. . . . We need it to preserve the fertility of our soil, and the time to prohibit the filled-milk traffic is now, before it has done greater damage to our health or to one of our basic and indispensable industries.[105]

Through procedural devices, the bill was rushed through the Senate, insuring that it could become law on March 4, 1923, the final day of the legislative

---

[101] 64 Congressional Record 3949 (February 19, 1923) (remarks of Senator Ladd, North Dakota).
[102] *ibid.*
[103] See Senate Rep. No. 987, 67th Cong., 4th Sess. (1923 Committee on Agriculture & Forestry). For an example of a label for filled milk which advised against using for baby formula, see 74 *Literary Digest* 20 (July 8, 1922), 20.
[104] "Filled Milk Legislation," H.R. Rep. No. 355, 67th Cong., 1st Sess., (1921 Committee on Agriculture).
[105] Senate Rep. No. 987, 67th Cong., 4th Sess., (1923 Committee on Agriculture & Forestry). For a less emotional survey of the importance of the dairy industry see Report of the Federal Trade Commission on Milk and Milk Products, 1914-1918, (1921).

session, when President Harding made the dramatic gesture of going to the Capitol to sign the last-minute bills.[106]

In spite of the law, the Carolene Products Corporation continued to manufacture the product, under license from the Carnation Milk Company.[107] The company won its first federal victory when a district judge declared the statute unconstitutional.[108] On review, however, the Supreme Court reversed the district court and held that the statute was constitutional. On remand, the company was found guilty and fined $1,000.[109]

The federal statute is still on the books, though no longer enforced.[110] Indeed, milk reinforced with vegetable oil (now primarily soybean oil) has come to be recognised as superior to regular milk, with its high percentage of animal fat. A federal district court has even declared the 1923 act to be unconstitutional.[111] And, in the greatest of all ironies, the Milnot Company which won that decision was once known as Carolene Products.[112] In June 1988, Milnot introduced a new packaging, with a red banner declaring that the milk was "cholesterol free".[113] The label also boasts that "if cows could, they'd give Milnot". Milnot is sold primarily in the Midwest and South.[114]

8. Conclusion

With its decision in *Carolene Products*, the Supreme Court announced a 180-degree turn away from the by now familiar economic regulation. In the late 1930s, the Court had little sense of the tasks ahead of it. But the Court had provided the vocabulary for dealing with those tasks. It only remained for subsequent justices to complete the lexicon.

---

[106] *New York Times*, March 5, 1923, 2, col. 7. See also *id.*, February 26, 1923, 17, col. 8 (prediction of events of final week of legislative session).

[107] The success came in spite of legislative efforts to prohibit the product. The state's supreme court twice declared laws unconstitutional: *People v. Carolene Products Co.*, 345 Ill. 166, 177 N.E. 698 (1931); *Carolene Products Co. v. McLaughlin*, 365 Ill. 62, 5 N.E.2d 447 (1936).

[108] *United States v. Carolene Products Co.*, 7 F. Supp. 500 (S.D. Ill. 1934).

[109] The procedural events are recounted in *Litchfield Creamery Co. v. Commissioner*, docket no. 110318, 2 T.C.M (CCH) 929 (October 19, 1943). For the affirmance of the fine see 104 F.2d 969 (7th Cir. 1939).

[110] In 1973, the Food & Drug Administration announced that it would no longer seek to enforce the statute. 38 *Federal Register* 20, 748 (1973).

[111] *Milnot Co. v. Richardson*, 350 F. Supp. 221, 224 (S.D. Ill. 1972).

[112] 350 F. Supp. at 222. Actually, the company which became Milnot in 1974 was the old Litchfield Creamery Co.; the change of name occurred when Canteen Corporation acquired Litchfield. *Chicago Tribune*, July 12, 1988, 4 of "Business" section.

[113] 90 *Dairy Foods Magazine* 48 (March 1989).

[114] *Chicago Tribune*, July 12, 1988, 4 of "Business" section.

AN EVERYDAY STORY OF COUNTRY FOLK (NOT!)
GREALISH V. MURPHY (1946)

ROBERT CLARK*

1. INTRODUCTION

One of the most interesting features of contemporary contract law is the extent to which some of the courts, in jurisdictions that are historically part of the common law family, are, increasingly perhaps, declining to follow the persuasive jurisprudence of the House of Lords.[1] This is not, however, a very significant feature of recent Irish case-law in the contract field, even though one Supreme Court judge appeared to damn *Barclays Bank v. O'Brien*[2] with faint praise when he regarded the decision as "helpful".[3] Irish law has, historically, been deeply protective of certain equitable doctrines that have sought to give the judiciary quite sweeping powers to grant relief against gift transfers and contractual transactions that are, broadly speaking, oppressive or unwise. While terminology shifts around somewhat, with undue influence, unconscionable bargain, improvident transaction and unequal bargain being used to describe aspects of the general jurisdiction, Irish case-law supports judicial intervention in situations that go beyond the limits countenanced by the Privy Council in *Hart v. O'Connor*,[4] and by the House of Lords in both *National Westminster Bank plc v. Morgan*[5] and *O'Brien*.[6] It is also significant that the influence of Irish judicial decisions in this area of equitable jurisprudence extends far beyond these shores. If we take the landmark nineteenth century Irish decision in

---

*Associate Professor of Law, University College Dublin; Consultant, Arthur Cox & Co.

[1] *E.g. Nelson v. Nelson* (1996) 184 C.L.R. 538 (H.C.A.), in which the High Court of Australia mapped out a new approach to statutory illegality, declining to follow *Tinsley v. Mulligan* [1994] 1 A.C. 340 (H.L.). This is not to suggest that the House of Lords is incapable of innovative decisions, but even some recent judgments can appear tentative *e.g. Malik v Bank of Credit and Commerce International S.A* [1998] A.C. 20 (H.L.).

[2] [1994] 1 A.C.180 (H.L.).

[3] *Bank of Nova Scotia v. Hogan* [1996] 3 I.R. 239 (S.C.) 246; [1997]1 I.L.R.M. 407, 413 *per* Murphy J.

[4] [1985] A.C.1000 (P.C.); see also *Boustany v. Pigott* (1993) 69 P.&C.R. 298 (P.C.).

[5] [1985] A.C.686 (H.L.).

[6] [1994] 1 A.C. 180 (H.L.).

Slator v. Nolan,[7] perhaps the most expansive statement on the equitable jurisdiction to control bargains which are struck on unequal terms, it is noteworthy
that later judges in Canada, Australia and New Zealand used this and other
Irish cases to build and sustain this jurisdiction, applying the principle to a
broad range of transactions such as separation agreements, sales of property at
undervalue, business partnerships, insurance settlements, and so on. A few
illustrations will suffice to emphasise the role of Irish case-law. In New Zealand, *Slator v. Nolan* was cited with approval in *K v. K*.[8] Many of the early
Canadian decisions[9] are improvidence transactions that ultimately lead to the
decision in *Waters v Donnelly*,[10] an important case in which Boyd C. cites
Slator v. Nolan as being a distillation of the earlier English and Irish case-law
on contracts made between persons not on equal terms. Post-*Waters v. Donnelly*
decisions in Canada are also supportive and although some of these cases have
been largely ignored[11] they underpin the view that the equitable jurisdiction to
relieve against improvident transactions is broadly based, goes beyond undue
influence and appears to be distinguishable from the unconscionable bargain
jurisdiction.[12] Irish case-law does not feature as a significant element in the
leading Australian case of *Blomley v. Ryan*[13] and it is the *O'Rorke v.
Bolingbroke*[14] line of authority that is most influential in this, and in later Australian decisions, such as *Amadio v Commercial Bank of Australia*.[15] These
converging lines of authority are a significant feature of *Grealish v. Murphy*[16]
and the combined effect of these Irish, New Zealand, Canadian and Australian
decisions should suggest to the English judiciary that it is English law that is
out of step with the broader equitable jurisdiction, and that abominable deci-

---

[7] (1874) I.R. 11 Eq. 367; the other late nineteenth century Irish cases that stand out are *Butler v.
Miller* (1867) I.R. 1 Eq. 195 and *Rae v. Joyce* (1892) 29 L.R. (Ir.) 500; see also the early
twentieth century case of *Kelly v. Morrisroe* (1919) 53 I.L.T.R. 145. *Rae v. Joyce* truly distinguishes the improvident bargain transaction from the unconscionable bargain because here the
weaker party was fully aware of the improvident nature of the transaction; the lender was imposing upon her needy circumstances and the legal advice given advised against the transaction.
[8] [1976] 2 N.Z.L.R. 31 (O'Regan J.).
[9] *e.g. Fallon v. Keenan* (1866) 12 Gr. 388; *Crippen v. Ogilvie* (1869) 18 Gr. 253; *Watson v.
Watson* (1876) 23 Gr. 70; *Traviss v. Bell* (1881) 29 Gr. 150.
[10] (1884) 9 O.R. 391
[11] *e.g. Hagarty v. Bateman* (1889) 19 O.R. 381; *Inglis v. Paw* (1907) 3 E.L.R.556; *Gladu and
Blair v. Edmonton Land Co.* (1914) 8 A.L.R. 80; *Birkett v. Ott* (1918) 57 S.C.R. 608; *Chartrand
v. Morin* [1922] O.W.N. 149; *Mitchell v. Mitchell* [1946] 3 W.W.R.670; *Wood v. Wood* [1976]
W.W.R. 113; *Beach v. Eames* (1976) 82 D.L.R. (3^d) 736n.
[12] *Doan v. I.C.B.C.* (1987) 18 B.C.L.R. 286. Note that some judges in Canada have used *Fry v.
Lane* (1888) 40 Ch.D. 312 (C.A.) to produce a similar result; see *Hrynyk v. Hrynyk* [1932] 1
D.L.R. 672; *Hnatuk v. Chretian* (1960) 31 W.W.R. 130; *Morrison v Coast Finance* (1965) 54
W.W.R. 257; *Fusty v. McLean Construction Ltd* (1978) 6 Alb. L.R. (2^d) 216.
[13] (1956) 99 C.L.R. 362 (H.C.A.).
[14] (1877) 2 App.Cas. 814; see text with and in n. 43 below.
[15] (1983) 151 C.L.R. 447 (H.C.A.); see, in particular, 474, *per* Deane J.
[16] [1946] I.R. 35 (H.C.).

sions such as *Hart v. O'Connor*[17] need to be reviewed afresh. Fortunately, there are signs[18] that a more radical approach maybe emerging, an impression which has been greater strengthened by Lord Millett's extra-judicial observation that substantive unfairness *per se* may be a trigger for relief from an unconscionable bargain.[19]

If this reassessment comes about the Irish case-law will be of renewed importance.[20] *Grealish v. Murphy* in particular provides support for the view that a bargain may be overturned without the need to show procedural unfairness.

2. THE ACTION

2.1 The Claim

The plaintiff, Peter Grealish, sought to set aside an indenture of settlement, created in October 1942, on the ground that it was improvident or, in the alternative, because of his own mental infirmity and incapacity to understand the deed, coupled with the undue influence of the beneficiary, Thomas Murphy. This formed the basis of the primary claim to relief, but the plaintiff also claimed sole title to a bank deposit of £2,000 which stood in the joint name of the parties, and to two sums of £500 of £645 which were claimed from the defendant as being monies improperly obtained from the plaintiff by the defendant. The plaintiff also sought to have an account taken as between himself and the plaintiff.

2.2 The Facts Surrounding These Dealings

These are colourful indeed. The folksy tales of Synge, Summerville and Ross and J.B. Keane are pale things indeed when matched against Gavan Duffy J.'s telling of the story behind this singular case.[21] In essence, Peter Grealish was a bachelor farmer of very limited intellectual capacity who had the need of a reliable manager for his two farms in the Oranmore district of County Galway. He had tried to solve this problem by marrying off one of two of his nieces, or a cousin, to Fox, a local man, who would bring in a marriage portion (payable to the plaintiff) and who would manage the farms until the plaintiff's death, the

---

[17] [1985] A.C. 1000 (P.C.).
[18] *Crédit Lyonnais Bank Nederland NV v. Burch* [1997] 1 All E.R. 144 (C.A.); *Royal Bank of Scotland v. Etridge (No.2)* [1998] 4 All E.R. 705 (C.A.).
[19] "Equity's Place in the Law of Commerce" (1998) 114 *L.Q.R.* 214, 220.
[20] See generally Capper, "Unconscionable Bargains" in Dawson, Greer and Ingram, (eds.), *One Hundred and Fifty Years of Irish Law* (SLS, Belfast, 1995) 45.
[21] [1946] I.R. 35 (H.C.). The case was heard over three days in July 1944 and the decision handed down on October 16, 1944.

big farm passing to Fox upon his death. A deed giving effect to this plan was executed on December 3, 1941, but the Grealish/Fox settlement was frustrated when, hardly surprising perhaps, the lady involved in the arrangement turned Fox down in late December 1941. In the following month the plaintiff recalled to mind a family that lived some distance away, in Headford Co. Galway, and he invited one of the sons of that family, the defendant Thomas Murphy, to travel to see him. They had not met before, but the plaintiff took a shine to Thomas Murphy and after explaining that he had need of someone to manage the farm and reside there with him, the plaintiff offered the defendant a settlement of Carnmore, the big farm, and other financial assistance, if he would act for the plaintiff in business matters in general. This the defendant agreed to, subsequently acting for him in relation to litigation brought by Fox in relation to the December 3rd 1941 agreement. In October 1942 the parties executed a deed of settlement, drawn up by a new solicitor who had not been responsible for the Fox settlement of December 1941. The new solicitor explained the nature and effect of the settlement to the plaintiff, his client, and the settlement, which effectively reserved for the plaintiff a life estate and passed effective control of his affairs to the defendant, came into operation shortly thereafter. Local opposition to the arrangement intervened however and the parties fell out. The agreement was at an end by June 1943.

2.3 Gavan Duffy J.'s Characterisation of the Main Actors in the Drama

As we shall see, the Court was unable to use the equitable concept of undue influence in relation to the primary action. The seamless way in which Gavan Duffy J. was nevertheless able to integrate the concept of improvident bargain into resolution of the action owes much to the way in which he used language to describe the parties.

(a) The Plaintiff – Peter Grealish

Gavan Duffy J. is intent upon painting a picture of the plaintiff as a reckless and yet feckless individual, unlettered and reliant upon others, a person who needed protection against the result of the considerable disadvantages he laboured under:

> he is a bachelor in the sixties; he is a man of generous turn, but obstinate; he can hardly read and he signs as a marksman; he is afflicted with a worse than Boeotian[22] headpiece and a very poor memory; a long life has not taught him sense, . . .[23]

---

[22]Notoriously stupid people, notable for "swine rather than wit" Ross, *Greek Society* (Heath, Lexington, 1992), 105.
[23][1946] I.R. 35, 37.

and

> Peter, for as Peter he is known[24] , had a couple of labouring men sleeping
> under his roof, but otherwise lived alone on a remote farm . . . neglected
> by his relatives and almost bereft of friends, . . .[25]

and

> he felt, as I surmise, that he could not by himself hope to hold his own in
> any considerable purchases or sales of cattle . . . and needed and realised
> that he needed, a reliable factotum as manager and as protector.[26]

Gavan Duffy J. also explained why Peter was, on the evidence not merely
simple-minded but was intellectually very feeble:

> I must go with the medical evidence to the extent of classifying him among
> the mentally deficient, though I should not myself assimilate him to a
> child of twelve. I cannot measure his deficiency in scientific terms and I
> need say no more than this, as I appraise him, the brain, while it must
> have developed with time, has never since childhood attained the normal
> powers of an adult; and he is liable to be erratic, especially outside the
> daily routine of his life at home. The trial threw occasional side-lights on
> Peter's faculties; for instance, he can read the clock, but cannot tell the
> time; Murphy virtually admitted that Peter was unable to count £2,000 in
> £50, £10 and £5 notes; and, having made to Murphy in October, 1942, an
> astounding present of, as Murphy says, £700, Peter was unable, as I must
> necessarily infer from the pleadings, to give his advisors in this action
> any instructions whatever on the matter, which came to light only through
> a question in Murphy's cross-examination.[27]

The circumstances in which the plaintiff subsisted with his neighbours are also
mentioned. The plaintiff's inability to defend himself from being imposed upon
is attested by the fact that several neighbours had apparently taken stretches of
his land in conacre, Peter having no ability to resist. He gave others to understand that his land was "boycotted" by his neighbours although Gavan Duffy J.
thought this too strong a term.[28] Nor were his relatives any more supportive of

---

[24]Recall the faithful retainer Peter Cadogan in the *Irish RM* books (the first being published in
  1899) also rather slow and also known by his first name, also Peter: see *e.g.* Somerville & Ross,
  The Irish R.M. (Abacus, London, 1989).
[25][1946] I.R. 35, 37.
[26]*ibid.*
[27][1946] I.R. 35, 39.
[28][1946] I.R. 35, 44.

the old man, concerned only to let him live out his wretched life in the hope and expectation that upon his death they would take the benefits of the family ties without having endured the obligations and disadvantages. This theme sometimes emerges in improvident transaction litigation. It is often a desire to spite or frustrate "expectant heirs" that helps to explain the one sided nature of the bargain,[29] but even so judicial intervention will still be possible because of the improvident nature of the transaction.

However, Gavan Duffy J. gives two instances of family hostility to Peter's needs: the first, the reluctance of one of two of his nieces to marry Fox as being too high a price to pay for financial security, and the second being a reference to sibling antipathy to Peter's business dealings with Murphy:

> Local hostility had declared itself against Murphy as early as October [1942], but, after his arrival, a quite unforeseen and particularly unpleasant series of attacks came from one of Peter's sisters, a bedlam, living some three miles away, who would descend in wrath upon Carnmore at intervals, giving tongue to loud maledictions upon the grabber of their brother's land. Murphy, I think, actually went in fear of his life from some of the local roughs, a number of whom had stoned his car, and he found the onslaughts of the termagant almost equally hard to endure.[30]

(b) The Defendant – Thomas Murphy

Bear in mind Gavan Duffy J.'s observation above that what the plaintiff needed was "a reliable factotum as manager and as protector".[31] The judge goes on to set out the circumstances that implicitly attest to the fact that the defendant did not meet this description.

Firstly his description of the plaintiff's reckless and impetuous nature contrasts with that of the defendant:

> Murphy, who comes of farming stock, had been a road worker and he was a haulier in a small way, with a car and lorry of his own . . . he was only 32 years of age . . . the golden prospect was that he would be a rich man after a few years of not too arduous labour and surely he could well bear any little passing troubles that the venture might entail. Murphy accepted Peter's proposal, but did nothing at this time [January 1942] to rush the old man. [32]

---

[29]See in particular the Northern Ireland case of *McCrystal v. O'Kane* [1986] N.I. 123 (C.A.).
[30][1946] I.R. 35, 41.
[31][1946] I.R. 35, 37.
[32][1946] I.R. 35, 39-40.

When some nine months later the settlement was drafted upon Peter's instructions the evidence indicated that the defendant was still playing the "cute hoor";[33] after a summer of driving the old man around from fair to fair, for which the old man was grateful and rewarded him with monies (partly to thwart "the apprehended machinations of a rapacious Estate Duty Office"[34]) the evidence was that in dealings with Dr. Comyn, Peter's solicitor, Murphy "never uttered a word".[35] Gavan Duffy J. said of "Peter's dumb attendant"[36] that "if this persistent silence is an example of western caution, it suggests tactical caution carried too far".[37]

The second element that is used to suggest this business dealing was something of a mis-match springs from the fact that Murphy's silence was a factor which pointed towards Dr. Comyn's role as advisor to Peter alone. But this did not mean that Murphy was acting without advice. He had discovered from his own solicitor about the Fox settlement and the litigation and was in receipt of legal advice from his own solicitor throughout the entire affair. Once the settlement had been executed and the plaintiff's intentions made legally "irrevocable and his alienation irretrievable",[38] the defendant's schemes were now on firm ground. What was ultimately fatal to Murphy's ambitions was local hostility to him, his lack of fidelity to the plaintiff, and the inventiveness of Gavan Duffy J.

The third element in Gavan Duffy J.'s characterisation of Murphy, the defendant, centres around the defendant's conduct after the execution of the settlement. Murphy pressed Grealish into depositing £2,000 into a bank account in their joint names. He also engaged in cattle sales without Grealish's knowledge or consent. This is at the heart of the £645 restitution claim, although it must be said that the evidence does not for example hint at the cattle sale being improvident. What does appear is the likelihood that the sale of the cattle was asset-striping by the defendant who in turn pocketed the cash proceeds. When these arguable breaches of duty are recalled, together with the activities of Peter's sister and a gun attack on the house where Murphy lodged within the area – Murphy was also under police protection for a time – it is hardly surprising that the relationship between the parties had collapsed by June 1943.

2.4 The Law – Undue Influence

This appears to be the primary legal ground for challenging the settlement, but

---

[33] See Gavan Duffy J.'s description of the defendant's actions at [1946] I.R. 35, 40; see also [1946] I.R. 35, 48.
[34]*ibid*. See also: "the imaginary terrors of Dublin Castle" ([1946] I.R. 35, 46).
[35][1946] I.R. 35, 43.
[36][1946] I.R. 35, 47.
[37][1946] I.R. 35, 43.
[38][1946] I.R. 35, 47.

Gavan Duffy J. was emphatic in rejecting undue influence as being at all relevant on these facts. In reading this judgment one is reminded of the speech of
Lindley L.J. in *Allcard v. Skinner*:[39]

> What then is the principle? Is it that it is right and expedient to save
> persons from the consequences of their own folly? Or is it that it is right
> and expedient to save them from being victimised by other people? In my
> opinion the doctrine of undue influence is founded upon the second of
> these two principles. Courts of Equity have never set aside gifts on the
> grounds of folly, imprudence or want of foresight on the part of the do-
> nors.[40]

While we will return to the issue of jurisprudential revisionism later, the decision on undue influence in *Grealish v. Murphy* is a classical instance of the
plea failing because of the absence of victimisation, at least in relation to the
October 1942 settlement. Recall that Peter had sought out the younger man
and that no blood link or business link existed. In the January-October 1942
period, the younger man had ingratiated himself with Peter as chauffeur and
"dumb attendant". At the time of the settlement there was no hint of undue
influence, real or imputed. All we have is a foolish, imprudent and short-sighted
old man entering into a foolish, imprudent and short-sighted agreement, the
very circumstances that Lindley L.J. referred to as being *invalid* factors in trig-
gering relief *via* undue influence.

However, although undue influence was not regarded as a runner, these
somewhat ill-drawn pleadings had referred to Peter's mental incapacity and
the very improvidence of the transaction. The trial judge regarded these assertions as alluding to a separate and distinct line of equity. Furthermore, the very
factors that were said *not* to trigger relief *via* undue influence played a central
role in giving the court the basis for setting aside the settlement via the improvidence jurisdiction. This is a point of central importance for these pleas of
undue influence, on the one hand, and improvidence/unconscionable bargain
on the other, are all too often regarded as complementary pleas. *Grealish v.
Murphy* suggests that they can often produce quite distinct results and operate
on different circumstances.

2.5 Improvidence

For a judge who prided himself so much upon establishing and maintaining
Irish precedents,[41] taking pride in Celtic ingenuity over Anglo-Saxon consist-

---

[39] (1887) 36 Ch.D. 145 (C.A.).
[40] (1887) 36 Ch.D. 145, 161 (C.A.); *cf.* the decision of Cotton L.J. ((1887) 36 Ch. D. 145, 171) in
the same case, approved in *Carroll v. Carroll* [2000] 1 I.LR.M. 210 (S.C.) 222 *per* Denham J.
[41] See Golding, *George Gavan Duffy* (Irish Academic Press, Dublin, 1982).

ency,[42] it is interesting to note that the authority selected to support equitable intervention in this case was primarily Lord Hatherley L.C.'s speech in *O'Rorke v. Bolingbroke*.[43] The view that a court of equity may intervene to protect persons who have not entered a transaction on equal terms in described by Gavan Duffy J. as a "rescue"[44] principle that has, as a corollary, the proposition that "the court must inquire whether a grantor, shown to be unequal to protecting himself, has had the protection which was his due by reason of his infirmity, and the infirmity may take various forms".[45]

While the trial judge clearly stated that this proposition applied to grants and contracts for value, the latter being overturned by a court with greater hesitation, the short catalogue of cases instanced to anchor the equitable principle are predominantly English. Yet in chronological terms none of these cases came within an ass's roar of the twentieth century and, more importantly, there were several Irish cases that mark the principle much more emphatically than a dissenting speech in a somewhat obscure decision that, in reality, is a part of the now fossilised line of authority that provided protection to the landed gentry of England and Ireland *via* the expectant heir doctrine.[46]

3. IRISH IMPROVIDENCE CASES

Improvidence, or unconscionable bargain case-law in Ireland is rich, and, more importantly, is somewhat continuous when contrasted with English case-law. I have summarised the decisions elsewhere[47] but in this context it is worth pointing out that there are a number of important twentieth century improvidence cases in Ireland, at least one of which[48] was decided before *Grealish v. Murphy*.

---

[42]Recall the pride with which, in *Kirby v. Burke and Hollaway* [1944] I.R. 207 (H.C.) 215, he cited the description of the result in *Donoghue v. Stevenson* [1932] A.C. 532 (H.L.) as being "a Celtic majority . . . against an English minority"; on this, see Hedley *"M'Alister (or Donoghue) (Pauper) v. Stevenson* (1932)" above, 64, esp. text with and in n.7.

[43](1877) 2 App. Cas. 814; it is an expectant heir case (see text with n. 46 below) on appeal from Ireland to the House of Lords, and for that reason it is described as an "Irish case" in Keane *Equity and the Law of Trusts in the Republic of Ireland* (Butterworths, London, 1988) p.242, para. 29.10; the one important Irish decision that Gavan Duffy J. cited, but almost in passing, is *Slator v. Nolan* (1876) I.R. Eq. 367, 409-10.

[44][1946] I.R. 35, 49: "Equity comes to the rescue whenever the parties to a contract have not met on equal terms . . .".

[45]*ibid*

[46]The expectant heir cases eventually dry up in *Permanent Trustees of N.S.W. v. Bridgewater* (1936) 36 S.R.N.S.W. 643, a Privy Council decision, but in more republican Tribunals than the English courts the principle has been doubted, see Dawson, "Economic Duress – An Essay in Perspective" (1947) 45 *Mich. L. Rev*. 253, 274; see also Clark, *Inequality of Bargaining Power* (Carswell, Toronto, 1987) 16-23.

[47]Clark, *Inequality of Bargaining Power* (Carswell, Toronto, 1987); Clark, *Contract Law in Ireland* (4th ed., Round Hall Sweet & Maxwell, Dublin, 1998) 298-302.

[48]*Kelly v. Morrisroe* (1919) 53 I.L.T.R. 145.

One of the important aspects of *Grealish v. Murphy* is the fact that the jurisdiction, separate and distinct from undue influence, has been maintained in both Irish jurisdictions. While some of the improvident transaction cases are based upon the fact that the transaction is executed between members of a family, this is clearly not a precondition to relief if *Grealish v. Murphy* is an improvident transaction case. But, one wonders, if the case could be pleaded afresh, is improvidence the key element? I think the answer is both yes and no.

Firstly, on the issue of improvidence alone as a vitiating factor, if the transaction had been challenged as a unconscionable bargain one must doubt whether Murphy could be said to have been guilty of any sharp practice, or procedural unconscionability. We are told by the Privy Council that both procedural and substantive unconscionability should be present to trigger relief from an unconscionable bargain, and the facts of the leading case of *Hart v. O'Connor*[49] suggest to me that unconscionability (at least in the English courts) would not be a runner on the facts of *Grealish v. Murphy*. This is not a position that the Northern Ireland courts have taken, for *Rooney v. Conway*[50] specifically negatives the need to show improper behaviour or equitable fraud by the benefiting party. On the issue of an alternative plea, I would suggest that, on the facts of *Grealish v. Murphy*, the post-contractual conduct of Murphy could well be interpreted as a repudiatory breach or breach of fiduciary duty.[51] However, rather than going down this particular route, Gavan Duffy J. completed a very difficult course by using the very rude navigational instruments afforded to him by the plaintiff's pleadings. The merit of the judgment is that the Court was able to revive from these quite exceptional facts an equitable jurisdiction that, in law and justice, is an important part of Equity's armoury.

4. IMPROVIDENCE AND UNCONSCIONABILITY

In an important article[52] David Capper has recently argued that the unconscionability doctrine is cast in broader terms than undue influence and that unconscionability can be used to absorb the undue influence jurisdiction. In making this argument Capper leans towards the view that unconscionable conduct by the party trying to retain the gift or consideration in question is a *sine qua non* to relief being granted. Capper goes on to point out that the degree of reprehensibility shown from the decided cases fluctuates considerably.[53] This is certainly true, but the cases also suggest that at one end of the spectrum

---

[49][1985] A.C.1000 (P.C.).
[50][1982] N.I.J.B. No.5; see also *Buckley v. Irwin* [1960] N.I. 98; however, in *Strange v. Johnson* [1997] N.I.J.B. 56, 68 Girvan J. favours the stricter test found in *Hart v. O'Connor*.
[51]*e.g. King v. Anderson* (1874) 8 I.R. Eq. 625.
[52]"Undue Influence and Unconscionability: A Rationalisation" (1998) 114 *L.Q.R.* 479.
[53](1998) 114 *L.Q.R.* 479, 494-495.

the person benefiting from the transaction often is not guilty of any real unconscionable dealing. No real "victimisation" is shown. Capper seems to cite *Hart v. O'Connor* and the procedural/substantive unconscionability test advanced by Lord Brightman with approval.[54] It is my view that *Hart v. O'Connor* would not be decided by an Irish Court in the same way and I cannot agree that *Hart v. O'Connor* is in sympathy with the broader equitable jurisdiction that cases such as *Grealish v. Murphy* represent. The Irish cases are clear about the fact that undue influence and unconscionable bargain are distinct doctrines. Some of the cases also support the view that even without any real evidence of "victimisation", there remains a slender but ancillary jurisdiction to protect persons who contract when not on equal terms, the contracts being improvident, or, to put it another way, to relieve against contracts that on their face appear to be so unreasonable that no person of average intelligence would enter into it. These cases traverse the centuries and if one were to pick only three Irish decisions they would be *Slator v. Nolan,*[55] *Grealish v. Murphy*[56] and *Carroll v. Carroll.*[57] The critical elements in each of these cases is the existence of "relational imbalance"[58] as between the parties and the fact that the bargains were, in their own terms, unwise because each involved contingent events that could and did rebound against the weaker party. These improvidence cases often involve a debate about the quality of legal advice given to the weaker party, the background knowledge of the legal adviser, the status of any legal counsellor as a truly independent adviser and the nature of the transaction. These are often cases in which no victimisation takes place and where no imputation of bad faith is made, but the transaction is nevertheless overturned upon proof of disparity and because of the improvident nature of the transfer. Some decisions[59] clearly contemplate improvidence as being a distinct doctrine – a "third way", to use a contemporary expression – and it is explained very succinctly by O'Byrne J. in *Lydon v. Coyne*[60] when responding to the argument that a solicitor seeking to advise a client whose personal history was unknown to him faces a difficult task: "solicitors must often protect parties against themselves".[61] Seen in this light perhaps, Lord Denning's principle of inequality of bargaining power is not altogether dead; it simply needs to be regarded as a residual doctrine that has specific application to specific facts. These include contractual

---

[54]*ibid.*
[55](1874) I.R. 11 Eq. 367.
[56][1946] I.R. 35.
[57][2000] 1 I.L.R.M. 210 (S.C.).
[58]Capper (1998) 114 *L.Q.R.* 479 uses the phrases "relational inequality" and "transactional imbalance".
[59]In *Smyth v. Smyth* High Court, unreported, November 27, 1978, Costello J. examined a plea for relief by reference to three distinct headings; (1) undue influence, (2) *Grealish v. Murphy*, (3) unconscionable bargain/sales by reversioners. On the facts relief was not forthcoming.
[60](1946) 12 Ir. Jur. Rep. 64.
[61](1946) 12 Ir. Jur. Rep. 64, 66.

imbalance, improvident terms that are generally contingent in nature, the absence of complete advice on the nature of the transaction, and some evidence that the person who is at a disadvantage may not have understood the significance or effect of the transaction. This is where the recent decision of the Irish Supreme Court in *Carroll v. Carroll* comes into the picture.

5. IMPROVIDENT TRANSACTIONS – INTO THE NEW CENTURY

The argument advanced in this paper is that *Grealish v. Murphy* has served a pivotal role in the retention of a vibrant Irish equitable jurisdiction to relieve against improvident transactions. This is not just a historical curiosity that can be attributed to cultural values that are particularly deep seated in rural Ireland; Gavan Duffy J. pointed to the "cardinal principle" of equity which insists that equity "comes to the rescue whenever the parties to a contract have not met upon equal terms",[62] and it should be noted that of the nine decisions cited by the learned judge, only two of them are Irish and that one of them, the leading decision in *O'Rorke v. Bolingbroke*[63] was ultimately a decision of the House of Lords.

A recent decision of the Supreme Court, handed down as the twentieth century came to an end, has reinforced the significance of *Grealish v. Murphy* as marking an enduring and important line of equity jurisprudence. In *Carroll v. Carroll*[64] two sisters sought to set aside a transfer of ownership of licensed premises made by their father, in favour of their brother, on the grounds of undue influence and/or improvident transaction. The circumstances surrounding the transfer were held to raise a presumption of undue influence which the donee could not on the facts rebut. While the decision of the Supreme Court represents an extremely cogent statement on undue influence, particularly in regards to the differences to be attributed to presumed undue influence and express undue influence, as well as providing clear guidance upon what may be required to rebut the presumption, it is the significance of Denham J.'s treatment of the improvident bargain plea that is most noteworthy in our present context.

By the findings of fact made by Shanley J. at trial of the action, it was concluded that Carroll Junior did not exercise actual undue influence over Carroll Senior. Nor was there evidence of lack of mental capacity on the part of Carroll Senior. Counsel for the estate of Carroll Junior (who had since died) argued that in relation to improvident transactions "it is necessary to show

---

[62][1946] I.R. 35, 49.
[63](1877) 2 App. Cas. 814, see text with and in n.43 above.
[64][2000] 1 I.L.R.M. 210 (S.C.), affirming the decision of Shanley J. at [1998] 2 I.L.R.M. 218. (H.C.).

some unconscientious use of power by the stronger against the weaker".[65] It is clear from Denham J.'s judgment that this proposition, taken from *Hart v. O'Connor*, does not represent the law in Ireland. Denham J. followed *Grealish v. Murphy* and drew significant parallels with Gavan Duffy J.'s treatment of the facts and the appeal before her. While Carroll Senior was not, like Peter Grealish, mentally deficient, the loss of his wife and ill health were factors that contributed to the depression and general debilitation that affected Carroll Senior. Like Peter Grealish's solicitor, the solicitor acting in the Carroll transfer was not aware of the underlying circumstances; indeed the solicitor was in essence working for Carroll Junior and he failed for this reason to read over the transaction and explain it to Carroll Senior. Finally, the Carroll transaction was clearly improvident. The "consideration" provided by Carroll Junior (clearance of V.A.T. debts from the trading profits of the business) was inadequate, and the fact that Carroll Senior did not retain a right of maintenance and support mirror the significance of Peter Grealish's failure to make the transfer to Murphy contingent or revocable in nature.[66] Denham J., citing with apparent approval[67] Counsel's submissions on the relevance of the facts in *Grealish v. Murphy* to the instant case, said:

> [Counsel] submitted that the improvidence argument revolves around *Grealish v. Murphy* with the adjustment of a single fact one can demonstrate the improvidence. If Thomas Carroll Senior survived until today, when his daughter-in-law had remarried and had a family, then Thomas Carroll Senior would be a sick, depressed and disabled man with no security for his care or medical care.[68]

There is a further parallel with *Grealish v. Murphy*. It has been argued above that it would have been possible for that transaction to be set aside because of repudiatory breach of the contract by Murphy; his conduct in managing the affairs of the plaintiff in such a way as to dissipate the plaintiff's assets could, in my view, have been a separate ground for granting rescission of the contract. In *Carroll v. Carroll* the physical and emotional state of Carroll Senior constituted a level of disability that could raise a suspicion that he was unaware of the financial situation the business was in, and unable to properly appreciate

---

[65] [2000] 1 I.L.R.M. 210, 219 referring to *Hart v. O'Connor*.
[66] This was a significant feature in *Lydon v. Coyne* (1946) 12 Ir. Jur. Rep. 64; see also *J.H. v W.J.H* High Court, unreported, December 20, 1979, Keane J.; *Noonan v. O'Connell*, High Court, unreported, April 10, 1987, Lynch J.
[67] [2000] 1 I.L.R.M. 210, 219 *per* Denham J.
[68] [2000] 1 I.L.R.M. 210, 221 *per* Denham J. In *Gregg v. Kidd* [1965] I.R. 183 (H.C.), Budd J., having set aside a transfer from an uncle to a nephew on the grounds of undue influence, went on, like Denham J. in *Carroll*, to hold that the transaction was also improvident ([1965] I.R. 183, 205-207); see also *O'Flanagan v. Ray-Ger* (1963-1993) Ir.Co.L.Rep. 289 (H.C.) 300 *per* Costello J.

the essential nature of the disposition made to his son. The failure of the solicitor to read over the instrument to him (because he was acting on the instructions of Carroll Junior) and the subsequent conversations with his daughters, assuring them that they would be provided for, reinforce this inference. It is certainly arguable that the facts provide fertile ground for a plea of *non est factum*, and *Carroll v. Carroll* has significant points of contact with a recent High Court decision that left open a plea of *non est factum* to a depressed businessman signing a document while in a low mental and physical condition.[69] This point of contact further underlines the fact that cognitive failure and the substantive unfairness of the exchange are at the heart of the improvident bargain transaction jurisdiction, and that this does not necessarily involve or require a finding of victimisation or equitable fraud by the person benefiting under the transaction.

6. IMPROVIDENCE AND *O'BRIEN*

While the House of Lords, in *Barclays Bank v O'Brien*,[70] resisted the opportunity to resolve difficult areas of matrimonial law by carving out a specific equity for married persons and those in similar relationships, preferring instead to look to the concept of constructive notice, it may be that the *O'Brien* line of authority is already too complex to be intelligible, is somewhat inconsistent given its extension into relationships such as that in *Crédit Lyonnais Bank Nederland NV v. Burch*,[71] and is under attack for the limited number of cases in which relief is forthcoming. Perhaps *Grealish v. Murphy* affords an opportunity for a fresh start. If we begin from the proposition that *O'Brien* is only one kind of relationship in which an improvident transaction may result, and that the approach to be adopted by a court in deciding whether the parties (whether they be two party or three party transactions, the third party often being a lending institution) we can find much of utility in Gavan Duffy J.'s paternalism, even if his conclusion on the quality of legal advice needed to uphold an im-

---

[69] *Ted Castle McCormack & Co. Ltd. v. McCrystal* High Court, unreported, March 15, 1999, Morris P.

[70] [1994] 1 A.C. 180 (S.C.). The only reported Northern Ireland case in which *O'Brien* has been applied is *Northern Bank Ltd. v. McCarron* [1995] N.I. 258. It is submitted that the application of the improvident transaction jurisdiction into *O'Brien* relationships would have resulted in the *McCarron* case being decided differently. On this see Millett, above, n.19; see also Mee, "Consents, Guarantees and the 'Badge of Shame'" (1994) 16 *D.U.L.J.* (n.s.) 197.

[71] [1997] 1 All ER 144 (C.A.). It is significant that in this case Millett L.J. explored the usefulness of unconscionable bargain case-law but in so doing he focused on factors that are relevant to improvident transaction case-law, in particular the extent to which the security taken by the bank lacked proportionality, the disparity in terms of knowledge and expertise and the fact that the substantive nature of the transaction was breathtakingly one-sided.

provident transaction can be said to over-egg the pudding.[72] It is extremely significant that the High Court of Australia, in *Garcia v. National Australia Bank*[73] has declined to apply the "bright line" reasoning in *O'Brien*, preferring instead to examine the facts at bar for evidence of a failure to understand the transaction or some other cognitive failure. This *Garcia* approach is not an unconscionability doctrine in any real sense.

7. CONCLUSION

Grealish v. Murphy keeps alive that separate and distinct jurisdiction which protects the weak and the feckless from over-extending themselves via gifts and contracts that in their own terms are unwise and improvident, that are transactions that no person of ordinary intelligence would enter. The reason why the defendant was deprived of his bargain was because in the period between the agreement and its execution he clearly became aware of Peter's disability. Let us hope that the lessons of this singular case, taken from an Ireland that is in fact largely disappearing,[74] can be used in more modern everyday situations and that the improvident bargain jurisdiction is again seen as a broad and jurisdictionally representative line of authority across the common law world.

---

[72] See [1946] I.R. 35, 45-48 for the judge's explanation of what the solicitor should have been aware of for him 'properly' to advise Peter.

[73] (1998) 194 C.L.R. 395 (H.C.A.), giving new life to *Yerkey v. Jones* (1939) 63 C.L.R. 649 (H.C.A.); see Stone "Infants, Lunatics and Married Women: Equitable Protection in *Garcia v. National Australia Bank*" (1999) 62 *M.L.R.* 604.

[74] Though it has not yet entirely disappeared: in *Toibin v. Cassidy* High Court, unreported, November 3, 1998, Keane J. (sitting as a High Court Judge, on Circuit) held that a transaction by which a young man with a much younger mental age transferred his farm to a much older man was improvident.

DUSTING DOWN EQUITY'S ARMOUR
HIGH TREES (1947) IN PERSPECTIVE

OONAGH BREEN*

1. INTRODUCTION

> It is a principle of justice and equity. It comes to this: When a man, by his words or conduct, has led another to believe that he may safely act on the faith of them – and the other does act on them – he will not be allowed to go back on what he has said or done when it would be unjust or inequitable for him to do so.

Thus stated Lord Denning in his book, *The Discipline of the Law*,[1] summing up the significance as he saw it of the case of *Central London Property Trust Ltd v. High Trees House Ltd*[2] and the principles which have grown from this case. The concept of promissory estoppel encapsulated in Lord Denning's summary nowadays may not seem very remarkable in legal terms – being a principle that students of equity almost take for granted and something with which contract students have had to learn to live. However, in 1947, when Denning J., newly appointed to the King's Bench, handed down this decision, it caused quite a controversy and much academic ink, if not blood, was spilt debating its merits and significance.[3] Some critics claimed the decision was a direct threat to the doctrine of consideration and would undermine the fundamental basis of enforcement of contractual obligations.[4] Others played down its importance relegating the comments of Denning J. (as he then was) to mere *obiter dicta* – a point not lost on Lord Denning himself.[5]

---

*Lecturer in Law, University College, Dublin.

[1] Denning, *The Discipline of the Law* (Butterworths, London, 1979) 223.
[2] [1947] 1 K.B. 130 (Denning J.).
[3] See, for instance, the rather entertaining academic skirmishes between Megarry and Morris on the issue: "Notes" (1947) 63 *L.Q.R.* 278 (Megarry); "The Authority of the Central London and High Trees Case" (1948) 64 *L.Q.R.* 28 (Morris reply); and (1948) 64 *L.Q.R.* 29 (Megarry riposte).
[4] See, for instance, Spencer Bower and Turner, *Estoppel by Representation* (3rd ed., Butterworths, London, 1977) 383.
[5] In his memoirs, he noted "Whenever I speak to students, someone is sure to call out – '*High Trees*'. It is greeted with acclaim. This is very different from the reception it used to get in days past from the higher judiciary. Some of them treated it with reserve. Others with suspicion, even with silent disapproval. To this day, there are still traces of it." Denning, above n. 1, 199.

The sword once pulled from the stone, however, could not be sheathed and in unleashing the power of equity – often described initially as 'quasi-estoppel' or '*High Trees* estoppel', although ultimately becoming more universally known as 'promissory estoppel' – Denning gave new life to an equitable remedy which had lain virtually unnoticed since its debut appearance in *Hughes v. Metropolitan Railway Company* in 1877.[6] This reawakening was not limited to contract law, nor to the concept of promissory estoppel itself. Arguably, *High Trees* lit the spark which set lawyers and judges alike on a path of rediscovery of the nature of equitable estoppel and the scope and breadth of the remedy available to deserving litigants.

There is no doubt that a case from humble beginnings has weathered the storm of time and arguably earns its place in the annals of the leading cases of the twentieth century. It is a fitting tribute to Lord Denning that in his hundredth (and sadly, his last) year, no less than two of his judgments are listed on the roll call of honour for the century.[7]

2. THE CASE OF *HIGH TREES*

In common with other great cases of our time,[8] the facts which led to *High Trees* were very simple. In 1937 the defendants entered into a lease of a block of flats for 99 years at a rent of £2,500 per annum. With the outbreak of war, and unable to find tenants for the flats, they experienced difficulty meeting the rent. Following negotiations the landlord agreed in writing to reduce the rent to £1,250. By September 1945, with the tenants' return to London the flats were fully let once more and the landlord sought to recover the full rent of £2,500 from that date onwards. The defendants disputed the landlord's claim on a number of grounds: first, it was pleaded that the agreement for the rent reduction was to operate for the entire duration of the lease agreement. Second, they claimed that the landlord was estopped from demanding rent at the higher rate

---

[6] (1877) 2 App. Cas. 439 (H.L.); *cf.* the comments of Keane in *Equity and the Law of Trusts in the Republic of Ireland* (Butterworths, London, 1988) 323 where he notes that it would be an over simplification to say the principle remained completely dormant until Denning J.'s decision in 1947. On the other hand, a perusal of Kiely's *Principles of Equity* (Fodhla Printing Co. Ltd., Dublin, 1936) reveals not a single chapter on estoppel much less a mention of *Hughes* or the later case of *Birmingham and District Land Co. v. London and North Western Rly Co.* (1888) 40 Ch. D. 268 (C.A.).

[7] See *Mareva Compania Naviera S.A. of Panama v. International Bulk Carriers SA* [1975] 2 Lloyd's Rep. 509 (C.A.) discussed in Capper "The *Mareva* Injunction – From Birth to Adulthood. *Mareva Compania Naviera S.A. v. International Bulk Carriers* SA (1975)" below, 255–274.

[8] One need only mention the unsuspecting snail in the bottle of ginger beer which revolutionised the law of negligence (*Donoghue v. Stevenson* [1932] A.C. 562 (H.L.) discussed in Hedley "*McAlister (or Donoghue) (Pauper) v. Stevenson* (1932)" above, 64–79); or the fluoridation of water which opened up the expanse of unenumerated fundamental rights (*Ryan v. Attorney General* [1965] I.R. 294 (H.C. and S.C.)).

or, alternatively had waived its right to do so in respect of arrears prior to the date of its letter in September 1945.

The core issue for the Court was the enforceability and scope of the landlord's promise to accept a lower rent. Being an agreement ostensibly without consideration meant no remedy lay for the defendants in contract. The law on the matter left no room for doubt in so far as payment by a debtor of a lesser sum for a greater, even if accepted by a creditor, did not amount to satisfaction of the debt and to this extent did not bind the latter.[9] With regard to the law of estoppel as it then stood, it was well established that an estoppel could only arise in relation to a representation as to existing fact.[10] The representation in this case was a promise not to insist upon full payment in the future and thus related not to existing fact but rather to a future representation. Thus two seemingly insurmountable common law barriers appeared to bar the tenants' claim in reliance on the landlord's promise – the rule in *Pinnel's Case* and the authority of *Jorden v. Money*. In spite of this, Denning J., while holding that the plaintiff was entitled to the full rent from the date of its September letter onwards, opined that had the landlord sought to claims arrears for the entire period in breach of the original promise it would have been unsuccessful. It is this finding which caused all the controversy – an *obiter dictum* of a first instance judge, flying in the face of the established law, which not alone has been cited as persuasive precedent in many foreign jurisdictions but which undoubtedly has influenced the rebirth and consequent development of the principle of equitable estoppel.

3. GROUND BREAKING IN ITS TIME? – THE LAW BEFORE *HIGH TREES*

Before embarking on an examination of the reasoning in *High Trees* it is instructive to note the weight of judicial precedent against such a result. Denning J.'s decision was far from inevitable. Indeed, it must be remembered that both *Pinnel* and *Jorden* survived not only *High Trees* but many later forays in the judicial arena,[11] although it may be said that the problems created by them have all but been overcome, given the development of the doctrine of promissory estoppel.[12]

---

[9] See the rule in *Pinnels Case* (1602) 5 Co. Rep. 117a. It was applied in Ireland in *Drogheda Corporation v. Fairtlough* (1858) 8 Ir.C.L.R. 98 (Q.B., Ir.) and approved by the House of Lords in *Foakes v. Beer* (1884) 9 App. Cas. 605 (H.L.).

[10] *Jorden v. Money* (1854) 5 H.L.C. 185.

[11] See, for example, the decision of the Court of Appeal in *D & C Builders Ltd. v. Rees* [1966] 2 Q.B. 617 (C.A.) where the majority of the Court applied *Foakes v. Beer*, and more recently *Re Selectmove* [1995] 2 All E.R. 53 (C.A.), cited in Clark, *Contract Law in Ireland* (4th ed., Round Hall, Sweet & Maxwell, Dublin, 1998) 59.

[12] Note the comments of Deane J in *Waltons Stores (Interstate) Ltd. v. Maher* (1988) 164 C.L.R. 387 (H.C.A.) 452 that *Jorden v. Money* no longer represents good law in Australia.

The rule in *Pinnel's Case*, although originating in the 1600s, received the approval of the House of Lord's in 1884 in the case of *Foakes v. Beer*, surviving intact subject to certain exceptions,[13] none of which were relevant in the situation arising in *High Trees*. The rationale underlying the rule in *Pinnel* is the necessity for consideration – the debtor already owing the creditor does not provide any new consideration through the part payment of an existing debt.[14]

The decision in *Jorden* is rather more problematic. It will be recalled that in this case the unfortunate plaintiff, Mr Money, had married his fiancée on the strength of the defendant's oral promise not to enforce a debt against him. Upon her subsequent revival of the judgement against him, Money went to the Chancery Courts essentially pleading estoppel. While his claim was successful before Lord Romilly MR, the Court of Appeal split, Knight-Bruce L.J. siding with Lord Romilly while Cranworth L.J. was in favour of allowing the appeal. The House of Lords by a majority, consisting of Lord Brougham and Lord Cranworth (who had been elevated in the meantime and therefore afforded another opportunity to put forward his view) found against the plaintiff, while Lord St Leonards vigorously dissented. As Meagher, Gummow and Lehane[15] point out: even though the plaintiff carried with him Lords Romilly, Knight-Bruce and St Leonard, as opposed to Lords Brougham and Cranworth (who favoured the defendant), at the end of the day judgment still went in favour of the latter, given Lord Cranworth's second bite at the cherry in the House of Lords – prompting the above writers to comment that "such a decision can have little to recommend it as a precedent".[16] This view has found favour with academics from other quarters.[17]

---

[13] Such as where a creditor's claim is disputed (*Cooper v. Parker* (1885) 15 C.B. 822 (Ex.Ch.)); where an unliquidated claim is involved (*Wilkinson v. Byers* (1834) 1 A.&E. 106 (K.B.)); or where there has either been part payment by a third party on behalf of the debtor or the debtor has refrained from enforcing a cross-claim of his or her own on the strength of the creditor's promise to accept part payment. On this latter point see *Brikom Investments Ltd. v. Carr* [1979] Q.B. 467 (C.A.) below.

[14] It must be said that Denning J.'s apparent flight in the face of the rule in *Pinnel's Case* in *High Trees* has been the source of much criticism by common law lawyers who cast a very jaundiced eye on *High Trees* as an authority on this ground. Indeed, Denning J. recognised in "Recent Developments in the Doctrine of Consideration" (1952) 15 *M.L.R.* 1, 4 that *Pinnel* as affirmed in *Foakes v. Beer* must still be applied in determining the "strict legal rights of the parties". However, he went on to cast doubt on his critics, critically commenting that "strict legal rights are always capable of being modified by the interposition of equity and that this what has happened in the discharge of contracts. The courts have repeatedly invoked equitable principles so as to neutralise ill effects of the common law doctrine of consideration."

[15] *Equity, Doctrines & Remedies* (3rd ed., Butterworths, Sydney, 1992).

[16] *ibid.*, 410. Indeed, more alarming still is the anecdotal evidence that Lord Brougham, on one of his sporadic visits from Cannes, missed some of the actual hearing himself!

[17] Sutton, *Consideration Reconsidered* (University of Queensland Press, 1974) 49 highlights the "logical difficulties implicit in the decision of *Jorden v. Money*" from the sheer impossibility of drawing a valid distinction between representations of fact and intention in some cases to the pertinent question as to what is the logical justification for drawing such a distinction, assuming

4. The Judgment in *High Trees* – Time Waits for No Man

4.1 The judgment itself

Using the opportunity presented to him, Denning J. did not limit his comments to the actual claim made by the plaintiffs in *High Trees*.[18] Instead, he considered what would have been the position if the plaintiff had claimed for arrears right back to date of the original promise. The learned judge stated,

> The law has not stood still since *Jorden v. Money*. There has been a series of decisions over the last fifty years which, although they are said to be cases of estoppel are not really such. They are cases in which a promise was made which was intended to create legal relations and which, to the knowledge of the person making the promise, was going to be acted on by the person to whom it was made, and which was in fact so acted on.[19]

Further on in his judgment, he explained why these instances constituted examples of promissory estoppel:

> The courts have not gone so far as to give a cause of action in damages for the breach of such promise, but they have refused to allow the party making it to act inconsistently with it. It is in that sense, and that sense only, that such a promise gives rise to an estoppel.[20]

Clearly, the principle relied upon by the learned judge was not new law, but rather had lain virtually dormant for over half a century. The cases referred to concerned contractual relations in which subsequent dealings between the parties had resulted either in acquiescence or waiver in respect of legal rights by

---

that it can be done. Moreover, he points to the fact that the majority decision in *Jorden* was not immediately accepted, running counter as it did to the accepted wisdom at the time (as illustrated by a line of authority, starting with *Hammersley v. De Biel* (1845) 12 Cl.&F. 45 (H.L.)), that the courts could indeed give effect to "representations of intention inducing action in reliance thereon to his detriment by the representee" (44-45). *cf.* the more recent views of Atiyah in *Essays on Contract* (Clarendon Press, 1986) where he comments that "*Jorden v. Money*, far from being (as the new orthodoxy would have it) a difficult obstacle in the way of recognition of promissory estoppel, is a clear indication that promissory estoppel was never necessary at all" (238). He argues that *Money*, unable to produce written evidence of Jorden's promise in consideration of marriage, as required by the Statute of Frauds, sought to evade the Statute by reliance on estoppel. Justifying the House of Lord's rejection of the plaintiff's claim he concludes that such a decision was necessary to avoid untold damage to the Statute, noting that, "[h]ad *Jorden v. Money* gone the other way, the result might well have been to confine the Statute of Frauds to executory contracts" (235).

[18] The landlords in friendly proceedings sought only to recover arrears from the date on which they had informed the defendants of their intention to require payment of the full rent.

[19] [1947] 1 K.B. 130, 134.

[20] *ibid.*

one party or acts of forbearance which made it inequitable for that party now to insist upon his or her legal rights. Interestingly enough, half of them had arisen in the context of landlord and tenant law.[21]

Perhaps the classic statement of promissory estoppel had been laid down 70 years earlier in the House of Lords decision in *Hughes v. Metropolitan Railways* – decided four years after the passing of the Judicature Act and twenty years after *Jorden*. In October 1874, the landlord had served repair notices on the respondent tenants allowing six months for certain work to be carried out. The tenants in November of that year offered to surrender their interest to the appellant for £3,000. While there was no consensus on the amount, the appellant indicated his willingness to enter into negotiations on the matter. With the negotiations proving unfruitful and just two days of the notice period remaining the tenants opted to carry out the necessary repairs. The landlord, however, claimed upon the expiry of the remaining days that they had forfeited the lease for breach of the covenant of repair as the six months lapsed. Against this forfeiture the respondents sought relief.

At the time of *Hughes*, in the absence of special circumstances, such as mistake or fraud, equity had no jurisdiction to grant relief against forfeiture incurred in such circumstances.[22] On the evidence, no such special circumstances were present in this case. Nevertheless, the House of Lords, upholding the Court of Appeal's decision, found that because the appellant had unconditionally entered into negotiations with the respondents and even though there was no intention on its part to mislead them, its actions had placed it in a position where it would be inequitable to insist on its strict forfeiture rights. The House of Lords led by Lord Chancellor Cairns, held that,

> [I]t is the first principle upon which all Courts of Equity proceed, that if parties who have entered into definite and distinct terms involving certain legal results – certain penalties or legal forfeiture – afterwards by their own act or with their own consent enter upon a course of negotiation which has the effect of leading one of the parties to suppose that the strict rights arising under the contract will not be enforced, or will be kept in suspense, or held in abeyance, the person who otherwise might have enforced those rights will not be allowed to enforce them where it would be inequitable having regard to the dealings which have thus taken place between the parties.[23]

---

[21] Of the four cases cited in this regard, two, *Buttery v. Pickard* (1945) 174 L.T. 144 (K.B.), and *Fenner v. Blake* [1900] 1 Q.B. 426 (Q.B.), concerned landlord and tenant disputes.

[22] The case was decided a good seven years before s.14 of the Conveyancing Act 1881 was enacted, which provided not only for the service of forfeiture notices setting out the breach and how it may be remedied, but also for relief against such forfeiture in appropriate circumstances (s.14(2)).

[23] (1877) 2 App. Cas. 439, 448. See also (1877) 2 App. Cas. 439, 452 *per* Lord Blackburn.

Given the absence of authority in the judgment for this proposition, it is arguable that this is the *fons et origo* of the principle. Shortly after *Hughes*, the Court of Appeal in *Birmingham and District Land Co. v. London & North Western Railway* further developed the concept making it clear that the principle was applicable to contract law generally and not just limited to cases of forfeiture for breach of covenant.[24] Moreover, their Lordships introduced the notion of *restitutio integrum* as a defence to the imposition of an estoppel, though notably in both cases the word 'estoppel' is not mentioned by their Lordships.

Five years prior to *High Trees*, Denning himself, had unsuccessfully advanced a similar argument himself as King's Counsel in *Salisbury (Marquess) v. Gilmore* to the effect that, "if a person with a contractual right against another induces that other to believe that it will not be enforced, he will not be allowed to enforce that right without at any rate putting that other party into the position that he was in before".[25] MacKinnon L.J., while sympathetic to the arguments before him, felt bound by what he referred to as the 'voices of infallibility' in the House of Lords in *Jorden*.

As a judge, however, Denning had more success. Placing his reliance both on the fusion of equity and law under the Supreme Court of Judicature Act, 1873 and the authority of *Hughes* to overcome the difficulties of *Jorden* and *Pinnel*, he experienced little difficulty in holding that the written promise between the parties was binding. Arguably, the language used by both Cairns L.C. and Bowen L.J. in *Hughes* and *Birmingham District Land Co* respectively, was broad enough to encapsulate representations as to future facts. Of course, the House of Lords in both would have been very much bound by *Jorden* – hence Denning J.'s necessity to couch these earlier cases not so much as estoppel cases (and thereby governed by the tenets of *Jorden*), but rather as promissory cases – a separate but related category to which more lenient rules could and indeed did apply.[26]

---

[24](1888) 40 Ch. D. 268, where Bowen L.J. quoted Lord Cairns and continued:
   The truth is that the proposition is wider than cases of forfeiture. It seems to me to amount to this, that if persons who have contractual rights against others induce by their conduct those against whom they have such rights to believe that such rights will either not be enforced or will be kept in suspense or abeyance for some particular time, those persons will not be allowed by a Court of Equity to enforce the rights until such time has elapsed, without at all events placing the parties in the same position as they were before. That is the principle to be applied. ((1888) 40 Ch. D. 268, 286).

[25][1942] 2 K.B. 38 (C.A.) – yet another landlord and tenant case.

[26]Denning J.'s penchant for skirting legal authorities contrary to his own viewpoint is well documented. Indeed, the judge has commented extra-judicially that, "I never say 'I regret having to come to this conclusion but I have no option.' There is always a way round. There is always an option – in my philosophy – by which justice can be done". *The Family Story* (Butterworths, London, 1981) 208.

4.2 The Scope of the Promise

Finding the promise to be binding, the judge turned his attention to its scope. Holding that in the circumstances the reduction was intended as a temporary arrangement to alleviate prevailing tenancy conditions, he found that these circumstances had changed by 1945 and significantly the promise was understood by all parties only to apply in this manner. Therefore, while the plaintiff could properly claim the full rent from the date the flats were full, had it sought to claim arrears prior to this date, Equity would have prevented such recovery. The judge concluded by reiterating the principle that "a promise intended to be binding, intended to be acted on, and in fact acted on, is binding so far as its terms properly apply". [27]

And thus was reborn the principle of promissory estoppel.

5. THE DECISION OF DENNING – THE VIEW FROM THE FLOOR

It is interesting to note the initial reaction of writers to the *High Trees* decision. Blundell, for instance, considered that it should be studied "as a leading case on the principles of contract law".[28] Stating that Denning's decision had provided "much food for thought"[29] he pondered whether the decision if considered sound law, would result in "a not inconsiderable break [being] made in the traditional doctrine of consideration and a way found of enforcing a gratuitous promise to take part of a debt in lieu of the whole".[30] Megarry, on the other hand, was much more scathing. An interesting feature of the case, according to him, was that all the important bits were *obiter*, causing him to comment, "Such a decision seems scarcely reportable, much less epoch making"![31] Cheshire and Fifoot, for their part, writing in 1947, welcomed the decision on the whole.[32] Noting that equity was concerned with justice being done and unlike the common law "refuse[d] to be diverted by doctrinal and technical difficulties",[33] they viewed *High Trees* as a simplification of the principles relating to waiver, forbearance and variation. Embracing the decision, they stated that:

---

[27][1947] 1 K.B. 130, 136.

[28]"Landlord and Tenant Cases" [1946] *Conveyancer* 128, 128.

[29]*ibid.*, 131.

[30]*ibid.*, 131.

[31]"Notes" (1947) 63 *L.Q.R.* 278. Indeed, Megarry goes on to refer to *Buttery v. Pickard* (1945) 174 L.T. 144 (K.B.), in which he points out the issue actually arose and that Humphreys J. "held that the landlord could not subsequently claim rent at a rate higher than the reduced rate". Commenting on the fact that the case was never fully reported, he stated that this was "no doubt [because] the *ratio* expressed in that case was less striking than the *obiter* excursion in the later case [of *High Trees*]'. *cf.* the views of Wilson on the authority of *Buttery* in "Recent Developments in Estoppel" (1951) 67 *L.Q.R.* 330, 343.

[32]"*Central London Property Trust Ltd. v. High Trees House Ltd.*" (1947) 63 *L.Q.R.* 283.

[33]*ibid.*, 300.

Equity must be administered in all courts, and as we have seen equity holds a contracting party to a forbearance that he has granted, whenever the other party has assumed it to be a firm undertaking and has proceeded on that assumption. This equitable principle is capable, if resolutely followed, of making this part of the law intelligible without resort to artificial distinctions, and in particular of circumventing the unnecessary and technical distinction between fact and promise which has confined the doctrine of estoppel within arbitrary limits.[34]

The commentary engendered by the decision in *High Trees* is quite remarkable[35] when one considers that it was a first instance decision by a judge of six months, delivered ex tempore, in which the main comments of note were arguably unnecessary to decide the issue in question.[36] And yet the comments of Denning J. (as he then was) appeared to act as a catalyst in academic and judicial circles. Lawyers began to debate anew the very fundamentals of contract law which had appeared to be set in stone at the turn of the twentieth century. Issues ranged from the need for contractual promises to be supported by consideration; the criteria which should apply in the discharge of such contracts; and whether those standards should vary depending on the means of discharge adopted – namely variation, forbearance or waiver. The debate did not remain within the remit of the English courts, however, a fact to which the law reports bear witness. Not all of the cases approved of *High Trees*. In fact, very many did not. However, *High Trees* was the starting point and from it was hewn the principle with which we are familiar today.

6. THE VIEW FROM THE BENCH – REVIVED FROM THE EMBERS BUT NOT CAST IN STONE

As with any new legal concept, following *High Trees*, promissory estoppel became for a time, the great New Hope for all potential litigants.[37] Perhaps the judiciary was wary of this, considering its potential to undermine contract law; perhaps a period of time was necessary for its implications to pan out. Whatever the reason, the opinion of one Irish writer that there prevailed a certain

---

[34] *ibid.*, 300-301.

[35] Apart from those writers cited above, see also Wilson, "Recent Developments in Estoppel" (1951) 67 *L.Q.R.* 330; Sheridan, "Equitable Estoppel Today" (1952) 15 *M.L.R.* 325; and Denning himself "Recent Developments in the Doctrine of Consideration" (1952) 15 *M.L.R.* 1.

[36] *cf.* the views of Morris, "The Authority of the Central London and High Trees Case" (1948) 64 *L.Q.R.* 193.

[37] Very much in the same way in which legitimate expectation is now frequently pleaded by litigants since the Supreme Court's decision in *Webb v. Ireland* [1988] I.R. 372 (S.C.).

judicial conservatism and resistance to change carries weight when the authorities are considered.[38]

One of the first restatements came about in *Combe v. Combe*,[39] when the Court of Appeal, was forced to reaffirm the very boundaries of the principle. The plaintiff sought to enforce a promise, made by her divorced husband between the decree *nisi* and the decree absolute, to pay her £100 a year maintenance. In reliance upon this promise but not in consideration of it, the wife had forborne from seeking maintenance in court. The defendant failed to pay and seven years later the plaintiff sued for arrears. Was the defendant estopped from denying the promise on the basis of *High Trees*? The Court of Appeal, in reversing the High Court's decision, held that he was not.[40] Stating the importance of not stretching *High Trees* principle too far, "lest it should be endangered",[41] Denning L.J. pointed out that the principle did not create new causes of action where none had existed before. The absence of consideration at the time of the promise meant that there was nothing for the court to enforce. Re-emphasising the need for consideration in cases of this ilk, and stating that that doctrine would well withstand the onslaught of *High Trees*, "being too firmly fixed to be overthrown by a sidewind",[42] Denning commented that:

> Its ill-effects have been largely mitigated of late, but it still remains a cardinal necessity of the formation of a contract, though not of its modification or discharge.[43]

In spite of the Court of Appeal's restatement in *Combe v. Combe*, the disinclination on the part of the House of Lords to follow it four years later is clear from the comments of Lord Simonds in *Tool Metal Manufacturing Ltd*, who in the course of his judgment stated:

> I would not have it supposed, particularly in commercial transactions, that mere acts of indulgence are apt to create rights, and I do not wish to lend the authority of this House to the statement of the principle which is to be found in *Combe v. Combe* and may well be far too widely stated.[44]

---

[38] See Brady, "A Case of Promissory Estoppel in Ireland" (1970) V *Ir. Jur. (n.s.)* 296.

[39] [1951] 2 K.B. 215 (C.A.). The case is a good illustration of the maxim which law students quote at will, namely that promissory estoppel acts as a shield and not a sword. It was followed in the New Zealand case *P. v. P.* [1957] N.Z.L.R. 854, discussed text after n. 55 below.

[40] It was not an insignificant fact that the plaintiff commanded a far larger salary than the defendant did and so there was no apparent injustice in denying her the arrears she sought. Denning L.J. made the point that if her financial situation were to change in the future she could make an application for maintenance to the divorce court. Such an application would have been pointless at the date of the action given the parties' respective salaries.

[41] [1951] 2 K.B. 215, 219.

[42] *ibid.*, 220.

[43] *ibid.*

[44] *Tool Metal Manufacturing Ltd v. Tungsten Electric Co. Ltd.* [1955] 1 W.L.R. 761 (H.L.) 764.

Indeed, Atiyah has commented that given Lord Simonds' remarks, "the success of the *High Trees* principle may well have depended on the fact that it did not reach the House of Lords while [he] held sway".[45]

Similarly, the *High Trees* principle ran the gauntlet of judicial conservatism in *Brikom Investments Ltd v. Carr*.[46] In this case, certain tenants and their assignees were sued for contributions in respect of roof repairs carried out by the landlords which the latter claimed were due under the express terms of the lease. The defendants claimed an estoppel based on the plaintiffs' representations that they would bear the cost of the repairs on this occasion, particularly given that on the basis of these assurances, the tenants had entered into 99-year leases. While Lord Denning M.R. was happy to uphold the decision of the County Court by applying *High Trees*, he was equally prepared to extend the principle to cover not only the original promisees but also anyone who took in good faith from such a person. In his inimitable style, he explained:

> It was suggested that if assignees are able to rely on an oral or written representation (not contained in the deeds) it would cause chaos and confusion among conveyancers. No one buying property would know where he stood. I am not disturbed by those forebodings. I prefer to see that justice is done: and let the conveyancers look after themselves. Suppose that the landlords here...had assigned their reversion to a purchaser: and then that purchaser had sought to recover the contribution from the tenant – contrary to the promise made by the original landlords. It would be most unfair if he could go back on the promise. Equity would not allow him to do it. Now if the assignee of the reversion takes subject to the *burden* of the estoppel, so also the assignee of the tenant should take subject to the *benefit* of it.[47]

In complete contrast, however, Roskill L.J. (with Cumming-Bruce L.J. concurring for the most part) made great efforts to distance himself from what he referred to as "the somewhat uncertain doctrine of promissory estoppel".[48] Disagreeing that the benefits and burdens of the promise in this case "ran down both sides",[49] he was satisfied to find for the defendants on the ground that there existed between the parties a perfectly good collateral warranty in relation to the repairs.

---

[45]This seems to be in spite of the fact that Lord Simonds was responsible for *Re Porter* [1937] 2 All E.R. 361 (Ch.D.), upon which Denning relied in *High Trees*! See Atiyah, "Contract and Tort" in Jowell & McAuslan, (eds.), *Lord Denning: the Judge and the Law* (Sweet & Maxwell, London, 1984) p. 29 at p. 33. In *The Discipline of the Law* Denning remarked that such an appeal could have ruined everything (above n. 1, 205).
[46][1979] 1 Q.B. 467 (C.A.).
[47][1979] 1 Q.B. 467, 484.
[48][1979] 1 Q.B. 467, 490.
[49][1979] 1 Q.B. 467, 486.

It is worthwhile to note the views of Roskill L.J. on promissory estoppel. It would seem from his comments in *Brikom* that he very much viewed the doctrine to be yet another creation from Denning's stable of law reform, bred not from precedent but rather from that unruly strain of justice *inter partes*. Citing Cairns L.C. in *Hughes*, he described the former's comments as more "an illustration of contractual variation of strict contractual rights",[50] although he did concede that one might view it as "an illustration of equity relieving from the consequences of strict adherence to the letter of the lease".[51] Roskill L.J. was prepared to accept that the courts would not allow a promisor to suddenly seek to enforce his rights where he had led a party to believe that the strict legal terms of a contract will not be enforced against him. He argued, however, that this result would be the same in both common law and equity and could be achieved without resort to promissory estoppel. One could reasonably wonder whether this is not just estoppel by another name?

The difficulties espoused in *Brikom* in relation to promissory estoppel were not isolated. Indeed, the House of Lords itself had similarly expressed its reservations with regard to the development of the doctrine, seven years earlier. Commenting on its expansion in *Woodhouse v. Nigerian Produce Ltd,* Hailsham L.C. remarked:

> I desire to add that the time may soon come when the whole sequence of cases based on promissory estoppel since the war, beginning with *Central London Property Trust Ltd v. High Trees House Ltd* may need to be reviewed and reduced to a coherent body of doctrine by the courts. I do not mean to say that they are to be regarded with suspicion. But as is common with an expanding doctrine they do raise problems of coherent exposition which have never been systematically explored.[52]

The subsequent exploration of this 'expanding doctrine' has led some jurisdictions to advocate and indeed implement a merger of the different forms of estoppel under the common banner of 'equitable estoppel'. This turn of events, while supported by some English judges has not received overwhelming support.[53] Similarly in Ireland, the jury is still out on the advisability of such a move, although current writers seem very much opposed to such a development.[54]

---

[50] [1979] 1 Q B 467, p.489.

[51] *ibid.*

[52] [1972] A.C. 741 (H.L.) 758.

[53] *cf.* current academic opinion in Australia where such a development has been welcomed: Parkinson, "Equitable Estoppel: Developments after *Walton Stores (Interstate) v. Maher*" (1990) 3 *J.C.L.* 50; Clark, "The Swordbearer has Arrived: Promissory Estoppel and *Waltons Stores (Interstate) v. Maher*" (1987-89) 9 *U.T.L.R.* 68.

[54] See Coughlan, "Swords, Shields and Estoppel Licences" (1993) 15 *D.U.L.J.* (*n.s.*) 188; Mee, "Lost in the big house: where stands Irish law on equitable estoppel?" (1998) XXIII *Ir. Jur.*

7. THE ACCEPTANCE OF HIGH TREES IN OTHER JURISDICTIONS

The same reluctance to take on board *High Trees* was not evidenced in other jurisdictions and there developed a corpus of case law radiating from the promissory estoppel doctrine espoused by Denning. This acceptance was not uncritical, however, and many of the later authorities refined the situations in which estoppel could be said to arise. The true significance of *High Trees*, in this respect, would seem to be that it provided a platform for the revitalisation of the doctrine. The scope of this revival was not limited to landlord and tenant law, neither was it strictly restricted to promissory estoppel itself but embraced the much wider concept of equitable estoppel. Nowhere was this more evident than in Australia and New Zealand where the judiciary from a very early stage realised the potential of such a doctrine.

In *P. v. P.*,[55] the New Zealand High Court applied the principles set out in *High Trees* in a matrimonial dispute. In this case, a husband had agreed to pay maintenance to his wife under a deed of separation. Upon their subsequent divorce, the Public Trustee wrongly informed the husband that the order cancelled his obligation to maintain his insane ex-wife, save for any arrears owing prior to the date of the court order. The husband therefore, paid off the remaining balance and took no further action. Upon the Public Trustee's discovery of his mistake, some four and a half years later, he sought to recover additional arrears from the husband. McGregor J. approached the case by asking three questions: firstly, could the defendant point to a representation made by the plaintiff that her strict contractual rights would not be enforced; if yes, could the defendant show he had acted upon such a representation. If both requirements could be satisfied by the person setting up the estoppel, in the words of the learned judge, "it is then for the court to decide whether it would be inequitable to allow the party seeking so to do to enforce the strict rights which he has induced the other party to believe will not be enforced."[56] As Sheridan points out in his case note on *P.*, the approach adopted by McGregor J. has the advantage of allowing the court decide cases on an individual basis without the creation of an inflexible rule.[57] While English Chancery lawyers were arguably far

---

(*n.s.*) 187. *cf.* the views of O'Dell, "Estoppel and *Ultra Vires* Contracts" (1992) 14 *D.U.L.J.* (*n.s.*) 123.

[55] [1957] N.Z.L.R. 854 (H.C. N.Z.).

[56] *ibid.*, 859.

[57] Sheridan, *"High Trees* in New Zealand" (1958) 21 *M.L.R.* 185, 186: "Doubtless promissory estoppel will most frequently succeed where there is detriment to the promisee in reliance on the original representation. It is submitted, however, that enforcement of the original obligation may be inequitable without any detriment (in the narrow sense), and that the categories of what is inequitable can never be closed." The truth of Sheridan's comments can be seen in *High Trees* itself, as Denning has himself commented extra-judicially that it is difficult to find any detriment where the tenant there remained on faith of the landlord's promise. If anything it was a benefit to the latter: Denning, above n.14, 6.

too conservative in their approach to equitable principles at the time,[58] there is no evidence of a similar reserve in the judgments of their foreign counterparts.

Indeed, as early on as 1956, the New Zealand courts made use of *High Trees* to breathe life into another form of equitable estoppel – proprietary estoppel. In *Thomas v. Thomas,*[59] the plaintiff brought an action under the Married Women's Property Act 1952 seeking to have her husband's interest in the family home transferred to her. The house had been purchased in their joint names but shortly after they moved in the defendant deserted the plaintiff informing her that she could have the house. The plaintiff took over payment of the mortgage instalments and the issue before the court was whether the plaintiff could claim entitlement to the property or whether she would have to wait for the husband to return and seek repossession before an estoppel would arise in her favour. The Supreme Court found in the wife's favour. Gresson J. on behalf of the court cited the case of *Dillwyn v. Llewelyn,*[60] an authority which along with that of *Ramsden v. Dyson*[61] had been much over-looked by the courts in the intervening years. Describing *Dillwyn* as a "case of equitable estoppel by acquiescence"[62] the judge held it to be a good authority for the use of estoppel as a sword and not merely as a shield. The fact that the promise to the wife was verbal and unsupported by consideration at the time of its making was not fatal to her case. It was intended to be binding, intended to be acted upon and most importantly the wife had subsequently acted upon it in paying the mortgage and other associated outgoings. In ordering a transfer of the property into the sole name of the plaintiff, Gresson J. stated:

> I think therefore that I can decide this case upon a principle well recog-
> nised in equity and akin to the principle explained by Lord Cairns in
> *Hughes v. Metropolitan Rly* and emphasised in *Central London Property
> Trust Ltd. v. Hightrees House Ltd,* [*sic.*] and justifying me in holding that
> a supervening equity in favour of the wife arose from the expenditure of
> money by her on the faith of the husband's abandonment to her of his
> interest in the property. If the transaction had been one between strangers
> where an owner surrendered his property to another by parol and that
> other on the strength of that surrendering built upon it, equity would not
> allow such owner to act inconsistently with the agreement. It would in
> fact give any support to such an arrangement short of giving a cause of

---

[58] By way of illustration one need only refer to Baker's comments in "The Future of Equity" (1977) 93 *L.Q.R.* 529 where he noted with satisfaction that the minority in *Donoghue v. Stevenson* had trained at the Chancery Bar.
[59] [1956] N.Z.L.R. 785 (N.Z. S.C.).
[60] (1862) 4 De G.F.&J. 517 (H.L.).
[61] (1866) L.R. 1 H.L. 129.
[62] [1956] N.Z.L.R. 785, 793.

action for damages for breach of it. . . . Estoppel in equity gives rise to substantive right in that it may operate to divest a party of title.[63]

It is interesting to note that these Antipodean equity decisions were prepared to consider both promissory and proprietary estoppel authorities almost interchangeably from the very start. The significance of this is that attention is focused on the creation of a supervening equity, the protection of which requires equitable relief, regardless of whether promissory or proprietary estoppel is pleaded. Arguably, this view of equity's role, focussing as it does upon the inequitable or perhaps even unconscionable conduct of the party rather than the form of action, paved the way for the merger of equitable estoppel in Australia in the late 1980s.

Interestingly, the decision credited in Australia with the express acceptance of promissory estoppel, *Legione v. Hateley*, was only handed down in 1982 by the Australian High Court.[64] In the course of their judgment, Mason and Deane JJ. in reviewing not only those early English authorities but also early Australian pronouncements[65] on the doctrine of estoppel, commented:

> The clear trend of recent authorities, the rationale of the general principle underlying estoppel in pais, established equitable principle and the legitimate search for justice and consistency under the law combine to persuade us to conclude that promissory estoppel should be acceptable in Australia as applicable between parties in such a relationship. [66]

The Australian courts are singular in their commentary in that they disavow any "forced reconciliation"[67] of the law existing prior and subsequent to *High Trees*. In the words of Mason and Deane JJ. a choice has to be made between the situation prevailing in *Jorden* and "the clear acceptance... of a doctrine of promissory estoppel which may operate to preclude the enforcement of rights at least between parties in a pre-existing contractual relationship".[68] In pragmatic terms, there is much to recommend such a view. The very operation of promissory estoppel results in a departure from the *Jorden* scenario. Moreover,

---

[63] *ibid.*, 794.

[64] (1983) 152 C.L.R. 406 (H.C.A.).

[65] *Thompson v. Palmer* (1933) 49 C.L.R. 507 (H.C.A.) and *Grundt v. Great Boulder Pty. Gold Mines Ltd.* (1937) 59 C.L.R. 641 (H.C.A.) – both cases preceding *High Trees* in which Dixon J. considered the nature of estoppel and the circumstances in which it operated. While the principles put forward in these cases are conceptually similar to that in *High Trees*, the High Court was quick to point out in *Legione* that it is not fully clear whether Dixon J. meant his references to extend to situations of future fact, particularly given the 'compelling authority' of *Jorden v. Money* at the time.

[66] (1983) 152 C.L.R. 406, 434-435.

[67] (1983) 152 C.L.R. 406, 434.

[68] (1983) 152 C.L.R. 406, 434.

true instances of promissory estoppel have no detriment requirement, although evidence of the latter will make a case much more arguable.

Other Commonwealth jurisdictions equally took note of the resurgence of promissory estoppel. Thus, in *John Burrows Ltd v. Subsurface Surveys,*[69] the Supreme Court of Canada considered that the effect of *High Trees* was merely to restate the *Hughes* principle. Citing *Combe*[70] and *Tool Metal,*[71] Ritchie J. on behalf of the Court held that the party claiming an estoppel must produce evidence to the effect that the other party intended legal relations created by contract to be altered as a result of the intervening negotiations.[72]

Similarly, the Federal Supreme Court of Nigeria (and upon appeal, the Privy Council) had cause to consider *High Trees* in *Ajayi v. Briscoe (Nigeria) Ltd.*[73] Lord Hodson, in reliance on *Tool Metal,* stated that the principle as revived in *High Trees* could not be extended so as to create rights in the promisee for which no consideration had been advanced. In particular, he stated that,

> The principle . . . is that when one party to a contract in absence of fresh consideration agrees not to enforce his rights an equity will be raised in favour of the other party. This equity is, however, subject to the qualification (a) that the other party has altered his position, (b) that the promisor can resile form his promise on giving reasonable notice which need not be a formal notice, giving the promisee a reasonable opportunity of resuming his position, (c) the promise only become final and irrevocable if the promisee cannot resume his position.[74]

The limitations implicit from Lord Hodson's judgment and indeed from many of the other cases cited above, was that promissory estoppel, if it truly existed as an independent species of estoppel, arose only in relation to waiver of *existing* contractual rights. No such limitation was placed on the principle however, when it arose for consideration in the Irish Courts in 1962.

---

[69](1968) 68 D.L.R. (2d) 354 (S.C.C.). See also the earlier Supreme Court decision in *Conwest Exploration Co Ltd. et al. v. Letain* (1964) 41 D.L.R. (2d) 198 (S.C.C.).

[70]*Combe v. Combe* [1951] 2 K.B. 215; [1951] 1 All E.R. 767 (C.A.).

[71]*Tool Metal Manufacturing Co. Ltd v. Tungsten Electric Co. Ltd.* [1955] 2 All E.R. 657 (H.L.).

[72]He stated: "It is not enough to show that one party has taken advantage of indulgences granted to him by the other for if this were so in relation to commercial transactions . . . it would mean that the holders of such notes would be required to insist on the very letter being enforced in all cases for fear that any indulgences granted and acted upon could be translated into a waiver of their rights to enforce the contract according to its terms" ((1968) 68 D.L.R. (2d) 354, 360-361).

[73][1964] 3 All E.R. 556 (P.C.); yet another unsuccessful attempt to defend a claim (this time under a hire purchase agreement) by way of promissory estoppel.

[74][1964] 3 All E.R. 556, p. 559.

8. Promissory Estoppel – The Irish Approach

In *Cullen v. Cullen,*[75] Kenny J. employed promissory estoppel in a situation where there were no contractual relations in existence at all. Holding that the plaintiff in a family dispute was estopped by his conduct from denying his son's right to land upon which the latter had built his house, the judge cited *High Trees* as the authority for such a proposition. Unfortunately Kenny J., constrained by the limitations of the doctrine, felt unable to order a transfer of the land into the defendant's name.[76] His misfortune was compounded by the fact that promissory estoppel was his last resort when his forays into the richer doctrine of proprietary estoppel had proved equally unfruitful, given the judge's failure to appreciate the second branch of *Ramsden v. Dyson.*[77]

Further inspirational use of promissory estoppel was made again by Kenny J. in *The Revenue Commissioners v. Moroney*[78] in spite of Counsel's noted lack of enthusiasm to argue the point before him and the fact that the Supreme Court did not feel the need to address the issue.[79] By an *inter vivos* deed acknowledging receipt of £16,000 the deceased had conveyed his pub to himself and his sons to hold as joint tenants. However, no money had ever exchanged hands and this clearly had been the parties' intention in executing the deed.[80] Upon the Revenue Commissioner's discovery of this state of affairs it claimed that death duty was payable on two-thirds of the property being an asset of the deceased. Moreover, it sought to exclude the defendants' extrinsic evidence to the contrary, including an affidavit by the solicitor, now deceased, who had drawn up the deed.

In the High Court Kenny J. raised the issue as to whether the sons could succeed on a plea that their father would have been estopped from claiming any part of the purchase money. Reviewing the English authorities from *Hughes* to *High Trees* and right through to the statements in *Ajayi* and *Tool Metal,* Kenny J. concluded that in his view,

there is no reason in principle why the doctrine of promissory estoppel

---

[75] [1962] I.R. 268 (H.C.).

[76] The learned judge commented, "While the estoppel created by the plaintiff's conduct prevents him asserting a title to the site, it does not give [the defendant] a right to require the plaintiff to transfer the site to him: if I had jurisdiction to make such an order I would do so, but I do not think I have" (p. 292).

[77] (1866) L.R. I H.L. 129. Kenny J. referred only to Lord Cranworth's mistaken stranger principle in his discussion of *Ramsden,* failing to appreciate the common expectation principle laid down by Lord Kingsdown in his dissenting judgment.

[78] [1972] I.R. 372 (H.C. Kenny J., and S.C.).

[79] [1972] I.R. 372, p. 378.

[80] Kenny J. took judicial notice of the fact that assessment of stamp duty on voluntary deeds was notoriously tiresome whereas those deeds expressed to be for consideration "passe[d] through the hazards of the Stamp Duty Office in about an hour" ([1972] I.R. 372, 376).

should be confined to cases where the representation related to existing contractual rights. It includes cases where there is a representation by one person to another that rights which will come into existence under a contract to be entered into will not be enforced.[81]

The learned judge thereby indicated his rejection not only of *Ajayi* but also of *Jorden v. Money*! In the Supreme Court, Walsh J. found it unnecessary to express a view on the doctrine, holding that as no indebtedness arose on the facts, promissory estoppel did not apply. In many ways it is a shame that the Supreme Court did not find it appropriate to express a view on the issue. More recently, judicial discussion of promissory estoppel has arisen mainly in the context of legitimate expectation,[82] a public law doctrine owing its origins, in Ireland at least, to the doctrine of estoppel.[83] While legitimate expectation has been viewed by some as surpassing the boundaries of promissory estoppel,[84] many of these decisions have done no more than accept the principles laid down in *High Trees*,[85] or the refinements made to it by later cases.[86] Arguably, legitimate expectation is limited to representations made by a public authority and thus has not supplanted the place of promissory estoppel in private law.[87]

9. THE FUTURE OF PROMISSORY ESTOPPEL: THE MERGER DEBATE

So how does promissory estoppel look at the close of the century? Arguably, given the wealth of case law, the concept now has developed a certain coherence. Yet for every limitation imposed upon it, invariably it finds a Court willing to grant it a new lease of life. Has it reached its zenith? Will its success in a

---

[81] [1972] I.R. 372, 381.

[82] See for instance, *Kenny v. Kelly* [1988] I.R. 457 (H.C.); *Duggan v. An Taoiseach* [1989] I.L.R.M. 710 (H.C.); *Wiley v. Revenue Commissioners* [1993] I.L.R.M. 482 (H.C. and S.C.); *Abrahamson v. Law Society of Ireland and the Attorney General* [1996] 2 I.L.R.M. 481 (H.C.).

[83] See *Webb v. Ireland* [1988] I.R. 372 (S.C.).

[84] See *Abrahamson v. Law Society of Ireland and the Attorney General* [1996] 2 I.L.R.M. 481 (H.C.) 494-495, where McCracken J. remarked that legitimate expectation while being similar to and "probably founded upon" the doctrine of promissory estoppel has now "been extended well beyond the bounds of that doctrine".

[85] See for instance, *Kenny v. Kelly* [1988] I.R. 457 (H.C.).

[86] For example, *Association of General Practitioners and others v. Minister for Health* [1995] 2 I.L.R.M. 481 (H.C.) 492 where O'Hanlon J. considered the application of *Combe v. Combe* [1951] 2 K.B. 215; [1951] 1 All E.R. 767 (C.A.) in Ireland.

[87] *cf.* the recent Circuit Court decision in *O'Rourke v. Gallagher* (Circuit Court, unreported, February 17, 2000) where in succession law proceedings Judge Deery sitting in Letterkenny made an order in favour of the plaintiffs (foster children of the Testator) on the basis that they had a "legitimate expectation" of inheritance because of promises made by the Testator to them during his lifetime. With due respect, this decision could more correctly be viewed as an instance of proprietary estoppel, notwithstanding the Judge's express reference to the doctrine of legitimate expectation.

strange way bring about its demise, given the calls for a merger of the various strains of estoppel? While there has been sporadic support for a merger of the various types of estoppel in England, the matter has never really been fully debated, despite the high profile of some of its proponents.[88] The Australian courts, however, have embraced the idea and in the seminal case of *Waltons Stores (Interstate) Ltd v. Maher*,[89] the High Court not only accepted the use of promissory estoppel in cases where there was no existing contractual relationship,[90] but more importantly sanctioned the use of such estoppel as a sword.[91] Mason C.J. and Wilson J. in reviewing the history of promissory estoppel in both Australia and England stated:

> One may discern in the cases a common thread which links them together, namely, the principle that equity will come to the relief of a plaintiff who has acted to his detriment on the basis of a basic assumption in relation to which the other party to the transaction has 'played such a part in the adoption that it would be unfair or unjust if he were left free to ignore it'. . . . Equity comes to the relief of such a plaintiff on the footing that it would be unconscionable conduct on the part of the other party to ignore the assumption.[92]

Unconscionability is the Court's touchstone.[93] Its presence creates an equity in favour of the aggrieved party, the extent of which is determined by the detriment suffered by that party. Subsequent pronouncements of the Australian High Court have further expanded on this.[94] Other jurisdictions have shown no real

---

[88] See Scarman L.J. in *Crabb v. Arun District Council* [1976] Ch. 179 (C.A.), where he opined that the while the distinction between proprietary and promissory estoppel might be valuable to law lecturers, he did not believe that putting the law into categories in other situations was of the slightest assistance at all. In *Amalgamated Investment & Property Co Ltd. (in liquidation) v. Texas Commerce International Ltd.* [1982] Q.B. 84, similar views in support of the amalgamation of the different estoppels were expressed by Goff J. in the High Court ([1982] Q.B. 84, 103 – expressing his dislike for the restriction of equitable estoppel "to certain defined categories") and by Lord Denning in the Court of Appeal ([1982] Q.B. 84, 122).

[89] (1988) 164 C.L.R. 387 (H.C.A.).

[90] This in itself is something with which the Irish Courts would have no difficulty – see above *Cullen v. Cullen* and *Revenue Commissioners v. Moroney*.

[91] The majority of the Court rejected the sword/shield analogy. For Brennan J., there was "no logical distinction to be drawn between a change in legal relationships affected by a promise which extinguishes a right and a change in legal relationships effected by a promise which creates one. Why should an equity of the kind to which *Combe v. Combe* refers be regarded as a shield but not a sword?" ((1988) 164 C.L.R. 387, 425-426).

[92] (1988) 164 C.L.R. 387, 404.

[93] For another example of unconscionability, which – in the guise of improvidence -has taken more root in Irish law, see Clark, "An Everyday Story of Country Folk (Not!). *Grealish v. Murphy* (1946)" above, 149.

[94] *Foran v. Wright* (1989) 168 C.L.R. 385 (H.C.A.) 411 where Mason C.J. accepted that a representation as to future conduct could in appropriate circumstances found an estoppel at common

enthusiasm to embark on a similar path. In New Zealand, recent case law, while noting the Australian developments, has opted for the traditional doctrine.[95]

Similarly, closer to home there has been no serious consideration of the issue by the English courts.[96] The one departure into this area by an Irish Court made no reference to the rationale for its decision or to the then emerging Australian principles, making it more likely to be an instance of judicial pragmatism than a concerted effort to introduce the merger debate into Irish law.[97]

For the moment, therefore, the distinct doctrine of promissory estoppel seems set to make it into the twenty-first century intact.

10. CONCLUSION

What started out as, in Atiyah's phrase, perhaps a dubious "accident of litigation", has endured and taken root so that we have now reached a stage where the overturning of the doctrine of promissory estoppel would result in as many protestations as were made by those who feared that Denning was out to destroy consideration. And yet time has shown that *High Trees* did not extinguish the need for the latter – if anything it clarified its role and its usefulness in the law of contract. It is surely the sign of a landmark case that despite over fifty years of intervening jurisprudence – with the refinements such judicial consideration inevitably involve – the fundamental *High Trees* principle is still taught to law students both as a foundation stone in Contract law and in Equity. Hayton has written of Denning in the following terms:

> If statutory provisions provoked by Lord Denning are left out of account, the judgment of posterity may well turn out to be that Lord Denning stirred and muddied the waters but when the waters settled the bedrock of Chancery law remained as before. Time alone will tell. It does however, already seem clear that Lord Denning's development of the injunction in a commercial context will be of lasting significance.[98]

---

law, apart from in equity. See also *Commonwealth v. Verwayen* (1990) 170 C.L.R. 394 (H.C.A.) where Mason C.J. notes (p. 413) that "there is only one doctrine of estoppel, which provides that a court of common law or equity may do what is required . . . to prevent a person who has relied upon an assumption . . . from suffering detriment in reliance upon [it] as a result of the denial of its correctness".

[95] See Hammond J. in *Rodney Aero Club Inc. v. Moore* [1998] 2 N.Z.L.R. 192 (H.C. N.Z.) 197.

[96] See further, Lunney "Towards a Unified Estoppel: The Long and Winding Road" [1992] *The Conveyancer* 239.

[97] *Re J.R.* [1993] I.L.R.M. 657 (H.C.). See further Coughlan and Mee, above n.54; *cf.* Clark, above n.11, 69 (stating that *Re JR* asserts that the distinction between promissory and proprietary estoppel remains valid).

[98] Hayton, "Equity and Trusts" in Jowell and McAuslan, (ed.), *Lord Denning: The Judge and the Law* (Sweet & Maxwell, London, 1984) 81.

Surely, his contribution to the doctrine of estoppel is worthy of the same tribute.

ACROSS THE CHEROKEE FRONTIER OF IRISH CONSTITUTIONAL JURISPRUDENCE

THE *SINN FÉIN FUNDS* CASE: *BUCKLEY V. ATTORNEY GENERAL* (1950)

THE HON. MR. JUSTICE RONAN KEANE*

Since I chose *Buckley & Ors. v. The Attorney General & Anor.*[1] – universally and in this article also referred to as the "*Sinn Féin Funds* case" – as one of the leading cases of the 20th century, I can hardly complain if, on a first re-reading, I was assailed with serious doubts as to whether it could justifiably claim that status.

Neither the High Court nor Supreme Court judgment purported to state any novel principle of law. They did not develop the existing law as reflected in earlier precedents. They did not even authoritatively restate the principles on which the existing law was based as they emerged from previous authorities. If it is, indeed, a leading case, it may well be unique in that there is not a single reference to any authority in either of the judgments. Unlike *Donoghue v. Stevenson*[2] it is devoid of human interest. It did not remedy any injustice, un-less the spending of the overwhelming bulk of the funds the subject of the litigation on legal costs, can be thought of as a desirable result. Unlike *Clinton v. Jones*[3] it cannot be said, at least on the surface, to have influenced even the course of Irish history, let alone world history. I find no reference to it in the standard works on the period.[4]

After that unpromising beginning, it may seem surprising that I am still prepared to defend its claim to inclusion in this collection, but I think a closer examination of the case and its historical background leads to the conclusion that not merely was my original choice justified, but that the omission of the *Sinn Féin Funds* case from even the most confined selection of the leading Irish cases of the century would be inexcusable.

One begins with the fact that the case is somewhat unusual in the sequence

---

*Chief Justice of Ireland.

[1] [1950] I.R. 67 (H.C., and S.C.).

[2] [1932] A.C. 562 (H.L.), on which see Hedley, "*M'Alister (or Donoghue) (Pauper) v. Stevenson* (1932)" above, 64.

[3] 520 U.S. 681; 117 S.Ct. 1636; 137 L.Ed.2d 945 (1997).

[4] Lee, *Ireland 1912-1985. Politics and Society* (C.U.P., Cambridge, 1990); Keogh, *Twentieth Century Ireland. Nation and State* (Gill & Macmillan, Dublin, 1994).

of great Irish constitutional law decisions in being concerned with *two* areas of huge importance, the separation of powers and the extent to which parliament may interfere with the private property rights of the citizen. It is in the first area that I believe the true significance of the decision lies. Let me begin my survey of the historical background far from the quiet backwaters of Ireland in the aftermath of the Second World War.

In 1832 the case of *Worcester v. The State of Georgia*[5] came before the United States Supreme Court. The Government of the United States, as in the case of other Indian tribes, had entered into a treaty with the Cherokee Nation. This ensured that they would retain a form of autonomy which respected their nationhood, although they accepted the sovereignty of the United States Government. The State Government in Georgia, however, contemptuously ignored the treaty between Washington and the Cherokees and the confrontation culminated in two clergymen being imprisoned for residing in the Cherokee nation without a licence from the State of Georgia. The subsequent proceedings ended in the Supreme Court, where Chief Justice Marshall ringingly rejected any attempt by Georgia to interfere in a treaty entered into between the Federal Government and the Cherokee Nation. The reported comment of President Andrew Jackson, an undisguised supporter of the Georgians' attitude, has gone down in history:

John Marshall has given his judgment: now let him enforce it.

No doubt emboldened by the reports of the President's response to the court's judgment, the Government in Georgia set about the task of driving the Cherokees from their territory and ultimately succeeded.[6] Their fate was a striking illustration of the fact that at that early stage of its history, the court, possessing the power neither of the sword nor of the purse, which were vested in the President and the Congress, could only rely on its moral authority and might do so in vain.

The Marshall court had, of course, in an even more celebrated case, held in *Marbury v. Madison*,[7] that the court possessed the power to strike down laws enacted by the Congress as being unconstitutional, although no such power had been expressly conferred on them by the Constitution. However, it was not until the following century that potentially the most serious conflict emerged with President Franklin Roosevelt's threats to pack the court if it struck down his "new deal" legislation.[8] That menacing confrontation was, of course, suc-

---

[5] 31 U.S. 51 (1832).
[6] Debo, *A History of the Indians of the United States* (University of Oklahoma Press, Norman, 1970; reprinted: Pimlico, London, 1995), 121-4.
[7] 1 Cranch (5 U.S.) 137 (1803).
[8] On which see Pratt, "A New Vocabulary for a New Constitutional Law. *U.S. v. Carolene Products* (1938)" above, 125.

cessfully defused and by the time *Brown v. Board of Education*,[9] invalidating racial segregation in public schools, was decided in 1954, the wheel had come full circle and the Federal Government was ultimately prepared to send in its marshals to enforce the Court's decision in the more obdurate southern states.

The judicial scene in post union Ireland was very different. The advanced transatlantic concept of the separation of powers had no place in a constitution resting unequivocally on the absolute sovereignty of the Crown in parliament. In Ireland, the relationship of the judiciary to the Dublin Castle Executive was notoriously close. Some judges thought it perfectly proper to drop into Dublin Castle on their way home from the Four Courts to hob-nob with the members of the Executive.

It would, however, be unfair to portray all the pre-1921 Irish judges as being unduly subservient to the Government. The two most celebrated figures on the bench during the period from the Union to the Treaty provide an instructive contrast. At the beginning of the period there is Lord Norbury, Chief Justice of the Common Pleas, forever remembered as the judge who presided at the trial of Robert Emmet, and the target of some of Daniel O'Connell's fiercest invective: he described him, on his departure from the bench, as "a sanguinary buffoon" who had been "bought off the bench by a most shameful traffic." (He had been advanced in the peerage and given a huge retiring pension by way of inducing him to vacate his seat, when his unfitness for office, always apparent, had become even more evident in old age). Norbury had been at the centre of an earlier political storm when a letter to him from the Attorney General, William Saurin, came to light in which the latter had encouraged Norbury, when travelling on Circuit, to persuade in private the members of the grand juries to resist the campaign for catholic emancipation.[10]

In contrast, Christopher Palles as Chief Baron was respected, not merely for his profound intellect and knowledge of the law, but also for his robust capacity to take on the executive where he thought this was demanded by the interests of justice. Nor was he alone among Irish judges in the last three decades under the Union in enjoying the respect of the nationalist majority: judges such as Holmes, Dodd and Ronan were also held in high esteem. It should be remembered, too, that on the very eve of the truce in 1921, the Master of the Rolls, Sir Charles O'Connor, ordered the general officer commanding the Crown forces in Ireland to appear before him to show cause why he should not be committed to prison for contempt, he having declined to release two IRA prisoners in response to an order of *habeas corpus*.[11]

---

[9] 347 U.S. 483 (1954).
[10] *Dictionary of National Biography* (2nd ed., O.U.P., Oxford & London, 1953-1961) vol. 19, 293; O'Connell (ed.), *The Correspondence of Daniel O'Connell* (The Blackwater Press for the Irish Manuscripts Commission, Dublin, 1972-1980) vol. 3, 323.
[11] The episode is dealt with in more detail by the writer in "'The Will of the General': Martial Law in Ireland 1535 – 1924" (1991-92) XXV-XXVII *Ir. Jur. (n.s.)* 150.

188 *Leading Cases of the Twentieth Century*

Although the decisions of Irish judges did not, on the whole, create any embarrassing problems for successive Irish Governments in the first quarter century of the new State's existence, that could not be ascribed to any undue subservience on the part of judges. Two factors were at work, the first of which was that the Constitution of the Irish Free State could be amended by the Oireachtas, not merely in the first seven years of its existence, but indefinitely, as the Supreme Court held in *The State (Ryan) v. Lennon*.[12] The second was the innate reluctance of judges who had been bred in the English constitutional tradition to overstep what they saw as the traditional limitations on the role of the courts. Although a number of the judges in the Supreme and High Courts during that period were from a unionist background, some judges whose political sympathies before appointment had been regarded as nationalist were equally conservative in their approach, an outstanding example being James Murnaghan.[13]

When the new Constitution was enacted in 1937, there was little immediate prospect of change, since it also could be amended in the first three years of its existence by legislation. It seemed unlikely that, even when that period came to an end, governments would have much cause for concern: the striking language in which Gavan Duffy J. invoked the provisions of the Constitution to invalidate powers of internment in *The State (Burke) v. Lennon*[14] found no echo in the judgment of the Supreme Court when the Oireachtas passed legislation designed to circumvent the effect of that decision.[15] Patrick McGilligan, in his lectures as Professor of Constitutional Law in University College Dublin in the early 1950s, was wont to point to the latter decision as representing the lowest point in Irish constitutional jurisprudence: the high point at that time, for him, was the *Sinn Féin Funds* case.

The factual background to the case is fully set out in a fascinating recent article by Dr. Gerard Hogan.[16] The Sinn Féin movement which at its zenith in the years before 1921 had been home to every shade of nationalist opinion, from the dual monarchy school of Arthur Griffith to the most dedicated adherents of physical force tracing their lineage to the Fenians, had melted away in the 1940s to a small group without any representatives in the Dáil. The catastrophic divisions in the wake of the Treaty had ultimately led to the formation of the two political parties which were to dominate the scene for decades to

---

[12][1935] I.R. 170 (H.C. and S.C.); on which see Hogan, "A Desert Island Case Set in the Silver Sea: *The State (Ryan) v. Lennon* (1935)" above, 80.
[13]His judgment in *The State (Ryan) v. Lennon* (above, n.12) was as positivist in its conclusion, if not in its tone, as that of Fitzgibbon J.
[14][1940] I.R. 136 (H.C.).
[15]*In re Article 26 and the Offences Against the State (Amendment) Bill, 1940* [1940] I.R. 470 (S.C.).
[16]Hogan, "The Sinn Féin Funds Judgment Fifty Years On" (1997) 2(9) *Bar Review* 375 [hereafter Hogan].

come, Fianna Fáil and Fine Gael. There remained a small number who still styled themselves as Sinn Féin and, more relevantly, claimed to be entitled to the funds of the original organisation which had been lodged in the High Court to the credit of the trusts of the organisation in 1924. When the proceedings began in 1942, there was approximately £24,000 standing to the credit of the suit, equating to several million pounds in present day values. The action was instituted by officers of the Sinn Féin organisation against the Attorney General and the personal representative of the surviving trustee of the trust monies, Mrs. Wyse Power, claiming a declaration that the trust monies were the property of their organisation. The Taoiseach, Eamonn De Valera, who had, of course, been president of Sinn Féin at the time of the Treaty, was not happy at the prospect of the ownership of the funds being determined by the litigation and his government secured the passage into law of the Sinn Féin Funds Act 1947.

Section 10(1) provided that all further proceedings in the action were to be stayed and subsection (2) went on:

> The High Court shall, if an application in that behalf is made *ex parte* by or on behalf of the Attorney General, make an order dismissing the pending action without costs.

The funds were then to be transferred to the Board, the Chairman of which was to be the Chief Justice[17] or another judge nominated by him, and were to be paid to persons who had been members of a number of specified bodies, including the I.R.A. during "the critical period", *i.e.* from the 1st April 1916 (the approximate date of the Easter Rising) to the 11th July 1921 (the date of the Truce) or their dependants.

The advice of the Attorney General, Cearbhall Ó Dalaigh, had naturally been sought when the Bill was drafted. His view, in general, was that the Constitution did not prohibit legislation which was retroactive in its effect, except to the extent that it prohibited acts being declared to be infringements of the law which were not so at the date of their commission (Article 15.5).[18] As Dr. Hogan points out,[19] however, he surprisingly failed to advert to the singular feature of this legislation, *i.e.* that it purported to compel the court to decide a case then actually before them in a particular way. He also considered himself supported in his view of the Bill's constitutionality by the decision of the U.S. Supreme Court in *Ex Parte McArdle*[20] in which the Supreme Court had refused to strike down a statute precluding an appeal in a case then pending.

---

[17] The Chief Justice at the time, Conor Maguire, discussed the provisions of the Bill as they affected him or his nominee with the Attorney General and, presumably for that reason, did not sit as a member of the court which ultimately decided the case; Hogan, 379.

[18] Sinn Féin Funds File (SR 11/41), Public Record Office National Archives.

[19] Hogan, 377-378.

[20] 74 U.S. 7 (1869).

This all naturally seems extraordinary to us, given the enormously influential role played by Ó Dalaigh as Chief Justice in the 1960s in the development of a new constitutional jurisprudence but again the very different ambience must be borne in mind. Apart from *The State (Burke) v. Lennon*, the only two cases in which legislation passed by the Oireachtas had been found invalid at that time were *In re Article 26 and The School Attendance Bill, 1942*[21] and *National Union of Railwaymen v. Sullivan.*[22]

Junior counsel for the Attorney General,[23] accordingly, had little reason to anticipate the storm which was about to break when, on a fateful summer morning in 1947, he went into the chancery court to apply for the *ex parte* order dismissing the action. He found that Gavan Duffy who was by now the President of the Court, had clearly anticipated the bringing of the application and had directed that it was to be made to him. There is reliable authority for the story long current in the Law Library that, having heard what counsel had to say, the President produced from his inside pocket a judgment which he had already prepared.[24] He was unsparing in his language:

> I am solemnly asked in this court, sitting as a court of justice, independent in the exercise of its functions, instead of giving a judicial decision in the action, to make a summary order dismissing the pending action out of court, without hearing the plaintiffs on the merits of their claim and without even listening to anything they have to say against this unprecedented application. . . .
>
> This court cannot, in deference to an Act of the Oireachtas, abdicate its proper jurisdiction to administer justice in a cause whereof it is duly seized. This court has been established to administer justice and therefore it cannot dismiss the pending action without hearing the plaintiffs: it can no more dispose of the action in that arbitrary manner at the instance of the Attorney General than it could give judgment for the plaintiffs without hearing the Attorney General against their claim. . . .[25]

Interestingly, the High Court judgment contained only a passing reference to the possibility that the section might also be vulnerable because of a conflict with the private property rights guaranteed by the Constitution. The reverse

---

[21] [1943] I.R. 334 (S.C.).
[22] [1947] I.R. 77 (S.C.).
[23] Andrias Ó Caoimh, subsequently Attorney General, Judge of the Supreme Court, President of the High Court, and Judge of the European Court of Justice.
[24] Hogan, 379, 381, n. 30.
[25] [1950] I.R. 67, 70-71. Such unsparing language was characteristic of Gavan Duffy; for another example, see Clark, "An Everyday Story of Country Folk (Not!). *Grealish v. Murphy* (1946)" above, 149.

happened in the Supreme Court, where, because the validity of an Act of the Oireachtas was being decided, only one judgment was delivered (by O'Byrne J.), the greater part of which was devoted to the private property issue.

So far as that part of the case is concerned the surprising feature of the case is not so much the judgment of the court, as the astonishing breadth of the proposition advanced on behalf of the Attorney General. It was argued that the effect of Article 43.1.2 was merely to prevent the total abolition of the right of private property, that the State was entitled to take away the property rights of any citizen without compensation and that whether such a measure was required by the "exigencies of the common good" referred to in the article was exclusively a matter for the Oireachtas. Such a reading of the Constitution could have had far reaching consequences if accepted. Extraordinarily, no attempt seems to have been made to present an alternative argument that the provisions of the Act were in any event reconcilable with the exigencies of the common good. Thus, it could have been pointed out that the private property rights of the plaintiffs only arose in a secondary and indirect manner, since they were in effect trustees for the members of the organisation known as Sinn Féin, whoever they might have been, and the only certain consequence of the litigation would be the dissipation of this relatively huge sum in legal costs (which is what actually happened).[26] It could reasonably have been regarded as being in the public interest that those funds, subscribed as they had been by large numbers of people who wished to support the old Sinn Féin movement, should be applied by an impartial body in favour of the survivors of the original movement and their dependants.

Thus, while the case is of some significance as being the first in which the private property articles were successfully invoked – in *Pigs Marketing Board v. Donnelly Limited*[27] Hanna J. had famously dismissed the references to "social justice" as "nebulous"[28] and an attempt to challenge the powers of the Land Commission in this area had also failed before Gavan Duffy J. in *Fisher v. Irish Land Commission*[29] – its importance in the long-term in this context may have been exaggerated. It was after all highly unlikely that so radical a proposition as that advanced on behalf of the Attorney General would have commanded acceptance. In *Blake v. Attorney General*[30] a fuller analysis was provided of the protection of property rights afforded by Article 40.3.2 and Article 43 and it is to that, and subsequent decisions, that lawyers will turn to find the extent to which the powers of the Oireachtas are circumscribed in

[26]The case itself was subsequently heard in the High Court by Kingsmill Moore J. and is reported *sub. nom. Buckley & Ors. v. Attorney General & Anor.* (1950) 84 I.L.T.R. 9. The learned judge concluded that the plaintiffs had not established their claim to be entitled to the funds.
[27][1939] I.R. 413 (H.C.).
[28][1939] I.R. 413, 418.
[29][1948] I.R. 3 (H.C.).
[30][1982] I.R. 117 (H.C. and S.C.).

abridging private property rights rather than to our case. In practical terms, the decision in *Blake* can be seen as having a particularly important effect in inhibiting attempts in the 1970s to deal with the problem of the price of building land and, specifically, as underlying the failure to implement the Kenny Report on that subject in 1973.[31]

However, although the other issue was disposed of relatively briefly in the judgment of O'Byrne J., the upholding by the Supreme Court of Gavan Duffy P.'s spirited defence of the separation of powers principle undoubtedly gave a clear signal to future governments that they would trespass on the judicial domain at their peril. Not only was there no subsequent attempt by the Oireachtas to intervene in cases actually at hearing, successive governments were punctilious in the extreme when exercising their undoubted right, left untouched by the *Sinn Féin Funds* case, to reverse by legislation the consequences of judicial decisions, to do so only in such a manner as to ensure they did not in any way fall foul of the separation of powers principle so robustly asserted in that case. Their caution in this area, indeed, led to unexpected consequences, as was demonstrated by what may be fairly called the *Pine Valley* saga.

That arose out of the decision by the Supreme Court in *The State (Pine Valley Developments Limited) v. Dublin County Council*[32] that the Minister for Local Government, in whom the appellate functions under the planning code were at the relevant time vested, had no power to grant a planning permission which contravened the development plan of the planning authority for the area in which the lands were situated. A significant number of planning permissions of that nature had been granted by successive Ministers for Local Government since the coming into force of the relevant legislation in 1964 and the implications in the case of property purchased or built in the belief that such permissions were valid were, of course, far reaching. It was against that background that the Oireachtas enacted the Local Government (Planning and Development) Act 1982, section 6 of which provided that such permissions were not to be regarded as being, or ever having been, invalid because they contravened the development plan.

Subsection (2), however, provided that:

> If, because of any or all of its provisions, subsection (1) of this section, would, but for this subsection, conflict with the constitutional right of any person, the provisions of that subsection shall be subject to such limitation as is necessary to secure that they do not so conflict but shall be otherwise of full force and effect.

---

[31] For a full discussion of the jurisprudence in relation to the private property articles, see Hogan and Whyte, *Kelly's The Irish Constitution* (3rd ed., Butterworths, Dublin, 1994) 1068 *et seq.*
[32] [1984] I.R. 407 (H.C. and S.C.).

In subsequent proceedings, brought by the developers against the Minister, it was accepted on their behalf that this subsection excluded them from the benefit of the retrospective validation of such planning permissions. They claimed, however, to be entitled to damages for breach of their constitutional rights resulting from the grant by the Minister to them of a permission which he should have known to be illegal. That claim, however, was rejected by the High Court, whose decision was upheld by the Supreme Court.[33] The plaintiffs then sought relief in the European Court of Human Rights on the ground that they had been subjected to discrimination which was a violation of the European Convention on Human Rights and Fundamental Freedoms.

The proceedings in the European Court took an unusual turn: the Irish Government contended that, although two of the judgments in the Supreme Court (those of Henchy and Lardner JJ.) indicated that subsection (2) was intended to avoid any unconstitutional invasion of the judicial domain, the effect of section 6 was nonetheless to validate the permission granted to the developers in that case. The European Court, however, did not accept that approach and held that the developers had indeed been subjected to discrimination in breach of the Convention.[34]

It is understandable that governments have been hesitant in seeking by legislation to reverse the effect of judicial decisions. While there could clearly be no constitutional objection to the Oireachtas altering the general law, setting aside a specific adjudication by a competent court was another matter. It was possibly open to argument that legislation having that effect was not necessarily invalidated by the *Sinn Féin Funds* decision, but there is undoubtedly judicial authority to the contrary in the *dicta* already referred to in the second *Pine Valley* case.

It is interesting to note, however, that, whatever be the position under our Constitution, the European Court of Human Rights has taken a relatively relaxed view of legislation which, while not formally interfering with existing litigation, nevertheless has the effect of making particular proceedings unwinnable. In *National and Provincial Building Society & Ors. v. United Kingdom*,[35] they rejected a complaint by the three applicant building societies that legislation enacted by the Westminster parliament had wrongfully interfered with their right of access to the courts, in that it had altered the law at a time when they had proceedings in being in a manner that ensured that those proceedings would be unsuccessful.

That was a case in which the three building societies were seeking to take advantage of a lacuna in revenue law that had been revealed in lengthy pro-

---

[33] *Pine Valley Developments Limited v. Minister for the Environment* [1987] I.R. 23 (H.C., and S.C.).
[34] *Pine Valley Developments Limited v. Ireland* Series A No. 222; (1992) 14 E.H.R.R. 319.
[35] (1998) 25 E.H.R.R. 127. I am grateful to Dr. Hogan for drawing my attention to this decision.

ceedings brought by the Woolwich Building Society against the Revenue which had ultimately been determined by the House of Lords in favour of that building society.[36] The legislation did not seek to interfere with the judicial decision which had brought that particular litigation to an end, but it did ensure that the proceedings instituted by the three applicant building societies were, in effect, unwinnable. While the court addressed the dangers inherent in the use of retrospective legislation which had the effect of rendering pending litigation against the State unwinnable, they also concluded that there were circumstances, of which this was one, where such legislation could be unexceptionable in terms of the Convention. It remains to be seen whether such an approach would be adopted by our courts or would be regarded as excluded by the *Sinn Féin Funds* case.

One cannot help wondering what would have been the result if the Government in dealing with the funds had adopted less of a sledge-hammer approach. They might, for example, have initiated a private Bill in the Oireachtas giving Sinn Féin – which had always been an unincorporated voluntary association – some form of corporate status and declaring that any property to which the unincorporated body was entitled should be vested on an appointed day in the new corporate body. That body, at the same time, could have been required to apply the funds for the same objects as had been set out in the ill-fated Act. If it had not been challenged, such legislation would have given the pending litigation the character of a moot, but would not have purported to deprive the court of its jurisdiction to deal with the case. It would have been not dissimilar to legislation in relation to military service pensions which had been applied by the Supreme Court two years earlier and which, while not expressly interfering with the jurisdiction of the courts, effectively ensured that pending litigation was decided in a particular way.[37] It was, as much as anything else, the peremptory legislative command directed to the courts – unprecedented, as Gavan Duffy P. pointed out – that sealed the fate of the Act.

Are we to conclude then that, generally speaking, the effects of the Sinn Féin funds case on the evolution of Irish constitutional law in the last fifty years have been less than is generally supposed? Experience would suggest that, if actual citation of the decision in subsequent cases is the criterion, it cannot compare in significance with – to take but a few examples – *Ryan v. Attorney General*[38] (the doctrine of unremunerated rights), *East Donegal Co-Operative v. Attorney General*[39] (presumptions of constitutionality), *In re*

---

[36] See *R. v. I.R.C. ex parte Woolwich* [1990] 1 W.L.R. 1400 (H.L.); *Woolwich v. I.R.C.* [1993] 1 A.C. 70 (H.L.); this latter decision has been followed in Ireland: *O'Rourke v. Revenue Commissioners* [1996] 2 I.R. 1 (H.C.).
[37] *The State (O'Shea) v. Minister for Defence* [1947] I.R. 49 (S.C.).
[38] [1965] I.R. 294 (H.C. and S.C.).
[39] [1970] I.R. 317 (S.C.).

Haughey[40] (fair procedures) and *The State (Healy) v. Donoghue*[41] (due process). While the practical consequences of the decision were relatively limited, however, its symbolic importance was considerable. Because the existence of any dissenting judgment could not be disclosed, it cannot be assumed that the court was unanimous. But given that all the judges came from the same conservative generation, the decision must undoubtedly have come as a severe jolt to politicians who were not accustomed to taking the Constitution seriously into account. In that sense, it undoubtedly heralded the judicial activism of a later era and deserves to retain its status as the case in which Irish constitutional jurisprudence crossed the Cherokee frontier.

The Act itself was never repealed, presumably because it was assumed that, as a result of the decision, it ceased to have any legal effect. If that was the assumption, it was technically incorrect. Section 14 empowered the Board to accept gifts for the purposes of the Act and O'Byrne J. was careful in his judgment to say that, in so far as it was confined to the administration of such gifts by the Board, the Act was "unobjectionable".[42] The Act also provided in Section 16 that, when the trust fund was, by reason of payments thereout, exhausted, the Board was to send a Certificate to that effect to the Government who could thereupon dissolve the Board. But since the fund was never vested in the Board, that section never became operative. The Chief Justice, accordingly, in addition to having many other responsibilities, remains in theory the chairman of a ghostly board, a metaphorical reminder to the Oireachtas and the Executive of the limitations on their powers imposed by the provisions of the Constitution and so dramatically demonstrated by this historic decision.

[40][1971] I.R. 217 (S.C.).
[41][1976] I.R. 325; (1976) 110 I.L.T.R. 29 (H.C. and S.C.); on this *cp.* Rumann, "The Indigent's Right to Counsel. *Gideon v. Wainwright* (1963)" below, 208.
[42][1950] I.R. 67, 84.

THE POWER TO PUNISH
REFLECTIONS ON *DEATON v. A.G.* (1963)

TOM O'MALLEY[*]

1. INTRODUCTION. THE CONSTITUTION AND SENTENCING

Although the Constitution of Ireland has had a profound impact on most aspects of criminal procedure, it is generally assumed to have few, if any, serious implications for the sentencing process. There is a fair degree of truth in this assumption; sentencing remains almost entirely governed by statutory and common-law rules. From the early 1960s, right down to the early 1990s, the Supreme Court issued several leading judgments which effectively "constitutionalised" criminal procedure, particularly in relation to matters such as bail, the admissibility of evidence, the provision of criminal legal aid, the presumption of innocence and similar matters.[1] Remedies such as *habeas corpus*, available at both pre- and post-conviction stages were also strengthened largely as a result of a dynamic judicial interpretation to Article 40.4 of the Constitution which protects personal liberty. Sentencing, however, remained largely immune from this process of constitutionalisation, but not entirely so. One of the earliest decisions of the Supreme Court at beginning of the 1960s when the so-called constitutional revolution was getting under way, established firm boundary lines between the sentencing functions of the various branches of government. This was the case of *Deaton v. Attorney General and the Revenue Commissioners*[2] which categorically outlawed any role for the executive branch of government in the selection of punishment. There is, however, a tendency to read too much into *Deaton*. It is often interpreted as prohibiting any legislative

---

[*]Lecturer in Law, National University of Ireland, Galway.

[1] Leading cases include: *The People (Attorney General) v. O'Callaghan* [1966] I.R. 510; (1968) 102 I.L.T.R. 45 (S.C.) (bail), *People (Attorney General) v. O'Brien* [1965] I.R. 142 (S.C.) (exclusion of unconstitutionally obtained evidence); *The State (Healy) v. Donoghue* [1976] I.R. 325; (1976) 110 I.L.T.R. 29 (H.C. and S.C.) (legal aid; on which *cp.* Rumann, "The Indigent's Right to Counsel. *Gideon v. Wainright* (1963)" below, 208); *O'Leary v. Attorney General* [1993] 1 I.R. 102; [1991] I.L.R.M. 454 (H.C.) (presumption of innocence). For a critical account of a similar "constitutionalisation" of criminal procedure in the United States, see Amar, *The Constitution and Criminal Procedure: First Principles* (Yale U.P., New Haven, Conn., 1997).

[2] [1963] I.R. 170 (H.C. and S.C.).

effort to curtail or structure judicial sentencing discretion. The central argument of this essay is, that far from curtailing the legislative sentencing function, *Deaton* may be criticised for having too readily accepted the power to prescribe mandatory sentences. In order to identify the possible constraints that the Constitution (or the common law) may impose on this power, we must look to the emerging law on proportionate punishment which, on one view at least, derives from the due process provision of the Constitution (Article 38.1).

2. THE FACTS AND HOLDING IN *DEATON*

The plaintiff in *Deaton* had been charged with offences relating to the importation of butter in contravention of section 186 of the Customs Consolidation Act 1876. This section provided that any person found guilty of such an offence "should forfeit either treble the value of the goods, including the duty payable thereon, or one hundred pounds, at the election of [the Revenue Commissioners]". The plaintiff sought a declaration to the effect that this provision was inconsistent with the Constitution as it purported to confer upon the Revenue Commissioners the power to administer criminal justice, a function which the Constitution reserves solely to the Courts.[3] It is well known that the plaintiff succeeded in the Supreme Court, but it is often forgotten that he failed in the High Court, where Kenny J. had held that the power of the Revenue Commissioners to select a penalty did not amount to the administration of justice. The important point, in his view, was that the courts retained exclusive jurisdiction over the determination of guilt or innocence, and that certainly did amount to the administration of justice. The executive power to select penalty did not come into play until a verdict of guilty had been returned in accordance with law. Kenny J. saw no substantial difference between this arrangement and the legislative stipulation of mandatory sentences which had existed throughout much of the history of Irish and British criminal law. Indeed, at the time he was writing, all murders carried the death penalty.[4] In the present case, the executive was, in effect, entitled to choose between one of two mandatory sentences, and Kenny J. did not see any significant difference between this arrangement and the traditional mandatory sentences specified by statute.

This reasoning failed to find favour with the Supreme Court which allowed the plaintiff's appeal, although it was at pains to stress the constitutionality of

---

[3] Article 34.1. Article 37, which allows for the exercise of limited judicial functions by persons or bodies other than courts, does not apply to "criminal matters". See *Keady v. Garda Commissioner* [1992] 2 I.R. 197; [1992] 2 I.L.R.M. 312 (S.C.); *Goodman International v. Hamilton (No 1)* [1992] 2 I.R. 542; [1992] I.L.R.M. 145 (S.C.).

[4] The death penalty for "ordinary" murder was abolished by the Criminal Justice Act 1964 and was abolished for all offences by the Criminal Justice Act 1990. Nobody had actually been executed for a capital offence since 1954.

the legislative power to prescribe mandatory sentences. Ó Dalaigh C.J., who delivered the judgment of the Court, said:

> There is a clear distinction between the prescription of a fixed penalty and the selection of a penalty for a particular case. The prescription of a fixed penalty is the statement of a general rule, which is one of the characteristics of legislation; this is wholly different from the selection of a penalty to be imposed in a particular case.[5]

He proceeded to say that once a choice of penalty was conferred by statute, the matter passed from the legislative to the judicial domain. In such a case, "the individual citizen who has committed an offence is safeguarded from the executive's displeasure by the choice of penalty being in the determination of an independent judge".[6] He said that the selection of punishment is an integral part of the administration of justice and, as such, cannot be committed to the hands of the executive.[7] Consequently, the impugned statutory provision was inconsistent with the Constitution as it authorised an impermissible executive intrusion into the judicial domain.

3. The Reception of *Deaton*

The Supreme Court's judgment in *Deaton* has been remarkably influential, not only in Ireland[8] but throughout the common-law world. Ironically, however, in other jurisdictions it has been used as often to uphold the constitutionality of mandatory sentences as to support the exclusivity of the judicial role in the selection of sentence. In *Wynbyne v. Marshall*,[9] for example, the Supreme Court of the Northern Territory of Australia relied heavily on *Deaton* and on other authorities which had been influenced by it to uphold the constitutionality of a law which prescribed a mandatory minimum sentence of 14 days' imprisonment for every property offence. Mildren J., delivering the principal judgment in *Wynbyne*, concluded that there was nothing in any of these authorities to suggest that merely because a court was mandated to record a conviction and impose a minimum sentence of imprisonment, that there is an interference with judicial independence. He did, however, accept the fundamental principle in *Deaton* that the selection of punishment, when there is a selection to be made, must remain a judicial task. But his decision is a stark reminder of the continu-

---

[5] [1963] I.R. 170, 182.
[6] [1963] I.R. 170, 183.
[7] *ibid.*
[8] Irish cases in which it has been applied include *The State (O) v. O'Brien* [1973] I.R. 50 (S.C.) and *Curtis and Geough v. Attorney General* [1986] I.L.R.M. 428 (H.C.).
[9] (1997) 117 N.T.R. 11; (1997) 7 N.T.L.R. 97; [1997] N.T.S.C. 120.

ing political power to strip the courts of discretion, or substantially curtail their discretion, whenever governments find it expedient to do so. This, however, may not be the last we hear of *Wynbyne* and similar cases from the Northern Territory. A group of London lawyers has recently lodged a complaint against the Australian Government with the United Nations Human Rights Committee in Geneva over the operation of the Northern Territory's mandatory sentencing laws.[10] They argue that these laws discriminate against Aborigines who are most affected by them. There has apparently been a huge rise in the number of Aborigines imprisoned for very minor property offences, such as stealing £9 worth of biscuits in one case. The complaint to the UN Committee has not yet been formally considered, but already the Secretary General of the UN, Kofi Annan, is reported to have put pressure on the Australian Government to over-rule the law in question.[11] This entire episode points to the limitations of the *Deaton* ruling which, as will be argued presently, is of itself insufficient to protect convicted persons from suffering disproportionate punishments.[12]

In *Hinds v. The Queen*,[13] which is now a treated as a leading common law case on the separation of powers, the Privy Council relied heavily on *Deaton* when finding that part of a law establishing a special gun court in Jamaica con-travened that country's constitution. The law in question was clearly intended to deal with the serious public disorder that had resulted from the widespread availability and misuse of firearms. It provided for the establishment of a spe-cial court to deal with firearms offences. Every person convicted by that court had to be detained "at hard labour during the Governor-General's pleasure". In deciding when to release such a detainee, the Governor-General was required to act on behalf of and in accordance with the advice of a five-member review board. Only one member of that board was a judge. Delivering the judgment of the Privy Council, Lord Diplock said that he "would not seek to improve upon what was said by the Supreme Court of Ireland in *Deaton v. Attorney General and Revenue Commissioners*",[14] namely that parliament was entitled to pre-scribe a fixed penalty but that the selection of punishment cannot be commit-ted to the hands of the executive. He therefore held that the provision of the Jamaican law conferring power on the review board to decide on the length of sentence was contrary to the Constitution. He said that there was no suggestion that the board would not perform its duties responsibly and impartially, but if such an arrangement were upheld, it might "open the door to the exercise of arbitrary power by the executive in the whole field of criminal law".[15] This

---

[10]*The Times*, July 13, 2000, 4.

[11]*ibid.*

[12]For more detailed analyses of mandatory sentencing in Australia see the contributions to (1999) 5 (1) *U.N.S.W.L.J. Forum* (January).

[13][1977] A.C. 198; [1976] 1 All E.R. 353 (P.C.).

[14][1977] A.C. 198, 226; [1976] 1 All E.R. 353, 370.

[15]*ibid.*

indeed is the strength of the *Deaton* principle. It places a definite curb on executive power. The approach of Kenny J. in the High Court had a certain logical coherence. His reasoning was that what the legislation effectively did was to give the executive the right of election between two mandatory sentences which, he felt, did not amount to granting any meaningful executive discretion in the choice of punishment. The Supreme Court's approach was probably the more prudent. Had it not called a halt to the type of statutory arrangement challenged in *Deaton*, the legislature might have begun to expand the range of options from which the executive branch could choose, thereby creating the kind of arbitrariness feared by Lord Diplock in *Hinds*.

One of the more interesting applications of the *Deaton* principle occurred recently in *Browne v. The Queen*,[16] another Privy Council decision. The defendant, who was appealing from the Court of Appeal of the Eastern Carribbean States, had been convicted of murder when he was 16 years of age and sentenced to be detained "until the pleasure of the Governor-General be known". As it happens, the sentence should have been "during the Governor-General's pleasure". Delivering the judgment of the Privy Council, Lord Hobhouse of Woodborough said that in view of the separation of powers provision in the Constitution of St. Christopher and Nevis (in which the appellant was convicted), the sentence passed, even after the correction of the verbal error, was unlawful. The Governor-General is part of the executive and not part of the judiciary. He should not therefore be allowed to determine the length of sentence to be served by the appellant. This is clearly similar to the reasoning of the Irish Supreme Court in *State (O) v. O'Brien*,[17] and particularly the reasoning of Walsh J. in that case when he held that the duration of the detention of a person sentenced to be detained "during his Majesty's pleasure" under section 103 of the Children Act 1908 was a matter to determined exclusively by the Courts. On the other hand, a person found guilty by insane in respect of a criminal charge must be committed to the Central Mental Hospital or a similar institution and detained there for so long as the Government decides.[18] The courts have held that the decision on release is an executive as opposed to a judicial function on the (rather technical basis) that a finding of guilty but insane amounts to an acquittal which means that the subsequent detention cannot be treated as a sentence.

---

[16][2000] A.C. 45 (P.C.).
[17][1973] I.R. 50 (S.C.).
[18]*Application of Gallagher* [1991] I.R. 31; [1991] I.L.R.M. 339 (S.C.). See, generally, Barton, "Insanity in the Supreme Court" (1991) 13 *D.U.L.J.* (*n.s.*) 127.

4. THE LIMITS OF *DEATON*

Deaton has occasionally been invoked to support the view that any legislative attempt to structure judicial sentencing discretion would be unconstitutional. In fact, there is little in the judgment itself or in the Privy Council and Commonwealth judgments it has influenced to support this view. One of the more remarkable features of *Deaton* is the general benediction that it gives to mandatory sentences.[19] As noted earlier, the Supreme Court of the Northern Territory in *Wynbyne*[20] relied on *Deaton, Hinds* and similar cases to arrive that the conclusion that "merely because a court, having found the appellant guilty of an offence, is mandated to record a conviction and impose a minimum sentence of imprisonment, that is [not] an interference with the independence of the judiciary".[21] *Deaton* itself therefore provides no explicit protection against the more widespread use of mandatory sentences or, perhaps, as shown by *Wynbyne*, the more widespread use of mandatory minimum sentences. Admittedly, the Supreme Court in *Deaton* did not have to confront the problem very directly. At the time, the only mandatory sentence of any consequence on the statute books was the death penalty for murder, and while many found that objectionable, it was not considered so disproportionate to the extent of being unconstitutional. In fact, the Constitution explicitly acknowledges the existence of the death sentence in Articles 13.6 and 40.4.5. The death penalty has now been abolished, not only in Ireland but in most other Western countries, the United States being a notable exception.[22] But there is a growing demand for mandatory sentences and penalties, and governments are showing themselves increasingly willing to give into those demands. In Ireland, for example, the Criminal Justice Act 1999 was flaunted by the Government as introducing a mandatory minimum10-year prison sentence for certain drug offences. In fact, all it does is to introduce a presumptive 10-year sentence as the courts have a reasonably wide discretion to impose a lower sentence in a variety of circumstances.

Mandatory sentencing can be a major source of injustice. It sacrifices individuation to consistency and often leads to the imposition of disproportionately severe sentences in individual cases. It is scarcely surprising therefore that whenever mandatory sentences are introduced, they are soon resisted through the adoption of various informal strategies to save offenders from the full rigour of the law. The history of this phenomenon has been well char-

---

[19] On the constitutionality of mandatory sentences, Hogan and Whyte, *Kelly's The Irish Constitution* (3rd ed., Butterworths, Dublin, 1994), 368 and 371.

[20] Above, n.9.

[21] *ibid., per* Mildren J.

[22] See Hood, *The Death Penalty: A Worldwide Perspective* (2nd ed., Oxford, 1996); Council of Europe, *The Death Penalty: Abolition in Europe* (Strasbourg, 1999); Schabas, *The Abolition of the Death Penalty in International Law* (2nd ed., Grotius Publications, Cambridge, 1993).

tered.[23] Between the late seventeenth and early ninetheenth centuries, for example, more than 200 felonies were made capital offences. Strictly speaking, therefore, everybody convicted of such a crime had to be sentenced to death. In reality, however, execution rates were remarkably low. Victims were often reluctant to press charges if they knew that an offender might suffer the death penalty as a result. Juries often acquitted even in the face of strong evidence or brought in a verdict on a lesser, non-capital charge. And, of course, the executive powers of pardon and clemency were widely used to commute the death penalty to some other form of punishment. The same patterns have been evident in recent years in the United States where mandatory sentences and guidelines have been introduced on a widespread basis during the past decade or two, particularly for drug and firearms offences. Informal neurtralisation strategies such as those described cannot, however, guarantee that all offenders will be spared the injustice of mandatory sentences. So long as mandatory sentences exist, they will be used. Sometimes they may be deserved but in many cases they will be both excessive and counter-productive. Every effort should, of course, be made to structure sentencing discretion so as to eliminate as many disparities as possible. But it is widely agreed that mandatory sentencing is a crude and ineffective way of achieving this goal. It is far better to leave discretion to the courts, while requiring or encouraging them to develop their own guidelines to ensure consistency of approach. Indeed, there is now some evidence here in Ireland, as a result of *Cox v. Ireland*,[24] that it is not every mandatory sentence or penalty that will be tolerated by the courts.

5. TOWARDS A PRINICPLE OF PROPORTIONALITY IN SENTENCING

In *Cox* the Supreme Court struck down a general sentencing provision on the ground that it was overinclusive to the point of being discriminatory. The plaintiff successfully challenged section 34 of the Offences Against the State Act 1939 which provided that a person convicted of a scheduled offence by the Special Criminal Court was to forfeit any office or employment remunerated from public funds, and was to be ineligible to hold any such employment for a period of seven years after the date of conviction. He also lost any pension rights earned before conviction. The plaintiff had lost his teaching job on foot of this section. In the High Court, Barr J., in finding for the plaintiff, had held that the penalties imposed by section 34 were "patently unfair and capricious in nature".[25]

---

[23] See Tonry, "Mandatory Penalties" (1992) 26 *Crime and Justice: A Review of Research* 243; Hay, "Property, Authority and the Criminal Law" in Hay *et al.*, (eds.), *Albion's Fatal Tree* (Pelican, London, 1975); McGlynn, *Crime and Punishment in Eighteenth-Century England* (Routledge, London, 1987).
[24] [1992] 2 I.R. 503 (S.C.).
[25] [1992] 2 I.R. 503, 513.

They amounted, he said, to an unreasonable and unjustifiable interference with the plaintiff's constitutionally-guaranteed personal rights, including the right to earn a livelihood. The Supreme Court did not, unfortunately, analyse the constitutional issues in any great detail, but found nonetheless that the impugned section failed to protect the constitutional rights of the citizen and were therefore impermissibly wide and indiscriminate. What the court found most objectionable was the automatic application of section 34 to those who happened to find themselves charged with a scheduled offence (which might be minor or serious in nature) and tried before the Special Criminal Court, as opposed to one of the ordinary criminal courts. The section did not allow for any account to be taken of the defendant's motive, the circumstances in which the offence was committed or the extent, if any, to which it threatened public peace or security.

On the basis of this reasoning, the Constitution would seem to require some degree of individuation of punishment. It does not inevitably follow from *Cox* that the mandatory sentence for murder is unconstitutional or that other mandatory penalties, such as those provided for certain road traffic offences, are automatically suspect. In the case of murder, the mandatory sentence might, in theory at least, be justified by the unique gravity of the offence. The pressing social interest in maintaining a high level of road safety might be invoked to justify the mandatory penalties for, say, drunken driving. Before reaching such a conclusion, however, the courts would need to be satisfied that none of the sentences or penalties in question is likely to be disproportionately severe in any particular case. In other words, to impose, say, a 12-month disqualification on a person convicted of drunken driving may be have a very severe impact on a particular offender, but not to the point of being disproportionate when one considers the countervailing public interest in road safety. Let us suppose, however, that the law was changed so as to provide for a mandatory 10-year prison sentence for every person, without exception, convicted of drunken driving even if the person had not been involved in an accident or caused any actual injury. Would this be constitutional? There is nothing in *Deaton* or in the line of Commonwealth decisions it has inspired to suggest that it would not be. *Cox*, with its implied emphasis on individuation of punishment, might provide a more promising ground of attack. But we cannot be confident of successfully challenging any mandatory sentence unless there is a firm constitutional basis for proportionality of punishment.

The Constitution of Ireland has no equivalent to the Eighth Amendment of the United States Constitution which prohibits, among other things, the imposition of cruel and unusual punishments. We may be reasonably confident, however, that cruel and unusual punishment is implicitly prohibited by the Irish Constitution by virtue of the protection it accords to bodily integrity, due process and personal liberty. In the United States, there have been several challenges to heavy non-capital sentences, such as life imprisonment without the possibility of parole for relatively minor offences, on the ground that they were so disproportionate as to amount to cruel and unusual punishment. These challenges have met with mixed success.[26] At one point in the 1980s, the Supreme Court seemed willing to interpret the Eighth Amendment as imposing a general requirement of proportionate punishment.[27] By the early 1990s, however, the Court, with a more conservative membership, was less receptive to such arguments and now seems unwilling to regard any non-capital punishment as violating the Eighth Amendment unless it is proved to be both cruel *and* unusual.[28] And, imprisonment, according to the Court is not unusual. In Ireland, a more promising line of proportionality jurisprudence has begun to emerge, with its roots in the due process provisions of the Constitution rather than in any implied prohibition on cruel and unusual punishment.

The first major authority adopting this line of argument is *The State (Healy) v. Donoghue*[29] in which it was held that persons facing trial on serious criminal charges were constitutionally entitled to free legal aid if they were unable to pay for their own legal representation. However, Henchy J., in one of those classic judgments which established him as one of the great Irish jurists of modern times, went on to say that the constitutional guarantees to due process, personal liberty and related fundamental rights necessarily implied:

> . . . a guarantee that a citizen shall not be deprived of his liberty as a result of a criminal trial conducted in a manner, or in circumstances, calculated to shut him out from a reasonable opportunity of establishing his innocence; or where guilt has been established or admitted, of receiving a sentence appropriate to his degree of guilt and relevant personal circumstances.[30]

Thus, Henchy J. was clearly of the opinion that the Constitution required proportionality between, on the one hand, the gravity of the offence and the personal circumstances of the offender, and on the other, the amount of punishment imposed. Equally significantly, he derived this principle primarily from the due process and personal liberty provisions of the Constitution. His stress on the need to individuate punishment (through his reference to the offender's personal circumstances) is also noteworthy; it foreshadowed later authorities, including *Cox* which we have already considered, to the same effect.

---

[26] Among the leading analyses of the history and meaning of the Eighth Amendment to the US Constitution are Granucci, "'Nor Cruel and Unusual Punishments Inflicted': The Original Meaning" (1969) 57 *Calif.L.Rev.* 839 and Baker and Baldwin, "Eighth Amendment Challenges to the Length of a Criminal Sentence: Following the Supreme Court from 'Precedent to Precedent'" (1985) 27 *Ariz.L.Rev.* 25.

[27] *Solem v. Helm* 463 U.S. 277 (1983).

[28] *Harmelin v. Michigan* 501 U.S. 957 (1991).

[29] [1976] I.R. 325 (S.C.).

[30] [1976] I.R. 325, 353.

It was not until the mid-1990s that these principles began to be applied by the superior courts in a concrete sentencing context. In *The People (DPP) v. W.C.*[31] Flood J. said that:

> ... the selection of the particular punishment to be imposed on an individual offender is subject to the constitutional requirement of proportionality. By this I mean that the imposition of a particular sentence must strike a balance between the particular circumstances of the commission of the relevant offence and the relevant personal circumstances of the offender.[32]

This reference by Flood J. to the constitutional basis of proportionality was taken up by Denham J .in *The People (D.P.P.) v. M.*,[33] one of the few Supreme Court judgments to date dealing exclusively with sentencing principles. In *M.*, the Court reduced from 18 years to 12 years the term of imprisonment imposed on a religious brother convicted of several sexual offences committed against children. Judgments were delivered by Egan and Denham JJ., and the other three members of the Court, including Finlay C.J. agreed with both. The judgment of Denham J. is the more germane for our present purposes. She said that sentences must be proportionate to both the gravity of the offence and the personal circumstances of the offender, which for this purpose includes the way he has responded to the charges. She referred to the judgment of Walsh J. in *The People (Attorney General) v. O'Driscoll*[34] in which he had said that in passing sentence, the courts must have regard not only to the particular crime, but also to the particular criminal.[35] She then went on to say that "[i]n a similar vein there is constitutional protection", quoting the statement of Henchy J. in *The State (Healy) v. Donoghue.*[36]

Taken together, the line of cases just considered (*Cox, Healy, W.C.*, and *M*) provides strong authority for the proposition that the requirement of proportionality in sentencing has a constitutional as well as a common-law foundation. The court in *O'Driscoll* did not refer to the Constitution as a basis for the principle of individuated sentencing, although it is significant that Denham J. in *M.*, when referring to the constitutional dimension, looked to *O'Driscoll* for support. It is reasonably safe to conclude, therefore, that when a judge has discretion as to the sentence to be imposed in a specific case (as she will have in respect of virtually every offence except murder), she must have regard to the principle of proportionality as defined in the cases just mentioned. In other

---

[31] [1994] 1 I.L.R.M. 321 (H.C.); better known as the *Lavinia Kerwick Case.*
[32] [1994] 1 I.L.R.M. 321, 325.
[33] [1994] 3 I.R. 306 (S.C.).
[34] (1972) 1 Frewen 351 (C.C.A.).
[35] (1972) 1 Frewen 351, 359.
[36] [1976] I.R. 325, 353 set out text with n. 30 above.

words, she is under an obligation to select a sentence which reflects both the gravity of the offence and the personal circumstances of the particular offender. This general principle is, admittedly, of little assistance in terms of identifying the kind or amount of punishment (if any) appropriate in a specific case. But it does strongly suggest that a judge cannot be guided solely by instrumental concerns such as the protection of the public or the need to show an example to others. These concerns can, of course, be reflected in the assessment of the gravity of the offence, but they must be tempered by consideration for the needs and circumstances of the offender.

The remaining, and more difficult, question is where this leaves mandatory sentences. Are the courts constitutionally entitled to strike down a mandatory sentence if they are convinced that its purpose or effect is to leave offenders liable to disproportionately heavy punishment? The cumulative effect of *Cox* and the later decisions in *W.C.* and *M* would seem be that the courts are so entitled. *Cox* showed that the Constitution will not tolerate the indiscriminate application of penalties and disqualifications to offenders without regard to their motivation for offending or their degree of guilt. The later cases were, admittedly, concerned primarily with the manner in which punishment is to be selected when there is a judicial selection to be made. But, the proportionality principle so strongly articulated in *W.C.* and *M* would be robbed of much of its meaning if the legislative branch of government was free to stipulate manda- tory sentences for a wide range of offences without regard to the variety of circumstances in which such offences may be committed. It is submitted, there- fore, that there is a constitutional requirement of proportionate punishment in Ireland and that this extends to prohibiting the statutory stipulation of manda- tory sentences which might result in the infliction of excessive sanctions. In- deed, if further support be needed for this proposition, one need only recall the relatively recent statement of Hamilton C.J. in *Rock v. Ireland*[37] (a case deal- ing with the constitutionality of restrictions on the right to silence) that the principle of proportionality "is by now a well-established tenet of Irish consti- tutional law".[38] There is no reason why the application of this principle should be confined to the assessment of statutory restrictions on constitutional rights or the legality of administrative action. It should be equally applicable to sen- tencing practices.

6. CONCLUSION

Its limitations notwithstanding, *Deaton* remains a leading case of the twentieth century. It is difficult to think of another Irish case that has exercised such an

---

[37] [1998] 2 I.L.R.M. 35 (S.C.).
[38] [1998] 2 I.L.R.M. 35, 49.

influence over the remainder of the common-law world. That alone would be a source of distinction, as relatively few Irish judgments, to use the language of the music industry, "make it on to the international scene". (There is an interesting study to be made of the international reception of Irish case law; it has never been quite clear why some Irish cases, such as *Deaton* and *People (Attorney General) v. Whelan*,[39] are frequently cited in foreign judgments and academic writings, while many other leading cases are not). The real significance of *Deaton*, however, is that it unambiguously consigned the selection of punishment to the judicial branch of government. By so doing, it has saved many defendants and offenders, not only in Ireland, but in many other parts of the world, from the arbitrary use or abuse of executive power. Were it not for the *Deaton* principle, for example, the appellant in *Browne v. The Queen*[40] might still be detained at the pleasure of the Governor-General of St. Christopher and Nevis. The principle has, in all probability, influenced the legal structure of sentencing in many Commonwealth countries with constitutions corresponding to the "Westminster model" (meaning that they provide for the separation of powers).

The Supreme Court in *Deaton* made a valiant effort to balance the exclusivity of the judicial role in the selection of punishment with respect for the democratic mandate of the legislature to enact rules of general application. This explains its apparently unquestioning acceptance of mandatory sentences. However, even within the text of the judgment may be found the germ of an argument to counter, possibly even on constitutional grounds, the more widespread use of such sentences. Ó Dalaigh C.J. stated quite emphatically that the selection of punishment was an integral part of the administration of justice.[41] One could argue that if the legislature were to provide mandatory sentences for a wide range of offences, it would, in effect, be selecting punishment for those offences and, therefore, in a sense engaging in the administration of justice. In a case decided some years after *Deaton*, Henchy J. held (in the High Court) that sentencing is not only part of the administration of justice but part of the trial of an offence.[42] If this so, then it follows that by virtue of the constitutional right to a fair trial, the convicted offender also has the right to a fair sentence.

---

[39] [1934] I.R. 518 (C.C.A.). *Whelan* is widely accepted as providing the standard definition of duress as a criminal defence. See also *People (Attorney General) v. Edge* [1943] I.R. 115 (S.C.) (kidnapping).

[40] [2000] A.C. 45 (P.C.).

[41] [1963] I.R. 170, 183.

[42] *The State (Woods) v. Attorney General* [1969] I.R. 385. See also *Application of Neilan* [1990] 2 I.R. 267 (C.C.A.) 287.

THE INDIGENT'S RIGHT TO COUNSEL
GIDEON V. WAINWRIGHT (1963)

CELIA RUMANN*

1. INTRODUCTION

In 1963, the United States Supreme Court ruled, for the first time, that the "right of an indigent defendant in a criminal trial to have the assistance of counsel is a fundamental right essential to a fair trial".[1] That ruling forever changed the administration of American justice and the view of what is essential for a fair trial. It recognised what legal commentators had asserted for years. That is, "[o]f all the rights that an accused person has, the right to be represented by counsel is by far the most pervasive, for it affects his ability to assert any other rights he may have".[2]

As Robert F. Kennedy noted, the Court's ruling was not pre-ordained. "If an obscure Florida convict named Clarence Earl Gideon had not sat down in his prison cell . . . to write a letter to the Supreme Court . . . the vast machinery of American law would have gone on functioning undisturbed. But Gideon did write that letter, the Court did look into his case . . . and the whole course of American legal history has been changed".[3]

In this article, I will discuss the factual background of the *Gideon* case and review the development of relevant case law which led to the decision. I will next examine the decision itself and trace some of the interpretations of the decision in subsequent litigation. Finally, I will discuss the continuing importance of this case.

2. *GIDEON*: CASE BACKGROUND

The facts of the *Gideon* case could not have been simpler.[4] It is perhaps the

---

*Assistant Federal Public Defender, District of Arizona; Adjunct Professor of Law, Arizona State University.

[1] *Gideon v. Wainwright*, 372 U.S. 335 (1963).
[2] Schaefer, "Federalism and State Criminal Procedure" (1965) 70 *Harv. L. Rev.* 1, 8.
[3] Lewis, *Gideon's Trumpet* (Vintage Press, New York, 1964) Rear Cover.
[4] For a full discussion surrounding the background and ruling of *Gideon*, see the groundbreaking work of Anthony Lewis in *Gideon's Trumpet, ibid.*

most ironic aspect of the story of *Gideon v. Wainwright* that such an important ruling should come from such a seemingly routine and uneventful case.

Clarence Earl Gideon had been "charged in a Florida state court with having broken and entered a poolroom with the intent to commit a misdemeanour".[5] This was a felony offence under Florida law.[6] Gideon appeared in court "without funds and without a lawyer" and asked the trial court to appoint counsel for him. That request was denied.[7]

At trial without counsel, "Gideon conducted his defence about as well as could be expected from a layman".[8] After his conviction, Gideon was sentenced to five years in the state prison.[9] He filed a filed a habeas corpus petition attacking his conviction and sentence in the Florida State Supreme Court, which was denied. He then filed an *in forma pauperis* petition for cert in the United States Supreme Court, which the Court granted on the question: "Should [the] Court's holding in *Betts v. Brady*, 316 U.S. 455, be reconsidered?"[10]

From this humble background arose one of the most important developments in American jurisprudence, the right to counsel for indigent people charged with crimes.

3. *GIDEON*: LEGAL BACKDROP

The case which the Supreme Court was reconsidering in *Gideon*, *Betts v. Brady*,[11] had set the standard for when appointment of counsel in state criminal cases was necessary. *Betts* was decided twenty years before *Gideon*. The *Betts* Court rejected the contention that the due-process clause of the Fourteenth Amendment provided a flat guarantee of counsel in state criminal trials. In so doing, the Court denied that the Sixth Amendment applied to the states wholesale. The Sixth Amendment provides, "In all criminal prosecutions, the accused shall enjoy the right . . . to have the Assistance of Counsel for his defence".[12] However, on its face, the Sixth Amendment only applies to the actions of the federal government. It could only be made applicable to the states, if at all, through the Fourteenth Amendment to the United States Constitution.

In *Betts*, the Court ruled that under the Fourteenth Amendment, a lawyer was only constitutionally required if the denial of counsel amounted to a "de-

---

[5] *Gideon*, 372 U.S., at 336.
[6] *ibid.*
[7] 372 U.S., at 337.
[8] *ibid.*
[9] *ibid.*
[10] 372 U.S., at 338.
[11] 316 U.S. 455 (1942).
[12] U.S. Const. amend VI.

nial of fundamental fairness". The Fourteenth Amendment states, in relevant part, "No State shall make or enforce any law which shall abridge the privileges or immunities of citizens of the United States; nor shall any State deprive any person of life, liberty, or property, without due process of law; nor deny to any person within its jurisdiction the equal protection of the laws".[13] It was the interaction between the Sixth and Fourteenth amendments that the Supreme Court analysed in both *Betts* and *Gideon.*

Instead of incorporating the Sixth Amendment requirement of counsel and making it applicable to the states, the Court in *Betts* laid out the "special circumstances" test for determining the necessity of counsel. The Court said:

> Asserted denial of due process of law is to be tested by an appraisal of the totality of facts in a given case. That which may, in one setting, constitute a denial of fundamental fairness, shocking to the universal sense of justice, may, in other circumstances, and in the light of other considerations, fall short of such denial. In the application of such a concept there is always the danger of falling into the habit of formulating the guarantee into a set of hard and fast rules the application of which in a given case may be to ignore the qualifying factors.[14]

Thus, under the "special circumstances" test, counsel was only required if there was something about a case or defendant that made it particularly complex. The courts considered such factors as the age and education of the defendant, the complexity of the offence, the conduct of the court and prosecutors, and defendant's familiarity with the criminal justice system. Consideration by various courts of these factors resulted in confusing precedent with counsel being required in one case and not so in another, with little meaningful legal or factual differences.[15]

In many ways, *Betts* had been something of an anomaly in the United States Supreme Court decisions regarding the application of the right to counsel. Ten years before it, the Court had decided *Powell v. Alabama.*[16] In *Powell*, the Court ruled on the necessity of the assistance of counsel for defendants charged with capital offences in state court.[17] For the first time, the Supreme Court in *Powell* invalidated a state criminal conviction for failure to comply with federal standards of justice.[18]

In determining that counsel was necessary under the facts of the *Powell* case, the Court recognised:

---

[13]U.S. Const. amend XIV, sec. 1.
[14]*Betts,* 316 U.S. at 462.
[15]*Gideon,* 372 U.S., at 350-351 (Harlan, J., concurring).
[16]287 U.S. 45 (1932).
[17]*Powell,* 287 U.S., at 49.
[18]*Gideon's Trumpet,* 108.

The right to be heard would be, in many cases, of little avail if it did not comprehend the right to be heard by counsel. Even the intelligent and educated layman has small and sometimes no skill in the science of law. If charged with crime, he is incapable, generally, of determining for himself whether the indictment is good or bad. He is unfamiliar with the rules of evidence. Left without the aid of counsel he may be put on trial without a proper charge, and convicted upon incompetent evidence, or evidence irrelevant to the issues or otherwise inadmissible. He lacks both the skill and knowledge adequately to prepare his defence, even though he have a perfect one. He requires the guiding hand of counsel at every step in the proceedings against him. Without it, though he be not guilty, he faces the danger of conviction because he does not know how to establish his innocence. If that be true of men of intelligence, how much more true is it of ignorant and illiterate, or those of feeble intellect.[19]

The *Powell* case has been interpreted to stand for the proposition that in a capital case, the failure of the trial court to appoint counsel is a denial of due process within the meaning of the Fourteenth Amendment.[20]

The *Powell* case was followed by the decision in *Johnson v. Zerbst*,[21] which announced an absolute rule that the Sixth Amendment required the appointment of counsel for all who could not afford it, in federal felony criminal cases. In so ruling, the Court again recognised the unfairness in forcing a defendant to face a criminal prosecution without the assistance of counsel. It noted:

[T]he average defendant does not have the professional legal skill to protect himself when brought before a tribunal with power to take his life and liberty, wherein the prosecution is represented by experienced and learned counsel. That which is simple, orderly and necessary to the lawyer, to the untrained layman may appear intricate, complex and mysterious.[22]

Against the backdrop of these cases, the *Betts* case was in many ways "an anachronism when handed down".[23] This anomaly was recognised by Justice Douglas' concurrence in *McNeal v. Culver*,[24] (which was joined by Mr. Justice Brennan), wherein he stated:

---

[19] *Powell*, 287 U.S., at 68-69.
[20] See *Hamilton v. Alabama*, 368 U.S. 52 (1961) (holding that in a capital case, a defendant need make no showing of particular need or of prejudice resulting from absence of counsel and that henceforth assistance of counsel was a constitutional requirement in capital cases).
[21] 304 U.S. 458 (1938).
[22] *Johnson*, 304 U.S., 463.
[23] *Gideon*, 372 U.S. 345.
[24] 365 U.S. 109, 119 (1961).

Betts v. Brady requires the indigent, when convicted in a trial where he has not counsel, to show that there was fundamental unfairness . . . This is a heavy burden to carry, especially for an accused who has no lawyer and cannot afford to hire one. It is a burden placed on an accused solely by reason of his poverty. Its only sanction is *Betts v. Brady*, which is so at war with our concept of equal justice under law that it should be overruled.[25]

Furthermore, the *Betts* case was decided by a six to three majority of the Court, with Justice Black writing for the dissent, in which he concluded that no person should be "deprived of counsel merely because of his poverty. Any other practice seems to me to defeat the promise of our democratic society to provide equal justice under the law".[26] This defeat of the promise of equal justice under the law is exactly where the matter stayed for twenty-years, until the *Gideon* decision was handed down.

4. *GIDEON* RULING

In *Gideon*, Justice Black's vision of what constituted 'equal justice under the law,' became the law of the land. Writing for the Court, Justice Black penned the decision that overruled *Betts*. Though there were four opinions, the Court's and three concurrences, the decision to overrule *Betts* was unanimous.

After a discussion of the apparent conflict between the Court's rulings in *Powell* and *Johnson* with the *Betts* decision, the Court decided:

Not only these precedents but also reason and reflection require us to recognise that in our adversary system of criminal justice, any person haled into court, who is too poor to hire a lawyer, cannot be assured a fair trial unless counsel is provided for him. This seems to us to be an obvious truth. Governments, both state and federal, quite properly spend vast sums of money to establish machinery to try defendant's accused of crime. Lawyers to prosecute are everywhere deemed essential to protect the public's interest in an orderly society. Similarly, there are few defendants charged with crime, few indeed, who fail to hire the best lawyers they can get to prepare and present their defences. That government hires lawyers to prosecute and defendants who have the money hire lawyers to defend are the strongest indications of the widespread belief that lawyers in criminal courts are necessities, not luxuries. The right of one charged with

---

[25] *ibid.*
[26] *Betts*, 316 U.S., at 477 (Black J., dissenting).

crime to counsel may not be deemed fundamental and essential to fair trials in some countries, but it is in ours.[27]

Through these words, the United States Supreme Court recognised the fundamental nature of the role of counsel in criminal cases.

5. *GIDEON*: INTERPRETATIONS OF THE RIGHT TO COUNSEL SINCE 1963

Left unanswered by the *Gideon* decision were all the practical application issues inherent in the ruling. What does it mean to be indigent? Was the ruling retroactive? Does the right to counsel apply to misdemeanours? What about for appeals? What does it mean to have counsel? For the last forty-five years in the United States, defendants, lawyers, legislatures and courts at all levels, have struggled with questions such as these and the implementation of the *Gideon* decision. A search of any legal database reveals that literally hundreds of appellate decisions that have discussed the issue in some form or other.[28]

Perhaps the first issue that arose was to ensure that all states provided counsel at trial to those charged with felony offences. This was not as troublesome as might have been the case. Though not required before the *Gideon* case, many states already supported the notion that appointment of counsel was necessary, and many states provided counsel.

Those states demonstrated their support through the filing of amicus briefs on the counsel issue in *Gideon*.[29] Twenty-three states and the American Civil Liberties Union filed amicus briefs asking that *Betts* be overturned.[30] Only two states, Alabama and North Carolina filed amicus briefs urging affirmance of *Betts*.[31] Thus, many states clearly supported the proposition urged by *Gideon*.

The same day that the Supreme Court decided *Gideon*, it ruled affirmatively on the question of whether indigent defendants have the right to counsel for their first appeal as a matter of right.[32] Later however, the Court declined to extent the right to counsel beyond such appeals in *Ross v. Moffit*.[33] *Ross* held that states did not have a duty to appoint counsel for indigent state prisoners seeking discretionary review of their convictions.[34]

In late 1999, the Supreme Court was again faced with the question of the

---

[27] *Gideon*, 372 U.S., at 344
[28] This article does not attempt to answer all the questions raised by the *Gideon* decision; rather, included here are some of the highlights of the subsequent resolution of these issues.
[29] *Gideon's Trumpet*, 141-144.
[30] *Gideon*, 372 U.S., at 336.
[31] *Gideon*, 372 U.S., at 336.
[32] *Douglas v. California*, 372 U.S., at 353 (1963).
[33] 417 U.S., at 600 (1974).
[34] *ibid.*

right to counsel on appeal. In *Smith v. Robbins*, the Court addressed the question of the validity of a procedure allowing defence counsel, upon concluding an appeal would be frivolous, to file a 'brief' that summarises the procedural and factual history of the case, but makes no substantive legal arguments. Instead, counsel requests that the court independently examine the record for arguable issues. Over a dissent of four of the justices, the Court upheld this procedure.[35]

Left unanswered in *Gideon*, was whether the right to assistance of counsel was claimable by all defendants charged with misdemeanours or serious misdemeanours as well as felonies. The Supreme Court's most recent word on this issue came in *Scott v. Illinois*, which held that the right to counsel applies only to misdemeanour cases in which imprisonment is imposed.[36]

This rule was a modification of the holding in *Argersinger v. Hamlin*.[37] In *Argersinger*, the Court held that appointment of counsel was required if imprisonment was possible for the offence charged. The *Scott* Court stepped back from this ruling to limit the requirement to those cases in which jail time was actually imposed.

In a further limitation of the impact of the *Gideon* decision, in *Nichols v. United States*,[38] the Supreme Court ruled that convictions so obtained, without the assistance of counsel, can be used as a basis to enhance sentences for subsequent convictions so long as counsel is provided in that later case.[39] The *Nichols* decision overruled the case of *Baldasar v. Illinois*,[40] in which the Court had ruled that a prior uncounseled misdemeanour conviction, constitutional under *Scott*, could not be used collaterally to convert a second misdemeanour conviction into a felony under the applicable Illinois sentencing enhancement statute.[41]

Perhaps the area involving the most frequent and contentious litigation to arise as a result of the *Gideon* case is that of what it means to have 'counsel.' Does the right to counsel mean merely the right to have a warm body, licensed in the practice of law, stand by, while the system processes human fodder for prison cells, or does it mean something more than that? The Court answered this question by ruling that "the right to counsel is the right to the effective assistance of counsel".[42] However, this did not end the inquiry.

Though the Sixth Amendment right to counsel is the right to effective assistance of counsel, what does this mean and how is 'effectiveness' measured?

---

[35] *Smith v. Robbins*, 528 U.S. 259, 120 S.Ct. 746 (2000).
[36] *Scott v. Illinois*, 440 U.S. 367 (1979).
[37] 407 U.S. 25 (1972).
[38] *Nichols v. United States*, 511 U.S. 738 (1994).
[39] *ibid.*
[40] 446 U.S. 222 (1980).
[41] *ibid.*
[42] *McMann v. Richardson*, 397 U.S. 759, 771 n. 14 (1970).

These questions were answered by the Supreme Court in the case of *Strickland v. Washington*.[43]

In *Strickland*, a capital case, the Court analysed the question of what is necessary to reverse a trial and sentence based on a claim of ineffective assistance of counsel. The Court concluded that in order to reverse a conviction or set aside a death sentence, a defendant must show, first, that counsel's performance was deficient and, second, that the deficient performance prejudiced the defence so as to deprive the defendant of a fair trial.[44]

The Court further explained that the proper standard for judging whether the attorney's performance was deficient was based on a totality of circumstances analysis, comparing counsel's performance with that of "reasonably competent attorney".[45] With respect to the second prong of the analysis, in order to show prejudice, the defendant was required to show that there was "a reasonable probability that, but for counsel's unprofessional errors, the result of the proceeding would have been different".[46]

As Justice Marshall lamented in his dissent, the test laid out in *Strickland* effectively means that the "Sixth Amendment is not violated when a manifestly guilty defendant is convicted after a trial in which he was represented by a manifestly ineffective attorney".[47] This analysis of the effect of the *Strickland* holding on the dream of equal justice under the law has been echoed by judges, lawyers and legal commentators since it was decided.[48]

6. CONTINUING IMPORTANCE

Gideon remains one of the most important American cases of the 20th Century. "A month after the decision [United States Supreme Court] Justice Clark called *Gideon* an "historic case," one that would "possibly have more physical impact on the administration of justice than any decided by the Court".[49] Time and history have proven the prophetic nature of Justice Clark's comments. The impact is felt by every indigent person accused of crime, when they are called before a court and have the protection of counsel to speak on their behalf and protect their interests.

This enhanced protection for criminal defendants in the United States stands in contrast not only to those provided under many international law covenants such as the European Convention on Human Rights and the International Cov-

---

[43] 466 U.S. 668 (1984).
[44] 466 U.S., at 687.
[45] *Strickland*, 466 U.S., at 687.
[46] 466 U.S., at 669.
[47] 466 U.S., at 711 (Marshall, J. dissenting).
[48] See, S. Bright, *Glimpses at a Dream Yet to be Realized*, 22-Mar Champion 12 (1998).
[49] Anthony Lewis, *Gideon's Trumpet*, 201.

enant on Civil and Political Rights and but also to the position in Ireland. These seem to be more akin to the rule laid down in the *Betts* decision, which *Gideon* overruled. For example, Article 6(3)(c) of the European Convention on Human Rights provides for free legal services only "when the interests of justice so require", a requirement which has been interpreted in much the same way as the "special circumstances" analysis rejected by the *Gideon* Court: the interests of justice are measured by "considering the case as a whole, including the complexity of the issues".[50] In Ireland, the Criminal Justice (Legal Aid) Act, 1962 provides for free legal aid in criminal proceedings for indigent defendants, where the gravity of the charge or "exceptional circumstances" make legal aid essential in the interests of justice. In *State (Healy) v. Donoghue*, the Supreme Court held that the due process and fundamental rights provisions of the Constitution (Articles 38.1, 40.3 and 40.4) generated safeguards for indigent criminal defendants, so that District Justices must inform criminal defendants appearing before them that such legal aid was available. Since the applicants had not been so informed, it was a violation of their constitutional rights to be convicted in the absence of legal aid, their convictions were quashed:

> A person who has been convicted and deprived of his liberty as a result of a prosecution which, because of his poverty, he has had to bear without legal aid has reason to complain that he has been meted out less than his constitutional due. This is particularly true if the absence of legal aid is compounded by factors such as a grave or complex charge; or ignorance, illiteracy, immaturity or other condition rendering the accused incompetent to cope properly with the prosecution; or an inability, because of detentional restraint, to find and produce witnesses; or simply the fumbling incompetence that may occur when an accused is precipitated into the public glare and alien complexity of courtroom procedures, and is confronted with the might of a prosecution backed by the state. As the law stands, a legal-aid certificate is the shield provided against such an unjust attack.[51]

Though the statutory language is reminiscent of *Betts*, the reasoning of the Court in *Healy* is reminiscent of *Gideon*. In particular, underlying both *Healy*

---

[50] *Granger v. UK* Series A, No. 174 (1990) 12 E.H.R.R. 469.

[51] [1976] I.R. 325 (H.C. and S.C.) 354 *per* Henchy J. See also [1976] I.R. 325, 350-351 *per* O'Higgins C.J. referring to *Gideon*; [1976] I.R. 325, 357 *per* Griffin J.; *cp.* [1976] I.R. 325, 363-364 *per* Kenny J. See also *McGorley v. Governor of Mountjoy Prison* [1996] 2 I.L.R.M. 331 (H.C.); Supreme Court, unreported, 24 April 1997. However, the statutory entitlement to legal aid applies to trials and appeals, but not to the earlier or ancillary stages of criminal proceedings (*State (O.) v. Daly* [1977] I.R. 312 (S.C.)); and the defendant may expressly or implicitly waive the right to legal aid (*State (Sharkey) v. McArdle* Supreme Court, unreported, 4 June 1981). See also *O'Neill v. Butler*, unreported, High Court, 26 November 1979, McMahon J.; *Cahill v. Reilly* [1994] 3 I.R. 547 (H.C.); *Byrne v. McDonnell* [1997] I.R. 392 (H.C.).

and *Gideon* is the concern that perhaps the most intrusive form of government conduct is an attempt by the government to take away a person's life or liberty through a criminal prosecution. *Gideon* forever changed the balance of power in such cases, tipping the scales of justice closer to level between the state and an accused person. For the first time, no person would face jail in the United States without a lawyer of his or her own to meet the experienced and able attorneys representing the state.

Though subsequent case decisions suggest that the Court is hesitant to expand the right to counsel or meaningfully evaluate the quality of the representation provided, so long as counsel was physically present during the proceedings, the right to counsel remains bedrock law and continues to have a tremendous impact on the criminal justice system.

The import of *Gideon* becomes clearer when one considers the astronomical rise in the numbers of prosecutions and the rate of incarceration in the United States. Statistics gathered by the United States Department of Justice reveal that at midyear 1998, one in every 150 U.S. residents was incarcerated, with an estimated 1,802,496 men and women held in the country's prisons and jails.[52] This was an increase of more than 76,700 inmates during the preceding 12 months, up 4.4 percent. Overall the incarceration rate has more than doubled in the past 12 years.[53]

A 1996 report on indigent defence in the United States published by the Department of Justice, Bureau of Justice Statistics further demonstrates the importance of the *Gideon* decision. It reports that though States and localities use several methods for delivering indigent defence services: public defender programs, assigned counsel, and contract attorney systems, 28 percent of State court prosecutors reported in 1992 that their jurisdiction used public defender programs exclusively to provide indigent counsel.[54]

Due to the rising numbers of criminal prosecutions, the financial cost of *Gideon* is increasing. In 1990, State and local governments spent approximately $1.3 billion on public defender services. In 1979, this figure was about $300 million. In constant 1990 dollars, State and local expenditures doubled for public defence from 1979 to 1990.[55] Furthermore, about three-fourths of the inmates in State prisons and about half of those in Federal prisons in 1991 received publicly-provided legal counsel for the offence for which they were serving time. In 1992 about 80% of defendants charged with felonies in the Nation's 75 largest counties relied on a public defender or on assigned counsel for legal representation.[56]

---

[52]Department of Justice, Bureau of Justice Statistics, Press Release, March 14, 1999.
[53]*ibid.*
[54]Dept. of Justice, Bureau of Justice Statistics Selected Findings, Indigent Defense, February 1996, NCJ-15890.
[55]*ibid.*
[56]*ibid.*

Those attorneys providing indigent representation are often hindered in their attempts to provide effective representation by the systems in which they accept appointment. Such limitations arise from the method of appointment, payment limitations and assistance for expenses. For example, in New York state, private attorneys accepting appointment of non-capital cases are paid 40 dollars per hour for in-court time and 25 dollars per hour for out-of-court time.[57] Payment on misdemeanour cases is capped at $800, while payment on felonies is capped at $1200 by the same statutory scheme in New York.[58]

And New York is not alone. In such states as Alabama, compensation for any "reasonable" out-of-court work by counsel is limited to 30 dollars per hour.[59] Though the situation is improving somewhat, as Yale Law Professor Stephen Bright has noted, "[t]he court-appointed lawyer in Alabama who spends the time required to prepare properly for a capital trial, or many other serious cases, may earn less than the minimum wage. A lawyer can make more money flipping hamburgers at a fast food restaurant than defending a capital case that takes several hundred hours of preparations".[60]

Such seemingly arbitrary "capping" of fees results in a disincentive for lawyers to go beyond providing minimal assistance. Knowing that her work will not be compensated if she spends any additional time on a case, a lawyer, aware of approaching a cap, is forced to risk providing free services or no services. No other participant in the criminal justice system faces this type of dilemma. Given the costs of handling such cases, in not only economic terms, but also in intellectual and emotional terms, payment schemes such as this often result in qualified and capable lawyers refusing to accept appointment of indigent cases.[61]

The reality is that the importance of *Gideon* is measured by every attorney who stands up to represent an indigent person charged with an offence for which they face imprisonment or death. If that attorney takes his or her obligation to that client as they would someone who was paying for their services themselves and if the courts provide the necessary financial support for services such as experts and investigation, the importance of *Gideon* is immeasurable. Whether the defendant is convicted or acquitted, Justice Black's vision for 'equal justice under the law' is strengthened, and so too is the entire justice system. If, on the other hand, that attorney, whether through inexperience, overwork, economics or apathy, fails to provide the effective assistance of counsel, irrespective of the prejudice to the client, the entire system of justice diminished. Likewise, if the legislatures and courts fail or refuse to provide the

---

[57] See Liotti, "Does *Gideon* Still Make a Difference?" (1998) 2 *N.Y.CityL.Rev*. 105, 124.
[58] *ibid.*
[59] Ala. Code § 15-12-21(d) (1999).
[60] S. Bright, *Glimpses at a Dream Yet to be Realized*, 22-Mar Champion 12 (1998), 14.
[61] Liotti, above n. 57, 132.

necessary support systems to counsel, through adequate funding for experts and investigation, justice suffers.

7. CONCLUSION

Legal commentators have long recognised that "[t]he most innocent man, pressed by the awful solemnities of public accusation and trial, may be incapable of supporting his own cause. He may be utterly unfit to cross-examine the witnesses against him, to point out the contradictions or defects of their testimony, and to counteract it by properly introducing it and applying his own".[62] The United States Supreme Court recognised this truism and the need to unequivocally counteract it for the first time in its 1963 decision of *Gideon v. Wainwright*. Though it has been almost 40 years since the *Gideon* decision, its importance increases daily as the number of those accused increases.

"It will be an enormous social task to bring to life the dream of *Gideon v. Wainwright* – the dream of a vast, diverse country in which every man charged with crime will be capably defended, no matter what his economic circumstances, and in which the lawyer representing him will do so proudly, without resentment at an unfair burden, sure of the support needed to make an adequate defence".[63] Those words of Anthony Lewis aptly spelled out the challenge of 'equal justice under the law.' It is a challenge not only to the lawyers assigned to represent the indigent, but upon the entire system of justice to provide the necessary support. But it is a dream that can be fulfilled and made reality due to the vision and courage of the United States Supreme Court in ruling as it did in the *Gideon* case. No case did more in the last century to make that dream possible.

---

[62]Rawle, *A View of the Constitution* (Philadelphia, 1825) 127-8.
[63]*Gideon's Trumpet*, 205.

THE DANGEROUS IDEA OF EUROPE?
VAN GEND EN LOOS (1963)

NIAL FENNELLY*

1. INTRODUCTION

The notion of a leading case as a primary source of law sits uneasily with the French rule forbidding the judges from interpreting the laws.[1] Montesquieu thought that: "The judges of the nation are but the mouthpiece of the law; inanimate beings who may neither moderate its strength nor its rigour".[2] *Van Gend en Loos*[3] was decided in 1963 when, even though the language of the case was Dutch, it was, of course, drafted in French and the "frequently oracular tone"[4] of French legal style prevailed at the Court of Justice. Citation of earlier decisions as authority – so systematically practised today – was unknown.

The ruling of the Court of Justice in *Van Gend en Loos* constituted, by the common accord of both its admirers and its critics, a major constitutional step in the development of the European Community. Its core element is the ruling that the Treaty of Rome represents more than a mere international agreement imposing obligations, at the level of international law, as between the contracting States. It confers rights on individuals which become part of their legal heritage and which national courts are bound to protect. From this central proposition the Court then or later deduced many of the main principles of Community law.

Professor Sir Patrick Neill, in his much publicised polemic, "The European Court of Justice: A Case Study in Judicial Activism", described the Court as:

---

*Judge of the Supreme Court.

[1] See West *et al.*, *The French Legal System. An Introduction* (Fourmat Publishing, London, 1992) 41, quoting from *Discours préliminaire du Code Civil de 1804 par Portalis*.
[2] See Arnull, "Interpretation and Precedent in European Community Law" in Andenas and Jacobs, (eds.), *European Community Law in the English Courts* (Clarendon Press, Oxford, 1998) 128. See Montesquieu, *De l'esprit des lois*, Livre XI, Chapitre 6: "Mais les juges de la nation ne sont . . . que la bouche qui prononce les paroles de la loi; des êtres inanimés qui n'en peuvent modérer ni la force ni la rigueur".
[3] Case 26/62, [1963] E.C.R. 1.
[4] Giuseppe Federico Mancini, Judge at the Court of Justice, "Crosscurrents and the Tide at the European Court of Justice" (1995) 4 *I.J.E.L.* 121.

"a court with a mission; . . . not an orthodox court"; as "a potentially dangerous court – the danger being that inherent in uncontrolled judicial power".[5] The starting point of his attack is the "seminal decision" in *Van Gend en Loos*, wherein he saw the Court as having already adopted its characteristic approach to interpretation.

2. THE BACKGROUND

2.1 Context

Van Gend en Loos was decided on February 5, 1963, barely five years after the entry into force of the Treaty of Rome. The Community was composed only of the six founding Member States. This foundation stone of European unity was laid three weeks to the day after President de Gaulle had unilaterally pronounced his notorious veto of the first United Kingdom negotiations on entry to the Community and one week after their breaking off.

The Community was to be based, at least in its first stages, on a customs union whose proclaimed objective was "the prohibition between Member States of customs duties on imports and exports" (Article 9[6]). The programme of progressive abolition of duties laid down by Articles 13 to 15[7] was not to be achieved until the end of the transitional period, *i.e.*, the end of 1969. The realisation of the ultimate internal market project would, however, have been inconceivable without a customs union between the Member States.

The progressive establishment of the customs union was underpinned by an essential standstill provision, Article 12[8], the meaning and applicability of which provided the bone of contention for *Van Gend en Loos*. It obliges Member States to "refrain from introducing between themselves any new customs duties on imports or exports . . . *and from increasing those which they already apply in their trade with each other*" (emphasis added).

There could not have been any doubt about the content, as distinct from the

---

[5] "The European Court of Justice – A Case Study in Judicial Activism" by Sir Patrick Neill Q.C., Warden of All Souls College Oxford presented as written evidence to the House of Lords Select Committee on the European Communities (HL Paper 88, Session 1994-1995 18th Report 1996 Intergovernmental Conference, 218-245); see reply by David Edward, Judge at the Court of Justice, "Judicial Activism – Myth or Reality?" in *Essays in Honour of Lord Mackenzie-Stuart* (Trenton Publishing, 1996) 29, (hereafter "Edward"). The word "task" is the English translation of the French "*mission*". See Articles 164 and 166 of the Treaty Establishing the European Community, 1957, referred to throughout as "the Treaty". Articles 164 and 166 have since been renumbered as Articles 220 and 222 respectively following the Treaty of Amsterdam 1997.

[6] Article 9 has since been renumbered as Article 23.

[7] These articles have since been repealed.

[8] Article 12 has since been renumbered as Article 25.

application, of this provision.[9] It imposes an express negative obligation. Any increase in an existing customs duty on a specific product would be in breach of the Member State's Treaty obligations. The issue was not whether that provision could be invoked at the international level of the Court of Justice against a defaulting Member State but whether an affected individual could claim to do so in his national court. That is the issue that enabled the increase of a duty to produce a great constitutional judgment.

2.2 The facts

The Dutch company, Van Gend en Loos, in September 1960, imported a consignment of ureaformaldehyde from the Federal Republic of Germany into the Netherlands. It claimed that the import duty applied to it, as of January 1, 1958, the date of entry into force of the Treaty, had been three per cent *ad valorem*. Between these two dates, the three Benelux countries had adopted as between themselves, by the Brussels Protocol, a new tariff classification, applying the Brussels Nomenclature, which led to the same product being assigned to a newly created sub-head subject to a duty of eight per cent. In simple terms, the duty was increased from three to eight per cent, in direct breach of Article 12.

It has often been overlooked that the Dutch Government maintained that the correct duty as of January 1, 1958, according to the former classification, was not three but ten percent. The Court of Justice left this outstanding matter, which was of course crucial to the claim of Van Gend en Loos, to the further inquiry of the national court. If it had been decided by the referring court, as the Dutch Government maintained it should have been, the matter would never have arisen.

Van Gend en Loos challenged the eight per cent tariff before the Tariefcommissie, the responsible administrative court, which referred two questions to the Court of Justice using only for the second time the preliminary reference procedure[10] provided by Article 177 of the Treaty.[11] The first question asked:

> Whether Article 12 of the EEC Treaty has direct application within the territory of a Member State, in other words, whether nationals of such a state can, on the basis of the article in question, lay claim to individual rights which the courts must protect . . . .

---

[9] It is true that the Netherlands contended that the provision did not apply to an increase consequent on a reclassification; this was rejected both by the Advocate General and the Court.

[10] The first was Case 13/61, *De Geus v. Bosch* [1962] E.C.R. 45.

[11] Article 177 has since been renumbered as Article 234.

3. THE PROCEDURE BEFORE THE COURT

3.1 Observations received

The Court of Justice received observations from Van Gend en Loos itself as well as the Commission and three Member State Governments, the Netherlands, Belgium and the Federal Republic of Germany. Only the Commission supported the position of Van Gend en Loos. However, none of the Member States shared the rigid dualist tradition regarding the force of international agreements, so firmly enshrined in Article 29.6 of the Irish Constitution[12] and which represents the historic common law approach.[13]

3.2 The plaintiff

There were three central planks to the Van Gend en Loos argument:

– Article 12 imposed a negative obligation and required no act of incorporation into the law of the Member States;

– Article 12 equally did not require any act of implementation at Community level;

– the Article protects individuals adversely affected by Member State action infringing it and must, consequently, have direct effect.

Clearly, the third point was the crucial one.

3.3 The Commission

The Commission, in a far-reaching submission supported these arguments, but also emphasised the importance of the case for the viability of the Treaty. The Treaty had established a system of Community law, which must be applied uniformly throughout the Community. Consequently, interpretation, as distinct from application, could not be left to the national courts. It also followed that national courts must ensure that Community law prevail over conflicting national law. Article 12, in particular, was capable of having direct effect.

---

[12] Article 29.6 provides that: "No international agreement shall be part of the domestic law of the State save as may be determined by the Oireachtas". This appears, read in the light of the reservation of "the sole and exclusive power of making laws for the State . . ." to the Oireachtas by Article 15.2.1, to mean that such effect can only be given by legislation. See, *inter alia, Norris v. Attorney General* [1984] I.R. 154 (S.C.)

[13] Lord Denning M.R. said in *McWhirter v. AG* [1972] C.M.L.R. 882 (C.A.) 886: "Even though the Treaty of Rome has been signed it has no effect as far as these courts are concerned, until it is made an Act of Parliament". See discussion in Birkinshaw, "European integration and United Kingdom Constitutional Law" in Andenas, (ed.), *English Public Law and the Common law of Europe* (Key Haven Publications, London, 1998).

3.4 Member States

None of the three intervening Member States took a stand against the very principle of direct effect. Belgium, for example, merely said that Article 12 was not "one of the provisions" which can have direct effect. The Court had, of course, significantly, decided less than one year before, in *De Geus v. Bosch* that certain of the competition rules of the Treaty, Article 85[14] in particular, had direct effect.[15] Germany accepted direct effect though limited to measures taken by the institutions: Article 189[16] provides that regulations are to "be binding in [their] entirety and directly applicable in the Member States".

It was clear, moreover, that the issue could not be debated in isolation from the question of the respective roles and jurisdictions of the national courts and of the Court of Justice. Direct effect would be meaningless without a competent jurisdiction to give it effect. Individuals had no direct access to the Court of Justice in respect of infringements of the Treaty by the Member States. Article 173[17] of the Treaty allowed individuals to challenge Community acts affecting them directly. They had to rely on their national courts in respect of national acts. Article 177 was the only procedure by which meaning could be given to their claims based on Community law.

The Netherlands Government argued that only the Commission, pursuant to Article 169[18] of the Treaty, or a Member State, pursuant to Article 170[19], could complain of an infringement by a Member State. The Court of Justice certainly could not be asked a question about such an infringement through the mechanism of the Article 177 procedure, since that Article is concerned not with application but with interpretation. This raised the issue of what could be the purpose of providing for the interpretation of the Treaty at the behest of national courts if the latter had no power to apply the answer?

The Belgian Government adopted a slightly different approach. It saw the problem as one of national, *in casu* Dutch, constitutional law. It was for the Dutch courts to decide on issues arising between the terms of two international agreements which, according to that country's approach, were part of national law. On such a national constitutional question the Belgian Government argued that the Court of Justice had no role to play.

---

[14] Article 85 has since been renumbered as Article 81.
[15] *De Geus v. Bosch*, n.10 above.
[16] Article 189 has since been renumbered as Article 249.
[17] Article 173 has since been renumbered as Article 230.
[18] Article 169 has since been renumbered as Article 226.
[19] Article 170 has since been renumbered as Article 227.

4. The Advocate General's Opinion

4.1 On direct effect

Advocate General Roemer was not prepared to accept what he acknowledged to be the very impressive argument of the Commission that "judged by the international law of contract and by the general legal practice between States, the European Treaties represent[ed] a far-reaching legal innovation . . .". He accepted that the Community did not consist solely of contractual relations between States, since it had established its own independent institutions. He also accepted that some provisions of the [Rome] Treaty were "intended to be incorporated into national Law", notably the competition rules found in Articles 85 and 86.[20] He also foresaw that certain articles, such as those dealing with free movement of persons, would have direct effect in the future.

However, the Advocate General followed the line of the Member States regarding the question of the possible direct effect of the great bulk of the Treaty. Both the wording and the context of most provisions showed that they were intended only to lay obligations on the Member States. Article 169, combined with Article 171,[21] provided for a "supranational approach", by allowing the Commission to bring infringement proceedings in the Court of Justice against Member States. Following a declaration by the Court, the Member State was bound to comply, but there was, he stressed, no provision permitting it to make a declaration of nullity of national legal rules. This, in his view, would have been essential if it had been intended to make the direct application of the Treaty prevail over national law.

Advocate General Roemer reviewed in some detail the complexities, as he saw it, of permitting Article 12 to have direct effect, given the continued functions of the Member States and the changing Community-law environment. He thought that "the effect of an international agreement depends in the first place on the legal force which its authors intended its individual provisions to have, whether they are to be merely programmes or declarations of intent, or obligations to act on the international plane or whether some of them are to have a direct effect on the legal system of the Member States".[22] Thus, without ruling out on grounds of principle the possibility of direct effect, the Advocate General thought that Article 12 was not, on its own merits, a suitable candidate.

4.2 Constitutions of Member States

It is perhaps in his review of the constitutional implications of a contrary ruling that the Advocate General confronted the issue of greatest long term impor-

---

[20] See text with n.10 above. Article 86 has since been renumbered as Article 82.
[21] Article 171 has since been renumbered as Article 228.
[22] [1963] E.C.R. 1, 19.

tance for Community law and for the role of the Court of Justice. This was, in reality, the nettle which the Commission was asking the Court to grasp so firmly in its judgment. This is why, even if the Advocate General's Opinion was not followed, it is important to understand its legal and constitutional context, particularly the review of the relationship between national law and international agreements in the constitutions of the original six Member States. None of them contained a negative formulation such as that expressed in Article 29.6 of the Irish Constitution, in effect making implementing legislation a pre-condition for any domestic-law effect. In all, with the possible exception of Federal Republic of Germany, mere ratification of an international agreement sufficed to give it internal legal force. Accordingly, the ratification of the Treaty in accordance with the Treaty's own provisions (Articles 247 and 248)[23] was probably, though coincidentally, all that was required for it to have that effect.

The following, is the essence of the Advocate General's review of the laws of the Member States on the subject: Article 66 of the Netherlands Constitution, gave international agreements, subject to their own terms, precedence over national law; neither the Luxembourg, Belgian nor Italian Constitutions contained any express provision, but the courts of each State accorded effect to the terms of ratified international agreements. Article 55 of the French Fifth Republic Constitution of October 4, 1958, which creates no special category for the European Treaties, accorded such agreements precedence over laws, subject to reciprocity by the other contracting States. Article 25 of the German Basic Law provided that the general rules of international law should take precedence over legislation and created rights in favour of individuals, though the Advocate General expressed doubt concerning the case of a clash with later laws; on the other hand the basic law also provided expressly for cases of transfer of sovereignty, as had been done in the case of the Treaty of Rome.[24]

4.3 On Article 177

The Advocate General thought these variations too significant to permit the uniform application of Community law. Article 177 provided no answer, since, as suggested by the Belgian Government, that Article did not provide for the application of the Treaty, but only for its interpretation. According to this view, the Court had no function to interpret a Treaty provision where the issue was its application in national law, a function reserved to the national courts. In substance, the Advocate General made a firm choice in favour of considering the Treaty according to established principles of public international law.

---

[23] Articles 247 and 248 has since been renumbered as Articles 313 and 314.

[24] See [1963] E.C.R. 1, 23. It is, for example, Art. 25 of the German Basic Law which permits the European Convention on Human Rights to have direct internal effect.

5. THE JUDGMENT

5.1 The new legal order

The brevity of the judgment comes as something of a shock to those accustomed to the discursiveness of the great common law judgments, with their frequent dissenting opinions. Indeed it is a fairly open secret that the judges were narrowly divided in their decision. The most significant passages cover two pages.[25] Of these, the most deservedly quoted is that which reads:

> [T]he Community constitutes a new legal order of international law for the benefit of which the states have limited their sovereign rights, albeit within limited fields, and the subjects of which comprise not only Member States but also their nationals. Independently of the legislation of Member States, Community law therefore not only imposes obligations on individuals but is also intended to confer upon them rights which become part of their legal heritage. These rights arise not only where they are expressly granted by the Treaty, but also by reason of obligations which the Treaty imposes in a clearly defined way upon individuals as well as upon the Member States and upon the institutions of the Community.[26]

The Court rejected the more cautious public international law approach of the Advocate General in favour of the innovative view of the Commission. The Community was and still is *sui generis*. The keystone of this particular arch is, however, on closer analysis, the finding that the ambit of the Treaties was not limited to the Member States, but encompassed their nationals as subjects of obligations and beneficiaries of rights. From this all the rest follows. I propose to examine both the genesis and the progeny of this idea. How, firstly, did the Court arrive at this conclusion? Secondly, what follows from it?

5.2 Interpretation of the Treaty

The Court began by adopting, as its rule of interpretation, that which applied to international agreements, namely that:

> To ascertain whether the provisions of an international treaty extend so far in their effects [*i.e.* so as to involve direct effect] it is necessary to consider the spirit, the general scheme and the wording of those provisions.[27]

---

[25] [1963] E.C.R. 1, 12-13.
[26] [1963] E.C.R. 1, 12.
[27] [1963] E.C.R. 1, 12.

This test does not differ essentially from that proposed by the Advocate General.[28] The Vienna Convention on the Law of Treaties is dated 1969 and post-dates *Van Gend en Loos* but is usually considered as representing, at least in part, a declaration of existing principles of international law. Article 31.1 of the Convention provides:

> A treaty shall be interpreted in good faith in accordance with the ordinary meaning to be given to the terms of the Treaty in their context and in the light of its object and purpose.

The Court has, indeed, invoked the Vienna Convention[29] when interpreting international agreements between the Community and third countries, but not when interpreting the Treaties themselves.[30] An agreement of that kind, it says in its Opinion on the draft agreement creating the European Economic Area, "merely creates rights and obligations between the Contracting Parties and provides for no transfer of sovereign rights".[31]

5.3 The Court's reasons

The interpretative principle does not answer the concrete question of whether the Treaty should be interpreted as conferring rights directly on individuals.

The Court's reasoning, as reproduced in English falls into two parts. As Judge Edward[32] points out, the structure of the judgment, in French, is important to understanding its reasoning. The first English paragraph corresponds to a recital of four provisions referring in some fashion to individuals. I have inserted before each the introductory conjunction which is standard in French judgments.

> [*attendu que*] The objective of the EEC Treaty, which is to establish a Common Market, the functioning of which is of direct concern to interested parties in the Community, implies that this Treaty is more than an agreement which merely creates mutual obligations between the contracting states. [*que cette conception se trouve confirmée*] This view is confirmed by the preamble to the Treaty which refers not only to governments but to peoples. It is also confirmed more specifically by the establish-

---

[28] See text with n.22 above.
[29] Opinion 1/91 on the EEA Agreement [1991] E.C.R. I-6079, I-6101, para. 14; Case C-432/92, *R. v. Minister for Agriculture, Fisheries and Food, ex parte Anastasiou and Others* [1994] E.C.R. I-3087, I-3132, para. 43.
[30] It has to be recalled that France has not signed the Vienna Convention. See *Droit communautaire et constitutions nationales,* Rapport d'information no 2630. Assemblée nationale 11 mars 1996.
[31] [1991] E.C.R. I-6079, I-6102, para. 20.
[32] Edward, above n.5, 47.

ment of institutions endowed with sovereign rights, the exercise of which affects Member States and also their citizens. [*qu'il faut d'ailleurs remarquer*] Furthermore, it must be noted that the nationals of the states brought together in the Community are called upon to co-operate in the functioning of this Community through the intermediary of the European Parliament and the Economic and Social Committee.[33]

The second concerns essentially the function of the Article 177 procedure:

[*qu'en outre*] In addition, the task assigned to the Court of Justice under Article 177, the object of which is to secure uniform interpretation of the Treaty by national courts and tribunals, confirms that the states have acknowledged that Community law has an authority which can be invoked by their nationals before those courts and tribunals.[34]

5.4 Direct effect – a comment

The first of these paragraphs, taken alone and read in English, is not overwhelmingly persuasive. The fact that an international agreement is likely to affect individuals or their interests, or that "peoples" are referred to in the preamble do not seem to identify any cogent interest of individuals in the legal content of the agreement. Still more, the voluntary character of individual participation in the elective process seems to fall short of creating a framework for the invocation of legal rights.

However, three Treaty provisions at least appear indisputably to affect individuals:

– Articles 173 and 174[35] expressly provide for actions against Community institutions by natural or legal persons;

– Articles 85 and 86, by necessary implication affect individual action in the sphere of competition;

– a regulation, by virtue of Article 189 is "binding in its entirety and directly applicable in all Member States".

5.5 On Article 177

In my view, however, the core of the reasoning is in the second paragraph. The Court drew attention to "the task assigned to the Court of Justice under Article 177" and observed that "the object of [this Article] is to secure uniform

---

[33] [1963] E.C.R. 1, 12.
[34] *ibid.*
[35] Article 174 has since been renumbered as Article 231.

interpretation of the Treaty by national courts and tribunals . . .". Having regard to the content of Article 177, it is difficult to quarrel with this. Every
national court or tribunal may request a ruling from the Court of Justice "if it
considers that a decision on that question is necessary to enable it to give judgment". Where a Community law point is raised before a court or tribunal "against
whose decisions there is no remedy under national law", it is placed under an
express obligation to "bring that matter before the Court of Justice". This provision by its language imposes an obligation directly on national courts. Unlike even Article 12 it is not addressed to the Member States. Thus it indisputably
penetrates the veil of national sovereignty. More cogently still, the scheme of
Article 177 implies an invasion of Community law into the domain of national
courts. Firstly, those courts are implicitly given power to interpret (with the
assistance of the Court of Justice) and necessarily, therefore, apply provisions
of Community law. No other reason could explain their being concerned in the
interpretation of the Treaty or secondary legislation. Secondly, the Article purports to impose an obligation to refer questions directly on national courts of
final appeal. Thirdly, this scheme of discretion and obligation is explicable
only as serving a purpose of uniform interpretation of Community law in the
national courts, a scheme which would be without purpose if those courts were
not empowered by the Treaty to apply Community law. Put otherwise, the Treaty
envisages the national courts as the first instance courts of Community law so
far as Member State actions are concerned.

Once Community law is to be considered, interpreted and applied by national courts, it is but a short step to conclude that individuals should have the
right to invoke its provisions. Consequently, the role of Article 177 seems to
speak more eloquently for the rights of individuals to flow from the Treaty than
the more general considerations first cited by the Court. The structure of the
Treaty, rather than vaguely expressed aspirations, provide the coherent rationale for a system of co-operating courts at national and Community level, with
the individual as one of the principal beneficiaries.

5.6 What individuals?

The judgment does not assist us in identifying the range of affected individuals. It speaks variously of "interested parties", "individuals", "nationals" and
"citizens" (of Member States). The corporate character of *Van Gend en Loos*
clearly did not present a problem. The diversity of nationality and citizenship
in the laws of the Member States was not addressed.[36] It seems implicitly to be
sufficient for a legal or moral person to have the capacity to sue before the

---

[36]The nationality of an individual is determined by national law. If he possesses the nationality of
   a Member State, another Member State may not dispute his status on the ground that he also has
   the nationality of a third country. Case C-369/90, *Micheletti and Others* [1992] E.C.R. I-4239.

national courts. Even now, it must be said, the contours of the notion of citizen-ship promulgated in the Treaty on European Union remain undefined.

The first and most immediate consequence of the recognition of rights as residing in individuals took the form of the Community-law notion of "direct effect". The entire debate would, of course, have been without purpose, if the fortunate community "nationals" did not benefit in a concrete form. It is ines-capable that some provisions of Community law have direct affect. As already noted, the Court had so decided in respect of Article 85. It could scarcely have done otherwise. Article 85(2) states bluntly the agreements or decisions pro-hibited by Article 85(1) are "automatically void". Article 189 gives "binding" effect to Regulations. The Court thus applied itself to laying down some rules which have become familiar for the purpose of identifying provisions which have direct effect. It found that "Article 12 contains a *clear* and *unconditional* prohibition which is not a positive but a negative obligation". Furthermore, there was nothing to make "its implementation conditional upon a positive legislative measure enacted under national law". Thus the Court formulated the essentials of the test for direct effect, namely that the provision be suffi-ciently clear and precise and also unconditional. This test has been developed and extended to other situations and ultimately has permitted reliance, in particula,[37] on unimplemented directives.

6. DIRECT IMPLICATIONS OF THE JUDGMENT

6.1 Supremacy of Community law

The second great consequence of the *Van Gend en Loos* judgment is more implicit than explicit. It is the issue of supremacy of Community law. Accord-ing direct effect to a provision of Community law does not solve very much if it leaves open the question of its hierarchy in the internal law of the Member State. The Belgian Government, in particular, characterised the real issue as one of conflict between two international agreements enjoying equal status in national law. The Advocate General was concerned at the varying national-law status of international agreements. The Court merely identified the uncondi-tional character of the negative obligation imposed by Article 12 and the right of an individual to "plead infringements" by Member States before the na-tional courts. This, in turn, implies, without saying so expressly, that any in-crease in the duty, including – also implicitly – one enjoined by another international agreement could be held by the national court to be contrary to Community law.

---

[37] Case 8/81, *Becker v. Finanzamt Munster Innenstadt*: [1982] E.C.R. 53; Joined Cases C-6/90 and C-9/90, *Francovich* [1991] E.C.R. I-5357 (on which see Cahill "The Citizen, The State and the Continuing Construction of the European Legal Order. *Francovich, Bonifaci and Others v. Italy* (1991)" below, 425).

It was not until the following year in *Costa v. ENEL*[38] that the Court ruled explicitly on the precedence of Community law, stating:

> ... the law flowing from the Treaty, an independent source of law, could not, because of its special and original nature, be overridden by domestic legal provisions, however framed, without being deprived of its character as community law and without the legal basis of the community itself being called into question.[39]

The principle of supremacy was accorded its fullest amplitude in *Simmenthal* in 1978 where the Court held that national courts must set aside any provision of national law "which might prevent Community law from having full force and effect".[40]

6.2 Importance of Article 177

The third important consequence of the judgment is the life it breathed into the Article 177 procedure, which has indisputably become the cornerstone of Community law. Apart from assigning to that Article a role in the protection of the rights of individuals as an essential step in its reasoning on direct effect, it responded effectively to the arguments of the Member States and the Advocate General regarding the function of the Court in applying Community law. It adopted a functional distinction, whereby, in effect, the Court should interpret Community law, while the national court would apply it. Thus, for example, the Court repeatedly states that its role is to interpret Community law and to furnish the national court with such assistance as will enable it to decide the case before it. However, only a national court can declare a national law incompatible with the Treaty and thus inapplicable.

7. OTHER CONSEQUENCES OF THE JUDGMENT

Apart from these principal contributions, *Van Gend en Loos* contributed in the longer term to several of the most important future ideas of Community law. These include:

– the method of interpretation, usually described as "teleological" so constantly employed by the Court in the interpretation of Community-law texts.

---

[38] Case 6/64, [1964] E.C.R. 585.
[39] [1964] E.C.R. 585, 594.
[40] Case 106/77, *Amministrazione delle Finanze dello Stato v. Simmenthal* [1978] E.C.R. 629, 644, para. 32; see, however, Case 36/75, *Rutili v. Minister for the Interior* [1975] E.C.R. 1219, 1229, para. 16.

The preferred language of the Court remains close to the *Van Gend en Loos* formulation, namely that it is necessary to consider "the spirit, the general scheme and the wording", supplemented later by "the system and objectives of the Treaty",[41] varied later to read "not only its wording but also the context in which it occurs and the objects of the rules of which it is a part";[42]

– the idea of a constitutional charter was first clearly enunciated more than twenty years later in *Partie Ecologiste "Les Verts" v. European Parliament*, where the Court declared that the Community is one "based on the rule of law" and that the Treaty is its "basic constitutional charter";[43] however, the genesis of the notion of a Community constitution is clearly discernible in *Van Gend en Loos* in "the new legal order", the limitation of sovereign rights and the definition of the subjects of that order;

– in *Les Verts* also, the Court extrapolated further from the foundation of *Van Gend en Loos* to develop the notion of "a complete system of legal remedies and procedures . . .".[44] Articles 173 and 184[45] permit direct challenge to Community acts before the Court. However, the Court has no jurisdiction to entertain an action by an individual against a Member State for breach of Community law. Article 177 fills this gap by assuring the right of access to the national court linked with the potential to have any question of interpretation of Community law referred to the Court of Justice.[46]

– nor is it too fanciful to trace back to *Van Gend en Loos* the identification in the case-law of the Court in the 1970s of a Community interest in the protection of fundamental human rights.[47] At least, it left open a ready machinery in the form of its interpretation of Article 177. The notion of respect for the "fundamental democratic principle that the people should take part in the exercise of power" is implicit in the reference to the European Parliament[48] and has become important as the Court becomes more

---

[41]Case 6/72, *Continental Can* [1973] E.C.R. 215, para. 22.
[42]Case 292/82, *Merck v. Hauptzollamt Hamburg-Jonas* [1983] E.C.R. I-3781, I-3792,p ara. 12.
[43]Case 294/83, [1986] E.C.R. 1339, 1365, para. 23.
[44]*ibid.*
[45]Article 184 has since been renumbered as Article 241.
[46]See Koen Lenaerts, Judge of the Court of First Instance, "Legal Protection of private Parties under the EC Treaty" in *Scritti in onore di Giuseppe Federico Mancini*, (Milano, Dott. Giuffre Editore, 1998) vol. 2, 591.
[47]Case 29/69, *Stauder v. Ulm* [1969] E.C.R. 419; Case 11/70, *Internationale Handelsgesellschaft v. Einfuhr- und Vorratstelle Getreide* [1970] E.C.R. 1125; Case 44/79, *Hauer v. Land Rheinland-Pfalz* [1979] E.C.R. 3727.
[48]See, for example, Case C-392/95, *European Parliament v. Council* [1997] E.C.R. I-3213, I-3246, para. 14.

conscious of its constitutional role to ensure respect for the institutional
balance inherent in the structure of the Treaty.

8. CONCLUSION

The battle lines remain drawn about the merits and even the legitimacy of *Van
Gend en Loos* and its progeny, all those cases which assert the supremacy of
Community law and which, therefore, impinge on the sovereignty of the Member States. The critics include but are not limited to Sir Patrick Neill. Professor
T.C. Hartley has not minced his words stating, in 1986, that the Court "has not
hesitated to remodel the law even when this has entailed adopting a solution
different from that envisaged in the Treaties"[49] and, ten years later, of pursuing
"a settled and consistent policy of promoting European federalism, a policy
which includes the extension of the powers of the Court itself".[50]

The extra-judicial writings of some members of the Court occasionally provide such critics with ammunition. In 1995, the late Judge Giuseppe Federico
Mancini[51] explained how the expression "une certaine idée de l'Europe", a
phrase coined by former Judge Pierre Pescatore and based in turn on General
de Gaulle's "une certain idée de la France",[52] encapsulated the "synergy produced by the coming together of men who, though steeped in different cultures
and legal traditions, shared a common set of values".[53] Elsewhere he has written of the "preference for Europe" prompted by the EC Treaty objective of "an
ever closer union among the peoples of Europe".[54]

Writing in less visionary terms, the late Judge Fernand Schockweiler explained how "the Court had acted as an engine for the building of the autonomous Community legal order".[55] He thought that its most decisive contribution
was its choice from the very beginning of the teleological method of interpretation. According to Judge Schockweiler, "by favouring this method . . . [t]he
Court gave preference to the interpretation best fitted to promote the achievement of the objectives pursued by the Treaty".[56] Furthermore, it "allowed a

---

[49]Hartley, "Federalism, Courts and Legal Systems; the Emerging Constitution of the European
Community" (1986) 34 *A.J.C.L.* 229, 247.
[50]Hartley, "The European Court, Judicial Objectivity and the Constitution of the European Union" (1996) *L.Q.R.* 95.
[51]Mancini, n.4 above, 125.
[52]Charles de Gaulle, *Mémoire de Guerre, L'appel 1940-1942* (Librairie Plon, Paris, 1954), 1.
[53]Mancini, n.4 above, 125.
[54]Mancini and Keeling, "Democracy and the European Court of Justice" (1994) 57 *M.L.R.* 175,
186.
[55]See Judge Fernand Schockweiler, late Judge at the Court of Justice, "La Cour de justice des
Communautés européennes dépasse-t-elle les limites de ses attributions?", 18 Journal des
Tribunaux, Droit Européen 73, Brussels, April 20, 1995.
[56]*ibid.*

development beyond the literal meaning of the texts in a dynamic direction in the light of the purposes pursued by the [EC] Treaty in its entirety and in its context".[57] These are, of course, all personal views and it is important to note that the President of the Court has recently reasserted the role of the Court as a custodian of legality rather than as a "motor of integration", a perception of the Court which he firmly rejected.[58]

From the purely practical standpoint, which, of course, cannot satisfy those who criticise the Court from a purely textual point of view, it is difficult to disagree with Professor Arnull's assessment of *Van Gend en Loos*:

> The contrary view, that the effect of the Treaty in the national legal sys-
> tems should have been left to depend on the constitutional law of the
> country concerned, would have fatally undermined the common market.
> Had the effect of the Treaty been determined by national law, it would
> have had direct effect in some States but not in others. It is plain that the
> common market could not have functioned properly on that basis.[59]

Critics of the agenda of European integration should be invited to read the preamble to the Treaty which expresses the aspirations of the Member States to achieve: "an ever closer union among the peoples of Europe, . . . economic and social progress . . . by common action to eliminate the barriers which divide Europe, . . . the removal of existing obstacles . . . in order to guarantee steady expansion, balanced trade and fair competition . . .". As the Court stated in its Opinion on the EEA Agreement, "Article 1 of the Single European Act makes it clear moreover that the objective of all the Community Treaties is to contribute together to making concrete progress towards European unity".[60]

The most vocal critics of the Court tend to base themselves on common law principles of textual interpretation. It is odd to find them attempting retrospectively to place themselves sympathetically in the shoes of the Member States of 1963 in order to conclude that, in *Van Gend en Loos*, in particular, the Court exceeded the power which the Member States intended it to have. This reasoning is striking for two reasons. Firstly, the common law Member States cannot convincingly complain about an interpretation of the Treaty which was well established and which they accepted on joining the Community. Secondly, the Member States have repeatedly and most recently in the Treaty of Amsterdam not only failed to clip the wings of the Court, as some would have it, but have

---

[57] *ibid.* (Author's free translation of the text).
[58] Gil Carlos Rodríguez Iglesias, address on the occasion of the publication of the work of Professor Jean Victor Louis on the European Union and the future of its institutions (Brussels, January 16, 1997).
[59] Above n.2, 118.
[60] Opinion 1/91, [1991] E.C.R. I-6079, I-6102, para. 17.

implicitly and sometimes explicitly approved the *acquis Communautaire* including the case-law of the Court.

I will conclude by referring to that merciless transatlantic critic of judicial activism in all its forms, Judge Robert Bork. Speaking of the activism of Chief Justice Marshall, he confessed nonetheless to admiring him. "His activism", he argued, "consisted mainly in distorting statutes in order to create occasions for rulings that preserved the structure of the United States . . . . The survival of the union was probably in some part due to the centralising and unifying force of Marshall and his court".[61] Were the members of the Court wrong to pursue "une certaine idée de l'Europe" or should they, to quote the poet Sassoon, have manifested:

> The visionless officialized fatuity that once kept Europe safe for Perpetuity.[62]

---

[61] Bork, *The Tempting of America. The Political Seduction of the Law* (Sinclair-Stevenson, London, 1990) 21.

[62] From "On Reading the War Diary of a Defunct Ambassador" Siegfried Sassoon.

JUDICIAL ACTIVISM, CONSTITUTIONAL INTERPRETATION AND THE PROBLEM OF ABORTION *ROE v. WADE* (1973) AND *X v. A.G.* (1992)

DR. NEVILLE COX*

1. INTRODUCTION

A case may be described as being leading for a number of reasons. Perhaps it is an especially interesting or well-argued one. Perhaps it creates a significant development in the law. Perhaps it marks an important turning point in social policy. Or, perhaps it is a leading case for all the wrong reasons. Perhaps it marks the beginning of a great injustice. Indeed, like the two cases that are the subject of this chapter – the American case *Roe v. Wade*[1] and the Irish case *A.G. v. X*[2] – perhaps it stands out because of the dangerous precedent that it creates.

These two cases involve constitutional deliberation in respect of what is, in their respective jurisdictions, a matter of the utmost social controversy namely the question of legal control of abortion.[3] In neither case could what was seen as the right result be achieved by anything other than brazen judicial activism. Yet the Supreme Courts in both cases were not daunted by this fact and used their position as guardians of their Constitutions to create what they felt was desirable social policy, in one case by an adventurous interpretation of what was a silent Constitution and in the other by ignoring the express terms of a constitutional provision.[4]

Paradoxically, however, this is actually the reason why both cases are of such perennial significance. Ireland and America are common law legal sys-

---

*Lecturer in law, Trinity College, Dublin

[1] 410 U.S. 113 (1973).

[2] [1992] I.R. 1 (S.C.).

[3] Ronald Dworkin says of abortion "[I]t is tearing America apart . . . it is also distorting its politics and confounding its constitutional law". See Dworkin, *Life's Dominion* (HarperCollins, London, 1993) [hereafter Dworkin] 4. See also Tribe, *Abortion: The Clash of Absolutes* (Norton, N.Y. & London, 1991) [hereafter Tribe].

[4] See Bork, *The tempting of America; The Political Seduction of the Law*, (Free Press/SinclaI.R. Stevenson, London, 1990) [hereafter Bork].

tems. In such countries a recurring question concerns the proper limitations of the judicial power to make law[5] and in *Roe v. Wade* and *AG v. X* the respective Supreme Courts exceeded such limitations in spectacular and high profile fashion. More than anything, it is the dangerous precedents which they set in this regard which marks them out as "leading" cases of the twentieth century.

2. *ROE V. WADE* AND THE FUNDAMENTAL RIGHT TO AN ABORTION

2.1 The Background to the Case

Roe v. Wade concerned a 19th century Texan anti-abortion statute which had been enacted as part of a general move to prohibit abortion throughout the U.S.A. between 1821 and 1900.[6] The prohibitive nature of such statutes had come under increasingly vocal criticism since the 1950s both because of the rise to social prominence of the feminist movement and also because of a more general moral horror at the tens of thousands of unsafe and often fatal illegal abortions carried out annually. Furthermore, the thalidomide scandal[7] and the rubella epidemic of 1964-1965 (both of which resulted in the births of thousands of seriously deformed babies with minimal life expectancy) generated a concern with quality of new-born life rather than with such life *per se* which appeared to give a moral authority to the call for abortion reform.[8]

Moreover proponents of such reform had a powerful constitutional weapon in their armoury namely the unenumerated constitutional right to privacy, recognised in 1965 in *Griswold v. Connecticut*,[9] and transformed in 1972 in *Eisenstadt v. Baird*[10] from a right of a married couple not to have state surveillance of their sex life to an individual right of reproductive privacy. This malleable right appeared sufficiently wide to include a (privacy based) right to have an abortion and feminist lawyers were looking for an opportunity to test it. All that was needed was a suitable plaintiff, and she was eventually found in the person of Norma McCorvey, a 21 year old working class divorcee, pregnant,

---

[5] Thus Hogan comments that "If the legitimacy of judicial review is to continue to be accepted decisions in major constitutional cases must be seen to represent more than the personal opinions of judges". "Constitutional Interpretation" in Litton (ed.) *The Constitution of Ireland 1937-1987* (Institute of Public Administration, Dublin 1988) 188.

[6] Mohr, *Abortion in America* (Oxford University Press, New York, 1978) [hereafter Mohr]. See also Tribe, 27-52.

[7] Thalidomide was a morning sickness drug marketed in the early 1960s which, when taken by pregnant women, resulted in appalling deformities of new-born babies who had a minimal life expectancy.

[8] See Tribe, 37-38. See also Veitch & Treacy, "Abortion in the Common Law World" (1974) 22 *A.J.C.L.* 152, 166.

[9] *Griswold v. Connecticut*, 381 U.S. 513 (1965). For a commentary on this case see Emerson, "Nine Judges in Search of a Doctrine" (1965) 63 *Mich.L.Rev.* 232 (1965).

[10]405 U.S. 438 (1972).

allegedly as the result of a gang rape (an allegation which she later retracted) and denied an abortion under Texan state law.

The case was argued in December 1971 and re-argued in October 1972, and a decision was finally handed down in January 1973, in which a majority of the Supreme Court ruled that a *fundamental* constitutional right for women to have an abortion flowed inevitably from the *Griswold* right to privacy and accordingly that the Texas statute and all other statutes like it were unconstitutional. It should be noted that within American rights jurisprudence a sharp distinction is made between mere "liberty interests" or non-fundamental rights and the far stronger fundamental rights which may only be set aside if this is necessary to service a "compelling state interest". The fact that the court in *Roe* had concluded that access to abortion was a *fundamental* right meant that the defendants were required to find a compelling state interest, which would justify restricting this right. Not surprisingly it was argued that such compelling interest existed in the protection of the fœtus. Blackmun J. for the court, however, rejected such argument on the basis that the fœtus was not, nor had it ever been considered a constitutional person. He did feel, however, that whereas state concern for fœtal life was not a *compelling* interest, it was nonetheless a *legitimate* interest that could at a certain point in pregnancy become compelling as also would the need to protect maternal health.

In order to balance these conflicting interests against the fundamental right, he divided pregnancy into three equal temporal trimesters. In the first, no legitimate interest was sufficiently compelling to justify any restriction on the right to abortion. In the second, where abortion became more dangerous for a woman, the *legitimate* interest of protecting a mother's health became *compelling* such that the abortion right might be regulated if this was necessary to ensure that the mother's health was not adversely affected by the abortion. In the third trimester, and specifically at the point when the fœtus achieves independent viability,[11] the *legitimate* state interest in its life was deemed to become *compelling* and thus at this stage of pregnancy abortion was prohibited unless the mother's life or health would be injuriously affected by enforced childbirth.[12]

There were two dissenting judgements, from Rehnquist and White JJ. Rehnquist J. felt that like all fourteenth amendment based rights, the right to choose to end pregnancy simply was not fundamental.[13] It was a form of liberty certainly, but one that merited no greater protection than any other liberty abridged by routine social and economic regulation. White J. also in dissent felt that what had to be at issue was the type of pregnancy which was unwanted

---

[11] 405 U.S. 438, at 163.
[12] The majority judgement was concurred in by Burger C.J. and Douglas, Stewart, Brennan, Marshall and Powell JJ.
[13] 410 U.S. 438, at 172-174.

for reasons of convenience, family planning, economics, dislike of children, gender selection and the social stigma of illegitimacy. He was opposed to any interpretation or balance that meant that the ". . . Constitution of the US values the convenience, whim or caprice of the putative mother more than the life or potential life of the fœtus".[14]

1.2 Criticisms of the Decision

Beyond simple opposition to the legalisation of abortion, which is not the concern of this chapter, the criticisms which are traditionally made of *Roe v. Wade* tend to fall into four principal categories,

– Criticism relating to the judicial activism inherent in the discovery of the fundamental right to abortion,

– Criticism relating to the status and value of the fœtus,

– Criticism relating to the trimester scheme,

– Other Miscellaneous criticisms.

Because it is the most important for present purposes, the first of the above criticisms – the undemocratic nature of the courts approach – will be considered last. The others will now be considered in turn.

(a) Criticisms relating to the Judicial Treatment of the Fœtus

The first major criticism of the decision in *Roe v. Wade* concerns the lack of significance which the Supreme Court attached to unborn life. The Court had insisted that because there was no unanimity of opinion theological, medical or philosophical on the question of when life began, therefore constitutional non-determination of this question was necessary, being morally neutral. Hence individual states were prohibited from imposing "one theory of life" on their citizens.[15]

Three immediate points arise. First, and rather obviously, the decision in *Roe* on this question was certainly *not* morally neutral, in that it endorsed one "theory of life", namely that the fœtus has no legal status until viability. Secondly, the restraint of the court in *this* area of moral controversy sits uneasily with its rampant activism in answering the equally controversial question of whether or not a right to abortion existed in the first place. Thirdly, as Tribe points out, the question of the point at which any society provides an individual fœtus with legal protection, albeit religiously, philosophically and medically

---

[14]410 U.S. 438, at 221.
[15]410 U.S. 438, at 152.

informed, is an entirely legal one, answered arguably by policy considerations.[16]

The court's predominant concern was with the question of whether the fœtus was or was not a constitutional person. It answered this question in the negative noting that all mention of "persons" in the Constitution referred to born persons.[17] It concluded then that as foetuses were *not* constitutional persons therefore they could not enjoy constitutional rights. As Dworkin points out,[18] this was a hugely important conclusion because if the fœtus *had* been deemed to be a constitutional person, then any law permitting even limited abortion would have fallen foul of the 14th amendment equal protection clause.

It is beyond the scope of this chapter to examine whether an individual fœtus is a "person". Indeed it is probable that any such examination is futile in that no certain result can be achieved. Nonetheless two points should be made about the Court's analysis in this regard. First, even if a fœtus is not deemed to be a *natural* person, this does not necessarily mean that it cannot be a *legal* person. Destro[19] suggests that it is anomalous that a legal fiction known as a corporation should be deemed a legal person whereas "the unborn offspring of human beings" should not.

Secondly, it is arguable that even if the fœtus is not a "person" legal or natural and possesses no constitutional rights, nonetheless the social commodity of unborn life is still inherently valuable and should therefore receive some degree of legal protection.[20] The Supreme Court's failure to address this point in *Roe* is little short of remarkable. Destro[21] points out that even in cases of federal discrimination, where black people were deemed not to be citizens for example, it was never suggested that such non-citizenship meant that they were entitled to *no* legal protection.[22]

---

[16] See also Callahan, "The Fœtus and Fundamental Rights" in Baird and Rosenbaum (eds.), *The Ethics of Abortion* (Prometheus Books, Buffalo N.Y., 1989) [hereafter Baird and Rosenbaum] 115. For an analysis of this point in the context of the British abortion law see Keown, "The Offence of Child Destruction" (1988) 104 *L.Q.R.* 120.

[17] In fact as Ely points out (Ely, *"Roe v. Wade* And The Wages of Crying Wolf" 82 *Yale L.J.* 920 (1973) [hereafter Ely] 925-926), the constitutional references to persons all refer to adult persons.

[18] Dworkin, 109-116. See also by the same author "The Great Abortion Case", June 29, 1989 *New York Review of Books* 47, 50.

[19] Destro "Abortion and the Constitution" (1975) 63 *Calif.L.Rev.* 1250 [hereafter Destro] 1335.

[20] This is what Dworkin terms the "detached" approach to opposition to abortion. See Dworkin, chap. 2.

[21] Destro, 1336.

[22] On this basis it has been suggested that *Roe* is entirely distinguishable from the cases on contraception for as Regan says, "Whether or not the cases from Meyer to Eisenstaadt establish a right of family related freedom of choice, none of these cases involves a state interest remotely like the interest in protecting "potential" but already conceived human life". See Regan "Revisiting *Roe v.* Wade" (1979) 77 *Mich.L.Rev.* 1569 [hereafter Regan] 1641-1642. See also Destro, 1250 and Ely, 926.

(b) Criticisms of the Trimester Scheme and the Significance Attached to Fœtal Viability[23]

There are two major criticisms of the construction of the trimester scheme created by the Supreme Court. The first is that it is just another blatant instance of judicial activism. What was devised was essentially a detailed abortion statute beyond the scope of the case. Tribe[24] disagrees with this assertion, pointing out that the courts have explored the complex ramifications of other rights (for example the 4th amendment ban on unreasonable searches and seizures) in the context of constitutional cases. It has also been suggested that the scheme was merely a judicial balancing of competing rights and interests, which was followed too rigidly in later cases.[25]

The second criticism in this area relates to the significance that the Supreme Court appeared to attach to fœtal viability. According to the court, protection of fœtal life became a compelling objective at viability because at that point, the "fœtus .... presumably has the capacity of meaningful life outside the mother's womb".[26] There are three principal objections to this argument. First, as Ely says,[27] viability is a completely arbitrary point on the line between conception and birth, and there seems to be no good reason why fœtal life, valueless prior to viability become compelling after that point.[28] Secondly it is argued that medical technology, if it continues to advance in the area of pregnancy and fœtal care, may mean that in time to come independent existence outside the womb may occur earlier than seven months, and indeed possibly very shortly after implantation[29] – developments with obvious consequences for the Trimester Scheme. Finally as Noonan points out,[30] the basis of the trimester approach is that legal recognition of the viable fœtus derives from its capacity to exist independently of its mother but,

> The most important objection to this approach is that dependence is not ended by viability. The fœtus is still absolutely dependent on someone's

---

[23] In practice the trimester scheme has had a very limited effect on the reality of the abortion situation in America. Dworkin (4) points out that only 0.01 % of all abortions occur after 7 months.

[24] Tribe, 109-110.

[25] Dworkin, "The Future of Abortion", September 28, 1989 *New York Review of Books*, 49.

[26] *Roe*, 163.

[27] Ely, 924-925.

[28] As Professor Glanville Williams points out, there is simply no point in the continuum between fertilisation and birth at which the beginning of protection of unborn life would not seem arbitrary; see Williams, "The Fœtus and the 'Right to Life'" [1994] *C.L.J.* 71, 73.

[29] Thus in *City of Akron v. Akron Centre for Reproductive Health*, 462 U.S. 416 (1983) O'Connor J. said (419) that, as medical technology progressed to ensure safe abortion at a later stage, and viability at an earlier stage, *Roe* might be on a collision course with itself.

[30] Noonan, (ed.), *The Morality of Abortion* (Harvard University Press, London, 1970) [hereafter Noonan] 52.

care in order to continue existence; indeed a child of one or three or even five years of age is still absolutely dependent on another's care for existence. . .The insubstantial lessening of dependence at viability does not seem to signal any special acquisition of humanity.

There are two answers to these criticisms. First, if the Supreme Court felt compelled to set time limits on the legal availability of abortion, then, by virtue of the nature of human gestation, the selection of any point between fertilisation and birth was always going to be arbitrary. Viability was no more arbitrary than any other point and, as in many areas of law, if a line had to be drawn then the appearance of arbitrariness in the drawing of that line is not a conclusive criticism.[31] Secondly, viability may legitimately be seen not as the *reason* for the final part of the trimester scheme, but merely as a *justification* for it. Dworkin[32] argues that by the seventh month of pregnancy a woman has had ample time to make an informed decision and exercise her right, and social concern for the value of life requires some protection to be afforded to a now mature fœtus. In other words, at this stage all the relevant rights are correctly balanced, and abortion may legitimately be prohibited.

(c) Miscellaneous Criticisms

Tribe's only criticism of the case is that the court in setting out its general principles went beyond the facts of the case, and while this is not necessarily illegitimate, nevertheless ". . . the sensitivity of the abortion question counselled more restraint than the Court exhibited in *Roe*".[33] Morgan seems to agree,[34] saying that no general principles on abortion should have been laid down by the court in *Roe* because the issue had had no resolution in political circles, but was still being hotly debated, and furthermore because the privacy right itself had not received sufficient judicial consideration.

A second miscellaneous criticism is that the decision undemocratically transferred control of the abortion question from individual state legislatures to the realms of federal constitutional jurisprudence.[35] This is, however, easily coun-

---

[31] On the other hand, it is arguable that where it is necessary to draw a line for legal purposes, then this should be done even where line drawing may appear arbitrary at any and all points. See Dyibikowski, "Lord Devlin's Morality and its Enforcement" (1975) *Proceedings of the Aristotelian Society* 89, 102.

[32] Dworkin, *New York Review of Books*, June 29, 1989, 52

[33] Tribe, 110.

[34] Morgan, "*Roe v. Wade* and the Lessons of the Pre-*Roe* Caselaw" (1979) 77 *Mich.L.Rev.* 1724, 1726-1730

[35] The states of Rhode Island, Connecticut and Utah immediately responded to *Roe* by enacting legislation which, in that it afforded the unborn a full right to life from conception was clearly incompatible with *Roe*. These laws were all deemed to be unconstitutional by the Federal District Court; see: *Doe v. Israel*, 358 F. Supp. 1193 (1973), *Abel v. Markele*, 369 F. Supp. 807 (1973) and *Doe v. Rampton*, 366 F. Supp. 189 (1973).

tered by the argument that if the Constitution *did* contain a fundamental right to have an abortion, then this should be enforced, irrespective of the opinions and objections of a legislature in an individual state.[36]

A further, emerging criticism of *Roe*, emanating from the feminist movement, is that the right to abortion should not derive from the dangerously limited right to privacy, which has been the basis for the refusal of congress to provide state medical funding to women seeking abortions, but rather from the constitutional guarantee of equality.[37] There are two bases on which this argument works. First, as Tribe[38] and indeed Frances Olsen[39] (who argues that abortion laws are framed from the limited perspective of the male viewpoint and fail to take into account the thinking of pregnant women) suggest, pregnancy is a state of affairs produced by a man and a woman, which affects only the latter party in any direct way, and to an enormous extent. Hence, a law banning abortion and thereby effectively limiting the constitutional right to reproductive autonomy of a woman while leaving the man's corresponding right untouched, violates the constitutional guarantee of equality before the law.

Secondly, Eileen McDonagh[40] argues that if the pro-life contention that the fœtus is a person is to be accepted, then because the burden which it imposes on a woman is so severe that if it were imposed by any "born" human on another person that person could insist on its removal (if necessary by killing in self defence), a law which prohibits abortion discriminates unfairly between born and unborn humans. Moreover, in her view, approaching the issue via equality rights rather than privacy rights would mean that a woman could justifiably claim the right to state funding of an abortion operation. Once again, the limited ambit of this paper means that analysis of these theories is inappropriate.

(d) Criticisms relating to the proper ambit of the Judicial Role in Constitutional Interpretation

The major concern of this chapter is with the proper role of the judiciary in resolving matters of social controversy and for many commentators, the decision in *Roe v. Wade* represented blatant and unwarranted judicial activism. This

---

[36]Tribe, 194-195.
[37]See Tribe, 151-159. See also Vinovskis, "The Politics of Abortion in the House of Representatives in 1976" (1979) 77 *Mich.L.Rev.* 1790; and Appelton, "The Abortion Funding Cases" (1979) 77 *Mich.L.Rev.* 1688.
[38]Tribe, 132.
[39]Frances Olsen, "Comment – Unravelling Compromise" (1989) 103 *Harv.L.Rev.* 105 [hereafter Olsen] 121.
[40]McDonagh, *Breaking the Abortion Deadlock; From Choice to Consent* (Oxford University Press, N.Y. & Oxford, 1996) [hereafter McDonagh] chaps. 2-5.

is for two reasons; first, because it was based on the right recognised in *Griswold v. Connecticut* – itself arguably the product of judicial lawmaking. Analysis of *Griswald*, however, could form the basis of another chapter in this book and will not be undertaken here. Secondly, it is felt that even if *Griswold was* a valid decision, the right to privacy recognised in that case simply did not translate into a fundamental right to abortion with the inevitability that the court in *Roe* seemed to accept.

One of the first notable critical commentaries on *Roe v. Wade* came from Professor John Hart Ely, who, while he wished to see a situation where abortion was freely available, nonetheless felt that *Roe* was a bad decision. In his view, whereas the *Griswold* decision was acceptable and recognised the existence of a most important right, it was important that its limits were carefully enforced. In *Roe* the privacy right was extended well beyond its previous limitations such that life itself, albeit in a controversial category was not strong enough to justify its restriction. Thus he concluded,[41]

> [*Roe*] is a very bad decision. Not because it will perceptibly weaken the court – it won't – and not because it conflicts with any idea of progress. . .it doesn't. It is bad because it is bad constitutional law. Or rather because it is *not* constitutional law and gives almost no sense of an obligation to try to be.

Professor Lawrence Tribe,[42] in one of the most important books written on the subject, argues on the other hand that not just is the right to abortion an inevitable concomitant of the right to privacy but the effect of pregnancy on a woman is so significant that the decision whether or not to have an abortion is one which should of itself be protected by the Constitution independently of the privacy right. This may well be so, but it does not deal with the fundamental point at stake namely that in a democracy the job of deciding on appropriate social policy is not that of the judiciary.[43] In common law countries this point may be more blurred than in civil law jurisdictions, but nonetheless it exists. It is entirely arguable that the court in *Roe* invented a constitutional right and in Ely's words, ". . .used it to superimpose its own view of wise social policy on that of the legislature",[44] just as in *Lochner v. New York*[45] and cases like it, the

---

[41]Ely, 947.

[42]Tribe, 92-104

[43]Professor Glendon has suggested that the decision in *Roe v. Wade* interrupted what was an inevitable move towards legislatively sponsored liberalisation of abortion laws, leading to a situation with the same practical result as that reached in *Roe*, but with less controversy. See Glendon, *Abortion and Divorce in Western Law* (Harvard University Press, London, 1989) 48-49. See Tribe, 49-51 for a criticism of this assertion.

[44]Ely, 937.

[45]198 U.S. 45 (1905).

Supreme Court in the early decades of this century had used the vague heading "liberty of contract" to invalidate what it regarded as socially unmeritorious legislation.

This criticism is not an endorsement of the type of originalist approach to constitutional interpretation favoured by Robert Bork and criticised by Ronald Dworkin.[46] Nor indeed is it a statement that the whole concept of unenumerated rights is anti-democratic, or an argument that *Griswold v. Connecticut* falls into this category. The point is that *Roe v. Wade* involves something very different to *Griswold*. The *concept* of a right to privacy (as distinct from the degree to which it may be restricted) is not controversial in modern democratic thought. In the terms used by Cardozo J. it can legitimately be seen as *implicit in the concept of ordered liberty*,[47] and hence may easily be classified as fundamental. The application of the privacy right to the abortion situation on the other hand is entirely controversial and is not easily reconciled with any of the usual definitions of a "fundamental right" within the American constitutional experience. It is hard to resist the conclusion that in recognising such a "right" the Supreme Court were simply imposing their view of wise social policy in an area which should have been legislatively and hence democratically controlled.

2.3 Conclusions on *Roe v. Wade*

Despite these criticisms, the decision in *Roe* has formed the basis of American abortion law from 1973 until the present day. Equally, it remains the source of enormous conflict in America. Its future has come under significant threat in two cases in 1989[48] and 1992,[49] during the course of which the fundamental status of the abortion right and the rigidity of the trimester framework appear to have been disregarded by a Supreme Court packed with Republican Party nominees. The right remains in place but restrictions on it which do not constitute an *undue burden* on its operation (for example second trimester fœtal viability checks) are permitted.[50] *Roe v. Wade*, however, whatever the social merits of the conclusions it reached, remains open to the criticisms listed above. As a judicial resolution of a matter of controversial social policy it is inherently undemocratic.

---

[46]Dworkin, chap. 5.
[47]*Palko v. Connecticut* 302 U.S. 319 (1937) 325.
[48]*Webster v. Reproductive Health Services,* 492 U.S. 490 (1990).
[49]*Planned Parenthood of SE Penn v. Casey* 120 L.Ed 2d 674, (1992).
[50]O'Connor J. in her dissent in the *City of Akron* case (n. 29 above) first proposed this test.

3. ATTORNEY GENERAL V. X AND OTHERS[51]

3.1 The Background to the Case

In 1974 in the seminal case *McGee v. A.G.*,[52] the Irish Supreme Court interpreted Article 40.3 of the Constitution as including an unenumerated constitutional right to marital privacy, encompassing the right to have access to contraceptives.[53] Elements within Irish society argued that this development was the first step in the process of judicial activism that, in America had led to the recognition of a right to abortion and that it would inevitably have the same result here.[54] It was true that the Offences Against the Person Act, 1861 criminalised abortion but an activist Supreme Court of the type that made the decision in *Roe* could judicially review this statute. Equally, it should be noted that a far easier source of relief for women seeking abortion in Ireland is the option of having recourse to an abortion in England (an option taken by over 6,000 Irish women annually) and hence the likelihood of such an action been taken was minimal.

Nonetheless, in a pre-emptive attempt to negate such a possibility, Article 40.3.3°, the eighth amendment to the Irish Constitution, was passed by popular referendum in September 1983. The wording of this amendment, criticised *inter alia* for being vague and sectarian, was as follows:

> The State acknowledges the right to life of the unborn and, with due regard to the equal right to life of the mother, guarantees in its laws to respect, and as far as practicable, by its laws to defend and vindicate that right.

Between 1983 and 1992, this constitutional provision was used by the Su-

---

[51] See Hogan and Whyte, *Kelly: The Irish Constitution* (3rd ed., Butterworths, Dublin 1994), 790-810 [hereafter Kelly]; Kingston, Whelan, & Bacik, *Abortion and the Law* (Roundhall Sweet & Maxwell, Dublin, 1997) [herafter Kingston, Whelan, & Bacik]; Sherlock, "The Right to Life of the Unborn and the Irish Constitution" (1989) XXIV *Ir. Jur.* (*n.s.*) 13 [hereafter Sherlock]; Whyte, "Abortion and the Law" (1992) *Doctrine and Life* 253 [hereafter Whyte]; Hesketh *The Second Partitioning of Ireland* (Brandsma Books, Dublin, 1990) [hereafter Hesketh]; Byrne and Binchy *Annual Review of Irish Law 1992* (Roundhall Press, Dublin 1994) 154-208 [hereafter Byrne and Binchy].

[52] *McGee v. A.G.* [1974] I.R. 284 (S.C.).

[53] In *Ryan v. A.G.* [1965] I.R. 294 (H.C. and S.C.), the Irish courts first accepted that Article 40.3.1 of the Irish Constitution protected certain unenumerated rights.

[54] See Kelly, 791; Casey "The Development of Constitutional Law under Chief Justice O'Dálaigh" [1978] *D.U.L.J.* 1, 10; O'Reilly, "Marital Privacy and Family Law" (1977) 65 *Studies* 8. See also Binchy, "Marital Privacy and the Family Law: A rely to Mr O'Reilly" (1977) 65 *Studies* 330. Fears were also expressed about the possibility of Ireland being required to liberalise its abortion laws by virtue of its membership both of the Council of Europe and the E.E.C. See Sherlock, 17-20.

preme Court on three occasions, (at the behest of both the Attorney General and the Society for the Protection of the Unborn Child) to justify the granting of injunctions against two counselling agencies and various Students Union magazines, preventing the supply to Irish women of information in respect of legal abortion facilities in the United Kingdom.[55] Such injunctions were deemed by the European Court of Human Rights to be in violation of Article 10 of the European Convention on Human Rights.[56] Moreover had their been any commercial connection between the suppliers of the information and the abortion clinics in question, it is probable that the European Court of Justice would have found the injunctions to be in violation of European Community Law.[57] It was against this background that the infamous *X* case arose.

3.2 The Facts of the Case

In December 1991, a then 14 year old girl, who had allegedly been sexually assaulted and raped by the father of a close friend for some time, discovered that she was pregnant by this man. She told her parents about the abuse that she had received and after some discussion, the family members agreed that she should have an abortion rather than continue with the trauma of this unwanted pregnancy. They went to England for this purpose, but prior to their departure her father enquired of police officials in Ireland whether DNA samples taken from the aborted foetus would be admissible in court as evidence of paternity in a criminal prosecution of the alleged rapist. The information that the girl was planning to have an abortion was sent to the D.P.P.'s office and hence to the Attorney General Mr Harry Whelehan, who felt that he was constitutionally obliged to seek an injunction to prevent the young girl from travelling for an abortion.[58]

3.3 The High Court Decision

On Monday February 17, 1992, Costello J. in the High Court granted the injunction sought, stating that he was constitutionally obliged to do so irrespective of the cause of the pregnancy, the age of the mother or the fact that she was allegedly suicidal. He said that under the terms of Article 40.3.3 he was required to draw a balance between competing but *equal* rights to life of mother and foetus – clearly an impossible task where such rights were in direct con-

---

[55] See *A.G. (S.P.U.C.) v. Open Door Counselling* [1988] I.R. 593 (S.C.); *S.P.U.C. v. Coogan* [1989] I.R. 734 (S.C.) and *S.P.U.C. v. Grogan* [1989] I.R. 753 (S.C.).

[56] *Open Door Counselling v. Ireland* Series A, No. 246; (1993) 15 E.H.R.R. 244.

[57] Case C-159/90 *Grogan v. Ireland* [1991] E.C.R.-I 4685. For a criticism of this decision see Phelan, "The Right to Life of the Unborn versus the Promotion of Trade and Services; the European Court of Justice and the Normative Shaping of the European Union" (1992) 55 *M.L.R.* 670.

flict. In this case, however, such a balance would have to favour the fœtus, because,[59]

> The risk that the defendant may take her own life if an order is made, is much less and is of a different order of magnitude than the certainty that the life of the unborn will be terminated if the order is not made.

It is arguable that use of this test was the only possible interpretation of a constitutional clause that expressly required a balance between what it deemed to be "equal" rights to life. After all, if the rights *were* equal, then assessment of the magnitude of the respective threats to these rights seemed like a good approach.

Less easy to justify, however, are Costello .J's conclusions in relation to E.C. law.[60] It was submitted in *X* that in as much as abortion is protected as a medical service under E.C. law,[61] therefore the injunction, in denying the girl the right to travel to receive services which were lawfully available in another member state, amounted to a violation of Articles 49 and 50 (ex Articles 59 and 60) of the Treaty. Costello J. accepting the bulk of these arguments, noted, however, that Article 8 of Council Directive 73/148/EEC allows a member state to derogate from the facilitation of such freedoms *inter alia* on the basis of public policy.[62] He felt that the highly controversial nature of abortion meant that it was an issue regarding which individual member states would be entitled to a wide margin of appreciation under community law. As such he concluded that the restriction on freedom of services which the proposed injunction would constitute was justifiable under community law as a proportionate act, necessary to safeguard a fundamental aspect of Irish public policy.[63]

This is a perfectly legitimate argument as to why E.C. law could not require Ireland to legalise abortion internally. On the other hand, given that what was at issue in *X* was an applicant's freedom merely to travel to receive a service which was perfectly legal under English law it is unlikely that Ireland's derogation powers would apply here. Indeed in the *Grogan* case, Advocate General

---

[58]On hearing that such an injunction had been sought, the family members returned to Ireland. In this context, their quite exemplary behaviour should be mentioned especially as Irish law suggests that the inevitable failure of an injunction is a sufficient ground for a judge in his discretion to refuse to grant it. See *Kutchera v. Buckingham* [1988] I.L.R.M. 1 (H.C.); [1988] I.L.R.M. 501 (S.C.). See also *A.G. v. Guardian Newspapers* [1990] 1 AC 109 (H.L.) (*Spycatcher (No. 2)*).

[59][1992] I.R. 1, 12. Hogan comments (*Irish Times,* February 19, 1992) that, "It has to be conceded that in view of earlier judicial pronouncements on Art. 40.3.3. Mr. Justice Costello's reasoning has a certain inevitability about it".

[60]Deirdre Curtin, "Claiming Rights to Abortion Under EC law", *Irish Times,* February 14, 1992.

[61]Case C-159/90 *Grogan v. Ireland* [1991] E.C.R.-I 4865; [1991] 62 C.M.L.R. 849

[62]See case 30/77, *R v. Bouchereau* [1977] E.C.R. 1999, 2014.

[63][1992] I.R. 1, 16. Costello J. stressed that the very existence of Art. 40.3.3 was ample evidence that opposition to abortion was bedrock of Irish public policy.

van Gerven had suggested that such a travel restriction would fall foul of E.C. law.[64]

3.4 The Supreme Court Decision

Because of its practical impact, Costello J.'s decision was widely condemned both in Ireland and abroad and to the relief of many, the case was appealed to the Supreme Court. On 26 February 1992, the court discharged the injunction, stating that it would explain its reasons for doing so later, but stressing that the issue had been decided on the basis of domestic and not European law. It was generally assumed that the Supreme Court had decided merely to allow the young girl to travel for an abortion,[65] but when the judgements were given it transpired that four of the five judges on the court had interpreted Article 40.3.3 as containing a right to have an abortion *in Ireland*, albeit in limited circumstances.[66]

Finlay C.J. argued that by virtue of its Preamble, the Irish Constitution had to be interpreted in accordance with concepts of prudence, justice and charity.[67] He considered the value to society of both of the competing lives in this case and, despite the fact that Article 40.3.3 specifically deems the two rights to life to be *equal* he appeared to conclude that the mother's life was worthy of more constitutional protection than that of the unborn.[68] Clearly convinced that the risk of the girl committing suicide was both real and imminent, he concluded that Costello J's test of balancing the degree of threat to the respective lives was inappropriate, and suggested an alternative, namely,[69]

> If it is established as a matter of probability that there is a real and substantial risk to the life as distinct from the health of the mother which can only be avoided by the termination of the pregnancy, such termination is permissible.

A slight extension to this test was given in the judgement of Egan J. He pointed

---

[64] [1991] E.C.R. I-4685, I-4719, para. 26.

[65] See for instance the comments of Professor Binchy, *Irish Times*, February 27, 1992. For the opposite conclusion see the comments of Dr. Gerard Hogan in the same newspaper.

[66] That the Supreme Court felt able to do so may be explained by the fact that Peter Shanley S.C. representing the Attorney General had conceded that Art. 40.3.3 allowed a right to abortion in limited circumstances.

[67] For a criticism of this conclusion see Byrne and Binchy, 170.

[68] Thus he said ". . . in vindicating and defending as far as practicable the right of the unborn to life, but at the same time giving regard to the right of the mother to life, the court must, amongst the matters to be so regarded concern itself with the position of the mother within a family group, with persons on whom she is dependent, with, in other instances, persons who are dependent upon her and her interaction with other citizens and members of society in the areas in which her activities occur" [1992] 1 I.R. 1, 53

[69] [1992] 1 I.R. 1, 53-54.

out that the term "laws" is mentioned twice in Article 40.3.3 and argued that this meant that the legislature was intended to have two functions within the terms of that article. It was required first to give unqualified *respect* to the right to life of the unborn and secondly to vindicate that right but only *as far as practicable*. Prohibiting abortion in this case would exceed the bounds of practicability in such vindication.

McCarthy J. argued that if there *was* a real and substantial risk to the life of the mother, then it would not be practicable to vindicate the right to life of the unborn by preventing abortion. Moreover, in such circumstances, McCarthy J. appeared to argue that a hierarchy of constitutional rights should be deemed to exist with the mother's right to life being more valuable than that of the fœtus. Such a conclusion is patently at variance with the express terms of the relevant constitutional clause, which speaks of the rights as equal. McCarthy J's. judgment is, however, perhaps best remembered for his attack on the legislative inertia that he felt had caused the present constitutional crisis. In his words,

> In the context of the eight years that have passed since the amendment was adopted and the two years since *Grogan's* case, the failure by the legislature to enact the appropriate legislation is no longer just unfortunate, it is inexcusable. . . . It is not for the courts to programme society; that is, partly at least, the role of the legislature.[70]

This is of course the thesis of this chapter. Nonetheless there is a certain inconsistency in McCarthy J's conclusion that "it is not for the courts to programme society", and the activist nature of the rest of his judgment. Moreover, this criticism of legislative inertia is arguably unfair. The 8th amendment was presented as an anti-abortion measure and had consistently been interpreted by the highest court in the land as an absolute ban on all manifestations of abortion. On this basis, the legislature could be forgiven for concluding that there was little need for clarifying legislation.

The sole dissenting judgement came from Hederman J. and was predominantly based on his opinion that in order for the constitutional right to life of the unborn to be set aside, there would need to be cogent evidence of a genuine threat to the mother's life. In this case, the fact of a risk to maternal life had been established by the uncontested and unquestioned testimony of one psychiatrist, giving it as his opinion that the girl was liable to commit suicide if forced to carry her pregnancy to term. Scant evidence indeed on which to set aside a constitutional right. It is difficult if not impossible to envisage any other situation where another constitutional right might be set aside on the basis of such an unevidenced assertion.[71]

---

[70][1992] 1 I.R. 1, 82.
[71]The evidence is summarised at [1992] 1 I.R. 1, 64-70 *per* Hederman J. However, one criticism

3.5 Criticisms of the Case

Criticisms of the Supreme Court decision in this case come essentially at two levels. First, there was a good deal of concern as to the practical implications of the decision, specifically that on one view of the decision, any woman claiming to be suicidal could now have an abortion at any time during pregnancy.[72] Secondly, it was suggested that as a piece of constitutional interpretation, this was a woefully short-sighted decision, and one where the admittedly hard facts of the case forced the judges to establish a very dangerous precedent within the realm of constitutional interpretation.[73]

(a) Criticisms as to the Consequences of the Decision

The complaint of the Irish anti-abortion movement following the *X* case, was that the Supreme Court had essentially found a right to abortion on demand latent within the terms of Article 40.3.3°. After all, anyone who wished an abortion could now claim to be suicidal and on the basis of the *X case*, this simple assertion might be enough. This situation was compounded by the fact that, unlike the US Supreme Court in *Roe v. Wade*, the Irish Supreme Court had not suggested that the "right to abortion" might become weaker or indeed non-existent at a later stage of pregnancy.

The latter point as to time limits is arguably not a strong one. The fact that the Court in *X* mentioned no such limits is undoubtedly a flaw in the majority judgments, but it is scarcely determinative of the issue.[74] Given the terms both of Article 40.3.3 and indeed of the Constitution generally, it would be fully legitimate for a hospital, a future court or indeed, if the context arose, the legislature to impose even quite strict time limits on the new abortion right.

The point about the acceptance of a threat of suicide as a justification for abortion is a more telling one and for two reasons. First, because if a woman wanted to have an abortion in Ireland, then, under the ruling in *X*, an allegation of suicidal tendencies supported by one psychiatrist would appear to give constitutional support to her claim.[75] The UK abortion experience is testimony to the fact that a badly worded limited exception to a prohibition on abortion can

---

of his judgment is that it is questionable whether, on an appeal, a judge may legitimately base his judgement on a different view of the facts to that found in a lower court.

[72] See Binchy writing in the *Irish Times*, March 6, 1992. See also Riordan, "Abortion, the Aftermath of the Supreme Court's decision" (1992) 80 *Studies* 293.

[73] Thus Dworkin (6) comments that "The furor [the High Court decision] created – protests broke out not only in Ireland but in London and New York as well – made the Irish Supreme Court eager to find some way to life the injunction, which it did".

[74] See Whyte, 261; and Kingston, Whelan, & Bacik, 94.

[75] Indeed in November 1992 when a referendum was put to the people proposing that abortion would be allowed where a mother's life was threatened by pregnancy, the risk of suicide was specifically excluded because of the possibility of abuse of such an exception. See 423 *Dàil Debates* Col. 1898 (1992). This proposed amendment was defeated

lead to abortion on demand.[76] Secondly, it is quite remarkable to have a situation where A's right to violate B's constitutional right to life should stem from a threat of self-destruction by A. It is arguable that the problem in this regard stems from the grant of the status of constitutional personhood to a fœtus, but where the Supreme Court in *Roe v. Wade* had no clear law, constitutional or otherwise on which to base their judgement, the court in *X* were required to give effect to a law which imbued the fœtus in the *X* case with constitutional personhood, irrespective of its mother's age, state of mind or of the manner by which it was conceived. The judges in the case may have disliked this law, but they were, nonetheless required to apply it.

(b) Criticisms of the Technique of Constitutional Interpretation Used

This leads on to the more far reaching criticism of this case, namely that it is a bad piece of constitutional interpretation. There are four points to be made in this regard.

First, despite the fact that a Thomistic view of Natural law had been informing the process of constitutional interpretation in Ireland for most of the previous thirty years[77] its significance received no mention from the majority judges in this case.

Secondly, it seems quite clear that Article 40.3.3° was seen by those who voted for it as an "anti-abortion" amendment. Although an originalist reliance on the intentions of those who voted the Constitution into place has not held much sway in Irish constitutional jurisprudence,[78] nonetheless it seems odd that an interpretation should be made which was patently at variance with the intentions of an electorate only nine years previously. This criticism is reinforced by the fact that in the next major abortion case in Ireland in 1995[79] a

---

[76] See Kennedy and Grubb, *Medical Law* (Butterworths, London, 1994) 864 *et seq.*

[77] See *inter alia, Ryan v. AG, McGee v. AG,* and *Norris v. AG* [1984] I.R. 36 (S.C.). See also Clarke, "The role of Natural Law in the Irish Constitution" (1982) XVII *Ir. Jur. (n.s.)* 187; O'Hanlon, "The Judiciary and the Moral Law" (1993) 11 *I.L.T. (n.s.)* 8. However, the decision in *In re Article 26 of the Irish Constitution and the Regulation of Information (Services Outside the State for the Termination of Pregnancies) Bill 1995* [1995] 1 I.R. 1; [1995] 2 I.L.R.M. 81 (S.C.), is seen by some as marking the end of the impact of natural law in the field of Irish constitutional interpretation. See, for example, Twomey, "The death of the Natural Law?" (1995) *Irish Law Times* 270. *cp.* Hogan, "A Desert Island Case Set in the Silver Sea. *The State (Ryan) v. Lennon* (1935)" above, 80, at text with nn. 30-45.

[78] See Kelly, cix-cxiii. For examples of judicial reliance on the state of the law and public opinion at the time of the enactment of the Constitution as an aid to its interpretation, see *In re the Offences Against the State (Amendment) Bill 1940* [1940] I.R. 470 (S.C.); *Ryan v. A.G.,* [1965] I.R. 294 (H.C.); *Conroy v. A.G.* [1965] I.R. 411; *State (Rollinson) v. Kelly* [1984] I.R. 248 (S.C.); and *McGee v. A.G.* [1974] I.R. 287 (HC., O'Keeffe J.; and S.C.) 293 *per* O'Keeffe J. (though *cf.* [1974] I.R. 287, 308 *per* Walsh J.).

[79] *In re Article 26 of the Irish Constitution and the Regulation of Information (Services Outside the State for the Termination of Pregnancies) Bill 1995* [1995] 1 I.R. 1; [1995] 2 I.L.R.M. 81 (S.C.)

constitutional contradiction within the terms of the newly amended Article
40.3.3° was expressly justified by the Supreme Court by reference to the intentions of the electorate in amending the Constitution in this manner.[80] Thirdly,
the interpretation in *X* was radically inconsistent with all other earlier interpretations of Article 40.3.3°.

Most extraordinarily, however, the interpretation of Article 40.3.3°. which
the Supreme Court in *X* gave is clearly at variance with the, admittedly impossible terminology of equal rights used therein. Finlay C.J. criticised the balancing test which Costello J. had employed in the High Court on the basis that it
would mean that in practical terms the right to life of the unborn would always
receive priority over that of the mother. Nonetheless there is a strong argument
for the view that if the rights in question are indeed equal, then the only legitimate approach for a court charged with balancing them when they are in direct
conflict (and there is a case for saying that in *X* the rights were not in direct
conflict in that the threat to the mother's life derived not from the unborn but
from herself), is to assess the comparative magnitude of the respective threats.
The net result reached by the Supreme Court in *X* – namely that the young girl
in the case should not be forced to carry to term a pregnancy which she did not
wish and which was the product of a criminal act – was undoubtedly what was
desired by a good deal of public opinion. Moreover, in moral terms it may well
be the "right" result.[81] Nonetheless in legal terms, in *X* as in *Roe v. Wade*, the
"right" result was reached by an inappropriate judicial intervention in an area
of extreme moral controversy, which struck at the very heart of democratic
government. Indeed the judicial activism in *X* is even more insidious than that
in *Roe*. In *Roe* the court merely invented a right which was not in the Constitution; in *X* the court made an interpretation of a constitutional provision which
was in clear and direct violation of the terms of that provision. Abortion politics aside, this is a dangerous approach to constitutional law and one which
sets a precedent with breathtaking potential. It is because both *Roe* and *X* set
such precedents that they may be viewed as leading cases of the twentieth
century.

---

[80][1995] 1 I.R. 1, 45; [1995] 2 I.L.R.M. 81, 108-109.
[81]Thompson, writing in 1971 said that, ". . . a sick and desperately frightened 14-year-old school-
girl pregnant due to rape may of course choose an abortion and . . . any law which rules this out
is an insane law". See Thompson, 65.

THE *MAREVA* INJUNCTION – FROM BIRTH TO ADULTHOOD
MAREVA COMPANIA NAVIERA S.A. v. INTERNATIONAL BULKCARRIERS S.A. (1975)

DAVID CAPPER

1. INTRODUCTION

"You cannot get an injunction to restrain a man who is alleged to be a debtor from parting with his property", roundly proclaimed James L.J. during the course of argument before the Court of Appeal in *Robinson v. Pickering*[1] in 1881. This pronouncement, not repeated in any of the judgments in that case, pithily summarised the received wisdom of almost every lawyer in the common law world until May 22, 1975 at the earliest. On that date Japanese shipowners asked the Court of Appeal in London for an *ex parte* injunction to restrain defendant charterers from removing any of their assets from the jurisdiction, pending the hearing of an apparently unanswerable claim for unpaid charter hire. The case in point, *Nippon Yusen Kaisha v. Karageorgis,*[2] began what Lord Denning, perhaps a little self servingly, described as "the greatest piece of judicial law reform in my time".[3] In a one page judgment for a unanimous Court Lord Denning M.R. said:

> It seems to me that the time has come when we should revise our practice. There is no reason why the High Court or this court should not make an order such as is asked for here. It is warranted by section 45 of the Supreme Court of Judicature (Consolidation) Act 1925 which says that the High Court may grant a mandamus or an injunction or appoint a receiver by an interlocutory order in all cases in which it appears to the

---

Senior Lecturer in Law, Queen's University Belfast; Barrister of the Inn of Court of Northern Ireland.

[1] (1881) 16 Ch.D. 660 (C.A.) 661.

[2] [1975] 1 W.L.R. 1093 (C.A.).

[3] Lord Denning, *The Due Process of Law* (Butterworths, London, 1980) 134. In his preface to Steven Gee Q.C.'s *Mareva Injunctions and Anton Piller Relief* (4th ed., Sweet & Maxwell, London, 1998) [hereafter, Gee] Lord Hoffman referred to the subject of this paper as "probably . . . the most remarkable example of judicial creativity in this century" (Gee, xiii).

court to be just or convenient so to do. It seems to me that this is just such a case. There is a strong prima facie case that the hire is owing and unpaid. If an injunction is not granted, these moneys may be removed out of the jurisdiction and the shipowners will have the greatest difficulty in recovering anything. Two days ago we granted an injunction *ex parte* and we should continue it.[4]

There was no further analysis, no reference to previous authority, and no acknowledgement that there might be any formidable obstacles in the way of this "change in practice".

The leading case presented in this essay is not the one just mentioned. This essay is concerned with the second reported case where an injunction of this kind was granted. It was the second case, *Mareva Compania Naviera S.A. v. International Bulkcarriers S.A.*,[5] which gave the name *Mareva* injunction to *ex parte* orders of this kind. Why it should have been the second case is not altogether obvious. It might be that one swallow does not make a summer and that the first case could have been seen as a one-off aberration not to be repeated. It might be that the reasons in the first case were too briefly stated and that a christening had to wait for a grander occasion when there was time to make a better job. That said, it is curious that the related procedure of the *Anton Piller* order also had to wait until its second reported case before it could be christened. The judgment of Brightman J. in *EMI Ltd v. Pandit*[6] was no less fully reasoned than that of the Court of Appeal in *Anton Piller KG v. Manufacturing Processes Ltd*,[7] although there may have been some reluctance to name a revolutionary new procedure after a first instance judgment.

This essay traces the development of the *Mareva* injunction from its birth to the mature adulthood which it enjoys today. First, there will be an analysis of the *Mareva* case itself. This will concentrate upon the Court of Appeal's efforts to demonstrate that the new injunction they were granting was consistent with previous authority. What will be apparent, however, is that even after this landmark case the life of the *Mareva* injunction hung very much in the balance. There were several occasions during the years which followed the *Mareva* case when the new procedure could have died. This essay explains the efforts of Lord Denning and others to keep it alive, and how it grew through childhood and adolescence to become one of major features of modern civil litigation. It is an exciting story, well worth telling in the year that Lord Denning passed away just six weeks after his hundredth birthday. It will not be possible to tell of all the developments which have taken place in the last quarter cen-

---

[4] [1975] 1 W.L.R. 1093, 1095.
[5] [1975] 2 Lloyd's Rep. 509.
[6] [1975] 1 W.L.R. 302.
[7] [1976] Ch. 55 (C.A.).

tury but the major landmarks of that time should be sufficient to justify the inclusion of *Mareva v. International Bulkcarriers* as one of the leading cases of the twentieth century. There will be some brief discussion of two areas where further development of the *Mareva* principle might be possible and some assessment will be made of the nature and extent of the revolution in civil procedure which the *Mareva* injunction has occasioned. The essay will concentrate upon developments in England and Wales, but some Irish[8] developments will be briefly considered since the *Mareva* injunction has been adopted in Ireland as in other jurisdictions throughout the common law world[9] in imitation of the English position.

2. THE BIRTH OF THE *MAREVA* INJUNCTION

Mareva Compania Naviera S.A. v. International Bulkcarriers S.A.[10] was another ship's charterparty case. Shipowners let their vessel to charterers on a time charterparty for a voyage to the Far East and back. The charterers let the vessel on a voyage charterparty to the President of India. Hire was payable under the charterparty half monthly in advance and the first two instalments were paid on time. The charterers defaulted on the third instalment and an exchange of telexes between the parties made it clear that the charterers were unable to pay. The shipowners treated this as a repudiation of the charterparty and issued a writ for unpaid hire and damages for repudiation. They also applied *ex parte* for an injunction to restrain the charterers from removing from the jurisdiction any moneys the latter had received from the President of India under the voyage charter. Donaldson J. was referred to the *Nippon Yusen* case but felt considerable doubt about it because the Court of Appeal had not been referred to its earlier decision in *Lister v. Stubbs*.[11] Accordingly he only granted the injunction for a limited time to enable an appeal to be brought to the Court of Appeal.

Consideration of the appeal requires some analysis of *Lister v. Stubbs*. That case concerned certain commissions which the plaintiffs' agent (Stubbs) acquired from customers as rewards for placing the plaintiffs' business with them. The plaintiffs laid a proprietary claim to certain investments which Stubbs ac-

---

[8] On the Irish position generally see Courtney, *Mareva Injunctions and Related Interlocutory Orders* (Butterworths, Dublin, 1998) [hereafter, Courtney].

[9] Except the United States. In *Grupo Mexicano de Desarrollo SA v. Alliance Bond Fund Inc*, 527 U.S. 308, 119 S.Ct. 1961, (1999) the United States Supreme Court ruled by a 5-4 majority that the federal courts in the United States had no power to grant *Mareva* type relief. In brief the Court's reasons were that the Judiciary Act of 1789 conferred on the federal courts the power to grant equitable relief possessed by the English Court of Chancery at that time. The English Court of Chancery then had no power to grant *Mareva* type relief and the federal courts' assumption of it would be an unjustifiable usurpation of Congress' legislative authority.

[10] [1975] 2 Lloyd's Rep. 509 (C.A.).

[11] (1890) 45 Ch. D. 1 (C.A.).

quired with the commissions and sought an injunction to compel him to hand those over to them. The principal issue in *Lister v. Stubbs* was whether the plaintiffs had any proprietary claim to the investments and the Court of Appeal answered that they had not.[12] The relationship between the plaintiffs and Stubbs was one of debtor-creditor, not trustee and *cestui que trust*. While this had nothing to do with the question whether the plaintiff was entitled to a pre-judgment injunction interfering with the defendant's freedom to use his assets as he pleased, a further question before the Court was concerned with this. This was the plaintiffs' application for a further injunction to compel Stubbs to pay the investments into court even if their relationship with him was debtor-creditor. The Court of Appeal refused this relief too but it is clear that this was because an order for payment into court would have converted the plaintiff into a secured creditor.[13] Nothing was said in *Lister v. Stubbs* about whether the plaintiff could obtain an injunction operating *in personam* and restraining the defendant from disposing of assets in any way. *Lister v. Stubbs* thus presented no major obstacle to the grant of what became known as *Mareva* relief.

In spite of this apparently obvious escape route the Court of Appeal's efforts to distinguish *Lister v. Stubbs* were curiously schizophrenic. Lord Denning M.R. adopted a broad brush approach, basing his judgment on what he described as the very wide power contained in section 45(1) of the Supreme Court of Judicature (Consolidation) Act 1925 to grant interlocutory injunctions in all cases where it appeared to the court to be just and convenient to do so, and making hardly any effort to distinguish *Lister v. Stubbs* at all.[14] Roskill L.J. was much more cautious and was reluctant to explore difficult legal questions in the absence of argument from both sides. He believed that had the defendants been represented before the court they would have contended that *Lister v. Stubbs* precluded the court, not as a matter of jurisdiction but as a matter of practice, from granting the injunction. Should it be necessary to distinguish *Lister v. Stubbs* this could be done via clause 18 of the charterparty which gave the shipowners a lien on cargoes and sub-freights for all sums due under the charterparty.[15]

This is all there was to the case which gave its name to the *Mareva* injunction; an *ex parte* appeal occupying little more than three pages of the Lloyd's Law Reports. Clearly the first *inter partes* challenge to the new procedure was going to be crucial. This came in *Rasu Maritime S.A. v. Perusahaan*

[12]*Lister v. Stubbs* was effectively overruled on this point in *Attorney General for Hong Kong v. Reid* [1994] 1 A.C. 324 (P.C.).
[13]In the words of Cotton L.J.: "I know of no case where, because it was highly probable that if the action were brought to a hearing the plaintiff could establish that a debt was due to him from the defendant, the defendant has been ordered to give security until that has been established by the judgment or decree" ((1890) 45 Ch. D. 1, 6).
[14][1975] 2 Lloyd's Rep. 509, 510.
[15][1975] 2 Lloyd's Rep. 509, 511.

Pertambangan ("The Pertamina"),[16] the importance of which was threefold. First, by discharging the injunction on the ground that the hardship likely to be suffered by the defendant was out of all proportion to any benefit which the plaintiff was likely to derive, the Court of Appeal demonstrated that the *Mareva* injunction could be controlled. Secondly, the refusal of the injunction on this discretionary ground forestalled an appeal to the House of Lords, where the new procedure would have met with an uncertain fate. Thirdly, in affirming the legitimacy of the new procedure the Court of Appeal had to confront more than one cited authority which strongly suggested that an injunction could not be granted to interfere in any way with the rights of persons to deal with their assets before judgment had been obtained against them.[17] One of these authorities, *Lister v. Stubbs*, has already been shown to be distinguishable on the ground that the plaintiff was seeking security for a debt. In others the relief sought was *in personam* but there was no explicit argument that the defendant was going to dissipate assets so as to put them beyond the plaintiff's reach. However, the last three of these cases concerned applications by wives to restrain their husbands from putting assets beyond the reach of maintenance proceedings which the wives had commenced. Along with the fraudulent conveyance this is one of the oldest debt-dodging tricks in the book. Thus it is clear that prior to the *Mareva* injunction the courts had at least some awareness of the risks of defendants stultifying legal proceedings by rendering themselves judgment proof. However it is not without significance that statutory provisions enabling spouses to seek orders restraining the other spouse from disposing of assets which might otherwise be available to meet a claim for financial provision were enacted before the *Mareva* injunction was invented.[18] Hence it is just about arguable that the courts did not fully appreciate the risk of defendants in different kinds of cases making themselves judgment proof.

Against this background the reasoning of the Court of Appeal appears to be somewhat superficial. Both Lord Denning M.R. and Orr L.J. relied on the width of the power conferred by section 45(1) of the 1925 Act. But only Lord Denning M.R. dealt with the cases cited by the defendant against the grant of interlocutory orders restraining the disposal of assets. He said that those authorities did not apply where a foreign based defendant was alleged to be on the point of removing assets from the jurisdiction.[19] In hindsight it perhaps looks strange

---

[16][1978] Q.B. 644 (C.A.).

[17]*Mills v. Northern Railway of Buenos Aires Co.* [1870] L.R. 5 Ch. App. 621 (Lord Hatherley L.C); *Robinson v. Pickering* (1881) 16 Ch. D. 660 (C.A.); *Lister v. Stubbs* (1890) 45 Ch. D. 1 (C.A.); *Newton v. Newton* (1885) 11 P.D. 11; *Burmester v. Burmester* [1913] P.D. 76; *Scott v. Scott* [1951] P. 193 (C.A.).

[18]The power to grant this relief goes back at least to the Matrimonial Causes (Property and Maintenance) Act 1958, s.2; the current power is found in the Matrimonial Causes Act 1973, s.37. In Ireland see Family Law Act 1995, s. 35(2); Family Law (Divorce) Act 1996, s. 37(2).

[19][1978] Q.B. 644, 659.

to limit an injunction directed against litigants rendering themselves judgment proof to one kind of defendant resorting to just one method of making itself judgment proof. But this fails to appreciate the huge departure from the universally accepted understanding of the law which Lord Denning was undertaking and the very real risk that had the Court of Appeal moved too quickly a conservatively minded House of Lords might have rejected the entire experiment.

3. From Childhood to Adolescence – The Survival of the *Mareva* Injunction

In *Siskina (Cargo Owners) v. Distos Compania Naviera ("The Siskina")*[20] the precocious young *Mareva* injunction survived a potentially fatal childhood illness. The plaintiffs were apparently seeking nothing more than the usual *Mareva* relief of that time, an injunction to restrain the removal of assets from the jurisdiction by a foreign based defendant. However there was just one crucial difference. The plaintiffs had no cause of action within the territorial jurisdiction of the English courts. They sought to serve a writ out of the jurisdiction under R.S.C. Order 11 rule 1(1)(i) (now rule 1(1)(b)) claiming an injunction restraining the defendants from doing something within the jurisdiction. But what they sought to injunct the defendants from doing was removing assets from the jurisdiction. This was no part of the relief which the plaintiffs were claiming at trial so, unsurprisingly, the House of Lords came to the conclusion that the writ could not be served. As the plaintiffs were not entitled to any substantive relief at trial they were not entitled to any ancillary relief in the form of a *Mareva* injunction. The rule here applied (in the United Kingdom practically obliterated now by statute) actually did very little damage to the *Mareva* procedure. But the appeal could have been fatal as the House of Lords might have taken the opportunity to declare the new procedure invalid. That it was not fatal owed much to counsel for the defendants, Anthony Lloyd Q.C. (now Lord Lloyd of Berwick), who chose not to attack the legitimacy of the *Mareva* principle, merely arguing that it did not apply unless the plaintiff had a cause of action within the jurisdiction.[21]

Although *The Siskina* may appear now to have been something of a setback for the *Mareva* injunction, its effect at the time was entirely different. Lord Denning confessed that he had a fear that the House of Lords would overrule the entire *Mareva* principle.[22] So when *The Siskina* came before the Court of Appeal he must have felt that he was somewhere between the devil and the deep blue sea. Would he grant the plaintiffs relief and provoke the defendants

---

[20][1979] A.C. 210 (C.A. and H.L.).
[21] See Lord Denning, *The Due Process of Law* (Butterworths, London, 1980) 145.
[22] *ibid.*

into an appeal to the House of Lords, or would he uphold the defendants' arguments and provoke the plaintiffs into an appeal? This time there could be no side stepping of the problem by deciding the case on some discretionary ground; a matter of fundamental legal principle was in issue. Faced with that dilemma it is perhaps no wonder that his Lordship invoked divine intervention. Contending that the courts could not afford to wait for legislative reform of the rule that a plaintiff could only get an interlocutory injunction where it had a claim for substantive relief at trial, Lord Denning M.R. said:

> The Judges have an inherent jurisdiction to lay down the practice and procedure of the Courts: and we can invoke it now to restrain the removal of these insurance moneys. To the timorous souls I would say in the words of William Cowper:
>
> > Ye fearful saints, fresh courage take,
> > The clouds ye so much dread
> > Are big with mercy, and shall break
> > In blessings on your head.
>
> Instead of "saints", read "Judges". Instead of "mercy", read "justice". And you will find a good way to law reform. . . .[23]

Since an appeal to the Lords was probably inevitable there may have been little point in deciding the case conservatively. Historically what is important about *The Siskina* is that the *Mareva* injunction went to the House of Lords and got out alive. Far from being a setback this may even have given the courts more confidence to extend the procedure into new areas. One such area was the extension of the *Mareva* injunction to defendants based within the jurisdiction. In *The Siskina* Lord Hailsham had drawn attention to the unsatisfactory distinction between English and foreign defendants,[24] and suggested that either the restriction to foreign defendants or the entire *Mareva* principle would have to be reviewed. When their Lordships declined the opportunity to review the *Mareva* principle it was probably more likely that the restriction to foreign defendants would be reviewed. Within two years three decisions – *Chartered Bank Ltd v. Daklouche*,[25] *Barclay-Johnson v. Yuill*,[26] and *Rahman v. Abu-Taha*[27] – firmly established that a *Mareva* injunction could be granted against defendants based within the jurisdiction as well as against foreign based defendants.

---

[23][1979] A.C. 210, 236.
[24][1979] A.C. 210, 261.
[25][1980] 1 All E.R. 205 (C.A.).
[26][1980] 3 All E.R. 190 (Ch.D.).
[27][1980] 1 W.L.R. 1268 (C.A.).

The final significant act of this most crucial stage of the *Mareva* injunction's life was the enactment of section 37(3) of the Supreme Court Act 1981,[28] which removed any doubts which may have remained about the courts' powers to grant *Mareva* injunctions and confirmed the extension to defendants based within the jurisdiction.

In Ireland, there is no such specific statutory authority to grant *Mareva* injunctions and there has been no significant judicial debate about the procedure's juridical basis. Essentially the courts have followed the English lead and based the power to grant this relief on the general jurisdiction to grant interlocutory injunctions.[29] However one area where Irish practice may be significantly different from that in England and Wales relates to the test for disposal of assets. As a result of the cases discussed above, and the subsequent decision of the Court of Appeal in *The Niedersachsen*,[30] it is clear that in England and Wales a *Mareva* injunction will be granted to restrain a defendant from disposing of its assets for reasons other than sound business purposes if the likely result of this is that the defendant would render itself judgment proof. The difference between this and the Irish position appears in the next section

4. A DISTINCTIVELY IRISH DOCTRINE?

The Irish courts accepted the *Mareva* injunction in four cases decided in the 1980s.[31] The most notable feature of these cases is that they contained *dicta* suggesting that to obtain the grant of a *Mareva* injunction in Ireland, the plaintiff had to produce evidence showing that the defendant would probably dispose of assets *with the intention* of making itself judgment proof. Two decisions of the 1990s, *Countyglen plc v. Carway*[32] and *O'Mahony v. Horgan*,[33] contain similar judicial statements to those in the earlier Irish cases although the present author has challenged whether they represent an attempt by the Irish courts to create their own distinctive *Mareva* jurisprudence.[34] That said, the leading commentator on *Mareva* injunctions in Ireland is clearly of the view that the

---

[28] Discussed in section 5 below.

[29] Contained in the Supreme Court of Judicature (Ireland) Act 1877, s. 28(8), as applied to the present High Court by the Courts (Supplemental Provisions) Act, ss. 8(2) and 48(3). See Courtney, paras. 2.02 and 2.16-2.17.

[30] [1984] 1 All E.R. 398 (C.A.); see also Gee, 198-200.

[31] *B.H. v. W.H.* [1983] I.L.R.M. 419 (H.C., O'Hanlon J); *Harry Fleming v. Ranks (Ireland) Ltd.* [1983] I.L.R.M. 541 (H.C., McWilliam J.); *Powerscourt Estates v. Gallagher* [1984] I.L.R.M. 123 (H.C., McWilliam J); *Serge Caudron v. Air Zaire* [1986] I.L.R.M. 10 (S.C.). On the early cases, see Harpum, "*Mareva* Injunctions in the Irish Courts" (1984) 6 *D.U.L.J.* (*n.s.*) 131.

[32] [1995] 1 I.R. 208.

[33] [1995] 2 I.R. 411.

[34] See Capper, "*Mareva* Injunctions: A Distinctively Irish Doctrine?" (1995) 17 *D.U.L.J.* (*n.s.*) 110.

Irish cases should be taken at face value.[35] The most recent Irish authority, *Bennett Enterprises Inc. v. Lipton*,[36] takes the same line as before and contains the baffling statement that ". . . if any dissipation of assets were to occur in the ordinary course of business, this of itself would not justify the granting of a *Mareva* injunction".[37] With respect, it is possible *either* to dissipate assets *or* to dispose of them in the ordinary course of business, but not possible to do both at the same time. The muddle caused by statements like these suggests that Irish courts have failed to understand that it is the threat of dissipating assets, and not the defendant's intention to defeat judgment, which is the true test plaintiffs must satisfy. One can infer an intention to defeat judgment from a probability of dissipating assets but why then insist on specific proof of an intention to defeat judgment?

5. ADOLESCENCE TO ADULTHOOD – THE GROWTH OF THE *MAREVA* INJUNCTION

The enactment in England of section 37(3) of the Supreme Court Act 1981 appears to have been a major catalyst in the development of the *Mareva* injunction during the 1980s. Prior to this enactment the usual *Mareva* order restrained the transfer of assets out of the jurisdiction *and* the disposal of assets within the jurisdiction. The reference to disposals within the jurisdiction was to make sure that the defendant could not evade the restraint on transfer of assets from the jurisdiction by alternative means, such as transferring assets to a collaborator who could then remove them from the jurisdiction.[38] It was necessary for the applicant to show a risk that the defendant would render itself judgment proof by the transfer of assets out of the jurisdiction. A risk that the defendant would only dispose of assets within the jurisdiction was insufficient.[39]

Although Lord Denning M.R. attempted to extend the *Mareva* injunction

---

[35] See Courtney, chap. 6.

[36] [1999] 2 I.R. 221; [1999] 1 I.L.R.M. 81 (H.C., O'Sullivan J).

[37] [1999] 2 I.R. 221, 228; [1999] 1 I.L.R.M. 81, 89. This echoes the judgment of Hamilton C.J. in *O'Mahony v. Horgan* [1995] 2 I.R. 411, 419 where the following statement is found: "It is not sufficient to establish that the assets are likely to be *dissipated in the ordinary course of business or in the payment of lawful debts*" (emphasis added).

[38] See the orders made in *Nippon Yusen Kaisha v. Karageorgis* [1975] 1 W.L.R. 1093; *Montecchi v. Shimco* [1979] 1 W.L.R. 1180 (C.A.); *Barclay-Johnson v. Yuill* [1980] 3 All E.R. 190.

[39] See *Barclay-Johnson v. Yuill* [1980] 3 All E.R. 190, 194 where Megarry V-C said: "It seems to me that the heart and core of the Mareva injunction is the risk of the defendant removing his assets from the jurisdiction and so stultifying any judgment given by the courts in the action...if the assets are likely to remain in the jurisdiction, then the plaintiff, like all others with claims against the defendant, must run the risk, common to all, that the defendant may dissipate his assets, or consume them in discharging other liabilities, and so leave nothing with which to satisfy any judgment."

to risks of disposal of assets solely within the jurisdiction,[40] his views were not shared by other judges[41] and the matter only became settled after the enactment of section 37(3) of the Supreme Court Act 1981, which provides as follows:

> The power of the High Court under subsection (1) to grant an interlocutory injunction restraining a party to any proceedings from removing from the jurisdiction of the High Court, or otherwise dealing with, assets located within that jurisdiction shall be exercisable in cases where that party is, as well as in cases where he is not, domiciled, resident or present within that jurisdiction.

The crucial words here are "otherwise dealing with", which in *Z Ltd v. A-Z and AA-LL*,[42] a case decided after the enactment of section 37(3), Lord Denning M.R. regarded as extending previous practice. Whether these words were intended to have this effect may be doubted since the Supreme Court Act 1981 was a consolidating Act and section 37(3) basically reproduced the usual wording of *Mareva* orders of that time.[43] The issue is largely academic now since case law has effectively established that *Mareva* injunctions can be granted to prevent the disposal of assets within the jurisdiction in the absence of any risk of disposal out of the jurisdiction.[44] Viewed as a question of principle, however, it is probably better that all disposals of assets situated within the jurisdiction can be restrained as the limitation to disposals out of the jurisdiction was never a particularly convincing way of distinguishing pre-*Mareva* case law. Once the power to grant *Mareva* injunctions was placed on a statutory footing the courts would have felt a great deal more confidence about where they could take the new procedure, and would not have had to settle for moving forward in short pragmatic steps.[45]

Also during the 1980s the courts developed a number of ancillary orders to support the operation of the *Mareva* procedure. The first to be developed was an order requiring the defendant to disclose the nature, value and whereabouts of its assets within the jurisdiction. Many plaintiffs knew that their defendants had assets within the jurisdiction but did not know where those assets were and

---

[40] See *Rahman v. Abu-Taha* [1980] 1 W.L.R. 1268, 1273.
[41] See *Faith Panton Property Plan Ltd. v. Hodgetts* [1981] 2 All E.R. 877 (C.A.) 882 *per* Waller L.J. and 885 *per* Brandon L.J.; *AJ Bekhor and Co Ltd. v. Bilton* [1981] 2 All E.R. 565 (C.A.) 573 *per* Ackner L.J.
[42] [1982] 1 Q.B. 558 (C.A.) 571.
[43] See Harpum "*Mareva* – Toward The Unknown" (1983) 3 *O.J.L.S.* 136, 140-143.
[44] *CBS (UK) Ltd. v. Lambert* [1983] 1 Ch. 37; *PCW (Underwriting Agencies) Ltd. v. Dixon* [1984] 1 All E.R. 398.
[45] Ireland has no statutory provision like s.37(3) applying specifically to *Mareva* injunctions. When the Irish courts accepted the *Mareva* injunction the English courts had already decided to extend the new procedure to disposals of assets within the jurisdiction. Ireland whizzed through all the above stages in one go. See Courtney, paras. 6.09-6.12.

therefore could not guarantee their preservation for judgment by serving the injunction on third party banks holding those assets. In granting discovery orders the courts reasoned that if they had power to grant *Mareva* injunctions they had ancillary power to make them effective.[46] However this development, important though it undoubtedly was, owed very little to section 37(3) since the major cases recognising the power to grant discovery orders pre-dated that provision.[47]

A bolder development, which might not have happened but for the explicit statutory recognition of the *Mareva* principle, was the grant of an order to restrain the defendant in person from leaving the jurisdiction and taking his assets with him. The immediate impetus for this came from attempts to revive the ancient writ of *ne exeat regno*, the extant nature of which had been recognised by Megarry J. in *Felton v. Callis*[48] six years before the grant of the first *Mareva* injunction. This writ is technically useless in the *Mareva* context because it requires proof that the defendant's absence from the jurisdiction would materially hamper the plaintiff in the prosecution of his action, as opposed to the enforcement of judgment.[49] The deficiency here was remedied in *Bayer v. Winter*[50] where the plaintiffs had already obtained a *Mareva* injunction when they became aware of circumstances which suggested that the defendant was going to evade execution of the order by leaving the jurisdiction, taking his assets with him. The Court of Appeal granted an injunction requiring the defendant to deliver up his passport and restraining him from leaving the jurisdiction until the *Mareva* injunction had been executed. The Lords Justices reasoned in similar fashion to the discovery cases – if there was power to grant a *Mareva* injunction to prevent the court's process being rendered nugatory there was power to grant ancillary orders to ensure the injunction was effective. The juridical basis of this power was said to be section 37(1) of the Supreme Court Act 1981, Fox L.J. relying upon the following dictum of Jessel M.R. in *Smith v. Peters*:

> I have no hesitation in saying that there is no limit to the practice of the Court with regard to interlocutory applications so far as they are necessary and reasonable applications ancillary to the due performance of its

---

[46]See *A v. C* [1980] 2 All E.R. 347 (Q.B.D.); *A.J. Bekhor and Co Ltd. v. Bilton* [1981] 2 All E.R. 565 (C.A.).
[47]The Irish law on ancillary orders, including discovery, is substantially the same. See Courtney, chap. 10.
[48][1969] 1 Q.B. 200 (Q.B.D.).
[49]This was overlooked in *Al Nahkel for Contracting and Trading Ltd. v. Howe* [1986] 1 All E.R. 729 (Q.B.D.) where the writ appears to have been granted to prevent the defendant from frustrating judgment. However it proved fatal to the applicant's case in *Allied Arab Bank Ltd. v. Hajjar* [1987] 3 All E.R. 739 (Q.B.D.).
[50][1986] 1 All E.R. 733 (C.A.).

functions, namely, the administration of justice at the hearing of the cause.[51]

Although these words describe the extent of the courts' powers to grant inter-locutory orders prior to the Supreme Court Act 1981, it is suggested that without the explicit recognition in section 37(3) that *Mareva* injunctions fell within section 37(1), it might have been difficult for the courts to have taken the quantum leap necessary to grant orders of this kind.[52] In Ireland, by contrast, the development of *Bayer* orders owes nothing to a section 37(3) equivalent because none exists in this jurisdiction. However, all Irish *Bayer* orders post-date the original English case.[53]

The next development chronologically was the use of *Mareva*-type injunctions to freeze the proceeds or alleged proceeds of crime. This matter will be postponed until consideration is given to two massive developments in *Mareva* jurisprudence, the extension of the procedure to assets located outside the territorial jurisdiction of the courts and the legislative abolition of the rule in *The Siskina*[54] that the plaintiff had to have a cause of action within the same territorial jurisdiction, which occurred in the 1980s and 1990s respectively. The first of these developments, the acceptance that it was appropriate for the courts to grant *Mareva* relief in respect of assets located in another jurisdiction, occurred in four Court of Appeal decisions within a short time of each other in the year 1989 – *Babanaft International Co S.A. v. Bassatne*,[55] *Republic of Haiti v. Duvalier*,[56] *Derby & Co. Ltd v. Weldon (No. 1)*,[57] and *Derby & Co. Ltd v. Weldon (Nos. 3 & 4)*.[58] What is clear from all of the judgments in these cases is that the Court of Appeal, while recognising the exceptional nature of the relief it was granting, never flinched from the conclusion that the general power to grant interlocutory injunctions contained in section 37 of the Supreme Court Act 1981 amply justified the conclusion that the courts had jurisdiction to grant relief of this kind. Most of the debate before the Court was concerned with practical considerations, particularly how to ensure that third parties holding the defendant's assets were not required to breach legal obligations in the country where the assets were located as the price of complying with the injunction.[59]

---

[51] [1875] L.R. 20 Eq. 511, 512-513; quoted at [1986] 1 All E.R. 733, 737.

[52] Subsequent instances of orders of this kind include *Re Oriental Credit* [1988] Ch. 203; *B v. B* [1996] 1 W.L.R. 329; *Morris v. Murjani* [1996] 1 W.L.R. 848.

[53] See *Re J Ellis Pharmaceuticals*, *The Irish Times*, August 13, 1988 (H.C., Blayney J.); *Re Mark Synnott (Life and Pensions) Brokers Ltd.*, *The Irish Times*, July 4, 1991 (H.C., Carroll J.); *Re TSD Ltd.*, *The Irish Times*, February 14, 1992 (H.C., Murphy J.).

[54] [1979] A.C. 210.

[55] [1990] Ch. 13 (C.A.).

[56] [1990] Q.B. 202 (C.A.).

[57] [1990] Ch. 48 (C.A.).

[58] [1990] Ch. 65 (C.A.).

[59] This is usually achieved through use of the so called "*Babanaft*" proviso, which is worded something like the following:

It is probable that once again the statutory recognition of the *Mareva* injunction in section 37(3) of the 1981 Act was an influential factor in the courts' assumption of this jurisdiction. "World-wide" *Mareva* injunctions have been accepted in Ireland, and similar principles to England and Wales seem to apply.[60]

The other of these two massive developments was in many respects the converse of the "world-wide" *Mareva* injunction just described. Instead of the plaintiff having a cause of action within the jurisdiction and the defendant's assets being out of the jurisdiction, the defendant has assets within the jurisdiction but the plaintiff's cause of action is in another jurisdiction. In *The Siskina*[61] the House of Lords had ruled that the plaintiff was not entitled to *Mareva* relief unless it had a cause of action within the jurisdiction. This principle was first weakened by the enactment of the Civil Jurisdiction and Judgments Act 1982 (implementing the Brussels Convention), section 25(1) of which states that the High Court may grant interim protective measures (which includes *Mareva* injunctions) in aid of legal proceedings which have been or are to be commenced in another Convention territory.[62] It appeared to have been further weakened by certain *dicta* of the House of Lords in two post *Siskina* cases – *South Carolina Insurance Co v. Assurantie Maatschappij "De Zeven Provincien" NV*[63] and *Channel Tunnel Group Ltd v. Balfour Beatty Construction Ltd*[64] – which strongly suggested that the power to grant injunctions was not limited to cases where the plaintiff had a substantive right within the jurisdiction of the court. However hopes for a judicial departure from *The Siskina* were dashed by the advice of the Privy Council in *Mercedez-Benz AG v.*

"Provided that, in so far as this order purports to have any extraterritorial effect, no person shall be affected thereby or concerned with the terms thereof, until it shall be declared enforceable or be enforced by a foreign court and then it shall only affect them to the extent of such declaration or enforcement unless they are:
(a) a person to whom this order is addressed or an officer of, or an agent appointed by a power of attorney of such a person, or
(b) persons who are subject to the jurisdiction of this court and:
    (i) have been given written notice of this order at their residence or place of business within the jurisdiction, and
    (ii) are able to prevent acts or omissions outside the jurisdiction of this court which assist in the breach of the terms of this order."
See *Derby & Co Ltd. v. Weldon (Nos. 3 & 4)* [1990] Ch. 65, 84. For further detail on these "worldwide" *Mareva* injunctions see Capper, "Worldwide Mareva Injunctions" (1991) 54 *M.L.R.* 329.
[60] See Courtney, paras. 7.35-7.38; *Bennett Enterprises Inc. v. Lipton* [1999] 2 I.R. 221; [1999] 1 I.L.R.M. 81.
[61] [1979] A.C. 210; see section 3 above.
[62] The Civil Jurisdiction and Judgments Act 1991 extends the 1982 Act to Lugano Convention countries.
[63] [1987] 1 A.C. 24 (H.L.) 44-45 *per* Lord Goff, with whom Lord Mackay L.C. agreed.
[64] [1993] A.C. 334 (H.L.) 340-341 *per* Lord Goff and 341 *per* Lord Browne-Wilkinson with whom Lords Keith and Goff agreed.

Leiduck.[65] The circumstances there were very similar to those in *The Siskina* –
the plaintiff was trying to get a *Mareva* injunction over assets in Hong Kong in
support of an action it was pursuing in Monaco. Lord Nicholls' minority advice picked up the lead offered by the *South Carolina* and *Channel Tunnel*
cases and ruled that the courts could grant injunctions even where a plaintiff
has no substantive right within the jurisdiction; from there it was a short step
towards serving the proceedings out of the jurisdiction because the term "injunction" as Lord Nicholls had explained it was broad enough to ground service under RSC Order 11 rule 1(1)(b). The majority, whose advice was delivered
by Lord Mustill, approached the two questions addressed by Lord Nicholls in
reverse order. They reasoned that the defendant could not be served with proceedings because a *Mareva* injunction was *sui generis* and not the kind of
injunction which fell within RSC Order 11 rule 1(1)(b); therefore it did not
matter whether the general power to grant injunctions was exercisable in the
absence of a substantive right within the jurisdiction.[66] This reasoning unin-
tentionally exposed a severe problem in international commercial litigation,
graphically described by Lord Nicholls in his dissenting advice:

> The first defendant's argument comes to this: his assets are in Hong Kong,
> so the Monaco court cannot reach them; he is in Monaco, so the Hong
> Kong court cannot reach him. That cannot be right. That is not accept-
> able today. A person operating internationally cannot so easily defeat the
> judicial process. There is not a black hole into which a defendant can
> escape out of sight and become unreachable.[67]

On the other hand some reassurance can be derived from the sign that the
courts did not regard the liberating effect of section 37(3) of the Supreme Court
Act 1981 as giving them an unlimited jurisdiction to grant *Mareva* relief.

Ultimately the departure from *The Siskina* principle came through legislation. The Civil Jurisdiction and Judgments Act 1982 (Interim Relief) Order
1997,[68] made under section 25(3) of the 1982 Act, extended the power of the
courts to grant interim protective measures to legal proceedings in countries
not party to either the Brussels or Lugano Conventions. By way of footnote to
this development the Court of Appeal, in *Credit Suisse Fides Trust S.A. v.
Cuoghi,*[69] has now granted a *Mareva* injunction in a case where neither the

[65][1996] A.C. 284 (P.C.).
[66]For a more detailed discussion of *Mercedez-Benz v. Leiduck* see Capper, "The Trans-Jurisdictional Effects of *Mareva* Injunctions" (1996) 15 *C.J.Q.* 211, 226-232.
[67][1996] 1 A.C. 284, 305.
[68]S.I. No. 302 of 1997.
[69][1997] 3 All E.R. 724 (C.A.).

plaintiff's cause of action nor the defendant's assets were located within the territorial jurisdiction of the court.[70]

The Irish position, however, lags some way behind England. Power to grant interim protective measures in aid of proceedings in other Brussels or Lugano Convention countries exists in section 13(1) of the Jurisdiction of Courts and Enforcement of Judgments Act 1998. But there is no Irish equivalent of the 1997 Order so *The Siskina* principle will still apply outside Brussels or Lugano Convention territory.[71] There are no Irish cases like *Cuoghi* but equally there are no reasons to believe that Irish courts would not ever grant similar relief in respect of Brussels or Lugano Convention countries.[72]

The last major development from this period in the life of the *Mareva* injunction was the attempt to utilise *Mareva* type injunctions to freeze the alleged proceeds of crime in advance of a criminal trial, with a view to their preservation for the making of compensation orders and the like. In *Chief Constable of Kent v. V*[73] such an injunction was granted by a majority of the Court of Appeal (Lord Denning M.R. and Donaldson L.J., Slade L.J. dissenting) but on different bases. Lord Denning M.R. relied on the general power to grant injunctions in all cases where it was just and convenient to do so.[74] Donaldson L.J. held that a legal or equitable right to freeze assets had to be demonstrated but found this in the police power to seize the proceeds of crime.[75] In his dissent Slade L.J. agreed with Donaldson L.J. about the need for a legal or equitable right but held that the police power to seize the proceeds of crime did not extend to freezing a bank account.[76] In a subsequent case, *Chief Constable of Hampshire v. A*,[77] a majority of a differently constituted Court of Appeal preferred the approach of Donaldson L.J., although an injunction was refused as a matter of discretion. There is a degree of artificiality about regarding the police right to detain stolen property as a legal or equitable right so to the extent that this is necessary to get a *Mareva* injunction in this area the approach of Slade L.J. should be preferred. In the light of the *South Carolina*[78] and *Channel Tunnel*[79] cases described above, neither of which was undermined in *Mercedez-Benz v. Leiduck*[80] as the appeal there was decided on the question of

---

[70]On this and the other development discussed in this paragraph, see Capper, "Further Trans-Jurisdictional Effects of *Mareva* Injunctions" (1998) 17 *C.J.Q.* 35.
[71]*Serge Caudron v. Air Zaire* [1986] I.L.R.M. 10 confirms the applicability of *The Siskina* principle in Ireland.
[72]See Courtney, para. 4.62.
[73][1983] 1 Q.B. 34 (C.A.).
[74][1983] 1 Q.B. 34, 42.
[75][1983] 1 Q.B. 34, 47.
[76][1983] 1 Q.B. 34, 50-52.
[77][1985] 1 Q.B. 132 (C.A.) 137 *per* Oliver L.J. and 139 *per* Purchas L.J.
[78][1987] A.C. 24.
[79][1993] A.C. 334.
[80][1996] A.C. 284.

service, the approach of Lord Denning M.R. has more going for it. However there are more fundamental objections to the grant of *Mareva* injunctions in this area, to do with the legitimacy of using the civil process with its lower standard of proof as a support for the criminal law. *Mareva* injunctions are not much utilised in this area now following the enactment of extensive legislative provisions enabling pre-trial restraint and post conviction confiscation orders to be made in relation to most serious offences.[81] With the advent of these provisions the judicial attitude to applications like those described above appears to be summed up in the words of Hoffman J. in *Chief Constable of Leicestershire v. M* that "the courts should not indulge in parallel creativity by the extension of common law principles."[82] It is nonetheless highly probable that what the courts began in this area the legislature has carried on. In Ireland there appear to be no common law examples of *Mareva*-like orders in aid of the criminal law but similar statutory powers to England and Wales have been enacted.[83]

6. WHAT NEXT FOR THE *MAREVA* INJUNCTION?

An injunction which is obtainable against foreign and domestic defendants, in respect of assets within and outside the jurisdiction, and whether the plaintiff has a cause of action within the jurisdiction or in another country, has clearly reached a considerable degree of maturity and does not have a great deal of scope for further growth. Two areas of possible further development will be considered in this section – whether a *Mareva* injunction can be granted when the plaintiff has, as yet, no legal right which can be infringed but is clearly going to have a legal right in the near future which almost certainly will result in an immediate cause of action; and whether a *Mareva* injunction can be granted where the plaintiff has a legal right but not one which can be the subject of High Court proceedings.

The first of these rather abstract conceptions can best be explained by way of a description of the typical fact scenario in which it arises. Suppose a plaintiff who has agreed to buy a ship from the defendant, the exchange of documents and payment of the balance of the purchase price to take place by a certain time tomorrow. The plaintiff strongly suspects that the ship will be defective in some way, not sufficiently that she will be unseaworthy but enough to give the plaintiff a strong claim for damages. It may be commercially impossible for the plaintiff to pull out of the sale, for example because the plaintiff has chartered the ship to a third party on a time or voyage charterparty com-

---

[81] See particularly the Criminal Justice Act 1988 and the Drug Trafficking Offences Act 1994.
[82] [1989] 1 W.L.R. 20, 23.
[83] Criminal Justice Act 1994; Proceeds of Crime Act 1996.

mencing in a short period of time. A deposit may also have been paid which might not be recoverable if the plaintiff abandons the contract. The plaintiff fears that if it hands over the balance of the purchase price and takes delivery of the ship, the defendant will remove the balance from the plaintiff's reach and, having no other assets anywhere in the world, the plaintiff will be unable to enforce any judgment it obtains in respect of the defects in the ship. So it tries to obtain a *Mareva* injunction over the balance of the purchase price a short time before completion of the sale so that when the contract is completed and the plaintiff sues for damages there will be assets available against which judgment can be enforced. But the difficulty is that at the time of applying for the injunction the plaintiff has no cause of action; it does not even have the right to seek a *quia timet* injunction because, there being no contract until completion, the plaintiff has no present legal right which can be infringed. Despite Saville J., in *A v. B*,[84] granting an "anticipatory" *Mareva* injunction to come into force and be notified to the defendant on completion of the contract, in *Veracruz Transportation Inc v. VC Shipping Co Inc ("The Veracruz I")*[85] the Court of Appeal disapproved of this practice. Although there is something unsavoury about the plaintiff going behind the defendant's back to get an injunction while the contract is completed, and then serving the injunction as soon as the balance of the purchase price has been paid, there may be no other way of the plaintiff protecting itself against serious losses if it cannot do this. It will not always be an effective answer to say that the plaintiff should not commit itself to other commercial obligations until sure that the ship it is buying is sound. If your business is chartering ships you need to acquire ships and these cannot be taken off a supermarket shelf just whenever they are needed. The *Veracruz* decision is widely regarded as unjust[86] and it is respectfully suggested that if the Court of Appeal gets another opportunity to look at this problem it should accept that in the light of the *South Carolina*[87] and *Channel Tunnel*[88] cases the power to grant injunctions is sufficiently flexible to enable an injunction of this kind to be granted. Whether it should do so in a particular case, and whether it should continue one if the defendant applies to discharge it, are separate questions; much will depend here on whether the plaintiff has got itself into a bind of its own making.[89]

---

[84] [1989] 2 Lloyd's Rep. 423 (Q.B.D.).

[85] [1992] 1 Lloyd's Rep. 353 (C A)

[86] See Collins, "The Legacy of *The Siskina*" (1992) 108 *L.Q.R.* 175; Marshall, "The Conditional or Anticipatory *Mareva* Injunction" [1992] *L.M.C.L.Q.* 161; Aitken, "The End of the "Anticipatory" *Mareva*?" (1992) 66 *A.L.J.* 542; Wilde, "Jurisdiction to Grant Interlocutory (*Mareva*) Injunctions" [1993] *L.M.C.L.Q.* 309.

[87] [1987] A.C. 24.

[88] [1993] A.C. 334.

[89] There appears to be no Irish authority on this question and Courtney seems to assume that the English rule would apply in Ireland. See Courtney, paras. 4.26-4.27.

The other area where there may be room for further development is where the plaintiff has a substantive right but no cause of action determinable by the High Court. Once again an example may illustrate what is meant. In *Department of Social Security v. Butler*[90] the Department had obtained a maintenance order under the Child Support Act 1991 against the father of a child following his separation from the child's mother. The Department also had the statutory responsibility for taking any action necessary to ensure that the order was enforced. Arrears of some £4,000 built up and the Department sought a *Mareva* injunction to restrain the father from disposing of his share in the proceeds of sale of the former matrimonial home. In refusing the injunction the Court of Appeal accepted that the power to grant a *Mareva* injunction under section 37 of the Supreme Court Act 1981 might not be restricted to cases where the plaintiff had a cause of action determinable by the High Court.[91] But the Child Support Act 1991 impliedly excluded any such power because, in the opinion of the court, it provided a fully comprehensive system for the recovery of maintenance arrears. The two recovery methods available to the Department were to make an attachment of earnings order against the father, or to apply to the Magistrates Court for a liability order, following which the usual methods of enforcement of a judgment were available. With respect, these methods do not constitute a fully comprehensive system for the recovery of arrears, either individually or together. An attachment of earnings order is useless against persons not in employment; and it is not unknown for persons liable to pay maintenance to find themselves without a job when called upon to honour their obligations. A liability order is perfectly satisfactory where the respondent is not going to dissipate his assets but that risk was the very reason the Department was seeking a *Mareva* injunction in the first place. The only recognition given to this risk was the suggestion made by Simon Brown L.J. that the Department should make more efficient use of the machinery in the Child Support Act 1991 by not allowing substantial arrears to build up.[92] Single mothers are not likely to be much reassured by that. The implications of *Butler* are disturbing given the enormous range of legal proceedings transacted by inferior courts and tribunals. In the absence of a statutory High Court action[93] or specific statutory powers for the High Court to grant injunctions in support of other legal proceedings, for example the power to support arbitration proceedings under section 44 of the Arbitration Act 1996, section 37 is the only source of protection for persons concerned that they might be unable to enforce their rights. The only crumb of comfort is that the Court of Appeal did not reject the

---

[90] [1995] 1 W.L.R. 1528 (C.A).
[91] Compare *Securities and Investment Board v. Pantell SA* [1989] 2 All E.R. 673 where a *Mareva* injunction was granted in aid of SIB's action under s. 6 of the Financial Services Act 1986.
[92] [1985] 1 W.L.R. 1528, 1542.
[93] See *Securities and Investment Board v. Pantell SA* [1989] 2 All E.R. 673 (Ch.D.).

idea that section 37 could be the source of such power, so it remains open to a party in later proceedings to argue that the specific statute under which it seeks a remedy does not by implication exclude *Mareva* relief.[94]

7. CONCLUSION – AN EVALUATION OF THE *MAREVA* DECISION

This short and deceptively simple *ex parte* appeal gave birth to a procedure of enormous importance and effected a revolution in the conduct of civil litigation. The focus of litigation today is much less on the trial and much more on interlocutory proceedings, designed in the case of *Anton Piller* orders to ensure that there remains some point in having a trial and in the case of *Mareva* injunctions that any judgment obtained can be enforced. This came about because, as Lord Hoffmann has observed extrajudicially, in the 1960s "it became apparent that civil law remedies were inadequate to deal with cases in which there was often no serious dispute: the problem was simply the enforcement of the law against a party who was determined to evade it".[95] The first serious attempt to develop a remedy against someone intent on dissipating assets came in the report of the Payne Committee in 1969, which recommended that the courts should have power to restrain a party to legal proceedings, either before or after judgment, from removing assets from the jurisdiction or otherwise disposing of them.[96] Predictably, perhaps, the legislature did nothing and six years passed before there took place a coincidence between counsel who were brave enough to ask for relief of this kind and judges who were bold enough to grant it.

In the development of the *Mareva* injunction what was the significance of the *Mareva* case itself? Leaving aside the point that it was not, strictly speaking, the first case where this kind of injunction was granted, its importance lies mainly in the recognition that without it the developments described in this paper might not have happened. Of course something like them might still have happened because the need to develop procedures like these was clear before the *Mareva* case was decided. In that light the importance of *Mareva v. International Bulkcarriers* is that it kick-started the process described in this essay. In evaluating the full extent of *Mareva's* importance, however, it is important to recognise that there were several times during the first few years of its life when the new procedure might have died. *The Pertamina*[97] was an important case because it showed that the new remedy was not to be granted

---

[94] In the absence of specific Irish authority on this question the Irish position is probably the same as in England. See Courtney, para. 2.38.
[95] Preface to Gee, xiii.
[96] *The Enforcement of Judgment Debts* (Cmnd. 3909), para. 1253.
[97] [1978] Q.B. 644.

just because it was asked for. *The Siskina*[98] was important because it might have resulted in the premature death of the child. Throughout this story an absolutely vital role was played by statute. Without the statutory recognition provided by section 37(3) of the Supreme Court Act 1981, would the *Mareva* have been extended to the disposal of assets within the jurisdiction, or to assets outside the jurisdiction? Statutes were decisive in removing the need for a plaintiff to show that it had a cause of action within the jurisdiction, something which the courts had stubbornly refused to do. Other statutes, particularly those providing for the pre-trial restraint and post conviction confiscation of proceeds of crime, were as much inspired by the *Mareva* injunction as they were an indispensable part of its development. They did not, however, account for the extension to English based defendants, which occurred before 1981. Another factor which simply cannot be displaced is one of personality, particularly the personality of Lord Denning. Had the late Master of the Rolls died or retired at seventy, as one journalist has suggested might have better served his reputation,[99] this unique achievement of his judicial career (begun during Lord Denning's seventy-seventh year) would never have happened. Overall the importance of *Mareva Compania Naviera v. International Bulkcarriers* is that, without that case, the developments described in this essay might not have happened at all and certainly would not have happened in the same way. It did not, however, accomplish all of those developments by itself.

---

[98] [1979] A.C. 210.
[99] A.N. Wilson, "If only Lord Denning had died at seventy", *The Independent on Sunday,* March 7, 1999.

UNTYING THE GORDIAN (JURISDICTIONAL) KNOT *BIER V. MINES DE POTASSE* (1976)

T P KENNEDY*

1. INTRODUCTION

The European Court of Justice decision in *Handelskwekerij GJ Bier BV and Stichtung Reinwater Foundation v. Mines de Potasse d'Alsace SA*[1] (*"Bier"*) is one of the most important decisions of that Court on the interpretation of the Brussels Convention on Jurisdiction and the Enforcement of Judgments 1968.[2] In a valuable combination of judicial subtlety and pragmatism *Bier* introduced clarity into the interpretation of Article 5(3) of the Convention and established a framework for ascertaining jurisdiction in multinational tort disputes.[3] This framework has been deployed and developed by the Court in subsequent decisions. The combination of Article 5(3) and the line of Court decisions starting with *Bier* have been remarkably successful. The approach espoused by the Court in *Bier* has found international acceptance and the negotiations on a proposed world-wide jurisdiction and judgments convention through the auspices of the Hague Conference on Private International Law have suggested an Article 5(3) equivalent for tort. Would this have been advocated without the certainty introduced by *Bier*? It is in the context of this international commendation and its being a template for others to follow that *Bier* can truly be considered as one of the leading judgments of the twentieth century.

2. THE CONVENTION

Article 5 of the Convention sets out a number of exceptions to the general

---

*Director of Education, Law Society of Ireland.

[1] Case 21/76, [1976] E.C.R. 1735.
[2] For more general commentaries on the Convention see Collins, *The Civil Jurisdiction and Judgments Act 1982* (Butterworths, London, 1983) [hereafter Collins]; Kaye, *Civil Jurisdiction and Enforcement of Judgments* (Professional Books, 1987) [hereafter Kaye]; Lasok & Stone *Conflict of Laws in the European Communities* (Professional Books, 1987) [hereafter Lasok & Stone]; and Mayss & Reed, *European Business Litigation* (Ashgate, Aldershot, 1998) [hereafter Mayss & Reed].
[3] For a view of the potential development of the law in non-Convention cases, see Swan, "The Future of the Conflict of Laws. Can *Morguard* (1990) Point the Way?" below, 405.

jurisdictional rule established by Article 2 – that persons domiciled in a contracting state be sued in the courts of that state. One of the most significant of these exceptions is that for torts contained in Article 5(3). It provides:

> Article 5: A person domiciled in a contracting state may, in another contracting state, be sued . . . (3) in matters relating to tort, delict or quasi-delict, in the courts for the place where the harmful event occurred . . .

A plaintiff thus has a choice of jurisdictions in a tortious dispute. He can elect to bring an action in the state of the defendant's domicile[4] or in the courts of "the place where the harmful event occurred". In many cases, it is relatively easy to point to a single harmful event occurring in a single state. However, in the case of a transnational tort the phrase is more ambiguous. The phrase was left intentionally vague by the drafters of the Convention. The Jenard Report states that:

> The Committee did not consider it appropriate to specify expressly whether account should be taken of the place in which the act causing the damage was effected or on the other hand of the place in which the damage had occurred; instead the Committee considered it preferable to employ wording adopted by various national legal system (Germany and France).[5]

Thus it was left open to a number of different interpretations. Where elements of the harmful event take place in more than one jurisdiction, which one takes jurisdiction? It could be the place where the principal act took place, where the damage was suffered, the jurisdiction with which the tort had its closest connection or the jurisdiction where the last of a series of tortious acts occurred.

3. *Bier*

This was the question that came squarely before the European Court of Justice in *Bier*. The case concerned cross-border pollution. Mines de Potasse d'Alsace SA allegedly discharged 11,000 tons of chloride into the river Rhine on a daily basis. GJ Bier BV ran large garden nurseries near Rotterdam in the Netherlands using water from the Rhine to water and irrigate its seedbeds. The high salinity of the Rhine due to the presence of the chlorine in the water damaged Bier's seedbeds. It also had to incur considerable expense in limiting the damage. Bier, supported by the Stichtung Rheinwater Foundation (a body charged

---

[4] As defined for Convention purposes – Article 52 of the Convention leaves domicile to be determined by the laws of the contracting states.

[5] Jenard Report. Para. A1.111.

with the task of improving the water quality of the Rhine), brought an action against Mines de Potasse in the Dutch courts. The French defendant argued that a Dutch court was not competent to hear the dispute. Under Article 2 of the Convention the defendant should be sued in the courts of its own domicile. If a tort had been committed, the place of the harmful event was France where the alleged pollutant had been discharged into the Rhine. Thus, if Article 5(3) could be invoked, France was the place of the harmful event. This argument was successful, at first instance. Bier appealed to the Hague Court of Appeal, which referred the matter to the European Court of Justice.[6] The Dutch court asked whether "the place where the harmful event" occurred was to be construed as meaning the place where the damage occurred or where the event which caused the damage took place.

3.1 The Dilemma

The parties, supported by the French and Dutch governments, advanced a number of theories of interpretation. The European Commission advanced arguments in favour of five alternative interpretations. Indeed, the importance of the issue to be decided was marked by the number of parties who made written and oral submissions and possibly marked also by the bewildering variety of theories and suggestions advanced.

The defendant and the French government argued in favour of the place of the occurrence of the harmful event rather than the place where damage occurred. They argued that it was best placed to establish the relevant facts related the allegedly wrongful act. They also argued that this jurisdiction would concentrate litigation in one state rather than exposing the defendant to several different actions in different states. Otherwise multiple actions would spring from the one tort in a number of different states. The French government, in particular, argued that the possibility of a multiplicity of fora was contrary to the purpose and scheme of the Convention. One of the central purposes of the Convention was the rational administration of justice and plaintiffs having a choice of multiple jurisdictions would not achieve this. Finally, they argued that the place where the damage occurred would be the domicile of the plaintiff and he would be placed in a more favourable situation than the defendant. The Commission argued that the concept of acting or failing to act is the essential ingredient of the tortious act. Damage is a mere consequence of the act or the failure to act. The person who performs or fails to perform the act is aware of the legal obligations in his state – it is unnecessary that he should be aware of obligations elsewhere in the world.

---

[6] Pursuant to Article 3 of the Luxembourg Protocol, 1971 annexed to the Brussels Convention, which allows the Court to give preliminary rulings on the interpretation of the Convention, at the request of the courts of the Contracting States.

The plaintiffs and the Dutch government supported the place of damage. They argued that damage was the predominant element of the tort, particularly in cases of pollution. Damages are easier to assess in the place where the damage occurred. The place of the causal event is likely to be the jurisdiction of the defendant and is therefore possessed of jurisdiction in any event – making the application of Article 5(3) unnecessary. In the alternative, they argued that different jurisdictional criteria might be appropriate for different torts. In the case of pollution several defendants may have contributed to the problem. Thus, it is appropriate to allow the victim to bring all his actions concerning the matter before the one court. The Commission argued that the advantage of this is that it looks to the last link in the chain of elements comprising the tortious act.

The Commission also outlined other jurisdictional approaches. It proposed ". . . the place in which the essential aspect of the legal sphere of the tortious . . . act is located".[7] It also considered the place most favourable to the party who has suffered the damage. Finally, it argued for the concurrence of several connecting factors.

Thus, the Court faced a multiplicity of jurisdictional approaches – many of them justified by strong argument. As Capotorti A.G. put it when starting his discussion of Article 5(3): "The imprecision to which I have referred is not fortuitous".[8]

3.2 Advocate General's Opinion – Confusion worse confounded

Interestingly, Capotorti A.G. recommended against the course of action taken by the Court. After reviewing the private international law rules of the Contracting States he argued that the interpretation ultimately taken by the Court was contrary to the letter and spirit of the Convention. However, he conceded the advantages of this interpretation saying:

> we should accept that the cumulative solution, which would leave the plaintiff free to choose between the court of the place where the act was committed and the court of the place where the event occurred, may appear by its very liberality fairer and better able to accommodate the characteristics of the various types of unlawful act.[9]

However, he went on to say that he felt it at odds with both the letter and the spirit of the Convention. Article 5(3) refers to the court of the place where the harmful event occurred. He felt that this was a reference to a single court and a single country, thus ruling out the possibility of more than one place or more

---

[7] [1976] E.C.R. 1735, 1742.
[8] [1976] E.C.R. 1735, 1751.
[9] [1976] E.C.R. 1735, 1755.

than one court being taken into consideration. It was contrary to the spirit of the Convention as it is designed to divide jurisdiction in such a way as to reduce rather than increase the scope of jurisdiction of each state.

Capotorti A.G. recommended the place where the damage occurred as the correct jurisdiction under Article 5(3). He felt that the nature of a civil wrong for its existence presupposes that damage should be established. A civil wrong is only legally complete when the injury to the legal rights of the person suffering it occurs. This is the most satisfactory outcome for the injured party, as it will generally coincide with the State in which he usually resides.

3.3 Judgment – The Gordian Knot United

The Court disagreed. It firstly held that "the place where the harmful event occurred" was to be given an independent interpretation. It looked to its previous decision in *LTU v. Eurocontrol*[10] and said that in reaching such an interpretation the Court must look at the objectives and scheme of the Convention. The general rule of the jurisdiction is that of the defendant's domicile in Article 2. The Court noted that the special jurisdictional grounds in Article 5, which exist by way of an exception to Article 2, were introduced due to the existence:

> . . . in certain clearly defined situations, of a particularly close connecting factor between a dispute and the court which may be called upon to hear it, with a view to the efficacious conduct of the proceedings.[11]

The meaning of "the place where the harmful event occurred" was unclear in the context of a tort which took place in more than one jurisdiction. The Court held that there was a significant connection in relation to both the place of the causal event and the place of injury as each could be helpful in relation to the necessary evidence and the conduct of the proceedings. The Court found it inappropriate to opt for one jurisdiction to the exclusion of the other, as there were significant connecting factors to both. The Court held therefore that:

> Where the place of the happening of the event which may give rise to liability in tort, delict or quasi-delict and the place where that event results in damage are not identical, the expression 'the place where the harmful event occurred', in Article 5(3) . . . must be understood as being intended to cover both the place where the damage occurred and the place of the event giving rise to it.
>
> The result is that the defendant may be sued, at the option of the plaintiff, either in the courts for the place where the damage occurred or

---

[10]Case 29/76, [1976] E.C.R. 1541.
[11][1976] E.C.R. 1735, 1746, para. 11.

in the courts for the place of the event which gives rise to and is at the origin of that damage.[12]

The Court went on to justify its decision. If the place where the harmful event occurred was interpreted as the place of the causal event this would cause some confusion between the scope of Article 5(3) and Article 2. As both Articles would be specifying the same jurisdiction, Article 5(3) would lose its effectiveness. If the place of damage was exclusively chosen, this would exclude "a helpful connecting factor . . . particularly close to the cause of the damage".[13] Finally the decision reached was in conformity with the approach taken in the national private international law rules of several of the Contracting States.[14]

The plaintiff has the option of suing the defendant in either the place where the damage occurred or in the place of the causal event giving rise of the damage. The Court in a simple yet subtle manner accepted the arguments of both the plaintiff and defendant. Like Alexander it untied the Gordian knot in the simplest and most surprising manner.

4. THE LIMITATIONS OF THE RULE

The rule in *Bier* can be criticised as giving rise to fragmentation of jurisdiction. In a number of decisions the Court has advocated caution in the use of the rule. It has limited the opportunities for forum shopping and brought the rule into line with the primary purpose of the Convention – to ensure certainty in the allocation of jurisdiction.

The Court in *Dumez Bâtiment and Tracona v. Hessische Landesbank*[15] made it clear that consequential financial loss suffered in one jurisdiction as a result of a tort in another jurisdiction did not found a claim under Article 5(3). Ricochet victims are thus excluded. In that case, a French parent company claimed for damages on the basis of losses suffered by its German subsidiary. The parent company claimed that the conduct of a German banks in its dealing with a German subsidiary of the plaintiffs from carrying out certain contracts had resulted in financial loss to the plaintiffs (as the anticipated profits would have been sent back to the French parent company). The German bank had withdrawn credits to a German property developer. This had caused the halting of a building programme resulting in the insolvency of the German subsidiary. Dumez argued that France was the place of the harmful event and Germany was the place of the causal event. The Court held that the French companies

---

[12][1976] E.C.R. 1735, 1748-1749, paras. 24-25.
[13][1976] E.C.R. 1735, 1746, para. 17.
[14]Reviewed by Capotorti A.G., [1976] E.C.R. 1735, 1752–1755.
[15]Case 220/88, [1990] E.C.R. I-49.

were not entitled to bring the action. The victims of the act were the German subsidiaries and only they would be able to sue under Article 5(3). The Court held:

> the . . . 'place where the harmful event occurred' contained in Article 5(3) of the Convention may refer to the place where the damage occurred, the latter concept can be understood only as indicating the place where the event giving rise to the damage, and entailing tortious, delictual or quasi-delictual liability, directly produced its harmful effects upon the person who is the immediate victim of that event.[16]

The Court made a similar finding in *Marinari v. Lloyds Bank Plc.*[17] The plaintiff had lodged promissory notes with a branch of Lloyds in London. The bank refused to honour the notes or return them. They then advised the police of the existence of the notes and that they were of uncertain origin. The plaintiff was arrested and the notes were sequestrated. After his release he brought an action in Italy against Lloyds seeking compensation for refusal to pay on the notes, for breach of contract, or damage to his reputation and for damage suffered due to his arrest. Lloyds argued that the damage had occurred in Italy. The plaintiff argued that the Italian court could have jurisdiction under Article 5(3) as that was where he suffered economic loss as a result of the events in London. The ECJ held:

> Whilst it is recognised that the term 'place where the harmful event occurred' within the meaning of Article 5(3) of the Convention may cover both the place where the damage occurred and the place of the event giving rise to it, that term cannot, however, be construed so extensively as to encompass any place where the adverse consequences of an event that has already caused actual damage elsewhere can be felt.
> Consequently, that term cannot be construed as including the place where, as in the present case the victim claims to have suffered financial loss consequential upon initial damage arising and suffered by him in another Contracting State.[18]

In the context of international trade the Court in *Réunion Européenne Sa & Ors v. Spliethoff's Bevrachtingskantoor BV and the Master of the vessel Alblasgracht V002*[19] looked to *Bier* but applied it cautiously. The case con-

---

[16][1990] E.C.R. I-49, para. 20.
[17]Case C-364/93, [1995] E.C.R. I-2719. See Reed & Kennedy, "The Europeanisation of Defamation" (1996) 5 *I.J.E.L.* 201.
[18][1995] E.C.R. I-2719, 2739-2740, paras. 14-15.
[19]Case C-51/97, ECJ, unreported, October 27, 1998.

cerned the application of Article 5(3) in a case involving the transportation of goods by sea. The Dutch company Spliethoff's Bevrachtingskantoor BV carried 5,199 cartons of pears from Australia to Rotterdam aboard its vessel "Alblasgracht V002" under a bill of lading. They were unloaded there and transported by road to France. On arrival, it was discovered that the pears were damaged – they had ripened prematurely owing to a breakdown in the cooling system. The French courts refused to accept jurisdiction over the Dutch defendants. The ECJ was asked to identify the place of the harmful event. The Paris Court of Appeal asked whether it was the place of final delivery where the damage was discovered.

The Court referred to *Bier* where it had held that the place where a harmful event occurs confers jurisdiction both on the place where the causal event takes place and the jurisdiction where damage is actually suffered. Both these state can assume jurisdiction due to the existence of a particularly close connecting factor between them and the dispute. However the Court noted that:

> In *Marinari*, . . . the Court made it clear that the choice thus available to the plaintiff cannot however be extended beyond the particular circumstances which justify it, since otherwise the general principle laid down in the first paragraph of Article 2 of the Convention that the courts of the Contracting State where the defendant is domiciled are to have jurisdiction would be negated, with the result that, in cases other than those expressly provided for, jurisdiction would be attributed to the courts of the plaintiff's domicile, a solution which the Convention does not favour since, in the second paragraph of Article 3, it excludes application of national provisions which make such jurisdiction available for proceedings against defendants domiciled in the territory of a Contracting State.[20]

The Court held that "the place where the event giving rise to the damage occurred" ". . .cannot be construed so extensively as to encompass any place where the adverse consequences can be felt of an event which has already caused damage actually arising elsewhere".[21] In this case the place of the causal event was difficult and might even be impossible to determine. Thus, the consignee of the goods should bring the carrier before the court for the place where the damage occurred. This could not be either the place of final delivery, which could be changed in mid-voyage, or the place where the damage was ascertained. To use either would in most cases be giving jurisdiction to the courts of the plaintiff's domicile. It would also be placing reliance on uncertain factors. This is incompatible with the objective of the Convention, which is to provide for the clear and certain attribution of jurisdiction. The place where damage

---

[20] *ibid.*, para. 29.
[21] *ibid.*, para. 30.

arose in a transport operation of this nature could only be the place where the carrier was to deliver the goods. This jurisdiction is certain and foreseeable and has a particularly close connection to the main dispute. The Court concluded ". . .the attribution of jurisdiction to the courts for that place is justified by reasons relating to the sound administration of justice and the efficacious conduct of proceedings".[22]

5. DEVELOPMENT OF THE RULE

The harm in *Bier* was material property damage. However, it is clear that the decision in *Bier* is not confined to cases of nuisance against land. The principle extends to all torts involving a physical injury to person or property and was arguably of wider application. In subsequent decisions the Court has extended the rule to cases involving other torts and modified it in its application to multi-state tortious disputes involving economic loss.

5.1 *Shevill* (*Bier* – Mark Two)

The key decision in the development of the doctrine in *Bier* is that of *Shevill v. Presse Alliance*.[23] It extends and develops *Bier*. In the context of multi-state torts, the two decisions must be taken together. Though *Shevill* was decided in the context of multi-state defamation it clearly has a much wider application. *Shevill* marks the second phase of the development of the *Bier* principle.

The first plaintiff, Fiona Shevill, domiciled in England with her main residence in Yorkshire, was employed at a bureau de change operated by the fourth plaintiff, Chequepoint SARL. Chequepoint SARL is a French enterprise operating a number of bureaux de change in France and elsewhere in Europe. The defendants publish the newspaper, "France Soir", a daily evening newspaper, which has a large circulation in France, in excess of 200,000 copies daily, and a smaller daily circulation of approximately 15,500 copies outside France. In relation to this latter circulation, it was claimed that only 230 copies were sold in England and Wales, notably only 5 in Yorkshire where the first plaintiff resided.

The plaintiffs claimed damages for harm caused by the publication of a defamatory newspaper article in "France Soir" on September 27, 1989. It referred to an alleged investigation by French police into the laundering of money obtained from the sale of drugs by, in particular, the Paris bureau de change in

---

[22]*ibid.*, para. 36.
[23]Case C-68/93, [1995] E.C.R. I-415; [1995] 2 A.C. 18. For a more detailed analysis of the implications of this case see Reed & Kennedy, "*Shevill* and International Torts: The Ghost of Forum Shopping Yet to Come" [1996] *L.M.C.L.Q.* 108

which Ms Shevill was temporarily employed for three months in the summer of 1989, and to whom reference by name was made in the article. In November 1989, the defendants published a retraction and apology in respect of Ms Shevill and Chequepoint SARL. The action, subsequent to amendments to the statement of claim, related solely to publication in England and Wales, not France. The defendants sought to strike out the claim arguing that there was no jurisdiction as no harmful event had occurred in England.

Before the Court of Appeal, it was argued by counsel for the defendant that none of the plaintiffs had suffered any actual damage so as to constitute a harmful event within the jurisdiction. There was no evidence that there was anyone who could possibly have been affected who knew Ms Shevill or who had access to any copies of the offending newspaper. These submissions were based upon the necessity of demonstrating for the purposes of Article 5(3) of the Convention that damage had been actually suffered, an approach which was inconsistent with the English law, which assumed that damage, had been suffered once the libel had been established.

Defamation, a generic term applicable to both libel and slander, consists of the publication of material which reflects on a person's reputation so as to lower the plaintiff in the estimation of right thinking members of society generally, or which would tend to cause her to be shunned or avoided. A libel consists of a defamatory statement or representation in permanent form, and is actionable per se, *i.e.* without proof of special damage (loss of money or of some temporal or material advantage estimable in money); a slander is more transient, and special damage must be proved except in a limited number of cases.

It was the acknowledgement by the Court of Appeal of the peculiar nature of English libel law, contrary to the defendant's submission, which was vital to its actual decision. Purchas L.J. stated:

> The only idiosyncratic aspect arising from the law of England and Wales is the assumption of damage. I do not recognise this as a jurisdictional point. Whether or not there may be detected a publishee in England who both knew the plaintiff and read and understood the French evening newspaper may well arise in the course of the action and be relevant to the assessment of damages. In my judgment, however, to restrict the exercise of jurisdiction to cases where the existence of such a person is established would not be correct.[24]

It was held by the Court of Appeal that, since the action was restricted to publication of the defamatory article in England and Wales, the court could as-

---

[24] [1992] 2 W.L.R. 1 (C.A.), 13; [1996] A.C. 959 (C.A. and H.C.) 976.

sume jurisdiction under Article 5(3) of the Convention once it was shown that there was an arguable case on which each plaintiff could rely to establish a publication carrying with it the presumption of damage.

The defendant appealed to the House of Lords arguing that the French courts had jurisdiction in the dispute under Article 2, and that the English courts did not have jurisdiction under Article 5(3) as the "place where the harmful event occurred" was France and no harmful event had taken place in England. The House of Lords, considering that the proceedings raised questions of interpretation of the Convention, decided to stay the proceedings pending a preliminary ruling by the European Court of Justice.

Darmon A.G. in his opinion pointed out that in a case of this nature it is difficult to establish where the harmful event took place. On a review of national defamation laws, he identified twin criteria of printing and communication. He referred to *Bier* where the Court had held that the place of damage would be either the place where it arose or the place where the event giving rise to it took place. In that case, there was a single instance of damage, whereas defamation potentially gives rise to multiple instances of damage. Damage to a person's reputation arises in every state where a defamatory statement is communicated to third parties. The Advocate General said that the cause of action could not be confined to one jurisdiction, as to do so would undermine the consistency of the Court's case law.

The second issue was whether the courts of every state in which there was damage could make an award for the whole of the damage, including that which arose in other states. The courts of the place of printing (pursuant to Article 5(3)) and those of the defendant's domicile (pursuant to Article 2) are the two central fora, having unlimited jurisdiction, given that there is a close connecting factor between these fora and the dispute. Courts of places where damage is suffered are best placed to assess the harm to the plaintiff's reputation in that state and to decide the extent of compensation. As each court is best placed to do this in its own jurisdiction, no one can be competent to award compensation for the entire harm done by the defamatory remark.

The Advocate General considered whether the English rules on jurisdiction in defamation (with the presumption of harm) met the requirement of a "harmful event" under Article 5(3). He was of the opinion that an attack on a person's reputation was a potentially harmful event and that it is for national courts, using their own national rules, to determine when damage arises. When a court is satisfied that damage arises a harmful event has taken place and the court will then have jurisdiction.

Léger A.G. gave a second opinion, broadly agreeing with Darmon A.G. He struck a more cautious note, warning of the dangers of forum shopping if universal jurisdiction was given to every state in which damage was suffered.

Arising from the questions referred to it by the House of Lords, the Court identified two fundamental matters of interpretation. Firstly interpretative guidance was needed on "the place where the harmful event occurred" in Article 5(3), with a view to establishing which court(s) had jurisdiction to hear an action for damages for harm caused to the victim following distribution of a defamatory newspaper article in several contracting states. Secondly, it had to be decided whether, in determining if it had jurisdiction as court of the place where the damage occurred pursuant to Article 5(3), the national court was required to follow specific rules different from those laid down by its national law in relation to the criteria for assessing whether the event in question was harmful and whether specific rules were needed in relation to the evidence required of the existence and extent of the harm alleged by the victim of the defamation.

The court firstly examined the concept of "the place where the harmful event occurred". Article 5(3) of the Convention provides special jurisdiction, by way of derogation from the general principle in the first paragraph of Article 2 of the Convention that the courts of the Contracting State of the defendants domicile have jurisdiction.

The Court examined in some detail its decision in *Bier* as an interpretative aid to establish the place of the harmful event in the international libel context. The harm in *Bier* was material property damage whereas in *Shevill* at issue was non-pecuniary damage to reputation. Nevertheless, the Court by parity of reasoning applied a similar analysis to Article 5(3) irrespective of the type of damage involved. It expressly stated in *Shevill* that identical principles apply, and the place of the event giving rise to the damage no less than the place where the damage occurred could constitute a significant connecting factor from the point of view of jurisdiction. Each of them, depending on the circumstances, could be particularly helpful in relation to the evidence and the conduct of the proceedings. The Court held that:

> In the case of a libel by a newspaper article distributed in several contracting states, the place of the event giving rise to the damage, within the meaning of those judgments, can only be the place where the publisher of the newspaper in question is established, since that is the place where the harmful event originated and from which the libel was issued and put into circulation.[25]

The court of the place where the publisher is established has jurisdiction to hear the whole action for all damage caused by the unlawful act. That jurisdiction will, as the Court noted, generally coincide in any event with the Article 2 jurisdiction based on the defendant's domicile.

The courts of the Contracting State in which the publication was distrib-

---

[25][1995] E.C.R. I-415, I-460–I-461, para. 24. Hence, when the matter returned to the House of Lords ([1996] A.C. 959 (C.A. and H.C.)) the decision of the Court of Appeal was affirmed.

uted and in which the victim claims to have suffered injury to his reputation have jurisdiction to rule on the injury caused in that state to the victim's reputation. The Court held that the state in which the defamatory publication is distributed and in which the victim claims to have suffered injury to his reputation is best suited to assess and determine the corresponding damage.

The underlying thread that runs through the Court's decisions on Article 5(3) in *Bier* and *Shevill* is the establishment of a close connecting factor between a dispute and the court, which should hear the matter on the basis of sound administration of justice.[26] The Court in *Bier* identified this when it stated that the basis of the special jurisdiction provided for in Article 5 was that:

> ... this freedom of choice was introduced having regard to the existence, in certain clearly defined situations, of a particularly close connecting factor between a dispute and the court which may be called upon to hear it, with a view to the efficacious conduct of the proceedings.[27]

In *Shevill*, Darmon A.G. said that the jurisdiction of the courts of the place where damage arose was founded on the idea of "a particularly close connecting factor between a dispute and the court which may be called upon to hear it, with a view to the efficacious conduct of the proceedings".[28] Léger A.G. even more robustly, emphasised the importance of the connecting factor, using it to base his finding that the courts of the place where harm is suffered cannot have universal jurisdiction. This emphasis follows the approach of the Jenard Report, which gives the justification of the special jurisdictional rules in Article 5, as being that there must be a close connecting factor between the dispute and the court having jurisdiction to resolve it.

The second limb of the judgment focused on whether a national court was required to follow specific rules different from those laid down by its national law in relation to the criteria for assessing whether the event in question is harmful and in relation to the evidence required of the existence and extent of the harm alleged by the victim of defamation. The defendants argued that the plaintiff had not suffered any damage so as to constitute, "a harmful event". There was no evidence that the plaintiff's reputations had actually been harmed or that those who knew the plaintiff had access to any copies of the newspaper. The defendants argued that the principles in English law that assumed that damage is suffered once a libel is established should be disregarded in favour of a common European interpretation of Article 5(3) and thus proof of actual

---

[26] However, a close connecting factor is not invariably needed to establish jurisdiction under Article 5. See Case C-288/92, *Custom Made Commercial v. Stawa Metallbau* [1994] E.C.R. I-2913, I-2955-I-2959.

[27] [1976] E.C.R. 1735, 1735, para. 11.

[28] [1995] E.C.R. I-415, I-431, para. 70.

288 *Leading Cases of the Twentieth Century*

damage to qualify England as the place where the "harmful event" occurred. The Court observed that the object of the Convention was not to unify the rules of substantive law and of procedure of the different contracting states. This was clear from the Convention itself and a number of the Court's decisions.[29] The effect was that it was for the substantive English law of defamation to determine whether the event in question was harmful and the evidence required to the existence and extent of the harm.

5.2 The Rejection of Alternative Jurisdictional Approaches

In the course of *Shevill* as in *Bier* a number of jurisdictional approaches were examined. The basic *Bier* principle was relatively easy to apply in a case involving only two jurisdictions. The judgment, however, did not resolve the difficulty of multi jurisdictional torts. In the case of a transnational libel a defendant could suffer damage to her reputation in each contracting state. A strict application of *Bier* could lead to a multiplicity of actions. This spectre of celebrity forum shopping caused many to recoil from a strict application and argue that *Bier* could not be applied to defamation.

Some commentators felt that *Bier* did not preclude the eventual adoption of specific rules for particular torts, such a rule that in defamation, the place where the harmful event occurred would be that of publication to a third party.[30] No such rule was ever adopted. Another wrote of a defamatory statement written, broadcast or posted in one state, published in a second and causing damage to reputations in a third. He said that it is the defendant's act in the first state, which should be held to be the harmful event.[31]

In *Shevill*, the defendant argued that Article 5(3) gives special jurisdiction only to the single court, which has the greatest connection with the cross border tort. This would have been France, owing to the very small circulation of the newspaper in England. This most significant connection test has been commended in an analysis of the Court of Appeal's decision.[32] However, Capotorti A.G. in *Bier*[33] had rejected it. Purchas LJ in the Court of Appeal also rejected the test, citing the opinion of the Advocate General.

In the course of the arguments before the European Court of Justice, the

---

[29] Most notably Case 365/88, *Hagen v. Zeehage* [1990] E.C.R. 1845, where the Court stated: "The object of the Convention is not to unify procedural rules but to determine which court has jurisdiction in disputes relating to civil and commercial matters in intra-Community relations and to facilitate the enforcement of judgments. It is therefore necessary to draw a clear distinction between jurisdiction and the conditions governing the admissibility of an action" ([1990] E.C.R. 1845, 1865, para. 17).
[30] Lasok & Stone, 232.
[31] Kaye, 561.
[32] Carter, "Jurisdiction in Defamation Cases" [1992] *B.Y.I.L.* 519, 521.
[33] [1976] E.C.R. 1735, 1756-1757.

United Kingdom argued that to accept such an interpretation would give rise to the kind of uncertainty that the Convention was designed to avoid. Darmon A.G., in his opinion, pointed to the two available fora – the courts of the place where the causal event occurred and those where the danger arose. He said that preference should not be given to either and to exclude one in certain cases and the other in other cases could undermine the consistency of the Court's case law. The Court held that an action could be brought either where the newspaper was published or where it was distributed. The Court did not entertain the argument that one forum or the other should have exclusive jurisdiction on the basis of a more significant connection.

Another alternative considered was giving the courts of the plaintiff's domicile jurisdiction over the whole loss. It would have been contrary to the whole tenor of the Convention if the plaintiff had been allowed to unilaterally always sue in their peculiar domicile. It was stressed by Advocate General Warner A.G. in *Ruffer* that:

> It was never suggested . . . much less held by the Court, that the place where the harmful event occurred could be the place where the plaintiff company had its seat or the place where the amount of the damages to its business was quantified . . . to hold that the place where the plaintiff has its seat could be regarded as being 'the place where the harmful event occurred' . . . would be tantamount to holding that, under the Convention, a plaintiff in tort had the option of suing in the courts of his own domicile, which would be quite inconsistent with the scheme of Article 2 *et seq.* of the Convention.[34]

Advocate General Darmon in *Shevill*[35] similarly stressed that to sanction the jurisdictional application of the plaintiff's forum would be equivalent to conferring jurisdiction on the forum actoris, an attribution to which, as the court has pointed out on numerous occasions, the Convention is hostile. The Court observed in its judgment in *Dumez* that:

> . . . the hostility of the Convention towards the attribution of justice to the courts of the plaintiff's domicile was demonstrated by the fact that the second paragraph of Article 3 precluded the application of national provisions attributing jurisdiction to such courts for proceedings against defendants domiciled in the territory of a Contracting State.[36]

The simple attribution of jurisdiction to the courts of the plaintiff's domicile

---

[34] Case 814/79, [1980] E.C.R. 3807, 3836.
[35] [1995] E.C.R. I-415, I-426.
[36] Case C220/88, [1990] E.C.R. I-49, 79, para 16. See also Case C-89/91, *Shearson Lehman Hutton* [1993] E.C.R. I-139, I-187, para. 17.

does not accord with the sound administration of justice or efficacious conduct of proceedings.

The judgment in *Shevill* does not impose an obligation on the plaintiff to sue in each separate member state where damage occurred. The plaintiff always retains the right to sue the defendant for the whole loss in the courts of the Member State where the defendant is domiciled (Article 2). No doubt in the international libel situation there are extreme disadvantages in such an approach but irrespective of the demerits the primacy of Article 2 within the scheme of the Convention has been maintained in *Shevill*.[37]

6. Application of the Rule

The observations made in *Bier vis-à-vis* physical or pecuniary loss or damage, have now been expressly applied to a case involving injury to reputation and the good name of both natural and legal persons due to a defamatory publication. In a libel scenario where a newspaper article is distributed in several Contracting States then, according to the Court, the place of the event giving rise to the damage (causal event), can only be where the miscreant publisher is established i.e. the place where the harmful event originated and from which the libel was issued and put into circulation. The court of the place where the publisher is established has jurisdiction to hear the whole action for all damage caused by the unlawful act. That jurisdiction will, as the Court noted, generally coincide in any event with the Article 2 jurisdiction based on the defendant's domicile.[38]

By similar reasoning to *Bier* co-existent jurisdiction, at the option of the plaintiff, was also held to exist in the place where the damage occurred, otherwise Article 5(3) of the Convention would be rendered superfluous. Where does the damage occur in the case of an international libel, published for example, throughout each individual Member State? The Court has answered this question by stating that the damage caused by a defamatory publication occurs in the places where the publication was distributed and where the victim claims to have suffered injury to her reputation.[39] A multiplicity of different fora will have jurisdiction over the harmful events within their own particular territory. The Contracting State in which the publication was distributed and in which the victim claims to have suffered injury to his reputation have jurisdiction to rule on the injury caused in that state to the victim's reputation. The underlying rationale for such a conclusion was founded by the Court on the sound administration of justice in that the State in which the defamatory publication was

---

[37] See [1995] E.C.R. I-415, I-461, para. 29 where this point was noted by the ECJ in its judgment.
[38] *ibid.*
[39] [1995] E.C.R. I-415, I-463–I-464, para. 34-41.

distributed and in which the victim claims to have suffered injury to his reputation is best suited to assess and determine the corresponding damage.

The acceptance of *Bier* as applying outside the sphere of torts where physical damage can be established is illustrated by the decision of the English High Court in *Domicrest v Swiss Bank Corp.*[40] The case was decided in the context of the parallel rules in the Lugano Convention on Jurisdiction and the Enforcement of Judgments in Civil and Commercial Matters[41] to those in the Brussels Convention. The alleged tort in question was that of negligent misstatement. The plaintiff was an English company. It supplied goods to a Swiss company after receipt of a payment order from the defendant. Bank officials had assured the plaintiff that the payment order was an assurance by the bank that payment would be made. The order was not honoured, as there was insufficient funds in the company's accounts. The plaintiff brought an action in England claiming damages in tort for negligent misstatement. It argued that England had jurisdiction under Article 5(3) as that was where it had suffered damage. The defendant argued that Switzerland was the place where the harmful event giving rise to the damage took place and that the damage was suffered in Switzerland and Italy where the goods were released.

The case turned on the interpretation of *Bier* as developed by *Shevill*. Rix J. pointed out that the damage was pure economic loss but held that nonetheless the rule in *Bier* applied. He first sought to identify the place where the harmful event occurred. In this respect he looked to the judgment of the ECJ in *Shevill*. Rix J. held:

> . . .the place where the harmful event giving rise to the damage occurs in a case of negligent misstatement is, by analogy with the tort of defamation, where the misstatement originates. It is there that the negligence, even if not every element of the tort, is likely to take place; and for that and other reasons the place from which the misstatement is put into circulation is as good a place in which to found jurisdiction as the place where the misstatement is acted on.[42]

He held that Switzerland was the place of the harmful event as it is the negligent speech of the representor rather than the hearer's receipt of it, which identifies the harmful event, which sets the tort in motion.

He then went on to consider the place where the damage occurred. This is likely to be the place where the misstatement is heard and relied on. However, in this case he held that the damage occurred in Switzerland and Italy. These were the jurisdictions in which the goods were released without prior payment.

---

[40][1998] 3 All E.R. 577.
[41]September 16, 1988, [1988] O.J. L. 3119/9.
[42][1998] 3 All E.R. 577, 594.

It is by reference to the loss of those goods that the damages were primarily pleaded. He said that was consistent with the approach of the Court in *Marinari*. England was an inappropriate forum as it was a jurisdiction in which "collateral damage" was suffered.

This case represents a classic application of the rule in *Bier*. The Court looks to *Bier* to identify the two relevant jurisdictions and then applies the refinements of the rule in *Shevill* to establish the appropriate jurisdictions.[43]

The *Bier* formula is the rule applied for the allocation of jurisdiction in tortious disputes within the European Union. It has been applied to defamatory material broadcast on television[44] and will apply to new categories of tortious liability arising from torts committed on the Internet[45] as well as to existing torts.

7. CONCLUSION

The rule in *Bier* has been remarkably successful. It has provided certainty and a flexible yet limited choice of jurisdiction for plaintiffs. It can stake a claim as one of the leading cases of the twentieth century. European private international law[46] is a new offshoot of private international law and European law but one, which has a remarkable success story. Article 5(3) of the Brussels Convention as interpreted and applied by *Bier* and subsequent cases is at the forefront of this development. The appropriateness of the rule in *Bier* contrasts favourably with the lack of clarity[47] and somewhat contrived solutions,[48] which

---

[43] A similar conclusion was reached by Kelly J. in the combined cases of *Gerry Hunter v. Gerald Duckworth & Co Ltd and Louis Blom Cooper* and *Hugh Callaghan v. Gerald Duckworth & Co Ltd and Louis Blom Cooper* High Court, unreported, December 10, 1999.

[44] In *Ewin & Ors v. Carlton Television* [1997] I.L.R.M. 223 (H.C.). Barr J applied the rule to defamatory material broadcast in the UK that was received by television viewers in Ireland. He held that harm had been done in Ireland. Damages in the case would be limited to the harm done to their reputations in Ireland. The only universal jurisdiction where compensation on a worldwide basis could be claimed is the jurisdiction where the publisher is established. The plaintiffs had a choice of jurisdiction under Article 5(3) and were free to choose Ireland.

[45] See *Mecklermedia Corporation v. DC Congress GmbH* [1997] 3 W.L.R. 479 (Ch.D.) where the English High Court held that an action brought by an English plaintiff against a German defendant for passing off on the Internet, could be heard by the English courts. England was the jurisdiction where the harmful event occurred as the harm caused to the plaintiff was damage to its goodwill in England. The assumption of jurisdiction was based on Article 5(3) and the *Bier* principle.

[46] Though given that the revised Brussels Convention will be released in the form of a regulation, this area of law may be subsumed into the mainstream of EU law.

[47] For instance over the scope of the Article. See in particular *Kleinwort Benson Ltd v. Glasgow City Council* in which the Court of Appeal ([1996] Q.B. 678 (C.A.)), by a majority, had held that Article 5(1) was sufficiently broad to cover claims for restitution of benefits transferred pursuant to void contracts, but the House of Lords ([1999] 1 A.C. 153 (H.L.)), also by a major-

the Court has reached in dealing with the special jurisdiction in Article 5(1) for contractual disputes.[49] The effect of the ruling in *Bier* will be with us well into the twenty first century if not beyond.

ity, reversed. In *Atlas Shipping v. Suisse Atlantique Société* [1995] 2 Ll. Rep.188, the English High Court had applied Article 5(1) to a restitutionary claim.

[48] For instance, the conflict of decisions of the Court on the phrase, "the obligation in question" in Article 5(1). See Hill, "Jurisdiction in Matters Relating to a Contract under the Brussels Convention" (1995) 44 *I.C.L.Q.* 591.

[49] Novy, "Article 5(1) of the Brussels Convention: the Unworkability of Special Jurisdiction in 'Matters Relating to a Contract'" (2000) 1 *Hibernian L.J.* 69.

THE TRIUMPH OF "INEXORABLE LOGIC"
D.P.P. v. MORGAN (1976)

SIR JOHN SMITH[*]

1. INTRODUCTION: THE LAW BEFORE *MORGAN*

From its publication in 1902 until the early 1960s Kenny's *Outlines of Criminal Law* was the unrivalled textbook on the subject. Deservedly so, for it was an elegant, clear, accurate text that it was pleasure to read. Probably almost all undergraduates and candidates for professional examinations learnt their criminal law from *Kenny*. The book must have had an enormous influence on their opinions and decisions. Law learnt as a student tends to stick, and the influence of *Kenny* can still occasionally be detected in the pronouncements of senior judges.

In his first edition *Kenny* discussed the question of mistake operating as "a defence" by negativing *mens rea*. He said that it did so only when three conditions are satisfied. First, "the mistake must be of such a character that, had the supposed circumstances been real, they would have prevented any guilt from attaching to the person in doing what he did". That is, the mistake must negative the *mens rea* of the crime. Secondly, he said, the mistake must be a reasonable one; and, thirdly, it must be a mistake of fact, not law.[1] That passage, like most of Kenny's work, continued unchanged right through to, and including, the fifteenth edition which was not superseded until 1951 when the "Entirely New Edition," as the book's new editor, J.W.C. Turner, described it, appeared. Even then, the proposition that "the mistake must be a reasonable one," with which I am concerned, survived,[2] though it was now qualified, perhaps inconsistently, by the statement that "Examination of the cases will reveal that this rule is fundamentally a matter of evidence".

When the law student moved into the world of practice of the criminal law, his bible became *Archbold* and here he found confirmation of what he had learnt from *Kenny*. The 35th edition of *Archbold* in 1962 continued to state: "Ignorance or mistake of *fact* may in some cases be allowed as an excuse for the inadvertent commission of a crime where the defendant acted under an

---

[*]Emeritus Professor of Law, University of Nottingham.

[1] Kenny *Outlines of Criminal Law* (1st ed., C.U.P., Cambridge, 1902) 65-69.
[2] Turner *Kenny's Outlines of Criminal Law* (16th ed., C.U.P., Cambridge, 1952) 47.

honest and reasonable belief in a state of things which if true would have justified the act done".[3]

The long accepted wisdom was then that only a reasonable mistake, negativing *mens rea*, would excuse. So in 1949 in *Younghusband v. Luftig*[4] Lord Goddard C.J. held that the accused had a defence to a charge of wilfully and falsely using the title, "M.D.", contrary to section 40 of the Medical Act, 1854, where he believed honestly and on reasonable grounds that he was justified in so describing himself. Lord Goddard said, "He must of course have a reasonable ground for his belief".[5] In this case where the accused in fact had reasonable grounds for his belief, Lord Goddard regarded it as axiomatic that the reasonable grounds were an essential element in the defence. But, only two years later, in *Wilson v. Inyang*,[6] when faced with a similar case in which the accused did not have reasonable grounds for his belief, Lord Goddard held that the accused had a defence. He conceded that "a man may honestly believe that which no other man of common sense would believe";[7] and he explained that, in *Younghusband v. Luftig* the court was "pointing out that, in considering whether a defendant has acted honestly, the magistrate ought to take into account the presence or absence of reasonable grounds of belief".[8] Glanville Williams greeted the decision with great enthusiasm, hailing it in a note in the *Modern Law Review*[9] as "[t]he most important contribution ever made to criminal jurisprudence by an English Divisional Court"[10] – and as one repudiating "in general terms the hoary error that a mistake of fact to afford a defence to a criminal charge must be reasonable".[11]

Even Lord Goddard himself, if he read the note, may have been surprised to find that he had made such an important contribution to criminal jurisprudence; and *Wilson v. Inyang* is now a forgotten case, not mentioned in *Archbold* or (I was slightly surprised to discover!) even in *Smith & Hogan*. But I cite it here as an indication of the great importance which Glanville Williams, the grandmaster of the criminal law, attached to the point of law which was to

---

[3] Butler and Garsia, (eds.), *Archbold. Criminal Pleading, Evidence and Practice* (35th ed., Sweet & Maxwell, London, 1962) para. 48.
[4] [1949] 2 K.B. 355; [1949] 2 All E.R. 72.
[5] [1949] 2 K.B. 355, 369; [1949] 2 All E.R. 72, 80.
[6] [1951] 2 K.B. 799; [1951] 2 All E.R. 237.
[7] [1951] 2 K.B. 799, 803. He is reported slightly differently in the All E.R. but the impact is the same: "[a] man may believe that which no other man of common sense would believe, but he yet may honestly believe it" ([1951] 2 All E.R. 237, 240).
[8] [1951] 2 K.B. 799, 803; [1951] 2 All E.R. 237, 240.
[9] "Mistake in Criminal Law" (1951) 14 *M.L.R.* 485. Professor Williams, in one his earliest articles on criminal law (turning his attention from public law and jurisprudence), "Homicide and the Supernatural" ((1949) 65 *L.Q.R.* 491) had already made clear his opinion that "We have no special rules relating to 'mistake'," the question being simply whether the prosecution had proved *mens rea* ((1949) 65 *L.Q.R.* 491, 493).
[10](1951) 14 *M.L.R.* 485, 485.
[11]*ibid.*

become the issue in the much more powerful authority of *Morgan* which is the subject of my present paper.

The balance of judicial authority in English law before *Morgan* undoubtedly supported the view that a defence of mistake of fact was good only if there were reasonable grounds for making the mistake. The judicial authority principally relied on was the case of *Tolson*[12] in 1890. Mrs. Tolson's husband was reported lost in a shipwreck. More than six years later, believing herself to be a widow, Mrs. Tolson remarried. Then, her husband turned up, alive and well. It may seem astonishing today that, not only was this perfectly innocent woman prosecuted and convicted of the serious offence of bigamy, a felony punishable with a maximum of seven years imprisonment, but that five judges of the Court for Crown Cases Reserved voted to uphold her conviction. That extraordinary fact can be explained only by the peculiar wording of the section under which she was charged. Happily, nine other judges took a different view. Mrs Tolson's honest belief that her husband had been drowned in a shipwreck was held to be a defence to bigamy, but only because it was a reasonable belief. If, say, a week after her husband's disappearance, she had consulted a fortune-teller, who gazed into her crystal ball and told her that her husband was dead, and she had then re-married, she would probably have been convicted, however sincere her belief in fortune-tellers and however strong her conviction that her husband was dead. Yet her only fault would have been her undue credulity, not an intention to flout or disregard the sanctity of marriage, which is the gravamen of the offence of bigamy.

Tolson was regarded as authority for a general principle, applicable not only to bigamy but throughout the criminal law, that only a reasonable mistake will excuse. The judges in the majority were, admittedly, emphatic in their assertion that they quashed the conviction only because the mistake was a reasonable one and so it is not surprising that this was considered an element in the *ratio decidendi*. The judges were not, however, actually confronted with a person who had made an undoubtedly honest yet unreasonable mistake; and, if they had been, they might, like Lord Goddard in *Wilson v. Inyang,* have been ready to qualify the stand they had taken earlier.

The "hoary error", as Glanville Williams believed it to be, was much too deeply rooted in the minds of lawyers to be eliminated by a judgment in the Divisional Court, even by so powerful a criminal lawyer as Lord Goddard. *Dicta* to the effect that only a reasonable mistake could excuse continued to flow and it seems likely that defendants were convicted on the grounds that

---

[12](1890) 2 Q.B.D. 168 (C.C.R.).

[13][1964] 1 Q.B. 285; [1963] 3 All E.R. 561 (C.C.A.). "Honest belief is not enough. There must be an honest belief on reasonable grounds" ([1964] 1 Q.B. 285, 283; [1963] 3 All E.R. 561, 565 *per* Lord Parker C.J., a Chief Justice less sympathetic to *mens rea* than the much-maligned Lord Goddard.

their mistakes were unreasonable, though the only clear reported decision was another bigamy case, *R. v. King*,[13] where the Court of Criminal Appeal held that the defendant's belief that his first marriage was void was no defence because it was an unreasonable belief. The *dicta* in *Tolson* became the *ratio decidendi* in *King*.

The rule in *Tolson* had a parallel in a supposed rule that a person is conclusively presumed to intend the natural and probable consequences of his act. If the result in question was a natural and probable result of what the accused did, that is, a reasonable man would have foreseen that it would probably happen, he was held to have intended it, whatever his actual state of mind might be. This rule was most authoritatively expressed in the notorious decision of the House of Lords, *DPP v. Smith*,[14] a case of the murder of a police officer. Smith, who was carrying stolen goods in his car, stopped at a traffic light where he aroused the suspicions of the officer. He drove off at high speed in order to avoid detection while the officer was clinging to the side of the car. The policeman was thrown off and killed. It was, in the opinion of the jury, a natural and probable consequence of his act that the officer would be killed or seriously injured, so Smith was guilty of murder, whether or not he realised there was any risk of death or serious injury. This case was very heavily criticised and referred to the Law Commission. The Commission agreed with the criticisms and proposed two clauses.[15] The first, which became section 8 of the Criminal Justice Act 1967[16] provides:

> A court or jury, in determining whether a person has committed an offence, –
>
> (a) shall not be bound in law to infer that he intended or foresaw a result of his actions by reason only of its being a natural and probable consequence of those actions; but
>
> (b) shall decide whether he did intend or foresee that result by reference to all the evidence, drawing such inferences from the evidence as appear proper in the circumstances.

This provision is of general application, throughout the criminal law, includ-

---

[14][1961] A.C. 290 (H.L.).

[15]*Imputed Criminal Intent: Director of Public Prosecutions v. Smith* (1966).

[16]In Ireland, a similar position had already been achieved by the terms of s.4(2) of the Criminal Justice Act, 1964, which provides that a "the accused person shall be presumed to have intended the natural and probable consequences of his conduct, but this presumption may be rebutted". On this section, see *The People (Attorney General) v. Dwyer* [1972] I.R. 416 (S.C.); O'Higgins and Ó Braonáin, "Section 4 of the Criminal Justice Act, 1964: The Redundant Presumption" (1991) 1 *I.C.L.J.* 113; O'Higgins and Ó Braonáin, "Section 4 of the Criminal Justice Act, 1964: A Constitutional Presumption" (1992) 2 *I.C.L.J.* 179; Stannard, "Murder, Intention and the Inference of Intention" (1999) XXXIV *Ir. Jur. (n.s.)* 202.

ing, but far from limited to, the law of murder. The Commission proposed a second clause, defining the *mens rea* of murder, which has never been enacted.[17] The *mens rea* of murder is still governed by the common law. All that section 8 can be taken to say about murder is that, if the law requires intention to cause, or foresight of, any result, that intention or foresight is not to be presumed but has to be proved by evidence; and section 8 says this about every offence. The section, however, is confined to "results", events which will happen in the future, not the facts or circumstances, although these may be equally essential elements of an offence. So the section did not affect the *Tolson* rule. Where awareness of fact and foresight of a result are elements in an offence, a person might be held liable because his unawareness of a fact was unreasonable; but he could not, after section 8, be held liable where foresight was required on the ground that his failure to foresee was unreasonable. It is not readily apparent why an unreasonable failure to be aware of facts should be thought culpable when an unreasonable failure to foresee results is not; but this seems to have been the state of the law when *Morgan* came before the courts.

2. THE DECISION IN *MORGAN*[18]

Morgan was a senior N.C.O. in the Royal Air Force. He invited three younger and junior members of that service to his house and suggested that they should have sexual intercourse with his wife. The young men, who did not know Mrs. Morgan, were at first incredulous but were persuaded by Morgan's stories of her sexual aberrations. They said that Morgan told them to expect some show of resistance on her part but not to take that seriously since it was a mere pretence that stimulated her own sexual excitement. Mrs Morgan's account was that she was wakened from sleep in the room she shared with her children and dragged struggling, screaming and shouting to her son to call the police. In another room the three young men, and then Morgan himself, each had intercourse with her without her consent. The three men gave evidence, completely contradicting that of Mrs. Morgan, evidence of such active co-operation and enjoyment on her part as to leave no doubt, if their testimony was true, that she was a consenting and willing party. The three younger men were convicted of rape and aiding and abetting rape, and Morgan was convicted of aiding and abetting rape, the rule being then that a husband could not be convicted of rape of his wife as a principal offender.

The trial judge, Kenneth Jones J., directed the jury in the clearest terms that

---

[17]However, in Ireland, a definition of the *mens rea* for murder as "an intention to kill or cause serious injury" is contained in s.4(1) of the Criminal Justice Act 1964.

[18][1976] A.C. 182 (C.A. and H.C.); [1975] 2 All E.R. 347 (H.L.); see McAuley, "The Grammar of Mistake in Criminal Law" (1996) XXXI *Ir. Jur. (n.s.)* 56.

the *mens rea* of rape was an intention to have sexual intercourse without consent. He said:

> . . . the prosecution have to prove that each defendant intended to have sexual intercourse with this woman without her consent. Not merely that he intended to have intercourse with her but that he intended to have intercourse without her consent. Therefore if the defendant believed or may have believed that Mrs Morgan consented to him having sexual intercourse with her, then there would be no such intent in his mind and he would not be guilty of rape but such a belief must be honestly held in the first place. He must really believe that.[19]

Nothing could be clearer than that; but then the judge went on:

> And, secondly, his belief must be a reasonable belief; such a belief as a reasonable man would entertain if he applied his mind to the matter.[20]

The convictions were upheld by the Court of Appeal[21] in a judgment delivered by Bridge J. That court distinguished between cases where there is an evidential burden on the accused and those where the evidential, as well as the burden of persuasion, rests on the Crown.[22] In the former class of case it was held that it is for an accused to show reasonable grounds for his alleged belief. So the Court of Appeal did recognise that sometimes an unreasonable mistake negativing *mens rea* might be defence. But Bridge J. then added:

> where the definition of the crime includes no specific mental element beyond the intention to do the prohibited act, the accused may show that though he did the prohibited act intentionally he lacked *mens rea* because he mistakenly, but honestly and reasonably, believed facts which, if true, would have made his act innocent.[23]

There was then no statutory definition of rape in English law. It was a common law offence. The prohibited act, however, was clear enough. It was having sexual intercourse with a woman who did not consent to it; and Bridge J. con-

---

[19] As set out in the speeches in the House of Lords; see, *e g* , [1976] A C. 182, 208; [1975] 2 All E.R. 347, 356 *per* Lord Hailsham; [1976] A.C. 182, 222; [1975] 2 All E.R. 347, 368-369 *per* Lord Edmund-Davies.

[20] *ibid.*

[21] *Sub nom. R. v. Morgan* [1976] A.C. 182 (C.A. and H.C.); [1975] 1 All E.R. 8 (C.A.).

[22] [1976] A.C. 182, 189-191; [1975] 1 All E.R. 8, 13-14, discussing, *inter alia, Woolmington v. D.P.P.* [1935] A.C. 462 (H.L.), on which see Stannard, "A Presumption and Four Burdens. *Woolmington v. D.P.P.* (1932)" above, 104.

[23] [1976] A.C. 182 191; [1975] 1 All E.R. 8, 14.

ceded that the prohibited act must be done intentionally. How then can it be
said, as the Court of Appeal did, that a man who believed honestly but unreasonably that the woman was consenting, intended to do "the prohibited act"?
Such a man, in fact, intends to have intercourse with a consenting woman. The
opinion of the Court can be explained only, it seems, by a course of reasoning
which runs:

1.   The accused intended to have intercourse with a woman.

2.   That woman did not consent to his doing so.

3.   Therefore, the accused intended to have intercourse with a woman who
     did not consent to his doing so, *i.e.*, he intended to do the prohibited act in
     rape.

And then, rules the Court, he has a defence only if he had reasonable grounds
for his honest belief that that she was consenting. The fallacy scarcely needs
further exposure. The actual intention of the person envisaged was to have
intercourse with a consenting woman, which is not, happily, an intention to do
a prohibited act.

The point of law certified for consideration by the House of Lords was:

> Whether in rape, the defendant can properly be convicted notwithstand-
> ing that he in fact believed that the woman consented if such belief was
> not based on reasonable grounds.[24]

In the House of Lords,[25] the point of law was decided, but only by a majority of
three to two, in favour of the appellants; but their appeal was dismissed under
the proviso to section 2 of the Criminal Appeal Act 1968. The jury had decided
the total conflict between the evidence of Mrs. Morgan and that of the appellants in Mrs Morgan's favour. Their verdict showed that they must have been
satisfied beyond reasonable doubt that she was speaking the truth and that the
appellants were lying; so if the jury had been correctly directed, they would
still, inevitably, have convicted. The judge had wrongly stated the law, but no
miscarriage of justice had occurred. Today, under the Criminal Appeal Act, as
amended, the proviso having been abolished, the House would say that the
conviction was "safe". The result would be the same. Justice was done on the
facts.

But it is the law with which we are concerned. As Lord Hailsham said, the
question was one of great academic importance in English law.[26] I would add
that it was also of great practical importance. "Academic" can be a loaded

[24][1976] A.C. 182, 192 ; [1975] 1 All E.R. 8, 15.
[25][1976] A.C. 182; [1975] 2 All E.R. 347.
[26][1976] A.C. 182, 204; [1975] 2 All E.R. 347, 353.

word. The principle established by the decision is that, once it is settled that the definition of a crime requires intention or subjective recklessness with respect to particular elements of the offence, a mistake of fact, whether reasonable or not, which is inconsistent with the existence of that intention or recklessness, is also incompatible with the guilt of the accused and must lead to his acquittal. In *Morgan* the trial judge, in the passage quoted above, stressed to the jury that the *mens rea* of rape was an intention, not merely to have intercourse with a woman, but an intention to have intercourse with a woman without her consent. Yet he went on to tell them that they could convict him if they found that he believed, but without reasonable grounds that the woman was consenting – that his intention was to have intercourse with a consenting woman. This, as Lord Cross pointed out, was to present the jury with two incompatible alternatives.[27] Lord Hailsham said:

> Once one has accepted, what seems to me abundantly clear, that the prohibited act in rape is non-consensual sexual intercourse and that the guilty state of mind is an intention to commit it, it seems to me to follow as a matter of inexorable logic that there is no room either for a defence of honest belief or mistake, or of a defence of honest and reasonable mistake. Either the prosecution proves its case or it does not.[28]

Here Lord Hailsham is distinguishing a simple denial of the prosecution's case from "a defence". The prosecution allege that the defendant intended to have sexual intercourse with a woman without her consent. He denies that, by claiming he honestly believed she did consent. The jury decides that he is, or may be telling the truth. The prosecution has failed to prove its case. This is different from a case where, for example, the defendant admits that he knew the woman was consenting, but claims that he was acting under duress – a gun was held to his head. He admits that he intended to have sexual intercourse with a woman without her consent, that he had the *mens rea* of the offence; but he pleads that he ought to be excused. If that is the correct analysis, that is a true defence.

With dissenting speeches by Lord Simon of Glaisdale and Lord Edmund-Davies, the decision was a close-run thing and it excited heated public controversy, particularly by some parties who thought it gave men a licence to commit rape. So the Home Secretary appointed an Advisory Group chaired by Mrs. Justice Heilbron to "give urgent consideration to the law of rape in the light of recent public concern and to advise the Home Secretary whether early changes in the law are desirable". The Group reported[29] within six months, concluding

---

[27][1976] A.C. 182, 203; [1975] 2 All E.R. 347, 361
[28][1976] A.C. 182, 214; [1975] 2 All E.R. 347, 352.
[29]*Report of the Advisory Group on the Law of Rape* (Cmnd. 6352, 1975). The Group made other important recommendations relating to evidence in rape cases, anonymity, and related matters.

that the law of rape had been correctly stated in *Morgan* and was right in principle. They recommended that the law should be put into statutory form. That recommendation was speedily implemented by the Sexual Offences (Amendment) Act 1976.[30] So far as the law of rape is concerned, *Morgan* is of only historical interest. It is no longer a live authority. The source of the law is now the statute.[31] But *Morgan* remains authority for a wider and much more important general principle. It really does, at last, repudiate what Glanville Williams condemned as "the hoary error" that only a reasonable mistake negativing *mens rea* could excuse. Even an unreasonable mistake excuses if it negatives the required *mens rea*. The decision does for awareness of circumstances what section 8 of the Criminal Justice Act 1967 does for foresight of consequences. So, we now we have two pillars of the subjectivist theory which prevails in English criminal law:

1. Section 8 of the Criminal Justice Act 1967: where the law requires intention or foresight of a result, the actual intention or foresight of the defendant must be proved.

2. *Morgan*: where the law requires knowledge of the existence, or possible existence of facts or circumstances, actual knowledge on the part of the defendant must be proved.

So much, I thought, was apparent at the time of the decision.[32] But it was not so readily apparent to the courts. So ingrained in the judicial mind was the rule that only a reasonable mistake could excuse that some lower courts were unable or unwilling to accept that that was no longer the law. The courts were inclined to say that *Morgan* was a decision on the law of rape and nothing more – like *Tolson*, a narrow decision. For a time, then, there was thought to be "a retreat from *Morgan*".[33] Perhaps the most striking example is the case of

---

[30]That provision has since been replaced by s.142 of the Criminal Justice and Public Order Act, 1994, s.142 which re-defines rape by substituting a new s.1 of the Sexual Offences Act 1956. It is now an offence for a man to rape a woman or another man. In Ireland, the Criminal Law (Rape) Act, 1981 achieved much the same position as the English 1976 Act while the Criminal Law (Rape) (Amendment) Act, 1990 achieves much the same extensions as the later English 1994 amendments.

[31]The relevant statute (s.1(1) of English 1976 Act; s.2(2) of Irish 1981 Act) provides: ". . . if at a trial for a rape offence the jury has to consider whether a man believed that a woman was consenting to sexual intercourse, the presence or absence of reasonable grounds for such a belief is a matter to which the jury is to have regard, in conjunction with any other relevant matters, in considering whether he so believed". In *People (D.P.P.) v. McDonagh* [1996] 1 I.R. 565 (S.C.) Costello P. traced the history of the English 1976 Act and of the subsequent introduction of the Irish 1981 Act, observing that each of the sections "deals specifically with the issue raised in *Morgan* and codifies the law in relation to mistaken belief . . ." ([1996] 1 I.R. 565, 572). On the legitimacy of Costello P.'s usage of legislative history, see Mullan, "Parliamentary History and Statutory Interpretation. *Pepper v. Hart* (1993)" below, 467, esp. at section 9.

[32]See commentary at [1975] *Crim. L.R.* 719.

[33]See Cowley, "The Retreat from *Morgan?*" [1982] *Crim. L.R.* 198.

Pheekoo.[34] The defendant was charged with an offence under section 1(3) of the Prevention from Eviction Act 1977:

> If any person with intent to cause the residential occupier of any premises (a) to give the occupation of any premises . . . [does certain acts, he commits an offence].

The defendant had done such acts to X and Y who were in fact residential occupiers. His defence was that he believed X and Y were not residential occupiers but squatters so he did not have the required intent.. The trial judge held that the alleged belief was no defence: he intended to evict X and Y, X and Y were in fact residential occupiers, therefore he had the necessary intent to evict the residential occupiers. His belief that they were squatters, whether reasonable or not, was no answer. The reasoning is the same as that discussed above in relation to rape and condemned as fallacious. The Court of Appeal allowed the appeal. This was a serious offence and *mens rea* was required. But then, in a fully considered *obiter dictum*, to give guidance to the courts, they held that only a reasonable belief would be a defence to the charge. Of *Morgan*, they said, ". . . it seems to us clear that this decision was confined and intended to be confined to the offence of rape".[35] *Tolson* was the applicable authority.

Now it is true that the House in *Morgan* showed no inclination to interfere with the bigamy cases of *Tolson* and *King*. For the majority, however, those cases could be reconciled only by strictly limiting the *mens rea* which must be proved in bigamy and this they did. Lord Fraser said, "bigamy does not involve any intention except the intention to go through a marriage ceremony".[36] Everyone who gets married, it appears, has the *mens rea* of bigamy. All that the prosecution need prove is that one of the parties was married already. The defendant is then guilty unless he introduces evidence which the jury thinks is, or may be, true, that he believed on reasonable grounds that neither of them was married. Lord Cross took a similar line: ". . . if the definition of the offence is on the face of it is 'absolute' and the defendant is seeking to escape his prima facie liability by a defence of mistaken belief, I can see no hardship to him in requiring the mistake – if it is to afford him a defence – to be based on reasonable grounds".[37] If the law of bigamy is indeed so draconian, there can be no quarrel with their Lordships' conclusions; but the offence in *Pheekoo* was not an absolute offence. The statutory definition expressly required an intention to

---

[34][1981] 3 All E.R. 84 (C.A.).

[35][1981] 3 All E.R. 84, 93. In *Kimber* [1983] 3 All E.R. 316 (C.A.) 320 Lawton L.J. said of this *dictum*: "We do not accept that this was the intention of their Lordships in *Morgan's* case. Lord Hailsham started his speech by saying that the issue as to belief was one of great importance in English law".

[36][1976] A.C. 182, 238; [1975] 2 All E.R. 347, 382.

[37][1976] A.C. 182, 202-203; [1975] 2 All E.R. 347, 352.

evict a residential occupier and it is submitted that the "inexorable logic"[38] of *Morgan* demanded that a person who believed the person he was evicting was not a residential occupier did not have such an intention, however unreasonable his belief might be. Unreasonableness could be no more than evidence, suggesting that the belief was not honestly held.

Pheekoo marked the limits of the retreat from *Morgan*. The tide turned in 1983 in *Kimber*.[39] The defendant was charged with an indecent assault on a woman. His defence was that he believed the woman consented to his actions. The judge directed the jury that his belief, reasonable or not, was no defence. On appeal, the Crown conceded that the direction was wrong but argued that the accused had a defence only if his belief was based on reasonable grounds. The court disagreed. They held that the *mens rea* of the offence was an intention to use violence to the woman, without her consent. If the defendant believed she was consenting, it followed that he did not have that intention. Lawton L.J. said:

> If, as we adjudge, the prohibited act in indecent assault is the use of personal violence to a woman without her consent, then the guilty state of mind is the intention to do it without her consent. Then, as in rape at common law, the inexorable logic, to which Lord Hailsham referred in *Morgan*, takes over and there is no room either for a 'defence' of honest belief or mistake, or of a 'defence' of honest and reasonable belief or mistake.[40]

3. *MORGAN* AND DEFENCES

In *Morgan*, as we have noticed, Lord Hailsham made clear his opinion that a defendant in a rape case, by asserting his belief that the victim was consenting, was not raising a defence, properly so called, but merely denying that the prosecution had proved its case.[41] The definition of a defence properly so-called may include a mental element, just as the definition of an offence does, but that was not seen to be the question in *Morgan*. It is true to say that *Morgan* decided nothing about mental elements in defences. Just as the substantive law may exclude a mental element in the definition of an offence, so it may in the definition of a defence but that was not in issue. Only Lord Edmund-Davies, dissenting, made a reference, and that a passing one, to defences, or what he looked upon as defences, asserting:

---

[38] [1976] A.C. 182, 214; [1975] 2 All E.R. 347, 352 *per* Lord Hailsham, above n.28.
[39] [1983] 3 All E.R. 316 (C.A.).
[40] [1983] 3 All E.R. 316, 319.
[41] [1976] A.C. 182, 214; [1975] 2 All E.R. 347, 361, above n. 28; Lord Edmund-Davies, dissenting, made the same point: [1976] A.C. 182, 229; [1975] 2 All E.R. 347, 375.

The law requires reasonable grounds for believing that physical action in self-defence or defence of another is called for. . . .[42]

There were numerous and consistent *dicta* in the authorities for this proposition regarding self-defence, but, strangely, no actual decision. The explanation for that may be that the proposition was considered too firmly established to merit a challenge so the point was never argued. Even the Criminal Law Revision Committee (hereafter C.L.R.C.) plainly thought that the law in this respect was unaffected by *Morgan*.[43] So when the question for the first time required an answer in the Divisional Court, I did not find it surprising that the Court applied those consistent *dicta*. In *Albert v. Lavin*,[44] Albert committed what we in England regard as the unforgivable sin: he jumped the bus queue. This intolerable act naturally provoked a hostile reaction and Lavin, a constable, off-duty and in plain clothes who happened to be present, apprehended a breach of the peace, which, as a peace officer, it was his right and his duty to prevent. He told Albert that he was a police officer but Albert continued to behave aggressively and hit Lavin who then arrested him for assaulting a constable in the execution of his duty. Albert's defence at his trial was that he did not believe Lavin was a police officer and that he was acting in self-defence by resisting assault and false imprisonment by a person who had no right to arrest him. If Lavin had not been a police officer he would have been acting unlawfully and the defence would have been good. The question for the Divisional Court was whether Albert was guilty of an offence if he used no more force then was reasonably necessary to protect himself from what he mistakenly and *without reasonable grounds* believed to be an unjustified assault and false imprisonment. The court, applying the unanimous *dicta* in the cases, held that he was guilty. The absence of reasonable grounds for his belief was fatal to the defence. The court distinguished between "the *mens rea* required for the basic elements of the offence and that required for a defence".[45] *Morgan* applied to the former but not the latter. And, though the section used the word, "unlawful", that added nothing and did not import unlawfulness into the definition of the offence. Hodgson J. said:

---

[42][1976] A.C. 182, 233; [1975] 2 All E.R. 347, 378. This objective theory would also seem to represent the law in Ireland with respect to murder (*The People (Attorney General) v. Dwyer* [1972] I.R. 415 (S.C.), on which see McAuley, "Excessive Defence in Irish Law" in Yeo, (ed.), *Partial Excuses to Murder* (Federation Press, Sydney, 1991) 194) but the subjectivist theory applies in the wide sphere of application of the Non-Fatal Offences Against the Person Act 1997 (ss.18-20 of that Act on which see n.51 below).

[43]"A few of us favour retaining a wholly objective test for self-defence, but most of us support a subjective test as to whether the defendant believed that he was under attack but an objective test as to the defendant's reaction to the threat". Fourteenth Report (Cmnd 7844, 1980) para. 283.

[44][1982] A.C. 546 (D.C., and H.L.); [1981] 1 All E.R. 628 (D.C.).

[45][1982] A.C. 546, 561-562; [1981] 1 All E.R. 628, 637.

. . .. no matter how strange it may seem that a defendant charged with assault can escape conviction if he shows that he mistakenly but unreasonably thought his victim was consenting but not if he was in the same state of mind as to whether his victim had a right to detain him, that in my judgment is the law.[46]

In *Kimber*,[47] the court found difficulty in agreeing with this reasoning, believing that the word "unlawful" did import an essential element into the definition of the offence. This was a momentous *dictum* because it paved the way for the court in the leading case of *Williams (Gladstone)*.[48] In that case, one, Mason, saw a youth rob a woman in a street. He caught the youth who escaped, then caught him again and knocked him to the ground. The appellant who saw only the latter stages of the incident, intervened. Mason said, falsely, that he was police officer but was unable to produce a warrant card when the appellant requested it. The appellant then punched Mason in order, he said, to save the youth from further beating. He was charged with assault occasioning actual bodily harm. The trial judge directed the jury that the appellant might have an excuse if he had a belief based on reasonable grounds, that Mason was acting unlawfully. The Court of Appeal, following *Morgan* as interpreted in *Kimber*, held that the word "unlawful," when used in the definition of an offence,[49] imports an essential element into that definition. Lord Lane C.J. said:

> The mental element necessary to constitute guilt [of assault] is the intent to apply unlawful force to the victim. We do not believe that the mental element can be substantiated by simply showing an intent to apply force and no more.[50]

When the law of assault is so interpreted, the only issue is, as Lord Hailsham said of the facts in *Morgan*, whether the prosecution has proved its case or not. There is no question of "a defence" properly so-called. When the prosecution charge assault, they allege that the defendant was acting unlawfully, *i.e.*, that he was not using reasonable force in defence of himself or – as in the instant case – in defence of another. So a person who believes in circumstances which would justify or excuse his conduct does not have the *mens rea* of assault. It is

---

[46][1982] A.C. 546, 562; [1981] 1 All E.R. 628, 639. When the case went to the House of Lords, the appeal was dismissed without a consideration the issue of belief ([1982] A.C. 546 (H.L.); [1981] 3 All E.R. 879). *Quaere* whether a similar result would be achieved in Ireland by virtue of s.18(6) of the Non-Fatal Offences Against the Person Act 1997?

[47][1983] 3 All E.R. 316, 320.

[48](1983) 78 Cr.App.Rep. 276.

[49]Section 47, unlike the definition of the offence in issue in *Kimber*, does not in fact use the word "unlawful." It simply refers to "any assault" and it is the common law "definition" of the offence of assault which is taken to incorporate the element of unlawfulness.

[50](1983) 78 Cr.App.Rep. 276, 280.

immaterial, applying *Morgan*, that he has no reasonable grounds for his belief. Lord Lane concluded his judgment by citing the recommendation of the C.L.R.C. – that "[t]he common law defence of self-defence should be replaced by a statutory defence providing that a person may use such force as is reasonable in the circumstances as he believes them to be in the defence of himself or any other person"[51] – and declaring that this already represents the present law as expressed in *Morgan* and *Kimber*. As the conviction in *Williams* had, in any event, to be quashed for misdirection on the onus of proof, it is arguable that all this was *obiter*, but it was very soon followed by other decisions, so as to establish it beyond all doubt at that level, and it has since received the approval of five Law Lords sitting in the Privy Council in *Beckford*.[52] Lord Griffiths said:

> Looking back, *D.P.P. v. Morgan* can now be seen as a landmark decision in the development of the common law, returning the law to the path on which it might have developed but for the inability [until 1898] of an accused to give evidence on his own behalf.[53]

So, somewhat belatedly, the judges have come to recognise the significance of the decision. A matter of doubt is the effect of *Morgan* on defences properly so called. *Morgan, Williams* and their successors were all concerned, or purported to be concerned, only with the *mens rea* specified in the definition of the offence. Lord Lane C.J., who so boldly and forthrightly rejected a hundred years (at least) of *dicta* in *Williams* had not taken the same approach in relation to duress. Here again, he is the author of the leading case, subsequently approved by the House of Lords. In *R. v. Graham*[54] where the defendant relied on duress, he said that the question was whether

> the defendant [was], or may . . . have been, impelled to act as he did because, as a result of what he reasonably believed King had said or done he had good cause to fear that if he did not so act King would kill him . . . ?[55]

---

[51] Fourteenth Report, para. 72(a); in Ireland, in the case of self-defence or defence of another or of property, or the prevention of crime, s.18(1) of the Non-Fatal Offences Against the Person Act 1997 provides that the "use of force by a person . . . *if only such as is reasonable in the circumstances as he or she believes them to be*, does not constitute an offence . . ."; while s.18(5) provides that "the question whether the act against which force is used is of a kind mentioned in . . . subsection (1) shall be determined *according to the circumstances as the person using the force believes them to be*" (emphasis added).

[52] [1988] 1 A.C. 130 (P.C.); see, *e.g.*, McAuley, "*Beckford* and the Criminal Law Defences" (1990) 41 *N.I.L.Q.* 158.

[53] [1988] A.C. 130, 145.

[54] [1982] 1 All E.R. 801 (C.A.). The case proceeded on the assumption, now known to be false, that duress could be a defence to murder.

[55] [1982] 1 All E.R. 801, 806.

308 *Leading Cases of the Twentieth Century*

Now this was two years before the decision in *Gladstone Williams* and Lord Lane was yet to undergo a conversion because, having compared duress with provocation, he went on:

> So too with self-defence, in which the law permits the use of no more force than is reasonable in the circumstances. And in general, if a mistake is to excuse what would otherwise be criminal, the mistake must be reasonable one.[56]

Morgan was not cited in *Graham*, and *Kimber* had yet to be decided. It is apparent, from the *dictum* cited above, that Lord Lane, in common with other judges (and counsel), had not, at that point, taken in the significance of *Morgan*. Would it have made any difference if *Morgan* had been cited in *Graham*? Murder, certainly no less than assault, must be unlawful. It is an unlawful killing with malice aforethought. The law is complicated by the fact that there need be no intention to kill, because an intention to cause grievous bodily harm is "malice aforethought". But there must be an intention unlawfully to cause (at least) grievous bodily harm. If it were not so, *Gladstone Williams* would not apply on a murder charge and everyone assumes, surely rightly, that it does – no less than on a charge of unlawfully and maliciously causing grievous bodily harm with intent contrary to section 18 of the Offences Against The Person Act, 1861. Does a person then intend *unlawfully* to cause grievous bodily harm if he does so because he believes that he himself will certainly be killed if he does not? If he does not intend an unlawful act, then by parity of reasoning with *Gladstone Williams* – and now *Beckford* – he ought to be acquitted whether his belief was reasonable or not. Is there a difference between the case (i) where the actual facts would ground self-defence and (ii) that where the actual facts would ground duress? Both should result in acquittal, but is the former justification, rendering the act not unlawful, and the latter a mere excuse, leaving the act, in some relevant sense "unlawful"? If so, the person believing (reasonably or not) in self-defence facts does not intend to do an unlawful act, the person similarly believing in duress facts does. It may be that in this way we can distinguish the two, but it has not been put to the test and, in view of the approval of *Graham* by the House of Lords, it is unlikely to be raised in the foreseeable future.

4. CONCLUSION: THE CONSEQUENCES OF *MORGAN*

I have equated *Morgan* with section 8 of the Criminal Justice Act 1967, asserting that *Morgan* did for awareness of circumstances what section 8 did for

---

[56] *ibid.*

foresight of results; and section 8 was certainly thought to be a landmark. However, neither section 8, properly interpreted,[57] nor *Morgan*, affect the nature of the *mens rea* which has to be proved to establish guilt of any particular crime. No one supposes that either of these developments signal the end of offences of negligence, like involuntary manslaughter, or of strict liability. So how important is it? After all, *Morgan* decided only that,

> where a state of mind is an element of an offence, a mistake of fact inconsistent with the existence of that state of mind is an answer to the charge.

You may say that this is self-evident, so blindingly obvious as to be hardly worth saying. If the law requires the prosecution to prove a particular state of mind and that state of mind is not proved, the prosecution must fail. "No big deal," is, I believe, the current jargon. To that I could only respond that the courts, by asserting that only a reasonable mistake would excuse, had been saying the contrary for many years, and the trial judge, the Court of Appeal and the dissenting Law Lords in *Morgan* itself were saying so, and, indeed, that some courts continued to say so after *Morgan* until more perceptive judges put them right.

Neither section 8 nor *Morgan* gets us anywhere unless the law of particular offences does require a subjective *mens rea*. That is of course a substantial limitation on the effect of both authorities. It is also a necessary limitation because the safety of society certainly demands the existence of offences of negligence and, most people probably think, of offences of strict liability. Nevertheless, *Morgan* is in my opinion of fundamental importance. Like section 8, it rids the law of a fiction, a pretence that a person has a guilty of state of mind which he did not have and that is a major step towards a rational criminal law.

---

[57] It was commonly supposed that the section changed the law of murder. This does not appear to be true. The provision intended by the Law Commission to change the law of murder was never enacted. It changed the way in which the *mens rea* of murder – as of very other crime requiring intention or foresight – must be proved; but that is all.

WHAT RULE OF REASON?
CASSIS DE DIJON (1979); A FLAWED *LOCUS CLASSICUS*

TOM CARNEY[*]

> *De ce que l'intelligence n'est pas l'instrument le plus subtil,*
> *le plus puissant, le plus approprie pour saisir le vrai,*
> *ce n'est qu'une raison de plus pour commencer par l'intelligence*
> *et non par l'intuitivisme de l'inconscient.*[1]

1. INTRODUCTION

Cassis de Dijon[2] is hailed as a milestone in the jurisprudence of the European Court of Justice. With *Dassonville,*[3] it lays the foundation for the Court's interpretation of the European Economic Constitution. *Cassis de Dijon*, allegedly, breathed fresh breath into the worn *Dassonville* doctrine, when the Court began its expansive interpretation of Article 28 (ex Article 30) of the EC Treaty, extending its net to catch any State measure capable of interfering with the market in respect of intra-Community trade in goods. Yet, what is important in *Cassis de Dijon* lies more in what is unsaid. While it explicitly introduced the idea that Article 28 includes the idea of mutual acceptance of goods, its celebrity is marked by the implicit introduction into the law of Article 28 of the so-called "rule of reason". Subsequent case law has, without apparent direction, built upon the implied reasoning of *Cassis de Dijon*. The Court's failure to set even basic parameters in *Cassis de Dijon* for the operation of its so-called "rule of reason" has generated confusion as regards the extent of Article 28's application, a confusion that persists today. Its legacy is most visible in the Sunday Trading cases,[4] and has led the Court, in *Keck and Mithouard*,[5] to purport to

---

[*]Legal Specialist, Office of the Director of Telecommunications Regulation, Ireland.

[1] Marcel Proust.
[2] Case 120/78, *Rewe-Zentral AG v. Bundesmonopolverwaltung fur Branntwein* [1979] E.C.R. 649.
[3] Case 8/74, *Procureur du Roi v. Dassonville et al.* [1974] E.C.R. 837.
[4] See, for comment, Arnull, "What shall we do on Sunday?" (1991) 16 *E.L.Rev.* 112
[5] Cases C-267 and 268/91, *Keck and Mithouard* [1993] E.C.R. I-6097.

clarify its rule of reason case law. This attempt has been recognised as an underwhelming and qualified success.[6]

From the time it was first reported in 1979, uncertainty has flowed through the cracks in the reasoning of *Cassis de Dijon*. The weaknesses in the judgment beg to be remedied by a clear and focused judicial statement regarding the exact nature and scope of Article 28's rule of reason.

2. THE SCOPE OF ARTICLE 28 OF THE EC TREATY

Article 28 of the EC Treaty prohibits quantitative restrictions on imports and measures having equivalent effect, while Article 29 (ex Article 34) condemns quantitative restriction on exports and all measures having equivalent effect. These prohibitions are subject to the possibility of justification under Article 30 (ex Article 36) of the Treaty.

The concept of what constitutes a quantitative restriction or "quota system" is well-established in international trade law. A typical example would be the numerical restriction placed by one state on specific imports from another. Non-tariff barriers are mechanisms commonly used to confer protection on domestic producers. The exact nature of a measure having equivalent effect to a quantitative restriction, though, is less clear cut. In theory, every non-fiscal state barrier to trade that is not a formal quota could be a measure having equivalent effect to a quantitative restriction. This, however, in practice, may not be a realistic approach to the treatment of every state measure that happens to have an effect on trade.

Distinctly applicable rules under Article 28 are national measures that are directed exclusively towards imports. Indistinctly applicable rules, meanwhile, apply equally to both imported and domestically produced products.

At an early point in the Community's development, the Commission believed that the concept of a state measure having equivalent effect to a quantitative restriction covered not only "legislative rules and administrative provisions" but also "administrative practices forming a barrier to importation or exportation that might otherwise take place, including those provisions and practices which render the importation and exportation more difficult in comparison with the sales of home production on the domestic market".[7] While it considered that domestic provisions which applied indiscriminately to imports and home products, as a rule, did not constitute measures having an equivalent effect to a quantitative restriction,[8] in Directive 70/50[9] the Commission gave a

---

[6] Case C-412/93, *Societe d'Importation Edouard Leclerc-Siplec v. TF1 Publicite SA et al.* [1995] E.C.R. I-179, 194 *per* Jacobs A.G.

[7] W.Q. 64/67 OJ 1967 169/12.

[8] In the 1969 Christmas package of directives, the Commission considered that provisions and restrictive practices which particularly affected imports and exports amounted in principle to

number of concrete cases in which equally applicable measures could fall foul of the prohibition contained in Article 28.

The Court did not follow the Commission's view of what constituted a measure having equivalent effect. For the Court, the precise legal form that such a measure takes is not of direct relevance and in *Dassonville* it held that "all trading rules enacted by Member States which are capable of hindering, directly or indirectly, actually or potentially, intra-Community trade are to be considered as measures having an effect equivalent to quantitative restrictions".[10] This all-embracing definition of measures having equivalent effect continues to be the Court's yardstick for the application of Article 28.[11] Similar to the concept of freedom found in the Commerce Clause of the US Constitution, free movement of goods in the Community is ensured by prohibiting, at least in principle, the Member States from adopting, or maintaining in force, any measure which, whether exclusively or not, touches on inter-state trade and makes intra-Community trade more difficult or distorts it.

Dassonville provides that in certain circumstances, in the absence of Community pre-emption, Member States may take measures to prevent unfair practices, so long as those measures are *reasonable* and that the means of proof required does not act as a hindrance to intra-Community trade and, should, in consequence, be accessible to all Community nationals. "Even without having to examine whether or not such measures are covered by Article [30], they must not, in any case, by virtue of the principle expressed in the second sentence of that Article, constitute a means of *arbitrary discrimination* or a *disguised restriction* on trade between Member States".[12] This is interpreted by Kapteyn and Van Themaat as the basis for the so-called "rule of reason" which was developed in *Cassis de Dijon,* and is viewed as the counterpart to the very wide interpretation given in *Dassonville* to the notion of measure having equivalent effect to a quantitative restriction.[13]

3. *Cassis de Dijon* – the Facts and the Finding

The facts of *Cassis de Dijon* are straightforward. Cassis is a blackcurrant liqueur containing 15 to 20 per cent alcohol by volume. It is commonly drunk

---

measures having equivalent effect to quantitative restrictions, but measures which applied equally to imports and domestic products did not. (OJ 1970 L 13).

[9] OJ English Special Edition 1970(I), 17.

[10] *Dassonville. op. cit.,* para 5.

[11] For examples, see Case 82/77, *Openbaar Ministerie v. Van Tiggele* [1978] E.C.R. 25; Case 132/80, *NV United Foods et. al v. Belgian State* [1981] E.C.R. 995, 1023; Case 207/83, *Commission v. United Kingdom* [1985] E.C.R. 1201; Case 182/84, *Miro BV* [1985] E.C.R. 3831.

[12] *Dassonville. op. cit.*

[13] Kapteyn and van Themaat, *Introduction to the Law of the European Communities* (3rd ed., Kluwer, 1998) [hereafter Kapteyn and van Themaat] 627.

with white wine and is lawfully produced in France. Prior to the decision, German law permitted the importation of the product but precluded the sale of any spirits of the category into which cassis fell, unless they were of at least 32 per cent alcohol content. A prospective importer initiated proceedings before the national courts to establish the incompatibility with Community law of the German rule. The European Court of Justice found that the rule violated Article 28. The measure, in its opinion, was one that was capable of hindering, directly or indirectly, intra-Community trade.

In *Cassis de Dijon,* the Court interpreted the *Dassonville* formula as catching all national measures, including those which are indistinctly applicable to both domestically produced and imported products. In so doing, it applied the concept of mutual recognition. It also introduced the idea that, where there has been no Community pre-emptive activity in a given area, Member States may impose indistinctly applicable measures that are necessary to satisfy a mandatory requirement recognised by the Court. The Court was conscious of the need for the Community to identify mandatory requirements upon which the Member States could rely and provided an inclusive list which it would recognise, stipulating that any trade barrier thus created must not be excessive in relation to the perceived threat against which it purports to act. Neither must it be possible for the Member State to deal with the matter by less restrictive alternative means.

4. The Flaws in the Reasoning of *Cassis de Dijon*

As stated, *Cassis de Dijon* extended the scope of the *Dassonville* formula to indistinctly applicable rules. Equally applicable national rules which do not provide for the mutual acceptance of goods are prohibited by Article 28. Such national rules, in some cases, may be "justified". They may be deemed "necessary" to protect mandatory requirements recognised by Community law.

The problems with this reasoning are many, given that the Court failed to set the parameters within which the "rule of reason" is supposed to operate. At best, it may only be implied from the judgment that the "rule of reason" applies solely to national measures which apply to both imported and domestically produced products. No other qualification for its operation is given. Clarity suffers. Reading the judgment, one could reasonably assume that the rule of reason might be applied to all equally applicable state measures that happen to have an effect on intra-community trade. Such an assumption, however, is incorrect, but is a direct result of the Court's vagueness. This is one of a number of flaws in the reasoning of the Court in *Cassis de Dijon* that we may now examine.

4.1 The parameter of "all equally applicable trading rules" is too broad

In Community law, Article 28 prohibits quantitative restrictions and *all* measures having equivalent effect. As we have seen in *Dassonville*, the term "*all* measures having equivalent effect" is deemed to include "*all* trading rules which have an effect, direct or indirect, actual or potential, on intra-Community trade". Briefly stated, Article 28, according to *Dassonville*, prohibits *all* national trading rules which happen to have an effect on trade between Member States. This theme is picked up in *Cassis de Dijon*, where the Court indicates the application of a rule of reason to all equally applicable trading rules.

To what extent can the Court, under Article 28, purport to prohibit *all* trading rules that happen to have an effect on intra-Community trade? The prohibition in Article 28 is directed to all measures of public authorities at local, regional or national levels and to public bodies or institutions for whose acts the Member State is responsible.[14] It also applies to all acts of the Community institutions.[15]

A wide interpretation of the notion of "measure having equivalent effect" can not be used to prohibit *all* trading rules that happen to have an effect on intra-Community trade in goods. In logic, even within Article 28 itself, a prohibition on quantitative restrictions is specifically provided for. At the very least, the term "all trading rules" does not include those national trading rules that happen to be classified as classical quantitative restrictions in Community law.

More importantly, the Treaty has specifically provided for a prohibition on national trading rules that impose customs duties and charges having equivalent effect to customs duties in Article 25 (ex Article 12). "[A]ny pecuniary charge, however small and whatever its designation and mode of application, which is imposed unilaterally on domestic or foreign goods by reason of the fact that they cross a frontier"[16] is condemned by the founding treaty. While the emphasis in the Court's jurisprudence lies in the hindering effect on the free movement of goods, fiscal and parafiscal obstacles to intra-Community trade are dealt with specifically under Article 25, and not under Articles 28 and 29. Article 25 applies in preference to Articles 28 and 29.[17] Not all trading rules which affect trade are treated by the Court itself as falling under the latter provisions.[18]

---

[14]Case 45/87, *Commission v. Ireland* [1988] E.C.R. 4929, 4962-4963, para. 12-17.

[15]Cases 80 and 81/77, *Societe Les Commissionnaires Reunis Sarl et al v. Receveur des Douanes* [1978] E.C.R. 927, 946-947, para. 35.

[16]Case 24/68, *Commission v. Italy* [1969] E.C.R., 193, 201, para. 9; Cases 2 and 3/69, *Sociaal Fonds voor de Diamantarbeiders v. SA Ch. Brachfeld and Sons et al.* [1969] E.C.R. 211, 222, para. 11-21.

[17]Case 46/76, *Bauhuis v. The Netherlands State* [1977] E.C.R. 5, 15, para. 12.

[18]The only exceptions mentioned in Title I of Part Three of the EC Treaty, dealing with the free movement of goods are those in Article 30. These relate only to Articles 28 and 29 and cannot be relied upon to justify charges falling under Article 25. See generally Case 46/76, *Bauhuis v. The Netherlands State* [1977] E.C.R. 5.

The Treaty, through Article 90 (ex Article 95) prohibits national rules which impose discriminatory or protective taxes. National rules that fall for adjudication under that provision can not be also caught under Articles 28 and 29. Article 90 will apply in preference to Article 28 and 29.

The *Dassonville* formula, therefore, should be read in light of the extent and scope of Article 28. It does not cover *all* trading rules that happen to have an effect, direct or indirect, actual or potential, on intra-Community trade in goods. It does not cover all equally applicable national trading rules. Rather, the notion of "measure having equivalent effect" excludes national rules that are quantitative restrictions in the strict sense or those national rules that impose fiscal or parafiscal charges caught by Articles 25 and 90. At its broadest, the rule of reason should only be considered for application to equally applicable measures that are specifically prohibited by Article 28 as measures equivalent to quantitative restrictions. Application of the rule, of course, would have to be subject to further conditions.

Interestingly, Maduro[19] notes that the Court, after *Cassis de Dijon,* abandoned its "trading rules" terminology.

4.2 The failure by the Court, under Article 28, to classify state measures according to their restriction on trade

The second flaw in *Cassis de Dijon*, a much more serious one, may be identified by reference to US interstate commerce law. In the United States, the Supreme Court in its dormant commerce clause jurisprudence has clearly identified, under three headings, state regulations that hinder interstate commerce. Under each category there are defined rules for the treatment of state measures which may have an effect on US commerce. The Court of Justice, in *Cassis de Dijon*, failed to put in place even a rudimentary model for the examination of national rules under Article 28.

In the United States, there are Federal limits on the power of the states to regulate the national economy. The commerce barrier to state action arises in two situations. In the first, Congress is silent: it has taken no action, express or implied, indicating its own policy on a given subject matter. In that situation, the objection to state authority rests entirely on the negative implications of the commerce clause of Article 1:8 of the US Constitution – on the unexercised commerce power and on the free trade value it symbolises. This situation is typically referred to as the operation of the "dormant" commerce clause. In the second situation, Congress has exercised the commerce power, and the challenge to inconsistent state action rests on both the exercise of the commerce power under Article 1:8 and the pre-emptive effect of the federal legislation of

---

[19]Maduro, *We, the Court. The European Court of Justice & the European Economic Constitution* (Hart Publishing, Oxford, 1998) [hereafter Maduro] 61.

Article VI of the Constitution. Our focus will be on the "dormant" commerce clause.

Under the "dormant" commerce clause, the US Supreme Court invalidates some "protectionist" state legislation even in the absence of congressional pre-emption. Modern dormant commerce clause decisions hold unconstitutional some, but not all, state regulations that burden interstate commerce and may be divided into three groups.

First, the Court has shown a clear antipathy to overt "discrimination" to out-of-state interests. A state law that, on its face, discriminates against out-of-state commerce is subject to an extra-ordinarily strong presumption of invalidity and will virtually always be struck down. Second, the Court has likewise invalidated laws in favour of local economic interests at the expense of out-of-state competitors even when they do not take the form of overtly discriminatory statutes. Overtly discriminatory laws are rare. But the Court has been willing to look behind state laws that are *prima facie* neutral towards outsiders in order to assess whether or not they have a forbidden, protectionist purpose. It has also looked to a law's protectionist effect, sometimes as evidence of protectionist purpose. A finding of "protectionism" is generally fatal to state regulation. Third, the Court has also struck down *prima facie* neutral laws that "unduly burden" interstate commerce, applying a rule of reason, a "balancing" approach. It has held that where a statute regulates even-handedly to effectuate a legitimate local public interest, and its effects are only incidental, it will be upheld unless the burden imposed on commerce is clearly excessive in relation to the putative local benefits. If a legitimate local purpose is found, then the question becomes one of degree. And the extent to which that burden will be tolerated will of course depend on the nature of the local interest involved, and on whether it could be promoted with less impact on interstate trade.[20]

The Community's treaty provisions for the free movement of goods resemble only in part the US regime. Even a cursory glance at the founding treaties of the European Community and the jurisprudence of its primary courts highlights the supra-national body's recognised lack of full sovereign state-like capacity. In international law, the European Community owes its identity, more or less, to the GATT Article XXIV 1994 exception to the most favoured nation principle.[21] The United States is a sovereign state. It is true that the Community has ambitions beyond that of a mere customs union, but these ambitions are tempered by the internationally binding treaties between the Member States founding and extending the Community. Any attempt to draw comparisons between the US and Community models for the free movement of goods must

---

[20] *Pike v. Bruce Church, Inc.*, 397 U.S. 137 (1970).

[21] Case 26/62, *Van Gend en Loos v. Nederlandse Administratie der Belastingen* [1963] E.C.R. 1; on which see Fennelly "The Dangerous Idea of Europe? *Van Gend en Loos* (1963)" above, 220.

be read with this basic fact in mind. In addition, the US and the Community display two different styles of judicial activism: market maintenance and market building.

In the US, market maintenance assumes that the dominant rationality of both the market agents and political systems has shifted to the larger economic and political spaces. The judiciary's focus is on reducing uncertainty that arises from the different economic and political fora within the new system and in regulating competition between the several states themselves, and between the states and the federal levels. In the Community, meanwhile, the main attention of the courts is devoted to national legislation and the need to harmonise the different national regulatory frameworks so as to create the foundations of the integrated market. Market building focuses on promoting the new set of rights brought by the larger integrated area and to break the path-dependence of actors from the national systems.[22]

Bearing these issues in mind, so much of what is important for the proper Community regulation of interstate trade is left unwritten in *Cassis de Dijon*. The judgment may be described as a blank blackboard over which the Court has scribbled its ideas for the building of the Community market. The Court has had to figure out, in later cases, what it had originally intended in *Cassis de Dijon*. No regime for the different treatment of distinctly applicable and indistinctly applicable rules is provided in *Cassis de Dijon*. It is implicit in the judgment that the scope of the judgment does not apply to national trading rules that are *distinctly* applicable to imported products. Member State rules, like the impugned rule of origin in *Dassonville* which on its face discriminated against the products of another Member State, will virtually always be struck down under a straight forward application of Article 28. *Cassis de Dijon* may only be invoked in the treatment of national rules that are *indistinctly* applicable to both imported and domestically produced products, but this statement requires to be refined below.

After several years of academic comment and judicial pronouncement on *Cassis de Dijon*, there appears to be little agreement on what is the exact scope of the *Dassonville* formula. Different theories have been put forward and can be divided into three categories on the basis of the tests proposed to guide the application of Article 28 in the review of State measures: (a) discrimination tests; (b) typological tests; and (c) balance or cost/benefit tests.[23] Until the decision of the Court in *Keck and Mithouard*, Article 28 jurisprudence was characterised by a progressive extension of its scope. With *Keck and Mithouard*, however, the Court retreated from the extensive scope given to Article 28 and tried unsuccessfully to face some of the problems and contradictions of its case

---

[22]Maduro, 88.
[23]*ibid.*

law in this area. As Maduro points out,[24] the Court still has not made up its mind as to the definite course to follow.

In logic, all trading rules (excluding quotas in the strict sense and national rules imposing fiscal or parafiscal charges) which have a direct or indirect, actual or potential effect on intra-Community trade in goods should be divided into two groups. The first group should include those rules that are overtly discriminatory and distinctly applicable to imported products. The second should include those rules that are indistinctly applicable to both imported and domestically produced products. This group may be further divided into two subgroups: first, rules which are indistinctly applicable in law to both imported and domestically produced products but materially discriminate against imported products; second, rules which are indistinctly applicable in law and in fact to both imported and domestically produced products.

4.3 Failure to specify clearly those national rules to which the "rule of reason" applies

Cassis de Dijon failed to specify those national measures to which the rule of reason should be applied. Neither did it lay down any ground rules for the operation of a rule of reason. Logically, not all trading rules are caught by the prohibition in Article 28. Neither should the rule of reason apply to all national trading rules.

Again borrowing from the US, one may identify the salient features of a model for any workable rule of reason. Section 1 of the Sherman Act 1890 broadly states that "every" contract, combination or conspiracy that restrains interstate trade is illegal. Taken literally, the extremely broad language in Sherman Act would prohibit virtually any business combination or agreement, including competitively desirable as well as undesirable arrangements. To avoid this absurdity, not surprisingly, the US courts have interpreted the statute far more narrowly, as prohibiting only those concerted practices that are "reasonably restrictive" of competitive conditions.[25]

On the one hand, in the United States, a measure which is "unreasonably restrictive of competitive conditions" is illegal under Section 1 of the Sherman Act. On the other, a measure which is not "unreasonably restrictive of trade" is not caught by the prohibition in Section 1, so there is no need for the defendant to justify it.

Two major separate lines of analysis have been developed to gauge the competitive reasonableness of particular practices challenged under Section 1. First, certain practices are treated as being so plainly anti-competitive and with-

---

[24] *ibid.*, 87.
[25] *Standard Oil Co. v. United States*, 221 U.S. 1, 65 (1911).

out redeeming virtue as to be *per se*, or conclusively, unreasonable. Secondly, those contracts, combinations or conspiracies in restraint of trade that are not deemed *per se* illegal are judged under what is termed "the rule of reason". As described by a series of decisions by the Supreme Court, the rule of reason broadly examines and balances the various competitive factors that bear upon whether or not a particular practice is "unreasonably restrictive of competitive conditions".[26] The so called "rule of reason" is not really so much a set standard of behaviour as it is a general inquiry into whether or not under "all the circumstances", a measure is "unreasonably restrictive of competitive conditions".

Despite being credited as the judgment that introduced the rule of reason into Article 28 jurisprudence, *Cassis de Dijon* does not provide a specific framework for the application of the rule of reason (mandatory requirements). It simply states that "[i]n the absence of common rules relating to the production and marketing of alcohol, . . . it is for the Member States to regulate all matters relating to the production and marketing of alcohol and alcoholic beverages on their territory. Obstacles to the movement within the Community resulting from disparities between the national laws relating to the marketing of the products in question must be accepted in so far as those provisions may be recognised as being necessary in order to satisfy mandatory requirements relating in particular to the effectiveness of fiscal supervision, the protection of public health, the fairness of commercial transactions and the defence of the consumer".[27]

Cassis de Dijon simply provides a non-exclusive list of those national provisions which may be recognised as being necessary in order to satisfy mandatory requirements. These rules are recognised as obstacles to the integration of the Community market. The true obstacle to market integration results from disparities in national laws. As a result, such national rules may only be adopted so long as there exists no Community pre-emptive action relating to production or marketing of a relevant product. The most important condition in the Article 28 rule of reason case-law is not clearly stated in *Cassis de Dijon*, but has been made explicit subsequently, namely that national measures have to be equally applicable in law and in fact, if they are to benefit from the rule of reason.[28]

To facilitate clarity, it is respectfully submitted that the Court should pronounce that national rules that are discriminatory and distinctly applicable are *per se* illegal. It needs to develop a clear policy for the application of a workable rule of reason to equally applicable rules.

---

[26] *ibid*. See also *National Society of Professional Engineers v. United States*, 435 U.S. 679, 687-91 (1978).

[27] [1979] E.C.R. 649, para. 8.

[28] See for example, Case 207/83, *Commission v. United Kingdom* [1985] E.C.R. 1201, 1212, paras. 20-22.

4.4 The failure of the Court to consider Article 30

In *Cassis de Dijon*, the Court failed to even mention Article 30, never mind try to explain any possible relationship between the so-called mandatory require-ments and the heads of justification given in the Treaty provision.

Article 30 offers a list of potential justifications and then issues a firm warn-ing that any purported justification will be carefully scrutinised in order to ascertain that it is genuine. Article 30 is the provision of the Treaty that permits the maintenance of barriers to intra-Community trade. It espouses a principle hostile to the fundamental principles of the free movement of goods within the Community. For that reason it is interpreted narrowly.[29] Member States, by law, are entitled to justify distinctly or indistinctly applicable rules through reliance on the heads of justification provided for in Article 30. The Court has always shown itself to be unwilling to extend the scope of the available heads of justification under Article 30 beyond those specifically laid down.[30]

In *Cassis de Dijon*, though, the Court found it necessary to allow rather greater latitude in justifying rules that apply to all products whether domestic or imported. Failing to even mention Article 30, the Court was not bound by the literal meaning to be given to the terms of that provision in their context and in light of its object and purpose. Instead it held that "obstacles to the movement of goods within the Community resulting from disparities between the national laws relating to the marketing of the products in question must be accepted in so far as those provisions may be recognised as being necessary to satisfy mandatory requirements relating in particular to the effectiveness of fiscal supervision, the protection of public health, the fairness of commercial transactions and the defence of the consumer".[31]

The first sentence of Article 30, through the term "justified" links the ex-ceptions listed therein to the prohibition contained in Article 28. The Court, in *Dassonville*, requires "justifiable" national measures to be "reasonable" while in *Cassis de Dijon* such measures have to be "necessary". Herein lies the ker-nel of the problem with the judgment.

The Treaty seeks to balance the needs of the common/internal market against the need to take into account general interests such as public health and public security. Article 28 prohibits all quantitative restrictions and measures having equivalent effect but, Article 30 permits "national laws to derogate from the principle of free movement of goods to the extent to which such derogation is and continues to be justified for the attainment the objectives referred to in that article".[32] Article 30 is not designed to reserve certain matters to the exclusive

---

[29] See second sentence of Article 30.
[30] Case 113/80, *Commission v. Ireland* [1981] E.C.R. 1625.
[31] [1979] E.C.R. 649, para. 8
[32] Case 35/76, *Simmenthal Sp.A v. Italian Minister of Finance* [1976] E.C.R. 1871, 1886, para. 14.

jurisdiction of the Member States. Where, in application of Articles 94 (ex Article 100) or 95 (ex Article 100a), the Community has adopted directives to provide for the harmonisation of the measures necessary to ensure the protection of one of the objectives mentioned in Article 30, recourse to that provision is no longer justified. The Community has competence in that field to the exclusion of the Member States.

In what Kapteyn and Van Themaat refer to as a second period of development,[33] the Court compensated for the application of Article 28 to equally applicable measures by the development of a rule of reason. In *Cassis de Dijon*, the Court equated the application of the rule of reason with reliance on a justification under Article 30. Indeed, the protection of public health was included among the examples of rule of reason "justifications" in *Cassis de Dijon*, but it is now accepted by the Court itself that public health protection falls exclusively under Article 30 itself.[34]

To date, the Court has indicated that national measures may be "justified" where *inter alia* they are enacted or enforced in the interests of; consumer protection,[35] fair commercial transactions,[36] the effectiveness of fiscal supervision,[37] environmental protection,[38] and the plurality of the media.[39] The development of the rule of reason has shown that there are other grounds not mentioned in the EC Treaty on which barriers to trade between Member States may be "justified", which may be felt to sit uncomfortably with the strict approach to Article 30 advocated in *Commission v. Ireland*.[40] It is not an application of the public policy provision in the first sentence of Article 30,[41] nor is it an expansion of the heads of the first sentence of Article 30. The major difference between the rule of reason and Article 30 is that "justifications" recognised under the rule of reason may only be relied upon in relation to national measures which apply equally in law and in fact to both imports and domestically produced products whereas Article 30 may be invoked by Member States to justify both distinctly applicable and indistinctly applicable national rules.[42]

---

[33] Kapteyn and van Themaat, 651.
[34] Cases C-1 and 176/90, *Aragonesa de Publicidad Exterior SA et al. v. Separtamento de Sanidad y Seguridad Social de la Generalitat de Cataluna* [1991] E.C.R. I-4151, I-4184, para. 13.
[35] This is *Cassis de Dijon* itself.
[36] Case 58/80, *Dansk Supermarket A/S v. A/S Imerco* [1981] E.C.R. 181, 194.
[37] *Cassis de Dijon*, [1979] E.C.R. 649, 662, para. 8; Case 90/82, *Commission v. France* [1983] E.C.R. 2011, 2030, para. 24
[38] Case 302/86, *Commission v. Denmark* [1988] E.C.R. 4607, 4630, para. 9.
[39] Case C-154/89, *Commission v. France* [1991] E.C.R. I-659, I-687–I-687, paras. 15-17.
[40] [1981] E.C.R. 1625, 1638, paras. 6-8; Case 46/76, *Bauhuis v. The Netherlands State* [1977] E.C.R. 5, 15, paras. 11-14.
[41] *ibid.*
[42] See, however, Case 2/90, *Commission v. Belgian State* [1992] E.C.R. I-4431 where the Court purported to apply the rule of reason to a national measure which was clearly a distinctly applicable rule.

The Court, in *Cassis de Dijon,* did not even consider, let alone foresee the difficulties that necessarily flow from the failure to consider the relationship between Article 30 and the rule of reason. As a result, it failed to identify the correct scope and effect of the operation of an Article 28 rule of reason. The consequence in subsequent case law has been confusion. Kapteyn and Van Themaat identify the legacy of the Court's failure to understand the scope of the rule of reason when it held that "there is now a category of measures which the Court formerly would have evaluated under the rule of reason, but now regard as not being caught by Article 28 at all, an approach which to say the least has been dogged by controversy, as much about the reasoning as the concrete result". [43]

The Court, in *Keck and Mithouard,* purported to clarify its rule of reason case law. This judgment has been criticised as "reasoning renounced". [44] *Keck and Mithouard* draws a distinction between national rules relating to the condition in which products are sold and domestic laws which govern selling arrangements. The positive approach of mutual acceptance of Member States' goods which was first laid down in *Cassis de Dijon* is followed. Rules governing the condition in which goods are sold on national markets, which are indistinctly applicable to domestically produced and imported products are still evaluated under Article 28 with application, as appropriate, of the "justifications" under either Article 30 or the "mandatory requirements". "Contrary to what was previously decided", [45] the Court found that "the application to products coming from other Member States of national provisions restricting or prohibiting certain selling arrangements is not such as to hinder directly or indirectly, actually or potentially, trade between Member States within the meaning of the *Dassonville* judgment, provided that those provisions apply to all affected traders operating within the national territory and provided that they affect in the same manner, in law and in fact, the marketing of domestic products and those from other Member States". [46] If "those conditions are fulfilled, the application of such rules to the sale of products from another Member State meeting the requirements laid down by that State is not by nature such as to prevent their access to the market or to impede such access any more than it impedes the access of domestic products. Such rules, therefore, fall outside the scope of Article 28 of the Treaty". [47] The approach in *Keck and Mithouard* was confirmed in *Hunermund.* [48]

---

[43] Kapteyn and van Themaat, 627.
[44] Gormley, "Prohibiting Restrictions on Trade within the EC" (1994) *E.B.L.R.* 63.
[45] [1993] E.C.R. I-6097, I-6131, para. 16.
[46] *ibid.*
[47] *ibid.*
[48] Case C-292/92, *Hunermund v. Landesapothekerkammer Baden-Wurttemberg* [1993] E.C.R. I-6787.

5. THE LEGACY OF *CASSIS DE DIJON*

There is something missing from the overall picture painted by *Dassonville, Cassis de Dijon* and *Keck and Mithouard*. There is a profound lack of logic that stands out like a sore thumb in *Keck and Mithouard*. A new category of measures exists which the Court formerly would have evaluated under the rule of reason, but now regards *as not being caught by Article 28*. This begs the purpose of having a rule of reason in the first place.

The jurisprudence of the Court so far has indicated that distinctly applicable measures are prohibited by Article 28. They may be justified under Article 30. In other words, indistinctly applicable domestic provisions remain caught by Article 28, but are exempted from the prohibition by virtue of the fact that they are justified under Article 30. An analogy with EU Competition law can be made. Collusive agreements are prohibited under Article 81(1) (ex Article 85(1)). Such agreements are void under Article 81(2) (ex Article 85(2)), unless exempted by the EC Commission under Article 81(3) (ex Article 85(3)). In Competition law decisions, the EC Commission goes to great pains to stress that agreements that are exempted under Article 81(3) remain subject to scrutiny under Article 81(1) should the terms of the exemption be breached.

Cassis de Dijon states that indistinctly applicable national provisions are also caught by Article 28. Later jurisprudence makes it clear that, in the absence of Community pre-emption, they may be justified under Article 30. In other words, these equally applicable measures remain caught by Article 28, but are exempted from the prohibition by virtue of the fact that they are justified under Article 30. Similarly, such measures may be "justified" under one of the headings recognised by the Court as a "mandatory requirement". This seems to indicate that these equally applicable measures remain caught under Article 28, despite benefiting from a so-called "rule of reason".

Since, *Keck and Mithouard*, the Court now seems to be saying that there is a category of indistinctly applicable national measures relating to selling conditions whose effects on intra-Community trade are so remote that they do not require to be exempted under Article 30 or "justified" under one of the "mandatory requirements" headings of *Cassis de Dijon*. Simply, they are deemed to fall outside the prohibition contained in Article 28.

Cassis de Dijon was supposed to have laid down the foundation stones for a rule of reason approach in Article 28. So why the need for terminology like "justification" or "justified" in the Court's language? Advocates of a rule of reason under Article 81(1) argue that agreements such as research and development projects have pro-competitive effects, so that they do not require justification under Article 81(3) and as such should be held to fall outside Article 81(1) altogether. In a series of important Competition law judgments, the Court has held that various restrictions on conduct do not amount to restrictions on competition; there have been several judgments of this kind, and this has encouraged the view that the Court may be moving towards the adoption of rule-of-reason analysis under Article 81(1).[49] Whether it is or is not is unimportant for the purposes of this argument. What is vital here is that where the Court considers a measure under Article 81(1), it has shown itself willing to balance the pro-competitive effects of an agreement against its anti-competitive effects. Where the agreement is found on balance not to infringe Article 81(1), there is no need for the matter to be justified under Article 81(3). Article 81 in its entirety is not applicable.

In US anti-trust law, as we have stated previously, agreements that are not illegal *per se* under the Sherman Act are analysed under the rule of reason whereby they are considered in their market context so as to ascertain whether or not they restrain trade. Anti-competitive and pro-competitive consequences of an agreement must be balanced against one another. The US courts have been prepared to undertake extensive economic analysis in order to establish whether or not an agreement is caught by the Sherman Act. If the agreement is deemed restrictive, depending on the nature of the illegality justifications may or may not be considered by the courts. If the agreement is not caught by Section 1, then it falls outside the Sherman Act altogether, without the courts needing to consider further "justifications".

Under the dormant commerce clause, the Supreme Court has also struck down *prima facie* neutral laws that "unduly burden" interstate commerce, applying a rule of reason, a "balancing" approach. However, to repeat what was written earlier, "where a statute regulates even-handedly to effectuate a legitimate local public interest, and its effects are only incidental, the statute will be upheld unless the burden imposed on such commerce is clearly excessive in relation to the putative local benefits. If a legitimate local purpose is found, then the question becomes one of degree. And the extent to which the burden will be tolerated will of course depend on the nature of the local interest involved, and on whether it could be promoted with a lesser impact on interstate activities".[50]

What seems evident from the application of various models of the "rule of reason" by the European Court of Justice in Competition law cases, and in anti-trust and dormant commerce clause cases by the US Supreme Court, is that where measures, public or private, are considered not to have adverse effects on trade or competition, they slip outside the area of prohibition. Once outside, no further judicial action is required to justify or exempt them.

In *Cassis de Dijon*-type jurisprudence, the Court of Justice purports to ap-

---

[49] Case 56/65, *Societe Technique Miniere v. Machinenbau Ulm* [1966] E.C.R. 235, 250; Case 258/78, *Nungesser KG v. Commission* [1982] E.C.R. 2015; Case 161/84, *Pronuptia de Paris v. Schillgalis* [1986] E.C.R. 353. See for general comment Whish, *Competition Law* (3rd ed., Butterworths, London, 1993) 208.
[50] *Pike v. Bruce Church, Inc.*, 397 U.S. 137 (1970).

ply a rule of reason, on the understanding that a state measure remains caught by the prohibition in Article 28 and requires to be justified under Article 30 or one of the mandatory requirements. This, to the writer, appears to be an incorrect understanding of the nature and purpose of a rule of reason. There should be no need to justify a measure which, if it benefits from a favourable finding under the rule of reason, ought properly to fall outside the prohibition in Article 28. Limited support for this argument may be derived from *Keck and Mithouard,* and from the EC Treaty itself, wherein it is provided that the list of "justifications" for obstacles to the free movement of goods is limited to those set out in Article 30. In EC law, the mandatory requirements cannot be treated as a set of further justifications. Their effect in law ought to be considered under a workable rule of reason.

6. A BASIC MODEL FOR ARTICLE 28'S RULE OF REASON

In Community law, all distinctly applicable rules that discriminate against imported products should be deemed illegal *per se.* They may, however, be justified under one of the heads listed in Article 30.

All indistinctly applicable rules should be considered under a rule of reason. The Court should develop a policy whereby it should consider *on a case-by-case basis* the true nature of the indistinctly applicable national measure.

The Court should be satisfied that the national measure, on its face, *in law,* applies equally to all goods, be they domestic or imported from another Member State. Once satisfied, it should classify the measure as one which is indistinctly applicable in law, and as such one that may benefit from a finding under the rule of reason.

The Court should then consider all the circumstances involving the application of the rule. In other words, the measure should be examined having regard to the economic and competitive context for application. Its effect on intra-Community trade should be examined through regard being had to the adverse effect on competition created for the imported good in the market of the Member State.

On the one hand, if the Court is satisfied that, having balanced all the issues surrounding the application of the rule against the effect, the measure discriminates *in fact* against imported products, then it should find that the measure infringes Article 28. The measure, however, may still be justified under Article 30.

On the other hand, if the Court, having regard to all the circumstances involving the application and effect of the state measure considers that it applies equally *in fact* to all domestically produced and imported products, then the Court should find that the measure does not infringe Article 28. Once the measure has been found, under the rule of reason, not to infringe Article 28, no justification under Community law is required. The rule does not infringe Community law.

7. Conclusion

A natural consequence of a Member State's reliance on a particular head of justification, be it under Article 30 or one of the mandatory requirements, is the need for positive intervention by the Community legislators to harmonise the national rules involved and to eliminate the obstacle to intra-Community trade. The practical result of *Cassis de Dijon* is that "it laid the foundations for the positive aspect of Article 28, namely that it involved not merely the prohibition of restrictions on trade between Member States, it also involved the idea of mutual acceptance of goods. That in turn was a substantial element in the revision of the Commission's approach to the harmonisation of laws and formed a central tenet of the White Paper *Completing the Internal Market* in particular as regards technical harmonisation and the approach to financial services".[51]

Identifying and treating in practice mandatory requirements as "justifications" for obstacles to the free movement of goods has allowed the Community to use *Cassis de Dijon* as one of the springboards for positive integration under Article 95 of the EC Treaty. Some of the heads of "justification" previously recognised under the so called "rule of reason" approach, like protection of the environment and protection of the consumer have now even obtained Treaty based status. While the results achieved in building the market may be lauded, it is now high time for the Court to tidy up its *Cassis de Dijon* jurisprudence and lay down some clear and precise conditions for the operation of a rule of reason which, *in law and in fact*, should be a rule a reason and not merely a disguised and blurred mechanism for the introduction by the Community judiciary of additional heads of justification in breach of the precise wording of Article 30.

---

[51] See Kapteyn and van Themaat, 628-629.

THE TAXATION OF MARRIED WOMEN
MURPHY v. ATTORNEY GENERAL (1982)

YVONNE SCANNELL*

1. INTRODUCTION

The Government is currently developing policies to encourage married women to remain in, or rejoin the work force. A shortage of skilled labour threatens the sustainability of the Celtic Tiger and married women are the only remaining indigenous source of labour. How times have changed. In 1976, only 3.5% of the workforce[1] were married women and the unemployment rate was 12.5%. This figure underestimates the true level of unemployment because most married women were not eligible for designation as unemployed at that time. In 1999, the percentage of married women in the Irish workforce is near the European average. Unemployment is a little over 4%.

There were several reasons for the low participation of married women in the workforce in the 1970's, the most important of which included the legal prohibitions on married women working in the civil service until 1973,[2] conventions and/or contractual arrangements requiring women to resign from their jobs on marriage in the private sector, lack of employment opportunities for all workers, especially women workers, a culture which disapproved strongly of married women working outside the home and not least, penal taxation of married woman who worked. This article is concerned about the last mentioned. It is the story of how tax discriminations against married women were removed in Ireland. It is a story of social reform shaped by the womens' movement and achieved by court action.

---

*Associate Professor of Law, Trinity College, Dublin.

[1] *Women and Employment in the UK, Ireland and Denmark* (EEC Commission 1974). The 1971 census stated that 39,000 married women were working but this figure included farmers or farmers' relatives working on the family farm. See *Irish Times*, April 30, 1996.
[2] This disability was removed by the Civil Service (Employment of Married Women) Act 1973.

2. THE TAXATION OF MARRIED COUPLES

2.1 Introduction

At common law, husband and wife were regarded as one person. A wife's legal personality merged with that of her husband upon marriage. So, for example, the property of a married woman vested in her husband until this rule was changed by the Married Woman's Property Acts, 1882-1907. This medieval view survived in Irish legislation particularly in legislation regulating economic rights such as taxation and social welfare entitlements. Amongst its most invidious reflections were sections 192-198 of the Income Tax Act 1967. Of these section 192 was the worst. This section provided:

> *General rule as to tax on husbands and wives.*
> **192.**—(1) Subject to the provisions of this Chapter, a woman's income chargeable to tax shall, so far as it is income for a year of assessment or part of a year of assessment during which she is a married woman living with her husband, be deemed for income tax (including sur-tax) purposes to be his income and not to be her income, but the question whether there is any income of hers chargeable to tax for any year of assessment and, if so, what is to be taken to be the amount thereof for tax purposes shall not be affected by the provisions of this subsection.
>
> (2) Any tax falling to be assessed in respect of any income which, under subsection (1), is to be deemed to be the income of a woman's husband shall, instead of being assessed on her, or on her trustee, guardian or committee, or on her executors or administrators, be assessable on him or, in the appropriate cases, on his trustee, guardian or committee, or on his executors or administrators.
>
> (3) References in this section to a woman's income include references to any such sum which, apart from this section, would fall to be included in computing her total income, and this subsection has effect in relation to any such sum notwithstanding that some enactment (including, except so far as the contrary is expressly provided, an enactment passed after the passing of this Act) requires that that sum should not be treated as income of any person other than her.

Expressed in plain English, the effect of this and other sections of the Act was that, on marriage, a married woman's income was deemed to be that of her husband and he was assessable to, and liable for, tax in respect of that income. All tax correspondence from the Revenue was addressed to the husband.[3] Tax

---

[3] Indeed, the standard tax form in 1977 carried the degrading instruction that a married woman's tax form should be filled in by her husband.

repayments on a married woman's income were payable to her husband. Married women had no privacy in respect of their financial affairs or investments. Most invidious of all, a wife's income became taxable at her husband's highest marginal rate.

In the 1970s taxation was much more onerous than it is now. For example, in 1974-5 the highest marginal tax rate was 80%! In 1975-6 it was 77%. This was reduced to 60% in the 1976-7 budget and it remained at this level until the 1990s. In addition to income tax, substantial social welfare contributions were levied on workers so that in 1975 over 90% of a married woman's income could possibly be deducted in tax and social welfare payments. If pension contributions were deducted, the figure could be higher. It was true that sections 197 and 198 of the Income Tax Act 1967 provided that married people could opt to be assessed separately for tax purposes but this would not have mitigated the overall tax burden on the couple: the section provided that the tax payable would be the same as if they had not opted for separate assessment. The only advantage of separate assessment was that it allowed for a more equitable internal distribution of the tax burden between the two partners in a marriage.

Until 1978, tax free allowances for married couples were also less favourable that for unmarried couples with the same incomes because a married couples allowance was less that the combined allowances of two unmarried people. Moreover, two unmarried cohabiting people could claim twice the mortgage interest and other reliefs available to a married couple.

2.2 Attitudes to and Effects of the Joint Taxation of Married Couples

Not unnaturally many married people, and especially many married women, resented this situation. In 1975, Ireland had the lowest percentage of women workers in the EEC and OECD countries. A study conducted by Margaret Fine Davies for the Department of Labour in 1974[4] found that the tax system was the second most important reason why married women did not engage in paid employment, the first being a desire to care for children. Dr. Fine Davies concluded that since all married women are subject to the tax situation, whereas only some have children, the tax reason would thus appear to be the greatest single overall deterrent to married women working.[5] Dr. Brendan Walsh in a study of women in employment surmised:

---

[4] Fine-Davis, *Attitudes to the Status of Women: Implications for Equal Employment Opportunity* (Report to the Department of Labour, February, 1977) (Department of Psychology, Trinity College, University of Dublin, 1977).

[5] The *Report of the Commission for the Status of Women* (Prl. 2760, 1972) 161 quoted a study by the Economic and Social Research Institute which found that 34% of working women in a non-farm sample felt that "the most helpful policy to assist married women who are interested in working would be a change in existing tax laws".

It is likely that some who are now deterred from working by the burden
of taxation at a high marginal rate, in addition to childcare etc. expenses,
would find it worthwhile to work if their tax liability were substantially
reduced.[6]

The *Report of the Commission on the Status of Women* also proposed the abolition of tax discrimination against married women stating that:

In the area of taxation, the question of the taxation of married couples is
the one which has been raised most often in the submissions received by
us and it is clearly an area in which there is a widespread sense of discrimination and grievance.[7]

The tax system therefore was demonstrably a deterrent to married women continuing in employment after marriage. It was also, although this was less de-
monstrable, a deterrent to people marrying. There was evidence that there had
been a 15% decline in the number of Irish marriages in the period 1973-8
although the number of people in their twenties had risen by 15% and although
a 30% increase in marriages could be expected.[8] Unfortunately, no surveys
had been carried out to determine why young people were not marrying at the
time. There was some anecdotal evidence that taxation was one of the main
reasons. I personally attempted to contract an illegal marriage in order to avoid
the tax penalty on marriage but the Archbishop of Dublin, John Charles
McQuaid, refused to participate in this tax avoidance scheme.[9]

In discussions on the optimal treatment of married couples in other jurisdictions, it was well recognised that a tax penalty on marriage was inappropriate in view of the general preference in most societies at the time of the
desirability of children being raised by married partners if possible.[10] By 1978,
the right to individual taxation had been granted in most OECD countries,
except Greece, Belgium and Switzerland and parts of the US. The International Fiscal Association declared at its congress in Amsterdam as far back as
1955:

---

[6] Walsh, *Women and Employment in Ireland: Results of a National Survey* (Paper No.69, ESRI, Dublin, 1973) 173.
[7] (Prl. 2760, 1970) 161.
[8] *Irish Times*, February 6, 1979.
[9] I devised a scheme whereby I would be married by a priest who would not enter the marriage in the civil register. Further research indicated that this scheme would not have succeeded but at least there would have been no public record of the nuptials!
[10] Nussbaum, "The Tax Structure and Discrimination against Working Wives" XXV *National Tax Journal* 183; Thorson, "An Analysis of the Sources of Continued Controversy over the Treatment of Family Income" XVIII *National Tax Journal* 130; Vickrey, *Agenda for Progressive Taxation* (New York, 1947) 282; Groves, *Federal Tax Treatment of the Family* (Brookings Institution, Washington, 1963) 76.

> . . .dans la grande majorité des cas, le fait du mariage n'a pa pur effet
> d'augumenter du moins dans l'immediat la capacité contributire d'époux
> jouissant l'un et l'autres de revenus personnels et qu'il est abnormal et
> malsain que le fait du mariage entraine une aggravation de la charge fis-
> cal des époux et mettre ceux-ci en état d'inferiorité fiscal *vis-à-vis* des
> manages irreguliers ou d'autres contributables vivant en commun.

It repeated this assertion at its Madrid Congress in 1972. Although joint taxation in itself was practised in some US jurisdictions Mr Justice Holmes had
stated *apropos* making a husband liable for his wife's tax in *Lucas v. Earl*[11]
that:

> Making a husband liable for the tax of a wife is an unfair burden on him
> and does not treat him equally with other citizens. The fruits are attrib-
> uted to a different tree from that on which they grew.[12]

3. THE FOUNDATION OF THE MPTRA

3.1 Background

The injustice of the taxation system as it affected married women inspired me
to research the position in other countries. This research revealed that the German, Italian and Cypriot courts had recently declared provisions similar to section 192 of the Income Tax Act 1967 unconstitutional under various articles in
their constitutions which guaranteed to protect the institution of marriage and/
or the equality of citizens. I had drafted an article for publication in the *Irish
Jurist* but then decided instead to challenge the constitutionality of sections
192-8 of the Income Tax Act 1967. At that time, I was a member of the Medico-
Legal Society, and Dr Declan Gilsenan, another member, and I, agreed to initiate an action funded by members of our respective professions affected by the
iniquitous tax. Almost simultaneously, on 1 June 1977, another group called
the Married Person's Tax Reform Association (MPTRA) was founded prior to
the 1977 general election to campaign against what became known as the Married Women's Tax. MPTRA's objective at that time was to conduct a *political*
campaign for change in the context of the forthcoming general election. A
letter from Maureen McHugh, secretary of the association, in the *Evening Press*
of 5 June 1977 invited members of the public to a meeting at the Hotel Peletier
in Harcourt Street where "representatives of the major political parties were
invited to present their policies in relation to tax inequity." The first public

---

[11] 281 U.S. 111 (1930).
[12] 281 U.S. 111, 115.

meeting of MPTRA was held in Harcourt Street on Saturday June 11. It was very well attended but no political party proved willing to commit to reforming the tax code. An *Irish Times* editorial of 13 June called for the political parties to "re-assess their policies in this area, and offer working married couples a fair deal." Declan Gilsenan and I decided to approach the MPTRA committee with a view to combining our efforts. A meeting was held in Wynne's Hotel the week after the Harcourt Street meeting. The MPTRA committee then consisted of a married couple, Mairead Ní Dubchon (Chairwoman) and Senan Ó Dubchon (PRO), both national school teachers, Maureen McHugh (secretary), a physiotherapist, and Ellen McCafferty (treasurer), a civil servant. The MPTRA committee was easily persuaded that the most effective way of meeting our joint objectives was to challenge the constitutionality of sections 192-8 but all agreed that the political campaign should also be pursued. I was co-opted to the committee as their legal adviser.

3.2 Organising the Constitutional Challenge

The process of challenging the constitutionality of sections 192-198 had to be handled carefully. Although it was theoretically possible to engage lawyers to take the case on a *pro bono* basis,[13] the committee agreed that it would be preferable to envisage paying for legal services rendered. Funds had to be raised for this. It was decided that the action would be taken on behalf of MPTRA and funded by the members of the Association who would all be required to pay a £2 membership fee and invited to contribute a sum towards legal expenses. The contribution would be refundable in whole or in part if the action succeeded.[14] The suggested contribution was 10% of the extra tax a couple was paying for the privilege of being married and a chart illustrating appropriate amounts was published. The possibility of being accused of maintenance or champerty, a possibility which inspired greater trepidation then than now, was mitigated by confining solicitations for funds to members of the Association although it was not at all certain that this strategy would succeed. In any case, MPTRA was prepared to take the consequences if it did not.[15] The committee was absolutely transparent about what it was doing in this respect. In so far as I am aware, this was the first time any Irish association or organisation had solicited funding for a constitutional action so explicitly and so publicly. The first public appeal for funds was published in the *Sunday Press* of 17 July 1977

---

[13] It is in fact very difficult to get good lawyers to take cases *pro bono*, contrary to the assertions of various members of the Bar Council from time to time. This is not to say that barristers do not donate their times and talents for the public good. They do, but *they* usually choose their cases when *they* are willing to take them.

[14] This is what happened in fact.

[15] Word was conveyed to me from a senior member of the judiciary that MPTRA was sailing very close to the wind in publicly soliciting funds for a constitutional action.

in an article written by Frances O'Rourke. It was subsequently repeated in many newspaper articles and on radio and television at every appropriate opportunity.

3.3 The Political Campaign

Needless to say, the political response to the campaign was not very encouraging. In 1977 the Women's Political Association circulated a questionnaire on the taxation of married couples to all members of the Oireachtas but only members of the Labour Party supported tax reform. Fianna Fáil, the government party, with the exception of Niall Andrews TD, was strongly against it. The only politician who gave the MPTRA wholehearted support and who joined the campaign was Senator Gemma Hussey, then an independent University member of the Senate. Surprisingly the press, particularly the *Irish Times*, was very supportive and the campaign benefited from a great deal of publicity from the very beginning. Almost all public meetings were extensively reported, even by provincial papers. Members of the committee were interviewed on radio and in the press as they worked tirelessly on the campaign addressing public meetings, writing letters, raising funds and preparing the brief for the case. No member claimed expenses for doing this. Membership of the association increased but very few paid the full contribution solicited. Fewer than 20 people paid £100 or more and those who did pay over £100 included members of the committee. The Trade Unions who had organised street marches in 1977 against excessive taxation were approached for financial and other support with disappointing results. The Irish National Teachers Organisation contributed the substantial sum of £500 at the second public meeting in the Belvedere Hotel. The Irish Nurses Organisation donated £10! The Irish Congress of Trade Unions sent nothing except a message communicated through the late Matt Griffin, general secretary of the INTO, that *their* legal advice was that the prospects for the case succeeding were remote. Fair taxation for married couples was ICTU policy at the time. With the exception of the INTO, no trade union provided any meaningful assistance to the campaign.

Fianna Fáil won the 1977 General Election. George Colley was appointed Minister for Finance. He was philosophically and personally opposed to reform. He expressed his views trenchantly on numerous occasions including in letters to the *Irish Times* on February 9 and March 7, 1978 and again on *This Week*, a popular RTÉ Sunday morning radio programme on 26 February where he debated the taxation of married women with Senator Gemma Hussey. Colley's main concern, apart from the alleged £60 million per annum which he had calculated that MPTRA demands would cost the Exchequer,[16] was that to con-

---

[16]This figure was quoted in the Dáil in response to a question from John Horgan TD. Since married women were only 3.5% of the workforce and since women generally at that time were much

cede the right to separate taxation for the "working wife" would discriminate against the non-working wife.[18] In this he had considerable public support to judge from the letter pages in the newspapers. Although its initial demands were for separate taxation for each partner in a marriage, MPTRA countered Mr Colley's objections by suggesting the adoption of income splitting, that is, a system by which *all* married couples would be taxed on all income generated by both spouses or by any one spouse as if each spouse had earned half of the total. This system can result in considerable tax saving for families with one income. It meant that *all* married couples, even those with one income, could enjoy two single persons' tax allowances and two tax bands. This suggestion was eventually adopted by Mr Colley although it discriminated against many two income married couples and single people.[18] Whatever the disadvantages of income splitting, at that particular time it would have been an enormous improvement on the existing situation and support for it deflected criticism of MPTRA.

Nevertheless, political opposition to MPTRA demands was sustained while it continued to raise funds for the constitutional case. Some members responded to muted opposition from the hierarchy, particularly Bishop McNamara in Limerick by supporting badges reading "Every Bishop a Wanted Bishop". Opposition from Fianna Fáil was particularly vehement but one particular incident ironically led to a huge increase in public support for the MPTRA. George Colley, responding to a motion from the Dublin Cabra branch of his party calling for "the removal of antiquated income tax laws pertaining to married women" at the January 1978 Fianna Fáil Árd Fhéis declared that he had "no sympathy with some well-heeled articulate married women [who] are pushing a solution to their problems which would cost £20 million a year and which would discriminate against one-income families". He told delegates that "whatever solution we find isn't going to downgrade the role of the married woman who stays at home to look after children". For months afterwards the words "well-heeled articulate" preceded references to married women in the media. MPTRA members gleefully referred to themselves by this appellation at every opportunity. The Cabra motion was defeated, but Mr Colley's ill-judged reference to the

---

worse paid than men, it was extremely unlikely that reforming the tax system could have cost this much. £60 million was over four times all the tax paid by farmers in 1977, and only £17.6 million less than the entire corporation tax paid that year. Mr Colley himself stated that there were 75,000 married women PAYE workers in 1977 (see letter to the *Irish Times,* March 3, 1978 by Rosheen Callender). Mr Colley subsequently reduced the figure to £20 million but even this figure was suspect. The citation of grossly misrepresentative figures by a respected member of the government was reprehensible and evidence of the very "low standards in high places" which Mr Colley himself had condemned in another context. See Bruce Arnold's article "Politics and Politicians: George Colley's Political Blunders" *Irish Independent,* April 4, 1978.

[17] This was the terminology Mr Colley used.

[18] See below, text with and in nn.78-82.

MPTRA campaigners had a similar effect to Padraig Flynn's reference on a popular radio programme to Mary Robinson's supposed deficiency as a mother in the 1990 Presidential elections.[19]

Mr Colley's remarks were deeply resented and they resulted in an immediate and measurable increase in MPTRA support. The Council for the Status of Women described Mr Colley's statement as "totally unjustified" and formally condemned it.[20] The Irish Housewives Association expressed itself as being "disappointed" at Mr Colley's remarks and called for the taxation of all persons as individuals and the provision of an adequate tax allowance for the married woman working in the home. It stated that each married woman should "have the choice as to whether she works at home, or outside ant that she should not be penalised in financial terms for exercising this choice".[21] The Irish Countrywomen's Association, a relatively conservative women's association, condemned Mr Colley at their winter council meeting in Killarney.[22] The press, particularly Christina Murphy in the *Irish Times* had a field day. On Sunday March 15 Mr Colley addressed a Fianna Fáil Ladies (*sic*) meeting in Dun Laoghaire, presumably in an effort to retrieve his diminishing reputation because the scheduled speaker was Dr Martin O'Donoghue. At that meeting he complained about the "emotional tone" evident in discussion of his comments and alleged that "prominent opposition supporters had seized the opportunity to attack him under the guise of organisations not linked with politics".[23] He admitted that he was referring to Gemma Hussey, an independent senator, Monica Barnes, chairwoman of the Council for the Status of Women, and Patsy Lalor, national president of the Irish Countrywomen's Association.[24] Informed that prominent Fianna Fáil members like Hillary Pratt and Dr Hazel Boland also supported tax reform, he commented that that he could only assume that they "had been misled into thinking that they are fighting for women's rights when in fact they are fighting to discriminate against the great majority of women in this country".[25] When Mr Colley's dogmatic views were publicly

---

[19]It is widely acknowledged that Mr Flynn's disparaging remarks contributed significantly to the defeat of the Fianna Fáil Presidential candidate and the election of Mary Robinson as President.

[20]*Evening Press*, January 20, 1978.

[21]*Irish Times*, February 21, 1978; *Evening Press*, March 3, 1978.

[22]*Irish Times*, February 23, 1978.

[23]"Colley hits back at his critics" *Irish Independent*, 4 March 1978. "Colley's Plan for fairer family tax", reporting on a speech by Colley to the Fianna Fáil Ladies' Club, Dun Laoghaire, *Sunday Press*, March 12, 1978; *Irish Times*, March 13, 1978.

[24]Subsequently all three women were heavily involved in Fine Gael politics but one of the reasons for this may have been that their public profiles were enhanced by the leadership they gave to the women's movement. They were attractive electoral candidates for any political party which could recruit them.

[25]See *Irish Press*, February 29, 1978.

rejected by the Fianna Fáil *ladies* in Dun Laoghaire,[26] it was clear that his vision of the role of married women was not universally shared, even in his own party. This was substantial progress for MPTRA and the women's movement.

Political realities now dictated that some concessions be made to married women. In the Finance Act 1978, the Fianna Fáil government increased the tax free allowances for all married persons to twice the single person's allowance but did not change the position with respect to marginal tax rates: a married woman would still be taxable at her husband's highest marginal tax rate. The measly £230 per annum allowance available to employed married women was not increased. This was mere tinkering with the system and was not sufficient to temper the opposition. It was suspected that doubling the tax allowances for married couples was a strategy to undermine part of the MPTRA legal case.[27] Mr Colley also announced in the Dáil that Ministerial notices were to be sent to employed married women by the Revenue notifying them that they had a right to be assessed separately for tax. There was an interesting response to these notices. Although separate assessment would not have improved the overall financial situation of any two income couple (and could have worsened that of some couples) by May 1978, nearly 5000 women in the Dublin area alone had opted for it.[28] Prior to that, only 750 wives had opted for separate assessment. This was concrete evidence that a substantial body of women wanted reform.

The Council for the Status of Women's response to Mr Colley's actions expressed disappointment that there was no change in the situation that the wife's salary is deemed to be part of her husband's salary for taxation purposes and stated that "this is the basic discrimination as it means that a wife's right to her own salary is not recognised".[29] Mairead Ní Dubchon of MPTRA declared that it would no longer rely on the political system for law reform and a that plenary summons would be lodged forthwith.[30]

On 1 March 1978, Gemma Hussey, Augustine Martin and Trevor West, all university senators, put down a motion in the Senate which read "That Seanad Éireann supports the legitimate activities of women's organisations which are seeking to redress the inequalities in the income tax code". The motion was not

---

[26]"Colley fiddles while women's tax row flares", *Hibernia* March 16, 1978. The article by Nuala Fennell reported that "Colley left the meeting, obviously angry and very upset while one woman gave him a standing ovation."

[27]The statement of claim in *Murphy* sought a declaration that the provisions of the Act were void in so far as they provided that a lower personal allowance was allowable as a deduction against taxable income in dealing with the combined incomes of husband and wife that would be allowable if they were not married to each other. Increasing the married persons allowance to twice a single person's allowance supported the argument that discriminatory taxation of married couples was justified because two income married couples could live cheaper than two single people and accordingly could afford to pay higher taxes.

[28]*Irish Times,* Editorial, May 7, 1979.

[29]*Irish Times*, February 2, 1978.

[30]*ibid.*

taken. But the momentum for tax reform increased and support came from many unexpected quarters.

On a broader economic front, other discriminations against women in the social welfare code were increasingly attracting attention. Single women and widows qualified for unemployment assistance for the first time in 1978. But married women remained ineligible for unemployment assistance. Their rights to unemployment benefits were less than the rights of all other workers: they could only claim it for a maximum of 155 days compared to a maximum of 390 days for all others. When this was raised in the Dáil, Mr Haughey, Minister for Social Welfare, "strongly"[31] advised all against taking action in the courts! But the genie was out of the bottle. An action group to do just this was established about this time and funds were openly solicited at meetings of women's organisations. The legal arguments relied on were exactly the same as those used against the taxation of married women.

By 1979, Mr Haughey had suffered a limited conversion to the notion of equality. In introducing an amendment to the Health Contributions Bill, 1978 to ensure that the incomes of a man and his wife would be treated separately for the purposes of that legislation, his stated purpose was to ensure "that neither the husband nor the wife should suffer any discrimination"![32]

3.4 Selecting Lawyers and Plaintiffs

In November 1977, MPTRA announced that it was ready to initiate legal proceedings,[33] and as the political campaign gathered momentum, the MPTRA fighting fund had increased substantially. Several solicitors were approached to take the case on a *pro bono* basis with assurances that I would do all the administrative work and briefing involved. It proved very difficult to get a solicitor to act for the Association. Eventually Alan Shatter who had been in College with me agreed to take it on the understanding that his prospects of recovering fees were remote if the case was lost. Rory O'Hanlon SC was recommended as a reputable senior counsel. Mr O'Hanlon readily and generously agreed to act for us. So also did Mary Robinson. Neither asked for fees and both appeared willing to forego any remuneration. MPTRA did indicate that we hoped to be in a position to pay modest fees. (At the time, it was naively calculated that the cost of losing the action would be about £10,000 which was the target set for the fighting fund).

So much for the lawyers. As for who the plaintiffs would be, logistical difficulties associated with bringing a representative action deterred MPTRA from doing this. Instead it was decided to search for the "ideal" plaintiffs. I

---

[31] *Dáil Reports*, April 13, 1978.
[32] *Dáil Reports*, February 21, 1979.
[33] See "Court Fight Over Wife Tax", *Evening Press* 14 November 1977. "Court Action to end Unfair Tax", *Irish Times* 15 November 1977.

could not be a plaintiff, partly because of ethical reservations about soliciting money for a case in which I would be the plaintiff, and also because many members of the public would have been unlikely to sympathise with the plight of a couple with our incomes, modest as they were. Other members of the MPTRA committee had children and were therefore deemed unsuitable plaintiffs. The ideal plaintiff, we decided, should be a childless married nurse. Nurses are very popular, many considered that they were grossly underpaid, and Article 41.2.2 of the Constitution could not be called in aid by the State if the plaintiff was not a mother. A suitable couple was found – a nurse married to a factory worker – but they lost their nerve and withdrew their offer to go forward. Considerable funds had been raised by late 1978 but it was proving impossible to find willing plaintiffs, still less ideal plaintiffs. Well into the campaign, Charlie Lennon, a member of the Teachers' Club in Parnell Square, suggested that Frank and Maura Murphy might be willing to take the case on behalf of the Association. Both were young national school teachers on modest salaries at the start of their careers. Most importantly, they were childless. Frank and Maura were approached, and they agreed to act as plaintiffs. Although they were not ideal occupationally, they were ideal in all other respects. At that stage of the campaign, it was clear that, thanks to the efforts of the Ó Dubchons and the support of the executive of the INTO, of which my father was a member, the bulk of the MPTRA support came from the teaching profession and in particular, from national teachers. Some support was also forthcoming from Women's Organisations, particularly from the members of the Women's Political Association, the Council for the Status of Women and some Fine Gael women politicians. The campaign for fair taxation for married women became a central part of the feminist agenda for the first time in 1977.[34] This was not an objective of the entire committee of the MPTRA which was anxious not to alienate male and non-feminist support, but it was one of my personal objectives although I was careful where and when I expressed it.

4. *MURPHY* IN THE COURTS

4.1 The High Court

The High Court hearing of *Murphy v. Attorney General* began on Tuesday July 10, 1979 almost exactly two years after MPTRA was founded. In the meantime, a great deal of research had been undertaken in order to brief counsel for the plaintiffs. The German and Italian cases on which they would rely were

---

[34]When the Irish Women's Liberation Movement was founded in 1970, it did not include fair taxation as one of its objectives. But by 1978, the Council for the Status of Women and the Women's Representative Council were lobbying the Minister for Finance for reform. See *Irish Times*, January 18, 1978.

translated free by the staff of the German and Italian departments in Trinity College, Dublin. The fighting fund had exceeded £10,000 but it was proving very difficult to get monetary support. Most contributions consisted of £2 donations. To our initial dismay, the Murphys had had a daughter, Orla, in early 1979, before the case was heard. This meant that the State could be expected to rely on Article 41.2 of the Constitution which could be interpreted as a constitutional preference for mothers who worked exclusively in the home. But it was too late to change plaintiffs and the case was also worth fighting for married women who had children, even if the prospects of success were somewhat diminished. The Murphys were represented by Rory O'Hanlon S.C. and Mary Robinson. The State had cautiously engaged two senior counsel, Donal Barrington S.C. and T.J. Connolly S.C., and John Cooke B.L. was the junior counsel. Mr Justice Hamilton presided. The hearing lasted a mere four days. The plaintiffs claimed:

- an order declaring that the provisions of sections 192 and 193 of the Income Tax Act 1967, as amended, was unconstitutional in so far as they provide that the income of a married woman living with her husband is deemed to be his income for income tax proposes and not to be her income,
- a declaration that the provisions of the Act are void in so far as they provide that a lower personal allowance is to be allowable as a deduction against taxable income in dealing with the combined incomes of husband and wife that would be allowable if they were not married to each other,
- an order declaring the provisions of the Act which give rise to an obligation on the part of a husband or wife in the circumstances referred to make returns concerning the income of the other party are repugnant to the constitution and
- a declaration that they are entitled to be assessed separately in each year for income tax purposes and entitled to make separate returns and entitled to the same reliefs and exemptions as if each of them was a single person and to have the rates of tax payable by them determined by reference to the income of each separately without aggregating their incomes for that purpose, and
- a declaration that each is liable only to make returns and payments in respect of his or her own separate income.

The plaintiffs relied in particular on the equality clause in Article 40.1 of the Constitution,[37] on Article 40.3 whereby the State guarantees in its laws to re-

---

[35] Article 40.1 provides:
   All citizens shall, as human persons, be held equal before the law.

spect, and, as far as practicable, by its laws to defend and vindicate the personal rights of the citizen, on Article 41.3 where the State pledges itself to guard with special care the institution of Marriage, on which the Family is founded, and to protect it against attack, and on Article 42.1 where the State acknowledges the Family as the primary and natural educator of the child and guarantees to respect the inalienable right and of parents to provide according to their means for the education of their children.

In court most reliance was placed on Article 41.3 because this was considered the strongest argument and it was deemed strategically easier to persuade the courts that the tax legislation represented a failure to protect the institution of marriage than to establish that it constituted sex discrimination which they had hitherto shown a very marked reluctance to declare unconstitutional. The main factual arguments advanced were that deeming a married woman's income to be that of her husband violated her right to equality before the law and to privacy in her financial affairs; that making her husband liable for her tax returns and payments violated his right to equality; that making it cheaper for a couple to "live in sin" than to get married undermined the institution of marriage, provided an incentive not to marry and failed to protect the family in its constitution and authority and that it discriminated against the family by detracting from the ability of parents to provide according to their means for the education and upbringing of their children. By way of illustration, the plaintiffs showed that a couple each earning £6000 per annum would have saved £1028 in 1978-9 by not getting married.[36] The plaintiffs themselves had paid an extra £512.70 in 1979 for the privilege of being married.

Precedents from Germany, Italy and Cyprus were relied on for the first time in Irish legal history.[37] In *Argiris Mikrommatis v. Republic of Cyprus*[38] the Cypriot Supreme Court declared unconstitutional section 19 of the Income Tax Law CAP323, a provision substantially the same as section 192 of the Irish Income Tax Act 1967, because it stated that in a situation where a married woman was not able, through the application of section 19 to enjoy, to the same extent as any married man, the income from her own labour "a married woman is placed in a disadvantageous position *vis-à-vis* a married man in the same occupation, trade or business. Such differentiation is not a reasonable distinction based on the intrinsic nature of the marriage nor is it otherwise

---

This shall not be held to mean that the State shall not in its enactments have due regard to differences in capacity, physical and moral, and of social function.

[36]   They would have to earn an extra £2,070 to make up this deficiency. The penalty on marriage was therefore £2,070 in this instance because the couple would have to earn that gross amount to gain a tax free £1,028. This was a considerable sum in 1978

[37] Kelly, "Equality Before the Law in Three European Jurisdictions" (1983) XVIII *Ir. Jur. (n.s.)* 259.

[38] (1961) 2 RSCC 125.

justified." The court held that section 19 amounted to a discrimination on the grounds of sex contrary to Article 28 of the Cypriot Constitution.[39]

In the *Valentini Libiana*[40] case in Italy, the *Corte Constituzionale* (Constitutional Court) held that the combined taxation of married couples discriminated against women because "combined income taxation does not encourage women to look for employment outside the family circle and this prevents the family from acquiring a modern structure in keeping with modern times, and prevents women from acquiring their rightful and autonomous place in society and achieving the economic independence which would allow them to be self-supporting in case of separation and divorce." The court found that combined taxation was contrary to the principle of equality of citizens of the State (Article 3 of the Constitution) and more specifically contrary to equality in marriage (Article 29 of the Constitution) in that taxation of combined incomes, as far as the wife is concerned, perpetuates the notion that she is her husband's property and this is incompatible with the social dignity of equal partners in marriage. (Article 29 of the Constitution). The court also held that "due to combined income taxation the family, as such, has to pay more income tax than an unmarried couple with the same jobs and income and this is obviously unfair and unconstitutional (contrary to Article 31 of the Constitution). It is damaging to the institution of marriage and it encourages cohabitation *more uxorio*".

The German Constitution also contained equality articles and articles guaranteeing to protect the institution of marriage. It most resembled the Irish Constitution.[41] In Germany also, the *Bundesverfassungsgericht* (Federal

---

[39] Article 28 reads as follows:
1. All persons are equal before the law, the administration and justice and are entitled to equal protection thereof and treatment thereby.
2. Every person shall enjoy the rights and liberties provided by this Constitution without any direct or indirect discrimination against any person on the ground of his community, race, religion, language, sex, political or other convictions, national or social decent, birth, colour, wealth, social class or any other ground whatsoever, unless there is express provision in this Constitution.

[40] Case No. 179/1976 (July 14, 1976). Article 3 of the Italian Constitution provides:
All citizens are invested with equal social status and are equal before the law, without distinction of sex, race, language, religion, political opinions and personal or social conditions.
Article 29 provides:
The State recognises the family as the natural association founded on marriage.
Marriage is based on moral and legal equality of husband and wife, within the limits laid down by the laws for ensuring family unity.
Article 31 provides:
The Republic facilitates, by means of economic and other provisions, the formation of the family and the fulfilment of the tasks connected therewith, with particular consideration for large families.
It safeguards maternity, infancy and youth, promoting and encouraging institutions necessary for such purposes.

[41] Article 3 of the Federal Constitution 1949 states:
1. All person shall be equal before the law.

Constitutional Court) had declared the combined taxation of married couples which penalised marriage unconstitutional[42] because it constituted a failure to protect marriage and the family contrary to Article 6 of the Constitution.

Only two expert witnesses were called by the plaintiffs, an accountant on the effects of the tax code on working married couples, and Dr Miriam Moore, a psychologist and author of a doctoral thesis on the effects on children of married women working outside the home. Dr Moore gave evidence that the fact that a mother worked outside the home was not detrimental to a marriage relationship or to the welfare of children. Both experts gave their evidence in less than an hour. The State did not call any expert witnesses.

The State's rebuttal was less than impressive. One suspected that it was reserving its best arguments for the inevitable Supreme Court appeal. As expected, its main case was based on Article 41.2 which provides:

1. In particular, the State recognises that by her life in the home, woman gives to the State a support without which the common good cannot be achieved.
2. The State shall therefore endeavour to ensure that mothers shall not be obliged by economic necessity to engage in labour to the neglect of their duties in the home.

It was an ancient and anachronistic argument. The thesis was that the social function of married women envisaged in the Constitution justified the treatment provided for in the Income Tax Act. Accordingly, legislative policy to confine women to the home was justifiable: that is their social function and a law which encourages this cannot be unconstitutional.

Judgment was delivered by Hamilton J. on October 12, 1978.[43] The High Court held that neither spouse had a constitutional right to privacy in respect of his or her income because the Constitution did not guaranteed this. (Nobody had alleged that it did guarantee this). The court appeared to hold that the obligation on spouses to reveal their incomes to each other was justified because of the special status of married couples and that the disclosure obligation

---

2. Men and women shall have equal rights.

3. No one may be either privileged or put at a disadvantage on account of his sex, his descent, his race, his language, his home and place of origin, his faith or his religious or political opinions.

Article 6 provides:.

1. Marriage and the family shall enjoy the special protection of the State.

2. The care and upbringing of children are a natural right of, and a duty primarily incumbent on, the parents.

The national community shall watch over their endeavours in this respect.

3. Every mother shall be entitled to the protection and care of the community.

[42] Case No.9 of 1957.

[43] [1982] I.R. 241 (H.C., Hamilton J.; and S.C.).

was justified in the interests of the common good, though the judgment did not say how the common good required this. The plaintiffs' arguments that section 138 of the Income Tax Act (under which tax free allowances for married couples were less than for two single people with the same incomes) was unconstitutional were dismissed apparently on the grounds that two can live more cheaply than one[44] and because the discrimination against them was justified by the differences in social function between a married couple and two unmarried people living together. No reasons were proffered as to what the difference in social function between married and unmarried couples was, or why the difference could justify treating the former *less* favourably. On the main argument – that the joint taxation of married persons was unconstitutional because of the extra taxation involved – after referring to US, German and Italian precedents, the court held that section 192 of the Income Tax 1967 was unconstitutional because "it was contrary to the principle of individual taxation of an individual's income".[45] It also held that since the aggregation of incomes applied only to married couples living together and in no other circumstances, it discriminated against married persons because it rendered them liable to pay more tax than other persons. Consequently, sections 192-198(1) of the Income Tax Act were declared unconstitutional having regard to the provisions of Article 41 of the Constitution. They were also declared unconstitutional having regard to the principles of Article 40.1 "as they discriminate invidiously against married couples, and the husband in particular, and cannot be justified on any ground".[46]

While this judgement left questions unanswered, it was a tremendous victory for the Murphys because the combination of their incomes making them liable to pay more tax than any unmarried couple was deemed to be a violation of Articles 41 and 40.1.

The judgement was widely welcomed in all the newspapers. One of the few grudging comments appeared in an *Irish Press* editorial of 13 October but the *Irish Press* had long been associated with Fianna Fáil interests and this was not surprising. The State appealed. (This is a reprehensible State practice when it is expensive to implement the law in a constitutional manner. Justice delayed represents a considerable saving for the Exchequer and it matters not to the State that this is also justice denied.) Hamilton J. stayed his order pending a Supreme Court appeal.

---

[44]Hamilton J. stated that ". . . the legislature is entitled to take into consideration the fact that when a husband and wife are living together certain expenditure is common to both" ([1982] I.R. 241, 267). In fact no evidence to this effect had been given and if the social function of married couples was deemed relevant it surely justified granting them *larger* allowances than single people because they were the basis of a family unit and would normally have child rearing expenses.

[45][1982] I.R. 241, 274.

[46]*ibid.*

4.2 The Supreme Court

Funding was less of a problem for MPTRA after the High Court victory. About £30,000 had been raised by the time of the Supreme Court hearing. MPTRA considered then that this was sufficient to cover all costs, even if the appeal succeeded.[47] To its dismay, Rory O'Hanlon S.C. was obliged to withdraw from the case as he was appearing in the lengthy Whiddy Island Tribunal. Word came that the State had briefed Frank Murphy SC to appear as a *third* Senior Counsel for the Supreme Court appeal. It was obviously worried because the convention was to employ only one or two seniors in constitutional cases.

MPTRA engaged two senior counsel for the Supreme Court appeal because of the heavyweight opposition. Alan Shatter briefed Kevin Liston SC, then the father of the bar. I felt that Mr Liston, a somewhat remote person with fixed views on the lawyer/client relationship (!) would not be philosophically attuned to the feminist undertones of the case but this proved to be a great advantage as he was adept at addressing the all-male Supreme Court in terms which they understood. The second senior counsel chosen was Dermot Gleeson S.C. Mr Gleeson had recently taken silk and was the youngest Senior Counsel in the history of the State since Isaac Butt. He had taught Constitutional Law in University College, Cork and was considered one of the finest lawyers of his generation. As in the High Court, Mary Robinson was the junior counsel. It was implicit that Dermot Gleeson and Mary Robinson were acting *pro bono* but MPTRA was prepared to pay Mr Liston's fees, if requested.[48] Mr Liston did not request any fees.

The State's case in the Supreme Court was much better argued than in the High Court. It justified the discriminations on the grounds of sex and marital status under Article 40.1 on the basis that the State was entitled to treat married couples differently because of differences of capacity and social function. However, the State did not provide any reasoned arguments as to what these differences were or how they could justify not only different treatment but treatment which places married couples in a position less favourable than that of unmarried couples. Giving married couples a tax free allowance less than that available to an unmarried couple was justified, argued the State "in as much as a wife ought not lightly to be encouraged to risk the neglect of what is normally her primary obligation – the care of her home and family".[49] The State also argued that the combined taxation of married couples did not fail to protect the institution of marriage because it was balanced by the other benefits which had been conferred on them under fiscal and other legislation which treated them

---

[47] In this we were very much mistaken as it transpired that it would barely have covered our own solicitors' costs!

[48] I learned afterwards that Mr Liston had taken great pride in being involved in *Murphy* and feel that he must also have been prepared to act *pro bono*.

[49] [1982] I.R. 241, 276.

much more favourably than unmarried couples. Examples of compensatory benefits given were the Capital Acquisitions Tax Act 1976, the Capital Gains Tax Act 1975, and the Finance Act 1975, which exempted married people from stamp duty on the transfer of land. (Most of this last mentioned legislation could only have been availed of by the relatively rich at that time). Provisions in the Succession Act 1965, the Family Home Protection Act 1976, the Family Law (Maintenance of Spouses and Children) Act 1976, were also described as leaving a married couple "by virtue of their social function, in a financially more advantageous position than two single individuals in receipt of identical incomes".[50]

Mr Gleeson robustly countered that it was not an answer to say that unconstitutionality in one part of the legislative code could be excused by a preference shown to married couples in another part: it had not been shown that under any other legislation £512.75[51] had flowed back into the Murphys' pockets in the past year. He stated that it was "small consolation for the large number of income-dependent families to be told that families especially well-endowed were being constitutionally treated" and that "if 20 advantages favoured married couples and a 21st discriminated against them and was not constitutional, the matter would not be salvaged by the applicability of the other 20 statutes".[52]

The Supreme Court judgment was delivered by Mr Justice Kenny on January 25, 1980. It was a single judgment. The judgment appeared to go against the plaintiffs until Mr Justice Kenny read the last nine lines. While the court accepted that in 1979 the assessment to income tax on a husband in respect of his wife's earnings "is not easy to justify"[53] it did not declare this unconstitutional. It expressly overruled Hamilton J.'s decision in so far it related to the principle of individual taxation on an individual's income on the basis that such a principle did not exist in Irish income tax legislation nor had it been acknowledged by any Irish court.[54] These were unconvincing reasons for finding that a husband should not be civilly and criminally liable in respect of his wife's tax liabilities. The very point of the case was to raise this issue, for the first time, before the courts. It would have been difficult for other courts to acknowledge a principle of individual taxation when they had never been invited to do so. The court itself admitted that making a husband liable for his wife's tax "was not easy to justify".

The Supreme court held that the inequality for income tax purposes between married couples living together on the one hand, and separated married

---

[50] *ibid.*
[51] This was the amount the Murphys paid in extra tax because they happened to be married.
[52] *Irish Times*, December 13, 1979.
[53] [1982] I.R. 241, 283.
[54] [1982] I.R. 241, 284 overruling [1982] I.R. 241, 274 (above, n.45).

couples or unmarried couples living together on the other, was justified by "the particular social function under the Constitution of married couples living together"[55] and that, having regard to the second paragraph of Article 40.1, an inequality will not be set aside as being repugnant to the constitution "if any state of facts exists which may reasonably justify it".[56]

While the court's meaning is not very clear, it appears that the "state of facts" which apparently justified treating married couples unfavourably under Article 40.1 was that the law made many (unquantified) favourable discriminations in their favour. It is pertinent to observe that the effect of this ruling was that it was permissible to tax the earned income of all married couples at a penal rate throughout their lives primarily because they could *possibly* avail of double the normal allowances if liable to capital gains tax and could transfer assets to each other without attracting liability for capital acquisition taxes or stamp duty! This is how the disadvantages of the discriminatory tax was were "balanced" by the Supreme Court.

The Supreme Court distinguished US, German and Italian precedents because of alleged differences between the various constitutional provisions involved. The Irish Constitution, the court held,[57] did not provide for "due process" in the sense in which it was applied in the US under the Fourteenth Amendment in *Hoepfer v. Tax Commission of Wisconsin*.[58] The German Constitution had, it said,[59] no clause like Article 41.2 of the Irish Constitution. Likewise, it said that the Italian Constitution had no clause similar to Article 40.1.2 of the Irish Constitution and that Article 29 was "quite different"[60] to Article 41 of the Irish Constitution. It considered that the Cypriot decision was based on different grounds to those argued in *Murphy* so that it had little or no relevance to the application of Article 40.1 in *Murphy*.

The failure to condemn double taxation and making a husband liable for his wife's unpaid tax under Article 40.1 was widely criticised in the academic literature. In an article in the *Irish Jurist*,[61] the late Professor John Kelly, at that time the foremost authority on Irish Constitutional Law, observed that equality before the law is guaranteed in the German and Italian constitutions in an identical phrase and that the Irish formula was exactly matched in the Italian and German texts. While the German and Italian constitutions, unlike the Irish one,

---

[55] [1982] I.R. 241, 283.
[56] [1982] I.R. 241, 283.
[57] *ibid.*
[58] 282 U.S. 206 (1931). In that case a majority of the U.S. Supreme Court held that the assessment of a husband to tax on his wife's income violated the due process clause in the Fourteenth Amendment.
[59] [1982] I.R. 241, 285.
[60] *ibid.*
[61] Kelly, "Equality Before the Law in Three European Jurisdictions" (1983) XVIII *Ir. Jur. (n.s.)* 259.

recite a number of criteria on which discrimination is specifically prohibited, this, he stated, is to be explained by the "anxiety to close a historical chapter of which the Second World War was the climax and in which official discrimination had been the basis from which unique horrors emerged: and on the Irish side, by the fact that some, at least of these specific types of discrimination are prohibited elsewhere in the constitution in settings which are more appropriate".[62] Professor Kelly pointed out that although the Italian Constitution differed from the Irish in reciting in association with the equality guarantee, a precept of social solidarity and progress, very similar objectives are prescribed in Article 45 (Directive Principles of Social Policy) of the Irish Constitution. And he stated that although Article 40.1 contained a qualification on the rights to equality, all it was doing was expressing "in summary form some fairly self-evident principles which . . . the German and Italian courts did not take long to establish in the course of judicial interpretation".[63] Professor Kelly's thesis was that there was no justification for the differences identified by the Supreme Court. In the next edition of his classic text, *The Irish Constitution,* Professor Kelly caustically observed that "to use a difference in social function, where the quality of the difference is acknowledged to be one expressly supported by the State, as the basis for less rather than more favourable treatment, verges on the eccentric".[64]

With respect to the arguments based on Article 41, the court accepted "the proposition that the State has conferred many revenue, social and other advantages and privileges on married couples and their children"[65] but continued:

> Nevertheless, the nature and potentially progressive extent of the burden created by s.192 of the Act of 1967 is such that, in the opinion of the Court, it is a breach of the pledge by the State to guard with special care the institution of marriage and to protect it against attack. Such a breach is, in the view of the court, not compensated for or justified by such advantages and privileges.[66]

Again, the court did not explain precisely how the State had broken its pledge to guard with special care the institution of marriage. When, in *Muckley v.*

---

[62](1983) XVIII *Ir. Jur.* (*n.s.*) 259, 261-262. Professor Kelly referred to Article 16.3 (no sex discrimination in laws disqualifying from Dáil candidacy or franchise); Article 40.6.2 (no political, religious or class discrimination in laws regulating the rights of association and assembly); Article 44.2.3.4 (no religious discrimination generally, or in the provision of State support for schools).
[63](1983) XVIII *Ir. Jur.* (*n.s.*) 259, 262.
[64]Kelly, *The Irish Constitution* (2nd ed., Jurist Publishing, Dublin, 1984) 456; see now Hogan and Whyte *Kelly: The Irish Constitution* (3rd ed., Butterworths, Dublin, 1994) 729.
[65][1982] I.R. 241, 287.
[66]*ibid.*

Attorney General,[67] a case which arose consequential on *Murphy*, the State submitted that *Murphy* was based on the court's acceptance that the unconstitutionality of sections 192-198 was because these sections constituted an inducement to couples not to get married, or if married, to separate,[68] the Supreme court stated that this was "to misunderstand the essential basis" of its decision in *Murphy*, which was that the invalid sections "penalised the married state".[69]

The quality of court's reasoning would certainly not justify the inclusion of *Murphy* in *Leading Cases of the Twentieth Century*. It can only be surmised that the five member court was divided on the basis on which to make its decision and that the judges had great difficulty in agreeing the reasons for the decision. Indeed, a reading of the judgment suggests that the decision of a majority to find for the plaintiffs was made at a very late stage and it has been speculated that one judge changed his mind at the last moment.

The Supreme Court order declared sections 192 to 198 of the Income Tax Act 1967 repugnant to the Constitution and sent the matter back to the High Court to deal with the accounts and to determine the dates from which the *Murphy* judgment was to take effect. These were matters the High Court had reserved to itself when judgment was given on October 10, 1978.

5. THE AFTERMATH

The Supreme Court decision was widely, but not universally, welcomed. Comments criticising the Supreme Court emanated from Parliamentary sources and were published in the press.[70] The Attorney General disassociated himself (but not those who made them) from these on January 31 when he requested the Supreme court "to speak to the minutes" of the order it had made and to rule on whether the decision ought to operate prospectively or retrospectively, and if retrospectively, whether it should apply from the date of the High Court judgment or from the date of the Supreme Court judgement.[71] The Attorney General stressed the urgency of the matter in view of the forthcoming budget which was scheduled for February 28. This type of application was virtually unprecedented. An aura of panic and unreality accompanied the application and the impression was conveyed that the Supreme Court was responsible for a national crisis.

---

[67] [1985] I.R. 472; [1986] I.L.R.M. 364 (H.C., Barrington J.; and S.C.).
[68] [1985] I.R. 472, 484; [1986] I.L.R.M. 364, 372.
[69] [1985] I.R. 472, 485; [1986] I.L.R.M. 364, 372.
[70] *Irish Press*, January 31, 1980: *Irish Times*, January 31, 1980.
[71] *Irish Times*, February 1, 1980.

The issue of retrospectivity had not been addressed in arguments before any court although it was one which had occurred to MPTRA which had made model summonses available and advised its members of the desirability of lodging these on their own behalf. The State was well aware of this because some members, including the Ó Dubchons, had lodged individual summonses. The Supreme Court had sent the matter of the accounts which would involve a determination of the date from which the Murphys were entitled to pay the same tax as single people back to the High Court which had reserved judgment on this matter when it made its judgment. But the Attorney General was asking the Supreme Court to tell the High Court how it should determine the matter!

All members of the Supreme Court, except Mr Justice Henchy, allowed the Attorney General's application although some considered that it would be impossible to give judgment by February 28. Mr Justice Henchy, dissenting on this point, would have declined the application holding that the Constitution provides, in Article 34, that a matter of first instance should be decided in the High Court and the Supreme Court by taking seisin of this matter would deprive the plaintiffs of their right to appeal the High Court decision to the Supreme Court.[72] The Chief Justice, Mr Justice Griffin and Mr Justice Kenny referred to previous instances when the Supreme Court had acceded to similar requests but did not cite any authorities for this in their decisions. It is difficult to escape the conclusion that the decision to allowing the application was unprecedented. The hearing on retrospectivity was scheduled for February 12.

On April 25, the Supreme Court held by a majority that sections 192 to 198 of the Income Tax Act 1967 were invalid from the date of their enactment.[73] Giving the lead judgment on this issue, Henchy J. held that in the absence of countervailing circumstances, the overpaid taxes were recoverable[74] "as money exacted *colore officii*, for the nature of PAYE collection of income tax is such that in the relevant period the plaintiff's salaries were subject to compulsory deduction by their employers of the income tax which was eligible under the now condemned statutory provisions. The payments were, therefore, involuntary to the point of being compulsory collections".[75] However, to this cause of action in restitution, Henchy J. held that the Government could rely upon a generous application of the defence of change of position, which had the effect of limiting the Murphy's claims and would have the effect of defeating most of the other claims which could have arisen from the unconstitutionality of sec-

---

[72] Article 34.4.1 of the Constitution states that "The Court of Final Appeal shall be called the Supreme Court."

[73] See *e.g.*, [1982] I.R. 241, 313, 324 *per* Henchy J. (Parke J. concurring), 331 *per* Griffin J., 333 *per* Kenny J.; *cf.* 300 *per* O'Higgins C.J. dissenting.

[74] [1982] I.R. 241, 316.

[75] [1982] I.R. 241, 317; see 331 *per* Griffin J. and 336 *per* Parke J. concurring; *cp.* 336 *per* Kenny J.; *cf.* 302 *per* O'Higgins C.J.: "Thus a payment may be voluntary although it is made unwillingly".

tions 192-198,[76] though the claims of other married couples would depend on the circumstances of each case.

Section 18 of the Finance Act 1980 provided for a new method of assessment to income tax for married persons for the year 1980, a system which still survives. The Act introduced a system for assessing married couples for taxation on their incomes as if they were single persons if they so wished and it provided that each spouse should be entitled to the same allowances and tax reliefs as if they were single persons from the tax year 1980-1 onwards. But section 20 provided that married couples could not recover tax paid or receive any credit for taxes paid unless, prior to the year 1989/80, they had instituted proceedings challenging the constitutionality of the 1967 Act.

Section 21 of the Finance Act 1980 purported to enable the Revenue to collect any arrears of unpaid taxes from working married couples under the old regime. The tax payable was to be calculated as if sections 192-8 had not been declared unconstitutional. In *Muckley v. Attorney General*[77] the Supreme Court foiled this manoeuvre and held section 21 unconstitutional. This was the correct decision although it had the effect of rewarding noncompliant taxpayers liable for arrears of tax and of penalising those who had paid their taxes on time.

After *Murphy*, several other sex discriminations were declared unconstitutional. In March 1984, in *O'G v. Attorney General*,[78] provisions in Adoption Act 1974, discriminating against a married man was expressly found to be repugnant to Article 40.1 of the Constitution. Although *Murphy* was not relied on, it may be surmised that negative reactions to the Supreme Court's failure in *Murphy* to condemn a sex discrimination under Article 40.1 must have helped to dissolve judicial reluctance to rely on it to condemn sex discriminations. Discriminations against married couples in social welfare legislation, which in practice impacted more severely on women than on men, were declared unconstitutional in *Hyland v. Minister for Social Welfare*[79] and *Healy v. Eastern Health Board*.[80] In *Hyland* a provision in the Social Welfare Act 1985, which provided that where each partner in a marriage was in receipt of social welfare and one or both was also in receipt of unemployment assistance, the combined income of both should be the same after the implementation of Directive 76/207/EEC[81] as it was prior to its implementation was declared unconstitutional on the grounds that this constituted a failure to protect the institution of mar-

---

[76][1982] I.R. 241, 317-321; see O'Dell "Bricks and Stones and the Structure of the Law of Restitution" (1998) 20 *D.U.L.J. (n.s.)* 101, 141-152.

[77][1985] I.R. 472; [1986] I.L.R.M. 364.

[78][1985] I.L.R.M. 61 (H.C.).

[79][1989] I.R. 624: [1990] I.L.R.M. 213 (H.C.).

[80]High Court, unreported, March 11, 1978.

[81]Directive 76/207/EEC on the implementation of equal treatment for men and women as regards access to employment, vocational training and promotion and working conditions.

riage. The effect of the section was to put married couples at a disadvantage to two cohabiting single people. Likewise in *Healy*, Keane J. in the High Court held that the State was not entitled to limit a wife's disability payments in an attempt to ensure that the family income of both partners did not exceed the amount which would have been payable to the wife if her husband and children had been regarded as her dependants for social welfare purposes. In both these cases, the High Court, relying on *Murphy*, extended the spirit of Directive 76/207/EEC by relying on Article 41 of the Constitution. The result is that, as Whyte observes, although the Directive only proscribes discrimination based on marital status where such discrimination is a disguised form of sex discrimination, Article 41 of the Constitution prohibits discrimination based on marital status where this impacts adversely on a married claimant *vis-à-vis* his or her single counterpart.[82] The practical difference is that may be easier to obtain a remedy for discrimination in some cases under the Irish Constitution than under European Law.

6. CONCLUSIONS

The selection of leading cases of a century is inevitably both a subjective and an objective exercise. Looking back twenty years later, *Murphy* is a leading case because of the profound legal, social and political changes which it engendered. It was the most important milestone on the road to securing the judicial recognition of equality before the law for women in Ireland. It secured the elimination of all the major economic discriminations in Irish fiscal legislation against married women, it vindicated their rights to work outside the home[83] and it set the stage for *O'G v. Attorney General* – the case in which sex discrimination was finally declared unconstitutional. Although the Supreme Court distinguished the cases from other European jurisdictions, it is tempting to speculate that their moral authority did influence its decision and, even if it did not, *Murphy* illustrated how much the Irish Constitution has in common with other European Constitutions, a lesson which had not previously been attempted. *Murphy* was the first case in Irish law where decisions from European jurisdictions outside the common law system were relied upon.[84] It has been relied on in at least 66 cases since it was delivered.[85]

---

[82]Whyte, "Council Directive 79/7/EEC in Ireland" in Whyte, (ed.), *Sex Equality, Community Rights and Irish Social Welfare Law* (I.C.E.L., Dublin, 1988) 39, 52-53.

[83]It is one of the reasons why married women in Ireland now constitute almost 20% of the workforce, a percentage which approaches the European average.

[84]The author modestly suggests that this case provides an excellent illustration of the role of the academic lawyer in advancing jurisprudence as few practitioners at that time would have had the time and facilities to uncover such apposite precedents in non common law jurisdictions.

[85]LEXIS search, May 5, 2000.

Murphy was also important in that it provided a focus for the women's movement in the late1970s, a focus which strengthened and united many Irish women in a common endeavour. It demonstrated the futility of the political technique of attempting to divide women against each other and of endeavouring to maintain political support by introducing a distracting "envy factor" into the debate. When the occasions demanded,[86] even those women's associations unlikely to be characterised as feminist at that time supported the rights of their sisters to equitable taxation.[87] The case is unique in that it was the first time constitutional rights were won by citizen action in the courts openly funded by donations which had been publicly and widely solicited. It also changed the language spoken in Ireland: since *Murphy* it is has become politically incorrect to describe a full-time home maker as a *non-working* wife. She is now commonly, and correctly, referred to a woman who works in the home. More deference is paid, albeit not yet economically, to her contribution to society. Unlikely supporters of women's' rights have emerged in the farming community where farms are now described as *family* farms because of the tax and other advantages the marital status of farmers attracts consequent upon *Murphy*. Perhaps most important of all, despite the limitations in its reasoning, *Murphy* is one of the great examples of how our courts, albeit mostly male and mostly conservative males, have upheld the Constitution, even when, and *especially* when, it was politically and economically unpopular to do so.

7. POSTSCRIPT: WHERE ARE THEY NOW?

Rory O'Hanlon S.C. later became a High Court judge and President of the Law Reform Commission. Mary Robinson later became President of Ireland and is now U.N. High Commissioner for Human Rights. Dermot Gleeson served as Attorney General. Frank Murphy is now a judge of the Supreme Court. Donal Barrington has recently retired from the Supreme Court; he was Ireland's first judge of the European Court of First Instance and was succeeded by John Cooke.

As to the MPTRA and the plaintiffs, Mairead Ní Dubchon is now a Labour Party politician. Gemma Hussey became a Government Minister. The Murphys separated soon after winning the case.

---

[86]Particularly after Mr Colley's speeches to the Fianna Fáil Árd Fhéis and the Dun Laoghaire Fianna Fáil Ladies Association.

[87]Their support was rewarded because income splitting ultimately conferred significant tax advantages on one-income married couples, advantages which are currently being re-assessed in the interests of inducing married women who work exclusively in the home back to paid work.

STILL SPEAKING WITH A FORKED TONGUE?
STREET V. MOUNTFORD (1985)

GERWYN LL. H. GRIFFITHS[*]

1. Defining Terms

Not 'great' cases, not 'famous' cases, but 'leading' cases. This apparently in-nocuous choice of adjective does, in fact, present a double-edged sword. That it gives flexibility cannot be denied – The Oxford Dictionary proffers no less than thirty seven meanings of the word – but all too easily this can also result in muddled terms of reference and consequent lack of focus.

In order to avoid these pitfalls, this paper adopts the following criteria which, it is suggested, provide an appropriate (albeit not definitive) yardstick by which a 'leading' case may be identified.

First among these is the immediate background to the decision. If a state of affairs exists which causes major concern or necessitates urgent judicial clari-fication, it is clear that an authoritative decision in this area will be of great significance.

Second, that the definition is not confined to cases which effect radical change. A return to orthodoxy or the undoing of a judicial heresy are equally worthy of being so described.

Third and of major significance, that the judgment or judgments, together with the analysis and reasoning therein, are logical, structured and proceed upon the basis of comprehensive consideration of all relevant, existing law.

Fourth, that the decision has provided and continues to provide a founda-tion for subsequent development and application of the law in the area in ques-tion. This will, inevitably, be closely linked to the third criterion in that principles established in the decision itself may be further refined and articulated in later cases.

Last, in the context of a collection of essays published in Ireland, the ques-tion of the relevance of a decision emanating from the courts in England and Wales must be addressed. As one writer has observed, not only has the concept of leasehold ownership played a central role in Irish history[1] but the existence or otherwise of a lease is an issue which has long exercised judicial minds on

[*]Senior Lecturer in Law and Head of Legal Research, the University of Glamorgan. The author wishes to thank Professor John Wylie for his comments on an earlier draft. All errors and omis-sions do, of course, remain those of the author alone.

both sides of the Irish Sea. Furthermore – and notwithstanding the view expressed by Kenny J. in *Gatien Motor Co. Ltd. v. Continental Oil Co. of Ireland Ltd.*[2] – while the existence of section 3 of the Landlord and Tenant Law Amendment Act Ireland Act 1860 (Deasy's Act)[3] does mean that there are significant differences within this area of the law, there are also instructive parallels and similarities.

It is in the light of all these criteria that the decision of the House of Lords in *Street v. Mountford*,[4] dealing as it does with the lease-licence distinction and the primacy of exclusive possession as a determinant thereof, now falls for consideration.

2. THE BACKGROUND

In Ireland, arguably influenced by section 3 of Deasy's Act and its insistence that the foundation of the landlord and tenant relationship is "the express or implied contract of the parties", great emphasis is placed upon the intention of the parties in ascertaining the existence of a lease and such an approach can be illustrated by numerous decisions. Indeed, as Henchy J. put it in *Irish Shell and BP Ltd v. Costello (No. 2)*:[5]

> in all cases it is a question of what the parties intended, and it is not permissible to apply an objective test which would impute to the parties an intention which they never had.

In contrast, in England and Wales, it was almost axiomatic that the right to exclusive possession, unless explicable on grounds such as freehold or copyhold ownership, led to the finding of a lease rather than a mere personal licence. If rent was paid, then the tenancy so created was categorised as periodic. If not, then a tenancy at will would result.[6] Thus, in the closing years of the nineteenth century, in *Lynes v. Snaith*,[7] Lawrence J. could say with complete justification:

---

[1] Wylie, *Irish Land Law* (3rd ed., Butterworths, Dublin, 1997) 899.

[2] [1979] I.R. 406 (S.C.) 420, in this respect rejecting counsel's argument that the law of the Republic of Ireland in this area differed from that in England and Wales.

[3] For a detailed discussion of the section, see Wylie, *Landlord and Tenant Law* (2nd ed., Butterworths, Dublin, 1998) 22-36.

[4] [1985] A.C. 809 (H.L.).

[5] [1984] I.R. 511 (S.C.) 517; see also, *Irish Shell and BP Ltd. v. Costello Ltd. (No. 1)* [1981] I.L.R.M. 66 (S.C.); *Kenny Homes and Co. Ltd. v. Leonard*, Supreme Court, unreported, June 18, 1998.

[6] *Doe d. Groves v. Groves* (1847) 10 Q. B. 486.

[7] [1899] 1 Q.B. 486, 488.

> I think it is clear that the defendant was a tenant at will and not a licensee, for the admissions state that she was in exclusive possession, a fact which is wholly inconsistent with her having been a 'mere licensee'.

Furthermore, perhaps influenced by the fact that, certainly so far as the parties themselves were concerned, the effects of finding a lease were relatively limited, the courts were happy to take the same approach in circumstances where, at first sight, there was no obvious tenancy.[8]

The twentieth century, or at least the middle years of it, presents a markedly different perspective. Against the background of increased statutory regulation[9] seeking to protect tenants by curtailing the landlord's right to recover possession and placing restrictions upon his ability to increase rent unilaterally, the view developed that the paramount factor in determining the existence or otherwise of a lease was now the contractual intention of the parties as it was evidenced by the face of the agreement itself.

Such a shift is evident from earlier authorities such as *Booker v. Palmer*[10] and also the judgment of Denning L J. as he then was, in *Facchini v. Bryson*.[11] It is received wisdom, however, (with which the present author concurs,) that this view is seen at the fullest extent of its development in the late nineteen-seventies when, in a series of decisions, the Court of Appeal appeared to give strong endorsement to the efforts of lease draftsmen to avoid the provisions of the Rent Acts in England and Wales by creating "non-exclusive occupation agreements".[12]

The first of these was *Somma v. Hazlehurst*[13] involving a young, unmarried couple seeking accommodation. Both were given a document which described itself as a "licence" and which purported to deny to the occupiers exclusive possession by reserving to the grantor the right to enter upon the premises himself or to introduce other "licensees" upon the property. It is unfortunate that it is not clear how far the decision is based upon the actual documents themselves or upon the factual background.[14] What is clear is that in a judgment later followed in *Aldrington Garages v. Fielder*[15] and other cases,

---

[8] See generally, Smith, *Property Law* (3rd ed., Longman, London, 2000) 331-332.

[9] The first Rent Act in England and Wales was, in fact, enacted in 1915: the Increase of Rent and Mortgage Interest (War Restriction) Act 1915. Over the next sixty years, there were numerous extensions, culminating for present purposes in the Rent Act 1977. For an example of statutory control of residential lettings in Ireland, see the Housing (Private Rented Dwellings) Act 1982.

[10] [1942] 2 All E.R. 674 (C.A.).

[11] [1952]1 T.L.R. 1986 (C.A.); see also *Errington v. Errington and Woods* [1952] 1 K.B. 29 (C.A.).

[12] For a discussion, see Partington, "Non-Exclusive Occupation Agreements" (1979) 42 *M.L.R.* 331.

[13] [1978] 1 W.L.R. 1014 (C.A.).

[14] Above n.12, 333.

[15] (1978) 247 E.G. 557; see also *Sturolson v. Wenitz* (1984) 272 E.G. 32.

Lord Denning endorsed the seeming demise of exclusive possession. There was, he said

> [n]o reason why an ordinary landlord . . . should not be able to grant a licence to occupy an ordinary house. If that is what both he and the licensee intend and if they can frame any written agreement in such a way as to demonstrate that it is not really an agreement for a lease masquerading as a licence, we can see no reason in law or justice why they should be prevented from achieving that objective.[16]

The issue was therefore clear. Which prevailed: professed intention or exclusive possession, classical contract theory or public policy? Mr Roger Street, solicitor in the English seaside resort of Bournemouth and admitted Rent Acts avoider,[17] provided the vehicle by which the House of Lords, notably in the person of Lord Templeman, sought to resolve the matter.

3. THE FACTS[18]

The case itself concerned an agreement made between the aforementioned Mr Street and Mrs Wendy Mountford under which she and her husband occupied two rooms, together with kitchen and bathroom and kitchen facilities, in a house owned by him situated in the picturesquely named St. Clements Gardens, Boscombe.

Notwithstanding that it conferred exclusive possession (a fact accepted without demur by the respondent) the agreement was, throughout, framed in terms of a licence. Thus, in addition to forbidding things as varied as paraffin stoves, pets, children and untidiness, the document described itself as a licence which was both personal and non-assignable and for which a "licence fee" of £37 per week was payable. It did, in addition, confer upon Mr Street the right of entry for numerous purposes and contained a statement signed by Mrs Mountford alone to the effect that she understood and accepted that there was no intention to create a tenancy protected by the Rent Acts.[19]

Despite these factors, Mrs Mountford sought the fixing of a "fair rent" on the basis that she was a tenant subject to the Rent Acts. Unanimously reversing the Court of Appeal[20] and confirming the original decision of the Bourne-

---

[16][1978] 1 W.L.R.1014, 1024-1025.

[17]Street, "Coach and Horses Trip Cancelled?: Rent Act Avoidance After *Street v. Mountford*" [1985] *Conv.* 328, 329.

[18]For a most useful exposition, see Tromans, "Leases and Licences in the Lords" [1985] *C.L.J.* 351.

[19][1985] A.C. 809, 815.

[20](1984) 49 P.&C.R. 324 (Griffiths and Slade L.JJ.); see also Kenny, "The Exclusive Licence" (1984) 81 *L.S. Gaz.* 2355.

mouth County Court, the House of Lords agreed.

Delivering a single judgment,[21] which not only gave wide consideration to English and Commonwealth cases[22] but also sought to stress the irrelevance of the Rent Acts to his reasoning,[23] Lord Templeman adverted firmly to the traditional view.

In England and Wales, unless exceptional circumstances were present, the major determinant of the existence of a residential tenancy was the right to exclusive possession. Furthermore, although if as a matter of fact and despite any artificial devices to the contrary, on its construction the agreement conferred this upon the occupier for a fixed term in return for periodic payments however labelled, they were not a lodger but a tenant. The actions of the parties in describing themselves otherwise was of no significance for, as his Lordship observed pithily:

> The manufacture of a five-pronged implement for manual digging results in a fork even if the manufacturer, unfamiliar with the English language, insists that he intended to make and has made a spade.[24]

There is, therefore, a divergence from the position in Irish law in a number of respects. One of these relates to the "exceptional circumstances" referred to above,[25] for while it is true that in Ireland as in England and Wales, there can be no tenancy without exclusive possession, because the requirement is much more equivocal as an indicator of the existence of a lease,[26] the number of situations where exclusive possession may be present but there will still be no lease is far more numerous.[27]

4. EVALUATION. THE JUDGMENT AND BEYOND

While it immediately becomes clear that the judgment focuses upon the three major elements of exclusive possession, a fixed period and the existence of rent, to confine any evaluation of its impact within these parameters ignores the scope and reality of its influence. Equally, since the full picture emerges

---

[21] Lords Scarman, Keith of Kinkel, Bridge of Harwich and Brightman concurring.

[22] Notably *Radaich v. Smith* (1959) 101 C.L.R. 207 (H.C.A.).

[23] [1985] 1 A.C. 809, 815. Note also the assertion on the same page that the decision does not curtail freedom of contract, a view not shared by Gray, *Elements of Land Law* (2nd ed., Butterworths, London, 1993) 273.

[24] [1985] 1 A.C. 809, 819.

[25] The issues of certainty of term and rent as a prerequisite are considered below.

[26] *Gatien Motor Co. Ltd. v. Continental Oil Co. of Ireland* [1979] I.R. 406, 420 *per* Kenny J. For a general discussion of this issue see Wylie, above n.3, 43-46.

[27] For example it is well settled that "lettings" in conacre and agistment do not, despite the terminology used, create a tenancy.

only in later cases,[28] these are considered where applicable in this part of the essay.

4.1 The Right To Exclusive Possession

(a) The Authorities Themselves

Although not aided by the somewhat interchangeable use of the terms "exclusive occupation" and exclusive possession",[29] it is entirely possible to discern a logical developmental structure in Lord Templeman's judgment.[30]

He dealt first with the arguments advanced by the occupier, namely the traditional view that the distinction between a lease and a licence lay in the grant of exclusive possession. Furthermore, it is clear that his Lordship himself viewed this as still being good law. His reasoning is strong in that it derives from a significant number of decisions during the nineteenth century and the early years of the twentieth. Notable among these are the decisions in *Glenwood Lumber Co. Ltd. v. Phillips*[31] and *Taylor v. Caldwell.*[32]

It must, however, be noted at the same time that several of these same cases involved fact situations differing from that in *Street* itself where all the characteristics of a tenancy were present but the language of the parties sought to negate this. It is not suggested that this destroys the authoritative nature of his Lordship's argument, merely that it may qualify it.[33]

(b) Legal Relations and Exceptional Categories

The judgment then moves on to focus upon the landlord's argument, which was essentially that the expressed intention of the parties was the overriding and all-important factor. In a chronological examination of the cases adduced to support this claim, one feature (or perhaps a number of manifestations of it) assumes central importance. This is that there may be circumstances or facts which, despite the existence of exclusive possession, negate the finding of a leasehold relationship.

It might therefore be the case that the parties did not intend to create legal relations. Or, to put it another way, there is no "right" to possession.[34] Utilising

---

[28]Bright and Gilbert, *Landlord and Tenant Law –The Nature of Tenancies* (Clarendon Press, Oxford, 1995) 325.
[29]A point noted by Gravells, *Land Law Text and Materials* (2nd ed., Sweet and Maxwell, London, 1999) 377.
[30]For perhaps the clearest judicial analysis see *Hadjiloucas v. Crean* [1988] 1 W.L.R. 1006, 1020-1022 *per* Mustill J.
[31][1904] A.C. 405 (H.L.).
[32](1863) 3 B.& S. 826; 122 E.R. 826 (Q.B.D.).
[33]The point is expertly argued in Hill, "Intention and the Creation of Proprietary Rights: Are Leases Different?" (1996) 16 *L.S.* 200.
[34]See Clarke, "Land Law and Trusts" [1985] *All E.R.Rev.* 190, 191-192.

this approach, decisions such as *Booker v. Palmer*,[35] *Cobb v. Lane*[36] and *Isaac v. Hotel de Paris*[37] were rationalised.

Then, continuing to endorse Lord Denning's view in *Facchini v. Bryson* that in "all the cases where an occupier has been held to be a licensee there has been something in the circumstances, such as a family arrangement, an act of friendship or generosity or such like to negate any intention to create a tenancy",[38] Lord Templeman had no difficulty in distinguishing other authorities, including that of *Errington v. Errington and Woods*,[39] as falling within these exceptions.

It is certainly true that, even before *Street* itself, the courts had recognised such exceptions. For example, the service occupier needing the accommodation for the better performance of his employment was regarded as a licensee[40] as was the person who received accommodation under an act of charity or goodwill.[41] Furthermore (and emphasising the continuing impact of his Lordship's judgment) this approach can still be seen. Thus, in *Norris v. Checksfield*,[42] an employee needing to live over the premises in order to fulfil a commitment that he drive his employer's vehicles was not regarded a s having acquired a lease, while in *Monmouth B. C. v. Marlog*,[43] an agreement under which a council house tenant shared his home with a woman and her two daughters on an informal basis did not operate to give her a sub-tenancy.

The foregoing account makes it difficult to challenge the efficacy or indeed the continuing influence of the noble Lord's use of these exceptional categories. A note of caution is, nevertheless, considered appropriate for two reasons. The first of these is that it is at least arguable that they do not constitute a separate principle but are rather a "working out"[44] of possession and might be explained by an absence of a significant degree of it.[45] In addition, it is entirely possible – as the courts appear to be aware[46] – that if it is not applied in a careful and logical manner the concept could effectively erode the critical mass of exclusive possession.

---

[35] [1942] 2 All E.R. 674 (C.A.).
[36] [1952] 1 T.L.R. 1037 (C.A.).
[37] [1960] 1 W.L.R. 239 (P.C.).
[38] [1952] 1 T.L.R. 1386, 1389.
[39] Above, n.7.
[40] *Smith v. Seghill Overseers* (1875) L.R.10 Q.B. 422.
[41] *Marcroft Wagons Ltd. v. Smith* [1951] 2 K.B. 496 (C.A.).
[42] [1992] 1 E.G.L.R. 159 (C.A.).
[43] [1992] H.L.R. 30 (C.A.); see also, Townsend, "Continuing Difficulties In Distinguishing the Lease from the Licence" (1995) 29 *The Law Teacher* 852.
[44] *Bretherton v. Paton* (1986) 18 H.L.R. 257, 263 *per* May L.J.
[45] *Radaich v. Smith* above, n.3 pp. 220, 223 *per* Taylor and Windeyer JJ.
[46] *Inter alia, Dellneed v. Chin* (1986) 53 P.&C.R. 172 (H.C.); but for an arguably more expansive approach see the House of Lords' decision in *Bruton v. London and Quadrant Housing Trust* [2000] 1 A.C. 406 (H.L.).

(c) Shams and Pretences

If the paramount status of exclusive possession constitutes a distinguishing factor in the approaches of English and Irish courts, then the way in which this is to be established presents an example of similarity of approach. As has been the case in Ireland,[47] in ascertaining what has been called "the factual matrix"[48] of exclusive possession, Lord Templeman was at some pains to stress the need to identify and disregard "sham devices and artificial transactions".[49]

Again, this concept did not spring fully formed from his judgment. As early as 1967 it is possible to see the Court of Appeal, in the person of Diplock L.J. (as he then was), overturning an agreement and thereby challenging contractual autonomy when

> acts done or documents executed by the parties . . . are intended by them to give to third parties or to the Court the appearance of creating between the parties legal rights and obligations different from the actual legal rights and obligations (if any) which the parties intend to create.[50]

The significance of *Street*, however, is that much evidence suggests it has stimulated a much wider interpretation of what kinds of terms will be struck out on this ground.[51] What is clear is that terms stipulating that the occupier be required to leave the premises for ninety minutes per day[52] or that a landlord reserves a multiplicity of rights to enter premises for a multiplicity of reasons or to introduce other occupiers at any time but in reality does neither,[53] will play no part in the final categorisation of the occupier's rights.

(d) Commerce, Lodgers and Multiple Occupation

The significance of the decision in *Street* receives further support from the fact that, despite the apparent restriction in Lord Templeman's judgment to residential leases,[54] the courts have been happy to apply the principles set out therein to commercial or business premises. Proof is to be found in the decision in *University of Reading v. Johnson-Houghton*[55] where Leonard L.J., in

---

[47] *Whipp v. Mackey* [1927] I.R. 372 (S.C.); *Texaco (Ir.) Ltd. v. Murphy*, High Court, unreported, July 17, 1991, Barron J.
[48] Above, n.28. p.128 .
[49] [1985] 1 A.C. 809, 825.
[50] *Snook v. London and West Riding Investments Ltd.* [1967] 2 Q.B. 786 (C.A.) 802.
[51] For a supporting view see Bright, "Beyond Sham and Into Pretence" (1991) 11 *O.J.L.S.* 136; a more circumspect view is taken by Smith, above, n. 8, 347-350.
[52] *Aslan v. Murphy (Nos. 1 and 2)* [1990] 1 W.L.R. 766 (C.A.).
[53] *Antoniades v. Villiers* [1990] 1 A.C. 417 (H.L.).
[54] For a discussion, see Bridge, *"Street v. Mountford –* No Hiding Place?" [1986] *Conv.* 344.
[55] (1985) 276 E.G. 1353 (C.A.).

concluding that a racehorse trainer who had taken out a trainer's licence some twenty-four years earlier and then held the gallops ever since under a series of agreements described as "licences" but which contained covenants that the University would grant no other trainers rights, was a tenant and not a licensee.

Even stronger support is, perhaps, to be seen in the judgment of Judge Paul Baker Q.C., who opined in *Associated Investment Trust Plc. v. Calow*:

> it seems to me that self-contained business offices stand in just the same case as do residential premises. Lord Templeman mentioned residence because that was the actual case that he was dealing with there. It was not meant to lay down a separate doctrine for residential properties as opposed to business properties.[56]

The courts' treatment of the lodger issue has not only been a relatively trouble-free aspect of Lord Templeman's formulation but again strikes a chord in both jurisdictions.[57] The application of his *dictum* that an occupier "is a lodger (and therefore not a tenant) if the landlord provides attendance or services which require the landlord or his servants to exercise unrestricted access to and use of the premises"[58] has, (albeit with one very recent dissenting voice[59]) been applied in an essentially straightforward manner. In almost all respects, the lodger is, of course, the quintessential licensee and, even before the decision in *Street*, it was possible to formulate a reasonably precise definition of this relationship whereby an individual sought a room in another person's home, shared bathroom ands kitchen facilities and received services such as cleaning and bed-linen.[60] This continued and does continue after *Street*. Thus, in *Markou v. Da Silvaesa*,[61] the existence in fact of extensive services by the owner indicated that there was no tenancy. Similarly, in both *Westminster City Council v. Clarke*[62] and *Brennan v. Lambeth L. B.C.*[63] arrangements whereby occupants of hostels for the homeless were not only supervised by a resident warden but subject to a requirement that they could be asked to change rooms if necessary were viewed as licences.

In this respect, therefore, while Lord Templeman's utterances cannot be

---

[56](1986) 280 E.G. 1252, 1256; *cf. Dresden Estates v. Collinson* (1987) 55 P.&C.R. 47 (C.A.); see also *Hunts Refuse Disposals Ltd. v. Norfolk Environmental Waste Services Ltd.* [1997] E.G.L.R. 113 (C.A.).

[57]*Waucob v. Reynolds* (1850) 1 I.C.L.R. 142; *Carroll v. Mayo County Council* [1967] I.R. 364 (H.C.) 367 *per* Henchy J.

[58][1985] 1 A.C. 809, 818.

[59]*Mehta v. Royal Bank of Scotland Plc.* (1999) 78 P.&C.R. D11, January 25, 1999 (H.C.).

[60]*Marchant v. Charters* [1977] 1 W.L.R. 1181 (C.A.); *Abbeyfield (Harpenden) Society Ltd. v. Woods* [1968] 1 W.L.R. 374 (C.A.).

[61](1986) 52 P.&C.R. 204.

[62][1992] 2 A.C. 288 (H.L.); see Cowan, "A Public Dimension to a Private Problem" [1992] *Conv.* 285; see also *Huwyler v. Ruddy* (1995) 28 H.L.R. 550 (C.A.).

regarded as ground-breaking they do provide an essential link, a clarification of this aspect of the lease relationship.

The author's contention at this stage of the work is that all the evidence so far shows a decision which, subject only to minor criticisms, has worked well. The picture does, however, change when attention turns to more than one occupier of the same premises.

This situation is, it is suggested, most usefully considered against the background of the joint appeal to the House of Lords in *AG Securities v. Vaughan* and *Antoniades v. Villiers*[64] which between them (although admittedly not exclusively)[65] illustrate the variations within the multiple occupation scenario. What becomes clear upon reading these decisions is that the courts in England and Wales identify three alternative ways of interpreting multiple occupation. In the first-as was exemplified by the flat –sharing agreement in *AG Securities* – whereby the occupants moved in at different times and paid different amounts of rent under separate agreements– there may in fact be a series of licences. Here, neither individually nor collectively do the occupants have the protection of a tenancy.

A second possible interpretation is that each occupier, while sharing some of the facilities, may have exclusive possession of some part of the premises (most usually a bedroom) giving him a lease of part with, of course, consequent statutory protection.[66]

Antoniades illustrates the final interpretation, that there is a joint tenancy of the whole. It is fundamental to this finding that the court is satisfied that the four unities of time, title, interest and possession are present. The unmarried couple in the case, having taken their flat in circumstances where the only unity apparently missing could be explained as a pretence, were so classified.

Ironically, since they also endorse his formulation in numerous ways,[67] these decisions undermine Lord Templeman's analysis in two respects.[68] The first of these is that in contrast to his clear insistence in *Street v. Mountford* itself that the Rent Acts had no part to play in the analysis utilised to establish a lease,[69] the multiple occupation issue sees him apparently adopting a much

---

[63](1997) 30 H. L.R. 481 (C.A.).

[64][1990] 1 A.C. 417 (H.L.); see also Harpum, "Leases, Licences and Shams" [1989] *C.L.J.* 19; Smith, "Those Who Do Not Remember the Past" [1989] *Conv.* 128.

[65]*Mikeover v. Brady* [1989] 3 All E.R. 618 (C.A.); *Stribling v. Wickham* [1989] 21 H.L.R. 381 (C.A.).

[66]Notably, the Housing Act 1988.

[67]Burn, *Maudsley and Burn's Land Law-Cases and Materials* (7th ed., Butterworths, London, 1998) 416.

[68]The present author's contention that the courts have exacerbated matters by utilising the joint tenancy as a distinguishing feature in a context other than that in which it originally developed is not considered relevant for present purposes!

[69][1985] 1 A.C. 809, 819.

more policy-based approach, leading him to comment that[70] "parties to an agreement cannot contract out of the Rent Acts, if they were able to do so, the Acts would be a dead letter".

Perhaps one of the attractions, in judicial terms, of Lord Templeman's judgment in *Street* was the simplicity of his finding that the individual occupier could be only one thing or the other: lodger or tenant. The second way in which the multiple occupation cases undermine his analysis is that they expose it as too simplistic. The ending of such a simple dichotomy is not, of itself, disastrous but does illustrate the fallibility of this particular pronouncement.

4.2 Fixed Periods and Rent

To the Irish lawyer, accustomed to a regime where the very foundation of the landlord and tenant relationship is the agreement of the parties with consequent relaxation of the requirement of certainty of term[71] but the existence of rent as a prerequisite for a lease coming within Deasy's Act,[72] the fact that the other two elements of Lord Templeman's formulation have not attracted the same amount of analysis and comment may be somewhat surprising. This state of affairs is, however, entirely explicable within its own context. Nevertheless, they do form a part of the judgment and any evaluation of its status must, necessarily, consider them.

Viewed from one standpoint, all of Lord Templeman's deliberations upon exclusive possession would have been as naught had the intrepid Mrs Mountford not agreed the period with reference to which she would pay her rent of £37 per week. Her troubles would have been much greater since the very characterisation of a tenure as a term of years in English law is "because its duration or continuance is bounded, limited and determined; for every such estate must have a certain beginning and certain end".[73]

The "fixed period" aspect of the judgment was, therefore, relatively unremarkable but Lord Templeman's insistence upon rent merits the following observations. Historically, the obligation upon a tenant to pay rent was indivisible from the tenurial relationship between lesssor and lessee. Quite simply the lease, being viewed as a property right, caused the rent naturally to "issue(s) out of the ground".[74]

Nowadays, however, for the majority of landlords the lease will be overwhelmingly a way of exploiting their land to create wealth. Such an approach

---

[70]*AG Securities v. Vaughan* [1990] 1 A.C. 417, 458.
[71]See, *inter alia*, *Wood v. Davis* (1880) 6 L.R. Ir. 50; *Holmes v. Day* (1874) I.R.8 C.L. 235.
[72]*Irish Shell and BP Ltd. v. Costello Ltd.,* [1981] I.L.R.M. 66, 71 *per* Griffin J. *Semble* this is not necessary if the relationship is one which is outside the Act, *e.g.* a mortgage by demise.
[73]Blackstone, *Commentaries* vol. II, 48.
[74]Holdsworth, *History of English Law* (2nd ed., Methuen, London, 1937) vol. VII, 262.

also dictates that rent will be a normal feature of a lease but it does, it is suggested, stop short of stipulating it as a necessary precondition as was suggested by Lord Templeman.

Furthermore, not only does the statutory definition of a term of years absolute specifically allow for a lease without a rent[75] but in *Ashburn Anstalt v. Arnold*,[76] the Court of Appeal held that rent was not required for a lease. Fox J. preferred instead to treat Lord Templeman's remarks as a pointer or strong indication of the existence of a tenancy. This, it is suggested, is the correct approach and certainly one which has been followed subsequently.[77]

5. CONCLUSION

When measured against the criteria set out at the commencement of this paper, *Street v. Mountford* is not a 'perfect' case.

So far as the background to it is concerned, there can be little argument that clarification was needed as to how the Rent Acts, particularly that of 1977, were to impinge upon or affect the existence and operation of residential leases. This did not, however, render the decision in the case inevitable.

It is entirely feasible that had he not steadfastly refused to acknowledge the significance of the Rent Acts, as he came to do in later years, Lord Templeman need not have considered many of the earlier authorities in a way which left their results intact but their reasoning battered.

Furthermore, even if it is quite properly acknowledged that, overall, the principles worked satisfactorily in the case of the single occupier, much greater difficulty was experienced in their application to multiple occupation.

These factors should not, however, be allowed to obscure the significant positive aspects of the case. It represented not only a return to orthodoxy when this was, in most ways, the means of clarifying a problematic situation.

To its further credit, it achieved this by disapproving only three existing authorities and, in so doing, restored the *Facchini v. Bryson* categories. Neither should the fact that it brought harmony once again to English and Commonwealth views of the lease be dismissed lightly.

Perhaps its greatest strength lies in the fact that, even though the present statutory regime has removed some of the reasons for its occurrence, it is still to the parameters laid down in the case that lawyers in England and Wales turn.

---

[75]Law of Property Act 1925, s.265(1)(xxvii).

[76][1989] Ch. 1.

[77]*Prudential Assurance Co. Ltd. v. London Residuary Body* (1991) 63 P.&C.R. 386 (C.A.) 397 *per* Scott L.J.; *Canadian Imperial Bank of Commerce v. Bello* (1991) 64 P.&C.R. 48 (C.A.) 55 *per* Ralph Gibson L.J.; *Skipton Building Society v. Clayton* (1993) 66 P.&C.R. 223, 230 *per* Slade J.

On the basis of this and all the other factors identified it must surely be regarded as a leading decision.

If, having begun with an analogy to a metal implement, the author may be allowed to end in a similar manner, we are still speaking with a forked tongue!

ACCOMMODATING THE SPECIAL NEEDS OF THE FINANCIAL MARKETS

R v. Panel on Takeovers and Mergers; Ex Parte Datafin plc (1987)

BLANAID CLARKE[*]

1. INTRODUCTION

In *R v. Panel on Takeovers and Mergers; Ex Parte Datafin plc*[1] ("the *Datafin* case"), the Court of Appeal held that decisions of the London Panel on Takeovers and Mergers ("the London Panel") are subject to judicial review.

1.1 The London Panel

The London Panel regulates conduct in the course of a takeover through the City Code on Takeovers and Mergers ("the City Code"). The City Code is a self regulatory code which operates to ensure fair and equal treatment of all shareholders in relation to takeovers and to provide an orderly framework within which takeovers can be conducted.[2] The City Code is intended to represent the collective opinion of those professionally involved as to good and fair practice. It is based upon ten General Principles which are described by the London Panel as "good standards of commercial behaviour".[3] These General Principles ensure that all shareholders of the same class of the target company are treated equally and are provided with sufficient information in time to make an informed assessment of the offer. The General Principles are expressed in broad terms and the spirit as well as the precise wording of the General Principles

---

[*]Senior Lecturer in Law, University College Dublin. The author would like to express her thanks to Mr. Kevin Costello and Mr. John O'Dowd of the Faculty of Law, University College Dublin for their comments and suggestions on earlier drafts of this article.

[1] [1987] 1 Q.B. 815; [1987] 1 All E.R. 564 (C.A.).

[2] The London Panel also administers the Rules Governing Substantial Acquisitions of Shares. The objective of these latter rules is to slow up the rate at which substantial holdings in shares may be built up. This will prevent the occurrence of what became known as "dawn raids".

[3] The City Code on Takeovers and Mergers – Introduction, A3.

and the ensuing rules must be observed.[4] As a result, the London Panel may modify or relax the effect of the precise wording of the General Principles accordingly. These principles are supplemented by a series of 38 rules some of which are expansions of the General Principles and examples of their application and others of which are provisions governing specific aspects of takeover procedure.

The City Code does not have the force of law. It is not created by Statute, or under an authority delegated by Parliament. This allows the London Panel to act quickly and flexibly. For example, it can react rapidly to new market developments by immediate amendment of the City Code. Rules can be fashioned to meet new contingencies. The operation of the City Code is however, recognised and supported by the Financial Services Act 1986 ("the 1986 Act") which provides the regulatory framework for the protection of investors and the conduct of the financial markets in the United Kingdom. Authorised bodies under the 1986 Act such as Financial Services Authority and the relevant self regulatory bodies impose rules providing that authorised firms should not act for clients who are unprepared to comply with the City Code (the "cold shouldering rule"). Furthermore, the Financial Services Authority requires authorised persons to co-operate with the London Panel in providing relevant information, documentation and assistance. In addition, where the London Panel reports a breach of the City Code by a practitioner to the appropriate authority which authorises that person under the 1986 Act the practitioner may be disciplined or have restrictions placed on his or her business.

1.2 The Facts of the *Datafin* Case

The *Datafin* case involved a contested takeover for McCorquodale plc, a company listed on the London Stock Exchange. Offers were made for the company both by Norton Opax plc and by Datafin plc. A stockbroking firm, Kuwait Investment Office ("KIO") subsequently purchased shares in the offeree at a price above the maximum which Norton Opax plc was permitted to pay under the City Code and committed these shares to the Norton Opax plc offer. The City Code prohibits an offeror from acquiring shares at prices higher that its offer price without increasing its offer price to match the higher prices. The City Code also prohibits an offeror from increasing an offer which has been made on the expressed basis that it would not thereafter be increased. Datafin plc complained that as Norton Opax plc and KIO were "concert parties" under the City Code, the restrictions on acquisitions applied equally to it. The London Panel determined that there was no evidence of any agreement or understanding providing for active co-operation between KIO and Norton Opax plc for the purpose of obtaining control in McCorquodale plc such as would render

---

[4] Introduction to the General Principles B1.

them concert parties. Datafin plc sought leave to apply for judicial review of the London Panel's decision and for consequential relief. This application was refused at first instance and the application was renewed to the Court of Appeal.

1.3 The Legal Issues

Two separate issues were considered by the Court of Appeal. Firstly, whether the Court had jurisdiction to entertain applications for the judicial review of decisions of the London Panel. Secondly, if the Court had jurisdiction, how in principle this jurisdiction ought to be exercised.

2. EXISTENCE OF JURISDICTION

2.1 *Datafin*

Counsel for the London Panel in the *Datafin* case argued that the court's supervisory jurisdiction only extends to bodies whose power is derived from legislation or the exercise of the prerogative. Counsel for the applicant argued that regard has to be had not only to the source of the body's power but also as to whether it operates as an integral part of a system which has "a public law character, is supported by public law in that public law sanctions are applied if its edicts are ignored and performs, what might be described as, public law functions."[5]

Because of the nature and history of judicial review, most of the actions to which it was traditionally directed were actions purportedly authorised by statute and discharged by bodies constituted by statute.[6] However, Donaldson M.R. relied on the dicta of Lord Parker C. J. in *R v. Criminal Injuries Compensation Board, ex parte Lain*[7] to the effect that the exact limits of the ancient remedy of certiorari had never been and ought not to be defined.

> The only constant limits throughout were that the body concerned was under a duty to act judicially and that it was performing a public duty. Private or domestic tribunals have always been outside the scope of certiorari since their authority is derived solely from contract, that is, from the agreement of the parties concerned.[8]

---

[5] [1987] 1 Q.B. 815, 836; [1987] 1 All E.R. 564, 575.

[6] *R v. Electricity Commissioners, ex p. London Electricity Joint Committee Co. (1920) Ltd.* [1924] 1 K.B. 171 (C.A.). See also Hogan and Morgan, *Administrative Law in Ireland* (3rd ed., Round Hall Sweet & Maxwell, Dublin, 1998) 770.

[7] [1967] 2 Q.B. 864 (Q.B.). See also *R v. North & East Devon Health Authority: Ex Parte Coughlan* [1999] Lloyds Rep. Med. 306 (C.A.).

[8] [1967] 2 Q.B. 864, 882.

It was noted that in *O'Reilly v. Mackman*,[9] a requirement to act judicially was deleted. Donaldson M.R. thus commented that in all the reports it was possible to find enumerations of factors giving rise to the jurisdiction. However, his Lordship opined that it would be a fatal error to regard the presence of all those factors as essential or indeed exclusive.

> Possibly the only essential elements are what can be described as a public element, which can take many different forms, and the exclusion from the jurisdiction of bodies whose sole source of power is a consensual submission to its jurisdiction.[10]

Lloyd L.J. noted that the source of power will often, perhaps usually, be decisive.

> If the source of power is a statute, or subordinate legislation under a statute, then clearly the body in question will be subject to judicial review. If at the other end of the scale, the source of power is contractual, as in the case of private arbitration, then clearly the arbitrator is not subject to judicial review. . . .But in between these two extremes there is an area in which it is helpful to look not just at the source of the power but at the nature of the power. If the body in question is exercising public law functions, or if the exercise of its functions have public law consequences, then that may, as counsel for the applicants submitted, be sufficient to bring the body within the reach of judicial review.[11]

Having regard to the wide-ranging nature and importance of the matters covered by the City Code and to the serious public consequences of non-compliance with the City Code, Donaldson M.R. stated that the London Panel was performing a public law function when prescribing and administering the City Code.

> It is without doubt performing a public duty and an important one. This is clear from the expressed willingness of the Secretary of State for Trade and Industry to limit legislation in the field of mergers and takeovers and to use the panel as the centrepiece of his regulation of that market. The rights of citizens are indirectly affected by its decisions, some, but by no means all of whom, may in a technical sense be said to have assented to this situation, e.g. the members of the Stock Exchange. At least in its determination of whether there has been a breach of the code, it has a

---

[9] [1983] A.C. 237 (H.L.).
[10] [1987] 1 Q.B. 815, 838; [1987] 1 All E.R. 564, 577.
[11] [1987] 1 Q.B. 815, 847; [1987] 1 All E.R. 564, 583.

duty to act judicially and it asserts that its raison d'être is to do equity between one shareholder and another. Its source of power is only partly based on moral persuasion and the assent of institutions and their members, the bottom-line being the statutory powers exercised by the Department of Trade and Industry and the Bank of England. In this context I should be very disappointed if the courts could not recognise the realities of executive power and allowed their vision to be clouded by the subtlety and sometimes complexity of the way in which it can be exerted.[12]

As a consequence, decisions of the London Panel were deemed subject to public law remedies including judicial review.

2.2 No Contractual Relationship

The extension of judicial review to bodies whose source of power lies neither in statute nor in the prerogative has left the courts facing the question of where to draw the boundary between public and private law, and on what basis.[13] In pure *Datafin* cases where the body has no visible means of legal support, judicial review has been held to apply.

> Indeed it would appear that the less means of support the better: a body with no statutory, prerogative or contractual power exercising a regulatory function is perhaps now one of the clearest cases for the availability of judicial review.[14]

For example, in *R v. Advertising Standards Authority Ltd., ex p Insurance Services plc*[15] Glidewell L.J. held:

> The Authority has no powers granted to it by statute or at common law, nor does it have any contractual relationship with the advertisers whom it controls. Nevertheless it is clearly exercising a public law function which, if the Authority did not exist, would no doubt be exercised by the Director General of Fair Trading.

In order to determine whether judicial review will lie, the main test would appear to be: has the legislature or executive entrusted on its behalf the ad-

---

[12][1987] 1 Q.B. 815, 838-839; [1987] 1 All E.R. 564, 577.
[13]Black, "Constitutionalising Self-Regulation" (1996) 59 *M.L.R.* 24, Costello, "When Is A Decision Subject To Judicial Review ? – A Restatement Of The Rules" (1998) XXXIII *Ir. Jur.* (*n.s.*) 91.
[14]Black, above, n.13, 33.
[15](1990) 2 Admin. L.R. 169 (Q.B.).

ministration of some important regulatory or social service function?[16] In *Murtagh v. Board of Governors of St. Emer's School,*[17] the High Court determined that a decision to impose a minor disciplinary punishment on a pupil attending a national school was subject to judicial review. The school in question was regulated by the Department of Education which formulated Rules with the concurrence of the Minister for Finance. Barron J. noted that these Rules governed every aspect of its existence including school discipline.

> The provisions for discipline are no different in character from any other of the Rules governing these schools. They are not consensual in nature.[18]

In *R v. Code of Practice Committee of the British Pharmaceutical Society, ex p Professional Counselling Aids,*[19] the Court had to determine whether a decision of the Code of Practice Committee of the Association of the British Pharmaceutical Industry ("APBI") was subject to judicial review. The Code of Practice Committee decided that a pharmaceutical related product manufactured by the applicant would be likely to bring discredit upon or reduce confidence in the pharmaceutical industry and its use would be contrary to the APBI's Code of Practice. Under the Medicines Act 1968, the Minister of Health was authorised to regulate advertisements and in pursuance of this authority the Minister introduced the Medicines (Standard Provisions for Licences and Certificates) Regulations, 1971. The APBI's Code of Practice had been drafted after consultation with the British Medical Association and the Department of Health and was amended in order to ensure compatibility with the Regulations. Acceptance and observance of the provisions of the Code of Practice was a condition of membership of the APBI. The applicant argued on the basis of *Datafin* that there was a public duty on the Committee because it was the voluntary self-regulating body and arm of the Department of Health, a statutory body. It was argued that the Committee was fulfilling an ancillary purpose which was part of the Department's public control of advertising. It was submitted that what the Committee was doing was part and parcel of a system operated in the public interest, namely the control of the advertisement of medicinal products. It was also noted that while the applicant was not in a contractual relationship with the respondents, he voluntarily submitted to their jurisdiction. Popplewell J. stated:

---

[16]See Costello, "The Identification of Organisations Subject to Judicial Review" (1995) 17 *D.U.L.J. (n.s.)* 89.
[17][1991] 1 I.R. 482 (H.C.). See also *The State (Hayes) v. Criminal Injuries Compensation Tribunal* [1982] I.L.R.M. 210 (H.C.).
[18][1991] 1 I.R. 482, 486.
[19](1990) 3 Admin. L.R. 697 (Q.B.).

In the end, the question which I pose to myself is, are these essentially domestic proceedings, or is there some public duty involved? In the end, having weighed up all the factors, I am driven in the light of the authorities, and particularly *Datafin*, to conclude that the court does have jurisdiction. I do so with the greatest reluctance, firstly because the extension of the law by *Datafin* seems to me to be likely to enlarge enormously the scope of those who are subject to judicial review with the consequential swamping of the courts in what are essentially domestic issues and an imposition on domestic bodies of a standard and code of conduct which it was never intended they should have. Secondly, the test which existed before Datafin was, if not entirely clear, a great deal clearer than the law now is.

2.3 Contractual Relationship

When a public body has a contractual source of power significant tensions arise. In *Murphy v. The Turf Club*,[20] an application was made for judicial review of a decision of the Turf Club to revoke a racehorse trainer's licence. The licence was issued by the Turf Club under the Rules of Racing and the Irish National Hunt Steeplechase Rules. Barr J. referred to the *Datafin* decision noting that it extended the scope of judicial review to encompass decisions made by bodies which do not derive their authority from statute or common law. However, Barr J. distinguished the case on the basis that the Turf Club was not the same kind of body as the London Panel in that it was not performing a public duty subject to public law remedies. The relationship between the racehorse trainer and the Turf Club was said to be derived from contract. Although there were statutory provisions relating to the Turf Club, they were deemed not to be relevant to the issue in question i.e. the decision to revoke a licence.[21] Furthermore, Barr J. stated:

> I am also satisfied that the respondent's duty to regulate the sport of horse-racing in Ireland, although having a public dimension, is not a public duty as envisaged by the Court of Appeal in [*Datafin*] and in purporting to revoke the applicant's training licence the respondent was not exercising a public law function. On the contrary its decision was that of a domestic tribunal exercising a regulatory function over the applicant, being an interested person who had voluntarily submitted to its jurisdiction.[22]

---

[20][1989] I.R. 171 (H.C.).
[21]Thus, a body may be subject to judicial review in respect of some of its functions but not all its functions.
[22][1989] I.R. 171, 174 – 175.

In reaching his decision, Barr J. relied on *The State (Colquhoun) v. D'Arcy*[23] where a divisional court of the High Court determined that the Court of the General Synod of the Church of Ireland derives its authority solely from the consent of the members of the Church and judicial review will not thus lie. Barr J. also relied on the Court of Appeal decision in *Law v. National Greyhound Racing Club Ltd.*[24] where Lawton L.J. held that the power of the stewards to suspend the plaintiff's license was derived from a contract between the plaintiff and the defendants.

> A steward's inquiry under the defendants' rules of racing concerned only those who voluntarily submitted themselves to the stewards' jurisdiction. There was no public element in the jurisdiction itself. Its exercise, however, could have consequences from which the public benefited, as for example by the stamping out of malpractices, and from which individuals might have their rights restricted by, for example, being prevented from employing a trainer whose licence had been suspended. Consequences affecting the public generally can flow from the decisions of many domestic tribunals. In the past the courts have always refused to use the orders of certiorari to review the decisions of domestic tribunals.[25]

Hogan and Morgan have pointed out that since the Turf Club enjoys a monopoly in respect of the granting of licences, the submission of the applicant to its jurisdiction could not be said to be absolutely voluntary.[26] Indeed, there is a very strong similarity between the role of the Turf Club under the Racing Board and Racecourse Act 1945 and the London Panel under the Financial Services Act 1986. Under the former Act the Turf Club and the Irish National Hunt Steeplechase Committee were empowered to exclude certain persons from racecourses. In addition, the consent of these two bodies was necessary in order for the statutory body, the Racing Board, to establish racecourses. In that sense, one could argue that what the Turf Club was doing was part and parcel of a system operating in the public interest.

The principle accepted in *Datafin* and *Law* that the consensual submission or contractual source of power excludes judicial review has dominated the reasoning in many subsequent UK cases. For example in *R v. Disciplinary Committee of the Jockey Club, ex parte Massingberd Mundy*,[27] the applicant, who had been chairman of a local stewards panel, was removed from the post

---

[23] [1936] I.R. 641 (H.C.).
[24] [1983] 3 All E.R. 300 (C.A.).
[25] [1983] 3 All E.R. 300, 303.
[26] Hogan and Morgan, above, n.6, 780.
[27] [1993] 2 All E.R. 207 (Q.B.).

of chairman. When he sought to challenge that decision, it was held by the Divisional Court that the decisions of the Disciplinary Committee of the Jockey Club were not subject to judicial review and reliance was placed on the decision in the *Law* case. Similarly, in *R v. Lloyd's, ex parte Briggs*[28] and *R v. Insurance Ombudsman, ex parte Aegon Life Assurance Ltd.*,[29] the contractual source of power was seen either to deny any public element by definition or to be the more dominant test. In *R v. Disciplinary Committee of the Jockey Club, ex parte Aga Khan*,[30] a decision to disqualify a horse which failed a drug test was not subject to judicial review as the source of the Jockey Club's power was deemed to be the consensual submission to the Club's jurisdiction. The applicants had argued that the Jockey Club had an effective *de facto* control of a significant national activity; that its functions were effectively public and; that its powers were of a nature and scope which affected the public. Farquharson L.J. responded to a similar argument by noting that:

> the fact is that if the applicant wished to race his horses in this country he had no choice but to submit to the Jockey Club's jurisdiction. This may be true but nobody is obliged to race his horses in this country and it does not destroy the element of consensuality.[31]

In *Beirne v. Garda Commissioner*,[32] it was suggested that where there is a contract between the parties, the necessity to demonstrate a public interest becomes more important. However, the Court determined that the particular functions of the Commissioner were not solely or even mainly derived from contract. In this case, the appellants argued that the decision to dismiss a Garda recruit is a decision arising from a contractual right vested in the Commissioner by virtue of the contract entered into between him and the applicant upon the acceptance of the applicant as a trainee. Finlay C. J. stated:

> The principle which, in general, excludes from the ambit of judicial review decisions made in the realm of private law by persons or tribunals whose authority derives from contract is, I am quite satisfied, confined to cases or instances where the duty being performed by the decision-making authority is manifestly a private duty and where his right to make it derives solely from contract or solely from consent or the agreement of the parties affected. Where the duty being carried out by a decision-making authority, as occurs in this case, is of a nature which might ordinarily

[28] [1993] Lloyds L.R. 176 (Q.B.).
[29] [1995] L.R.L.R. 101. (Q.B.).
[30] [1993] 2 All E.R. 853 (C.A.). See also *Jones v. Welsh Rugby Union*, Court of Appeal, *The Times*, January 6, 1998.
[31] [1993] 2 All E.R. 853, 873.
[32] [1993] I.L.R.M. 1 (S.C.). See also *Walsh v. Red Cross* [1997] 2 I.R. 478 (S.C.).

be seen as coming within the public domain, that decision can only be excluded from the reach of the jurisdiction in judicial review if it can be shown that it solely and exclusively derived from an individual contract made in private law.[33]

The majority of the Court found that the function of the Commissioner in admitting a recruit to training is not solely or even mainly derived from contract. Instead, it is a public statutory function regulated by statute and by statutory order.

Not only are these statutory duties exercised by the commissioner by virtue of his appointment to a public office, but they are duties which by the only other test of whether they fall within the public or private domain are, it seems to me, of the most intense interest to the public at large.[34]

By contrast, in *Rajah v. Royal College of Surgeons in Ireland*,[35] a decision not to allow a student re-sit an examination was held not to be subject to judicial review because the decision derived not from public law but from the contract which came into being when the applicant became a student in the college. In this case, the College was established by charter but this was held by Murphy J. in the High Court not to be sufficient to bring matters relating to the conduct and academic standing of its students within the ambit of judicial review.[36]

2.4 Governmental Interest

The "public power" test of *Datafin* appears to have been modified by subsequent caselaw. In *R v. Chief Rabbi, ex parte Wachmann*,[37] a ruling by the Chief Rabbi to the effect that Wachmann was not fit to hold office as a rabbi was not deemed to be subject to judicial review. Counsel for the applicant relied on the *Datafin* case arguing that the Court's jurisdiction should be extended to this case. It was argued that the applicant did not consensually submit to the Chief Rabbi's jurisdiction as he was pursuing his vocation. This was accepted by the Court. Simon Brown J. noted however that to regard the consensual submission to jurisdiction as a wholly distinct ground is artificial – "perhaps rather it shades into consideration of whether the body in question is fulfilling an essentially public duty and its decision is one having public law consequences".[38] It

---

[33] [1993] I.L.R.M. 1, 2.
[34] [1993] I.L.R.M. 1, 4.
[35] [1994] 1 I.R. 384 (H.C.). See also *Eoghan v. UCD* [1996] 2 I.L.R.M. 132 (H.C.).
[36] *cf. Browne v. Dundalk UDC* [1993] I.L.R.M. 328 (H.C.).
[37] [1993] 2 All E.R. 249 (Q.B.).
[38] [1993] 2 All E.R. 249, 254.

was also argued by the applicant that there is a clear "public element" to the decision. Referring to _Law_ and _Datafin_ however, Simon Brown J. stated:

> Their effect is clear enough. To say of decisions of a given body that they are public law decisions with public law consequences means something more than that they are decisions which may be of great interest or concern to the public or, indeed which may have consequences for the public. To attract the court's supervisory jurisdiction, there must be not merely a public but potentially a governmental interest in the decision-making power in question. And, indeed, generally speaking the exercise of the power in question involves not merely the voluntary regulation of some important area of public life but also what [counsel] calls a 'twin-track system of control'. In other words, where non-governmental bodies have hitherto been held reviewable, they have generally being operating as an integral part of a regulatory system which, although itself non-statutory, is nevertheless supported by statutory powers and penalties clearly indicative of government concern.[39]

Referring to _R v. Code of Practice Committee of the British Pharmaceutical Society, ex p Professional Counselling Aids_,[40] Simon Brown J. noted that it is feature of that case and similar cases that "were no self-regulatory body in existence, Parliament would almost inevitably intervene to control the activity in question".[41] His Lordship noted:

> It cannot be suggested . . . that the Chief Rabbi performs public functions in the sense that he is regulating a field of public life and but for his offices the government would impose a statutory regime. On the contrary, his functions are essentially intimate, spiritual and religious functions which the government could not and would not seek to discharge in his place were he to abdicate his regulatory responsibility.[42]

The Court thus refused to allow judicial review, stating that to do so would "involve a clear departure from and extension of the principles established by [the _Datafin_ case]".[43]

The "but-for test" was not accepted in the High Court in _Geoghegan v. Institute of Chartered Accountants_[44] where a decision by the Institute of Char-

---

[39] _ibid._
[40] (1990) 3 Admin L.R. 697.
[41] [1993] 2 All E.R. 249, 254.
[42] [1993] 2 All E.R. 249, 254-255. See also _R v. London Beth Din: Ex Parte Bloom_, Unreported 1988 COD 131 and _R v. Provincial Court of the Church of Wales: Ex Parte Williams_, unreported, Q.B.D., October 23, 1998.
[43] See also _Peters v. Collinge_ [1993] 2 N.Z.L.R. 554 (H.C. N.Z.).
[44] [1995] 3 I.R. 86 (H.C., Murphy J.; and S.C.).

tered Accountants ("the Institute") to proceed with disciplinary charges was deemed not to be subject to judicial review. The Institute was incorporated by Royal Charter in 1888 and the Royal Charter was amended by the Institute of Chartered Accountants in Ireland Act 1966 which provides *inter alia* that bye-laws made, altered or amended by the Institute will only be effective when approved by the Government. Bye-laws were then introduced and approved establishing disciplinary procedures. Relying on the decisions in *Murphy v. The Turf Club* and *R v. The Disciplinary Committee of the Jockey Club, ex p. Aga Khan*, Murphy J. held that the decisions were purely private questions governed by consent and not amenable to judicial review. This decision was reached despite the fact that evidence before the Court demonstrated that the disciplinary code had been agreed as appropriate by the Government in the absence of legislation. The Supreme Court appeared divided on the issue of the availability of judicial review. In determining that judicial review should be available in this case, Denham J. identified a number of important factors:

(1) This case relates to a major profession, important in the community, with a special connection to the judicial organ of Government in the courts in areas such as receivership, liquidation, examinership, as well as having special auditing responsibilities.

(2) The original source of the powers of the Institute is the Charter: through that and legislation and the procedure to alter and amend the bye-laws, the Institute has a nexus with two branches of the Government of the State.

(3) The functions of the Institute and its members come within the public domain of the State.

(4) The method by which the contractual relationship between the Institute and the applicant was created is an important factor as it was necessary for the individual to agree in a "form" contract to the disciplinary process to gain entrance to membership of the Institute.

(5) The consequence of the domestic tribunal's decision may be very serious for a member

(6) The proceedings before the Disciplinary Committee must be fair and in accordance with the principles of natural justice, it must act judicially.[45]

Whilst Egan J. agreed that the Committee's decision was subject to judicial review, O'Flaherty J., with whom Blayney J. concurred, agreed with the decision of Murphy J. in the High Court.[46]

---

[45][1995] 3 I.R. 86, 130.
[46]Hamilton C.J. reserved his position on this point.

However, the *Wachmann* decision was followed in *R v. Football Associa-tion, ex parte Football League*,[47] where Rose J. stated:

> I accept [counsel's] submission that *Datafin* extends judicial review to a
> non-statutory body which exists otherwise than as the result of the exer-
> cise of the prerogative and that the ratio of the decision is that a body may
> be subject to judicial review if it regulates an important aspect of national
> life and does so with the support of the state in that, but for its existence,
> the state would create a public body to perform its functions. But *Datafin*
> does not, in my judgment, impinge on the decision in *Law* which I have
> earlier sought to summarise. It is common ground that both *Law* and
> *Datafin* are binding on me.[48]

It was noted that *Law*, although not referred to in the judgments, was cited in
argument by both sides in *Datafin*. Rose J. stated that it could not, therefore,
have been overlooked or regarded as inconsistent by the Court of Appeal.

> I have crossed a great deal of ground in order to reach what, on the au-
> thorities, is the clear and inescapable conclusion for me that the FA is not
> a body susceptible to judicial review either in general or, more particu-
> larly, at the instigation of the League, with whom it is contractually bound.
> Despite its virtually monopolistic powers and the importance of its deci-
> sions to many members of the public who are not contractually bound to
> it, it is, in my judgment, a domestic body whose powers arise from the
> duties exist in private law only. I find no sign of underpinning directly or
> indirectly by any organ or agency of the state or any potential govern-
> ment interest, as Simon Brown J. put it in *Wachmann*, nor is there any
> evidence to suggest that if the FA did not exist the state would intervene
> to create a public body to perform its functions. . . .But, for my part, to
> apply to the governing body of football, on the basis that it is a public
> body, principles honed for the control of the abuse of power by govern-
> ment and its creatures would involve what, in today's fashionable par-
> lance, would be called a quantum leap. It would also, in my view, for
> what it is worth, be a misapplication of increasingly scarce judicial re-
> sources.[49]

---

[47] [1993] 2 All E.R. 833 (C.A.). See also *Andreou v. Institute of Chartered Accountants in Eng-land & Wales* [1998] 1 All E.R. 14 (C.A.).

[48] [1993] 2 All E.R. 833, 845. Counsel for the applicant had argued that, whereas in *Law* the question was whether the particular decision had a public law impact, in *Datafin* the question was whether the particular body was open to judicial review. Successive Divisional Courts had, he said, confused these two separate questions.

[49] [1993] 2 All E.R. 833, 848.

Unlike the *Datafin*, "public element test" which focuses on the nature of the power, the "governmental interest" test looks at the context of power, marking thus a narrowing of the *Datafin* test.[50]

2.5 Conclusion

Despite the coherent and logical judgments in the *Datafin* case, the extension of judicial review to bodies operating without "visible means of legal support" has led to some confusion both in the UK and Irish courts. Attempts to draw the line between public and private law and to define a "public law function" have led to apparent inconsistencies of treatment and resultant uncertainty. The importance of "governmental influence" as opposed to "public interest" remains to be absolutely determined. Particularly in cases where decisions involve some form of exercise of contractual powers, matters still remain unsettled.

3. How Jurisdiction Should Be Exercised

As a statutory body exercising powers conferred by statute, the jurisdiction of the courts to entertain applications for judicial review of a decision of the Irish Takeover Panel was likely to be more straightforward. Thus, the findings of the Court of Appeal in the *Datafin* case on the issue of the existence of the jurisdiction would not have been as relevant to the Irish Takeover Panel. The second part of this paper concentrates however, on the importance of the second issued to be discussed by the Court in *Datafin* – the practical issue. It considers the effect of the judgment on the drafting of the Irish Takeover Panel Act 1997 and the possible implications, if any, for the operation of the Irish Takeover Panel.

3.1 Irish Takeover Panel

The Irish Takeover Panel Act 1997 ("the Act") establishes the Irish Takeover Panel ("the Irish Panel") as the body responsible for the monitoring and supervision of takeovers and other relevant transactions in relation to securities in relevant companies in Ireland.[51] The Act applies to takeovers of Irish companies whose shares are currently being traded on a market regulated by a

---

[50]Black, above, n.13, 36. See also *Scott v. National Trust* [1998] 2 All E.R. 705 (Ch.D.).
[51]See generally Clarke, *Takeovers and Mergers Law in Ireland* (Round Hall Sweet & Maxwell, Dublin, 1999) chap.3; Clarke, "Teaching a New Dog Old Tricks – the Irish Takeover Panel Rules" (1997) 4 *Commercial Law Practitioner* 195; Clarke, "Ireland: The Irish Takeover Panel Bill, 1996" (1997) 18 *The Company Lawyer* 32; Clarke, "The Irish Takeover Panel" (1996) 3 *Commercial Law Practitioner* 252; Clarke, "The Irish Takeover Panel Act 1997 – A Further Cutting of the UK Regulatory Ties" [1998] 1 *Palmer's In Company* 1.

recognised Stock Exchange or whose shares were so traded in the five years prior to the takeover. The Act may also apply to any public limited company prescribed by the Minister "in order to secure more fully the protection of shareholders". To date, no additional companies have been prescribed. The Irish Panel commenced operations in Ireland with effect from July 1, 1997.[52] The Act grants the Irish Panel rule-making powers and on the July 1, 1997, the Irish Takeover Panel Act 1997 (Takeover) Rules 1997 ("the Rules") came into operation. The former substantially mirrors the City Code although minor changes in wording have been made in order to render the Rules suitable for their statutory format. In addition, many of the Rules now confer express discretion on the Irish Panel as to whether to apply the provisions. Similarly, the Act allows the Irish Panel to grant derogations from, or waive, any of these Rules in exceptional circumstances.

It was clear from the outset that statutory enforcement provisions would be a necessary feature of takeover regulation in Ireland. As noted above, the ultimate sanction for non-compliance with a ruling of the London Panel is the withholding of the facilities of the securities markets in the City of London. However, due to the separation of the London and Dublin Stock Exchanges in 1995, the threat of suspending or removing a Stock Exchange listing would not now be as effective especially for a large foreign multinational company. In order to ensure compliance with the General Principles and the Rules, the Act thus empowers the Irish Panel to give directions to any party to the takeover. This might include for example, a direction to acquire or dispose of securities or to make an offer on specified terms. The Irish Panel is also entitled to enquire into the conduct of any person where it suspects that a contravention of the Rules or the General Principles has occurred or may occur. In the exercise of these powers, the Irish Panel may conduct a hearing, exercising the same powers and privileges as a High Court judge in relation to compelling attendance, examination on oath, and compelling the production of documents. Refusing to co-operate with the Irish Panel or hindering the conduct of the hearing may give rise to a criminal prosecution involving a fine and/or a prison sentence. Where the Irish Panel feels that its ruling or direction is unlikely to be complied with, it may also seek a High Court enforcement order.

Section 13(1) of the Act expressly confers the right to apply for judicial review of a rule, a derogation or waiver of such a rule, or a ruling or direction of the Panel under Order 84 of the Rules of the Superior Courts.[53] Indeed, this is stated to be the sole method of questioning the validity of the foregoing. However, section 13(2) of the Act provides that a rule may only be challenged in a situation where the Panel has made a ruling or given a direction based on

---

[52] Irish Takeover Panel Act 1997 (Commencement) Order 1997 (S.I. No. 158 of 1997) and Irish Takeover Panel Act 1997 (Commencement) (No.2) Order 1997 (S.I. No. 255 of 1997).
[53] S.I. No.15 of 1986.

that particular rule, to which the applicant is party. Section 13 of the Act was stated to be designed to provide "a balanced approach to ensure that parties can protect their interests while at the same time ensuring that takeover activity is not unduly impeded".[54] Fears had been expressed that the availability of judicial review in the context of takeovers would lead to tactical litigation. This concern has been reduced by requiring an applicant for judicial review to seek leave under the Act before applying. This allows the Court to refuse unmeritorious applications which are made merely to delay matters. Section 13(3)(b) of the Act provides that leave to apply for judicial review is not to be granted unless the Court is satisfied that there are substantial grounds for contending that the rule, derogation, waiver, ruling or direction is invalid or ought to be quashed.[55] Section 13(6) provides that the decision of the Court on the application for leave to apply or on the judicial review itself is final and leave to appeal to the Supreme Court will only be granted where the Court certifies that its decision involves a point of law of "exceptional public importance" and that it is desirable in the public interest that an appeal should be taken.[56] Clearly however, this will not prevent an appeal being taken on the issue of the constitutionality of any law.[57] To date, no applications for judicial review have been sought under section 13.

3.2 Grounds For An Application for Judicial Review

The second issue to be considered in the *Datafin* case was the manner in which the Court's jurisdiction should be exercised given the nature of the London Panel's activities in the financial markets and the need for speed and certainty in its decisions. The grounds upon which an application for judicial review

---

[54] Vol.149 Seanad Debates, Second Stage Col.1692.

[55] The issue of what constitutes "substantial grounds" has been considered by the Irish Courts on a number of occasions. In *McNamara v. An Bord Pleanála,* [1995] 2 I.L.R.M. 125, 130, Carroll J. stated that: "In order for a ground to be substantial it must be reasonable, it must be arguable, it must be weighty. It must not be trivial or tenuous".

[56] Provisions such as those found in s. 13(3)(b) and s. 13(6) are common in licensing and planning legislation. In *Lancefort Limited v. An Bord Pleanála (No. 2)* [1999] 2 I.R. 270 (S.C.) Keane J. noted that because s. 82(3)(A) of the Local Government (Planning and Development) Act 1963 (inserted by the Local Government (Planning and Development) Act 1976) as amended by s. 19(3) of the Local Government (Planning and Development) Act 1992 requires an applicant to institute proceedings within a strict time limit, and to establish "substantial grounds" for contending that the decision in question is invalid before leave is granted and severely restricts the right of appeal from the decision of the High Court to the Supreme Court, "the Oireachtas has made plain its concern that, given the existence of an elaborate appeals procedure which can be invoked by any member of the public and the determination of the issues by an independent board of qualified persons, the judicial review procedure should not be availed of as a form of further appeal by persons who may well be dissatisfied with the ultimate decision, but whose rights to be heard have been fully protected by the legislation. The courts are bound in their decisions to have serious regard to that concern" ([1999] 2 I.R. 270, 309-310).

[57] Section 13(7).

could be based were seen by the Court to be limited. Such a finding is consistent with the London Panel's character as the controlling body for the self-regulation of takeovers and mergers. It was noted that:

> the Panel combines the functions of legislator, court interpreting the Panel's legislation, consultant, and court investigating and imposing penalties in respect of alleged breaches of the Code.[58]

Against this background, it is clear that it would be difficult to prove any wrongdoing on the London Panel's part.

Firstly, Donaldson M.R. stated that there could be:

> little scope for complaint that the Panel has promulgated rules which are *ultra vires*, provided only that they do not clearly violate the principle proclaimed by the Panel of being based on the concept of doing equity between one shareholder and another.[59]

The Court stated that the London Panel was unlikely to violate this, its guiding principle. The same could be said of the Irish Panel.

Secondly, Donaldson M.R. stated that it would be difficult to argue that the London Panel had erred in interpreting its own rules and he suggested that the London Panel was to be given "considerable latitude" both "because, as legislator, it could properly alter them at any time and because of the form which the rules take, *i.e.* laying down principles to be applied in spirit as much as in letter in specific situations". [60] A court might intervene, his Lordship believed only where the interpretation "were so far removed from the natural and ordinary meaning of the words of the rules that an ordinary user of the market could reasonably be misled".[61] Even in this case, it was suggested the court might decide that it was more appropriate to declare the true meaning of the rule, leaving it to the London Panel to promulgate a new rule accurately expressing its intentions than to quash the London Panel's original decision. Similarly, his Lordship stated that the London Panel's discretionary power to grant dispensations from the operation of the rules was fettered only by the obligation to seek equity between shareholders. As a result, the London Panel could only be challenged "in wholly exceptional circumstances" and there again he indicated the appropriate relief was likely to be declaratory rather than remedial. Although the Irish Panel is a statutory body, the Act attempts to imbue it with as much flexibility and discretion as possible. Section 8 of the Act endows the Irish

---

[58] [1987] 1 Q.B. 815, 841; [1987] 1 All E.R. 564, 579.
[59] *ibid.*
[60] *ibid.*
[61] *ibid.*

Panel with general and specific rulemaking powers. Only rules made in respect of the substantial acquisition of shares and the Mergers, Takeovers and Monopolies (Control) Act 1978 must be submitted to the Minister for Enterprise and Employment in advance and approved. Section 8(7) of the Act empowers the Irish Panel to grant derogations from, and waivers in respect of any rules in exceptional circumstances where the Irish Panel considers it appropriate to do so. In making this decision, the Irish Panel is required to take into consideration the General Principles.

Finally, the Court in *Datafin* noted that the London Panel's disciplinary function would be open to challenge only if a lack of *bona fides* could be proven and even then the appropriate remedy would again be a declaration.

3.3 *Certiorari* and *Mandamus*

Matters of evidence are not reviewable by way of *certiorari*. Donaldson M.R. noted that:

> it is not for a court exercising a judicial review jurisdiction to substitute itself for the fact-finding tribunal, and error of law in the form of a finding of fact for which there was *no* evidence or in the form of a misconstruction of the Panel's own rules would normally be a matter to be dealt with by a declaratory judgement. [62]

Indeed the only circumstances in which the learned Judge could anticipate the use of the remedies of *certiorari* and *mandamus* was in the unlikely event of the London Panel acting in breach of the rules of natural justice. Thus, Donaldson M.R. stated that the role of a court in an appropriate case is:

> "to review the decision of the Panel and to consider whether there has been 'illegality' *i.e.* whether the Panel has misdirected itself in law, 'irrationality', *i.e.* whether the Panel's decision is so outrageous in its defiance of logic or accepted moral standards that no sensible person who had applied his mind to the question to be decided could have arrived at it, or 'procedural impropriety', *i.e.* a departure by the Panel from any procedural rules governing its conduct or a failure to observe the basic rules of natural justice. ... [63]

In *R v. Panel on Takeovers and Mergers, ex. parte Guinness*,[64] Lord Donaldson elaborated further on the grounds for granting relief. He said:

---

[62] *ibid.*
[63] [1987] 1 Q.B. 815, 842; [1987] 1 All E.R. 564, 580.
[64] [1989] 1 All E.R. 509 (C.A.).

Illegality would certainly apply if the Panel acted in breach of the general law, but it is more difficult to apply in the context of an alleged misinterpretation of its own rules by a body which under the scheme is both legislator and interpreter. Irrationality, at least in the sense of failing to take account of relevant factors or taking into account irrelevant factors, is a difficult concept in the context of a body which is itself charged with the duty of making a judgement on what is and what is not relevant, although clearly a theoretical scenario could be constructed in which the Panel acted on the basis of considerations which on any view must have been irrelevant or ignored something which on any view must have been relevant. And similar problems arise with procedural impropriety in the narrow sense of failing to follow accepted procedures, given the nature of the Panel and of its functions and the lack of any statutory or other guidance as to its procedures which are intended to be of its own devising. Similarly, in the broad sense of breach of the rules of natural justice, what is or is not fair may depend on underlying value judgements by the Panel as to the time scale which is appropriate for decision, the consequences of delay and matters of that kind.[65]

In this case, the Court of Appeal also held that where a right of appeal from the decision-making body existed but was not exercised, the court would only grant relief by way of judicial review in exceptional circumstances.

3.4 The Time Factor

In the *Datafin* case, the jurisdiction of the Court was also said to be limited in terms of the time factor involved. Donaldson M.R. stated that in light of:

> the special nature of the Panel, its functions, the market in which it is operating, the time scales which are inherent in that market and the need to safeguard the position of third parties, who may be numbered in thousands, all of whom are entitled to continue to trade on an assumption of the validity of the Panel's rules and decisions, unless and until they are quashed by a court, the relationship between the Panel and the court has to be historic rather than contemporaneous.[66]

Section 13(3)(a) of the Act provides that the application for leave to apply for judicial review must generally be made in the case of a rule, within seven days of the date when the related ruling or direction is made, and in the case of a

---

[65][1989] 1 All E.R. 509, 512.
[66][1987] 1 Q.B. 815, 842; [1987] 1 All E.R. 564, 579.

derogation, waiver, ruling or direction, within seven days from the date the derogation, waiver, ruling or direction is granted, made or given. This is in effect a "partial ouster clause" which restricts the use of judicial review. This period may only be extended in circumstances where the delay was not caused by the default or neglect of the applicant or any person acting for them and where an extension would not cause injustice to any other party concerned in the matter. In considering whether injustice would be done, the Court must consider (a) the length of time which has elapsed since the completion of the takeover or relevant transaction or any substantial step in the effecting of such a takeover or relevant transaction and (b) the nature of the relief that could ultimately be granted to the applicant.[67]

The uniquely strict time limit set out in the Act demonstrates the commitment of the Legislature to a swift settlement of any disputes. It is entirely consistent with the acceptance of the Court in *Datafin* of "the special needs of the financial markets for speed on the part of decision-makers".[68]

His Lordship went on to explain that he would expect:

> the contemporary decisions to take their course, considering the complaint and intervening, if at all, later and in respect by declaratory orders which would enable the Panel not to repeat any error and would relieve the individuals of the disciplinary consequences of any erroneous findings of breach of the rules.[69]

This decision ensures that judicial review cannot be used as "a mere ploy" or a delay tactic in takeover battles. In *Datafin*, the Court suggested that the Panel and those affected should treat its decisions as valid and binding, unless and until they are set aside. The strict time limit imposed in the Act avoids the need for the parties to ignore any applications, as it is likely that the application will be settled within a short period.

4. CONCLUSION

In *Datafin*, Donaldson M.R. suggested that the Court should grant certiorari and mandamus only where there had been a breach of natural justice and that in all other cases contemporary decisions of the Panel should take their course and the relationship of the Court and Panel should be "historic rather than contemporaneous".[70] Clearly, there is an acceptance in the Act that the remedy

---

[67] Section 13(5).
[68] [1987] 1 Q.B. 815, 840; [1987] 1 All E.R. 564, 578.
[69] *ibid.*
[70] [1987] 1 Q.B. 815, 842; [1987] 1 All E.R. 564, 579.

of judicial review should not be lightly available, and that there should be a minimum degree of delay to the transaction. It remains to be seen however, whether the Irish Court in its choice of orders will limit itself to a declaration with prospective effect.

TAKING THE TREATY SERIOUSLY
New Zealand Maori Council v. Attorney General
(1987)

ANDREW S. BUTLER*

1. Introduction

"This case is perhaps as important for the future of our country as any that has come before a New Zealand Court."

"This case is of the greatest public importance . . . in its impact on racial relationships in New Zealand . . . ."

These, the opening lines of the judgments of, respectively, Cooke P. and Richardson J. (as they then were) in *New Zealand Maori Council v. Attorney-General* ("the *First Maori Council case*"),[1] almost of themselves self-select that case for inclusion as New Zealand's leading case of the century.[2] Indeed, reaction in the press reflected the importance of the case. It was referred to as a "landmark judgment",[3] which had "finally restor[ed] the Treaty of Waitangi to a central role in the legal system", with the result that "New Zealand had finally moved into a post-colonial era".[4]

The *First Maori Council case* involved an action by a Maori representative group for a declaration that any transfer of Crown assets to new state trading

---

*Barrister & Solicitor of the High Court of New Zealand; Senior Lecturer, Victoria University of Wellington. Many thanks to Nilay Patel for his research assistance.

[1] [1987] 1 N.Z.L.R. 641 (C.A) 651 *per* Cooke P., 668 *per* Richardson J.

[2] See also Somers J. *ibid.*, 686 who noted that the case "is of great importance not only to the parties to it but also for the impact it may have on the social future of the country"; the title of R. P. Boast's article, *"New Zealand Maori Council v. Attorney-General*: the case of the century?" [1987] *N.Z.L.J.* 240; Professor Sir Kenneth Keith (now Keith J.), "The Roles of the Tribunal, the Courts and the Legislature" (1995) 25 *V.U.W.L.R.* 129, 129 ("that most important decision"); and former Prime Minister and Professor of Law, Sir Geoffrey Palmer, "Where to From Here?" (1995) 25 *V.U.W.L.R.* 241, 242 ("the great constitutional case").

[3] "Historic Case Won by Maori" Editorial *Evening Post,* June 30, 1987.

[4] Remarks of (respectively) the Project Waitangi organisation, and Dr Ranginui Walker, Chairman of the Auckland District Maori Council, reported in "Maori people partnership role stressed" *Evening Post,* June 30, 1987, 5.

enterprises without a system in place to protect those assets which were the subject of land grievances from alienation would violate the "principles" of the Treaty of Waitangi ("the Treaty"). The Court of Appeal, interpreting the relevant statutory provisions, unanimously agreed and thereby initiated a flurry of litigation on Maori issues that has continued unabated for the last decade.

But as a leading public law case in a constitutional system centred on parliamentary sovereignty, the *First Maori Council case* displays the inherent tension between innovation and legal restraint demanded of judges. On the one hand, its attempt to give life in contemporary conditions to the spirit and principles of a treaty signed almost 150 years earlier have influenced the political and legal agenda and have given Maori a belief that their grievances can be heard in the legal as well as the political forum. On the other hand, however, the Court of Appeal's approach was doctrinally quite conservative. In particular, each judgment was premised on upholding traditional notions of parliamentary sovereignty and emphasised the limited domestic effect of the Treaty absent statutory recognition. Moreover, the decision appeared to leave the initiative for the recognition of rights flowing from the Treaty in the hands of Parliament: the courts would, and could, only intervene to the extent that Parliament explicitly provided.

2. Historical and Legal Context

2.1 Historical background to the Treaty of Waitangi[5]

From the beginning of the nineteenth century, contact between the Maori inhabitants of New Zealand and foreigners (known as *Pakeha* in Maori) started in earnest. Traders, whalers, missionaries and others came to New Zealand. This contact caused concern on all sides. There were concerns about the lawlessness of the foreigners who were outside the jurisdiction of their European homelands; fears by Maori for the peaceful enjoyment of their culture and lands; and so on. Among the European powers, competition for spheres of influence was increasing; and in Europe colonisation movements were seeking out new countries for settlement.

The British Government instructed Captain Hobson to engage in negotiations with Maori for the assumption of British sovereignty over the islands of New Zealand. On 6 February 1840, the Treaty was signed by representatives of the British Crown and about fifty North Island Maori chiefs. In May 1840, without having secured the signatures of all North Island chiefs and having secured no signatures by tribes of the South Island (he regarded the southern tribes to be uncivilised), Hobson issued two proclamations declaring British

---

[5] See generally Orange, *The Treaty of Waitangi* (Allen & Unwin, Wellington, 1987).

sovereignty over New Zealand. The first declared British sovereignty over the North Island on the basis of cession (through the Treaty). The second declared British sovereignty over the South Island by virtue of Cook's discoveries in the previous century. These proclamations appeared in the *London Gazette* on 2 October 1840 and have since been regarded as authoritatively establishing in international and colonial law Crown sovereignty over New Zealand.

2.2 The Terms of the Treaty

The Treaty was drawn up in English and Maori, but the two texts do not exactly correspond.[6] There has been continuing disagreement as to the exact meaning of the Maori text and the importance of its differences from the English text. Moreover, if it is recalled that many of the Maori signatories were unable to read and would have signed the Treaty based on the oral explanation of its terms given at particular signing meetings, it will be appreciated how difficult is the task of resolving the textual differences.

The Treaty is very short. By the first article of the Treaty, Maori gave "absolutely to [the Crown] for ever complete government [*Kawanatanga*] over their land."[7] By the second article the Crown guaranteed "the full exclusive and undisturbed possession of their Lands and Estates Forests Fisheries and other properties . . . so long as it is their desire to retain the same in their possession"[8] with an exclusive Crown right of pre-emption over those lands on terms to be agreed between Maori and the Crown. Under the third article the Crown extended to Maori its "royal protection and imparts to them the Rights and Privileges of British subjects".[9]

2.3 Traditional Treatment of the Treaty in Domestic Law

The *locus classicus* is Lord Simon L.C.'s opinion for the Privy Council in *Te Heuheu Tukino v. Aotea District Maori Land Board*.[10] The plaintiff challenged

---

[6] See also Walker, *Ka Whawhai Tonu Matou. Struggle Without End* (Penguin, Auckland, 1990) 263-6.

[7] Professor I. H. Kawharu's translation of Maori version of the text referred to in *First Maori Council case* [1987] 1 N.Z.L.R. 641, 663.

[8] Original English version of the text. Professor Kawharu's translation of the Maori version of art. 2 refers to the Crown's agreement "to protect the chiefs, the subtribes and all the people of New Zealand in the unqualified exercise of their chieftainship [*rangatiratanga*] over their lands, villages and all their treasures [*taonga*]." In Maori *taonga* is a broad concept embracing any treasured thing, tangible or intangible, such as for example the Maori language. The reader will readily see that there is a significant divergence in meaning between the English and Maori texts of art. 2, but space constraints prevent me from delving into the many interesting views expressed on the issue.

[9] *ibid.*

[10][1941] A.C. 308 (P.C.).

the power of the New Zealand legislature to impose a charge on Maori lands on the ground that the statute conflicted with the right of Maori to enjoy the exclusive and undisturbed enjoyment of their lands (Article 2 of the Treaty). The Privy Council dismissed the plaintiff's claim. First, for any rights under a treaty of cession to be cognisable by a court "they [have to] have been incorporated in the municipal law."[11] That had not occurred here. Second, even if Article 2 rights had been incorporated in New Zealand domestic law, such incorporation "would not deprive the legislature of its power to alter or amend such a statute by later enactments."[12] This much represented (and continues to represent) the standard legal view of the domestic effectiveness of treaties of cession in English colonies. But the existence of the Treaty, from the Maori perspective, was to have negative effects beyond its unenforceability.

Under traditional common law, where the Crown had assumed sovereignty over new territory, the radical title to the territory moved from the previous sovereign(s) to the Crown, but the title to use and enjoy land (communally or individually) previously recognised under native laws and customs remained in place (provided that the peoples were "civilised"), until extinguished by Crown purchase or ousted by statute.[13] This approach was reflected in an early decision of the New Zealand Supreme Court, *R. (McIntosh) v. Symonds*, which affirmed that "in solemnly guaranteeing the native title, and in securing what is called the Queen's pre-emptive right, the Treaty of Waitangi, confirmed by the Charter of the Colony, does not assert either in doctrine or in practice anything new and unsettled".[14] The common law "secures to them all the enjoyments from the land which they had before our intercourse . . .".[15]

Notwithstanding *Symonds*, from the late 1870s onwards[16] the local judiciary refused to give effect to customary native title absent a statute, saying that to do so would be in effect to enforce the terms of the Treaty contrary to the rules related to treaties of cession. In *Wi Parata v. Bishop of Wellington*,[17] Prendergast C.J. refused to recognise any aboriginal claim to land where the claimants did not hold a Crown-grant title pursuant to the Native Land Acts

---

[11] [1941] A.C. 308, 324.

[12] [1941] A.C. 308, 327.

[13] *St Catherine's Milling and Lumber Co. v. R.* (1888) 14 App. Cas. 46, (P.C.) 55; *Attorney-General v. John Holt & Co.* [1915] A.C. 599 (P.C.); *Amodu Tijani v. The Secretary, Southern Rhodesia* [1921] 2 A.C. 399 (P.C.). See generally, McNeil, *Common Law Aboriginal Title* (Oxford: Clarendon, 1989).

[14] (1847) [1840-1932] N.Z.P.C.C. 387 (S.C.) 390 *per* Chapman J.

[15] [1840-1932] N.Z.P.C.C. 387, 391.

[16] See generally McHugh, *Maori Magna Carta: New Zealand Law and the Treaty of Waitangi* (Oxford University Press, Auckland, 1991) and Hackshaw, "Nineteenth Century Notions of Aboriginal Title and their Influence on the Interpretation of the Treaty of Waitangi" in Kawharu, (ed.), *Waitangi: Maori and Pakeha Perspectives of the Treaty of Waitangi* (Oxford University Press, Auckland, 1989).

[17] (1877) 3 N.Z.Jur. (N.S.) S.C. 72.

1862 and 1865.[18] On this approach common law aboriginal title simply did not exist. Moreover, claimants could not seek to rely on the "so-called" Treaty as an alternative source of aboriginal land rights, because in law it was a "nullity".[19]

There followed a period of struggle between the local courts and the Privy Council over issues related to aboriginal land rights issues. In *Wallis v. Solicitor-General*,[20] their Lordships implicitly accused the Court of Appeal of refusing to grant appropriate relief for fear of conflict with the executive government. The response was an extraordinary "Protest of Bench and Bar" on 25 April 1903 in the course of which the local judiciary's view of the Treaty, as propounded in *Wi Parata,* was defended.[21]

The Native Land Act 1909, which provided that customary title was not available against the Crown, largely resolved the issue in favour of the local judges' approach. The impotence of the Treaty in this environment was confirmed by the Privy Council in *Te Heuheu Tukino* discussed above. It is not surprising then that Lindsay Buick in the preface to the second edition of his book, *The Treaty of Waitangi,* (1932) noted "a waning interest in the chief political incident in the history of our country".[22]

2.4 Maori Perspective on the Treaty[23]

The Maori perspective on the Treaty was altogether different from that of the settlers. While the significance of the Treaty was not much appreciated in its early days when Maori were still in the ascendancy, the influx of immigrants (soon outgrowing the dwindling Maori population), coupled with the establishment of a settler government in 1852, hastened tension between Maori and non-Maori, particularly in relation to land acquisition. After the Land Wars of the 1860s[24] resulted in the breaking-up of concerted Maori resistance to the settlers and also saw large tracts of Maori land being unjustly confiscated;[25] in light of the subsequent transformation of much Maori communal land to individual freehold titles through the Native Land Court established in 1867;[26]

---

[18]See the discussion in McHugh, above, n.16, 112-7.

[19](1877) 3 N.Z.Jur. (N.S.) S.C. 72, 78-9.

[20][1903] A.C. 173 (P.C.). The Court of Appeal's judgment is at (1902) 21 N.Z.L.R. 655 (C.A.).

[21]Reproduced in [1840-1934] N.Z.P.C.C. 730-760.

[22]Buick, *The Treaty of Waitangi* (Thom. Avery & Sons Ltd, New Plymouth, 1933) vii. See also Orange above, n.5, 234 who comments that from the 1880s until the 1930s, "Pakeha interest in the treaty . . . had been minimal."

[23]See generally, Walker, "The Treaty of Waitangi as the Focus of Maori Protest" in Kawharu, (ed.), above, n.16, 263-279.

[24]Belich, *The New Zealand Wars* (Penguin, Auckland, 1987).

[25]Rice, (ed.) *The Oxford History of New Zealand* (Oxford University Press, Auckland, 1992) 187 *et seq.*

with the spread of disease and the undermining of chiefly authority, the traditional Maori way of life was under severe threat.

For many, the Treaty was seen as a way of countering the degradation of
Maoridom. From the 1870s onwards various Maori parliaments and gatherings
were convened to consider how best to use the Treaty as a means of protecting
Maori. Between 1882 and 1924 no less than four Maori deputations went to
London to enlist the intercession of the English monarch (in whose name the
Crown's Treaty undertakings with Maori had been pledged) with the settler
government to secure Treaty compliance. All were unsuccessful. Efforts to
have the New Zealand Parliament enact a Maori Rights Bill failed (1896), as
did a petition to have the Treaty ratified by the same Parliament (1936). Despite these setbacks Maori continually and consistently invoked the Treaty as
the source of claims for equal treatment with non-Maori and as the source of
Crown obligations to protect their interests. Gradually in the 1970s Maori protests based on the Treaty became more concerted. The annual Waitangi Day
ceremonies at the Waitangi (meeting house) *marae* became a focal point of
protest and resulted in a large number of arrests. Finally some change occurred.
Of great significance was the passage in 1975 of the Treaty of Waitangi Act
designed to ensure that Treaty grievances could be dealt with.

2.5 The Waitangi Tribunal[27]

The Treaty of Waitangi Act 1975 established the Waitangi Tribunal "to make
recommendations on claims relating to the practical application of the principles of the Treaty and, for that purpose, to determine its meaning and effect and
whether certain matters are inconsistent with those principles . . .".[28] Originally section 6(1) of the 1975 Act restricted the "jurisdiction" of the Tribunal
to hearing claims that (1) enactments in force; (2) governmental polices or
practices currently in force or proposed to be adopted; or (3) any other acts
done or omitted, or proposed to be done or omitted by the Crown, were "inconsistent with the principles of the Treaty". In 1985 the Act was amended to
allow the Tribunal to investigate historical grievances dating back to the time
of the signing of the Treaty in 1840.[29] Importantly, the Tribunal's jurisdiction
was purely recommendatory and non-binding (section 6(3)).

The enactment of the 1975 Act, as Richardson J. observed in the *First
Maori Council case*, "pointed to the existence of a body of unmet grievances.

---

[26]Williams, *Te Kooti Tango Whenua: The Native Land Court* (Huia, Wellington, 1999); Boast,
   Ereuti and Smith, *Maori Land Law* (Butterworths, Wellington, 1999) ch. 2.
[27]See, *e.g.*, Durie, "Background Paper" (1995) 25 *V.U.W.L.R.* 97; Sorrenson, "Towards a Radical
   Reinterpretation of New Zealand History: the role of the Waitangi Tribunal" in Kawharu (ed.)
   above, n. 16, ch. 6.
[28]Long Title to the 1975 Act.
[29]S.3(1) of the Treaty of Waitangi Amendment Act 1985, inserting a new s.6(1) in the 1975 Act.

Its extension . . . to Crown conduct and events extending back to February 6, 1840 must have reflected a legislative intention that long-felt Maori grievances should and would be aired and findings made in a judicial forum".[30] While the Tribunal's initial impact was minor, the later work of the Tribunal has laid a solid foundation as to the meaning of the "principles of the Treaty". It has referred to the Treaty as "the foundation for a developing social contract"[31] designed "to provide a direction for future growth and development",[32] based on notions of partnership. As a partner the Crown has a duty not only to recognise Maori interests specified in the Treaty but also to actively protect them.[33] Moreover, the Tribunal has emphasised that "[p]ast wrongs can be put right, in a practical way, and it is not too late to begin again".[34] Moreover, the Tribunal's jurisprudence has recognised that the concept of treasure or *taonga* in art. 2 embraces economic and non-economic cultural assets and interests.

3. THE CASE: *NEW ZEALAND MAORI COUNCIL V. ATTORNEY-GENERAL*

3.1 State Owned Enterprises legislation and Treaty claims

As part of its reform programme the Fourth Labour Government elected in 1984 set about a radical overhaul of New Zealand's public sector enterprises, detaching many services from ministerial departments and constituting them as self-standing, corporate entities in which the state retained control through sole shareholdings. This was to be achieved through the State-Owned Enterprises Act 1986 ("S.O.E. Act").

Prior to the enactment of the S.O.E. Act the Department of Lands and Survey and the New Zealand Forest Service administered about 14 million hectares of land. It was proposed that about 10 million hectares of Crown land would pass to the fourteen S.O.E.s established under the 1986 Act. After the S.O.E. Bill was introduced into Parliament, a number of Maori (who had brought, or had hoped to bring, claims before the Waitangi Tribunal) expressed concern that if enacted, it would significantly reduce the amount of Crown land with which to redress Maori grievances proved before the Tribunal.

These claimants filed an urgent claim before the Tribunal to the effect that the Bill would violate the principles of the Treaty. The Tribunal in an interim report agreed.[35] The Tribunal recommended that protective measures be included in the S.O.E. legislation. As a result, the S.O.E. Bill was amended by the addition of two crucial provisions, sections 9 and 27.

---

[30] [1987] 1 N.Z.L.R. 641, 683.
[31] *Te Atiawa Report*, W.A.I. No. 6, March 17, 1983, 61.
[32] *ibid.*
[33] *Manakau Harbour Report*, W.A.I. No. 8, July 19, 1985, 95.
[34] *ibid.*
[35] *Claim No A23 Interim report*, December 8, 1986, 2.

Section 27(1) prevented the alienation of any S.O.E. land, except to the Crown, where the land was the subject of a Tribunal claim lodged prior to the Governor-General's assent to the S.O.E. legislation. Section 27(2) gave the Governor-General a discretionary power to order the resumption of S.O.E. land by the Crown (upon the payment of compensation) following a Tribunal recommendation in relation to a land claim. The section 27(2) power applied in respect of claims lodged both before and after the Governor-General's assent to the S.O.E. legislation.

Section 9 was a straightforward provision, which simply read:

> **9. Treaty of Waitangi** – Nothing in this Act shall permit the Crown to act in a manner that is inconsistent with the principles of the Treaty of Waitangi.

The Bill received the royal assent on December 18, 1986.

3.2 The Proceedings

In early 1987, the Prime Minister announced that Crown lands were about to be transferred to S.O.E.s. The New Zealand Maori Council and others, dissatisfied with the protection which the Crown appeared to be offering Tribunal claimants, applied for judicial review of the projected transfers, and sought appropriate declarations that any move by the Crown to transfer its lands to S.O.E.s would be contrary to section 9 of the S.O.E. Act. They also sought a declaration that the Crown was under a duty to consult with Maori in relation to each proposed transfer.

The claimants were of the view that Crown land which was the subject of a post-18 December 1986 claim and which was transferred by an S.O.E. into private hands would fall outside section 27 protection and not be recoverable to satisfy a Tribunal claim. Moreover, on interrogatories, the claimants secured an important admission from the Crown that it had not established any system to consider whether a Tribunal claim existed in relation to each asset passing from Crown hands into those of an S.O.E. This posed the danger that an inadvertent transfer into private hands of Crown land subject to Tribunal claims could in fact occur. This danger was unacceptable as land was a precious *taonga* (or treasure) which could not be replaced by the payment of money. The claimants submitted that in such cases the broadly worded section 9 of the S.O.E. Act could be relied upon to prevent any transfer of Crown land to S.O.E.s.

The Crown for its part accepted that the protective ambit of section 27 was limited in the manner suggested by the claimants, but argued that section 27 was a complete code as to the treatment of Crown land subject to Tribunal investigation: the limited protective ambit provided by section 27 could not be outflanked by reliance on the generally worded section 9.

3.3 Court of Appeal Decision

The Court of Appeal unanimously granted a declaration that the failure to put in place a system to check whether Crown lands being transferred to S.O.E.s were the subject of Tribunal claims was unlawful; required the Crown to submit a scheme of safeguards to the Court within 21 days from the date of the judgment; and further declared that no action by the Crown in relation to Crown assets under the S.O.E. Act was to be undertaken.[36] However, the Court refused to declare that the Crown was bound to consult with Maori.

3.4 The Statutory Interpretation Point

All judges rejected the Crown's submission that section 27 was exhaustive of Parliament's intention to protect Treaty claims to Crown land. If section 27 was intended to be a code, then enactment of section 9 would have been superfluous.[37] Acceptance of the Crown's argument would, said Casey J., reduce section 9 to "a token gesture of goodwill".[38] This view of Parliament's intention neither he, nor his colleagues, were prepared to accept. Bisson J. expressed his view strongly, stating:

> It is inconceivable that Parliament, after passing the extended provisions of the Treaty of Waitangi Act on 9 December 1985 [*i.e.* the Treaty of Waitangi Amendment Act 1985] with the intention of putting an end to long outstanding and legitimate grievances which had simmered in the breasts of Maoris from generation to generation since 1840 without a special tribunal being available to consider such grievances would on 30 September 1986, only 10 months later, introduce in the form of the State-Owned Enterprises Bill legislation which might deprive some claimants with legitimate grievances from attaining the very thing which was at the heart of their grievances, namely the recovery of the land still owned by the Crown, land in respect of which they had been wrongly deprived.[39]

Similarly, Cooke P. refused to accept the Crown's limited view of section 9. Such an interpretation "would go close to treating the declaration made by Parliament about the Treaty as a dead letter. That would be unhappily and unacceptably reminiscent of an attitude, now past, that the Treaty itself is of no true value to the Maori people".[40]

---

[36] See the proposed orders set out in the judgment of Cooke P.: [1987] 1 N.Z.L.R. 641, 666.
[37] [1987] 1 N.Z.L.R. 641, 658 *per* Cooke P.; 679-680 *per* Richardson J.; 695-6 *per* Somers J.; 701 *per* Casey J.; 708-710 *per* Bisson J.
[38] [1987] 1 N.Z.L.R. 641, 701.
[39] [1987] 1 N.Z.L.R. 641, 700.
[40] [1987] 1 N.Z.L.R. 641, 661.

In light of the rejection of the Crown's principal argument, the central issue became the scope and interpretation of section 9.

3.5 The Principles of the Treaty: Approach and Application.

The judges emphasised that what Parliament required by section 9 was that effect be given to the *principles* of the Treaty, not the literal text.[41] This enabled the Court to avoid the substantial controversy over the interpretation of the precise language of the Maori and English texts, which it did not have to resolve.

Next, all members of the Court preferred to adopt a generous approach to the interpretation of the Treaty, not pedantic, traditional legalism. In the words of Cooke P., "[w]hat matters is the spirit".[42]

The judges emphasised that the Treaty, though almost 150 years old, was a living document. While the principles of the Treaty might be the same today as they were when it was signed in 1840, what has changed, as Somers J. observed, are the "circumstances to which those principles are to apply".[43]

Cooke P. added a further element: that of interpreting the Treaty as "a document relating to fundamental rights", taking account of relevant developments in international human rights norms.[44]

The Court then had to determine what the *relevant* principles were in this case. That in turn called for "an assessment of the relationship the parties hoped to create by and reflect in [the Treaty], and an inquiry into the benefits and obligations involved in applying its language in today's changed conditions and expectations in the light of that relationship".[45] Deriving assistance from the work of the Waitangi Tribunal, the Court focussed on the concept of "partnership".[46] The principle of Treaty partnership was compared with fiduciary duties, and Cooke P.'s further comments were largely consistent with what one might find in such duty:[47] "the duty of the Crown is not merely passive but extends to active protection of Maori people in the use of their lands and waters to the fullest extent practicable".

In his judgment, Richardson J. regarded "the honour of the Crown"[48] as a relevant and important principle of the relationship created by the Treaty. His Honour explained it thus:

---

[41] See, *e.g.* [1987] 1 N.Z.L.R. 641, 662 *per* Cooke P.; 714 *per* Bisson J.
[42] [1987] 1 N.Z.L.R. 641, 663.
[43] [1987] 1 N.Z.L.R. 641, 692; see also 673 *per* Richardson J.
[44] [1987] 1 N.Z.L.R. 641, 655-6.
[45] [1987] 1 N.Z.L.R. 641, 702 *per* Casey J.
[46] See *e.g.* [1987] 1 N.Z.L.R. 641, 664 *per* Cooke P.; 715 *per* Bisson J.
[47] [1987] 1 N.Z.L.R. 641, 664.
[48] [1987] 1 N.Z.L.R. 641, 682.

Where the focus is on the role of the Crown and the conduct of the Government that emphasis on the honour of the Crown is important. It captures the crucial point that the Treaty is a positive force in the life of the nation and so in the government of the country. [49]

Applying the notions of partnership, of good faith, and of the honour of the Crown to the facts of the instant case, the Court concluded that the transfer of Crown lands to S.O.E.s was such a major initiative that, although it was within the Government's prerogative to so decide, as a reasonable Treaty partner it should take Maori into its confidence regarding the method by which to implement the policy. In particular, a partner would have put in place safeguards for claims already known to the Crown, whether or not they have yet been submitted to the Waitangi Tribunal. [50]

On the issue of consultation, however, the Court found against Maori. Cooke P. was of the view that such relief would be difficult to implement (who should be consulted?) and would "hold up the processes of Government". [51] Richardson J. for similar reasons held that "an absolute open-ended and formless duty to consult is incapable of practical fulfilment and cannot be regarded as implicit in the Treaty". [52]

3.6 Parliamentary Sovereignty

While the Court's analysis of the S.O.E. Act and its interpretation and application of the principles of the Treaty represented success, even "victory", for the Maori people, [53] the members of the Court were at pains to emphasise the limitations of the judicial role in giving effect to the Treaty. In particular, the Court clearly reaffirmed the position that the Treaty is not a supreme law bill of rights or overriding constitutional document, and that while the Treaty imposes solemn obligations on the Crown and Parliament, it does not qualify New Zealand's legislative sovereignty. Somers J. stressed that:

Neither the provisions of the Treaty of Waitangi nor its principles are, as a matter of law, a restraint on the legislative supremacy of Parliament. [54]

Second, the judges acknowledged the important initiatives taken by Parlia-

---

[49] [1987] 1 N.Z.L.R. 641, 682. See also 702 and 703 *per* Casey J.

[50] [1987] 1 N.Z.L.R. 641, 665 *per* Cooke P.; 704 *per* Casey J.

[51] [1987] 1 N.Z.L.R. 641, 665.

[52] [1987] 1 N.Z.L.R. 641, 683.

[53] [1987] 1 N.Z.L.R. 641, 667 *per* Cooke P. In an unusual addendum to the case, signalling the case's great significance, Cooke P. sought to explain the effect of the Court's decision. He clearly preferred to see the result as a success for Maori, but recognised that others might speak in terms of "victory".

[54] [1987] 1 N.Z.L.R. 641, 691.

ment which enabled the Court to be in a position to adjudicate upon the dispute. As Cooke P. observed (having referred to section 9 of the S.O.E. Act and the Treaty of Waitangi Act):

> If the judiciary has been able to play a role to some extent creative, that is because *the legislature has given the opportunity*.[55]

This made it clear that without parliamentary leash the ability of the Courts to redress historic Maori grievances and protect Treaty-related rights and interests was likely to be limited. Only Cooke P. held out the possibility that, "when interpreting ambiguous legislation" reference might be had to the Treaty even absent explicit mention of the Treaty.[56]

4. ASSESSMENT OF THE *FIRST MAORI COUNCIL CASE* ON ITS TERMS

Writing soon after the Court of Appeal judgments were released, respected Maori Law scholar Richard Boast commented that, "[t]o a very large degree, the judgments . . . are an exercise in utterly orthodox statutory interpretation . . .".[57] In terms of the resolution of the potential conflict between sections 27 and 9 of the S.O.E. Act this is plainly true. However, a very significant component of the decision related to the interpretation of the expression "principles of the Treaty of Waitangi". This exercise involved considerable reference to materials which are non-orthodox. In this regard, the Court was greatly assisted by the pioneering work of the Waitangi Tribunal.[58]

In addition, and very significantly, the rhetoric of the Court of Appeal judgments strikes a clear break with the past in several ways. First, there is a new judicial characterisation of the Treaty. The Treaty is no longer a "so-called treaty", nor a useful mechanism to pacify the natives, but rather a "solemn compact", dealing with "fundamental rights"; a "living instrument" setting out the "social contract" between Maori and the Crown, and premised upon notions of good faith "partnership" and "the honour of the Crown".

Second, the language of the judgments centred on the notion of a Maori-*Pakeha* partnership. This analysis of the relationship between Maori and *Pakeha* marks a shift in jurisprudential thinking about the nature of governance in New Zealand. No longer are Maori to be regarded as subjects, or as one interest group among many; rather Maori, being a Treaty partner, have direct access to

---

[55][1987] 1 N.Z.L.R. 641, 668, emphasis added.

[56][1987] 1 N.Z.L.R. 641, 656. On the expansive, non-literal, approaches to interpretation adopted by the Court of Appeal, *cp. Pepper v. Hart* [1993] A.C. 593 (H.L.) on which see Mullan, "Purposive Interpretation and Parliamentary Materials *Pepper v. Hart* (1993)" below, 467.

[57][1987] *N.Z.L.J.* 240, 242.

[58]Acknowledged at [1987] 1 N.Z.L.R. 641, 661 *per* Cooke P.; 702 *per* Casey J.

the Crown, and expectations in terms of how they will be treated, which are referable to the terms of the Treaty. While subject, like all New Zealanders, to the ultimate exercise of sovereignty by Parliament the principles of the Treaty require that a special status be accorded Maori.

Third, and closely related, the judges went out of their way to acknowledge the legitimate sense of Maori grievance. Cooke P. noted that, "[a]ll too clearly there have been breaches in the past".[59] Richardson J noted "a body of unlet grievances",[60] and referred to the Crown as "the lagging partner" which had been guilty of "neglect".[61] Somers J. acknowledged that the terms of the Treaty "were broken"[62] while Bisson J. referred to "long outstanding and legitimate grievances".[63] The judgments recognised Maori compliance with their Treaty obligations and identifies the Crown as the party which has failed to meet Treaty obligations. The importance of this rhetorical stance is that the Court of Appeal, while dispensing Crown justice, is nonetheless seen to distance itself from the executive. It is a bicultural Court, not in the sense that its composition is bicultural,[64] but rather in the sense that its perspective is bicultural. It favours neither the Crown nor Maori, but works for the betterment of the partnership upon which both Treaty partners embarked 150 years before. This is certainly a shift from the executive–bias evident in *Wallis*.[65]

Fourth, for many years New Zealand courts had not been welcoming forums for Maori claimants, particularly where the Treaty was involved. The *First Maori Council case* represented a major advance, indicating to Maori that the courts were willing to protect their rights and interests under the Treaty, once the law permitted. Moreover, the courts were prepared to be "creative"[66] in such endeavours (subject always to overriding constitutional grundnorms such as parliamentary sovereignty).

As regards the Court's actual decision, the application of the "principles" of the Treaty to the instant case steered a good course between empty gestures and radicality. Introducing extensive consultation requirements in a situation where a major plank of Government reform would likely be delayed would have been impolitic in the first case on section 9. Doubtless, it would also have posed some practical problems in terms of who should be consulted and how meaningful and lengthy that consultation should be (problems since reasonably well resolved). Moreover, it was unnecessary to insist on consultation

[59] [1987] 1 N.Z.L.R. 641, 667
[60] [1987] 1 N.Z.L.R. 641, 683.
[61] [1987] 1 N.Z.L.R. 641, 672.
[62] [1987] 1 N.Z.L.R. 641, 692.
[63] [1987] 1 N.Z.L.R. 641, 710.
[64] Eddie Durie, Chief Judge of the Maori Land Court and Chairman of the Waitangi Tribunal, was the first Maori appointed to the High Court bench. He was appointed in 1998.
[65] See text above, n.17.
[66] [1987] 1 N.Z.L.R. 641, 668 *per* Cooke P.

when the Crown had admitted to having failed to implement the straightforward safeguard of putting in place a system to monitor asset transfers for the existence of a Tribunal claim. The delay which the establishment of such a system involved was reasonable in the circumstances but also demonstrated that adequate but effective remedies would be available from the courts where section 9 was not respected by the Crown. At the same time, however, the Court was signalling to Government that it need not fear that the Treaty principles would be the source of impossibly onerous requirements on its activities.

However, while the rhetoric of the *First Maori Council case* may have marked a departure from the past, in a key area the decision is doctrinally conservative.

As we have noted, the Court clearly reaffirmed the approach of the Privy Council in *Te Heuheu Tukino* that the Treaty had no domestic life beyond that granted by Parliament. This is a very significant fetter on the effectiveness of the Treaty, making its operation entirely dependent on the goodwill of Parliament.[67] Cooke P. explicitly acknowledged that the Court's decision to block the transfer of Crown assets was possible because "the legislature has given the opportunity".[68] Such a statement, of course, signals to the legislature that if it wishes to put the brakes on curial resolution of Treaty claims parliamentary omission would be a good strategy. Moreover, it manifests a subordination of the solemn compact to an overly sensitive deference to Parliament, leaving that institution with huge powers of initiative in the field. Why do the courts need no parliamentary intervention to give effect to common law property and personal rights, as well as respect for natural justice, yet the document which lies at the foundation of the nation and which is the source of constitutional legitimacy, has no effect until Parliament decides otherwise? While it may have been understandable that the Privy Council in 1940 – still at that stage presiding over a vast colonial empire which the British were determined to keep intact on their terms only – would be keen to downplay the domestic effect of a treaty of cession, surely in New Zealand of the 1980s, a post-colonial society, the judiciary should have felt free to develop its own view of the domestic legal status of the Treaty.[69] Only an autochthonous development of New Zealand constitutional common law which recognises the legal effect of the Treaty (per-

---

[67] See in particular the judgment of Somers J. [1987] 1 N.Z.L.R. 641, 691-2 which is explicit on the point. See also Boast [1987] *N.Z.L.J.* 240, 245.

[68] [1987] 1 N.Z.L.R. 641, 668.

[69] It should be noted that while the *First Maori Council case* was being litigated, there were actually proposals that the Treaty of Waitangi would enjoy a significantly higher domestic legal status. In its 1985 White Paper entitled *A Bill of Rights for New Zealand* (Government Printer, Wellington, 1985), the Labour Government had proposed to enact a supreme law bill of rights, in which the Treaty was to receive a prominent position: see pp. 74-7. However, many Maori, for a variety of reasons, opposed the inclusion of the Treaty in a bill of rights, and when the bill of rights was enacted as an ordinary statute in 1990 (New Zealand Bill of Rights Act 1990) the Treaty was not incorporated.

haps subject to any specific legislation to the contrary) can truly reflect a "solemn compact"[70] which the Court was prepared to acknowledge as the "foundation" for a developing social contract between the "partners".[71] Looked at from another perspective, how in a mature democracy can such a foundational document be allowed to impose obligations only to the extent that the now-dominant descendants of the colonisers (and immigrants) permit, and yet retain the accolade of being "a positive force in the life of the nation"?[72] Surely it is only a positive force on the sufferance of the dominant group—hardly a source of positivity if one happens to be of the minority? Rhetoric is all well and good, but in a system of parliamentary sovereignty it is as easily wiped away as chalk from a blackboard.

In defence of the Court of Appeal's approach on this issue, it might be observed that the presence of a statutory affirmation of the Treaty obviated the need to undertake any reassessment of the parliamentary supremacy grundnorm. However, if this was the case then it would have been better if the Court had said nothing on the issue of sovereignty; by expressing the strong view that parliamentary sovereignty was unaffected by its decision, the Court was clearly reaffirming the cardinal importance of that doctrine in New Zealand constitutional law.

Tantalisingly, however, Cooke P. (alone of the judges) appeared to leave open the possibility of utilising the Treaty in interpreting "ambiguous legislation" and he accepted the submission that "the Court will not ascribe to Parliament an intention to permit conduct inconsistent with the principles of the Treaty."[73] Certainly, the use of the Treaty as an interpretative aid would be an improvement on the previous uses to which the Treaty could be put.

Overall, then, the Court of Appeal affirmed that the compass within which the principles of the Treaty could operate in New Zealand law was quite limited. The Court was not prepared to expand that compass, notwithstanding its recognition of the significance of the Treaty. However, within that narrow compass, the Court was prepared to recharacterise the Treaty and revolutionised the rhetorical terms in which courts would in the future speak of the Treaty. This in itself was progress. As could be expected, the new rhetorical register laid down as law was picked up by those in the political arena and has since shaped the regard in which the Treaty is held. Furthermore, the *First Maori Council case* was important because Maori won. After over a century of mainly negative results, the Court of Appeal's decision was not only an important vindication of the Maori view of the Treaty but also established that that view would be heard, and, in appropriate cases, accepted as legitimate by the courts. That was also progress.

---

[70] [1987] 1 N.Z.L.R. 641, 673 *per* Richardson J.
[71] [1987] 1 N.Z.L.R. 641, 702 *per* Casey J.
[72] [1987] 1 N.Z.L.R. 641, 682 *per* Richardson J.
[73] [1987] 1 N.Z.L.R. 641, 656.

5. FALLOUT FROM THE CASE[74]

The immediate fallout from the *First Maori Council* were amendments to the S.O.E. Act and to the Treaty of Waitangi Act to ensure that the lacunae identified in case were plugged. In particular the Waitangi Tribunal's powers were extended to permit it to make *binding* rulings on the resumption by the Crown (under powers of compulsory acquisition) of old Crown land wrongfully taken from Maori.[75]

More significantly, the success of the Maori Council in 1987 prompted further litigation relating to Treaty claims and the corporatisation and/or sale of state assets. A summary of that litigation and the Court of Appeal's current understanding of the Treaty and the principles of the Treaty is beyond the scope of this essay.[76] However, a number of features should be explored.

First, the rhetorical status of the Treaty has gradually increased such that by 1998 it had become "trite" that the Treaty was a *constitutional* document.[77]

Second, and in turn, this heightened status has both brought about and been manifested in a new doctrinal approach which holds that, "conformance with the principles of the Treaty by the Crown should be regarded as required unless there is reason from wording or context to consider otherwise. It is simply not acceptable, in modern thinking, to say there is no need to consider the Treaty".[78] The result is that in exercising their supervisory role on administrative decision making, the courts will hold that the Treaty is a mandatory relevant consideration unless context says otherwise – the presence of a statute is no longer necessary to bring the principles of the Treaty to bear on an issue.

Third, the Treaty's increased status has had ramifications for the common law rights of Maori.[79] For example, in the *Fisheries cases*,[80] arguments were

---

[74] For an extended, though somewhat sceptical, analysis of the impact of the *First Maori Council* case in later years, see Kelsey, "Judicialisation of the Treaty of Waitangi: A Subtle Cultural Repositioning" (1994) 10 *Aust J. Law & Soc.* 131.

[75] Treaty of Waitangi (State Enterprises) Act 1988.

[76] See Joseph, "Constitutional Review Now" [1998] *N.Z.L.Rev.* 85, 93-108.

[77] Upston-Cooper, "Slaying the Leviathan: Critical Jurisprudence and the Treaty of Waitangi" (1998) 28 *V.U.W.L.R.* 683, 683; *New Zealand Maori Council v. Attorney-General* [1996] 3 N.Z.L.R. 140 (C.A.) 185 *per* Thomas J.

[78] *New Zealand Maori Council v. Attorney-General* (HC Wellington, C.P. 40/96, March 29, 1996, McGechon J.), 18.

[79] Aside from specific Treaty-related litigation, there has been a resurgence of interest in, and recognition of, common law aboriginal rights of Maori, particularly in the non-land holding settings such as fishing rights. Developments in respect of native title to land such as those in Australia after *Mabo v. State of Queensland (No.2)* (1992) 175 C.L.R. 1 (H.C.A.) (on which see Tunney, "Native Title and the Search for Justice. *Mabo* (1992)" below, 445) are restricted by the statutory framework established in Te Ture Whenua Act 1993, the modern day successor to the Native Land Acts.

[80] *Te Runanga o Muriwhenua Inc v. Attorney-General* (C.A. 110/90, 28 June 1990); *Te Runanga o Muriwhenua Inc v. Attorney-General* [1990] 2 N.Z.L.R. 641 (C.A.); *Te Runanga o Wharekauri Rekohu v. Attorney-General* [1993] 2 N.Z.L.R. 301 (C.A.) 305, 306.

made to the Court of Appeal that a quota management system might interfere with traditional Maori fishing rights. The courts appeared ready to accept that the Crown was under fiduciary duties to protect such aboriginal rights, and that in New Zealand a source of these fiduciary duties could be the Treaty, particularly since the concept of Treaty partnership developed in the *First Maori Council case* reflected the sorts of considerations which would lie on the shoulders of a fiduciary at common law. Thus, the Treaty came full circle – from having been the reason why the Courts had refused to recognise aboriginal property rights, the Treaty has now become a source of common law rights.

On the other hand, the courts have continually emphasised the limits to which the Treaty can be put. First, it has been "stress[ed]" that the principles of the Treaty "are of limited scope and do not require a social revolution".[81] For a number of commentators this conceptualisation of the Treaty principles represents a capture – since on one view the Treaty promised Maori elements of self-government (*tino rangatiratanga* protected by article 2), yet the colonial/settler government ignored and overrode this undertaking leading to *Pakeha* domination a true performance of Treaty principles would require a revolution. Instead, the *First Maori Council* and its progeny have "legitimated and entrenched" *Pakeha* economic and political power[82] – offering partial recognition by the dominant *Pakeha* group but on its terms only.

Second, at a more micro-level, the Court of Appeal has emphasised that the principles of partnership do not require an equal sharing of all the benefits accrued on, or through the use of, assets which were the subject of a Treaty claim: "There may be assets in the building up of which, even if Maori have some fair claim to share, other initiatives have still made the greater contribution".[83] Again, the interests of the *Pakeha* majority will not be erased by the errors of previous generations.

Third, the Treaty can only be applied in the traditional manner on judicial review — the courts are not empowered to second-guess administrative decisions unless completely unreasonable.[84]

6. CONCLUSION

In concluding his article on the case, Richard Boast said that, "[t]he Maori council case has to be seen as but a part of the continuing process of constitutional change concerning the status of the Treaty, a process which is taking

---

[81] *Tainui Maori Trust Board v. Attorney-General* [1989] 2 N.Z.L.R. 543 (C.A.) 527 *per* Cooke P.

[82] Kelsey, "Rogernomics and the Treaty: An Irresolvable Contradiction" (1989) 7 *Law in Context* 66, 85.

[83] *New Zealand Maori Council v. Attorney General* [1989] 2 N.Z.L.R. 142 (C.A.) 152.

[84] See *e.g. New Zealand Maori Council v. Attorney-General* [1994] 1 N.Z.L.R. 513 (P.C.) 517, 524.

place simultaneously on a number of fronts".[85] That is as it inevitably will be, and probably should be, in a system such as New Zealand's governed by parliamentary sovereignty, based on participative democracy and constrained by stare decisis. In New Zealand, on current perceptions of public law, there is little room for bold initiatives such as those available to the Supreme Courts of the United States or Ireland.

The *First Maori Council case* is no *Brown v. Board of Education*. There was no judicial revolution; no cries of judicial licence; no accusations of judicial legislation; no protests in the street. Indeed, the judges subsequently emphasised that compliance with the Treaty did not require a social revolution.[86] It did not upset or challenge the hallowed notions of parliamentary sovereignty, which (because of the consistently far higher numbers of *Pakeha* in Parliament) had facilitated the perpetration of breaches of the Crown's Treaty undertakings. It did not revisit older jurisprudence which had refused to give common law rights status to Treaty-protected rights. Rather the *First Maori Council case* was a bold but well-judged move, in a relatively sympathetic environment, in a manner which parliamentarians may well have favoured. The decision may have delayed the implementation of a reform programme that was dear to the erstwhile Government, but it had no lasting negative effects on that programme. However, it did revolutionise the terms in which the Treaty is spoken of in the legal world; it did manifest a judicial commitment to the implementation of the Treaty partnership which was not apparent in previous jurisprudence; and it has shaped, and continues to shape, developments in the Treaty field. On that basis alone, the decision deserves recognition as probably New Zealand's leading case of the twentieth century.

---

[85] Boast [1987] *N.Z.L.J.* 240, 245.
[86] *Tainui* above, n.81, 527.

THE FUTURE OF THE CONFLICT OF LAWS CAN *MORGUARD* (1990) POINT THE WAY?

JOHN SWAN*

1. INTRODUCTION

It is the argument of this paper that the topic known as the Conflict of Laws has no right to exist and that all the problems that it is believed to exist to deal with can easily be dealt with by other and more natural methods. I am principally concerned to argue that choice of law rules of all types, whether of the traditional common law type or more modern variations, are wrongly conceived and unnecessary. I do not claim that concerns about the proper criteria for the taking of jurisdiction or the recognition or enforcement of foreign judgments are misconceived. I shall attempt to illustrate the relevance of those issues to the proper solution of what are now seen as problem of the "choice of law".

The principal alternative methods that I shall propose will be found in Constitutional Law – for those countries that have a federal constitution – or in the legislation of institutions like the European Union, in International Law or in the various domestic laws that exist to deal with problems of contract, tort, property, succession, marriage, *etc.*

It is obviously impossible for me to cover all the arguments that my claim entails and I shall be very selective in the examples that I shall explore. I claim that the arguments that compel me to the conclusion that I have stated are contained in the judgment of the Supreme Court of Canada in the case *De Savoye v. Morguard Investments Ltd.*[1]

2. THE FACTS AND JUDGMENT IN *MORGUARD*

Morguard was a simple case involving the enforcement in British Columbia of an *in personam* judgment of the court of Alberta. The respondents were mortgagees of land in Alberta. The appellant who then resided in Alberta, was originally guarantor but later took title to the land and assumed the obligations of mortgagor. Shortly afterwards, he moved to British Columbia. The mort-

---

*Professor of Law, McGill University; Stikeman, Elliott, Barristers & Solicitors, Montreal.

[1] [1990] 3 S.C.R. 1077; [1991] 2 W.W.R. 217; 76 D.L.R. (4th) 256 (S.C.C.) (hereafter *Morguard*).

gages fell into default and the respondents brought action in Alberta. The appellant was served with process in the action by double registered mail addressed to his home in British Columbia pursuant to orders for service by the Alberta court in accordance with its rules for service outside its jurisdiction. There were rules to the same effect in British Columbia.

The appellant took no steps to appear or to defend the action. There was no clause in the mortgage by which he agreed to submit to the jurisdiction of the Alberta court, and he did not attorn to its jurisdiction.

At the expiry of the redemption period, the respondents obtained an order for a judicial sale of the mortgaged properties. Judgment was entered against the appellant for the deficiencies between the value of the property and the amount owing on the mortgages. The respondents then each commenced a separate action in the British Columbia Supreme Court to enforce the Alberta judgment for the deficiencies. Judgment was granted to the respondents by the Supreme Court in a decision which was upheld on appeal to the British Columbia Court of Appeal.

At the time that the plaintiff commenced its action in Alberta and when it sought enforcement in B.C., the law governing the enforcement of foreign judgments in Canadian provinces was essentially the same as the common law rules enforced in England.[2] Those rules required that the defendant had either submitted to the foreign court or been personally served in the foreign jurisdiction and the enforcing court would apply its standards to those questions. Under these rules, Mr. De Savoye could not have been sued in B.C. on the Alberta judgment and it is almost certain that he had got advice saying precisely that.

The trial judge had enforced the judgment on clearly invalid grounds, *viz.*, that the Alberta court had properly exercised its jurisdiction under its rules. The Court of Appeal dismissed the appeal but adopted the argument that, since a B.C. court would have taken jurisdiction on the same facts, it should recognise the Alberta judgment. This is the argument for reciprocity and was based on the decision of the English Court of Appeal in *Travers v. Holley*.[3]

The Supreme Court rejected both these grounds and, instead, based its judgment on a number of factors. La Forest J. said:

> The world has changed since the above rules were developed in 19th century England. Modern means of travel and communications have made many of these 19th century concerns appear parochial. The business com-

---

[2] I shall ignore any statutory changes in England; they were not duplicated in Canada which, until *Morguard*, relied principally on *Emanuel v. Symon* [1908] 1 K.B. 302 (C.A.).

[3] [1953] P. 246; [1953] 2 All E.R. 794 (C.A.). The argument of reciprocity has superficial attractiveness but is fundamentally unprincipled: it merely says that, if we treat our defendants unfairly, we'll let you do the same. There is no justification for importing into the rules for the enforcement of foreign judgments *in personam*, the rules for dealing with the recognition of foreign divorces.

munity operates in a world economy and we correctly speak of a world community even in the face of decentralised political and legal power. Accommodating the flow of wealth, skills and people across state lines has now become imperative. Under these circumstances, our approach to the recognition and enforcement of foreign judgments would appear ripe for reappraisal. Certainly, other countries, notably the United States and members of the European Economic Community, have adopted more generous rules for the recognition and enforcement of foreign judgments to the general advantage of litigants.

However that may be, there is really no comparison between the interprovincial relationships of today and those obtaining between sovereign countries in the 19th century. Indeed, in my view, there never was and the courts made a serious error in transposing the rules developed for the enforcement of foreign judgments to the enforcement of judgments from sister-provinces. The considerations underlying the rules of comity apply with much greater force between the units of a federal state, and I do not think it much matters whether one calls these rules of comity or simply relies directly on the reasons of justice, necessity and convenience to which I have already adverted. . . .

In any event, the English rules seem to me to fly in the face of the obvious intention of the Constitution to create a single country. This presupposes a basic goal of stability and unity where many aspects of life are not confined to one jurisdiction. A common citizenship ensured the mobility of Canadians across provincial lines. . . . In particular, significant steps were taken to foster economic integration. One of the central features of the constitutional arrangements incorporated in the *Constitution Act 1867* was the creation of a common market. Barriers to interprovincial trade were removed by s. 121. Generally trade and commerce between the provinces was seen to be a matter of concern to the country as a whole; see *Constitution Act 1867*, s. 91(2). . . .

These arrangements themselves speak to the strong need for the enforcement throughout the country of judgments given in one province. But that is not all. The Canadian judicial structure is so arranged that any concerns about differential quality of justice among the provinces can have no real foundation. All superior court judges – who also have superintending control over other provincial courts and tribunals – are appointed and paid by the federal authorities. *And all are subject to final review by the Supreme Court of Canada, which can determine when the courts of one province have appropriately exercised jurisdiction in an action and the circumstances under which the courts of another province should recognise such judgments.* Any danger resulting from unfair procedure is further avoided by sub-constitutional factors, such as for example the fact that Canadian lawyers adhere to the same code of ethics throughout Canada.. . .

These various constitutional and sub-constitutional arrangements and practices make unnecessary a "full faith and credit2 clause such as exists in other federations, such as the United States and Australia. The existence of these clauses, however, does indicate that a regime of mutual recognition of judgments across the country is inherent in a federation. Indeed, the European Economic Community has determined that such a feature flows naturally from a common market, even without political integration. To that end its members have entered into the 1968 *Convention on Jurisdiction and Enforcement of Judgments in Civil and Commercial Matters.*[4]

Let me summarise what La Forest J. has said: the proper assertion of jurisdiction by one Canadian province forces another the recognise the judgment of the first province. The standards of fairness that the first province has to meet are national standards, subject to the supervision of the Supreme Court. In the Canadian context, it is possible to regard these standards and recognition requirements or obligations as constitutional norms, *i.e.*, as standards and obligations that find their justification and content in the Constitution. Regarding the standards and obligations in this light has some important consequences. The most obvious is that, as I have said, they are national. This fact does not mean that the provinces have to agree or that the federal parliament has jurisdiction to set them. The administration of justice is within the constitutional competence of the provincial legislatures.[5] But under *Morguard*, national standards are established by the Supreme Court in the exercise of its general power to hear appeals of provincial law and to interpret the provisions of the Canadian Constitution.

3. THE IMPLICATIONS

I have to say at the outset that the Supreme Court of Canada has emphatically denied that the implications that I shall argue should be drawn from *Morguard* and from the very important case of *Moran v. Pyle National (Canada) Ltd.*[6] which preceded it. This rejection occurred in *Tolofson v. Jensen; Lucas (Liti-*

---

[4] [1990] 3 S.C.R. 1077, 1098-1100; 76 D.L.R. (4th) 256, 270-272; emphasis added. For a discussion of a related aspect of that 1968 Convention, see Kennedy "Untying the Gordian (Jurisdictional) Knot,•: *Bier v. Mines de Potasse* (1976)" above, 275.

[5] *Constitution Act 1867*, s. 92(14).

[6] [1975] 1 S.C.R. 393; [1974] 2 W.W.R. 586; 43 D.L.R. (3d) 239 (S.C.C.).

gation Guardian of) v. Gagnon[7] the court, while rejecting the traditional choice of law rule in torts, the rule established in *Phillips v. Eyre*,[8] adopted an equally brutal and undiscriminating application of the *lex loci delicti* as the choice of law rule for torts on the basis that such a rule was required by the "vested rights" theory of conflicts – a theory not regarded as relevant for a very long time – and the demands of simplicity.[9]

The judgment of La Forest J. in *Morguard* at one level looks to be quite standard stuff and would not provide material for a radical exegesis where it not for some other things said by La Forest J. He finds support for his opinion in the earlier *Moran v. Pyle National (Canada) Ltd.*[10] That decision dealt with an argument that courts of Saskatchewan did not have jurisdiction over an Ontario manufacturer of light bulbs who had been sued in Saskatchewan in an action in negligence brought by the widow of a Saskatchewan resident who had been killed by the alleged negligent manufacture of a light bulb. The Saskatchewan legislation at that time required that, before leave to serve the writ *ex juris* could be granted, the plaintiff show that the tort had been "committed in Saskatchewan". In holding that the tort had been committed in Saskatchewan, Dickson J., giving the judgment of the Supreme Court said:

> Generally speaking, in determining where a tort has been committed, it is unnecessary, and unwise, to have resort to any arbitrary set of rules. The place of acting and the place of harm theories are too arbitrary and inflexible to be recognised in contemporary jurisprudence. In [*Distillers Co. (Biochemicals) Ltd. v. Thompson*[11]] and again in [*Cordova Land Co. Ltd. v. Victor Bros. Inc.*[12]] a real and substantial connection test was hinted at. Cheshire[13] . . . has suggested a test very similar to this; the author says that it would not be inappropriate to regard a tort as having occurred in any country substantially affected by the defendant's activities or its consequences and the law of which is likely to have been in the reasonable

---

[7] [1994] 3 S.C.R. 1022, [1995] 1 W.W.R. 609, 120 D.L.R. (4th) 289 (S.C.C.) (hereafter *Tolofson/ Gagnon*). There was a single judgment dealing with two cases, one, *Tolofson*, involving Saskatchewan and British Columbia, the other, *Gagnon*, involving Ontario and Quebec. Both actions involved intra-family claims arising out of motor vehicle accidents. The accidents happened in the more restrictive jurisdiction and were brought in the more generous one.

[8] (1870) L.R. 6 Q.B. 1.

[9] The decision has, as had to have been expected, recently led to cases in which lower courts are simply refusing to apply a choice of law rule that takes no account of the values at issue or the belief by the court that a mechanical rule leads to injustice. See, *e.g.*, the decision of the Ontario Court of Appeal in *Hanlan v. Sernesky* (1998) 38 O.R. (3d) 479, affirming (1997) 35 O.R. (3d) 603, and Black, "Crash, The Ontario Court of Appeal Bumps into *Tolofson*" (1998) 41 C.C.L.T. (2d) 170.

[10] [1975] 1 S.C.R. 393; [1974] 2 W.W.R. 586; 43 D.L.R. (3d) 239 (hereafter *Moran*).

[11] [1971] A.C. 458 (H.L.).

[12] [1966] 1 W.L.R. 793 (Q.B.D.).

[13] *Private International Law* (8th ed., Butterworths, London, 1970) 281.

contemplation of the parties. Applying this test to a case of careless manufacture, the following rule can be formulated: where a foreign defendant carelessly manufactures a product in a foreign jurisdiction which enters into the normal channels of trade and he knows or ought to know both that as a result of his carelessness a consumer may well be injured and it is reasonably foreseeable that the product would be used or consumed where the plaintiff used or consumed it, then the forum in which the plaintiff suffered damage is entitled to exercise judicial jurisdiction over that foreign defendant. This rule recognises the important interest a state has in injuries suffered by persons within its territory. It recognises that the purpose of negligence as a tort is to protect against carelessly inflicted injury and thus that the predominating element is damage suffered. By tendering his products in the market place directly or through normal distributive channels, a manufacturer ought to assume the burden of defending those products wherever they cause harm as long as the forum into which the manufacturer is taken is one that he reasonably ought to have had in his contemplation when he so tendered his goods. This is particularly true of dangerously defective goods placed in the interprovincial flow of commerce. [14]

Note what has happened: Dickson J. starts off talking about the issue of the place of the tort but, by the end of the passage he is talking what I can only call "pure" choice of law. He begins by justifying the taking of jurisdiction by Saskatchewan; he ends by justifying the application of Saskatchewan domestic law. That justification does not depend on any choice of law rule or on any special rule having to do with cases that present geographically complex facts, *i.e.*, "conflicts" cases, but on an analysis of the defendant's business and the risks that it must be held to have assumed. There is no tort choice of law rule,

---

[14][1975] 1 S.C.R. 393, 408-409. This passage was quoted by La Forest J. in *Morguard*, [1990] 3 S.C.R. 1077, 1107-1108; 76 D.L.R. (4th) 256, 276. The language of Dickson J. is startlingly similar to that in *World-Wide Volkswagen Corp. v. Woodson*, 444 U.S. 286; 100 S.Ct. 559 (1980). White J., writing for the majority said:

When a corporation "purposefully avails itself of the privilege of conducting activities with the forum State," ... it has clear notice that it is subject to suit there, and can act to alleviate the risk of burdensome litigation by procuring insurance, passing the expected costs on to customers, or, if the risks are too great, severing its connection with the State. Hence if the sale of a product of a manufacturer or distributor such as Audi or Volkswagen is not simply an isolated occurrence, but arises from the efforts of the manufacturer or distributor to serve directly or indirectly, the market for its product in other States, it is not unreasonable to subject it to suit in one of the those States if its allegedly defective merchandise has there been the source of injury to its owner or to others. The forum State does not exceed its powers under the Due Process Clause if it asserts personal jurisdiction over a corporation that delivers its products into the stream of commerce with the expectation that they will be purchased by consumers in the forum State (444 U.S., at 297-298).

no worrying about the characterisation of the issue or about any theory of the Conflict of Laws.

One other fact must be noted. Under the Canadian constitution, the *Constitution Act 1867*, the provinces have jurisdiction over "Property and Civil Rights in the Province" and "The Administration of Justice in the Province". It is accepted that this grant of power also limits the power of the provincial legislatures to legislate with extraterritorial effect. I shall not develop the argument here, but it does not take much imagination or require any radical re-casting of well-accepted constitutional arguments to be able to claim that there is a similar restriction on the power of provincial judges to adjudicate extraterritorially. This constitutional limit on provincial power can also be seen as reflected both in La Forest J.'s judgment in *Morguard* and in Dickson J.'s judgment in *Moran*.

What does the combination of *Moran* and *Morguard* achieve? It suggests that in a case of geographically complex facts – and for the moment I shall restrict the geographically complex facts to Canadian facts – the test whether the court properly took jurisdiction will be determined, broadly speaking, by a general standard of fairness, similarly the test of the law to be applied will be determined in much the same way and finally if these two steps have been properly performed, the resulting judgment will be entitled to recognition.[15] The "fairness" criterion of jurisdiction and "choice of law" will reflect the constitutional limits on provincial sovereignty[16] and these decisions will have been made under the general supervision of the Supreme Court. In other words, Canada could have a fully functioning system of the conflict of laws without any need to "talk" conflicts at all.[17] Other common law jurisdictions like Ireland could easily follow the lead offered by *Morguard*.[18]

---

[15]Professor Peter Hogg, the most respected constitutional scholar in Canada, has observed, *Constitutional Law of Canada* Loose-leaf ed., 13-17, 13-18:

While Canada does not have an equivalent to the due process clause of the fourteenth amendment for cases where only economic issues are at stake, in my view the due process test, as elaborated in [*Moran* and *Morguard*], could as easily serve as a test of extra-territoriality under the Constitution of Canada.

The argument that I have made is substantially that of Professor Hogg, Section 13.5.

[16]Canada is unusual, at least when compared to the United States and Australia, in having no explicit constitutional provisions dealing with matters that come within the scope of the Conflict of Laws, *viz.*, judicial jurisdiction or "full faith and credit".

[17]This statement is not qualified by the power of Canadian courts to determine that they are not the proper or most convenient forum. That power, while usually exercised in cases of geographically complex facts, is simply the expression of the concern that the court's process not be abused and in this sense is quite different from the concern expressed in the due process clause of the United States Constitution or in a case like *Moran*.

[18]In the leading case of *Grehan v. Medical Incorporated* [1986] I.R. 528; [1986] I.L.R.M. 627 (S.C.), Walsh J., for the Supreme Court, rejecting *Phillips v. Eyre* (1870) L.R. 6 Q.B. 1, held that "the Irish courts should be sufficiently flexible to be capable of responding to the individual issues presented in each case and to the social and economic dimensions of applying any particular choice of law rule to the proceedings in question" ([1986] I.R. 528, 541; [1986] I.L.R.M. 627, 638). Newman "Enforcement of Foreign Judgments in Non-Convention Cases" (2000) 5

4. A RE-WORKING OF *CHAPLIN v. BOYS*[19]

I would like to review the facts and solution to a famous case to illustrate how the approach outlined in *Moran* and *Morguard* might work. The facts in *Chaplin v. Boys* are well known but it is worth re-stating them. The plaintiff was injured in a road accident in Malta caused by the admitted negligence of the defendant. The plaintiff sustained serious injuries and sued for damages. Under the Maltese law, the plaintiff could recover only financial loss directly suffered, expenses incurred and lost wages together with a sum for ascertained future loss of wages with a right to make a further application to the court when the anticipated losses arose. He could recover no damages in respect of the injury itself for pain, suffering and loss of amenities. I shall ignore the fact that both parties were serving in the British armed forces at the time of the accident.

I shall make one temporary alteration in the facts to make the Canadian analysis more directly applicable; I shall assume that Malta is a Canadian province and that the action is brought in another Canadian province which I shall call Ontario and which, like England, has a tort regime that awards one time damages which include damages for pain and suffering and which represent the present value of the plaintiff's future losses.

If, as was the case in *Chaplin v. Boys*, the parties both reside in the same jurisdiction, there may be no issue of the power of the court to hear the case, both parties may, in fact, be quite content to have the matter litigated in a convenient forum. If the parties had no connection, or no substantial connection, with Ontario, the court may consider that it should decline to hear the case, but if the parties are both resident in the province and were, perhaps, habitually resident there, there may be no reason that the court would have any hesitation over taking jurisdiction. Note the obvious point that if the court refuses to hear the case, there will be no need to consider which of the two rules should be applied.

What then to do about the differing laws of the two jurisdictions? It is worth noting that the tort regime applicable in each province is both fair and rational; indeed variations on the Maltese scheme have been suggested in Canada and elsewhere and the Quebec "no-fault" scheme of compensation for motor vehicle accidents has some aspects of the Maltese scheme.

There are two aspects of the Maltese scheme that need to be considered: (i)

---

(7) *Bar Review* 354, argues that the *Grehan* approach "involves very similar considerations to those relevant to the *Morguard* test" (358) and points out that the Supreme Court "has recently demonstrated its willingness to reshape longstanding rules of private international law" (*ibid.*, referring to *W. v. W.*, [1993] 2 I.R. 476 (S.C.)); consequently he argues that "[i]n principle, the Court is free to assess the suitability of the established criteria in an appropriate case" (*ibid.*), and concludes that "in an appropriate case the Irish Superior Courts may very well be convinced to follow the Canadian approach" (359).
[19][1971] A.C. 356; [1969] 2 All E.R. 1085 (H.L.).

the denial of any damages for pain and suffering and (ii) the right of the plaintiff to seek further damages as losses are incurred.

It may well be the case that, since Malta is an isolated island, there is no interaction like that which occurs between Canadian provinces, American states and within Europe when cars are driven from one country to another and accidents with multi-national connections occur. If the Maltese situation is transposed into one where there is interaction or if, as is, of course, almost certain, interaction occurs, it is obvious that any insurer will have to cover the risks that non-Maltese parties may be injured and that litigation may be brought in more than one place and that the place where the insurance was taken out will not be the only place where litigation might occur.

I have suggested that *Moran* and *Morguard* require that an Ontario court consider whether its assertion of jurisdiction will be consistent with the limits on provincial legislative power under the *Constitution Act 1867*. The same test is applicable, as *Moran* states, to what I can call the choice of law issue. It is here that the principal difference between traditional conflicts and my new proposal begins to appear. Seen in the light of *Moran*, the Ontario court will consider, not an abstract choice of law rule of any kind, whether the appalling rule of *Phillips v. Eyre*,[20] the bastard form adopted by the House of Lords in *Chaplin v. Boys* or any of the American formulations as found in, for example, *Babcock v. Jackson*,[21] the Restatement or in various academic writings, but the simple question, should we apply our domestic law of torts or should we defer to the law, in this case, of Malta?

This approach is not to be regarded as similar to that of, say, *Phillips v. Eyre*.[22] That case justified the application of English law, regardless of any of the express limits on provincial power based on the Canadian Constitution or the kind of "due process" limit outlined by Dickson J. in *Moran*. The approach is "forum-centred" simply because a court has to have some perspective from which to look at any problem that comes before it. An Ontario court has to look at any case brought in Ontario from its own point of view; it can't look at a problem as a Maltese court would and some kind of abstract, "unlocalised" point of view is, if not literally inconceivable, likely to do little for practical legal analysis. A forum-centred point of view does not entail a refusal to consider whether the domestic solution of some other jurisdiction may not be a preferable solution in the facts of the case before it, a case that is, after all, one with geographically complex facts.[23]

---

[20] (1870) L.R. 6 Q.B. 1. *Phillips v. Eyre* was "applied" by the Supreme Court of Canada with bizarre results in *McLean v. Pettigrew* [1945] 2 D.L.R. 65. The irony is that the decision in the case is exactly correct, as the New York Court of Appeals pointed out in *Babcock v. Jackson* 12 N.Y. 2d 473; 191 N.E. 2d 279 (1963); [1963] 2 Lloyd's Rep. 286.

[21] *ibid.*

[22] (1870) L.R. 6 Q.B. 1.

[23] The author whose views are closest to mine was Albert Ehrenzweig. See Ehrenzweig, *Conflict*

All this being said, it can be argued that, in dealing with the issue of damages for pain and suffering, the Ontario court could say one of two things. The first would be to say:

> We consider that one of the purposes of the law of torts in Ontario law is to compensate plaintiffs for the intangible injuries that they might suffer. The application of this purpose in this case does not involve an improper or excessive assertion of our values over a person who acted in a foreign jurisdiction. We recognise that the defendant can fairly argue that he should be entitled to rely on the law of the place where he acted, but he[24] can equally fairly be taken to have faced the risk that what was done in Malta might have serious consequences for someone outside it. Accordingly, we award the plaintiff damages for his pain and suffering.

The second would be to say:

> The plaintiff chose to go into Malta. In so doing, he took the risk that he might be injured in a motor vehicle accident by a person whose home is there. That person, the defendant in this case, was entitled to rely on the measure of and types of damages that are awarded to people injured in motor vehicle accidents. It would be wrong for this court, whatever the extent of the plaintiff's rights under Ontario law to recover damages for pain and suffering, to impose on the defendant an obligation so much more extensive than he was justified in expecting from his activities in Malta. Accordingly, the plaintiff's claim for damages for his pain and suffering is dismissed.

While the first solution can be defended, the second seems to me to be far preferable in general. What is important is not the fact that I have suggested that the *lex loci delicti* should be applied, but that we can debate the purpose

---

of Laws (West Publishing Co., St. Paul, Minn., 1962) and Ehrenzweig, *Private International Law: A Comparative Treatise on American International Conflicts Law, Including the Law of Admiralty* (Sijthoff, Leyden; Dobbs Ferry, N.Y., 1969).

[24] I have to ignore the expectations of the defendant's insurer. There are two reasons for this. The first is that it is hard to see how an insurer has an independent interest that entitles its expectations to the considered; the insurer's liability is triggered because the insured is liable. (The provisions of the uniform Canadian *Insurance Act* reflect this point of view. See, *e.g.*, the Ontario *Insurance Act* R.S.O. 1990, c. I.8, s. 252, as does, or perhaps did, the European "green card" system). The second reason is that reliance by any insurer is an odd kind of reliance. Insurance rates are set on the basis of the insurer's or the industry's actual loss experience. Increasing the risks to which insurers are exposed means that their loss experience will be worse and, depending on ordinary market pressures, an individual insurer (or the industry) will or will not be able to increase premiums and pass the increased costs on to insureds. In either event, it is hard for an insurer to claim that it is caught by unfair surprise by being made liable where it had hoped or even expected that it would not be.

behind the competing rules and chose the one that respects the rights and expectations of the parties and, speaking very broadly, treats them fairly. In doing
so we are either talking constitutional law or torts; we are not talking conflicts.

The choice of Maltese law does not entail the choice of Maltese law in
every case in which a plaintiff is injured in Malta because there might well be
cases where it would not be improper or unfair to apply Ontario law. Perhaps
there was a pre-existing relation between the parties in *Chaplin v. Boys* that
make it reasonable and fair to say to the defendant that, as regards the claim of
the plaintiff, the defendant should have expected that the law of Ontario should
be applied. This solution is, of course, the solution adopted in cases like *Babcock
v. Jackson* and in *McLean v. Pettigrew*.[25] On the facts of *Chaplin v. Boys* that
we have, we can draw the inference that the parties had not gone to Malta on a
holiday or trip together or that there was any reason to regard the parties' relation as being one to which it would be appropriate to apply Ontario standards.

There are certain to be cases that are more finely balanced than the one I am
discussing – American courts have had to deal with many variations on the fact
pattern that I have analysed. My point is that we have to discuss those cases on
the terms and with regard to the values outlined or suggested in *Moran* and
Morguard. It cannot be a preferable method of deciding difficult cases to adopt
a choice of law rule *of any type* whose only purpose is to choose or justify the
choice of a solution without looking at the only factors that have to be important. That process has to operate so that the choice of a result that we would
regard – if we ignored conflicts – as correct will only occur by chance.

The second issue raised by the facts of *Chaplin v. Boys* is at this point
irrelevant but I shall, nevertheless, look briefly at it.

In traditional conflicts analysis the question of the method of calculating
and providing for the payment of damages would be characterised as a question of procedure to be governed by the *lex fori*. Exactly the same position can
be reached (and without the question-begging conclusion expressed in the statement that the issue is to be characterised as one of "procedure") by noting that
courts have different ways of dealing with the fact that the losses that the plaintiff may experience as a result of his injuries cannot be fully known at the date
of the trial. An Ontario court could properly note that it has no power to permit
the plaintiff to return to court to make further applications for compensation so
that, if it is to give any effective award, it will have to make a lump-sum judgment that attempts to express once and for all the extent of the plaintiff's losses.
It should also be noted that there are various devices available (particularly if
there are insurance companies involved) by which sums can be secured for the
payment, over time, of the compensation that the plaintiff is entitled to. The
effect of such structured settlements is likely to differ from that which a scheme

---

[25]This solution was rejected in *Tolofson/Gagnon*, above, n.7.

like the Maltese scheme might have, but the goal of both systems is the same and neither party can, I think, object that the application of one rather than the other would violate any idea of fairness or constitutional propriety. In other words, it would not be constitutionally wrong for an Ontario court, assuming of course, that it had power to make any award, to say to the defendant that he would have to meet his obligations in the only manner in which an Ontario court can express them.

It is worth noting again that the difficulties that a court might have in dealing with a very different tort regime may be reflected in the willingness of the court to take jurisdiction. Nothing that I have said about the *Morguard* test for taking jurisdiction affects the power of the court to say that it is not a convenient forum.[26]

Analysed in this way, the decision in *Chaplin v. Boys* can be seen to be one that does not respond to the problems that the facts raised. Had the House of Lords held that the English "connection" of the parties was sufficient to justify the imposition of the English rules for tort compensation along the lines of the first argument that I made, that decision could have been defended, criticised, analysed and developed. As it is, the decision justifies the application of English law without making any analysis of the impact of that decision on the defendant. It's not a question of asking whether "civil liability" does or does not exist under the foreign law, but how the rules of that jurisdiction work with those of England. This focus makes the existence of choice of law rules of the traditional type not only a source of confusion and distortion but simply unnecessary.

What is important about the analysis in the Canadian context is that the automatic application of or casual assumption that it is always justifiable to apply the *lex fori* can be shown to be wrong. If it is wrong (in the constitutional sense) for Ontario to apply its law beyond the limit set by section 92(13) of the *Constitution Act 1867*, it is equally wrong to be oblivious to these limits and their justification just because there are no constitutional criteria that the court has to acknowledge. All that will happen outside the constitutional context is that the criteria may be less clear and there will not be a Supreme Court to supervise the constitutional competence of the court.

The analysis that I have made in the Canadian context would be equally applicable in any other. The fact that there may be constitutional restrictions on the power of the Ontario court to apply its law to out-of-province defendants does not suggest that a court free of constitutional restraints should not acknowledge the same concerns. While a decision of the English court or some court of a sovereign country may not (absent the requirements of controls ex-

---

[26] See the decision of the Supreme Court of Canada in *Amchem Products Inc. v. British Columbia (Workers' Compensation Board)* [1993] 1 S.C.R. 897; [1993] 3 W.W.R. 441; 102 D.L.R. (4th) 96; 77 B.C.L.R. (2d) 62.

pressed in a treaty like the Brussels Convention) be subject to mandatory review, any court that behaves responsibly must have regard to concerns of fairness.[27]

My analysis discloses that *Chaplin v. Boys* is a relatively simple case in
which the English court should have either declined jurisdiction or refused to
apply English law. It is a case where, to use American terminology, there was a
"false conflict", *i.e.*, where there was an appearance of a conflict which, on
examination turned out not to exist as there was no justification for applying
English law or, to put the matter the other way round, there was no reason not
to apply Maltese law. There are more difficult cases which have been referred
to as cases where there is a "true conflict".

5. A More Difficult Case

I cannot here investigate just what is or is not a "true" or a "false" conflict[28] but
I shall illustrate the problem by taking another case in the Supreme Court of
Canada, *O'Connor v. Wray*.[29] I shall take the facts of that case as representing
a simple problem.[30] Take the case of an owner of a car, a resident of Montreal,
who lends his car to a friend to permit him to visit his mother in Quebec City.
The friend, however, does not go to Quebec City but drives into Ontario and
there injures an Ontario resident. The Ontario resident sues the owner and
driver, in Ontario, for damages for her injuries. The owner and driver are served
ex juris in Quebec. (The driver is impecunious and drops out of the action.)
The owner initially challenges the right of the Ontario court to hear the dispute
and to adjudicate on it. The owner loses on that issue: the Ontario Court (General Division) holds that Ontario is an appropriate forum for the resolution of

---

[27]The identification of certain assertions of jurisdiction as "exorbitant" under Article 59 of the
Convention is an analogous recognition that a court may have to recognise a claim that it acted,
if not unfairly, then at least in a way that does not compel universal respect.

[28]The origin of the terms, "false" and "true" conflicts is Brainerd Currie, "Married Women's
Contracts: A Study in Conflict of Law's Method" (1958) 25 *U.Chic.L.Rev.* 227. See also Cavers,
"A Critique of the Choice of Law Problem" (1933) 47 *Harv.L.Rev.* 173. In the context of Currie's
discussion, *Chaplin v. Boys* would be an example of a false conflict.

[29][1930] S.C.R. 231; [1930] 2 D.L.R. 899. This case probably comes as close as any to being a
"true conflict", *i.e.*, a case where the values behind each of the rules in conflict would be for-
warded by their application. Even so, it's an easier case than some because, while the Ontario
rule is a "positive" rule, intended to protect people injured by motor vehicle accidents, the
Quebec rule is a "negative" rule, one that is content to let the loss lie where it has fallen, rather
than a positive rule, seeking to protect one party. A more difficult case is *Lilienthal v. Kaufman*,
395 P. 2d 543, (Oregon S.C., 1964).

[30]I have developed this problem at more length in Swan, "Canadian Constitution, Federalism and
the Conflict of Laws" (1985) 63 *Can. Bar Rev.* 272, and Swan, "Federalism and the Conflict of
Laws: The Curious Position of the Supreme Court of Canada" (1995) 46 *South Carolina L. Rev.*
923.

the dispute and that the owner is not being unfairly treated by being sued in Ontario. At the conclusion of the trial, the trial judge gives the following judgment:

> The plaintiff relies on the Ontario *Highway Traffic Act*[31] which states:
>
> > **192(1)**   The owner of a motor vehicle . . . is liable for loss or damage sustained by any person by reason of negligence in the operation of the motor vehicle . . . on a highway unless the motor vehicle . . . was without the owner's consent in the possession of some person other than the owner or the owner's chauffeur, and the driver of a motor vehicle . . . not being the owner is liable to the same extent as the owner.
>
> The plaintiff points out that the expectation created by the specific purpose of the loan of the car, *viz.*, that it would be used only in Quebec, has been held by Ontario courts not to exclude the operation of s. 192. These courts have generally held that it is the giving of permission to drive rather than the restrictions upon that permission that is important in exposing the owner to liability. The defendant argues that, since Quebec law[32] does not impose liability on the owner in these circumstances, *i.e.*, where the driver does not comply with the limitation on the permission he has been given, an owner should not be subjected to liability in Ontario.[33]
>
> I am faced in this case with the classic situation in which two people, both equally without fault, each argue that the other should bear the loss caused by the wrongful act of a third person. Both claims are strong. The plaintiff, seriously injured in an accident by a person without assets, seeks recovery from the person on whom the law of the province where she lived and where the accident happened puts the risk of loss. The defendant, on the other hand, is caught by surprise by being subjected to liabil-

---

[31] R.S.O. 1990, c. H.8.

[32] At this point I have entered the realm of imagination. My assumption that Quebec would not impose liability on the owner is made for the purpose of illustrating the problem I want to discuss. The assumption that the laws of two provinces or two states could reasonably differ on the particular point I have raised is, I hope, a reasonable one. That fact is all that I need to make the point. The issue could not now arise between Ontario and Quebec as the latter province has a compulsory, state-run no-fault insurance scheme that precludes all civil actions for personal injuries arising from motor vehicle accidents.

[33] Though the attribution of views to Ontario and Quebec is partly imaginary, the issue that I have chosen as my example, *viz.*, vicarious liability and the possibility that two provinces or states may differ, is explored in the Restatement Second, Conflict of Laws, in the illustrations to § 174. The startling omission of any analysis of the case where the two parties may reasonably have strong claims to "protection" under their respective laws is indirect evidence to support the argument that I shall shortly elaborate that the Restatement Second is founded on a fundamentally false premise.

ity in circumstances that he had never expected and which impose on him a risk which, given the provisions of Quebec law, he had not contemplated.

In resolving this issue, I have to have special regard for the law of Ontario. That is the province of whose courts I am a member and with the legislature of which I share a responsibility to forward the values of Ontario society. I am acutely conscious of my responsibility to be both aware of and sympathetic to the values of Quebec and of the rights of its residents not to be unfairly subjected to the law of another province. Giving the matter the best thought that I can, I hold that I have to forward the loss distribution values of Ontario and impose the risk of loss on the defendant. I accordingly give judgment for the plaintiff.

This decision is appealed to the Ontario Court of Appeal which dismisses the appeal. The defendant seeks and obtains leave to appeal to the Supreme Court of Canada.

Meanwhile, an exactly similar case has been before the courts of Quebec. An Ontario plaintiff, injured in the same way as the plaintiff in the Ontario case, the case I have just discussed, has brought action in Quebec against a Quebec resident and owner of a car lent to a friend who has caused the plaintiff injury in Ontario. Since the action was brought in Quebec, there was no issue of the right of the Quebec courts to assert jurisdiction over the defendant. The trial judge in Quebec gave judgment for the defendant and explained her decision to do so on the following grounds:

I am conscious of the fact that, from the perspective of the plaintiff, his claim to be compensated by the defendant is strong, after all he never left his home province and under its laws he would have been entitled to shift the risk to the defendant. I note, however, that even in Ontario, the right of a person injured by a person driving a car to shift his or her loss on to the owner of the car is not absolute. It is clear, for example, that, under Ontario law as interpreted by the Ontario courts, a person who does not have the owner's permission to drive the car, a thief or joy-rider perhaps, will not expose the owner to liability if he or she injures another. The two provinces differ, not at any deep level of principle, but at a more superficial level of where the line is to be drawn between that situation where the owner will be vicariously liable for the torts of the person driving his or her car and that where the owner will not be so liable. In this situation I accordingly find for the defendant and dismiss the action.

This decision is appealed to the Quebec Court of Appeal and the appeal is dismissed. The plaintiff seeks and obtains leave to appeal to the Supreme Court of Canada.

The judges of the Ontario and Quebec courts have, as it will, I think, be readily admitted, behaved responsibly. Not only did each court behave responsibly in the application of its law and justified it as consistent with *Moran*, but a defence of the assertion of long-arm jurisdiction by the Ontario court could easily be justified on grounds that are responsive to all the values that are relevant to such a decision, values that we can accept as part of Canadian federalism and reflected in a case like *Morguard* or *Moran*.

It is worth asking whether anything would have been gained had the two judges "talked conflicts" and, for example, had said that the issue was to be "governed" by the *lex loci delicti* (*Tolofson/Gagnon*) some variant of *Phillips v. Eyre* or *Chaplin v. Boys* or by an inquiry into which jurisdiction the issue of vicarious liability was most closely connected to.[34] Any such analysis will have had to leave unarticulated the careful consideration that each court gave to the problem that it faced and the need, as each saw it, the be faithful to the values of the jurisdiction in which it was.

The problem that I want to focus on is that facing the Supreme Court. That court can do two things; it can allow one appeal and dismiss the other or it can dismiss both appeals. On what ground should it do the first? Before I deal with that question, it is important to note what even considering that alternative entails.

The decision to allow one appeal and dismiss the other requires the belief that there should be one solution to a similar problem before two courts, *i.e.*, that uniformity of decisions is required. If we pause for a moment to consider the problems of uniformity more carefully, the problems can be transformed. Is uniformity really desirable or necessary? The international legal order and every federal system must accommodate the right of states and, in the Canadian context, provinces, to make value judgments appropriate for themselves. Diversity is a fact in the world and in federal states like Canada. The purpose of a federal system is, after all, to permit each constituent part to make its own decisions on matters within its jurisdiction. What then is wrong with simply saying that the differences between the Ontario and Quebec courts are a reflection of the fact that the legislative schemes for the vicarious liability of owners of cars differ? There is no more reason for similar (or identical) judicial decisions on matters within provincial competence than there is for legislative decisions and we have already admitted that such uniformity is neither desired nor found in the world.

In the Canadian context, a uniform decision could only be found if there was some transcendent national standard for vicarious liability. The existence of such a standard is precluded by the fact that issues of vicarious liability are

---

[34] The comment that I made on the Restatement in the previous note is vivid proof that, even so thorough an attempt to make conflicts "work" as the Restatement Second, is unable to deal with the truly difficult cases.

matters exclusively within the power of the provinces. The Supreme Court could impose such a standard as part of the Canadian "common law" – the Supreme Court of Canada, unlike the United States Supreme Court, has power to determine provincial law – but Quebec is not a common law province and, even if the issue arose between two common law provinces, there can be no justification for the assumption that uniformity in this example is required while diversity is tolerated in the rest of the provinces' law. Of course, countries like Canada have federal legislation which establishes national rules as, in Canada's case and to take one example, those regarding the law of negotiable instruments.[35] The existence of such legislation (or similar legislation in an organisation like the European Union) simply demonstrates what we always knew, *viz.*, that uniformity in some things is desirable even as it is not sought in everything.

This analysis suggests that uniformity is not particularly important and that diversity is one of the consequences of a federal system. If uniformity is desirable, it will be obtained by the development of national values, the development, in other words, of a federal "common law". In either of these situations, *i.e.*, the imposition of uniformity or the acceptance of diversity, the solution will be reached by the application of what can only be regarded as constitutional values. Uniformity as such is either irrelevant because, from a constitutional point of view, diversity is acceptable, or imposed by the decision of the Supreme Court that one provincial value is better than another (or possibly, that both are to be subordinated to some "federal" value).

The judgment of the Supreme Court in *Morguard* makes plain in the Canadian context what is constitutionally explicit in the United States Constitution, *viz.*, that the recognition of the requirements of the due process clause entails the recognition of the resulting judgment under the "full faith and credit" clause. It would follow from this argument that the judgment of the Ontario court in the case that I have put would have to be enforced in Quebec.[36] There is nothing unusual in this; courts regularly enforce judgments that they might not themselves have given.

6. Uniformity as a Goal for the Conflict of Laws

All that I have said about the problem before the Supreme Court of Canada and within Canada applies *a fortiori* to the international scene. Diversity in the legal results reached by different states on similar cases is simply a conse-

---

[35] *Bills of Exchange Act* R.S.C. 1985, c. B-4.
[36] A judgment of the Supreme Court, affirming the judgment of the Ontario Court of Appeal, would be directly enforceable in Quebec under the *Supreme Court Act* without the need to bring proceedings for enforcement, though I know of no case where this provision has had to be considered.

quence of national legislatures and national differences and should be cause for nothing more than the study of comparative law or sociological inquiry. In such a world there can be no valid argument that, just because a case comes labelled as a "conflicts case", we have to abandon our usual, domestic approach to the solution of problems of fairness in our procedures and problems in torts, contracts, property, succession or any other area of the law and find another one that, for example, makes the Irish solution the same as the French solution.

The argument that the conflict of laws is necessary to ensure uniformity is, I think, both absurd and wrong-headed.[37] It is absurd to the extent that there is, as simple matter of fact, no uniformity in choice of law rules. There is not, for example, the faintest chance that the new choice of law rule for torts stated by the Supreme Court in *Tolofson/Gagnon* would ever be applied by an American court so that, while the Supreme Court can compel all Canadian courts to follow its rule, there is bound to be the risk of different results in international torts.[38] Moreover, even if there were uniformity in the formulation of choice of law rules, that does not lead to uniformity in decisions and that kind of uniformity is the only kind that matters – at least so far as clients are concerned. One only has to consider the different concepts of public policy and public order in the common and civil law systems to see how uniformity will not be achieved in practice, however similar choice of law rules are. Similarly, wildly differing understandings of "fundamental" concepts like domicile, make the goal of uniformity impossible in practice.

The aptly named "escape devices" of renvoi and characterisation, not to mention exotica like the "incidental question", are further clear evidence that the search for uniformity must be a chimera.[39]

I shall not explore here any other choice of law rules; I re-state my claim that such rules are unnecessary and all problems that the rules are supposed to exist to deal with can be better dealt with in other ways. Those ways have already been described. There will be easy cases in which the obvious and

---

[37] The principal exponent of the need for uniformity is Castel, *Canadian Conflict of Laws* (4th ed., Butterworths, Toronto & Vancouver, 1997).

[38] It is interesting and ironic that the case that has shown the inadequacy of the *Tolofson/Gagnon* rule, *Hanlan v. Sernesky*, above, n.9, involved a tort in which the *lex loci delicti* was Minnesota. The refusal of the Ontario courts to apply Minnesota law and to apply Ontario law in an intra-family tort may well have led to a result that the Minnesota courts would themselves have reached. *Hanlan* was followed in *Wong v. Wei* [1999] 10 W.W.R. 296, (B.C.S.C.) (accident in California, all the parties resided in British Columbia), but distinguished in *George v. Gubernowicz* (1999) 44 O.R. (3d) 247, (Ont. Ct. (Gen. Div.)) and *Buchan v. Non-Marine Underwriters, Members of Lloyds London, England* (1999) 44 O.R. (3d) 685, (Ont. S.C.J.) on the ground that *Hanlan* applied only to international torts.

[39] It is ironic that Castel, above, n.37, even as he states the need for conflicts to provide certainty and predictability and to discourage forum shopping (42–43) openly advocates "result-selective" characterisation (45).

correct result will be reached without the need for any choice of law rule; and there will be hard cases in which there may be no easy and obvious correct result. In these latter cases, the only hope for satisfactory conclusions is the careful examination of the reasons that make the case difficult and of the choices that there are. Choice of law rules do not contribute to this examination and are more likely to obscure the problems. It is bizarre to think that complex and difficult problems can be dealt with without actually examining them.

7. CONCLUSION

I have been saddened by the fact that the Supreme Court did not take the chance that the facts of *Tolofson/Gagnon* offered to develop what the court had so sensibly and, indeed, courageously done in *Moran* and *Morguard*. If the arguments of those cases are accepted, I believe that it is not possible to maintain that there is any need for the conflicts as that system deals with choice of law rules. Once it is admitted, as *Moran* makes clear, that a court can properly look at the world from its own perspective and consider in every case with geographically complex facts that comes before it whether and to what extent it can apply its own law, a criterion has been established to control the improper application of the *lex fori*. The inquiry required by the need to consider the proper application of the *lex fori* forces the court to treat responsibly the claims of a party to the protection or benefits of another law that may differ from that of the *lex fori*. The resulting analysis, as I hope the two examples that I have given illustrate, is one that applies the usual standards of judicial reasoning, focuses on the issues that have to be resolved and makes the development of the law a rational process.

It has to be one of the most serious charges against choice of law rules that they force courts into inquiries that are unnatural and fundamentally different from those that courts do in every case that is not labelled as a "conflicts" case. Indeed, when no such labelling is possible when there is no "conflicts" category into which the case can be put, the result is often pure common sense.[40]

We have got ourselves into this mess because we believe that we have to achieve "uniformity", even as we are quite unclear what uniformity might look like. At the same time as we hold fast to this belief, we ignore two obvious and inescapable facts: choice of law rules in the context within which they are and have to be applied simply cannot achieve uniformity and, what is far more important, uniformity is not even a goal that should be sought. We deny that uniformity is a valid goal by recognising the rights of independent states to

---

[40] See, *e.g.*, the judgment of McKinlay J.A. in *Québec (Sa Majesté du Chef) v. Ontario Securities Commission* (1992) 10 O.R. (3d) 577; 97 D.L.R. (4th) 144 (*sub nom. Re The Queen in right of Quebec and Ontario Securities Commission et al*).

make such rules as seem good to them, whether or not those rules are the same as those of other countries and, in federal states, the constitutional division of powers is specifically designed to permit the component parts of the federation to have different rules. Of course, states and provinces may agree that there should be uniformity but that simply means that, with respect to those matters that are to be uniform, the legislatures have agreed not to assert their right to differ.

I don't think that the courts can make the leap that is required all by themselves. They need the help of academics in first seeing what has to be done and then in working through what the new approach would entail. *Moran* and *Morguard* have, I believe, shown the way.

THE CITIZEN, THE STATE
AND THE CONTINUING CONSTRUCTION
OF THE EUROPEAN LEGAL ORDER
FRANCOVICH, BONIFACI AND OTHERS V. ITALY (1991)

DERMOT CAHILL*

1. *FRANCOVICH* – ANOTHER BUILDING BLOCK IN THE EUROPEAN LEGAL ORDER

In 1991, *Francovich, Bonifaci and Others v. The Republic of Italy*,[1] the European Court of Justice established that inherent in the European Community legal system is the principle of State liability for harm caused to individuals arising from the State's failure to fulfil it Community obligations. In establishing that such a principle existed, and that it is the duty of the national courts to vindicate that principle, the Court has further helped underpin the coherence and growth of the new order in international law that is the European Community legal system, a system whose efficacy and existence is dependent on the respect of Member States of its rules and principles based on law.

The implications of the judgment, one of the leading judicial decisions of the twentieth century, have been felt at many levels.[2]

First, in establishing the principle of State liability, *Francovich* promoted the role of the citizen in ensuring that EC law is enforced. The judgment has provided the citizen with an important legal tool to use against the State when seeking redress for harm caused because of the State's failure to comply with its EC obligations.

---

*Lecturer in European Union Law, University College Dublin.

[1] Joined Cases C–6 & 9/90, [1991] E.C.R. I–5357.

[2] For interesting and varied analyses the following are recommended as further reading: Oliver's commentaries on case law discussed in this article at (1997) 34 *C.M.L.Rev.* 635; Barav, "State Liability in Damages for breach of Community Law in the National Courts" in Heukels and McDonnell, (eds.), *The Action for Damages in Community Law* (Kluwer, 1997), 363; my own earlier contribution, "New Developments in Determining Criteria for Member State Liability" (1996) 18 *D.U.L.J.* (*n.s.*) 167; Van Gerven, "Bridging the Unbridgeable: Community and National Tort Laws after *Francovich* and *Brasserie*" (1996) 45 *I.C.L.Q* 507; Spink, "Contravening EC law: the Liability of the Member State" (1997) 48 *N.I.L.Q.* 111; Convery, "State liability in the United Kingdom after *Brasserie du Pêcheur*" (1997) 34 *C.M.L.Rev.* 603; Caranta, "Governmental Liability after Francovich" [1993] *C.L.J.* 272.

Second, the prospect of facing damages actions pursuant to the principle of State liability increases pressure on Member States to ensure that they implement EC law on time, and indeed respect their EC law obligations generally. The "global effect" of the judgment is to promote respect for Community obligations amongst Member State authorities, thus enhancing the force of the Community "rule of law".[3] Consequently, it can be expected that the prospect of damages actions may force the Member States to be more diligent in future.[4]

Third, the coherence of the Community's legislative and normative programmes in areas such as harmonisation must be greatly strengthened after the judgment. By 1991 the Community was engaged in a massive legislative programme of directives designed to implement the Internal Market programme. In this regard the Court's judgment certainly was timely. Furthermore, it became clear in subsequent judgments after *Francovich* that the State liability principle is not merely confined to applying to mere late implementation of directives, but may apply generally to many different kinds of State failure to respect Community obligations, such as *legislative enactment* or *administrative decision* contrary to EC law.[5]

Fourth, in the context of the need to have uniform protection of citizen's rights in the different Member State judicial systems, the establishment of the principle of State liability is forcing a reappraisal of whether it is sufficient for the European Court to leave it to the national courts to decide how best to accommodate vindication of the State liability principle within existing national remedies and procedures, or whether the time is approaching when either the Court or Community legislation will be required in order to ensure adequate vindication of the principle on behalf of the citizen.[6]

---

[3] For example, a glance at any of the recent annual reports of the European Commission to the European Parliament will demonstrate how some Member States are less than diligent when it comes to implementing EC law by the proper dates for implementation. In this regard see further Prechal, *Directives in European Community Law. A study of Directives and their Enforcement in National Courts* (Clarendon Press, Oxford, 1995), p.7 where that author observes that Commission statistics in 1993 revealed that the European Commission started 1, 140 infringement proceedings in respect of Member State failure to implement directives (the majority being for non-implementation) and 300 of these proceeded to at least the reasoned opinion stage.

[4] For example, in the Irish case of *Tate, Robinson and Others v. Minister for Social Welfare* [1995] 1 I.R. 418 (H.C.) the State was held liable to compensate a large group of litigants prejudiced by Ireland's failure to implement an EC equal treatment directive. It is estimated that the cost to the State of this single action could eventually amount to more than £250 million.

[5] See below Section 5 *et seq.* when the post-*Francovich* case law is considered in detail.

[6] See below at Section 8 when views of Van Gerven and others are considered.

2. THE PRE-*FRANCOVICH* ERA

In order to have some appreciation of the great step that was taken in the judgment, it is instructive briefly to refer to the enforcement tools that the Court had provided for the citizen in the pre-*Francovich* era. Probably more than any other Community institution, the Court has been methodically establishing principles over the previous thirty or so years to assist the citizen aggrieved by the State's failure to fulfil its Community obligations. Under the Treaty of Rome 1957, the establishment of supranational institutions was envisaged, as was the creation of the common market between the Member States. It was clear from the outset that relationships between the Member States would change irrevocably as their sovereign independence to control flow of trade across their borders would be altered. While not much explicit emphasis was put on the rights of the citizen by the words of the Treaty (which seemed to be directed to Member States), it became clear quite early in the life of the Community that Community Law granted rights and imposed obligations on the citizen under this new legal order. In order to encourage the new regime to flourish, the European Court of Justice played a central role in ensuring that the new legal order had a unity and coherence which could be acceptable to the Member States, in particular to their judicial organs. Central to that role has been the Court's part in promoting the use in the national courts of a set of legal tools for the benefit of the citizen affected by the State's failure to respect its obligations of membership.

For example, in cases such as *Van Gend en Loos*,[7] *Costa v. Enel*,[8] and *Simmenthal*[9] the Court quickly established the doctrine of supremacy, firmly laying down that where Community law and national law conflict, national courts must give effect to Community law. This was given more concrete expression in decisions such as *Walrave and Koch v. Association Union Cycliste Internationale*[10] and *Defrenne v. SABENA*[11] where the Court held that provisions of the Treaty of Rome may create legally invocable obligations not just between the citizen and the State, but furthermore, as between citizens *inter se*. Then came further developments when the Court applied similar reasoning to secondary legislation enforcement in seminal judgments such *Van Duyn*[12] and *Ratti*.[13] A directive could be invocable by way of "direct effect" whereby it

---

[7] Case 26/62, *NV Algemene Transporten Expeditie Onderneming van Gend en Loos v. Nederlandse Administratie der Belastingen* [1963] E.C.R. 1; on which see Fennelly, "The Dangerous Idea of Europe: *Van Gend en Loos* (1963)" above, pp.220 above.
[8] Case 6/64, *Flaminio Costa v. ENEL* [1964] E.C.R. 585.
[9] Case 106/77, *Amministrazione dell Finanze dello Stato v. Simmenthal SpA* [1978] E.C.R. 629.
[10] Case 36/74, [1974] E.C.R. 1405.
[11] Case 43/75, [1976] E.C.R. 455.
[12] Case 41/74, *Van Duyn v. Home Office* [1974] E.C.R. 1337.
[13] Case 148/78, *Pubblico Ministero v. Ratti* [1979] E.C.R. 1629.

could be the source of legally invocable rights by an individual in a dispute with the State even though the State had failed to implement the directive into national law by means of a domestic implementation measure.[14] In order to assist further the citizen affected by the State's failure to comply with its EC obligations, the Court widened the concept of the State in cases such as *Foster,*[15] and in cases such as *Von Colson and Kamann*[16] and *Marleasing*[17] exhorted the national courts to interpret national law in a manner that was harmonious with Community law.

A common feature of the Court's enunciation of all of the aforementioned tools (and which has now also featured in the Court's establishment of the State liability principle) is the notion that the various tools serve to promote the effectiveness of EC law. The Court has been anxious to ensure that neither the national courts nor the citizen are left with empty hands when faced with State failure to respect EC obligations. Such tools have been established by the Court for use by the citizen in the national courts, who have been urged by the Court to allow their use, in order to permit vindication of EC law based rights or obligations whose expression might otherwise be jeopardised by the failure of the State.

3. THE ESTABLISHMENT OF THE STATE LIABILITY PRINCIPLE

However, despite the availability of these useful legal tools, there was still a major weapon that was as yet unavailable to the citizen affected by Member State failure to respect its Community obligations: the action in damages based on EC law. In *Francovich, Bonifaci and Others v. The Republic of Italy*, that step was eventually taken.[18] In some respects, it is hard to believe that the European Court of Justice had not made such a useful tool available earlier than it did. Particularly noteworthy is the way in which the Court managed to command respect for the enforcement of EC law in co-operation with the national courts, even in the absence of such a useful tool as the damages action. Of course, the Court had made the other tools discussed above available to the disgruntled citizen, and had urged the national courts to allow use of such tools.

---

[14]Though the Court would not contemplate permitting EC secondary legislation to be directly enforceable as between private individuals, as in the case of EC Directives (Case 152/84, *Marshall v. Southampton and South West Hampshire Area Health Authority (No. 1)* [1986] E.C.R. 723). However, it is otherwise when EC secondary legislation is also "directly applicable", as is usually the position in the case of EC Regulations.

[15]Case C–188/89, *Foster and Oths v. British Gas plc.* [1990] E.C.R. I–3313.

[16]Case 14/83, *Von Colson and Kamann v. Land Nordrhein-Westfalen* [1984] E.C.R. 1891.

[17]Case C–106/89, *Marleasing SA v. La Comercial Internacionale de Alimentacion SA* [1990] E.C.R. I–4135.

[18]Joined Cases C–6 & 9/90, [1991] E.C.R. I–5357.

However, it was not until 1991 that the European Court of Justice finally crossed the bridge that had been in its sights for some time. The joined cases of *Francovich, Bonifaci and Others v. The Republic of Italy,*[19] presented the Court with an opportunity to decide whether a citizen had the right to obtain damages against the State in circumstances where the State had failed to implement EC law, thereby causing the citizen loss. Conscious that it was taking a bold step, the Court invoked the authority of seminal decisions such as *Van Gend en Loos*[20] and *Costa v. Enel,*[21] and pronounced that:

> The full effectiveness of Community rules would be impaired and the protection of the rights which they grant would be weakened if individuals were unable to obtain redress when their rights are infringed by a breach of Community law for which a Member State can be held responsible.
> The possibility of obtaining redress from the Member State is particularly indispensable where, as in this case, the full effectiveness of Community rules is subject to prior action on the part of the State and where, consequently, individuals in the absence of such action, individuals cannot enforce before the national courts the rights conferred upon them by Community law.
> It follows that the principle whereby a State must be liable for loss and damage caused to individuals as a result of breaches of Community law for which the State can be held responsible is inherent in the system of the Treaty.[22]

Whatever may have been the reason for the thirty year delay in the Court finally recognising that the principle of State liability was inherent in the Treaty, it had now recognised it. Furthermore it had made it clear that its existence is derived from the need to make Community rules fully effective in the Member States. In this regard, the *Simmenthal*[23] judgment was invoked in support. Furthermore, the Court made it clear[24] that the national courts will have the power to find that such liability is well founded. Article 5 of the Treaty was invoked in further support as the Court pointed out that Member States are obliged to do everything to nullify the unlawful consequences of a breach of Community law, including permitting the award of damages against the State where the State has not lived up to its Community obligations.[25]

---

[19] See n.1 above.
[20] See n.7 above.
[21] See n.8 above.
[22] Joined Cases C-6 & 9/90, *Francovich, Bonifaci and Others v. The Republic of Italy* [1991] E.C.R. I-5357, I-5414, paras. 33-35.
[23] See n. 9 above.
[24] [1991] E.C.R. I-5357, I-5415, para. 32.
[25] Article 5 has since been renumbered as Article 10 following the Treaty of Amsterdam 1997.

4. STATE LIABILITY AND NON-IMPLEMENTED DIRECTIVES

The significance of *Francovich* cannot be overestimated. Not only is it a seminal judgment in itself, but also it provided the seed for further development of the principle of State liability to take hold. Before concentrating on these later post-*Francovich* developments, first it is necessary to concentrate on *Francovich* itself in order to appreciate the great leap forward brought about by that judgment when viewed against the background of the legal dispute present in the case itself. Directives are the legal instrument used by the Community when it wishes to achieve a particular result but leaves it up to the Member State to decide, within a stipulated time frame, how best to achieve the objective desired. Essentially, what *Francovich* achieved is that it provided the citizen adversely affected by the State's failure to implement a directive on time with a new weapon. Before *Francovich*, a citizen attempting to enforce a non-implemented directive against the State might be thwarted by the fact that the national court was unable to construe the relevant directive in a directly effective fashion on grounds of lack of clarity or imprecision. However, *Francovich* now provides a remedy which, while it will not achieve a directly effective implementation of the unimplemented provision, nevertheless allows the citizen to sue the State for damages on the ground that the State's failure to implement is the cause of the citizen's deprivation of rights.

In *Francovich*, Directive 80/397[26] had not been implemented into Italian law by the due date for its transposition into national law. The purpose of the directive was to guarantee employees a minimum level of protection in the event that their employer became insolvent, by requiring Member States to provide for the setting up of guarantee funds to cater for employees' unpaid wages in the event that the employer was unable to meet their claims. However, the directive did not designate the bodies who were to administer such funds nor did it indicate that the Member State authorities were to assume such responsibility. The plaintiffs were employees who instituted proceedings against their respective former employers, and finding that the employers were insolvent, claimed to be entitled to payments from the guarantee funds. Unfortunately, no such funds existed as the Italian authorities had not implemented the directive. Hence, the local tribunals hearing the various employees' claims referred identical Article 177[27] references to the Court, which joined the cases as one. Essentially, the reference concerned two issues. First, whether the provisions of the directive were directly effective against the State even in the absence of a domestic implementation measure? Second, whether the Italian State could be liable in damages, in the event that the directive turned out not to be enforceable, because of the State's failure to implement the directive.

---

[26] O.J. [1980] L 283/23.
[27] Article 177 has since been renumbered as Article 234.

On the first issue, direct effect, the Court held that the relevant provisions of the directive were not capable of being directly effective. The plaintiffs could not invoke the directive as its terms were not sufficiently clear and precise. Particularly, the directive was not clear as to the identity of the guarantee institutions or the source of their finance. On the second issue – whether damages should in principle be possible against the State for its failure to implement EC law in circumstances where a citizen was thereby deprived of rights the directive intended him to have in the first place – the Court in a historic ruling recognised that State liability is required by Community law in such circumstances. The Court then set out the conditions for determining liability where a State has failed to take all the measures necessary to achieve the result prescribed by a directive: (1) was the aim of the directive to create rights for individuals?; (2) was the content of those rights ascertainable from the directive?; and (3) was there a causal link between the Member State's failure to implement and the damage that resulted to the injured party?

In establishing that State liability existed under Community law, the Court had yet again altered the nature of the relationship between the citizen and the State. Where the State had failed to implement EC law such that the citizen's rights were affected, the citizen was empowered to go before a national court and seek damages for loss thereby occasioned. The remedy, damages, could be granted by a national court even though the directive was not one that would have been capable of enforcement by way of direct effect.[28] However, the Court did attach a reservation to the availability of the remedy. It provided that in the absence of Community legislation, it is for the internal legal order of each of the Member States to designate the competent courts and lay down the detailed procedural rules for legal proceedings intended fully to safeguard the rights which individuals derive from Community law.[29] Furthermore, it added that following the principles laid down in the *San Giorgio* judgment[30] the substantive and procedural conditions for reparation and loss laid down by the national law of the Member States must not be less favourable than those relating to similar domestic claims and must not be so framed as to make it virtually impossible or excessively difficult to obtain reparation. These are known as the principles of effectiveness and equivalence.[31]

---

[28] Although unfortunately in the case of Mr. Francovich, it was ultimately determined that even after the directive was implemented into Italian law, compensation in his particular situation was not possible as the Court (in the second *Francovich* Article 177 ruling) interpreted the relevant directive as permitting Member States the right to exclude from any right to compensation employees in his particular situation: see Case C–479/93, *Francovich v. Italy (No. 2)* [1995] E.C.R. II–3843. For commentary see Barrett, "Mr. Francovich strikes again or when is an insolvency not an insolvency?" (1996) 18 *D.U.L.J.* (*n.s.*) 157.

[29] [1991] E.C.R. I-5357, I-5415–I-5416, paras. 42-43.

[30] Case 199/82, *Amministrazione delle Finanze dello Stato v. San Giorgio SpA* [1983] E.C.R. 3595.

[31] See further below at Section 8 where Van Gerven queries whether the application of such prin-

5. WHETHER STATE LIABILITY EXTENDED BEYOND STATE FAILURE TO IMPLEMENT
DIRECTIVES?

However, as is the case with so many leading cases, *Francovich* was setting the scene for a series of cases that were to soon follow it. At paragraph 38 of the judgment, the Court stated:

> Although State liability is thus required by Community law, the conditions under which that liability gives rise to a right to reparation depend on the nature of the breach of Community law giving rise to the loss and damage.

While it may not have been immediately apparent, the Court was signalling that the State liability principle may also be applicable to situations other than the mere failure to transpose directives into national law. With this paragraph the Court was setting the scene for issues to be resolved in future case law. While, as with many leading cases, *Francovich* did not provide all the answers, it certainly set the scene for others to follow. It would soon become clear that Court's judgment in *Francovich* covered more than just failure to implement a directive with the consequent loss of invocable rights. It had in fact recognised a general principle of State liability for failure to respect EC obligations.

5.1 State Liability in the Context of National Legislation Contrary to EC Law

The 1996 decision of the Court in the joined cases of *Brasserie du Pêcheur SA v. Federal Republic of Germany* and *R. v. Sec of State for Transport, ex p. Factortame Ltd*[32] ("*Brasserie du Pêcheur/Factortame 3*") demonstrates how the *Francovich* liability principle was applied to cover the situation where the State has *legislated* contrary to EC law.

In this decision, the Court was not faced with unimplemented directives but rather with plaintiffs who claimed damage as a result of Member States' maintenance of national laws which were, clearly on the basis of previous judgments of the Court, contrary to EC Law. The issue for the Court was of immense importance. In both cases, one emanating from Germany and the other from the UK, neither jurisdiction provided a legal basis for grounding an action in damages in national law in the circumstances. Hence, the issue was whether the Court would hold that the principle of State liability was also applicable to situations where the State had legislated contrary to EC law, in circumstances

---

ciples are sufficient to protect the citizen affected by the State's failure to comply with its membership obligations.

[32] Joined Cases C–46 & 48/93, [1996] E.C.R. I–1029.

where the State did not provide for a legal remedy in damages against the State under domestic law? And furthermore, if the Court was minded to find such a principle existed, would the three criteria for establishing State liability enunciated in *Francovich* apply?

5.2 Background

Before these crucial issues are discussed, first a brief synopsis of the factual background to the two cases may be helpful. In *Brasserie du Pêcheur*, the plaintiff claimed it had suffered loss when it had to discontinue beer exports to Germany. First, German law only allowed a product to be sold as "bier" when it was produced in a certain manner and consequently any beer produced by any other means was not allowed to be sold under such designation in Germany. Second, German law also prohibited the importation of beer containing additives.

Brasserie du Pêcheur instituted proceedings seeking damages for loss claiming that the national laws in question were contrary to EC law. Their case was a strong one as already in 1979 in the famous *Cassis De Dijon*[33] decision, the Court had promulgated principles under Article 30 which rendered national measures which operated in a similar fashion to the "bier" law restriction incompatible with Article 30.[34] Additionally, in 1987 in *Commission v. Federal Republic of Germany*[35] the Court had held that Germany's beer additives law was contrary to Article 30. However, the obstacle that the plaintiff faced was that German law[36] only permitted actions in damages to be taken against the public authorities where it could be demonstrated that they owed a duty to the specific litigant. German law did not provide for an action in damages to be taken merely because the State in legislating for the public as a whole, had caused damage to an individual litigant. The Member State argued that no specific duty was owed to Brasserie du Pêcheur. *Brasserie du Pêcheur* therefore presented the Court with an opportunity to pronounce on whether Brasserie du Pêcheur could invoke the principle of State liability based on EC law whereby the German State could be held liable in damages because it had maintained in force laws contrary to EC law which had allegedly caused Brasserie du Pêcheur loss.

R. v. Sec of State for Transport, ex p. Factortame Ltd ("*Factortame 3*")[37] presented similar issues. The applicants were owners of Spanish fishing ves-

---

[33] Case 120/78, *Rewe Centrale AG v. Bundesmonopolverwalthung fur Branntwein* [1979] E.C.R. 649, on which see Carney, "What Rule of Reason? *Cassis de Dijon* (1979); A Flawed *Locus Classicus*", above, 310.
[34] Article 30 has since been renumbered as Article 28.
[35] Case 178/84, [1987] E.C.R. 1227.
[36] Paragraph 839 of German Civil Code and Article 34 of German Basic Law.
[37] Joined Cases C–46 & 48/93, [1996] E.C.R. I–1029.

sels that had been prevented from fishing UK fishing quotas by the UK Merchant Shipping Act 1988, a law that had been earlier held to be contrary to EC law because it discriminated on the basis of nationality.[38] The Court of Justice was now asked pursuant to Article 177 whether an applicant could seek damages against a Member State, where it was alleged that the Member State had enacted a law that was contrary to EC law in circumstances where existing national law did not allow any damages remedy for a litigant allegedly affected by such a law.[39]

5.3 State Liability Principle Inherent in the Treaty

The Court proceeded to rule (in *Brasserie du Pêcheur/Factortame 3*) that the *Francovich* State liability principle was not just confined to situations where unimplemented directives were involved. It was a principle of much wider application. Referring to Article 215(2) of the Treaty, the Court held that Article 215(2) (which establishes the conditions for the non-contractual liability of the Community) is simply an expression of a general principle familiar to the legal systems of the Member States that an unlawful act or omission gives rise to an obligation on public authorities to make good damage caused in the performance of their duties.[40] Hence, the Court was establishing that the principle of State liability is not only based on the duties of the Member State to ensure that EC law can be effectively enforced (as elaborated upon in *Francovich* itself) but also it is inspired by the general principle found in Member State legal systems that unlawful activity must be permitted a remedy. The Court then stated that:

> . . . the Court held in *Francovich*, at paragraph 35, that the principle of State liability for loss and damage caused to individuals as a result of breaches of Community law for which it can be held responsible is inherent in the system of the Treaty.
>
> It follows that that principle holds good for any case in which a Member State breaches Community law, whatever be the organ of the State whose act or omission was responsible for the breach.[41]

---

[38] In an earlier decision in the *Factortame* litigation, Case C–221/89, *R. v. Secretary of State, ex p. Factortame* [1991] E.C.R. I–3905, the Court had held that the 1988 Act's nationality requirements were contrary to Article 52 EC (since renumbered as Article 43).

[39] Existing remedies in U.K. law such as the tort of misfeasance of public office were not invocable against the U.K. State in respect of Acts of the Parliament.

[40] Joined Cases C-46 & 48/93, *Brasserie du Pècheur SA v. Federal Republic of Germany* and *R. v. Secretary of State, ex p. Factortame Ltd* [1996] E.C.R. I-1029, I-1144, para. 29, Article 215 has since been renumbered as Article 288.

[41] [1996] E.C.R. I-1029, I-1144, paras. 31-32.

Francovich is the source of the Court's inspiration. As if it had not already been sufficiently clear, the Court then proceeded to make it clear that the principle of State liability will apply irrespective of a Member State's national constitutional division of powers. The Court stated, ". . . the obligation to make good damage caused to individuals by breaches of Community law cannot depend on domestic rules as to the division of powers between constitutional authorities."[42]

5.4 State Liability Possible Even Where EC Law Directly Effective

However, the impact of *Francovich* did not end there. The Court also ruled in *Brasserie du Pêcheur/Factortame 3* that *Francovich* could not be confined to allowing a remedy in damages where the provision of EC law in issue was not directly effective. As one may recall, in *Francovich* the EC directive in question was not directly effective. Now several Member States[43] intervened to argue that the *Francovich* principle of State liability should not apply where the provisions of EC law infringed were directly effective. Basically the Member States were arguing that as Article 30 was directly effective in the case of *Brasserie du Pêcheur*, and Article 52 in the case of *Factortame 3,* State liability in damages should not arise. The Court rejected this contention in strong language by holding that the *Francovich* principle of State liability also applies all the more where the State's infringement is of a directly effective provision.

5.5 Conditions for State Liability will vary According to the Nature of the Breach

The Court them proceeded to take up where it left off at paragraph 38 of *Francovich.* It now became clear what the Court had in mind when it had referred to the conditions for determining State liability varying *according to the nature of the breach* (emphasis added). Looking to Article 215(2) for inspiration, the Court held that when the liability of Community institutions was in issue, it was recognised that the existence of the Community's legislative function must not be hindered by the prospect of actions for damages whenever the general interest of the Community requires legislative measures to be taken even though individual interests may be adversely affected. In such situations, the Community institutions will only be held liable in damages where they have "manifestly and gravely disregarded" the limits on the exercise of their powers.[44] By analogy, the Court reasoned that similar considerations should

---

[42][1996] E.C.R. I-1029, I-1145, paras. 33.
[43]Germany, Ireland and the Netherlands.
[44][1996] E.C.R. I-1029, I-1029, I-1147–I-1148, paras. 44-45.

apply when attempting to determine whether a Member State should be subject to the State liability principle when the Member State is legislating or making economic policy choices in a field governed by EC law.[45] The justification given by the Court for this reasoning was that the protection of rights which individuals derive from Community law cannot, in the absence of particular justification, vary depending on whether national authority or a Community authority was responsible for the breach.[46]

The Court then held that where a Member State is acting in an area where it has a narrow discretion, such as where Community law obliges it to act in a manner which considerably reduces its discretion, or perhaps Community law obliges it to refrain from acting, then failure to comply with the limits placed on its discretion will render the State liable. However, where the State's margin of discretion is considerably wider, then liability principles apply as are similar to those that apply to Community institutions in similar situations.[47] According to the Court, in such circumstances, three conditions must be met. First, the Community law infringed must be for the protection of individuals. Second, the breach of Community law must be *sufficiently serious* (emphasis added). Third, there must be a direct causal link between the breach of the obligations resting on the State and the damage sustained.

Applying these principles to the case before it, the Court found that both Germany and Britain had found themselves in wide discretion situations. For example, it found in *Brasserie du Pêcheur* there was no Community harmonisation in existence at the time the German beer purity legislation was enacted, and so the German authorities had a wide measure of discretion to lay down beer purity requirements. Similarly, in *Factortame 3* the Court found that Community law had not removed jurisdiction from the UK to register fishing ves-

---

[45] Van Gerven disagrees that the same latitude rightly allowed to Member States when making policy choices should also be allowed when Member States are making legislative choices based on the interpretation of Community legal rules. See n.52 below.

[46] [1996] E.C.R. I-1029, I-1146–I-1147, paras. 41-42.

[47] *cf*. Waalbroek, "Treaty violations and liability of Member States: the effects of the *Francovich* case law" in Heukels and McDonnell, (eds.), (see n. 2 above), 335 who takes the view that, although the Court has said that the conditions for determining State liability should be the same for Member States as for Community Institutions under Art. 215(2), the approach taken by the Court in *Brasserie du Pêcheur/Factortame 3* may indicate that the Court may be prepared to apply a less rigorous approach to litigants seeking to establish State liability than it has traditionally applied to litigants attempting to establish Community liability. To support this, that commentator points to the fact that the Court did not elaborate the traditional strict language of Art. 215(2) liability to the same extent as it would when considering an Art. 215(2) application *per se*. Furthermore, Van Gerven, "Bridging the Unbridgeable: Community and National Tort Laws after *Francovich* and *Brasserie*" (1996) 45 *I.C.L.Q*. 507, 523-524 has drawn attention to the fact that in Francovich the Court indicated that if State liability was established then the measure of damages had to be equal to the loss, whereas in Art. 215(2) cases, compensation will only be awarded where the loss is beyond normal economic risks.

sels, and that furthermore that the EC's common fisheries policy does leave a measure of discretion to the Member State to regulate fishing matters.

However, the Court then proceed to give guidance[48] to the national courts to assist them to decide whether in either case before it, the Member State's breach of EC law was "sufficiently serious" in order to ground liability in damages. In the case of *Brasserie du Pêcheur*, the Court indicated that the "bier" requirement was manifestly contrary to EC law as there had been previous case law ruling upon the incompatibility of such rules with EC law.[49] However, on the other hand, the question of whether the German ban on importation of beer containing additives was compatible with Article 30 was not clear until the Court ruled on the matter in *Commission v. Federal Republic of Germany* in 1987.[50] In the case of *Factortame 3*, the Court held that the 1988 UK legislation which permitted only UK nationals to register fishing boats out of UK ports had already been held in earlier litigation in the *Factortame* saga to be contrary to Article 52 as it constituted direct discrimination on grounds of nationality.[51] However, in so far as the UK Act's requirements as to domicile were concerned, these also constituted a prime facie breach of EC law and the question for the national court to decide was whether such provisions constituted a sufficiently serious breach which would warrant an award of damages? In order to assist the national court decide this issue, the Court set out a number of factors for consideration by the national court: the legal disputes relating to certain features of the common fisheries policy, the attitude of the EC Commission and whether it had made its attitude known to the Member State in good time, the view of the national court as to the state of certainty of EC law, and whether the Member State had diligently complied with any interim relief that was ordered by the Court.

While the foregoing considerations were specifically intended for the national court's assistance in the *Brasserie du Pêcheur/Factortame 3* litigation, the Court also helpfully set out criteria to assist national courts generally to decide whether a "sufficiently serious" breach has occurred. It held that in deciding whether a Member State has committed a sufficiently serious breach, criteria that national courts may have regard to are: the degree of clarity of the Community rule breached; the measure of discretion left by that rule to the Member State authorities; whether the breach was intentional or involuntary;

---

[48]Though as this writer has previously noted elsewhere ("New Developments in Determining Criteria for Member State Liability" (1996) 18 *D.U.L.J.* (*n.s.*) 167, 177) the Court was going beyond its advisory role under Article 177 as it was leaving the national court with little doubt as to how it viewed the respective Member State measures. Oliver expresses similar sentiments in his commentary on the case at (1997) 34 *C.M.L.Rev.* 635, 645.

[49]Case 120/78, *Rewe Centrale AG v. Bundesmonopolverwalthung fur Branntwein* [1979] E.C.R. 649.

[50]Case 178/84, [1987] E.C.R. 1227.

[51]In the earlier Case C–221/89 *R. v. Secretary of State, ex p. Factortame* [1991] E.C.R. I–3905.

whether any error or law was involved, and if so was it excusable or not; whether a Community institution's actions contributed to the breach; or, whether the Member State had adopted or retained national measures contrary to EC law.[52]

Giving further guidance, the Court held that a breach would be sufficiently serious where a previous ruling of the Court had held the point in issue infringed EC law, or where a preliminary ruling existed on the point in issue, or where in settled case law the Court has taken a contrary positions to the national authorities.

Thus the impact of *Francovich* was now felt in the Member States beyond the mere failure to implement an EC directive scenario. Now the *legislature* of the Member States would have to be more careful when enacting legislation and would have to ensure that domestic legislation adopted contrary to EC law did not constitute a "sufficiently serious" breach of EC law.[53]

6. State Liability and Poorly Implemented Directives

A few weeks after the *Brasserie du Pêcheur/Factortame 3* judgment, the Court delivered its judgment in *R. v. H.M. Treasury, ex p. British Telecom.*[54] In *British Telecom* the Court was called upon to consider whether the applicant was entitled to plead the principle of State liability in a situation where the Member State had incorrectly transposed a directive into national law. *British Telecom* argued that the UK had implemented EC Directive 90/531[55] incorrectly as it had designated certain contracts for public tendering, whereas according to *British Telecom* the directive intended that entities such as *British Telecom*

---

[52] Van Gerven, "Bridging the Unbridgeable: Community and National Tort Laws after *Francovich* and *Brasserie*" (1996) 45 *I.C.L.Q.* 507, 527-9 comments that while such criteria are suitable for determining whether State liability is established where the State is making *policy choices*, he takes the view that the Court may have gone too far in providing that such criteria are also to be used to determine liability in the situation where the State has made an *erroneous interpretation of Community legal rules*. Van Gerven observes that "It may actually lead to virtual immunity for any kind of conduct on the part of the legislature which does not manifestly fly in the face of Community law, as in the case of direct discrimination." The writer sees merit in this view, and notes that this accords with the writer's own view expressed in "New Developments in Determining Criteria for Member State liability" (1996) 18 *D.U.L.J.* (*n.s.*) 167 that the burden of proof on a litigant seeking damages may be difficult to surmount because of the "sufficiently serious" criteria's demands.

[53] It should be noted that the domestic German tribunal ultimately determined in the *Brasserie du Pêcheur* litigation that no damages were to be awarded on the basis that there was no causal link demonstrated between any damage that may have been sustained by the litigant and the "bier" requirement. Furthermore, in the case of the additives legislation, the domestic authorities were found to have taken steps to abrogate any harmful effects *vis-à-vis* imports. The tribunal's finding on the additives issue has been criticised as being less than convincing: see Oliver, n.2 above.

[54] Case C-392/93, [1996] E.C.R. I-1631.

[55] O.J. [1990] L 297/1.

should have the right to designate. The Court held that the UK had indeed transposed the directive incorrectly, and thus was in breach of its Community obligations. However, the breach was not a sufficiently serious breach according to the Court, because the Court pointed to the lack of clarity and precision in a key article in the directive. The Court took the view that Article 8(1) of the directive was imprecisely worded and was reasonably capable of bearing, as well as the construction applied to it by the Court, the interpretation given to it by the UK in good faith. Furthermore, the Court pointed to the fact that several other Member States also took a similar interpretation of the directive. In addition, the Court pointed out that no guidance was available to the UK from the Court's previous case law on the matter at issue, and neither had the Commission raised any objections when the Member State had notified the implementing regulations to the Commission back in 1992.

From *British Telecom* it is evident that the Court has applied the *Francovich* State liability principle to the situation where the State has *mis-implemented* EC law, though the conditions for determining liability are not identical to those applied in *Francovich* itself. The reason for using the "sufficiently serious" criterion is that the Court was recognising that there is a distinction between the situation where there is State failure to implement a directive *at all* (*Francovich*), and the situation where the State implements *incorrectly* due to the directive's lack of precision or imprecise language (*British Telecom*). According to the Court's judgement in the later case of *Dillenkofer and Oths. v. Federal Republic of Germany*,[56] breach in both instances may be "sufficiently serious", though more readily apparent in the first situation. In other words, a failure to implement a directive is a sufficiently serious breach by itself, whereas a State acting in an area where it has discretion only commits a sufficiently serious breach where the surrounding circumstances demonstrate that it had a manifest disregard for the limits on its discretion.

7. STATE LIABILITY AND ADMINISTRATIVE ACTION

Francovich's State liability principle was further extended in 1996 in the Court's decision in *R v. Ministry of Agriculture, Fisheries and Food ex p. Hedley Lomas (Ireland) Ltd.*[57] In dispute was the UK's refusal to grant the applicant export licences to send sheep to Spain for slaughter. The UK refusal was based on the UK view that Spanish slaughter houses were not complying with humane slaughtering standards set out in Directive 74/577.[58] The UK authorities had no evidence on which to base the refusal decision apart from the opinions of animal

---

[56]Joined Cases C–178, 179, 188-190/94, [1996] E.C.R. I–4845.
[57]Case C–5/94, [1996] E.C.R. I–2553.
[58]O.J. [1974] L.316.

welfare activists. The Commission informed the UK that its actions were contrary to Article 34 of the Treaty and could not be justified pursuant to Article 36.[59] The applicant instituted proceedings in the UK courts seeking a declaration that Article 34 was breached, and a remedy in damages against the Member State.

An Article 177 reference was made to the Court which held that the refusal to award the export licence was contrary to Article 34. Also, it held that as the Community had legislated to harmonise the area by way of the directive, recourse to Article 36 was no longer possible. When the Court then considered the issue of State liability, its reasoning became "uncharacteristically circuitous"[60] in that the Court appeared to say that the Member State had a wide discretion in the early part of the judgment, only later to state that the Member State had very little or no discretion to act because the EC legal regime (i.e., the Directive) had removed such freedom. Ultimately, the Court found[61] that the UK's actions were of a sufficiently serious nature and it would be up to the national court to decide if the necessary element of causation was demonstrated. What is confusing about this decision is that the Court did not apply the *Francovich* criteria *simpliciter*, but instead applied the language of the *Brasserie du Pêcheur/Factortame 3* decision by using the "sufficiently serious" criteria. As other commentators including this author have written, why was it necessary to refer to *Brasserie du Pêcheur/Factortame 3* at all when the Court had concluded that the Member State was not acting in a wide discretion situation?[62]

The greater significance of course of *Hedley Lomas* was that it constitutes yet another example of where the *Francovich* State liability principle was invoked – on this occasion to an *administrative decision* taken by a Member State authority contrary to EC law in circumstances which allegedly caused loss to a corporate citizen. It provides an example of a yet further instance of where the State may be liable in damages for breach of EC law.

Whatever confusion may have existed after *Hedley Lomas* regarding the use of State liability principle terminology, the Court set about putting matters to right in *Dillenkofer and Oths. v. Federal Republic of Germany*[63] where the

---

[59] Articles 34 and 36 have since been renumbered as Articles 29 and 30 respectively.

[60] Oliver, "Commentary on the *Hedley Lomas* decision" (1997) 34 *C.M.L.Rev.* 666, 674.

[61] The writer uses the word "found" as that can only be how the Court's decision can be described, notwithstanding that the matter was before the Court pursuant to an Article 177 reference.

[62] Oliver, "Commentary on the *Hedley Lomas* decision" (1997) 34 *C.M.L.Rev.* 666, 673; Barav, "State Liability in Damages for breach of Community Law in the National Courts" in Heukels and McDonnell, (eds.), *The Action for Damages in Community Law* (Kluwer, 1997) 363; the writer's own contribution, Cahill, "New Developments in determining criteria for Member State liability" (1996) 18 *D.U.L.J. (n.s.)* 167, 181-183.

[63] Joined Cases C–178, 179, 188-190/94, *Dillenkofer and Oths. v. Federal Republic of Germany* [1996] E.C.R. I–4845.

Court, perhaps conscious that its terminology in *Hedley Lomas* was confusing, stated as follows:

> In substance, the conditions laid down in [*Francovich, Brasserie du Pêcheur, Factortame 3 and Hedley Lomas*] are the same, since the condition that there should be a sufficiently serious breach, although not expressly mentioned in *Francovich,* was nevertheless evident from the circumstances of the case.[64]

While this may well be correct, there is nevertheless a substantial difference in the threshold level of evidence required in order for an applicant to succeed in establishing State liability in cases where a wide discretion is allowed to the Member State, rather than where there is no or only little discretion (such as where there is a complete failure to implement a directive at all). Indeed in *Dillenkofer*, the Court expressly rejected contentions put forward by Germany (and by several other Member States in support) that Germany's failure to implement the directive on time was not a sufficiently serious breach as it had particular difficulties in making the necessary changes to its domestic law in light of the directive's requirements. Mere failure to implement was sufficiently serious and the Court stated that its judgment in *Francovich* demonstrated a similar example of such a situation. However, the same will not necessarily be the case where a litigant is attempting to establish State liability in circumstances where a Member State is considered to have a discretion to make legislative and policy choices. That this is now clear can be seen from the Court's pronouncement that:

> When the Court held that the conditions under which State liability gives rise to a right of reparation depended on the nature of the breach of Community law causing the damage, that meant that those conditions are to be applied according to each type of situation.[65]

It is submitted that because of this different threshold, *Francovich*, on its own terms, is more significant than ever, as the threshold that the litigant has to cross is far lower than under the "sufficiently serious" criteria as elaborated in *Brasserie du Pêcheur/Factortame 3*.[66] Furthermore, as Van Gerven has observed:

> One may wonder whether the criterion of "sufficiently serious breach" is

---

[64] [1996] E.C.R. I-4845, I-4879, para. 23.
[65] [1996] E.C.R. I-4845, I-4879, para. 24.
[66] As previously discussed by this writer in "New Developments in determining criteria for Member State liability" (1996) 18 *D.U.L.J.* (*n.s.*) 167, 184-185.

not too blunt to differentiate sufficiently between breaches of Community law, created as it first was for assessing the use of wide discretion in matters of policy or decision-making involving value judgments, and whether it will not in some instances limit the legal protection of injured persons too severely and in others impose too much of a burden on public authorities.[67]

8. STATE LIABILITY AND ITS FUTURE IMPACT ON REMEDIES AND PROCEDURES IN NATIONAL COURTS?

While it is undeniable that the Court recognised the principle of State liability in *Francovich,* and elaborated upon it in later cases, the work remains as yet unfinished. Convery puts it well when she observes that the question now is how this multi-faceted principle will operate before the national courts in its finer details. Particularly, whether the Member States will be required to provide a brand new tort, or whether existing torts cannot be amended in order to accommodate litigants.[68] To date, the Court seems content to rule that it is up to the national courts to regulate the availability of remedies for breach of EC law provided that the twin principles of effectiveness and equivalence are respected.[69] According to Craig and De Burca, the interaction between Community requirements and national rules remains one of the outstanding questions concerning the principle of State liability.[70] Van Gerven has written that:

> It does not suffice, however, that rights which EU citizens derive from Community law (hereafter "Community rights") are in each member State protected by judicial process *to some extent.* For that protection to satisfy the uniform application of Community law in the member States - which is "a fundamental requirement of the Community legal order" – it must also be sufficiently uniform, i.e. similar or of a comparable nature, in each of the member States. Only then is it possible to avoid judicial protection of Community rights varying considerably from one member State to another, thus depriving such rights of the equal substance which they

---

[67] Van Gerven, "Bridging the Unbridgeable: Community and National Tort Laws after *Francovich* and *Brasserie*" (1996) 45 *I.C.L.Q.* 507, 544.

[68] See Convery, "State liability in the United Kingdom after *Brasserie du Pêcheur*" (1997) 34 *C.M.L. Rev.* 610 where consideration is given to whether the existing UK torts may provide adequate avenues of providing relief, or whether a new form of tortious action is required.

[69] As set out in Case 199/82, *Amministrazione delle Finanze dello Stato v. San Giorgio SpA* [1983] E.C.R. 3595, and as also referred to in both *Francovich* and *Brasserie du Pêcheur/Factortame 3* (see Sections 4 and 5 above).

[70] Craig and De Burca, *EC Law. Text Cases and Materials* (2nd ed., Oxford University Press, London, 1998), 248.

are intended to have for all Community citizens alike. And indeed, it cannot be emphasised enough that equality of *rights*, and uniform application thereof throughout the Community, implies sufficiently harmonised *sanctions* guaranteeing the enforcement of those rights *and* sufficiently harmonised legal *remedies* enabling the enforcement of such rights and sanctions through the judicial process in an adequate *and* comparable manner in all the Member States.[71]

Of the aforementioned twin principles of effectiveness and equivalence which the Court had reiterated in *Francovich,* the learned author continued to observe that they:

> ... do not achieve ... the objective of an adequate and sufficiently harmonised level of judicial protection in all the Member States. That objective can only be achieved only if the European Court is willing, in the absence of action by the Community legislature, to lay down the procedural and, more important, the substantive conditions of legal remedies which are essential to guarantee the effective and (sufficiently) equal protection of the Community rights involved across the Community.[72]

9. CONCLUSION

It is suggested that *Francovich* is one of the leading cases of the twentieth century as it placed a valuable tool in the hands of the Community citizenry whose EC law based rights and obligations may be jeopardised by the State's failure to comply with its membership obligations. Particularly noteworthy is the Court's insistence that the principle of State liability is inherent in the system of the Treaty. In so providing, the judgment further bolsters the construction of the European Community legal order.

The principle of State liability adds an important compliment to the array of tools that had already been fashioned by the Court for the benefit of the Community citizen. Of striking significance is the way in which the Court moved quickly after *Francovich* to make it clear that the principle of State liability applied to different kinds of State breach of Community law, whether it be failure to implement Community legislation, or enactment of laws contrary to Community law, or administrative decisions taken contrary to Community law.

However, while much progress has been made in a short time, of concern is

---

[71](1996) 45 *I.C.L.Q.* 507, 513-4.
[72](1996) 45 *I.C.L.Q.* 507, 515.

the risk that national courts might seize on the "sufficiently serious" criteria in situations where the State has a wide discretion to act when making legislative or policy choices, in order to unfairly deny a remedy to the citizen adversely affected by the State's breach.

As the new century begins, it may be appropriate for the Court to consider whether some form of harmonisation is required, whether legislative or judicial, in order to ensure that uniform protection is provided throughout the Member States when citizens seek to vindicate the principle of State liability in the national courts, particularly in the case of certain jurisdictions which traditionally have not permitted, or made it excessively difficult for, the citizen to obtain damages against the State.

NATIVE TITLE AND THE SEARCH FOR JUSTICE
MABO (1992)

JAMES TUNNEY*

Because if Columbus had been met with signs saying: "Private Property" or "Keep Out" – he would simply have turned around and gone back to Spain.[1]

1. INTRODUCTION

The landscape and life of the Aboriginal peoples of Australia may seem a long way from the mind of the law student in the European common law world of eminent busts, musty books and dusty libraries. The islands in the Torres Straits are perhaps such places as students dream of when their minds wander while listening to the mystical principles of land law. In that general part of the world over a century ago when Krakatua erupted, it sent columns of ash 20 kilometres in the sky, causing a huge tsunami and leading to beautiful sunsets in far away parts of the globe. It was heard clearly from Alice Springs to Sri Lanka. The *Mabo* case was metaphorically of similar proportions.[2] It sent tremors that threatened to topple long established constructs of power, politics and law.

2. THE GENERAL LAWSCAPE. THE STRUGGLE FOR LAND AND SOULS

2.1 Old and New

Although *Mabo*'s central focus was about native title, the penumbra was wider. Title has a number of meanings, and contexts, of which land may seem to be the most significant. *Mabo* is most directly a product of the clash between Europe and the inappropriately named 'New World', and all that was part of colonialism and imperialism, from the scramble for Africa, to the search for El Dorado. Some would see it as part of a longer line, for example those that argue that the colonisation of Ireland preceded the assault on Native Ameri-

---

*Senior Lecturer in Law, University of Abertay, Dundee, Scotland.

[1] See Pelletier, *A Wise Man Speaks* (Department Of Indian Affairs, Quebec, 1985) 47.
[2] *Mabo v. State of Queensland (No.2)* (1992) 175 C.L.R. 1 (H.C.A).

cans and the enslavement of Africans, and identified a pattern of exploitation.[3] That *Mabo* was decided 500 years after Ferdinand and Isabella entered the Alhambra in Granada, defeating the Moors and supporting Columbus's voyage to the new world, was not a mere coincidence. Debates that would echo later in the cool, gloomy lecture halls of Salamanca University, inside the orange sandstone buildings, identified and anticipated the poles of potential legal analysis of title to the new world. Ironically enough, Cortés, who burnt his boats, marched on Tenochtitlan, conquered the Aztecs and destroyed Montezuma, went to Salamanca to study law exactly 500 years ago in 1499, but left from boredom.[4]

In the 'Old World' in Spain, legal analysis came largely from the discipline of theologians, who would later be described as international lawyers. Clearly opposing views of the legal right of the Spanish to the Americas emerged.[5] On the one hand were arguments which ultimately were to triumph, such as that of Bartolomé de las Casas in his treatise published in Seville in 1552.

> The kings of Castile and León are true princes, sovereign and universal lords and emperors over many kings. The rights over all that great empire and the universal jurisdiction over all the Indies belong to them by the authority, concession, and the donation of the said Holy Apostolic See and thus by divine authority. This and no other is the juridical basis upon which all their title is founded and established.[6]

This was quite moderate when contrasted with a multitude of examples of the xenophobic and racist, and general views which ascribed satanic characteristics to the native people. The first hand accounts of the bloody sacrifices of the Aztecs and of the gore-covered temples no doubt influenced some of these reactions. That general type of view was consistent with the introduction to the Institutes of Justinian in 533, which articulated explicitly the connection between conquest, God, authority and law over the 'barbarian nations'. On the other hand, Francisco de Vitoria, a professor of theology at the University of

---

[3] See for example, Kolchin, *American Slavery 1619-1877* (Penguin, London, 1993), 15.

[4] As well as classic historical studies such as Prescott, *History of the Conquest of Mexico*, (Swan Sonnenschein, London, 1843) and Pakenham, *The Scramble for Africa 1876-1912* (Abacus, London, 1991) there are also literary and cultural perspectives such as Said, *Culture and Imperialism* (Vintage, London, 1994). Anthropological studies include Nader (ed.), *Law in Culture and Society* (University of California Press, London, 1997). Many specific studies of Aboriginal experience in particular locations are emerging, such as Austen, *A Cry in the Wind: Conflict in Western Australia 1829-1929* (Darlington, Darlington W.A., 1998).

[5] For a convenient and accessible translation, see Englander, Norman, O'Day and Owens, *Culture and Belief in Europe 1450-1600: An Anthology of Sources*, (Blackwell, Oxford, 1994) [hereafter Englander *et al.*].

[6] De las Casas, "Aquí Se Contienen Trínta Proposiciones Muy Jurídicas" in Englander *et al.*, 327.

Salamanca, argued differently. In *Relectio de Indiis*, utilising the Bible and Aristotle as authority, he concluded,

> The upshot of all the preceding is, then, that the aborigines undoubtedly had true dominion in both public and private matters, just like Christians, and that neither their princes nor private persons could be despoiled of their property on the ground of their not being true owners.[7]

2.2 The Quest for Land

Title to land and sovereignty are often confused, as they are very closely related.[8] Although civilian law might argue that such arguments were canvassed long ago, unfortunately Vitoria's view was well and truly stillborn. Today, countries like Brazil are revisiting indigenous land title, and seeking legal accommodations, especially where tribes fled into the jungle areas to survive. Conquest gave title, as did adherence to Christianity, just as Islam had in North Africa and Spain itself for 800 years. Arguments such as that of John Winthrop (the Governor of Massachusetts) who in 1631 objected to the natives' lack of enclosure and proceeded to concoct a rationale based on analogy to the Israelites and Canaanites, were common enough.[9] It is true enough that there are plenty of precursors of title issues back to the rivers of Babylon, back to cities like Jericho and beyond in the Middle East, as soon as humankind began to cultivate wheat and the land. But as Shakespeare reminds us, the devil can cite scripture for his purpose. It is a little simplistic to impute undue instrumentality to the philosophical justifications the conquerors have recorded at the time. Nearly all peoples have struggled for land or its produce at some time. The history of the Middle East and the use of the horse in warfare to allow attacking armies to take the surfeit of agricultural produce of those settled civilisations, illustrate that contemporary debates are part of a long continuum. The exploits of Genghis Khan and the Mongol dynasty, the consolidations of Kublai Khan and Oljeitu and the transformation into Islam provide analogies.

The history of mankind has been one of struggle, conflict and dispossession. Native or indigenous peoples have not fared well as a general proposition, whether in Europe itself, in China, Asia or elsewhere, especially if they were nomadic. As a matter of rationalisation, the approach of the expanding common law systems to native peoples was perhaps put succinctly by John

---

[7] Vitoria, *De Indiis et de Iure Relectiones*, in Englander *et al.*, 337.

[8] *Mabo* (1992) 175 C.L.R. 1, 180 *per* Toohey J.; Reynolds, 'Sovereignty' in Peterson and Sanders (eds.), *Citizenship and Indigenous Australians: Changing Conceptions and Possibilities* (Cambridge University Press, Cambridge, 1998) 208.

[9] Weaver (ed.), *Defending Mother Earth: Native American Perspectives on Environmental Justice* (Orbis, New York, 1996), 108.

Marshall, Chief Justice of the United States Supreme Court, as follows, consistent with the tradition of law based on force,

> Conquest gives a title which the Courts of the conqueror cannot deny, whatever the private and speculative opinions of individuals may be, respecting the original justice of the claim which has been successfully asserted.[10]

This arguably contrasts with some classic studies of the law of indigenous or traditional people, such as the Zapotec, which emphasise the role of consensus and the community ownership of law and legal process. The complaints about the Aztec empire, from their contemporaries the Tlasacans, Cholulans and Totonacs, would warn about over romanticisation of all indigenous peoples. Conquest and the subsequent imposition of a legal establishment necessarily involved disregard of peoples, and of their legal systems.[11]

In Ireland, the struggles revolving around land tenure have helped define the departing millennium. The land annuities issue was one of the defining features of the post-independence establishment of nationhood. In the arts, the play 'The Field' by John B. Keane, is a draught brewed from the meaning of land and the historical, social, familial, psychological, emotional, religious and mystical bond it involves with those who come to settle it. Land involves deep, psychic attachments. As Scotland gets devolved power and is dismantling its feudal land system, at a time when communities are mobilising and buying out their feudal 'superiors' and even applying indigenous analyses to 'crofting', the universality of land tenure issues are plain to be seen.[12]

3. TREMBLINGS AND TREMORS. THE FORCES GATHER

But rumblings and plumes from the volcano began in the sixties, alongside the rise of rock and roll, as Dylan told the world that the times, they were a changin'. In the US, Native Americans took over Alcatraz and in Australia, actions by various groups such as the Yolngu at Yirrkala and the Gurindji pointed to a new dawn.[13] Specific activities such as mining were often the spur, in the mael-

---

[10] *Johnson v. McIntosh* (1823) 8 Wheat. 543 (U.S.S.Ct.).

[11] See Kenny, Preface to *Tristam Kennedy and the Revival of Irish Legal Training 1835-1885*, (Irish Academic Press, Dundalk in association with the Irish Legal History Society, 1996) noting the displaced Brehon Law in Ireland in the context of legal education.

[12] See also Ardrey, *The Territorial Imperative: A Personal Inquiry into the Animal Origins of Property and Nations* (Kodansha, London, 1997).

[13] In relation to the U.S. see Indians of All Tribes, "Planning Grant Proposal to Develop an All-Indian University and Cultural Complex on Indian Land, Alcatraz" in Moquin and Doren, (eds.), *Great Documents in American Indian History* (Da Capo, New York, 1995) 374.

strom of social and technological dynamics. A referendum in Australia in 1967 was hoped to mark a new chapter in indigenous-settler relations. Although attempts to harness the common law failed in a series of cases, the process of engagement with law had begun. Justice knows that the law sometimes lags behind it.

The law was grappling with a range of problems posed by the incorporation of those it has often excluded in Australia, as all legal systems have done at various times, whether it be on grounds of gender, race or religion. In *R. v. Anunga*,[14] for example guidelines were articulated to be applied in the context of questioning Aboriginal suspects. Various Commissions examined the need for legislative reform. But the legal focus of the campaign for Aboriginal rights began to settle on the land title issue, and cases such as the *Milirrpum*[15] were among the first arrows in the native title quiver, although it did not strike its target. Statutory intervention, such as the Aboriginal Land Rights (Northern Territory) Act 1976 began to tackle the emergent conflicts. By the start of the last decade of the twentieth century, the global environmental movement, the greater mobilisation of Aboriginal people, the symbolically important return of Aboriginal heads, the return of objects of symbolic significance such as a boomerang to the Wurrundjiri tribe,[16] the national re-examination of history and the consequent search for identity, created a head of pressure that was bound to bear down on some old constructs. Other countries were engaging in varying degrees in this dialogue with the past. The experience of Canada, bearing some similarities of size and demography, and the treatment of the indigenous people there, provided an uncannily close parallel.

Mabo was probably partly related to the crescendo of concern about environmental degradation associated with greenhouse gases and global warming. As part of the drive to reverse damage done to the environment, indigenous rights received closer attention at an international level. In this domain, law has been solidifying in favour of indigenous rights, often in tandem with the articulation of environmental rights.[17] As indigenous people found a more sensitised body of international law, it invited a look at long held legal truths.

Undoubtedly, those who are part of, and identify with, the common law system, may be proud of many of its undeniable achievements. The trajectory of treatment of indigenous people is not one of them however. The writing may have been on the rock face therefore, before the High Court had the opportunity which it took in the *Mabo* case. All great cases come out of the crucible of

---

[14](1976) 11 A.L.R. 412 (S.Ct.N.T).

[15]*Milirrpum v. Nabalco Pty.* (1970) 17 F.L.R 141 (S.Ct.N.T.).

[16]In general see Greenfield, *The Return of Cultural Treasures* (2nd ed., Cambridge University Press, Cambridge, 1996).

[17]See Weaver, n.9 above, and Sutherland, "Indigenous Peoples, Emerging New Legal Standards for Comprehensive Rights" (1997) 27 (1) *Environmental Policy and Law* 13.

their times and circumstances. This was the second of two cases involving Mabo and Queensland,[18] illustrating another feature of leading cases, namely, persistence, like the *Marshall* series of cases in the E.U.[19] Unfortunately also, like *Barber*, the principal plaintiff did not live to enjoy the fruits of victory.[20]

4. ERUPTION. FACTS AND JUDGMENT

Eddie Mabo was a descendant of the original inhabitants, the Meriam people, of the Murray Islands in the Torres Strait. Although Mabo brought the action along with Passi and Rice on their own behalf and others, there was the curious coincidence of the name 'Mabo' which housed within it the derogatory slang for the Aboriginal people, and perhaps the bones of 'maybe'. A poet might wonder what part such little things have in the making of history. They brought an action against the State of Queensland and the Commonwealth of Australia. They claimed that the Crown's sovereignty over the Islands was subject to the land rights of the Meriam people. The chronology of events from a common law analysis begins when the islands were annexed to the Colony of Queensland in 1879. In 1882 they were reserved by proclamation for the inhabitants of the colony, and one of the islands was leased by the Crown. In 1912 the Governor ordered the islands set aside for the Aboriginal peoples, apart from the leased part. In 1931 the Crown granted a 20-year lease (which was subsequently forfeited) of two of the islands for the establishment of a sardine factory. In 1939, the reserve (the islands) were put under the control of trustees. Three inhabitants sought declarations that the Meriam people were entitled to the Islands as owners, possessors, occupiers or as persons entitled to use and enjoy the lands, that the islands were not and never had been Crown Land within the meaning *inter alia*, of the Land Act of 1962 (Qld), and that the State of Queensland was not entitled to extinguish the title of the Meriam people.

The High Court held that the Crown's acquisition of sovereignty over the territory comprising Australia could not be challenged in an Australian court. A majority held that the Murray Islands did not constitute Crown Land under the Land Act. Upon acquisition of sovereignty the Crown acquired a radical or an ultimate title to land. Native title survived radical title. Native title to land and persons entitled to it were determined by the laws and customs of the indigenous people. The Meriam people were entitled, as against the whole world, to possession, occupation, use and enjoyment of the Murray Islands land. But the acquisition of sovereignty exposed native title to extinguishment by a valid

---

[18]*Mabo v. Queensland* (1988) 166 C.L.R. 186.
[19]Starting with Case 152/84, *Marshall v. Southampton A.H.A.* [1986] E.C.R. 723; [1986] 1 C.M.L.R. 688.
[20]Case C-262/88, *Barber v. G.R.E.* [1990] E.C.R. I-1889; [1990] 2 C.M.L.R. 513.

exercise of sovereign power inconsistent with the right to enjoy native title. There was a spectrum of opinion on other issues, in particular that of the method of extinguishment of title, although some of the debate was speculative, and is perhaps best explored by looking at subsequent cases.

Thus Australian law recognised a form of native title which, in cases where it was not extinguished reflects the entitlements of the indigenous people in accordance with their laws or customs to traditional lands. Apart therefore from certain leases, the land entitlement of the Murray Island inhabitants was preserved as native title, recognised under the law of Queensland, as the concept of native title was not inconsistent with Australian common law. Although it originated in traditional, indigenous law, traditional title was recognised by the common law. Native title existed over Australian lands and seas, where it had not been explicitly extinguished and where there was a real acknowledgement of traditional law and real observance of traditional culture.

In reaching its judgment the High Court rejected the view that Australia was *terra nullius*, reversing a long pedigree of legal argument. They also rejected the argument that Crown assumption of sovereignty rendered it the absolute beneficial owner of all lands therein. These crucial decisions are the obvious dimension that have registered in the international domain. The persistence of such unsustainable doctrines, and their toleration by generations of legal establishments (apart from being obviously offensive of the highest order to Aboriginal peoples) probably drove law students off to more enlightened and defensible pastures on graduation. Brennan J., with whom Mason C.J. and McHugh J. agreed, reiterated a number of times the incompatibility of the *terra nullius* doctrine with contemporary Australian common law, recognising the unique and increasingly independent role of the High Court. He did so in a series of almost rhetorical questions or by a statement of possible responses, where the implicitly or explicitly untenable one was the *status quo*. He recognised that the existing common law could be departed from where it did not "fracture . . . the skeleton of principle".[21] Brennan J. relied on the majority judgment in the International Court of Justice's decision in the *Advisory Opinion on Western Sahara*,[22] and held:

> If the international law notion that inhabited land may be classified as terra nullius no longer commands general support, the doctrines of the common law which depend on the notion that native peoples may be "so low in the scale of social organisation" that it is "idle to impute to such people some shadow of the rights known to our law" can hardly be retained. If it were permissible in past centuries to keep the common law in

---

[21] (1992) 175 C.L.R. 1, 30.
[22] (1992) 175 C.L.R. 1, 40-41. He also cites the Vice President citing the opinions advanced by the Republic of Zaire, which talk of the bond to land, as a playwright might.

step with international law, it is imperative in today's world that the common law should neither be nor be seen to be frozen in an age of racial discrimination.[23]

He went on:

Whatever the justification advances in earlier days for refusing to recognise the rights and interests in land of the indigenous inhabitants of settled colonies, an unjust and discriminatory doctrine of that kind can no longer be accepted. The expectations of the international community accord in this respect with the contemporary values of the Australian people. The opening up of international remedies to individuals pursuant to Australia's accession to the Optional Protocol to the International Covenant on Civil and Political Rights brings to bear on the common law the powerful influence of the Covenant and the international standards it imports. The common law does not necessarily conform with international law, but international law is a legitimate and important influence on the development of the common law, especially when international law declares the existence of universal human rights.[24]

Thus a common law doctrine which was founded on discrimination should not survive as being contrary to international standards, and the fundamental values of the common law.

Toohey J., who also relied on the *Western Sahara* case, also concluded that "[o]ne thing is clear. The Islands were not *terra nullius*".[25]

Deane J. and Gaudron J. were conscious of the special nature of the case. They stated that:

The acts and events by which that dispossession in legal theory was carried into practical effect constitute the darkest aspect of the history of this nation. The nation as a whole must remain diminished unless and until there is an acknowledgement of and retreat from, those past injustices. . . . The lands of this continent were not *terra nullius* or 'practically unoccupied' in 1788.[26]

They also justify their use of 'emotive' language, believing it to be unusual in a judgment.[27]

---

[23] (1992) 175 C.L.R. 1, 41-42.
[24] (1992) 175 C.L.R. 1, 42.
[25] (1992) 175 C.L.R. 1, 180.
[26] (1992) 175 C.L.R. 1, 109.
[27] (1992) 175 C.L.R. 1, 120.

5. THE BOOMERANG. THE LEGISLATURE AFTER *MABO*

5.1 A Step Forward. How Many Steps Back?

After the explosion, the lava began to settle in new shapes.[28] Questions about the impact of the case and the nature of native title were foremost against the chorus of disapproval by landowners, mining companies and others and the jubilation of some aboriginal advocates. The *Mabo* boomerang did not take too long to return. In October 1992, the Federal Government began consultations with relevant parties to deal with the consequences of the decision. Just over a year later the Native Title Act 1993 (Cth.) received the Royal Assent, coming into effect on the first of January 1994, and generally sought to uphold *Mabo*. It was to provide *inter alia*, for the recognition and protection of native title, to establish a mechanism for determining claims, and to set standards for future dealings with native title. Certain past acts were validated to accommodate the consequences of native title, with rights of compensation. It was seen to be necessary to avoid complexity and expense of claims. It established a National Native Title Tribunal to help determine Aboriginal title. It also provided for the recognition of State and Territory procedures consistent with criteria identified in the Act. In addition, there were various State Acts such as the Native Title (Queensland) Act 1993 (Qld.). Important cases had followed the 1993 Act, such as that of *Western Australia v. Commonwealth*[29] where the native title legislation was challenged. Western Australia unsuccessfully challenged the constitutionality of the legislation, while at the same time the Wororra and Yawuru peoples challenged the State legislative response to the Commonwealth legislation. In June 1996, the Federal Government introduced an Amending Bill to the Native Title Act. In December the High Court gave its decision in the *Wik* case.[30]

5.2 *Wik*

The major issue of 'pastoral leases' was not finally decided until the *Wik* case. Many had believed that the grant of a pastoral lease gave exclusive possession and thus extinguished native title. The High Court explored the doctrine of extinguishment articulated in *Mabo*. In *Wik*, the High Court recognised that pastoral leases were a peculiar feature of the Australian experience. The granting of pastoral leases did not necessarily extinguish native title. Extinguishment could only be determined by reference to particular rights which were asserted and established. Pastoral leases and native title could co-exist. Pasto-

---

[28]For a comprehensive list of relevant Australian legal literature, see *The Australian Digest* (The Law Book Co, Sydney 1997).
[29](1995) 183 C.L.R. 373 (H.C.A).
[30]*Wik Peoples v. The State of Queensland* (1996) 187 C.L.R. 1 (H.C.A).

ral leases gave rights of use to pastoralists. In the event of inconsistency, the statutory rights would prevail. *Wik* in many ways, from a popular perspective, may have stolen *Mabo*'s thunder, by underlining some of the exact impacts on pastoral interests and on mining rights. It was more sparks to the tinder. Again the High Court majority looked closely at English common law principles and their appropriateness for a completely different environment. The common law of Australia, was a different creature. The furore erupting as a result of the consequences of *Mabo* seemed to have been superseded in the Australian press by references to *Wik* (although the academic world did not desert *Mabo*). A period of judicial tranquillity might have been expected. In Europe, for example, the *Van Duyn* case on its facts may be explained as a cautious response because of the radical legal decision it involved.[31] But the Australian judiciary seemed to be marching to a different drumbeat. The *Wik* case was said to have doubled the area of Australia potentially subject to native title claims!

5.3 A Count of Ten

The Prime Minister responded with a 'Ten-Point Plan in' April-May 1997, said to be addressed to *Wik*, but going beyond it in reality. Indigenous interest advocates such as the National Indigenous Working Group on Native Title felt that it was an unfair response which benefited groups such as the pastoralists at the expense Aborigines.[32] Pastoralists would argue that they had a deep attachment to the land also. In September, the Native Title Amendment Bill, incorporating the proposed amendments of 1996 and some amendments in response to *Wik,* was introduced to the House of Representatives.[33] Controversy was fuelled by provocative and ill-founded characterisations of the practical consequences of judicial decisions and legislation. The Native Title Amendment Bill [No2] was re-introduced in early 1998. The Act received its royal assent in July 1998, after much political turmoil and horse-trading, and public convulsions. The Native Title Amendment Act of 1998 was seen to minimise Aboriginal rights, and was a setback to the indigenous movement and reconciliation. It was alleged to have gone beyond the contemplation of the common law by confirming the extinguishment of certain claims, decreasing rights by validation of "intermediate period title",[34] expanding the rights of pastoralists, diminishing rights to negotiate, and emasculating the application of the Racial Discrimination Act 1975. In response to the Ten-Point Plan and legislation,

---

[31] See Case 41/74, *Van Duyn v. Home Office* [1974] E.C.R. 1337; [1975] 1 C.M.L.R. 1.

[32] See National Indigenous Working Group, "Critique of the Ten-Point Plan" (1997) 4 (3) *Indigenous Law Bulletin* 10.

[33] See Clarke, "The Native Title Amendment Bill (1997)" (1997) 4 (6) *Indigenous Law Bulletin,* 10.

[34] Meaning between the N.T.A. 1993 and *Wik*.

actions for genocide were initiated in the Australian courts, against the main political sponsors amongst other things.

5.4 The International Eye

A freedom to act solely limited by the internal dynamics of a dominant law making group, is increasingly a thing of the past, as global connections form constantly, consistently and exponentially. The legislative response, and its difficult birth were seen by some to have diluted the positive possibilities created by the judges. The traditional tension between the common law and legislation arose. But the Australian situation cannot be equated with say the Thatcherite deconstruction of aspects of labour law, as a product of the British constitutional doctrine of parliamentary supremacy. An international dimension had emerged which sought to control somewhat the response to *Mabo* and *Wik*. The E.U. had become a player in international affairs. European Parliamentarians came to hear the *Wik* Senate debates. It had bound itself to promote indigenous rights.[35] In its dealings and exercise of external trade policy, many would have seen the Community as bound to advocate the protection of human rights as part of an overall dialogue. In the *Nold* case, the European Court of Justice had accepted that it has a duty to protect human rights as an inherent part of its competence and jurisdiction.[36] Indigenous rights are part of the fundamental rights that have to be respected.[37]

The '*Wik* Native Title' legislation as it became known, and the Ten-Point Plan were seen to be discriminatory on a racial basis and the United Nations Committee on Racial Discrimination were asked to visit Australia. It requested information about the native title legislation under Article 9 of the Convention and changes to the Native Title Act which it believed to be discriminatory. The Government argued that the common law protected native title, that the legislation respected it, ensured its protection, provided certainty for land management where there was competing interests, provided certainty for agreements, and provided certainty by providing a framework for dealing with native title through a claims process. They also argued that the Indigenous Land Fund provided assistance to help the purchase of land where native title has been extinguished. The Aboriginal and Torres Islander Commission, however, believed that the Amendments were discriminatory, in that as they preferred the rights of non-native title holders over native title holders, they failed to protect native title holders equally. The involvement of international bodies was a technique that groups such as the Cree and the Saami peoples have used quite

---

[35]See the Communication on the External Dimension of Human Rights Policy, COM (95) 567 final.

[36]See Case 4/73, *Nold K.G. v. Commission* [1974] E.C.R. 491, 507, para. 13.

[37]See in particular the *U.N. Draft Declaration on the Rights of Indigenous Peoples* UN Doc.E/CN.4/Sub.2/1994/56, 105 (1994); 34 I.L.M. 541.

effectively.[38] The climax of native title debates corresponded with the Stolen Generation report which exposed the assimilation practices in relation to Aboriginal children, as had happened in Canada.[39] By putting the *Mabo* line on a wider path of racial discrimination it showed how advances in the common law, inspired by international norms, are less susceptible to parliamentary deconstruction in a modern, liberal democracy, reflexively integrated into an interdependent world trading system.

6. POST-*MABO* CASE LINES AND CONTOURS ON LAND AND SEA

As has been mentioned, subsequent cases such as *Wik*, interacted reflexively with legislative responses to *Mabo*. Recently, there has been a flood of cases, arising from *Mabo* and the subsequent legislation.[40] In *Fejo* the High Court reaffirmed that extinguishment of native title by a grant in fee simple is irreversible.[41] Federal Court cases continue to explore the boundary of native title in the context of Aboriginal and mining interests, and there are interesting, recent examples of both failure and success, which help inform the assessment of *Mabo*. The *Yorta Yorta* case reveals some of the limitations of *Mabo*.[42] It was accepted that insofar as a claim establishes a clan who occupied the land prior to the Crown assertion of title, the nature of traditional laws, and the substantial connection with the land, then the claims must be recognised by the common law subject to extinguishment. Anthropologists, linguists, historians, elders and genealogists were called in aid, with massive mining, recreational and State opposition. Although descent was demonstrated, and the traditional laws were identified, there had been a severance of the necessary connection. The tide had washed away the link, as the unhelpful metaphor said. The nightmare history, and the torture of litigation in such cases may seem to lead to a crushing finality for the hopes of certain indigenous interests. Thus a native title application for large parts of Northern Victoria and Southern New South Wales, was rejected as the forbearers had long ceased to observe traditional practices indicative of spiritual attachment to it. This raises the double injustice criticism.[43] For example, because the requirement to establish native title at com-

---

[38] See also Singer, "Sovereignty and Power" (1991) 86 *Nw.U.L. Rev* 1.
[39] *The National Inquiry into the Separation of Aboriginal and Torres Strait Islander Children and their Families* (1997).
[40] An example of a recent case arising out of the subsequent legislation is the case of *Strickland and Another on Behalf of the Maduwongga People v. Native Title Registrar* (1999) 168 A.L.R 242 (F.C.A).
[41] *Fejo v. Northern Territory of Australia* (1998) 195 C.L.R 96 (H.C.A).
[42] Members of the *Yorta Yorta Aboriginal Community Case v. State of Victoria and Oths.* [1998] F.C.A. 1606, (Unrep, Olney J, December 18, 1998).
[43] See for example, Wolfe, "Nation and Miscegenation: Discursive Continuity in the Post-*Mabo* Era" (1997) 36 *Social Analysis* 93.

mon law an Aboriginal person clan or group must substantially maintain its traditional connection with the land, forcible removal could destroy the nexus.[44] In other cases rights to take abalone in exercise of native title rights have been rejected.

The *Ben Ward* case on the other hand, was a claim by the Miriuwung, Gajerrong and Balangarra peoples of East Kimberley under the Native Title Act 1993.[45] This was a mammoth action which involved the court utilising meteorological, geographical, historical, linguistic, economic, literary, archaeological, anthropological evidence as part of its analysis while treating with a whole list of respondents from electricity concerns, to tour operators, to fishery, nature reserves, air transport companies and boating interests. Some of the judiciary have been clearly uncomfortable with their new role as a roving commission at times. In *Yarmirr*, the Croker Island people applied for a native title decision under the 1993 Act.[46] The Mandilarri-Ildugji, the Murran, the Gadura-Minaga and the Nygaynjharr clans of Aboriginal people were held to possess communal title over the sea and sea-beds in the claimed area. Those rights were non-exclusive, but included the right to travel within, fish and visit sacred places in the relevant area, and were subject to Commonwealth, State laws and Crown leases. In *Yanner v. Easton* the High Court held that members of the Gunnamulla clan of the Gangalidda, were entitled to harpoon crocodiles as the Fauna Act 1974 had not extinguished native title rights.[47] There have also been successful claims by the Arrernte People to lands around Alice Springs.

7. AUSTRALIAN PARALLELS. BATTLE FOR OTHER LANDS OF THE SOUL

7.1 Aboriginal Art. Waterholes and Fountainheads

Another series of cases in Australia may help plot the trajectory of the *Mabo* case.[48] Intellectual Property (I.P) and issues in the penumbra of I.P, will often be the focus of contemporary legal disputes between indigenous peoples and others.[49] This is to be expected in a world where there is a huge shift from the value of the tangible to the intangible. By their nature, these disputes tend to derive from a clash between an indigenous cultural perspective of a motif,

---

[44] See *New South Wales Law Reform Commission Research Report. The Aboriginal Child Placement Principle* (March 1957, Sydney).

[45] See *Ward and Oths. v. State of Western Australia and Oths.* (1998) 159 A.L.R. 483; rvsd. sub. nom. *Western Australia v. Ward* (2000) 170 A.L.R. 159.

[46] *Yarmirr and Oths v. The Northern Territory and Oths.* (1998) 156 A.L.R 370 (F.C.A.).

[47] *Yanner v. Easton* (1999) A.C.L. Rep 5 H.C. 1.

[48] In general see Blakeney, "Communal Intellectual Property Rights of Indigenous Peoples in Cultural Expression" (1998) 1. *J.W.I.P.* 6.

[49] Tunney, "E.U., I.P., Indigenous People and the Digital Age: Intersecting Circles" [1998] *E.I.P.R.* 335.

458 *Leading Cases of the Twentieth Century*

image, object, construction, dance or performance and a western or commercial conception of them. The first major case in the Australian series was *Yumbulul*,[50] a pre-*Mabo* case. It involved the issue by the Reserve Bank of Australia of a banknote reproducing the design of a Morning Star Pole. The Morning Star Pole, which was created by the Aboriginal artist Yumbulul, played a crucial role in Aboriginal ceremonies. Yumbulul sought to set aside an assignment of copyright as a result of his role as guardian of the pole on behalf of his clan, the Galpu. Aboriginal law was held not to be relevant to the validity of an assignment of the copyright works by the creator. The judge recognised that Australia's copyright laws were inadequate in relation to Aboriginal claims to regulate reproduction and use of essentially works of communal origin. He mentioned that:

the question of statutory recognition of Aboriginal communal interests in the reproduction of sacred objects is a matter for consideration by law reformers and legislators.[51]

Blakeney suggests that *Mabo* was a significant development occurring in this line of cultural expression cases. *Mabo* had increased the calls for legislative treatment of other areas of Aboriginal law.[52] The next case on the graph was *Milpurrurru*.[53] The case concerned the importation of carpets from Vietnam into Australia, which bore Aboriginal artworks. Aboriginal law required the traditional owners to act to preserve the dreaming. This case established that in the event of unauthorised reproduction of works involving a breach of copyright, customary Aboriginal laws could be taken into account in the quantification of damage suffered. In *Bulul Bulun* the artist and members of the Ganalbingu took action to protect the copyright in Bulun Bulun's work "Magpie Geese and Water Lilies at the Waterhole", which had been reproduced on imported printed fabric.[54] In the course of their judgment, the Court did recognise that a fiduciary relationship existed between the artist and his people, based on the recognition of the consequences of the Ganalbingu customary law, for the particular factual situation. Although on the facts, this was not hugely helpful to the plaintiffs, it was important in recognising the mechanism of possible relevance of traditional law. The mechanism involved a fiduciary analysis, which originates in equity and in this type of case has been recognised in *Wik*, following Canadian case law. The presence of the *Mabo* mood can be discerned in the back-

---

[50] *Yumbulul v. Reserve Bank of Australia* (1991) 21 I.P.R 481 (F.C.A.).
[51] (1991) 21 I.P.R 481, 491.
[52] See for example, Brennan, "*Mabo* and its Implications for Aborigines and Torres Strait Islanders" in Stephenson and Ratnapala, (eds.), *Mabo: A Judicial Revolution* (University of Queensland Press, Brisbane, 1993) 1, 23-24.
[53] *Milpurruru & Oths. v. Indofurn Pty Ltd. & Oths.* (1995) A.I.P.C., 91.
[54] *John Bulun Bulun & Another v. R & T Textiles Pty Ltd.*[1998] 1082 F.C.A., September 3, 1998.

ground to these cases. They show how law becomes a theatre in which new cultural understandings and sensitivity may emerge from the still smouldering ashes of ignorance, hate and disregard.

7. 2 Re-Visiting Genocide

Aboriginal issues continue to surface, and the success of *Mabo* has justified a mining of the common law by Aboriginal interests, and a paradoxical quasi-colonisation of the courts of the coloniser. In *Kruger v. The Commonwealth*,[55] the High Court had to decide, in the context of an action for damages for false imprisonment and deprivation of liberty brought by Aboriginals who had been removed from their families, and a mother whose child was taken from her, whether the (NT) Aboriginal Ordinance 1918 was constitutionally valid. One of the bases which they rejected was the argument that it was invalid as it authorised acts of genocide as defined, *inter alia*, by the Genocide Convention of 1949. The Ten Point Plan had given rise to challenges on the basis of contemporary genocide levelled against the politicians involved. In the sad case of Wadjularbinna Nulyarimma, the genocide argument was raised and rejected, against the background of the evolving *Pinochet* case in the UK in the later stages.[56] In addition, representatives of the Arabunna people put forward a genocide claim based on failures associated with World Heritage applications. Genocide is accepted to have occurred in its purest, ghastly sense in the 1830's, for example. However the genocide argument had increasingly been advanced in relation to recent conduct, particularly after the Stolen Generation report.[57]

8. THE CANADIAN MIRROR

While New Zealand or South Africa may provide useful laboratories to test the parallels to, or the relevance of *Mabo*, Canada echoes closest the Australian context.[58] The US provides important analyses from a troika of cases, *Johnson, Cherokee Nation* and *Worcester v. Georgia*.[59] Furthermore, the US experience

---

[55] *Kruger v. The Commonwealth* (1996-7) 190 C.L.R 1 (H.C.A.).
[56] See *Nulyarimma and Oths. v. Thompson: Buzzacott v. Minister for the Environment and Oths.* (1999) 166 A.L.R. 621 (F.C.A). In relation to *Pinochet*, see Webber, "The *Pinochet* Case: The Struggle for the Realisation of Human Rights" (1999) 26 (4) *J.Law & Society* 523.
[57] See Tatz, *Genocide in Australia. Research Discussion Paper No.8*, (Australian Institute of Aboriginal and Torres Strait Islander Affairs, Canberra, 1999). Cuneen, "Criminology, Genocide and The Forced Removal of Indigenous Children from their Families" (1999) 32 (2) *A.N.Z.J.Crim.* 124.
[58] For a comparison between Australia and Canada see Lokan, "From Recognition to Reconciliation" (1999) 23 *Melb.U.L.Rev.* 68. For an excellent, comprehensive text containing a selection of all the major law material see Issac, *Aboriginal Law* (2nd ed., Purich, Saskatoon, 1999).
[59] *Johnson* (1823) 8 Wheat. 543; *Cherokee Nation v. Georgia* 5 Pet. 1 (1831); *Worcester v. Geor-*

of the question of oil extraction and environmental legislation in relation to tribal land, may become more relevant in future.[60] In New Zealand the Crown negotiated the Treaty of Waitangi with the Maoris.[61] Likewise in Canada there are treaties to look to, notwithstanding a history of lack of respect for them. [62] In addition, there is a constitutional entrenchment of Aboriginal rights. Section 35(1) of the Constitution Act of 1982, provides that,

> The existing aboriginal and treaty rights of the aboriginal peoples of Canada are hereby recognised and affirmed.

Canadian legal discourse in this area has been longer and constitutes a more dynamic legal construct because of the competing constituencies within it. The Royal Proclamation of 1763 acknowledged native title.[63] Although Quebec has received its fair share of international attention, the Native Peoples (or First Nations) of Canada had often been forgotten.[64] The First Nations have struggled in Canada for recognition, and are achieving some success, after a history of sorry treatment which is hopefully ending. The full extent of sufferings of the First Nations is only emerging relatively recently and the Residential School system, looms very large in the psyche of the indigenous peoples of Canada.[65] As the communities are finding their voices to articulate their pain, some of their people have climbed western academic ladders to add new perspectives.[66] The legal establishment have sought to engage in a re-evaluation, as the Report of the Royal Commission on Aboriginal Peoples reveals.

Native title in Canada is merely part of the legal construct of protection of the Aboriginal Peoples. There is a wider concept of Aboriginal rights, which exist independently of native title.[67] These might include hunting and fishing

---

gia 31 U.S. 530 (1832). This last case also figures elsewhere in this volume: see Keane, "Across the Cherokee Frontier of Irish Constitutional Jurisprudence. The *Sinn Féin Funds: Buckley v. A.G.* (1950)" above, 185.

[60] See Weaver, "Triangulated Power and the Environment" in Weaver, above, n.9 and see Wilson, *The Underground Reservation: Osage Oil* (University of Nebraska Press, Lincoln, 1985).

[61] See Wilson, "Beyond Waitangi: Comparative Issues in Native Title Dispute Resolution" (1996) 7 *A.D.R.J.* 271; see also Butler "Taking the Treaty Seriously: *New Zealand Maori Council v. Attorney-General* (1987)" below, 387.

[62] With regard to their breach in the U.S. see Vine Deloria, Jnr, *Behind the Trail of Broken Treaties; An American Declaration of Independence* (Delta, New York, 1974). 'Aboriginal' is used in Canada also of course, consistent with its Latin origins 'ab origine' from the beginning.

[63] R.S.C. 1985, App. 11, No.1.

[64] From the Quebec Act of 1774 onwards, there has been special attention given to the French speaking population.

[65] See for example, York, *The Dispossessed; Life and Death in Native Canada* (Vintage, London, 1990).

[66] See for example, McPherson and Rabb, *Indian from the Inside: A Study in Ethno-Metaphysics* (Centre for Northern Studies, Lakehead University, Thunder Bay, 1993).

[67] *R. v. Van der Peet* [1996] 2 S.C.R. 507 (S.C.C.).

rights. Some type of right to self-government is also emerging.[68] There have been recent Treaties such as the Nisga'a Treaty in British Columbia, in addition to the creation of the Inuit territory of Nunavut by the Nunavut Land Claims Agreement.[69]

The cumulative effect of the rights which are founded on alternative but complementary bases are believed by some to represent a movement towards legal rights associated with self-government, more consistent with a seepage of sovereignty towards self-determination. Canada's combined, comprehensive approach to Aboriginal rights, may provide lessons to Australia and elsewhere. Countries such as Indonesia may need to adopt similar approaches as democracy becomes more well established. When the bloody civil war in Algeria is settled, one wonders whether the Berber issue will rise again.[70] *Mabo* was more significant individually in that in Australian legal terms, all the eggs were in the native title basket.

9. On the Interpretations of Legal Dreams

9.1 The Rising Tide of Cultural Arguments

Native issues and cultural conflicts lead to confusing conceptual conundrums which test us philosophically. For example, should indigenous people on the West Coast of the United States be able to invoke traditional whaling rights despite current international bans? Such conflicts bring us to perhaps the greatest debate in the first century of the new millennium, namely the reconciliation of competing cultural constructs. Ultimately it will involve a re-examination of competing theologies. If lawyers think this is not an issue for them, they should look to the terrible strife in Nigeria and the Sudan, as well as the Balkans. Inevitably it seems to demand that a robust universality of principles is adhered to, which accommodates in a complex way, the competing cultural concerns. Ultimately, the benefit of universal protections, which indigenous people will obtain, will bind them to universal prohibitions also. The emerging global legal order has to reach accommodations to deal with multi-cultural situations. Many academics condemn cultural relativism while denying their own ontology and subjectivity beneath the emperors clothes of (often Euro-American) objectivity. There will be universal principles which are rendered operational by respect for competing cultural analyses. *Mabo*, seen in this context, is important in that it cuts a safety-line to the shore, and embarks on a great concep-

---

[68] See Wilkins, ". . . But We Need the Eggs: The Royal Commission, The Charter of Rights and the Inherent Right of Self Government" (1999) 49 *U.T.L.J.* 53.

[69] See Sanders, " "We Intend to Live Here Forever": A Primer on the *Nisga'a Treaty*" (1999) 33 *U.B.C Law Rev.* 103.

[70] See Brett and Fentress, *The Berbers* (Blackwell, Oxford, 1997).

tual voyage and attempts to navigate the undercurrents of competing cultural forces by modest and achievable reconciliation. But the courts are but a small bark on an unruly sea.

9.2 The Contest for Meaning

There are all sorts of views, perspectives and opinions of *Mabo*, from the hostile to the enthusiastic, from the racist to the reforming.[71] The High Court were clearly aware of its significance. The use of the word revolutionary is justifiable. From an Aboriginal perspective, it may be seen as falling far short of the real legal issue which is that of sovereignty, or absolute self-determination.[72] But complete sovereignty substitution is not going to happen. It is certainly located in common law evolution, informing the discussion of where it comes from, how it grows, corrects itself, adapts, relates to statute, international law, the future and the past, the divide between politics and law, and the relationship with culture and identity. It can be located in the context of explorations of judicial activism. It can be seen as part of the graph of a decade of Australian High Court activism, and innovative decisions relating to issues such as the exclusion of uncorroborated evidence, legal representation, rape in marriage and freedom of expression.[73] It can be seen as the product of a unique Australian law, akin to post-independent Irish law or any other post-independent State. It also seemed to come at a unique conjunction of national discourse, emerging global debate and the ascendancy of a narrative of national, academic debate. A post-modernist analysis would also spring to mind when one thinks of the possibilities of a multiplicity of legal rights and legal systems and exploration of identity engendered.[74] Law may ignite fuses to settlement of conflict.

Whatever markings one follows, involves an ineluctable return to the source of all debates about law. One fascinating arena of debate was among Australian feminist lawyers. Articles such as Povinelli, in "The Cunning of Recogni-

---

[71] See for example Bartlett, "Political and Legislative Responses to *Mabo*" (1993) 23 *U.W.A.L.Rev.* 352; Hanks, "A National Aboriginal Policy" (1993) 16 *U.N.S.W.L.J.* 45; Lumb, "Native Title to Land in Australia: Recent High Court Decisions" (1993) 42 *I.C.L.Q.* 84; McIntyre, "Aboriginal Title: Equal Rights And Racial Discrimination" (1993) 16 *U.N.S.W.L.J.* 57; Nettheim, " Judicial Revolution or Cautious Correction? *Mabo v. Queensland*" (1993) 16 *U.N.S.W.L.J.* 1; Reynolds, "The *Mabo* Judgment in the Light of Imperial Land Policy" (1993) 16 *U.N.S.W.L.J.* 27; Webber, "The Jurisprudence of Regret as Regards the Search for Standards of Justice in *Mabo*" (1995) 17 *Syd. L.R.* 5

[72] The right to self-determination as expressed for example in the Barunga Statement of 1988.

[73] Such as *R. v. L* (1991) 174 C.L.R. 371(H.C.A.); *R. v. McKinney* (1991) 171 C.L.R. 468 (H.C.A.); *Australia Capital Television v Cth.* (1992) 177 C.L.R. 106 (H.C.A.); *R. v. Dietrich* (1992) 177 C.L.R. 292 (H.C.A.); *Theophanous v. Herald & Weekly Times* (1994) 182 C.L.R. 104 (H.C.A.); *Stephens v. W.A. Newspapers* (1994) 182 C.L.R. 211(H.C.A.). In general see Kirby, "Judicial Activism" (1997) 27 *U.W.A.L.Rev.*, 1.

[74] See Stychin, "Relatively Universal: Globalisation of Rights Discourse and its Evolution in Australian Sexual and National Identities" (1998) 18 *Leg.St.,* 335.

tion: Real Being and Aboriginal Recognition in Settler Australia" and Sangeetha Chandra-Shekeran, "Challenging the Fiction of the Nation in the 'Reconciliation' Texts of *Mabo* and Bringing Them Home"[75] are examples. The latter is a formidable analysis which levels sound criticisms such as of the historical methodology while pointing to counter-narratives.[76] This is in tandem with most basic legal criticisms which are levelled against the legal logic which in effect penalises those who suffered the most, those who were most dispossessed. But there is an additional attack on the idea that *Mabo* represented justice performed. The author sees it is a "deft" nation– building exercise. At the time the piece was concluded in August 1998, the author said:

> The ascendancy of the One Nation party in the Queensland State election has clearly revealed that anti-aboriginal populist rhetoric mobilises grassroots support in a way that the politically correct language of reconciliation cannot. Within this atmosphere the 'victories' of Mabo and Bringing Them Home may appear as memories of halcyon days when there was promise and goodwill. The totalising charges of racism seem justified and the time for subtle critical analysis seem to be gone.[77]

It could be argued that this misses the point. A clever and worthwhile analysis became a total deconstruction, that seems to leave the writer unable to put it back together again. The juggernaut of law has limited mobility. Judges have often warned of the limitations they are under.[78] If a court can overturn a principle which is repugnant, it is difficult to criticise it because it has not done more. We might argue that all law pursues a relentless purpose of refinement. Law itself may be wrong, false, misguided or misinformed, but its substitutes may be poor, pale and problematic ones. The choice of wholesale acceptance or rejection of the monumental network of law, is not available to us, unless perhaps we are willing to storm the Bastille, which many academics are not. If we are to be totally cynical and conspiratorial, we might conclude that some of the islands which will revert as a result of *Mabo* will be sunk by global warming anyway! As has been said recently by Kader Asmal from his experience in South Africa, there is a path between the Gandhi and Kissinger view of world affairs.[79] More significant questions might be about what academics and practitioners have done to perpetuate injustice where it exists. Cuneen has raised the question of the flaws of the liberal paradigm of criminology, for example,

---

[75] Both in the *Australian Feminist Law Journal* (1998) Vol. 11.
[76] Such as Nyoongah Mudrooroo, *Master of the Ghost Dreaming* (Angus and Robertson, Sydney, 1991).
[77] (1998) 11 *A.F.L.J.*, 125.
[78] See *In the Matter of Citizen Limbo* (1990) 92 A.L.R 81 (H.C.A) 82-83 *per* Brennan J.
[79] Asmal, "Truth, Reconciliation and Justice: the South African Experience in Perspective" (2000) 63 *M.L.R.* 1, 5.

as a result of looking at the experience of Aboriginal people.[80] How many European law schools have had indigenous speakers, advocates or lecturers to visit or teach there?

10. THE RE-ENCHANTMENT OF JUSTICE IN A NEW LEGAL ENVIRONMENT?

10.1 Reflexivity

International law influenced the context in which this common law decision operated, and the common law will reflexively relate to the further development of international law, and the law of regional legal communities. In the E.U., for example, decisions such as *Nold*, provided conduits for the flow of rights from the international level into an enforceable regional context. Recent Australian cases such as the *Hindmarsh Bridge* case,[81] have shown a similar Australian approach. Some would see *Mabo* as a purely internal affair. However the attempts to utilise International Conventions on Racial Discrimination by the Saami, the Cree or the people of Polynesia, illustrate how the development of interdependent legal systems contribute to the promotion of universal legal values and the sovereignty of law while diminishing the opportunity for the success of short-term, reactionary forces.

Mabo raises important and deep issues, related to the universality of legal values and justice itself. Universality implies an inclusivity, which legal systems have not always demonstrated. This has important implications for emerging legal systems, most particularly that of the World Trade Organisation. Exclusive legal systems will sow a bitter harvest. Constructive movements may seek non-law solutions.[82] In Mexico a revolution by the Zapatistas is predicated partly on the failure of world trade developments to recognise the needs of the indigenous, local economy. The value of law is undermined if it cannot command the maximum support possible.

As the magic wand of tourism is being accused of (literally) enslaving indigenous peoples and promoting environmental devastation and the cell lines of a tribe in New Guinea have been patented, the indigenous people's struggle continues. The Bushmen (Khwe) of the Kalahari, one of the last remnants of stone age man are being eclipsed in Botswana, having been displaced progressively in the last centuries. Difficult ethical choices face us. We can be sure that the vitrified, vested interests of commercial forces will not let these choices be easily made. Car manufacturers (it would seem from their advertisements) would rather that vehicles roam the plains than people and animals.

---

[80] See Cuneen, n.57 above.

[81] See *Kartinyeri v. The Commonwealth* (1998) 195 C.L.R. 337 (H.C.A.).

[82] Posey and Dutfield, *Beyond Intellectual Property; Towards Traditional Resource Rights for Indigenous Peoples and Local Communities* (International Development Research Centre, Ottawa, 1996).

10.2 Re-Enchantment

But it is not just a story of brilliant scarlet twilights from volcanic activity on the other side of the world. Within the common law *Mabo* may have represented an occasion of re-interpretation of a profound type. While perhaps like Krakatau, it disappears and collapses itself with its own tremendous force, it seemed on many levels to herald a new approach. The *Ward* case,[83] for example, ironically seems to bring the common law back to its roving roots. The relaxation of the rules of practice, procedure and evidence, and the relaxed leave to intervene, could yield some lessons which could benefit law, to the same extent that equity modified the rigour of common law. The necessary engagement with the Aboriginal worldview, leading rationalist and materialist judges to talk of the dreamtime is an interesting confluence. Perhaps the common law itself has time to dream at the millennium's close and recuperate, as the advent of communications technology, the challenge of globalisation, and the need for greater enforceability, efficiency and effectiveness call for re-interpretations, not least, of the logic of law. It also points to the need to see law as a wide canvas, with colours supplied by other disciplines, as the Court of Appeal did when confronted with genetic engineering in a patent case or the European Court of Justice when faced with economics in competition cases.[84] It engaged with a wide range of disciplines without ever losing its identity of law, but did not shirk from taking a decision, which other analytic disciplines have the luxury to avoid. It seems to vindicate a Holmsian view of the path of law, a century ago.

> For every fact leads to every other by the path of the air. Only men do not yet see how, always. And your business as thinkers is to make plainer the way from some thing to the whole of things; to show the rational connection between your fact and the frame of the universe. If yours subject is law, the roads are plain to anthropology, the science of man, to political economy, the theory of legislation, ethics, and the several paths to your final view of life. To be master of any branch of knowledge you must master those which lie next to it and thus to learn anything you must know all.[85]

Mabo is no magic cure, but it is a great case. Why is it a leading case? It has become known. It swept aside a long line of precedent and reasoning, and was

---

[83] Above, n.44.
[84] In the case of the Court of Appeal, see *Genentech's Patent* [1989] R.P.C. 142 and in the case of the European Court of Justice, see joined Cases C 89, 104, 114, 116-117, 125-129/85, *A. Åhlström and Others v. Commission (Re Woodpulp Cartel)* [1988] E.C.R. 5193.
[85] Novick, *The Collected Works of Justice Holmes* (University of Chicago Press, Chicago, 1995) vol. 3, 472.

thus of significance actually and symbolically. It provoked outrage. It contributed to the definition of national identity. It provokes great debates about what law itself is. Thus it was an affirmation of law, of the sovereignty of law and its ability to construct a consensus of competing constituencies, which of all the modes of human endeavour has the potential to provide a roof over us, if built on firm foundations tempered in the fires of cultural awareness. It challenges this generation and the next, to produce a new crop of legal thinkers who can deal with the great issues that we do and will face, with powers of creativity, integration and imagination as well as the presently over-prized mechanistic mindset. *Mabo* was part of a move towards justice, which like the truth, may emerge very slowly sometimes. It is strong medicine. With increased globalisation, and the gradual erasure of the illusory line between peoples, law and legal systems, it might be better to talk of justice in the international legal environment.

PURPOSIVE INTERPRETATION AND PARLIAMENTARY MATERIALS
PEPPER V. HART (1993)

KENNETH MULLAN*

1. INTRODUCTION

The purpose of this paper[1] is to examine the impact of the decision of the House of Lords in *Pepper v. Hart*.[2] In that case the long-established rule that courts were not permitted to refer to parliamentary materials when construing legislation was abrogated and certain tests for the admissibility of *Hansard* as an aid to statutory interpretation were established. For that reason alone, the case may properly be regarded as a leading case of the twentieth century.

However, the restriction of the impact of the decision to the technical repeal of the exclusionary rule is miss the wider point that the ruling is representative of the modern purposive approach to statutory interpretation adopted by the courts to give effect to the true intention of Parliament. Such an approach, coming at the end of the century, is in sharp contrast to the rigid adoption of literal rules for the interpretation of legislation undertaken by the courts at the beginning of the century. Further the impact of the ruling on the fundamental work of the courts in discovering the meaning of legislative provisions has been substantial, indeed more significant that imagined by the House of Lords when the case's principles were formulated.

The immediate significance of the case has been examined in a number of articles.[3] The primary focus of the paper will be to analyse the background to *Pepper v. Hart* and to assess the use of the ruling and the application of the

---

*Appeal Tribunal Chairman, Appeals Service, Northern Ireland. The author is extremely grateful to Geraldine Fee for her assistance in the retrieval of some of the reference material described in the paper.

[1] Some of the material in this chapter has already been published in Mullan "The Impact of *Pepper v. Hart*" in Dickson & Carmichael, (eds.), *The House of Lords. Its Parliamentary and Judicial Roles* (Hart Publishing, Oxford, 1999).

[2] [1993] A.C. 593; [1993] 1 All E.R. 42 (H.L.).

[3] See, for example, Miers, "Taxing Perks and Interpreting Statutes: *Pepper v. Hart*" (1993) 56 *M.L.R.* 695; Davenport, "Perfection – But at What Cost?" [1993] 109 *L.Q.R.* 149; Oliver, "*Pepper v. Hart*: A Suitable Case for Reference to *Hansard*" [1993] *P.L.* 5; Styles, "The Rule of Parliament: Statutory Interpretation after *Pepper v. Hart*" (1994) *O.J.L.S.* 151

tests by the House of Lords in cases subsequent to the ruling. The paper will also address the approaches taken by the Irish courts to the issue of reference to parliamentary materials for the purpose of assisting the process of statutory interpretation.

The impact of *Pepper v. Hart* across the whole range of courts and tribunals in the United Kingdom has been significant and the number of House of Lords' cases in which the ruling has been applied is small in comparison with the number of cases in lower courts and tribunals. However a number of the House of Lords' cases were decided immediately after the ruling in *Pepper v. Hart*. The initial approach of the House of Lords was to have interpreted and applied the relaxed ruling in a liberal and permissive manner an approach which was followed by the lower courts and tribunals.

Following these decisions, the House, principally through Lord Browne-Wilkinson who gave the main speech in *Pepper v. Hart,* sought to reassert its authority and reaffirm that the ruling was meant to be to be implemented in a strict manner with the clear limits set out in the case. The recent approach of the House of Lords demonstrates that judges are taking a contradictory attitude towards the applicability and use of parliamentary materials, using them for certain defined purposes within the imposed limits, and for other purposes, outside those limits.

2. A CENTURY OF THE EXCLUSIONARY RULE

The exclusionary rule has a history which predates the beginning of the twentieth century. The first declaration of it was probably in the 1769 case of *Millar v. Taylor*[4] and was reaffirmed in the 1848 case of *Salkfield v. Johnson.*[5] By the beginning of the twentieth century the rule was firmly rooted in the practices and procedures of the English courts. Lord Lester[6] concludes that the adoption of the rule was based on two factors:

> The arid wasteland from which the exclusionary rules sprang insisted that the doctrine of legal precedent should be so rigidly inflexible that the supreme judicial authority . . . could not override their previous judgments, however wrong-headed or outmoded those previous judgments had become . . . By the same token, the Victorian Law Lords and their successors had adopted rigidly literal rules for the interpretation of Acts of Parliament. They had decided that, to avoid "making laws" they were compelled to give effect to the "plain and unambiguous language of a

---

[4] (1769) 4 Burr. 2303; 98 E.R. 201.
[5] (1848) 2 Exch. 256; 154 E.R. 487.
[6] "*Pepper v. Hart* Revisited" (1994) 15 *Stat. L. Rev.* 10.

statute", no matter that words are rarely plain or unambiguous in real life, and no matter how absurd might be the result of such a liberal interpretation. They had concentrated upon the letter rather than the purpose of the law, leaving it to Parliament to clear up the statutory mess, instead of seeking themselves to make best sense of what the legislation meant.[7]

Whatever the basis for the adoption of the rule, it was firmly adhered to for well over eighty years, despite the best efforts of Lord Denning to relax its rigidity. In the 1950 case of *Magor and St Mellons RDC v. Newport Corporation*, and based on an approach taken earlier,[8] he had favoured the relaxation of an "ultra-legalistic interpretation",[9] only to be firmly reprimanded by Lord Simonds when the case went to the House of Lords:

> It seems to me to be a naked usurpation of the legislative function under the thin guise of interpretation. And it is the less justifiable when it guess-work with what material the legislature would, if it had discovered the gap, filled it in. If a gap is disclosed, the remedy lies in an amending Act.[10]

Lord Denning fought many battles with the House of Lords over a wide range of issues related to judicial practices and procedures. One of these issues was the relaxation of the exclusionary rule, and the admonitions of Lord Denning's formal and informal approach to using extrinsic aids to construction led to the most forthright and authoritative statements of what the rule meant and why its use should be continued.

So for example in *Beswick v. Beswick*, Lord Reid had the following to say:

> For purely practical reasons we do not permit debates in either House to be cited. It would add greatly to the time and expense involved in preparing cases involving the construction of a statute if counsel was expected to read all the debates in *Hansard*, and it would often be impracticable for counsel to get access to at least the older reports of debates in Select Committees of the House of Commons; moreover, in a very large proportion of cases, such a search, even if practicable, would throw no light on the question before the court.[11]

In *Davis v. Johnson*,[12] in construing section 1 of the Domestic Violence and

---

[7] (1994) 15 *Stat. L. Rev.* 10, 12
[8] *Seaford Court Estates Ltd v. Newport Corporation* [1949] 2 K.B. 481 (C.A.)
[9] [1950] 2 All E.R. 1226 (C.A.) 1236 *per* Denning L.J. dissenting.
[10] [1952] A.C. 189 (H.L.) 191.
[11] [1968] A.C. 58 (H.L.) 74.
[12] [1979] A.C. 264 (C.A. and H.L.).

Matrimonial Proceedings Act 1976, Lord Denning looked at both the *Report of the House of Commons Select Committee on Violence in Marriage*[13] and the reports of Parliamentary debates in *Hansard*.[14] Lord Denning expressed some strong views on the use of the *Hansard* materials:

> Some may say – and indeed have said – that judges should not pay any attention to what is said in Parliament. They should grope about in the dark for the meaning of an Act without switching on the light. I do not accede to this view . . . And it is obvious that there is nothing to prevent a judge looking at these debates himself privately and getting some guidance from them. Although it may shock the purists, I may as well confess that I have sometimes done it. I have done it in this very case. It has thrown a flood of light on the position.[15]

Goff and Cumming-Bruce L.JJ. were not prepared to join the fun. Cumming-Bruce L.J. said:

> "I am not alarmed by the criticism that I am a purist who prefers to shut his eyes to the guiding light shining in the reports of Parliamentary debates in *Hansard*.[16]

When *Davis v. Johnson* went to the House of Lords, the rebukes were stinging and the reaffirmation trenchant, with all five Law Lords disagreeing with Lord Denning's statement. Lord Scarman's speech is most usually quoted:

> There are two good reasons why the courts should refuse to have regard to what is said in Parliament or by ministers as aids to the interpretation of a statute. First, such material is an unreliable guide to the meaning of what is enacted. It promotes confusion, not certainty. The cut and thrust of debate and the pressures of executive responsibility . . . are not always conducive to a clear and unbiased explanation of the meaning of statutory language And the volume of Parliamentary and ministerial utterances can confuse by its very size. Secondly, counsel are not permitted to refer to *Hansard* in argument. So long as this rule is maintained by Parliament (it is not the creation of the judges), it must be wrong for the judge to make any judicial use of proceedings in Parliament for the purpose of interpreting statutes.[17]

---

[13] *H. of C. Papers* (1974 75) 553-i.
[14] *H. of C. Official Report (1975-76) Standing Committee Domestic Violence Bill.*
[15] *ibid.,* 276-7.
[16] *ibid.,* 316.
[17] *ibid.,* 349-50.

Lord Denning was equally forthright in his judgment in *Nothman v. London Borough of Barnett*:

> The literal method is now completely out of date . . . In all cases now in the interpretation of statutes we adopt such a construction as "will promote the general legislative purpose underlying the provision". It is no longer necessary for judges to wring their hands and say: "There is nothing we can do about it". Whenever the strict interpretation of a statute gives rise to an absurd and unjust situation, the judges can and should use their good sense to remedy it – by reading words in, if necessary – so as to do what Parliament would have done had they had the situation in mind.[18]

Lord Denning's philosophical comments would no doubt gain respect from today's House of Lords. In 1978 they were soundly dismissed by the House of Lords on appeal.[19]

Interestingly Lord Denning tried further innovative methods of getting around the effect of the House of Lords ruling in *Davis v. Johnson*. In *R v. Local Commissioner for Administration (ex parte Bradford Metropolitan City Council)*,[20] he looked at a citation in a law book which contained quotations from *Hansard* in order to clarify the meaning of a phrase in section 26(2) of the Local Government Act 1974:

> According to the recent pronouncement of the House of Lords in *Davis v. Johnson*, we ought to regard *Hansard* as a closed book to which we as judges must not refer at all . . . By good fortune, however, we have been given a way of overcoming that obstacle. For the ombudsman himself in a public address to the Society of Public Teachers of Law quoted the relevant passages of *Hansard* as part of his address: and Professor Wade has quoted the very words in his latest book on administrative law[21] . . . And we have not yet been told that we may not look at the writings of the teachers of law. . . . I hope therefore that our teachers will go on quoting *Hansard* so that a judge may in this way have the same help as others have in interpreting the statute.[22]

Finally in *Hadmor Productions Ltd v. Hamilton*, Lord Denning had again re-

---

[18][1978] 1 All E.R. 1243 (C.A.) 1246.
[19][1979] 1 All E.R. 142 (H.L.), especially 151.
[20][1979] 2 All E.R. 881 (C.A.).
[21]Wade, *Administrative Law* (4th ed., Clarendon Press, Oxford, 1977) 821; see now Wade and Forsyth, *Administrative Law* (8th ed., Clarendon Press, Oxford, 2000) 137, n.82, which refers to the *Bradford M.C.C.* case but no longer qoutes the Ombudsman's address.
[22][1979] 2 All E.R. 881, 898

ferred to *Hansard* in the Court of Appeal[23] and was criticised for this when the case went to the House of Lords. Lord Diplock's speech is again the most often quoted:

> There are a series of rulings by this House, unbroken for a hundred years, and most recently affirmed emphatically and unanimously in *Davis v. Johnson,* that recourse to construed is not permissible as an aid to its construction.[24]

Support for the House of Lords' unequivocal position was to also to be found in the joint reports of the Scottish and English Law Commissions on reform of the principles of statutory interpretation,[25] the report of the Renton Committee,[26] and by the majority of those who participated in the debates of the House of Lords in considering Lord Scarman's Interpretation of Legislation Bills in 1980 and 1981.[27]

Support for the retention and continuation of the exclusionary rule was also to be found in the Irish courts. In *Minister for Industry & Commerce v. Hales,*[28] McLoughlin J., after reviewing a series of materials on the principles of statutory interpretation, had the following to say on the issue of the consideration of extrinsic evidence for the purpose of assisting the process of interpreting a statute:

> . . . What has to be interpreted is not the intention of the Minister but the intention of the legislature as expressed in the Act . . . the conclusion that such evidence is inadmissible is confirmed by the most compelling authorities . . . it would be departing very far this canon of interpretation if we were to admit evidence of contemporaneous circumstances which would result in giving an interpretation to a section of the statute. . . .[29]

Butler J., who also gave judgment in *Hales*, returned to the theme in *People (A.G.) v. Dwyer,*[30] approving the use of the exclusionary rule:

---

[23] [1981] 2 All E.R. 724 (C.A.) 731, 733.

[24] [1982] 1 All E.R. 1042 (H.L.) 1055.

[25] *The Interpretation of Statutes* (Law Com No 21; Scott Law Com No 11; 1969) paras.53-62.

[26] *Report of the Committee on the Preparation of Legislation* (1975, Cmnd. 6053) paras.19.20-19.26.

[27] 405 HL Deb., cols. 276-306 (February 13, 1980); 418 HL Deb., cols. 64-83 (March 9, 1981) and 1341-7 (March 26, 1981).

[28] [1967] I.R. 50 (H.C.).

[29] [1967] I.R. 50, 66-68

[30] [1972] I.R. 416 (S.C.), interpreting s.4 of the Criminal Justice Act, 1964 the effect of which is considered in Smith, "The Triumph of 'Inexorable Logic'. *D.P.P. v. Morgan* (1976)" above, 294.

The Court of Criminal Appeal seems to have interpreted the Criminal Justice Act, 1964 as being legislative approval of the form of direction given to the jury in the present case, and as a deliberate omission by the Legislature to amend the law in accordance with the principle expressed in *Howe's Case*. It is not, of course, permissible to enquire whether or not the matter was present in the mind of the legislature when the bill was passed. The intention of the legislature may only be gathered from an interpretation of the words used in the Act of 1964.[31]

In *The People (DPP) v. Quilligan*,[32] Walsh J. reaffirmed that:

... whatever may have been in the minds of the members of the Oireachtas when the legislation was passed, in so far as their intention can be deduced, as it must be, from the statute. . . .[33]

In the light of all of this, it is difficult to imagine the House of Lords taking such revolutionary action as to abolish the exclusionary within the subsequent ten years. It is important to identify the factors which allowed *Pepper v. Hart* to happen, because this background has demonstrated that it did not happen in isolation. What are they?

Several authors have formulated different theories. Lord Lester points to the growing European legal influence which encouraged a more purposive and less literal approach to the interpretation of legislation. The increasing interaction between the United Kingdom and European Courts (both Court of Justice and Court of Human Rights) has made the UK judges more aware of the advantages of considering the object and purpose of legislation instead of a literal interpretation.[34]

Ingman[35] agrees, arguing that the process of legitimising reference to *Hansard,* which culminated in *Pepper v. Hart*, began when the House of Lords took the lead in adopting a more relaxed approach towards its use in cases involving the construction of delegated legislation designed to give effect to our European Community obligations. Ingman argues that the justification for this development was that proposed delegated legislation, in the form of draft regulations. is not, unlike a Bill, subject to the Parliamentary process of consideration and amendment in committee. The case of *Pickstone v. Freemans plc*[36] is clear evidence of this approach. Lord Templeman and Lord Keith felt able to quote from the *Hansard* report of draft regulations which, when eventu-

---

[31] [1972] I.R. 416, 432 discussing *R. v. Howe* (1958) 100 C.L.R. 448 (H.C.A.).
[32] [1986] I.R. 495 (S.C.).
[33] [1986] I.R. 495, 511.
[34] Lester, *"Pepper v. Hart* Revisited" (1994) 15 *Stat.L.Rev.* 10, 13-14.
[35] *The English Legal Process* (7th ed., Blackstone Press, London. 1998) 269.
[36] [1988] 2 All E.R. 803 (H.L.).

ally made, added new provisions to the Equal Pay Act 1970. The regulations had been made under the authority of the European Communities Act 1972 in order to comply with a decision of the Court of Justice of the European Communities.

Lord Lester[37] also argues that the experience of a number of Commonwealth common law jurisdictions, including Australia, India, New Zealand, Canada, in modifying and relaxing the exclusionary rule within those jurisdictions[38] may have persuaded the UK courts and judges that the relaxation of the exclusionary rules does yield positive results and concurrently does not lead to excessive problems with access, recourse, over-quoting and cost. In particular the 1990 report of the New Zealand Law Commission[39] was well received.

Lord Lester also highlights that the gradual introduction of extrinsic material short of the official parliamentary record was also a determinative factor in the gradual erosion of the exclusionary rule. He points to cases such as *Black-Clawson Ltd v. Papierwerke Waldhoff-Aschaffenburg*,[40] where the House of Lords felt able to look at the report of an official committee for the purpose of discovering the mischief of a statute, and *Factortame (No. 1)*[41] where the Law Lords commented on the Government's decision not to give effect to a Law Commission recommendation. Ingman[42] agrees with the significance of these cases, arguing that by the time of *Pepper v. Hart*, the reports of the Law Commission, royal commissions, the Law Reform Committee and other official committees had all been looked at by the judges. Ingman also cites the cases of *R v. Ayres*,[43] where the House of Lords looked at a report of the Law Commission and *R v. Allen*[44] where it considered a report of the Criminal Law Revision Committee. Ingman also notes that in *Attorney-General's Reference (No. 1 of 1988)*[45] Lord Lowry quoted from a Government White Paper; in *Duke v.*

---

[37](1994) 15 *Stat.L.Rev.* 10, 14.

[38]In Australia through the cases of *Commissioner of Taxation (Cth) v. Whitford Beach Pty Ltd* (1982) 56 A.L.J.R. 240; *Re Australian Federation of Construction Contractors, ex p. Biling* (1986) 68 A.L.R. 416; and *R v. Bolton, ex p. Beane* (1987) 70 A.L.R. 225; in India through the case of *K.P. Verghese v. Income Tax Officer* A.I.R. (1981) S.C. 1922; in New Zealand through the cases of *Marac Life assurance Ltd v. Commissioner of Inland Revenue* [1986] 1 N.Z.L.R. 694; *Brown v. Doherty and Whangarie County Council* [1990] 2 N.Z.L.R. 63; and *Brown v. Langwoods Photo Stores Ltd* [1991] 1 N.Z.L.R. 173; in Canada through the cases of *Lyons v. The Queen* [1984] 2 S.C.R. 633; and *Canada (Attorney General) v. Young* (1989) 3 F.C. 647; all quoted by Lester, n.37 above. See also Kerr "Parliamentary History as an Aid to the Interpretation of Statutes" (1993) 11 *I.L.T.* (*n.s.*) 72, 72-73.

[39]Report No. 17 "A New Interpretation Act", December 1990

[40][1975] A.C. 591 (H.L.).

[41][1990] 2 A.C. 85 (H.L.).

[42]Above n.14, 267.

[43][1984] A.C. 447 (H.L.).

[44][1985] A.C. 1029 (H.L.).

[45][1989] A.C. 971 (H.L.).

GEC Reliance Ltd[46] Lord Templeman also referred to a White Paper; in *R v. Burke*,[47] Lord Griffiths looked at an official report.

A further important factor, identified by both Lord Lester and Ingman, was the abolition, in 1980, of the parliamentary rule which prevented counsel from citing *Hansard* in court. Lord Lester also sees the importance of greater access to parliamentary materials, particularly through the publishing of authoritative guides (such as Current Law) and textbooks and encyclopædia, in countering the early reasoning that relaxation of the exclusionary rule would pose too many practical recourse problems. Lord Lester also points to the debates which took place in the House of Lords, in its legislative capacity, in 1989.[48] The present Lord Chancellor, Lord Irvine of Lairg had instigated a debate on the modification of the exclusionary rule and had received significant support from a number of Law Lords.

One issue which arose in the parliamentary debates was the extent to which judges were already surreptitiously looking at parliamentary materials. Lord Lester has no doubt that the practice (although clearly unfair to the parties to the action) was reasonably widespread. Indeed he had joined in the practice by providing guides to judges as to when and where to find the relevant materials.[49] The relaxation of the exclusionary rule might therefore be seen as formalising an already informal practice.

Around the same time as the members of the Appellate Committee were preparing their speeches on *Pepper v. Hart*, another important Commission under the chairmanship of Lord Rippon was examining aspects of the legislative process. The eventual report of the Rippon Commission did not recommend any relaxation of the exclusionary rule but did make suggestions that the pertinence of it was debatable. Interestingly, one member of the Rippon Commission was Lord Browne-Wilkinson who gave the main speech in *Pepper v. Hart*.

One final factor which could be said to have played an important part in preparing the ground for *Pepper v. Hart* to happen was the change in the make up of the House of Lords in the 1980s and 1990s. Gordon has suggested that *Pepper v. Hart* is the first of a series of decisions, emanating from the Lords, which has articulated a strongly liberal viewpoint, so strong, in fact, that "it seems to represent a form of national conscience".[50] The other decisions noted by Gordon probably give more support for this theory but it could be agreed that he has a point. Much has been said recently about the personalities in the Lords. There is no doubt, as Gordon notes,[51] that there has been an infusion of

---

[46][1988] A.C. 618 (H.L.).
[47][1990] 1 A.C. 135 (H.L.).
[48]503 HL Deb., cols. 278-307, January 18, 1989.
[49]In *Charter v. Race Relations Board* [1972] A.C. 868 (H.L.) for example.
[50]"The Awakened Conscience of the Nation" (1994) *Counsel* March/April 10.
[51]*ibid.*, 12.

new talent which in turn is producing a body of innovative and creative case law.

Pepper v. Hart was a case waiting to happen. The seeds of doubt concerning the validity of the exclusionary rule had been sown. All that was needed was the correct bed of facts in which to nurture them.

3. WHAT WAS THE RULING IN *PEPPER V. HART*?

The facts and the decision in the case should now be well-known to lawyers and non-lawyers alike. However it is useful to remind ourselves of the specificity of the facts and the tests for the admission of parliamentary materials which were established in order to examine how they have been consequently applied.

Five speeches were given by the Lord Chancellor, Lord Bridge of Harwich, Lord Griffiths, Lord Oliver of Aylmerton and Lord Browne-Wilkinson. The opinions of the Lord Chancellor and Lord Browne-Wilkinson are referred to and quoted from most often; the former because Lord Mackay dissented on the main issue and the latter because his ruling is declared to be the most definitive. For these reasons, those two speeches are worth concentrating on.

Lord Mackay indicated that his major difficulty with the case was the submission of Mr Anthony Lester QC (as he then was) for the appellants that reference to parliamentary material should be allowed with the permission of the court and where the court was satisfied that the reference is warranted:

> (a) to confirm the meaning of a provision as conveyed by the text, its object and purpose, (b) to determine a meaning where the provision is ambiguous or obscure or (c) to determine the meaning where the ordinary meaning is manifestly absurd or unreasonable.[52]

The Lord Chancellor believed that virtually every case involving the interpretation of statutes could fall under one of these heads thereby adding considerably to the level, practice and cost of litigation – a practical objection of substance by which he was willing to stand. The greater significance which the quotation from Lord Mackay's speech has since assumed lies in the fact that he is the only panel member to allude to the possibility of using parliamentary materials to *confirm* the already-established construction of an ambiguous legislative provision. The other speeches concentrate on the proposed use of parliamentary materials to *determine* the meaning of obscure or ambiguous legislation. We shall see below that it appears that the House of Lords is now prepared to use *Hansard both* to determine and confirm meanings when the latter use is not

---

[52][1993] A.C. 593, 614; [1993] 1 All E.R. 42, 47 *per* Lord Mackay L.C..

permitted by the decision of the House as a whole and when the supposed basis for that use may even have been included in the judgment of the Lord Chancellor by error.[53]

Lord Browne-Wilkinson gave the leading judgement of the majority and it is his summary of the circumstances in which the exclusionary rule could be relaxed which is most often quoted as representing the *ratio* of the case:

> . . . the exclusionary rule should be relaxed so as to permit reference to parliamentary materials where: (a) legislation is ambiguous or obscure, or leads to an absurdity; (b) the material relied on consists of one or more statements by a minister or other promoter of the Bill together if necessary with such other parliamentary material as is necessary to understand such statements and their effect; (c) the statements relied on are clear. Further than this, I would not at present go.[54]

It is submitted that the words of Lord Browne-Wilkinson are clear and that the conditions which he formulates are specific. Each condition follows in sequence from the other so that there can be no reference to the parliamentary material unless the legislative provisions are ambiguous or obscure or leads to an absurdity (condition (a)). That condition must be satisfied *before* there can be any reference to the parliamentary materials. If condition (a) is satisfied then and only then do conditions (b) and (c) come into play. We shall see below that these conditions have not been interpreted in this manner by some judges and consequently are being applied in a different manner. In particular, some judges may be reviewing the parliamentary materials in order to decide whether the legislative provisions are ambiguous or obscure or may be using those materials to confirm a particular construction.

Lord Browne-Wilkinson gives an indication of what he means by "ambiguity" or "obscurity". The Finance Act 1976 was ambiguous or obscure precisely because he found that the statutory words, on their face, were capable of bearing one of two different, opposing meanings. That is a definition of ambiguity or obscurity which has been readily accepted as definitive in a large number of cases over a period of centuries. It is submitted further that the courts have centuries of experience in deciding whether a piece of legislation is obscure, ambiguous or could lead to an absurdity, on its face.[55] The House of Lords

---

[53]Lord Lester has indicated that while he had initially argued for recourse to parliamentary materials to confirm the meaning of legislative provisions, this argument was abandoned in submissions before the Appellate Committee. Apparently the Lord Chancellor was unaware of this change of position at the time of preparation of his speech. See further Lester, *"Pepper v. Hart* Revisited" (1994) *Stat. L. Rev.* 10, 21.

[54][1993] A.C. 593, 640; [1993] 1 All E.R. 42, 69.

[55]The analysis of any textbook on statutory interpretation will confirm this. See for example, Bell & Engle, *Cross on Statutory Interpretation* (2nd ed., Butterworths, London, 1987).

ruling does not add any novel test for the determination of the ambiguity, obscurity or absurdity of legislative provisions. We shall see that the definition of ambiguity or obscurity has since been extended by the House of Lords beyond the relatively simplistic and logical approach taken by Lord Browne-Wilkinson.

Lord Browne-Wilkinson limits the range of admissible parliamentary material to

> . . . one or more statements by a minister or other promoter of the Bill together if necessary with such other parliamentary material is necessary to understand such statements and their effect . . [56]

He makes it clear that the reason for this limitation is the avoidance of unnecessary searches through parliamentary materials in the hope of uncovering the "crock of gold", that is the clear indication of Parliament's intentions.[57]

In the substance of the case itself, Lord Browne-Wilkinson sets off a pattern of a liberal interpretation of the range of such extra materials by referring, in some detail, to a press release which was issued simultaneously with the statement of a minister on the context of the particular provisions and whose contents confirmed that minister's particular intentions. That pattern has been maintained by the House of Lords.

Lord Browne-Wilkinson gives some further guidance as to the basis on which clarity of statement should be determined. He states that parliamentary material should only be admitted where:

> . . . such material clearly discloses the mischief aimed at or the legislative intention lying behind the ambiguous or obscure words.[58]

Later in his speech he adds a further qualification which suggests that clarity also includes the requirement that the statement of the minister represents the intention of Parliament as a whole. In the present case he was satisfied that the minister's statement did represent the collective intention in that the matter was not raised again, certain amendments were withdrawn and no further amendment was made affecting the correctness of the minister's statement.[59] In the subsequent cases before the House of Lords, this requirement has not been elaborated upon.

One or two other aspects of the speech of Lord Brown-Wilkinson are worth noting at this stage. On the particular facts of the case he found that section 63 of the Finance Act 1975 was ambiguous and that if the relevant parliamentary materials on the point were reviewed he would favour a particular construc-

---

[56][1993] A.C. 593, 640; [1993] 1 All E.R. 42, 69.
[57][1993] A.C. 593, 637; [1993] 1 All E.R. 42, 67.
[58][1993] A.C. 593, 634; [1993] 1 All E.R. 42, 64.
[59][1993] A.C. 593, 642; [1993] 1 All E.R. 42, 71.

tion. If the parliamentary materials were not reviewed he would favour an opposing, literal construction of the provision. However he had arrived at this finding in his speech *after* having reviewed at length the parliamentary materials on the provision and before making the final decision of whether a reference is permissible. This illustrates the difficulty, discussed again below, of the potential influence of cited and sighted parliamentary materials on the decision to permit the admission of it. As Lord Browne-Wilkinson freely admits: "[h]aving once looked at what was said in Parliament, it is difficult to put it out of mind".[60]

In considering the issue of the potential increase in the volume and cost of litigation which might be brought about by a relaxation of the exclusionary rule, Lord Browne-Wilkinson indicates that any attempt to introduce materials which do not satisfy the tests which he has outlined ought to be met by orders for costs against the party who have improperly introduced the materials.[61] This warning about costs has been repeated in a Practice Direction on the citation of *Hansard* which was issued with the concurrence of the Lord Chancellor, the Lord Chief Justice, the Master of the Rolls, the President of the Family Division and Vice-Chancellor on December 20, 1994.[62] The purpose of the Direction is to compel any party intending to refer to any extract from *Hansard* in support of any argument to serve copies of the extracts on the court and all other parties to the action. Failure to comply with the Direction may lead to an order for costs. We shall see below that despite the fact that there are cases where Lord Browne-Wilkinson's tests were not satisfied – in that the legislation was not ambiguous or the minister's statement was unclear – the warning as to orders for costs has so far gone unheeded.

Finally it should be noted that despite the limitations imposed upon the relaxation of the exclusionary rule by Lord Browne-Wilkinson – including the warning that beyond those limitations he was not then prepared to go[63] – the application of the ruling in subsequent House of Lords cases has shown that the judges favour a liberal rather than a strict interpretation of the tests. It is also clear that the other courts and tribunals are following this example.

Having clarified the ruling in *Pepper v. Hart* and established the difficulties which have arisen in its application, it is now necessary to turn to the decisions of the House of Lords in which it has subsequently been referred to look at those difficulties in more detail.

Before doing so, it would be worthwhile to make some general observations about the complete series of cases in which the ruling in *Pepper v. Hart* has been referred to in judgments or has been cited in argument.

---

[60][1993] A.C. 593, 642; [1993] 1 All E.R. 42, 71.
[61][1993] A.C. 593, 637; [1993] 1 All E.R. 42, 67.
[62][1995] 1 W.L.R. 192.
[63][1993] A.C. 593, 640; [1993] 1 All E.R. 42, 69.

4. THE CASES

To date, there have been at least 295 cases in which the decision in *Pepper v. Hart* was either cited in argument or referred to in judgments.[64]

The 295 cases which were analysed in detail came from a wide variety of courts and tribunals and were concerned with a broad diversity of legislation. 16 of the cases were in the House of Lords; 70 were decisions of the Civil Division of the Court of Appeal; 19 were decisions of the Criminal Division of the Court of Appeal; 3 were decisions of the Northern Ireland Court of Appeal; 36 were decisions of the Chancery Division of the High Court; 79 were decisions of the Queens Bench Division of the High Court; 4 were decisions of the Family Division of the High Court; 1 was a decision of the Privy Council; 18 were decisions of the Employment Appeal Tribunal; 5 were decisions of the Court of Session; 10 were decisions of the VAT Tribunal; 22 were decisions of the Special Commissioners; 1 was a decision of the Registered Designs Appeal Tribunal; 5 were decisions of the Lands Tribunal; 1 was a decision of an Industrial Tribunal; 1 was a decision of the Supreme Court of Hong Kong, High Court; 3 represented the decisions in *Pepper v. Hart* itself and a further 1 related to the Practice Direction arising out of that case.

One case involving Ford Motor Company's application in relation to certain intellectual property rights was appealed from the Registered Designs Appeal Tribunal to the House of Lords and thus appeared four times on the list of cases. It is interesting to note that by the time the case had reached the House of Lords any discussion of the admissibility of *Hansard* had been abandoned.

A broad diversity of legislation was covered in these cases – too broad to mention in detail. However it is possible to state that the most troublesome type of legislation was that relating to taxation being involved in well over 50 of the cases; perhaps not surprisingly when this was the subject-matter of *Pepper v. Hart.*

5. WHAT HAS BEEN THE IMPACT OF *PEPPER V. HART* IN SUBSEQUENT HOUSE OF LORDS' CASES?

The ruling in *Pepper v. Hart,* was quickly applied in a number of subsequent House of Lords' cases,[65] including *R. Warwickshire County Council, ex parte Johnson,*[66] *Chief Adjudication Officer and another v. Foster,*[67] *Stubbings v.*

---

[64]LEXIS search, September 15, 2000, on the phrase "Pepper w/5 Hart".
[65]For a detailed analysis of the application of *Pepper v. Hart* in these cases see Mullan, above n.1.
[66][1993] A.C. 583 (H.L.).
[67][1993] A.C. 754 (H.L.).

Webb,[68] *Attorney-General v. Associated Newspapers Ltd and others,*[69] *Scher and others v. Policyholders Protection Board and others (No 2),*[70] and *Holden v. Crown Prosecution Service (No. 2).*[71]

A review of these cases shows that the initial decisions of the House of Lords do not appear to favour a strict interpretation of Lord Browne-Wilkinson's tests. A strict interpretation of those tests might mean that the three tests or conditions outlined by Lord Browne-Wilkinson must be applied in a sequential fashion. This would mean that the *first* task for the court would be to decide whether the legislation in question is ambiguous, obscure or leads to an absurdity. This would mean that this is a *preliminary* issue to be determined *without* argument about, or recourse to parliamentary materials. Counsel should not be permitted to cite passages from *Hansard* nor should the court have sight of it before the preliminary question of obscurity, ambiguity has been resolved. Counsel would be justified in arguing that the legislation was ambiguous or obscure or could lead to an absurdity such as to justify recourse to the parliamentary materials but should give no indication of the content of such materials.

Should the court determine that the legislation is neither ambiguous or obscure nor leads to an absurdity after having heard argument on the question of ambiguity, obscurity or absurdity then that should be the end of the matter and there should be no further reference to *Hansard*. If that approach is not followed it could lead to the situation where the court, in seeking to determine whether legislation is obscure or ambiguous or could lead to an absurdity so as to justify recourse to *Hansard* to ascertain it its true construction, might have recourse (either deliberately because it has had sight of it or innocently because it has been cited by counsel) to *Hansard*.

Should the court determine that the legislation is ambiguous or obscure or leads to an absurdity after having heard argument on the question of ambiguity, obscurity or absurdity then reference to *Hansard* to determine the second (the material consists of a statement by a minister or other promoter of the Bill) and third (the clarity of the statement) of Lord Browne-Wilkinson's tests or conditions should be permitted. At this stage counsel should be permitted to present argument on the existence and content of such material.

Initially, the House of Lords did not appear to favour such an approach. The application of the tests was not strict. Rather the House seemed to be prepared to consider parliamentary materials without giving a clear indication that it had found the legislation to be ambiguous or obscure. Occasionally the decision on ambiguity or obscurity had been based, not on a finding as such by

---

[68] [1993] A.C. 498 (H.L.).
[69] [1994] 2 A.C. 238 (H.L.).
[70] [1994] 2 A.C. 57 (H.L.).
[71] [1994] 1 A.C. 22 (H.L.).

the Law Lord concerned, but on the conclusion that the legislation must be ambiguous because of a difference of opinion in the courts below.

Often the House considered parliamentary material *de bene esse,* compelling itself to have regard to it because arguments on it had appeared in counsels' submissions. The result was that it often had sight of parliamentary material prior to a decision on its admissibility. The materials which had been seen include the statements of ministers and other ministers but the range of acceptable material had been extended since Lord Browne-Wilkinson's ruling.

Rarely did a consideration of the parliamentary material dispose of the issue of construction. More often than not the House used the statements found in *Hansard* to confirm a construction of legislation which had already been established by traditional methods. Use of parliamentary material for this purpose is not part of the original *ratio* of *Pepper v. Hart.*

The House appeared to be moving to a scenario where it felt empowered to have recourse to the use of *Hansard* without giving a clear exposition of the basis for doing so. The initial cases have shown that the Lords believe that they had such authority and that it was largely unfettered.

6. HAS THIS APPROACH BEEN MIRRORED IN THE DECISIONS OF OTHER COURTS AND TRIBUNALS?

An analysis of a large number of cases shows that the trends and patterns established by the House of Lords in its initial application of the ruling in *Pepper v. Hart* has been reflected in the lower courts and tribunals. There are instances where those courts do appear to be taking a strict line,[72] for example in *R v. Singleton,*[73] *R v. Stipendiary Magistrates Ex parte Director of the Serious Fraud Office,*[74] *R v. Moore,*[75] *R v. Dorset County Council Ex parte Rolls and another,*[76] and *Ford Motor Company Ltd.*[77]

What are the difficulties with the remaining cases? The difficulty is that the courts have either had the parliamentary materials cited to them in argument or have sight of them by other means. In some cases the judges have applied the maxim *de bene esse* to allow the submissions on the parliamentary materials to be heard or to have citations from *Hansard*; in other cases the judges are not explicit that they are hearing submissions *de bene esse* but that appears to have been their intention and in a number of cases the courts have given no reason

---

[72]For a detailed analysis of the application of *Pepper v. Hart* in these cases see Mullan, above n.1.
[73]*The Times,* June 22, 1994.
[74]*The Independent,* June 24, 1994.
[75]159 J.P. 101.
[76](1994) 92 L.G.R. 398.
[77][1993] R.P.C. 399.

for hearing submissions on the use of parliamentary materials or for having recourse to them.

Examples of this approach would be the cases[78] of *Ford Motor Company's Design Applications,*[79] *R v. Secretary of State for the Home Department Ex parte Okello,*[80] *Hassall and another v. Secretary of State for Social Security,*[81] and *Griffin (Inspector of Taxes) v. Craig-Harvey.*[82]

In a large number of the cases examined, the courts followed the initial lead of the House of Lords and were willing to consider submissions, hear arguments or consider the contents of parliamentary materials without giving an obvious reason for doing so or alternatively, after having considered the parliamentary materials, refrained from answering the question of their admissibility under the *Pepper v. Hart* principle.

Examples of this approach are to be found in the cases[83] of *Massmould Holdings Ltd v. Payne,*[84] *Connolly v. Secretary of State for Northern Ireland,*[85] and *R v. Jefferson.*[86]

Having seen the parliamentary materials in advance, the lower courts have often gone on to decide that the legislation was not ambiguous or obscure so as to invoke the principle in *Pepper v. Hart.* The difficulty lies in deciding whether or not the decision on ambiguity, obscurity or absurdity was influenced by the earlier access to the parliamentary materials on the issue. In some of these cases the courts declined to comment further on the matter but in some the courts went to make comments about what they had read or seen. In a number of the cases the courts, in a somewhat self-congratulatory manner, indicated that the parliamentary materials confirmed their initial construction of the legislation. For example, in *Petch v. Gurney (Inspector of Taxes),*[87] Millett L.J. gives a classic judgment in this category.

In certain cases the courts indicated that there was no assistance to be derived from the parliamentary provisions. Again this points to the obvious danger that the initial construction has been influenced by what was seen or read in the parliamentary materials.

In two[88] of the cases where the courts had access to the parliamentary materials apparently *de bene esse,* they eventually refused recourse to *Hansard*

---

[78]For a detailed analysis of the application of *Pepper v. Hart* in these cases see Mullan, above n.1.
[79][1994] R.P.C. 545.
[80][1994] Imm. AR 261.
[81]*The Times,* December 26, 1994.
[82][1994] S.T.C. 54.
[83]For a detailed analysis of the application of *Pepper v. Hart* in these cases see Mullan, above n.1.
[84][1993] S.T.C. 62.
[85]LEXIS Transcript.
[86][1994] 1 All E.R. 270 (C.A.).
[87][1994] 3 All E.R. 731 (C.A.).
[88]*R v. London Borough of Wandsworth, Ex parte Hawthorne* CO/2122/93 LEXIS Transcript, *Van Dyck and another v. Secretary of State for the Environment and Another* [1993] 1 P.L.R. 124.

under the third of Lord Browne-Wilkinson's tests *i.e.* that the statement of the Minister was not clear. The two cases are worthy of note for other reasons. In the *Hawthorne* case, there is the most extensive recourse to the materials in *Hansard* in any of the cases looked at. The materials which were looked at included statements by ordinary Members of Parliament. In the *Van Dyck* decision, the case was relisted after the original judgment had been given so that submissions on the applicability of *Pepper v. Hart* might be heard. Again the analysis of the parliamentary materials is fairly extensive. The eventual judgment is given in two chapters.

In one or two cases the reasons given for eventually disallowing recourse to *Hansard* under the principles in *Pepper v. Hart* could not be easily explained. In *Mendip District Council v. Glastonbury Festivals Ltd*,[89] the court allowed recourse to *Hansard* in relation to one piece of legislation in question without giving any reason for so doing and then indicated that no useful assistance could be gained from the materials found. In relation to the second piece of legislation which post-dated the commission of the criminal offences which were the subject of the case, the judge indicated that he doubted ". . . whether it is permissible to endeavour to construe an earlier statute, that in question, by reference to a later statute".[90]

In *R v. Newham London Borough Council Ex parte Barking & Dagenham London Borough Council, Ex parte University of East London*[91] we have probably seen the most illogical application of the ruling in *Pepper v. Hart* from a legal point of view. In this case, Potts J. is invited by counsel to look, under the principle in *Pepper v. Hart*, at certain parliamentary materials which, it is believed assist a certain construction of the legislation. After referring to all the conditions laid down by Lord Browne-Wilkinson, the judge indicates that "[i]n order to decide the point I looked at the Parliamentary material".[92] He is of the belief that the fact that he then discovers that the statement of the minister is not clear is sufficient to make it impermissible to have regard to the material in construing the statute.

In a number of the cases of the cases where the courts originally considered the parliamentary material, recourse to *Hansard* was permitted under the principles in *Pepper v. Hart*. For example, in *Botross v. London Borough of Hammersmith and Fulham*,[93] the court considered that the assistance which could be gained from the parliamentary materials fell within the limits of *Pepper v. Hart*. Having considered those materials the court is reassured to discover that

---

[89] [1993] Crim L.R. 701.
[90] LEXIS Transcript.
[91] [1994] R.A. 13.
[92] LEXIS Transcript
[93] *The Times*, November 7, 1994.

their construction of the legislation is confirmed by the statement of the government minister in accepting the amendment.

In *Sunderland Polytechnic v. Evans*,[94] the Employment Appeal Tribunal decided that on the basis of the submissions which had been made before them, the construction of the legislation was obscure. However in order to satisfy themselves that the approach which they were taking, based on an earlier judgment,[95] was correct, they would look at the parliamentary material. Once regarded that material did confirm that the earlier precedent was wrong and that they ought to move away from it.

It is equally clear that there is a range of cases where the courts are prepared to have recourse to *Hansard* without giving an explicit reason under the ruling in *Pepper v. Hart* and indeed without referring to that judgment at all.

7. *MELLUISH (INSPECTOR OF TAXES) V. BMI (No 3) LIMITED* – LORD BROWNE-WILKINSON REVIEWS *PEPPER V. HART*

In *Melluish (Inspector of Taxes) v. BMI (No 3) Limited and other appeals*,[96] Lord Browne-Wilkinson gave his first critique of the use of his prior ruling in *Pepper v. Hart*. His Lordship's comments about the admissibility of parliamentary materials in *Melluish* are critical and are reflective of a concern that the ruling, which was initially formulated in terms of strict limitation, is now being applied in a liberal and permissive manner.

Melluish, like *Pepper v. Hart*, is a case concerned with the interpretation of finance legislation. In particular the appeal raised the question of the capital allowances which could be claimed by taxpayers who carried on the business of purchasing plant and machinery and leasing it to relevant users. The particular difficulty in the case arose from the fact that the plant purchased by the appellant taxpayer companies, such as central heating, lifts, boilers and ventilation, was incorporated into the structure of the buildings owned by the lessees of the plant. As a result they became fixtures. Ordinarily they would then become the property of the owner of the land. However, in order to claim capital allowance under the Finance Acts of 1971 and 1985, the appellant taxpayer companies would have to show that the plant which had at all material times been affixed to the land "belonged" to the companies.

In his speech dismissing the appeals, Lord Browne-Wilkinson addressed the submissions of counsel for the Crown that his Lordship should have regard to statements made by ministers in the course of progress through Parliament

---

[94][1993] I.R.L.R. 196 (E.A.T.).
[95]*Home Office v. Ayres* [1992] I.C.R. 721 (E.A.T.).
[96][1996] A.C. 454 (H.L.).

of the 1985 Finance Bill. Applying that test to the present facts, his Lordship accepted that some of the language in the Finance Act 1985 was ambiguous or obscure. However the remaining tests for the admissibility of the parliamentary materials were not satisfied:

> The parliamentary materials sought to be introduced by the revenue in the present case were not directed to the specific statutory provision under consideration or to the problem raised by the litigation but to another provision and another problem. The revenue sought to derive from the ministerial statements on that other provision and other problem guidance on the point your Lordships have to consider . . . In my view this is an improper use of the relaxed rule introduced by *Pepper v. Hart* which, if properly used, can be a valuable aid to construction when Parliament has directly considered the point in issue and passed the legislation on the basis of the ministerial statement. It provides no assistance to a court and is capable of giving rise to much expense and delay if attempts are made to widen the category of materials that can be looked at. . . .[97]

His Lordship was further of the view that judges should be astute to check such misuse of the new rule by making appropriate orders as to costs wasted. In the present case, if the costs issue had been pertinent, he would have suggested disallowing some part of the costs of the Revenue for introducing such materials.

The significance of the critical remarks of Lord Browne-Wilkinson is twofold. Specifically, his remarks concerning costs reflect his view in *Pepper v. Hart* that, on the basis of a potential increase in the volume and cost of litigation which might be brought about by a relaxation of the exclusionary rule, any attempt to introduce materials which do not satisfy the tests which he has outlined ought to be met by orders for costs against the party who have improperly introduced the materials. Secondly, and more importantly, his remarks about the inappropriate use of the relaxed rule are indicative of a belief that the three tests or conditions for the introduction of parliamentary materials were meant to be applied in a strict manner and that deviance from such an approach should be penalised by the imposition of orders as to costs. The comments are also reflective of a concern that the current practice is permissive and indulgent, allowing for the submission of parliamentary rules outside the confines of the rule.

---

[97] [1996] A.C. 454, 481-482.

8. To What Extent has the House of Lords Heeded Lord Browne-Wilkinson's Second Warning?

The Secretary of State for Social Security and another v. Remilien, Chief Adjudication Officer v. Wolke[98] is the most recent decision of the House of Lords to consider the ruling in *Pepper v. Hart*, and gives a good indication of the current attitude of the House towards the ruling.

The facts were that the appellants were single mothers and nationals of member states of the European Community living in England and claiming Income Support. They received letters from the Home Office informing each of them that the Secretary of State was not satisfied that they were lawfully resident in the United Kingdom under European Community law in view of the fact that they were present in a non-economic capacity, had become a burden on public funds and that they should make arrangements to leave. An Adjudication Officer of the Department of Social Security subsequently decided that the appellants were no longer entitled to Income Support since they were persons who, for the purposes of Regulation 21(3)(h) of the Income Support (General) Regulations 1987, had been required by the Secretary of State to leave the United Kingdom. The Adjudication Officer terminated payment of Income support pursuant to Paragraph 17 of Schedule 7 of the 1987 Regulations.

The Adjudication Officer's decision against one of the appellants was quashed on her application for judicial review. A Social Security appeal Tribunal had upheld the Adjudication Officer's decision in relation to the other appellant. She appealed to a Social Security Commissioner and was successful. The Chief Adjudication Officer appealed to the Court of Appeal against both decisions. The Court of Appeal, by a majority, allowed the appeals, on the ground that the letters from the Home Office constituted a requirement to leave the United Kingdom which ended the appellant's entitlement to Income Support.

A five member Committee allowed the appeals, by a majority.[99] Lord Hoffman gave the only speech for the majority. On first reading, his references to the applicability of the ruling in *Pepper v. Hart* appear to show that he was prepared to be strict in limiting that application. As noted above, the main issue for consideration was the meaning of the phrase "required by the Secretary of State to leave the United Kingdom" in Regulation 21(3)(h) of the Income Support (General) Regulations 1987. Counsel for the Secretary of State and the Chief Adjudication Officer had sought to rely on a statement made by the Parliamentary Under-Secretary of State for Social Security to the House of Commons Standing Committee on Statutory Instruments on the meaning and

---

[98] [1998] 1 All E.R. 129 (H.L.).
[99] Lord Slynn dissented on the substantive issues. His speech contains to no reference to the decision in *Pepper v. Hart*.

intention of the relevant Regulation and had argued that the parliamentary material was admissible under the principle in *Pepper v. Hart*. Lord Hoffman, (perhaps mindful that his draft speech will eventually be read by Lord Browne-Wilkinson?), is clear on the point:

> One of the conditions for admissibility under that principle is that the statement must be clear . . . I do not think that the minister's statement passes this test. Nor, probably, did the departmental brief upon which it is based . . . I find the statement to be of no assistance.[100]

What is interesting about Lord Hoffman's speech is that while the above passage contains the only reference to the applicability of *Pepper v. Hart*, there are other excerpts which refer to the relevant parliamentary material. It is clear from those excerpts that Lord Hoffman did, in fact, find the statement to be of assistance.

An earlier submission by Counsel for the Secretary of State and the Chief Adjudication Officer related to the fact that Regulation 21(3)(h) had been passed, in part, to give effect to the decision in the case of *R v. Secretary of State, ex p Antonisse*.[101] In rejecting the substantive argument, Lord Hoffman had the following to say:

> . . . one cannot exclude the possibility that the Secretary of State (or, more realistically, his advisers) were simply muddled about what *Ex p Antonissen* had decided. There is some support for this view in the passage from the minutes of a statement made on 27 April 1993 by Mr Alistair Burt, Parliamentary Under-Secretary of State for Social Security to the House of Commons Second Standing Committee on Statutory Instruments *etc*, to which Mr Plender drew our attention. . . .[102]

This is the very parliamentary statement which Lord Hoffman had rejected under the third of Lord Browne-Wilkinson's tests for admissibility of parliamentary materials and from which he could "find . . . no assistance". No reason is given for reference to the parliamentary materials, beyond the fact that counsel made reference to them in his submissions. It is arguable that the inclusion or rejection of the relevant parliamentary materials made little difference to Lord Hoffman's overall conclusions on the meaning of the legislative provi-

---

[100] [1998] 1 All E.R. 129, 147. Lord Hoffman is obviously of the view that the first limb of Lord Browne-Wilkinson's test is satisfied *i.e.* that the legislative provision which he is being asked to interpret is ambiguous or obscure or leads to an absurdity. The sequential nature of the three limbs of the test demands that conclusion.

[101] Case C-292/89, [1991] ECR I-745.

[102] [1998] 1 All E.R. 129, 145

sions in these appeals and that he was able to arrive at a suitable construction on other substantive and unrelated grounds.

What is clear, however, is that judges are gaining sight of parliamentary materials, largely through the submissions of counsel. The approach to the applicability and use of those materials, once cited and sighted, appears to be contradictory. Once seen, the parliamentary materials are difficult put out of mind, and, as the speech of Lord Hoffman demonstrates, it is easy to use those materials for certain purposes, and not others.[103]

9. THE RELAXATION OF THE EXCLUSIONARY RULE IN IRELAND

As noted above, support for the retention and continuation of the exclusionary rule is to be found in a number of judgments in the courts in Ireland. To date, the most significant reaffirmation occurs in the case of *Howard v. Commissioners for Public Works*,[104] which is also regarded as the leading case on statutory interpretation in the jurisdiction. Finlay C.J. was clear on the issue:

> I am satisfied that it would not be permissible to interpret a statute upon the basis of either speculation, or indeed, even of actual information obtained with regard to the belief of individuals who either drafted the statute or took part as legislators in its enactment with regard to the question of the appropriate legal principles as applicable to matters being dealt with in the statute.[105]

Despite this, there are some indicators of the potential for a relaxation of the exclusionary rule along *Pepper v. Hart* lines. As far back as 1981, Costello J. was making some inroads. In *Wavin Pipes Ltd v. Hepworth Iron Co.*,[106] the judge referred to aspects of the parliamentary history of the Patents Act, 1964, to reinforce his earlier conclusions on its interpretation decided on traditional grounds. Referring to the case of *Bourke v. Attorney General*,[107] in which the Supreme Court had referred to the *travaux préparatoires* of the Council of Europe Convention on Extradition when considering aspects of the Extradition Act, the judge noted:

---

[103] Another recent House of Lords decision, in the case of *Inland Revenue Commissioners v. Willoughby* [1997] 1 W.L.R. 1071 (H.L.) demonstrates the extent to which judges will freely refer to parliamentary materials. In this case, Lord Nolan muses on how an earlier Committee might have decided an appeal, eventually reversed by a subsequent Committee, had it had access to relevant parliamentary materials. See further his comments at [1997] 1 W.L.R. 1071, 1073.
[104] [1994] 1 I.R. 101 (S.C.).
[105] [1994] 1 I.R. 101, 140.
[106] [1982] F.S.R. 32 (H.C.).
[107] [1972] I.R. 69 (S.C.).

If the courts can properly look at the history of the adoption of an international convention for the purpose of ascertaining the meaning of the words used in it, there would appear to be no reason in principle why in appropriate cases they should not be free when construing the words in a statute to obtain assistance from the history of its enactment by parliament.[108]

He added:

It would be difficult to find a clearer case than this to demonstrate how the parliamentary history of an enactment can assist in ascertaining the legislative intent.[109]

Hogan[110] indicates that Costello J. had taken a similar approach in *Beecham Group Ltd v. Bristol Meyers Co.*,[111] and also refers to the case of *F.F. v. C.F.*[112] where Barr J. had used parliamentary history as an aid to the construction of section 2 of the Statute Law Revision (Pre-Union Irish Statutes) Act 1962.

The move towards the relaxation of the exclusionary rule, as advocated by Costello J. in *Wavin* was generally welcomed. Casey,[113] after reviewing the arguments for and against the retention of the rule, concluded that the approach taken by Costello J. was appropriate, and he ended by indicating that it would be interesting to see whether the judge's colleagues would follow the lead which he had given. Kerr,[114] writing after the speeches in *Pepper v. Hart* were delivered, concludes that the Irish judiciary have been reluctant to do so. He analyses the decision of Judge Sheridan in *Conalty v. Tipperary (North Riding) County Council*,[115] in which the judge concluded that the law had not gone so far as to enable a court to bring into consideration, in interpreting a statute, the expres-

---

[108] [1982] F.S.R. 32, 40. On the issue of whether the judge was correct in this finding, on the related issue of whether the judge considered that this finding implicitly overruled the decision in the *Hales* case, and on the judgment in general see Casey, "Statutory Interpretation – A New Departure" (1982) 4 *D.U.L.J.* (n.s.) 110.

[109] [1982] F.S.R. 32, 41. The defendants had argued for a construction of the Act which had been expressly rejected by the Minister in declining to take an amendment which would expressly have had that effect. Hence, Costello J. continued that: "[t]he evidence relating to (a) the fact of the rejected amendment and (b) the reasons give for its rejection assists therefore in establishing that the words used in the statute should not be interpreted as the defendants suggest" (*ibid.*). Indeed, as Hogan and Whyte point out, "Costello J. was himself in the best position to take this point, as it was he who, when a member of the Dáil seventeen years previously, had moved this amendment"! Hogan and Whyte, *Kelly: The Irish Constitution* (3rd ed., Butterworths, Dublin, 1994) 473.

[110] "Statutory Interpretation – The Mullaghmore Case" (1993) 15 *D.U.L.J.* (n.s.) 243, 249, n.22.

[111] High Court, unreported, March 13, 1981.

[112] [1987] I.L.R.M. 1 (H.C.).

[113] "Statutory Interpretation – A New Departure" (1982) 4 *D.U.L.J.* (n.s.) 110.

[114] "Parliamentary History as an Aid to the Interpretation of Statutes" (1993) 11 *I.L.T.* (n.s.) 72.

[115] (1989) 7 *I.L.T.* (n.s.) 222.

sion of opinion of a Minister for State no matter how honestly given. In arriving at this conclusion, the judge preferred the decision of the divisional court in *Hales*, as reinforced in by the *dictum* of Butler J. in the Supreme Court in *The People (Attorney General) v. Dwyer*, and declined to follow the decision of Costello J.

After analysing other cases in which the potential for the relaxation of the exclusionary rule could have arisen, the practice and procedure of other jurisdictions and the decision in *Pepper v. Hart*, Kerr concludes that one would be hard pressed to find a clearer case than *Wavin* to show how the parliamentary history of an enactment can assist in discovering the legislative intent.[116]

Hogan, in supporting a relaxation of the exclusionary rule, concedes that the comments of Finlay C.J. in *Howard* and Walsh J. in *Quilligan*, most often cited in support of its retention, were essentially asides, and that the fundamental question of principle was neither fully argued before nor addressed by the Supreme Court.[117] However he argues that the well known practical advantages of a more relaxed approach, so evident in the *Howard* case, would support a case for further relaxation. In so doing, he also recognises a number of practical issues arising from the potential for such a move. Among these is the fundamental assumption that all existing legislation was drafted with knowledge that reference to parliamentary materials would not be permitted when it came to its interpretation in the courts.

Further there existed the possibility that the supporters or sponsors of legislation might make exaggerated claims as to its effect during enactment, in turn leading to the danger that the courts might be influenced by what the legislators contemplated rather than what the objective language of the statute actually said. Hogan concludes, however, that such difficulties might be overcome by permitting the relaxation of the exclusionary rule to be undertaken by the Oireachtas itself.[118]

Meanwhile Costello J. kept plugging away. Sitting as an additional judge in the Supreme Court in *People (D.P.P.) v. McDonagh*,[119] and without reference to the judgments in *Howard*, he stated:

> It has long been established that a court may, as an aid to the construction of a statute or one of its provisions, consider legislative history . . . It was urged on the appellant's behalf that the court should not consider the legislative history of [the relevant section] because the court can only do so when construing a section which is ambiguous, which this section clearly is not. I cannot agree with this submission; our courts do not and

---

[116] (1993) *I.L.T.* (*n.s.*) 72, 74.
[117] (1993) 15 *D.U.L.J.* (*n.s.*) 243, 251.
[118] *ibid.*, 253.
[119] [1996] 1 I.R. 565 (S.C.).

should not adopt such a rigid exclusionary rule . . . and it seems to me that
the court should have regard to any aspect of the enactment's legislative
history which may be of assistance . . . As the legislative history of the
section being considered in this case throws very considerable light on
its proper construction, it would be wrong of this Court to ignore it.[120]

He has been assisted by one of his High Court colleagues, Budd J. In *An
Blascaod Mór Teoranta v. Commissioners of Public Works*,[121] he stated:

> while I am aware of the stringency of the decision of the Supreme Court
> in the *Howard* case, nevertheless it seems to me that there must be some
> leeway for the relaxation of the exclusionary rule in considering a consti-
> tutional challenge involving as it does the double construction rule and
> other principles such as the rule about severability.[122]

There has also been some judicial consideration of the decision in *Pepper v.
Hart*. In *Wadda v. Ireland*,[123] it was submitted to Keane J. that he ought to
consider the statements made during the debates on the Guardianship of Infants Act, 1964 in the Dáil by the minister responsible for introducing the measure. This submission relied on the decision of Costello J. in *Wavin* and on
Pepper v. Hart for its authority. However, the judge did not think that the issue
needed to be considered as he held that the relevant statute was not ambiguous,
and hence that the reference to the legislative history did not arise.[124]

In the later *Crilly v. Farrington*[125] Geoghegan J. observed that the traditional exclusionary rule had been "changed somewhat"[126] by virtue of *Pepper
v. Hart* and *People (D.P.P.) v. McDonagh*, but he saw little point in analysis of
the former because he thought it clear that the Supreme Court in the latter had

---

[120] [1996] 1 I.R. 565, 570.

[121] High Court, unreported, July 1, 1997.

[122] It is arguable that the comments of Budd J. have to be treated with a degree of caution in
considering the overall issue of the permissible use of parliamentary materials to assist in the
process of statutory interpretation. Casey ("Statutory Interpretation – A New Departure" (1981)
4 *D.U.L.J.* (*n.s.*) 110, 112) has argued that there is a difference between cases concerned with
construction and cases concerned with constitutionality. In so doing, he questions the reliance
placed by Costello J. in *Wavin* on the cases of *McMahon v. Attorney General* [1972] I.R. 69
and *Maher v. Attorney General* [1973] I.R. 140 (H.C.).

[123] [1994] 1 I.L.R.M. 126 (H.C.).

[124] See also *Cronin v Murray*, High Court, unreported, December 17, 1998, where Macken J.
accepted counsel's submission, made with reference to *Howard*, that s.8 of the Adoption Act
1976 was clear and unambiguous and that she should not take into account the terms of any
Dáil debate on the matter. However, she continued that even if she "were permitted to do so,
and [counsel] agreed that I could look at the Dáil debates *de bene esse*, I am of the view that
these debates do not assist the Defendant[s'] . . . argument . . .".

[125] [2000] 1 I.L.R.M. 548 (H.C.).

[126] [2000] 1 I.L.R.M. 548, 557.

"gone much further".[127] He quoted the passage from the judgment of Costello J. in *McDonagh* set out above,[128] and continued:

> It would seem to me that nothing could be clearer than this statement. Not only is it possible for an Irish court to look at parliamentary papers to assist in the construction of a statute but it is not limited to doing so only where there is ambiguity. I do not think that that decision is in any way in conflict with *Howard v. Commissioners for Public Works* because in that case the question of introducing external elements such as parliamentary papers did not arise.[129]

Consequently, in his view, Irish courts were no longer "hidebound by some strict common law rule which forbids"[130] recourse the Dáil Debates, and would not be precluded from having such recourse "because the statutory provision was unambiguous using the traditional canons of construction".[131] This is plainly a much more radical position than that suggested by *Pepper v. Hart* and reasserted by Lord Browne-Wilkinson in *Melluish*, even if does reflect what seems to happen in practice in many lower courts in England. In any event, it is clear that there is room – perhaps even a necessity – for consideration by the Supreme Court in Ireland of the fundamental question of the relaxation of the exclusionary rule. To date, the question has neither been fully argued for nor addressed by this court in detail,[132] and the conflict between *Howard* and

---

[127] *ibid.*

[128] At n.120.

[129] [2000] 1 I.L.R.M. 548, 558; holding that it is "well within the spirit and intent of the passage cited [from the judgment of Costello J. in *McDonagh*] to deduce from it that he would have been of the view that in certain circumstances such a ministerial statement [*sc.* "an explanation as to the meaning of a section by the relevant minister when piloting the Bill through the Dáil"] could be availed of. This view would seem to correspond to that taken by Shanley J. in *In re National Irish Bank Ltd (No. 1)* [1999] 3 I.R. 45; [1999] 1 I.L.R.M. 321 and Kearns J. in *Lawlor v. Flood* High Court, unreported, 2 July 1999" ([2000] 1 I.L.R.M. 548, 558). Note that both of these cases have been appealed, (respectively: [1999] 3 I.R. 145; [1999] 1 I.L.R.M. 321 (H.C. and S.C.); and [1999] 3 I.R. 107 (S.C.);) and decided in the Supreme Court without reference to this point.

[130] [2000] 1 I.L.R.M. 548, 558.

[131] [2000] 1 I.L.R.M. 548, 559; in the event, he held that the minister's statement, and an inference as to what the members of the Oireachtas intended, confirmed him in the interpretation of s.2(1) of the Health (Amendment) Act 1986 at which he had independently arrived (*cp.* Millett L.J. in *Petch v. Gurney (Inspector of Taxes)*, above n.87).

[132] The only reference to *Pepper v. Hart* in the Supreme Court would seem to be in *D.P.P. (Ivers) v. Murphy* [1999] 1 I.R. 98 (S.C.), where Denham J. for a unanimous court (Barrington and Lynch JJ. concurring; Keane J. concurring in a short judgment; O'Flaherty J. concurring in the result) held ([1999] 1 I.R. 98, 109-111) that if a literal interpretation produced an absurd result, the court have regard to the "the purposive approach" to statutory interpretation, on which she quoted the observation of Lord Griffiths in *Pepper v. Hart* [1993] A.C. 593, 617; [1993] 1 All E.R. 42, 50 set out below (text with n.133).

McDonagh has not been properly resolved. An Irish *Pepper v. Hart* is undoubtedly waiting to happen; indeed, if and when the exclusionary rule re-
stated in *Howard* is finally and *expressly* departed from, then, after *McDonagh*
and *Crilly v. Farrington*, an Irish *Pepper v. Hart* may well go very much further than Lord Browne-Wilkinson did in that case.

10.   PEPPER V. HART – A LEADING CASE OF THE TWENTIETH CENTURY

For many reasons, *Pepper v. Hart* can rightly claim to be a leading case of the
twentieth century. The abrogation of a two hundred year old rule. The House
of Lords declining to follow three of its own previous decisions. Strong speeches
from a seven member Appellate Committee. The first in a series of decisions
reflecting new jurisprudence from new talent. A minor constitutional law issue.

What it should be remembered for is the culmination of a movement towards the adoption of a purposive approach to the process of statutory interpretation. Among the technical arguments relating to the abrogation of the rule
are some strong statements on the issue. Both Lord Griffiths and Lord
Browne-Wilkinson in their speeches stressed the merits of the purposive, as
opposed to the literal, approach to statutory interpretation. According to Lord
Griffiths:

> [t]he days have long passed when the courts adopted a strict constructionist
> view of interpretation which required them to adopt the literal meaning
> of the language. The courts now adopt a purposive approach which seeks
> to give effect to the true purpose of legislation and are prepared to look at
> much extraneous material that bears on the background against which
> the legislation was enacted.[133]

Lord Browne-Wilkinson (with whose opinion Lords Keith, Bridge, Ackner
and Oliver expressly agreed) said:

> [g]iven the purposive approach to construction now adopted by the courts
> in order to give effect to the true intentions of the legislature, the fine
> distinctions between looking for the mischief and looking for the inten-
> tion in using words to provide the remedy are technical and inappropri-
> ate.[134]

Stevens has indicated that this aspect of the ruling is the most significant:

> With that decision, no-one could now deny that a totally new approach to

---

[133] [1993] A.C. 593, 617; [1993] 1 All E.R. 42, 50.
[134] [1993] A.C. 593, 635; [1993] 1 All E.R. 42, 65.

interpreting statutes – and thus inevitably to the relative balance between courts and the legislature – has been accepted . . . another important source of judicial power has been created.[135]

It is equally arguable that the decision in *Pepper v. Hart* has given a lead to the judges in other jurisdictions such as Ireland to reconsider their own position in relation to this fundamental principle.

The ruling in *Pepper v. Hart* is one which was initially formulated in terms of strict limitations. "Beyond that I would not go" were the initial words of Lord Browne-Wilkinson, a warning which was primarily repeated by a number of other senior judges. This research has indicated that the House of Lords' initial approach to the interpretation and application of the rule in *Pepper v. Hart* was to relax the rule further. Judges were ready to hear submissions on and view the contents of parliamentary materials *before* they have made a decision to admit such materials under the ruling in *Pepper v. Hart*. The courts were using those materials to *confirm* the construction of the legislation which they had already discovered.

The judges appeared to be willing to extend the meaning of "ambiguity" and "obscurity" and to broaden the range of admissible parliamentary material by arguing that it was necessary to understand the statements of ministers and their effect. Further it was also clear that judges were willing to refer to *Hansard* without giving a clear basis for their decision to do so and without indicating that the basis for that recourse is the decision in *Pepper v. Hart*. The initial example which had been set by the House of Lords has been followed by the lower courts and tribunals.

The speech of Lord Browne-Wilkinson in *Melluish* shows that he is concerned about the manner in which his ruling has been interpreted and implemented. He has also issued a warning to legal advisers that the inappropriate use of parliamentary materials will be met with appropriate orders as to costs. A stringent, restrained approach to the use of extrinsic aids is not happening. Lord Browne-Wilkinson has had to lead the call to reaffirm the need to keep resort to *Hansard* within the distinct limitations which he had stated in *Pepper v. Hart*.

Despite this, the recent approach of the House of Lords demonstrates that judges are taking a contradictory attitude towards the applicability and use of parliamentary materials. It may be that Lord Browne-Wilkinson's triple locks for the admissibility of parliamentary materials are slowly being unpicked by the judiciary and that *Hansard* has become, or is becoming, an open book for guidance on the meaning and purpose of legislative provisions.

---

[135] Stevens, "Introduction to the House of Lords as a Supreme Court' in Dickson & Carmichael, (eds.), *The House of Lords Its Parliamentary and Judicial Roles* (Hart, Publishing, Oxford, 1999) 111.

PSYCHOLOGICAL SUFFERING AND PHYSICIAN-ASSISTED SUICIDE
CHABOT (1994)

DR. UBALDUS DE VRIES[*]

1. THE FACTS: NETTY'S STORY

This case concerns a psychiatrist, Dr. Chabot, whose patient was deeply and apparently hopelessly ill, and who wished to die.[1] The doctor provided her with a fatal poison, which she drank. The doctor, whose professional standing and motives are above question, reported what he had done to the proper authorities.

The history of the patient, Netty, is so tragic, so appalling, that it would require a Bronte or Dostoyevsky to do it full justice. She presented in 1991. Dr. Chabot diagnosed depression without psychotic symptoms.[2] The depression was a result of a complicated mourning process. Netty had married when she was 23. The marriage was unhappy. Two children were born. In 1986 her eldest son committed suicide. This affected her deeply, and her marital problems worsened. She started to express a death wish. However, she promised herself that she would not attempt suicide until her younger son was able to fend for himself. Meanwhile she underwent psychiatric treatment. She felt that this was of no help though. In 1988 Netty's father died. She left her husband and divorced him in 1990. In that year her younger son was involved in a serious road traffic accident. While he was in hospital, doctors discovered a malignant tumour in his brain. He died in 1991. On the eve of his death, Netty had bought four graves – two for her two sons, one for herself and another for her ex-husband. She planned to be buried between her two sons. Hours after her youngest son died, she attempted suicide. She failed. From then on she became totally preoccupied with her own death. However, she also wanted to die in a humane manner. Eventually she came into contact with Dr. Chabot, via the Dutch Society for Voluntary Euthanasia.

---

[*]Lecturer, Dublin City University.

[1] H.R. June 21, 1994, N.J. 1994, 656.

[2] Dr. Chabot relied on DSM III R (Diagnostic Statistical Manual), as used by the American Psychiatry Association. For more details about the case and the diagnosis; see: Chabot, *Zelf Beschikt* (Amsterdam, 1995).

For his part in her death, Dr. Chabot was prosecuted. He was acquitted at trial and by the Court of Appeal, but he was found guilty in the Supreme Court. No sentence was imposed.

2. THE CRIMINAL LAW CONTEXT

Article 294 of the Dutch Criminal Code renders it a crime intentionally to force another to commit suicide, to assist a person to commit suicide or provide to a person the means to commit suicide. Article 293 renders it a crime intentionally to take another person's life at his or her request.

Both crimes amount to what is termed euthanasia in the Netherlands. In the Dutch literature, it is defined as the deliberate commission or omission to shorten the life of a person at his or her request.[3] Thus, the person so requested by another, assists the other in the suicide, provides the means, or physically administers the means him or herself. Although these are fundamentally different courses of action, the Dutch courts have not distinguished between them when asked to rule on their lawfulness.

Since the 1970s a debate is ongoing as to whether doctors who carried out either crime should be exonerated from prosecution. In fact, as far back as 1973, the local court of Leeuwarden ruled on the lawfulness of euthanasia by a doctor.[4] Although the doctor was found guilty, the court referred to the defence of necessity as a possible means by which a doctor could be exonerated in the circumstances.

The defence of necessity arises under Dutch criminal law where the accused is under some physical or psychological constraint or duress to violate the law. The constraint or duress must be external and of such a degree that the accused felt compelled to give in, or was forced to give in, and violate the law. Thus, a person who is asked at gunpoint to hand over money he holds in trust for another can do so justifiably. In these situations, the free will of the accused is lost as the result of external pressure. Necessity can also arise in the absence of any external physical or psychological pressure. Here, the free will is not lost. Instead, the accused made a considered judgment to violate the law. The accused did so, however, to achieve a greater good. The accused had entered into a conflict of duties between which he or she made a choice. This choice is justified if the means used were proportionate to the aim and there were no alternative, less radical, means to achieve the aim. Thus, an optician who sold a pair of glasses, after the legal closing time, to a person who had lost his glasses and was completely helpless, made a justifiable choice to violate the

---

[3] *E.g.* Leenen, *Handboek Gezondheidsrecht – Deel 1: De Rechten van Mensen in de Gezondheidszorg* (3rd ed., Samson H.D. Tjeenk Willink, Alphen aan de Rijn, 1994), 266.
[4] Rb. Leeuwarden, February 21, 1973, N.J. 1973, 183.

law to fulfil a greater duty.[5] The court felt that the optician's professional obligation outweighed his legal obligations under the relevant legislation in this situation.[6]

3. EUTHANASIA AND THE DEFENCE OF NECESSITY

In 1984 the Dutch Supreme Court dealt with its first case of euthanasia.[7] In *Euthanasia I*, a medical practitioner was confronted with a death wish from a 95-year-old patient. Her wish to die stemmed from her unbearable and hopeless suffering. As far as the patient was concerned, her suffering could only be relieved if she was allowed to die in a humane manner. The doctor fulfilled her death wish. He administered a lethal dose of drugs. The doctor was prosecuted under article 293 of the Dutch Criminal Code.

In his submissions to the court, the doctor relied on the defence of necessity. He argued that the patient's death wish had confronted him with a conflict between two duties: (i) his legal duty to preserve life (as implied under articles 293 and 294) and (ii) his professional duty to relieve his patient's suffering. To discharge of the second meant that he had to fulfil his patient's death wish, thus breaching his first duty and commit a crime.

The choice would be justified if the means used were proportionate to the aim (to fulfil the patient's death wish) and if there were no alternative, less radical, means to relieve the patient's suffering. This depended on the circumstances of the case. Considering these, the court accepted the doctor's diagnosis. The patient's suffering was hopeless and unbearable. No other alternative treatment options were available to relieve the patient's suffering, which would not result in the patient's death. The patient's death wish was voluntary, sincere and persistent. In other words, the patient understood and accepted the only real option available to her. It could be argued that the death wish lay in her consent to the available option open to her. The doctor had consulted his assistant, and had come to his conclusions by reference to contemporary medical ethics and his medical skill and knowledge. In doing so, he had made a justifiable choice to break the law and achieve a greater good: to fulfil the patient's death wish.[8]

---

[5] H.R. October 15, 1932, N.J. 1923, 1329 (*Optician* case).

[6] At common law, the defence of necessity covers the first of these branches (constraint or duress) and may even reach cases where "it is excusable in an emergency to break the law if compliance would impose an *intolerable* burden on the accused" (*Perka v. R.* (1984) 13 D.L.R. (4th) 1, 12 *per* Dickson J., emphasis added) which may or may not extend in principle as far as the second branch contemplated by Dutch law. But even if does, it is clear that at common law, necessity cannot be pleaded in answer to a charge of homicide: *R. v. Dudley and Stevens* (1884) 14 Q.B.D. 273.

[7] H.R. November 27, 1984, N.J. 1985, 106 (*Euthanasia I* case).

[8] The decision in *Euthanasia I* was confirmed in H.R. October 21, 1986, N.J. 1987, 607 (*Eutha-*

4. The Position of the Royal Dutch Medical Association

It is important to consider briefly the position of the medical profession since it has played a dominant role in the discussion on the acceptability of euthanasia. The Royal Dutch Medical Association (R.D.M.A.) formulated its position in 1984.[9] It pointed out that most decisions surrounding life and death are part of the individual doctor-patient relationship. It stated that only medical practitioners are competent to deal with such decisions. They can answer questions that precede such wish – questions relating to the patient's illness and suffering and hope of alternative treatment or palliative care. In addition, a doctor is subject to peer review; apart from criminal proceedings, he or she can face disciplinary sanction if rules of conduct are not adhered to.

The medical profession has accepted euthanasia as an option for patients in circumstances where a patient's suffering is hopeless and unbearable and results in a death wish. The doctor must determine whether the death wish is voluntary, sincere and persistent. This depends on the nature and extent of the suffering that underlies the death wish and the availability of alternative treatment options. The doctor must also consult a colleague, for the latter to confirm the suffering and the merits of the patient's request.

The R.D.M.A. also pointed out that it is really irrelevant whether the suffering stems from a terminal illness. Nor does it ascribe an overriding importance to whether death is imminent. The Association believed that this would not sufficiently recognise how the patient experiences the suffering. Statistics, however, show that a great majority of patients whose death wish is fulfilled suffered from a terminal illness and had a life-expectancy of less than three weeks.[10]

5. The Statutory Reporting Procedure

The result of the case law discussed so far is that euthanasia remains a criminal offence under the Dutch law but the authorities do not prosecute medical practitioners in certain circumstances. To this end, in 1990, a non-statutory reporting procedure was put in place. In 1993 this procedure was incorporated into an amendment to the Burial Act, 1991.[11] The procedure obliges doctors to

---

nasia II case). However, since the common law does not accept the defence of necessity in the context of homicide (above, n.6), an Irish court would be unable to rely on similar reasoning.

[9] Report of the Euthanasia Committee "Vision on Euthanasia" in: R.D.M.A., (ed.), *Euthanasia in the Netherlands* (R.D.M.A., Utrecht, 1994), 12 *et seq.*

[10] For these, and other, statistics; see: Van der Wal & Van der Maas *Euthanasie en andere Medische Beslissingen rond het Levenseinde* (SDU, Den Haag, 1996); Centraal Bureau voor de Statistiek (C.B.S.) *Het Levenseinde in de Medische Praktijk* (C.B.S., Voorburg/Heerlen, 1996).

[11] Amendment to the Burial Act (Stb., 1993, 643).

state truthfully the cause of death. If euthanasia was carried out, the doctor is asked to comment on specific questions. These questions are listed in a Schedule attached to the amendment of the Act. The report is sent to the local coroner and district attorney. Prosecution will not follow if it is clear that the doctor had entered into a conflict of duties and made a justifiable choice to honour the death wish of the patient. The doctor is in such a position if the suffering is unbearable and hopeless, and the resulting death wish is voluntary, sincere and persistent. The doctor must have consulted a colleague who must have examined the patient if the suffering is psychological.[12]

6. The Decision in *Chabot*[13]

In previous cases, the courts were confronted with situations where the suffering stemmed from physical illness or trauma. Indeed, in most cases the patient suffered from a terminal illness. There was a certainty that death would follow. It also meant that the patients' suffering in these cases was predominantly physical. The death wish was based on this suffering. The suffering was both hopeless and unbearable. No other alternatives were available to relieve the patient's suffering in any real sense. In these cases, both the hopelessness of the illness and the hopelessness and unbearableness of the suffering could more readily be objectively determined by reference to medical practice and experience.

Thus, it is not the underlying condition – the terminal illness – that is a precondition for the lawfulness of euthanasia. Instead, the suffering, as experienced by the patient, appears to lead to a death wish.

The facts in *Chabot* confronted the Supreme Courts with a patient who suffered from a psychological illness. Her illness caused her to suffer so intensely that only death could relief her from this suffering, as far as she was concerned. This was subsequently confirmed by the psychiatrist. The extensive consultation between the patient and Dr. Chabot led him to conclude that in his clinical judgment the only way to relieve Netty's suffering was a course of treatment that would end her life. As far as he was concerned, this was the only treatment option left open to him and Netty. In this, his colleagues with whom he had consulted supported him. This so being, could Dr. Chabot maintain that he had entered into a conflict of duties?

The Court of Appeal of the district of Leeuwarden stated that the absence of any physical trauma or terminal illness was irrelevant to the fundamental questions that needed to be answered: Did a situation exist in which the patient

---

[12]See also Leenen, above. n.2; Dillmann & Legemaate "Euthanasia in the Netherlands: The State of the Legal Debate" in *Euthanasia in the Netherlands*, above, n.9, 81-87.

[13]For a translation of most parts of the Supreme Court judgment, see Griffiths, "Assisted Suicide in the Netherlands: the *Chabot* Case" (1995) 58 *M.L.R.* 232.

expressed voluntarily a sincere and persistent death wish? Was this the result of the patient's suffering? Did the doctor acknowledge the suffering as being unbearable and hopeless having regard to the present state of medical science and current medical ethics? Were alternative treatment options available?

To answer these questions, the court stated that in the absence of a physical, terminal illness a more careful analysis was warranted. The court accepted that Dr. Chabot had conducted such analysis. It accepted the evidence that the doctor was confronted with a voluntary and persistent death wish from a competent person whose suffering was hopeless and unbearable. This situation confronted him with the question whether to fulfil the death wish of the patient or to refuse his assistance and to maintain the life of the patient. All experts in court agreed that at all times the accused had balanced these duties with due care and by reference to current medical ethics and practice. Dr. Chabot was acquitted.

The prosecution appealed the decision. It argued that the Court of Appeal had erred in law on three accounts. First, it submitted that in the absence of a physical, terminal illness, physician-assisted suicide could never be lawful. Second, it submitted that, considering the patient's psychological suffering, the death wish could not have been arrived at in complete freedom – the death wish was not voluntary. Third, the doctor did not act with due care in failing to consult another doctor who had seen the patient for himself.

The Supreme Court accepted the third of these submissions, but rejected the first two, and it is in this rejection that the importance of the decision lies.

6.1 The Cause of Suffering

Should the cause of suffering be crucial to the lawfulness of euthanasia? The prosecution argued it should. It argued that where the trauma is otherwise than physical, the court should choose for the preservation of life.[14] Instead, the Court of Appeal accepted the necessity defence. It allowed the deliberate ending of life of other categories of patients in the absence of an inevitable terminal phase.

The Supreme Court rejected the argument. It stated that it could not allow such a general restriction to the necessity defence. It would undermine the very nature of the defence since its application depends on a *post facto* analysis. The function of this analysis is to determine the lawfulness of the doctor's clinical and professional judgment of the patient's suffering, not of the cause of the suffering. The cause does not bear any meaning on how the patient experiences the suffering. The Supreme Court agreed with the appellate court

---

[14]The prosecution felt supported by a decision of the Supreme Court in H.R. May 3, 1988, N.J. 1989, 391. However, this decision was not helpful to the prosecution, since the court was bound by the findings of fact made by the Court of Appeal in that case.

that this analysis must be conducted more carefully, because it is, objectively, more difficult to determine the hopelessness and unbearableness of psychological suffering.

Since the court refused to distinguish a physical condition from a psychological condition, the court, in effect, ignored the traditional distinction between body and mind, and between physical and psychological suffering. This was further explained by the Advocate General (A.G. Meijers) in his opinion. He added that philosophical and human experience regard a distinction between physical and psychological suffering artificial and unhelpful. The distinction does not contribute to answering the degree and extent of the suffering.[15] It relies on the Cartesian distinction between mind and body (*res extensa – res cogitans*) and disregards the fact that physical suffering can also have a psychological effect, which can influence the rationality of a decision. Similarly, psychological suffering does not necessarily undermine a person's rational powers.

6.2 The Voluntary Nature of the Request: A Careful Analysis

The Court of Appeal accepted the evidence that the death wish was voluntary. However, the prosecution argued that the mental state of the patient cast doubt on the voluntary nature of the death wish. Although the prosecution accepted that mentally ill patients can make autonomous decisions, it questioned whether, for the purpose of the necessity defence, Netty could have made the request in "complete freedom". To this end, it argued that the nature of the suffering is to be fundamental to determine whether the request was voluntary and autonomous. The prosecution referred to a decision of the Dutch Medical Disciplinary Council.[16] The Council stated that it remained difficult to determine whether the free will of a psychiatric patient who had expressed a death wish was influenced by the underlying psychological condition. It remained therefore almost impossible to determine whether the death wish stemmed from, related to, or formed part of the illness.

This led the prosecution to conclude that medical opinion is divided as to whether mentally ill patients, suffering from either a psychological illness or, as in Netty's case, psychological trauma, can fully express their free will. To rely on the necessity defence, the death wish must be completely voluntary. Since this can now be doubted, the Court of Appeal erred in law in allowing the defence.

This argument was also rejected by the Supreme Court. It rejected the submission that in relation to psychiatric patients a free and voluntary will cannot exist. It agreed with the opinion of the Court of Appeal that the death wish of a

---

[15]The A.G. followed Annotator 't Hart in H.R. May 28, 1991, N.J. 1991, 784.
[16]March 29, 1990; [1990] *Tijdschrift voor Gezondheidsrecht* 77.

psychiatric patient can stem from an autonomous decision and free self-determination. The A.G. added that the prosecution had failed to understand the nature of "human freedom": a complete freedom does not and cannot exist.

However, the prosecution argued that, even if this be so, the Court of Appeal could not justifiably have come to the conclusion that the patient's death wish stemmed from her free will in the absence of a careful analysis of the voluntary nature of her death wish. It argued that medical opinion was divided as to whether mentally ill patients can fully express their free will. The Supreme Court agreed with this argument, partly in the light of the prosecution's third submission: the absence of a second opinion.

6.3 Second Opinion

The prosecution relied on previous case law of the Supreme Court. In these cases, the court stated that insufficient consultation with a third party might lead to a guilty verdict.[17] These cases all dealt with terminally ill patients. Consequently, consultation with other doctors would even be more important in relation to psychiatric patients. The diagnosis may be more diffuse and the margin of judgment errors bigger. In addition, the death wish must be voluntary, considered and persistent. Therefore, the more the free will is in doubt, which is the case with psychiatric patients, the more conditions must be in place to avoid irreversible errors. This meant, according to the prosecution, that at least one independent third party – another doctor – must have seen and diagnosed the patient and confirm the findings of the treating doctor. The prosecution also referred to the amendment Bill to the Burial Act 1991.[18]

The accused's defence here, which was accepted by the Court of Appeal, was that a second opinion and diagnosis by a third party would have made no difference, as far as the patient was concerned. Therapeutic advantage would not have been achieved, nor would it have led to a different diagnosis. It was enough that the accused had consulted other specialists himself.

The Supreme Court stated that a second opinion is not always a necessary criterion for the necessity defence. However, in *Chabot*, a second opinion would have aided the court better to determine whether the defence of necessity could succeed. It would determine the validity of the professional and clinical judgment of the doctor. The absence of such an analysis by an independent expert precluded the Court of Appeal from making a judgment as to whether the accused was confronted with a conflict of duties between which he could make a justifiable choice. To this end, the Court of Appeal should have rejected the necessity defence.

Dr. Chabot was found guilty but no sentence was imposed.

---

[17]N.J. 1985, 106; N.J. 1988, 157; N.J. 1989, 391.
[18]The Bill has since been passed in Parliament; above n.11.

7. COMMENTARY

Dr. Chabot could not rely on the defence of necessity because he had not con-sulted another doctor who had seen the patient for him or herself. The Supreme Court did not reject the defence because of the different cause that belied the suffering. Instead, the court agreed with the Court of Appeal that the suffering must be abstracted from its cause. It is the compelling nature of the situation, not how the situation occurred, that determines whether a conflict of duties exists. In doing so, the court called into question the purpose of medical inter-vention. And, with it, the dilemma between preserving life and relieving suf-fering. The judgment recognises that the traditional mind-body distinction is artificial and, perhaps with the constant advances of medical technology, holds the distinction as untenable. At the heart of the judgment, the court makes clear that suffering is a definite subjective feeling. In some cases, as in Netty's, this leads to the patient realising that his or her life is no longer worth living, is untenable. The patient prefers death. If the patient is convinced of this and the doctor sees no alternative route of intervention, then the doctor's duty is to alleviate the suffering, no matter that in doing so, the necessary consequence is not only the relief of suffering, but also the death of the patient.

In doing so, the court has expanded the boundaries of the doctor-patient relationship within which euthanasia is lawful.

This leads to the question whether the court ruled on the lawfulness of euthanasia generally. Did the court in *Chabot*, for the fist time recognise a "right to euthanasia"? In abstracting the cause of the suffering, did the court justify that there are no grounds left to distinguish euthanasia from categories of patients who express a death wish but whose suffering is neither physical nor psychological, for example, people with *Lebensschemrz*? In other words, within a doctor-patient relationship, does the latter have the autonomy to de-cide the moment of his own death,[19] and to avail of the assistance of the doc-tor[20] under certain conditions?

---

[19] *Cf. In re a Ward of Court (No. 2)* [1996] 2 I.R. 79 (H.C., and S.C.). Here the Supreme Court, by a majority, held first, that had the ward been competent, in the exercise of her constitutional right to self-determination implicit in her rights to bodily integrity and privacy she would have had the right to forego or discontinue medical treatment *(cp. Cruzan v. Director, Mo. Dept. of Health*, 497 U.S. 261 (1990)) though not to have her life terminated; and second that it was in her best interests in the circumstances to discontinue her treatment *(cp. Airdale N.H.S. Trust v. Bland* [1993] A.C. 789 (H.L.)).

[20] *Cf. Washington v. Glucksberg*, 521 U.S. 702, 117 S.Ct. 2258 (1997); *Vacco, Attorney General of New York v. Quill*, 521 U.S. 793, 117 S.Ct. 2293 (1997). In *Cruzan*, above, n.19, the U.S. Supreme Court had held that a competent person has a liberty interest under the Due Process Clause of the Fourteenth Amendment in refusing unwanted medical treatment. In *Glucksberg*, however, the Court held that an examination of their nation's history and legal traditions led to the conclusion that the "right" to assistance in committing suicide, asserted by the respondents, is not a fundamental liberty interest protected by the Due Process Clause, so that Washington's prohibition against "caus[ing]" or "aid[ing]" a suicide did not violate that clause. The Supreme

Although this century has seen an increasing respect for patient autonomy, it cannot be accepted that the court in *Chabot* went so far as to say: "I, your doctor, wash my hands, and give you whatever you like".

Instead, in the case no alternative form of medical intervention was likely to be effective in the considered clinical judgment of the treating psychiatrist. The patient was clearly *in extremis*. In allowing the doctor to end the life of the patient quite deliberately, the court, perhaps, made a humane and realistic judgment. It gave recognition to a cautious professional approach to an extreme situation. In doing so, it demanded that the patient was carefully and properly informed of all the available options and allowed the patient to come independently to the decision to take the only available palliative option.[21]

Thus, the autonomy of the patient can be said to lie in his or her consent. The suffering is the kernel of the lawfulness of euthanasia. The doctor determines this suffering by reference to medical opinion. The death wish is an expression of the suffering the patient experiences. The doctor determines the alternatives that are available, which can relieve the patient's suffering. The options he proposes are, subsequently, consented to. It is a doctor's duty to ensure that this consent is a valid consent. In other words, the patient has been put in a situation that he or she could come to an informed consent. He or she is told about the nature of the treatment and its consequences. The patient, then, consents to treatment that can ultimately result, or does result, in ending his or her life. This is, perhaps, the real expression of the patient's death wish.

It means that the defence of necessity has been developed into a *medical* exception to articles 293 and 294 of the Dutch Criminal Code. This had already become evident after the court's judgments in *Euthanasia I*. The choice between the two conflicting duties was the expression of the doctor's professional autonomy. Subsequently, the validity of the choice was determined by reference to general medical practice and medical ethics. Kelk, annotating the judgment in *Euthanasia I*, stated that if this development took shape, medical practice itself could expand the boundaries within which euthanasia can be carried out lawfully.[22] And, indeed, this was accepted in *Chabot*.

In *Chabot*, the Supreme Court has for the first time recognised overtly what is really a matter of common medical knowledge. Conscientious doctors do and always have regarded the alleviation of suffering as one of their principal

---

Court of Canada had already reached a similar conclusion in *Rodriguez v. British Columbia* [1993] 5 S.C.R. 519. And in *Vacco*, decided on the same day as *Glucksberg*, the U.S. Supreme Court held that New York's prohibition on assisting suicide did not violate the Equal Protection Clause of the Fourteenth Amendment, on the grounds that the distinction between letting a patient die and making that patient die is an important, logical, rational, and well-established one which comports with fundamental legal principles of causation, and was recognised, at least implicitly, in *Cruzan*.

[21] Could it be that this decision represents a course of action that elsewhere, in the context of acute physical illness, is solved *sub rosa* by the use of the "double effect" hypothesis?

[22] See Kelk (1995) 44 Ars Aquie 330.

professional objectives. Though the usual paradigm in which this principle operates is the doctrine of "double effect". This double effect takes place at the latter stages of palliative care. Instead of leaving this as it is, the court made a general and humane point, that at some stages of acute suffering life should not be artificially continued.

8. CONCLUSION: WHY *CHABOT*?

It may be argued that there is something perverse in selecting the *Chabot* decision as one of the major cases of the Twentieth Century, since the decision was more of an apotheosis of preceding authority than a new departure. However, there are three reasons for doing so.

First, the decision extended in a significant way the symptoms for which a doctor could legitimately avail of the necessity defence. For the first time the court accepted a psychological illness within the ambit of necessity. In doing so, the court expressly refused to distinguish between the causes of suffering.

Second, the Supreme Court, by its judgment affirmed the role and function of the autonomy of professional judgment. It confirmed and emphasised that the defence of necessity is to be determined by reference to medical judgment alone. It ruled, in fact, on the lawful boundaries of the doctor-patient relationship.

Third, the Supreme Court recognised that the patient's own perceptions of the nature and extend of her illness required to be taken seriously. The case could at one level be taken as suggesting that the patient was sufficiently *compos mentis* to formulate her death wish, and that this wish should be respected. On another level, though, it could be suggested that the patient displayed sufficient capacity to consent to the sort of palliative treatment that actually ended her life.

One final point is that the case raises, for the first time in a legal context, the question whether death is "natural". Is death a consummation that arrives in its own good time? In considering this, the case recognises that death is a political, social and economic matter. Its effect is as to whether society can tolerate a situation where death is as an inevitable goal to be attained, with the maximum of dignity, care and painlessness, when all alternative methods of coping with life and its attendant inflictions have been exhausted. If so, then society must adjust its political, economic and religious prejudices to provide this particular form of palliative intervention.

UNBALANCING THE SEPARATION OF POWERS
CLINTON V. JONES (1997)

MICHAEL P. O'CONNOR*

1. INTRODUCTION

Choosing *Clinton v. Jones*[1] as one of the leading cases of this century is undoubtedly a controversial choice. The choice of any case decided two years ago would normally be quite presumptuous. However, *Clinton v. Jones* was not chosen merely to be provocative. In this paper, I will discuss how the direct consequences of this decision have already earned it a place among the leading cases of this century. In addition, the likely future consequences of this decision are so profound as to rival in importance any U.S. Supreme Court decision since *Marbury v. Madison*,[2] was decided nearly two centuries ago.

The issues presented to the United States Supreme Court in *Clinton v. Jones* were fairly straight-forward. On *certiorari* to the United States Court of Appeals for the Eighth Circuit, the Court was presented with the following questions:[3] (1) whether the litigation of a private civil damages action against an incumbent President must in all but the most exceptional cases be deferred until the President leaves office; and (2) whether a district court, as a proper exercise of judicial discretion, may stay such litigation until the President leaves office.[4] The first question presented for review, which was answered in the negative by the Supreme Court, is the one of most historical import. The Court denied the President's request to defer a pending civil suit until the expiration of his term in office. By virtue of this decision, the President was required to make a choice between settling a sexual harassment suit for damages or contesting the litigation. The President chose to contest the charges fully through litigation.[5]

---

*Attorney at Law; Legal Writing Professor, Arizona State University College of Law.

[1] 520 U.S. 681; 117 S.Ct. 1636; 137 L.Ed.2d 945 (1997).

[2] 1 Cranch (5 U.S.) 137 (1803).

[3] A petition which seeks discretionary review in the United States Supreme Court is styled as a petition for a writ of *certiorari* to the court below.

[4] *Clinton v. Jones*, 520 U.S. at 689, n.12; See also: Petition for Writ of Certiorari filed by petitioner, President William Jefferson Clinton, in the United States Supreme Court on May 15, 1996, Case No. 95-1853.

[5] In retrospect, this decision by the President was a fateful one. However, it is a decision that all future Presidents may have to face due to the Court's decision in *Clinton v. Jones*.

The details of this litigation subsequent to the Court's decision have been discussed in excruciating detail in the various media. For the purposes of this paper, it will suffice to note that allegations arose concerning whether the President testified truthfully in that litigation, and whether he obstructed justice by encouraging others to testify falsely.[6] These allegations resulted in only the second impeachment of a sitting President in United States history, and the first in over one hundred years. The factors which led to the President's impeachment are many, some of which will be discussed in detail later in this paper. These causal relationships between the various factors and the President's impeachment have been and continue to be hotly disputed by various parties. One fact, though, cannot be disputed: but for the Court's decision in *Clinton v. Jones*, the two articles of impeachment could not have been passed.

It is important to note that, to date, the allegations against President Clinton have not been proven in any tribunal. One of the articles of impeachment failed to obtain a simple majority in the Senate trial; the other failed to obtain the necessary two-thirds majority to result in conviction.[7] Whether these charges are ever proven in a court of law after the President's term is irrelevant to the fact that unproved allegations of misconduct during a civil trial preoccupied much of the energy and attention of two branches of the U.S. government for over one year.[8]

All actions of the President during this period were judged, in succession, through the lens of these allegations, possible impeachment, impeachment and the subsequent trial in the Senate. From presidential decisions on whether to hold press conferences, to the scheduling of foreign diplomatic trips, all were criticised as efforts to avoid answering questions concerning the allegations of misconduct in the *Jones* litigation.[9] Even the use of U.S. troops in Iraq was immediately criticised by members of Congress as having been done to obtain "political cover",[10] violating the long-observed unwritten rule that "politics stop at the water's edge".[11] The allegations against the President became an obsession in Washington, D.C., dominating the activities of the executive and legislative branches of government.[12]

Were *Clinton v. Jones* to have no further consequences, other than those

---

[6] Similar charges were repeated concerning the President's behaviour during the Independent Counsel's subsequent investigations of the President's actions in the civil case.

[7] Alison Mitchell, *"Clinton Acquitted Decisively," N.Y. Times,* February 13, 1999.

[8] In addition, the Chief Justice of the United States Supreme Court, William Rehnquist, was required to preside over the Senate trial of the impeachment charges, lasting several weeks.

[9] R.W. Apple, Jr., "No Reservoir of Credibility," *N.Y. Times,* December 17, 1998.

[10] Alison Mitchell, "Impeachment Vote in House Delayed as Clinton Launches Iraq Air Attack," *N.Y. Times,* December 17, 1998.

[11] Eric Schmitt, "G.O.P. Splits Bitterly Over Timing of Assault," *N.Y. Times*, December 17, 1998.

[12] Alison Mitchell, "Outlook for Political Dynamics: More of the Same," *N.Y. Times*, October 22, 1998.

alluded to above, it is already arguably one of the most important U.S. cases in the last one hundred years. The likely future consequences of this case, however, virtually assure that it will be regarded as one of the most significant cases of the 20th Century. These future consequences directly relate to and threaten the delicate balance of powers enumerated in the United States Constitution. Such dramatic consequences are possible because the decision in *Clinton v. Jones* provides an extra-constitutional check on the power and authority of the Presidency. Unwittingly or deliberately, the Supreme Court has shifted governmental power from the executive to the judicial branch and provided political enemies of any sitting President with a method of attacking the Presidency that is shielded from and, therefore, not governed by the political processes. The nature of politics, so well understood by the Framers of the Constitution, virtually guarantees that this method will be used to attack future Presidents, unless and until the Supreme Court reconsiders its decision in *Clinton v. Jones*.

In the following sections of this paper, I will discuss the separation of powers as defined by the U.S. Constitution and governmental practice over the last two centuries and the related doctrine of constitutional checks and balances. Finally, I will describe how the decision in *Clinton v. Jones* has upset that balance and provided a nearly limitless potential for political enemies of a sitting President to harass and undermine the office of the Presidency.

2. The Separation of Powers

Much has been written on the constitutional doctrine of separation of powers,[13] and this paper is not meant to be a dissertation on that subject. However, the issue of the separation of powers is critical to a proper understanding of the import of the Supreme Court's decision in *Clinton v. Jones*. Therefore, a brief recitation of some of the more relevant principles will be necessary.

The Framers of the U.S. Constitution were greatly concerned about the colonial history of tyranny under British rule. Therefore, they wanted to ensure that their own government would not concentrate too much power into the hands of those governing. James Madison commented that the governmental power "ought to be effectually restrained from passing the limits assigned to

---

[13]In an Irish context, see generally, Morgan, *The Separation of Powers* (Round Hall Sweet & Maxwell, Dublin, 1998). The division envisaged by the Irish Constitution between the executive, legislature and judiciary is in many ways similar to that envisaged by U.S. Constitution and sketched below, with the important difference that the executive in Ireland is the Government and not the President. On one of the crucial building blocks out of which the Irish version of the separation of powers is constructed, see Keane, "Across the Cherokee Frontier of Irish Constitutional Jurisprudence. The *Sinn Féin Funds* Case: *Buckley v. Attorney General*" above, 185.

it".[14] To that end, the Framers devised a system of limited government, controlled by a document that specifically enumerated those powers to be exercised by the various governmental authorities. The federal governmental powers enumerated in the Constitution were apportioned separately among the three branches of government: the legislative, the executive and the judiciary. [15]

Article I of the Constitution enumerates the legislative power of the government and apportions that power into the hands of the United States Congress.[16] Article II vests all executive authority of the United States Government into the hands of the President.[17] Article III concerns the judiciary, and vests judicial authority into the hands of the United States Supreme Court and those inferior courts "as the Congress may from time to time ordain and establish".[18] "The ultimate purpose of this separation of powers is to protect the liberty and security of the governed".[19] The United States Supreme Court again recognised this fact, in the last quarter century, when it noted that the Framers of the Constitution "viewed the principle of separation of powers as a vital check against tyranny".[20]

The Constitution, however, "by no means contemplates total separation of each of these three essential branches of government".[21] To the contrary, the framework of the U.S. government was designed so that "practice will integrate the dispersed powers into a workable government. It enjoins upon its branches separateness but interdependence, autonomy but reciprocity".[22] The Supreme Court has stated that it is "archaic" to think of the division of responsibility among the three branches of government as being "airtight".[23] In fact, it is the "degree of overlapping responsibility, a duty of interdependence as well as independence" which helps prevent "the accumulation of excessive authority in a single Branch".[24]

The Constitution most directly requires co-operation through the exercise

---

[14] James Madison, *The Federalist No. 48* (Cooke (ed.), Wesleyan U.P., Middletown, Conn., 1961), 332.

[15] For the purposes of this paper, we are discussing the division of power among the three branches of the federal government. We are not concerned here with the allocation of power between the federal government and the governments of the various states.

[16] U.S. Const., art. I.

[17] U.S. Const., art. II.

[18] U.S. Const., art. III, § 1.

[19] *Metropolitan Airports Authority v. Citizens for the Abatement of Aircraft Noise, Inc.*, 501 U.S. 252, 272 (1991). See also, generally: Office of Legal Counsel, "The Constitutional Separation of Powers Between the President and Congress," Memorandum for the General Counsels of the Federal Government, May 7, 1996.

[20] *Buckley v. Valeo*, 424 U.S. 1, 121 (1976).

[21] *Buckley*, 424 U.S., at 121.

[22] *Mistretta v. United States*, 488 U.S. 361, 381 (1989) (quoting *Youngstown Sheet & Tube co. v. Sawyer*, 343 U.S. 579, 635 (1952) (Jackson, J., concurring)).

[23] *Nixon v. Administrator of General Services*, 433 U.S. 425, 443 (1977).

[24] *Mistretta*, 488 U.S., at 381.

of overlapping responsibility in the following areas: (1) the requirements of bicameralism and presentment to the president for all pieces of legislation;[25] (2) the requirement that the appointment of ambassadors, federal judges and officers of the United States be made by the President with the advice and consent of the Senate;[26] and (3) the area of War Powers.[27] In these areas, the Constitution specifically identifies the co-ordinated roles to be played by the President and the legislators, providing a clear road map of what is permissible action by the particular branches of government involved.

In other areas of governmental action the roles to be played are not so clearly defined. In particular, the complex interaction between the executive and judicial branches is not very clearly defined in the Constitution. It is this relationship which lies at the heart of the separation of powers issue raised in *Clinton v. Jones*.

2.1 The Unique Role of the Chief Executive

"The President occupies a unique position in the constitutional scheme".[28] Unlike the delegations of power to the other branches of government, the Constitution vests all executive power in a single person, the President.[29] In both Constitutional and practical terms, the duties of the Presidency are unceasing.[30] While Congress is required to meet but "once in every year",[31] and the Supreme Court sits for a set term each year before adjourning,[32] the President must attend to Constitutional duties continuously throughout his tenure in office.[33]

In light of the unique constitutional role of the President, previous courts have been reluctant to find the President answerable to federal court jurisdiction, except in the most unusual of cases.[34] In 1833, Justice Story of the United

---

[25] See U.S. Const., art. I, §§ 1, 7. Any action taken by Congress that has "the purpose and effect of altering the legal rights, duties, and relations of persons . . . outside the Legislative Branch" must be passed by both houses of Congress and presented to the President for signature. *INS v. Chadha*, 462 U.S. 919, 952 (1983).

[26] See U.S. Const., art. II, § 2, cl. 2.

[27] The Constitution vests the President with the power of the Commander-in-Chief of the U.S. Armed Forces. *See*: U.S. Const., art II, § 2. But only Congress has the authority to declare war. *See*: U.S. Const., art I, § 8, cl. 11. The area of War Powers is one of the most contested and, arguably, the most flagrantly violated provisions of the U.S. Constitution. See Fisher, *Presidential War Power*, (University Press of Kansas, Lawrence, Kansas, 1995).

[28] *Nixon v. Fitzgerald*, 457 U.S. 731, 753 (1982.)

[29] U.S. Const. art II.

[30] See Amar and Katyal, "Executive Privileges and Immunities: The *Nixon* and *Clinton* Cases," 108 *Harv. L. Rev.* 701, 713 (1995).

[31] U.S. Const. art. I, § 4.

[32] Act of September 24, 1789, 1 Stat. 73.

[33] See U.S. Const. Amend. XXV (detailing elaborate procedures for carry out Presidential duties in the event the President is "unable to discharge the powers and duties of his office").

[34] See generally *Nixon v. Fitzgerald*, 457 U.S. 731 (1982).

States Supreme Court, himself an early Constitutional scholar, stated the following:

> The president cannot . . . be liable to arrest, imprisonment, or detention,
> while he is in the discharge of the duties of his office; and for this pur-
> pose his person must be deemed, in civil cases at least, to possess an
> official inviolability.[35]

This traditional reluctance to impose judicial authority on the Chief Executive
is rooted in the separation of powers doctrine. This fact was recognised by
Thomas Jefferson when he expressed his belief that the President, while in
office, could never be held accountable to judicial process.

> The leading principle of our Constitution is the independence of the Leg-
> islature, executive and judiciary of each other . . . But would the execu-
> tive be independent of the judiciary, if he were subject to the commands
> of the latter, and to imprisonment for disobedience; if the several courts
> could bandy him from pillar to post, keep him constantly trudging from
> north to south and east to west, and withdraw him entirely from his con-
> stitutional duties?[36]

While the Jeffersonian ideal of a Chief Executive who is in no way accountable to the judiciary has been modified over time, it remains true that
"Courts traditionally have recognised the President's constitutional responsibilities and status as factors counselling judicial deference and restraint".[37] In
fact, until *Clinton v. Jones*, no sitting President had ever been compelled to
testify in a civil proceeding.[38]

2.2 The Danger Inherent in Unnecessarily Subjecting a Sitting President to Judicial Process

There are times, of course, when a sitting President is subject to judicial process.[39] These times are when it is necessary for the proper functioning of government and the administration of justice.[40] However, history teaches that the

---

[35] Story, *Commentaries on the Constitution of the United States*, (1st ed., Hillard, Gray & Co., Boston, 1833) vol. 3, section 1563, 418-419; quoted in *Fitzgerald*, 457 U.S. at 751, n.31.

[36] *The Works of Thomas Jefferson* (Ford, (ed.), G.P. Putnam's Sons & The Knickerbocker Press, New York & London, 1904) vol. 10, 404; quoted in *Fitzgerald*, 457 U.S., at 751, n.31.

[37] *Fitzgerald*, 457 U.S., at 753.

[38] Brief for the United States as Amicus Curiae in Support of Petition, Drew S. Days III, Solicitor General, Case No. 95-1853 ("We know of no instance, however, in which a sitting President has been compelled to furnish evidence in connection with a civil proceeding").

[39] *United States v. Nixon*, 418 U.S. 683 (1974).

[40] *ibid.*

judiciary should move reluctantly in subjecting the President to the jurisdiction of the courts when to do so in no way advances the interests of governing the populace at large. The Courts had previously remained deferential to the office of the Presidency in part because of the very real concern about subjecting the President to the authority of a judge who has life tenure and is unaccountable to the political process. Distinguished delegates to the Constitutional Convention, such as John Adams and Oliver Ellsworth, agreed that "the President, personally, was not subject to any process whatever . . . For [that] would . . . put it in the power of a common justice to exercise any authority over him and stop the whole machine of government".[41] As the Supreme Court stated over seventy years ago, the constitutional boundaries between the branches must be determined "according to common sense and the inherent necessities of the governmental co-ordination".[42] The Court failed to heed this guiding principle in deciding *Clinton v. Jones*.

The Court's decision in *Clinton v. Jones* did not evince common sense as to the likely consequences of its decision.[43] It in no way advanced the necessities of governmental co-ordination. If anything, it did just the opposite. It must be remembered that the issue decided by the Court in *Clinton v. Jones* was not *whether* the President should be made to answer the civil charges against him in a court of law; the issue was *when* he was to be made to answer those charges. The Court's decision required a sitting President, for the first time in history, to be answerable to a civil suit for damages during the pendency of his term in office.

The danger inherent in requiring a sitting President to be subject to judicial process is clear. If the President is a litigant in front of a federal judge, that judge exercises power over the President. The court sets the calendar and requires the litigants to perform certain actions in adherence to the court's time-table, or suffer the consequences. Even if the particular judge presiding is deferential to the President's calendar concerns, there is a likelihood that, at some point during the litigation, the court will in some way exercise power over the President's ability to perform the executive functions of the office. This may take the form of requiring the President to appear in court for testimony. It may take the form of requiring the President to sit for depositions by a certain date, or it may take the form of ruling upon the President's request for a continuance. All of these normal, routine functions that a judge exercises during litigation have the potential of requiring the President to forego pressing

---

[41] *Journal of William Maclay* (Maclay, (ed.), D.A. Appleton & Co., New York, 1890) 167; quoted in *Fitzgerald*, 457 U.S., at 751, n.31.

[42] *J.W. Hampton, Jr. & Co. v. United States*, 276 U.S. 394, 406 (1928).

[43] "As for the case at hand, if properly managed by the District Court, it appears to us highly unlikely to occupy any substantial amount of petitioner's time". *Clinton v. Jones*, 520 U.S., at 702.

duties of the Chief Executive, or risk negative consequences of a dismissed action or a contempt citation.

Recently, the President was cited for contempt by the district court judge presiding over the Jones lawsuit.[44] Since this contempt citation was issued after the settlement of the President's suit, at a time when no proceedings were pending before the court, there is a substantial question as to whether the district court was within its power in issuing this citation. Irrespective of that question, however, is the dilemma caused by the court's action. If the President chose to disregard that citation, a grave constitutional crisis could precipitate. What remedy would be available to the court in this situation? Normally, the court would jail a litigant who refused to comply with a contempt citation. That two of the branches of the U.S. government could be brought to the brink of this type of confrontation, arising from a matter that is wholly unrelated to the proper functioning of government, underlines the danger inherent in the *Clinton v. Jones* decision.

Unnecessarily subjecting a sitting President to judicial process causes great strain upon and risks permanent damage to the very structure of government, which is one of separated powers. This is true because the Separation of Powers principle is violated not only when one branch performs those powers reserved to another, but also when the actions of one branch prevent the affected branch "from accomplishing its constitutionally assigned functions".[45] This is exactly the danger inherent in the Court's decision in *Clinton v. Jones*. The Court's decision in *Clinton v. Jones* offends the separation of powers principle and risks great harm to the structure of government in the United States because the decision places the executive branch under the discretionary authority of the judiciary.

3. CHECKS AND BALANCES

The Separation of Powers doctrine is inextricably intertwined with the principle of constitutional checks and balances. By separating the powers of the various branches but requiring them to work in conjunction with each other, the Constitution created a system wherein the several branches of government exercised checks against the accumulation of power in the other branches. James Madison articulated the rationale behind what he termed the "distributions of power" with the following words: "the constant aim is to divide and arrange

---

[44] John M. Broder and Neil A. Lewis, "Clinton Is Found to Be in Contempt on Jones Lawsuit," *N.Y. Times*, April 13, 1999.

[45] *Nixon v. Administrator of Gen. Servs.*, 433 U.S., at 443; *accord CFTC v. Schor*, 478 U.S. 833, 851, 856-57 (1986).

the several offices in such a manner as they each may be a check on the other".[46] This structural arrangement and the procedural requirements which derive from it, ensure that power is balanced among the several branches. The delicate balance thus achieved prevents any branch from exercising tyrannical power against the population.

The Constitutional system created by the Framers distributed power among the branches because the Framers understood the nature of politics. "The framers regarded the checks and balances they had built into the tripartite Federal Government as a self-executing safeguard against the encroachment or aggrandisement of one branch at the expense of the other".[47] The genius of the Framers of the U.S. Constitution lay in the recognition of human beings' political nature. The Constitution does not rely upon people in government to act nobly. The Framers of the document understood that people could not be counted upon always to act in the interests of the common good.[48] In fact, the system was designed to pit self-interest against self-interest, in the understanding that a government so divided would be less capable of acting tyrannically against the population.

The Supreme Court, itself, has recognised that each of the three branches of government have a strong tendency to grasp all available power for itself. In the past, the Court has described the necessity for "vigilance against the 'hydraulic pressure inherent within each of the separate Branches to exceed the outer limits of its power'."[49] Yet, in this case, the Court disregarded the realities of these pressures and stated that it has "confidence in the ability of our federal judges" to ensure that the Chief Executive is not prevented from effectively accomplishing the President's constitutionally assigned duties.[50] The Court also stated that their was little danger that its decision would lead to a rash of lawsuits against the President or that a lower federal court judge would act capriciously in exercising power over the President.[51]

The Court's expression of "confidence" that the members of the federal judiciary would do nothing to hinder the President from performing the duties of Chief Executive and Commander-in-Chief may merely be a sign of political naiveté.[52] However, it may be a sign of something more common to members

---

[46] James Madison, *The Federalist No. 51* (Cooke, (ed.), Wesleyan U.P., Middletown, Conn., 1961), 349; quoted in *Buckley*, 424 U.S., at 122-23.

[47] *Buckley*, 424 U.S., at 122-23.

[48] James Madison, *The Federalist No. 10* (Cooke, (ed.), Wesleyan U.P., Middletown, Conn., 1961).

[49] *Mistretta*, 488 U.S., at 382 (citation omitted).

[50] *Clinton v. Jones*, 520 U.S. at 708-709.

[51] *ibid.*

[52] One would have to be naive to believe that all federal judges in the United States, when exercising their discretionary powers over their respective calendars, would uniformly exercise this power in a noble manner, particularly when they have been granted authority to exercise this power over the President of the United States. It must be remembered that U.S. federal judges are appointed through a *political* process. Most federal judges, including those sitting on the

of each branch of government, namely "that hydraulic pressure . . . to exceed the outer limits of its power".[53]

Moreover, the expression of confidence in the judiciary in *Clinton v. Jones* is irrelevant to whether or not the principle of separation of powers has been violated. The Supreme Court has repeatedly held that it is "irrelevant for separation-of-powers purposes" whether the overreaching branch will actually act in a manner that violates the principle.[54] The proper analysis is to determine the extent to which the intrusion prevents the Chief Executive from performing the President's constitutionally assigned duties.[55] This analysis, however, was ignored by the Court's ruling in *Clinton v. Jones*.

A careful review of the power granted to the federal judiciary in *Clinton v. Jones* and the likelihood for abuse which is engendered by this ruling makes clear the danger that future Presidents will be prevented from performing their constitutionally assigned duties, unless and until the Supreme Court reconsiders its decision in this case.

4. UPSETTING THE BALANCED CHECKBOOK

The potential for abuse opened by the Supreme Court's decision in *Clinton v. Jones* is enormous. The Court's decision permits an extra-constitutional check on the authority of the Presidency. Whereas the Framers of the Constitution carefully structured the mechanisms for channelling the political animus of various parties through a finely crafted system of checks and balances, the Court's decision in *Clinton v. Jones* permits any political enemy of a sitting President to circumvent all of those procedural constraints. No longer must an aggrieved politician or party content themselves with political mechanism and debate between elections. Now, any political (or personal) enemy of a sitting President merely has to file a lawsuit to harass the Chief Executive and undermine the President's effectiveness in office.

As stated above, the Supreme Court expressed its confidence that the judiciary could and would prevent such lawsuits from being used to overwhelm the President. The Court cited the possibility that litigants seeking to harass the President would be hit with sanctions under Rule 11 of the Federal Rules of

---

U.S. Supreme Court, have been actively engaged in party politics throughout their careers before being appointed to the bench. While in almost all cases it should be presumed that the judges will be very deferential to the President, it only takes one judge in one case to upset the balance of power in government. It is the mere fact that a judge is given the discretionary power to exercise over the President that shifts the balance of power between the branches.

[53] *Mistretta*, 488 U.S., at 382.

[54] *Metropolitan Washington Airports Authority*, 501 U.S., at 269 n.15; see also *Bowsher v. Synar*, 478 U.S. 714, 774 (1986) (White, J., dissenting).

[55] *Morrison v. Olson*, 487 U.S. 654, 696 (1988).

Civil Procedure. The Court apparently believes that this would provide suffi-cient deterrent effect against the use of vexatious litigation. However, Rule 11 has been in existence for many years and has not prevented harassing litigation from being filed in other contexts.[56] In addition, the applicability of Rule 11 sanctions often do not become clear until after a significant amount of litiga-tion has occurred. Sanctions applied after the President has been required to respond to frivolous suits would do little to ensure that the President was not prevented from performing the constitutional duties of the Presidency.

The Court also noted that "most frivolous and vexatious litigation is termi-nated at the pleading stage or on summary judgment, with little if any personal involvement by the defendant".[57] The Court cited only to the Federal Rules of Civil Procedure, not to any evidence whatsoever, for its interesting assertion that "most frivolous and vexatious litigation" would be terminated at this stage. Of course, it is of little consolation to the nation that "most" litigation would be so dismissed if the President is tied up in lawsuits which are not so dismissed. Moreover, it must be noted with some irony that the Paula Jones lawsuit was dismissed by the district court.[58] No one could say credibly at this time that the suit filed by Ms. Jones did not consume a tremendous amount of the Presi-dent's time. Finally, it is of little significance to the public if the President is being drawn away from official duties by preoccupation with *any* lawsuit, whether meritorious or frivolous.

As the Supreme Court recognised in *Nixon v. Fitzgerald*, "diversion of [the President's] energies by concern with private lawsuits would raise unique risks to the effective functioning of government".[59] This is true because when faced with a lawsuit, "cognisance of . . . personal vulnerability frequently could dis-tract a President from his public duties".[60] The great jurist, Judge Learned Hand, noted, that he would "dread a lawsuit beyond anything else short of sickness and death".[61] Judge Hand's comment reflects accurately the type of overriding concern that a lawsuit can instil in a litigant, particularly a defend-ant. This concern likely would be heightened in a sitting President, a politician whose ability to govern may be affected by the degree to which allegations in a particular suit are proven true.

---

[56] Abby Goonough, "City Could Sharply Reduce Cost of Lawsuits, Study Says," *N.Y. Times*, Sep-tember 24, 1998.

[57] *Clinton v. Jones*, 520 U.S. 681, 708.

[58] The suit was dismissed by the district court on April 1, 1998, forty-seven months after it was filed. The district court's decision to dismiss the case was later appealed by Ms. Jones, and that appeal was only dismissed after the President agreed to a settlement during the pendancy of that appeal.

[59] *Fitzgerald*, 457 U.S., at 751.

[60] *Fitzgerald*, 457 U.S., at 753.

[61] Learned Hand, *Lectures on Legal Topics* (Association of the Bar of the City of New York, 1926) vol. 3, 105; quoted in *Fitzgerald*, 457 U.S., at 763, n.6 (Burger, C.J., concurring).

4.1 The Potential for Abuse

The knowledge that a sitting President may become preoccupied with a civil lawsuit will almost certainly lead to additional lawsuits being pressed against future Presidents. These lawsuits will attract the attention and efforts of political enemies of the President. An examination of the facts surrounding the prosecution of Paula Jones' civil suit make the foregoing assertions clear.[62]

At various times throughout the Jones' litigation against the President, people who are avowed enemies of Mr. Clinton's presidency played critical roles in sustaining that litigation.[63] The roles played by these individuals largely were hidden from view. Some of these individuals provided substantial legal advice and assistance, including writing briefs for Ms. Jones.[64] In addition, some of these individuals arranged for Ms. Jones to have representation when other counsel of record decided to drop the case.[65] Yet, due to their hidden roles in the case, these individuals and their motivations were not subjected to public scrutiny. The actions of these individuals provide a blueprint for the harassment of future Presidents by their political enemies.

Powerful people who are aggrieved by the outcome of a presidential election will be tempted to support litigation against the President which they believe may embarrass or distract the Chief Executive. A President so distracted will be less effective at governing, precisely the goal sought by political enemies of a President. It matters little to such individuals whether the allegations are true or false, able to be proven or not. If the result is a less effective President, the enemies of that President will mark it as a victory.

Whereas, in the past, the constitution formally channelled political animus through a public system of checks and balances, that animus can now be directed at Presidents *sub rosa*. When political confrontation is open, the parties seeking to attack a President must take their chances on alienating the electorate and suffering the consequences in the next election. No such consequences attach to a behind-the-scenes attack on a President through hidden support for civil litigation. In addition, Rule 11 sanctions, the deterrent relied upon by the Supreme Court, will have no effect on individuals who are neither litigants nor attorneys of record in a particular suit against the President. They are shielded, not only from public view, but from the sanctions from the court as well.

---

[62] Regardless of how one feels about the merits of the lawsuit filed by Paula Jones, it is clear that political enemies of the President assisted Ms. Jones in the prosecution of the case against the President. For the purposes of this article, it is assumed that all allegations made by Ms. Jones in her suit against President Clinton were true and provable.

[63] See David Johnston and Don Van Natta, Jr. "Inquiry to Ask Whether Reno was Misled by Independent Counsel," *N.Y. Times*, February 10, 1999.

[64] *ibid.*

[65] *ibid.*

5. CONCLUSION

The Supreme Court's decision in *Clinton v. Jones* will prove to be one of the most important U.S. cases of the Twentieth Century. But for that decision, the impeachment of President Clinton could not have occurred. The Jones' litigation and the allegations which flowed from it consumed the energies of two branches of the U.S. government for over one full year. Independent Counsel Ken Starr's office has reportedly concluded that the *Clinton v. Jones* decision also authorises the indictment of a sitting President.[66] The spectre of the Chief Executive of the United States under indictment during the President's term of office is one that has never before threatened the Republic. Even if Mr. Starr's interpretation of this decision is incorrect, as many legal scholars believe it to be,[67] the short-term consequences of this decision have already been more dramatic than that of any decision in recent constitutional history.

The long-term consequences of this decision are likely to prove even more dramatic. The delicate balance of power has been shifted heavily away from the executive to the judiciary. Future Presidents will find themselves subjected to the dictates of federal district court judges who would be able "to exercise any authority over him and stop the whole machine of government".[68]

More dangerous, perhaps, are the purely political realities which attend this decision. The politics of power in the United States have long been characterised by personal attacks, long memories and revengeful counter-attacks.[69] It is naive to believe that a tactic which proved capable of limiting President Clinton's effectiveness in office will not be used by others to limit the effectiveness of future Presidents. The ramifications of *Clinton v. Jones* threaten to undermine the stability and productivity of the United States government. Until this decision is reconsidered and reversed, it will remain one of the most important decisions of the Twentieth Century.

---

[66]Don Van Natta, Jr., "Starr is Weighing Whether to Indict Sitting President," *N.Y. Times,* January 31, 1999.

[67]Robert H. Bork, "Clinton, Out of Reach," *N.Y. Times*, February 3, 1999.

[68]*Journal of William Maclay* (Maclay (ed.), D.A. Appleton & Co., New York, 1890), 167; quoted in *Fitzgerald*, 457 U.S., 751, n.31.

[69]See Alison Mitchell, "Bitter Clash on Timing of Impeachment," *N.Y. Times*, December 18, 1998 (Republicans raise Watergate and Vietnam to justify impeachment); see also Alison Mitchell, "Outlook for Political Dynamics: More of the Same," N.Y. Times, October 22, 1998.